"I can either hide and do nothing, or kill...you wouldn't let me hide."

RED

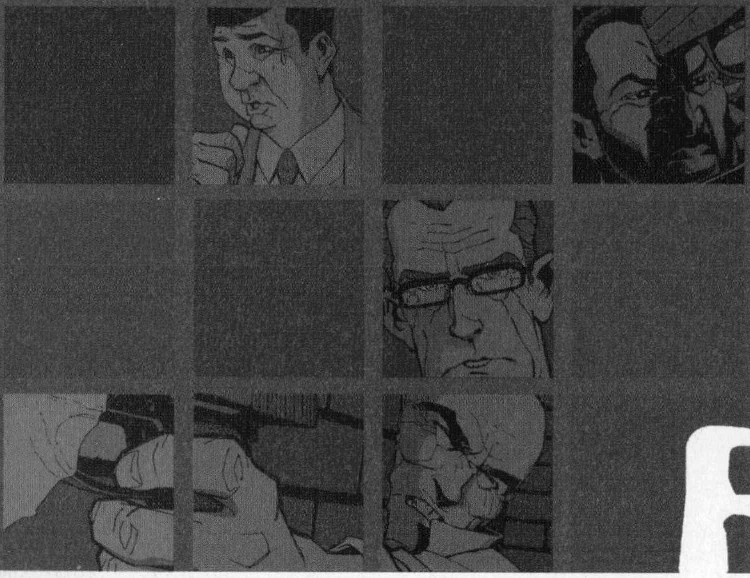

RED

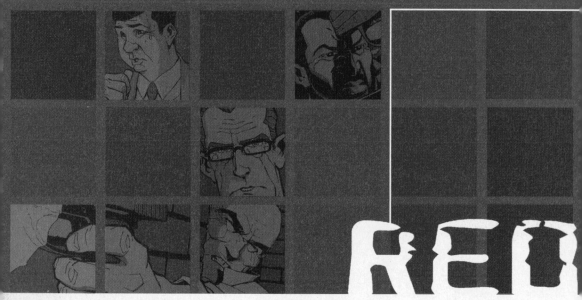

Writer:
Warren Ellis

Artist:
Cully Hamner

Colors:
David Self

Letters:
John Costanza

Editor:
Ben Abernathy
with John Layman

Covers by:
Hamner

Red Book Design by: Larry Berry

I promise you that everyone at the CIA who knows my name is going to die."

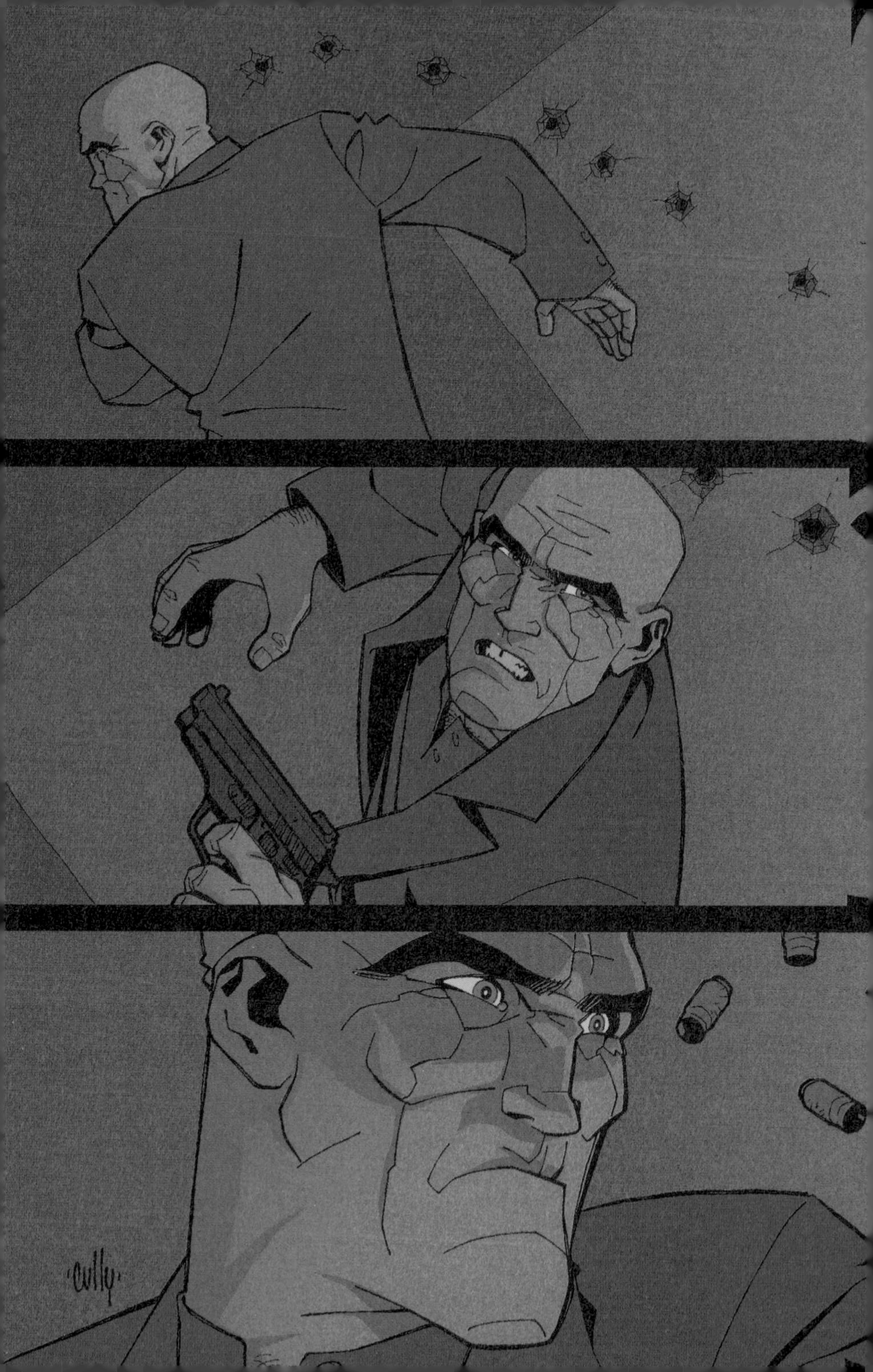

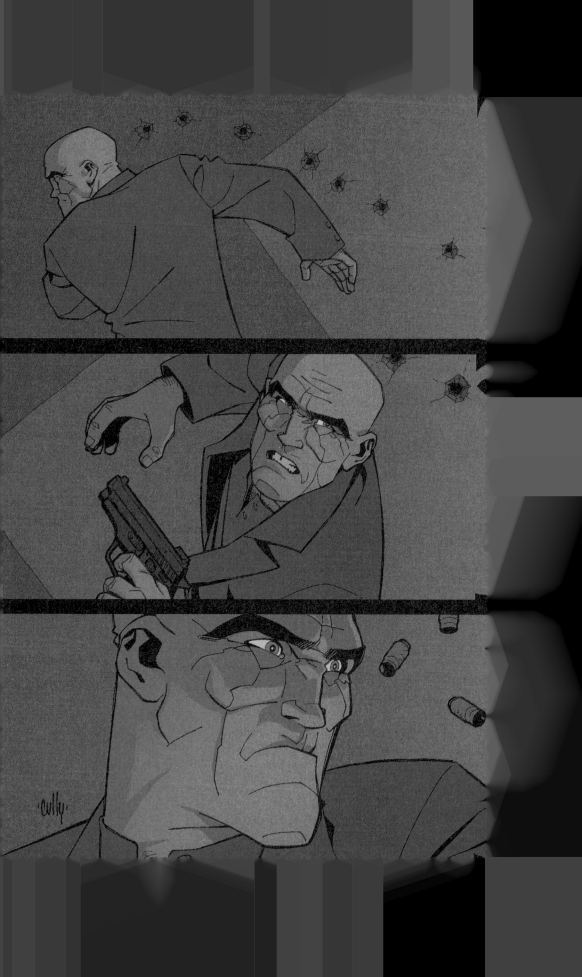

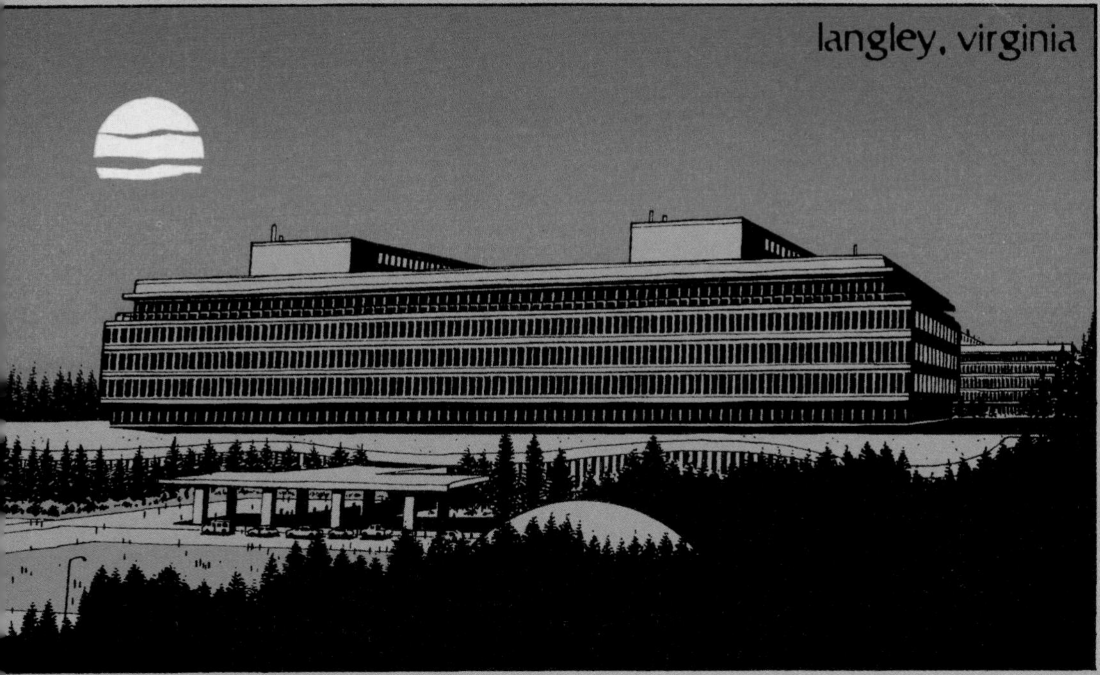
langley, virginia

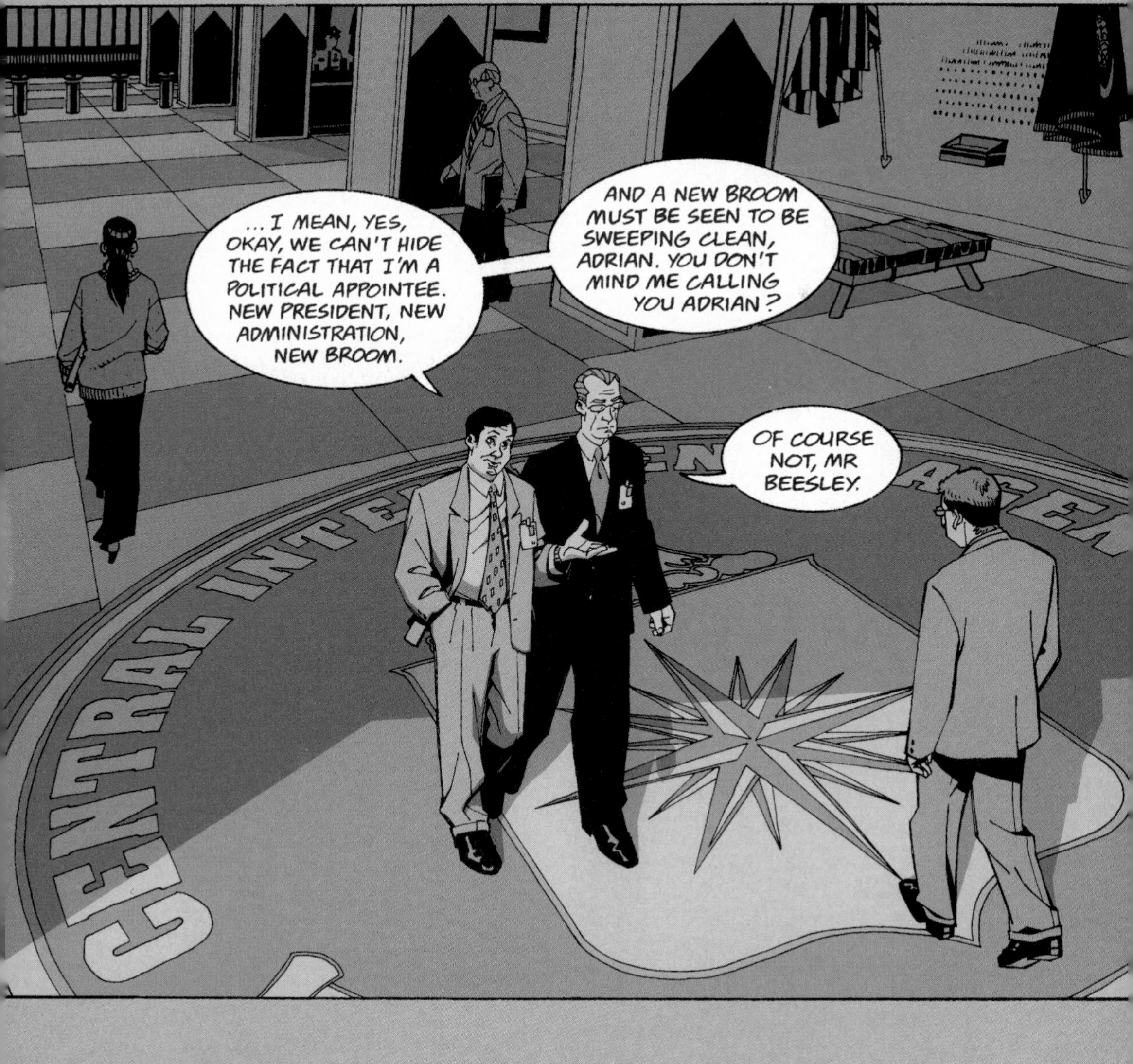
... I MEAN, YES, OKAY, WE CAN'T HIDE THE FACT THAT I'M A POLITICAL APPOINTEE. NEW PRESIDENT, NEW ADMINISTRATION, NEW BROOM.
AND A NEW BROOM MUST BE SEEN TO BE SWEEPING CLEAN, ADRIAN. YOU DON'T MIND ME CALLING YOU ADRIAN?
OF COURSE NOT, MR BEESLEY.
CENTRAL INTELLIGENCE AGENCY

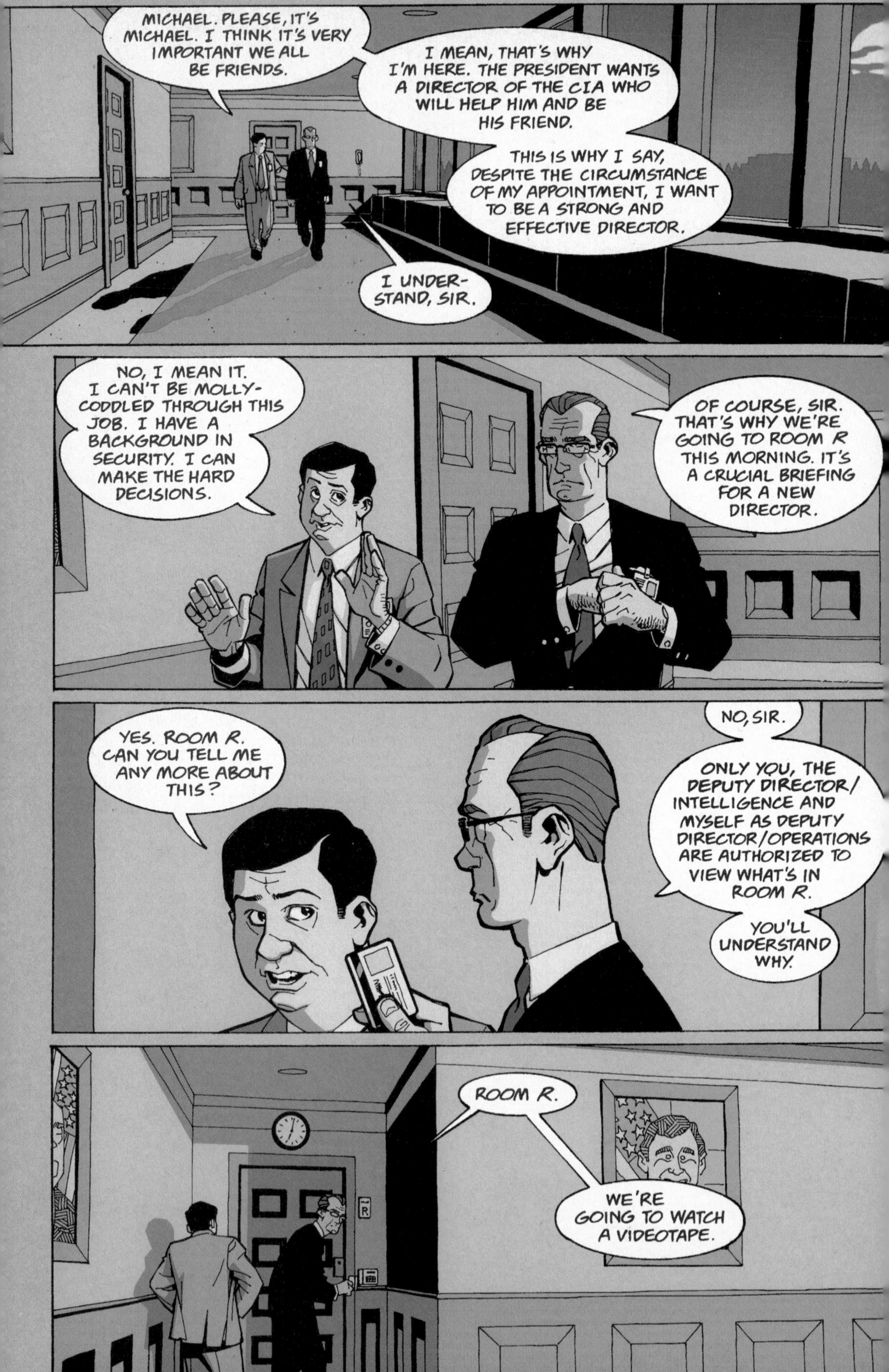
MICHAEL. PLEASE, IT'S MICHAEL. I THINK IT'S VERY IMPORTANT WE ALL BE FRIENDS.
I MEAN, THAT'S WHY I'M HERE. THE PRESIDENT WANTS A DIRECTOR OF THE CIA WHO WILL HELP HIM AND BE HIS FRIEND.
THIS IS WHY I SAY, DESPITE THE CIRCUMSTANCE OF MY APPOINTMENT, I WANT TO BE A STRONG AND EFFECTIVE DIRECTOR.
I UNDERSTAND, SIR.
NO, I MEAN IT. I CAN'T BE MOLLY-CODDLED THROUGH THIS JOB. I HAVE A BACKGROUND IN SECURITY. I CAN MAKE THE HARD DECISIONS.
OF COURSE, SIR. THAT'S WHY WE'RE GOING TO ROOM R THIS MORNING. IT'S A CRUCIAL BRIEFING FOR A NEW DIRECTOR.
YES. ROOM R. CAN YOU TELL ME ANY MORE ABOUT THIS?
NO, SIR.
ONLY YOU, THE DEPUTY DIRECTOR/INTELLIGENCE AND MYSELF AS DEPUTY DIRECTOR/OPERATIONS ARE AUTHORIZED TO VIEW WHAT'S IN ROOM R.
YOU'LL UNDERSTAND WHY.
ROOM R.
WE'RE GOING TO WATCH A VIDEOTAPE.

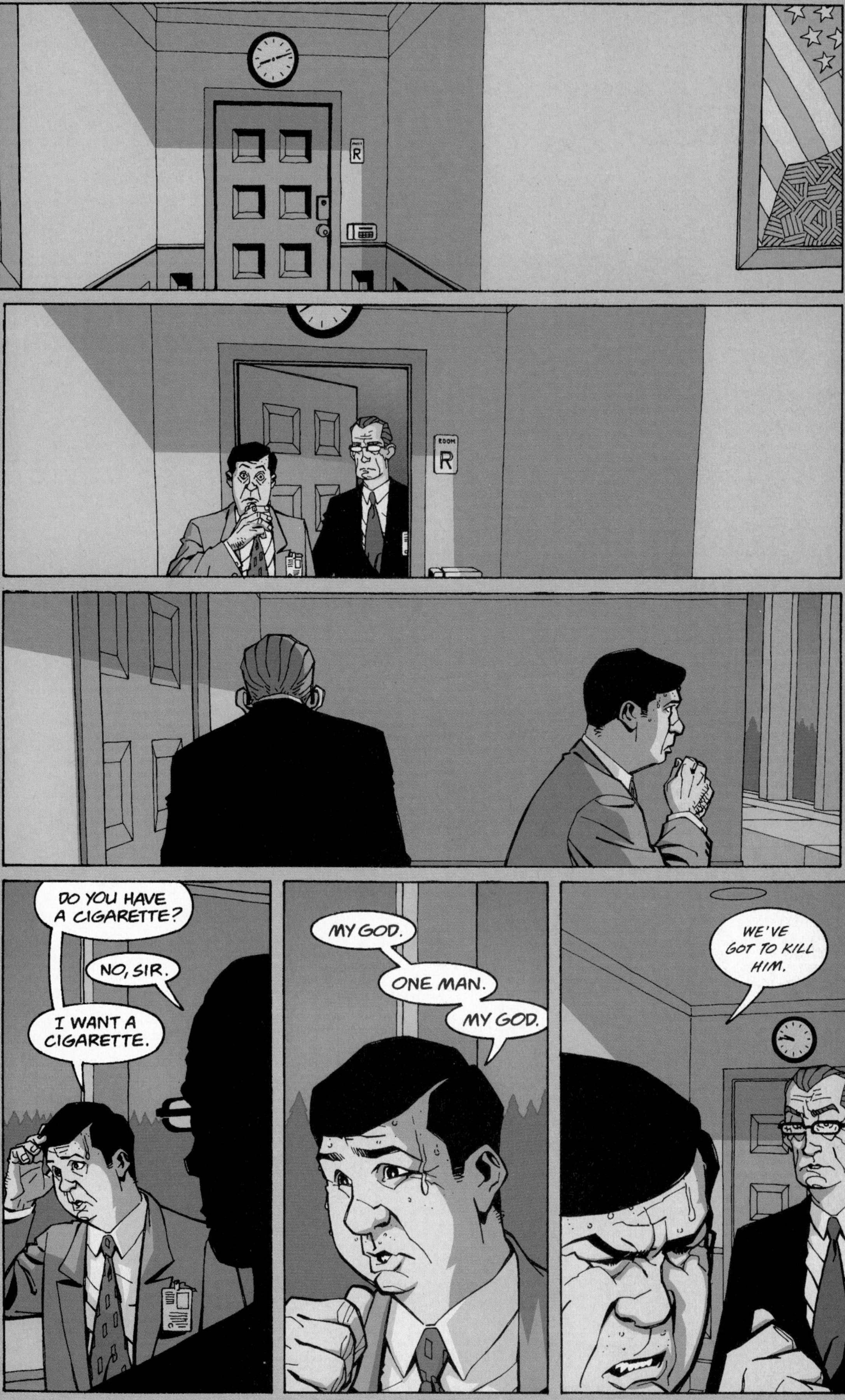
DO YOU HAVE A CIGARETTE?
NO, SIR.
I WANT A CIGARETTE.
MY GOD.
ONE MAN.
MY GOD.
WE'VE GOT TO KILL HIM.

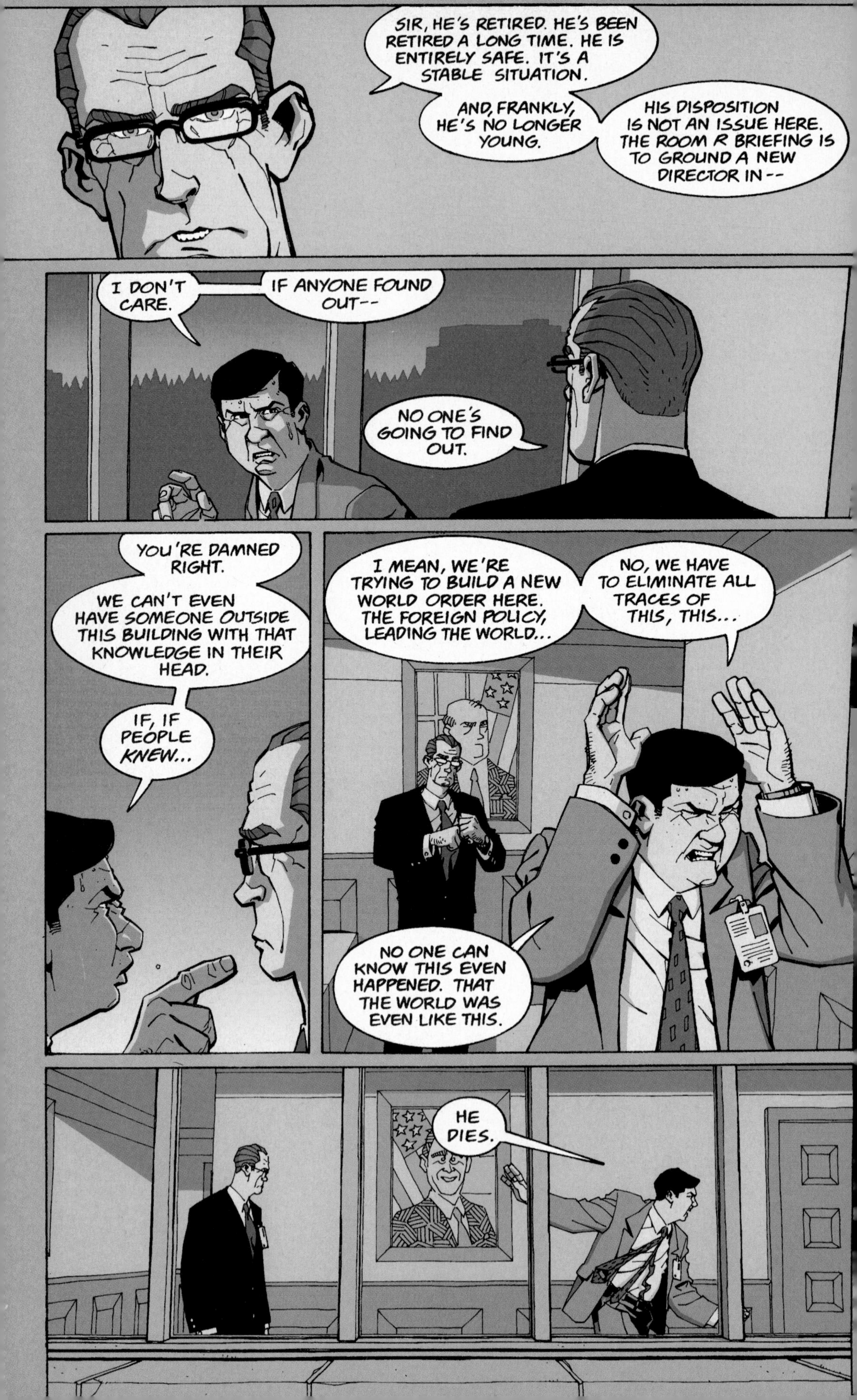
SIR, HE'S RETIRED. HE'S BEEN RETIRED A LONG TIME. HE IS ENTIRELY SAFE. IT'S A STABLE SITUATION.
AND, FRANKLY, HE'S NO LONGER YOUNG.
HIS DISPOSITION IS NOT AN ISSUE HERE. THE ROOM R BRIEFING IS TO GROUND A NEW DIRECTOR IN--
I DON'T CARE.
IF ANYONE FOUND OUT--
NO ONE'S GOING TO FIND OUT.
YOU'RE DAMNED RIGHT.
WE CAN'T EVEN HAVE SOMEONE OUTSIDE THIS BUILDING WITH THAT KNOWLEDGE IN THEIR HEAD.
IF, IF PEOPLE *KNEW*...
I MEAN, WE'RE TRYING TO BUILD A NEW WORLD ORDER HERE. THE FOREIGN POLICY, LEADING THE WORLD...
NO, WE HAVE TO ELIMINATE ALL TRACES OF THIS, THIS...
NO ONE CAN KNOW THIS EVEN HAPPENED. THAT THE WORLD WAS EVEN LIKE THIS.
HE DIES.

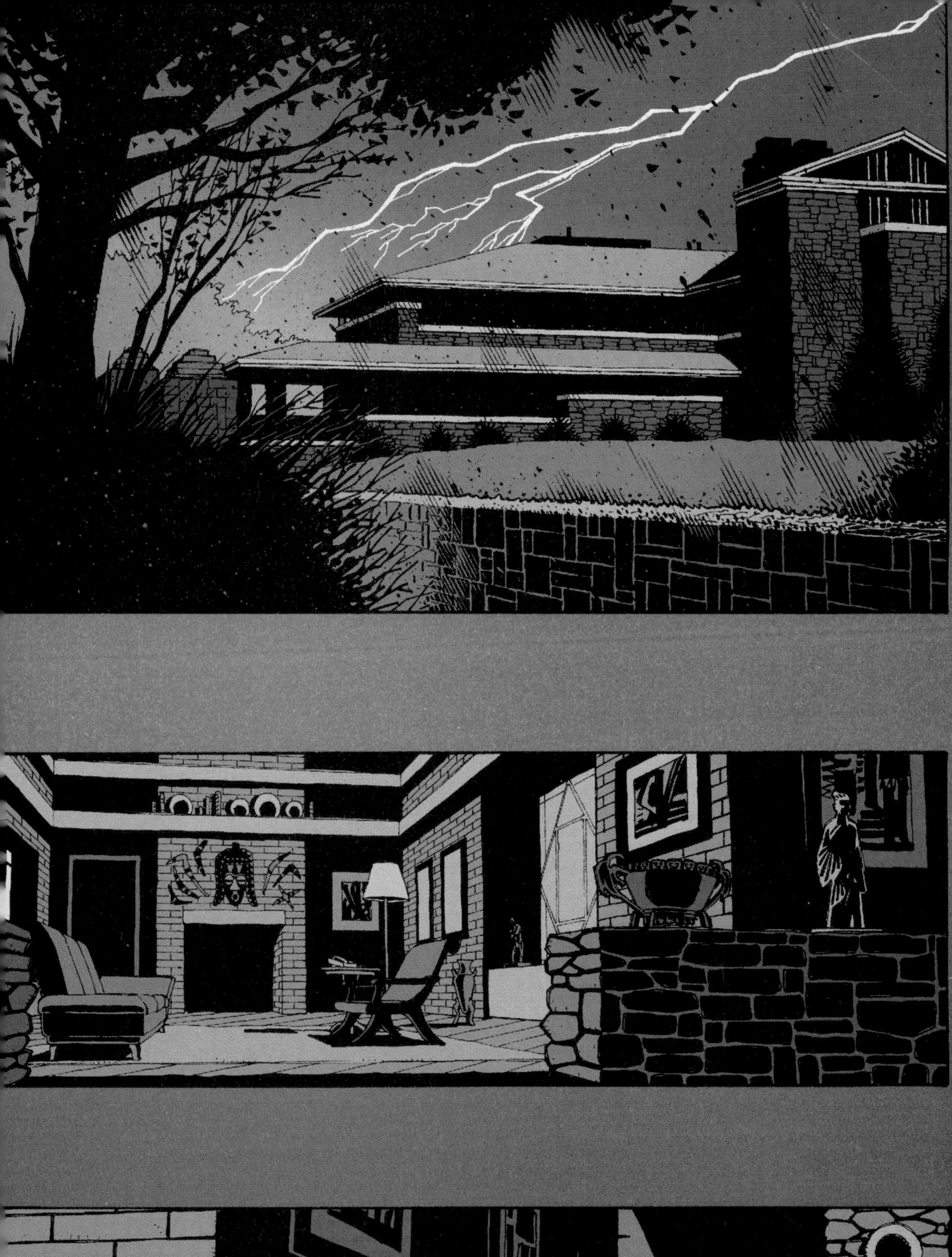

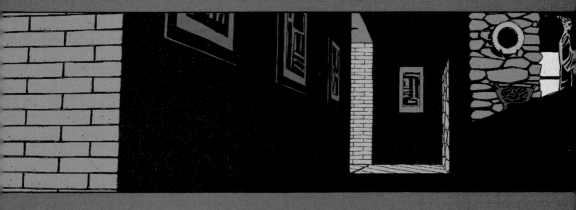

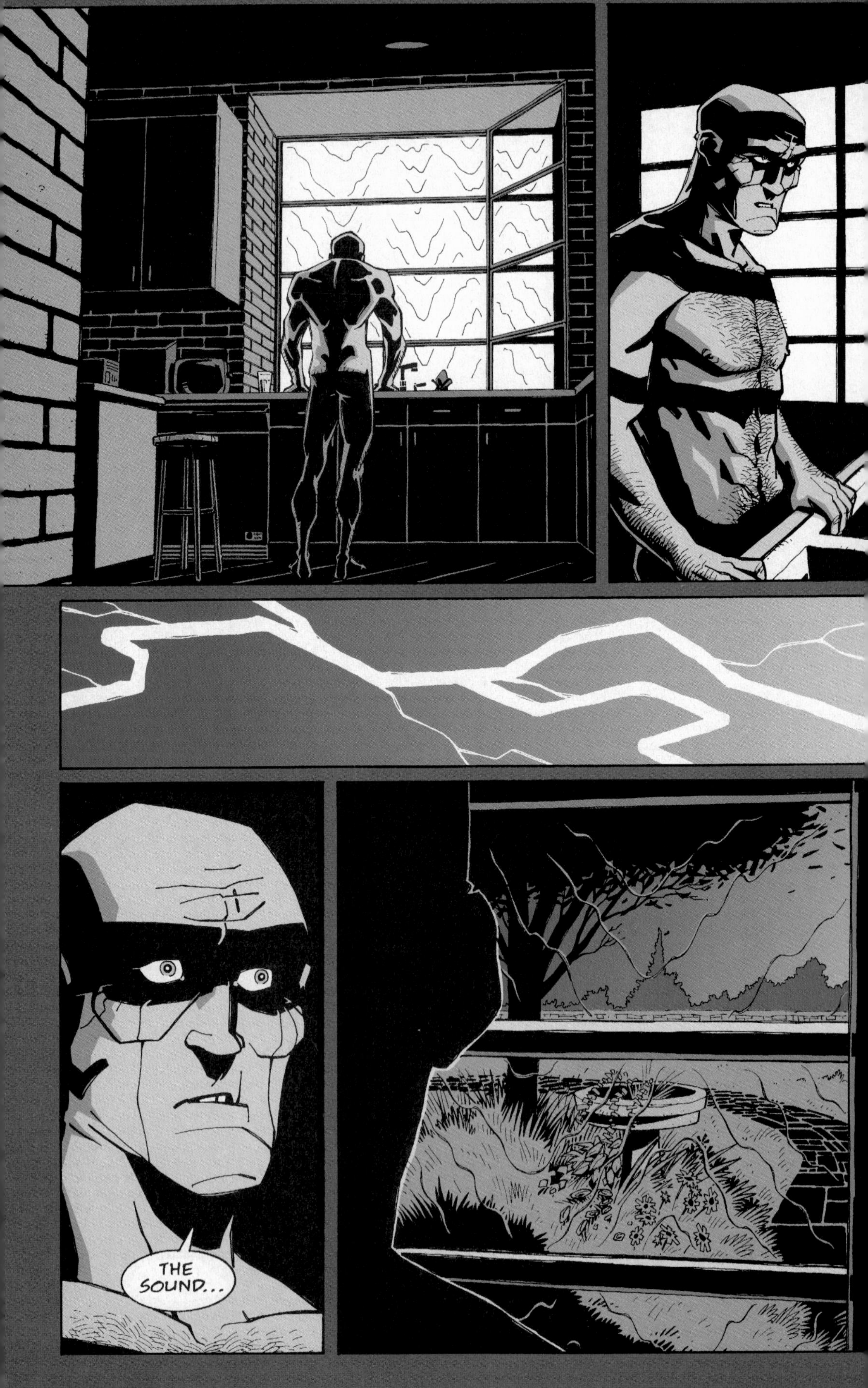
THE SOUND...

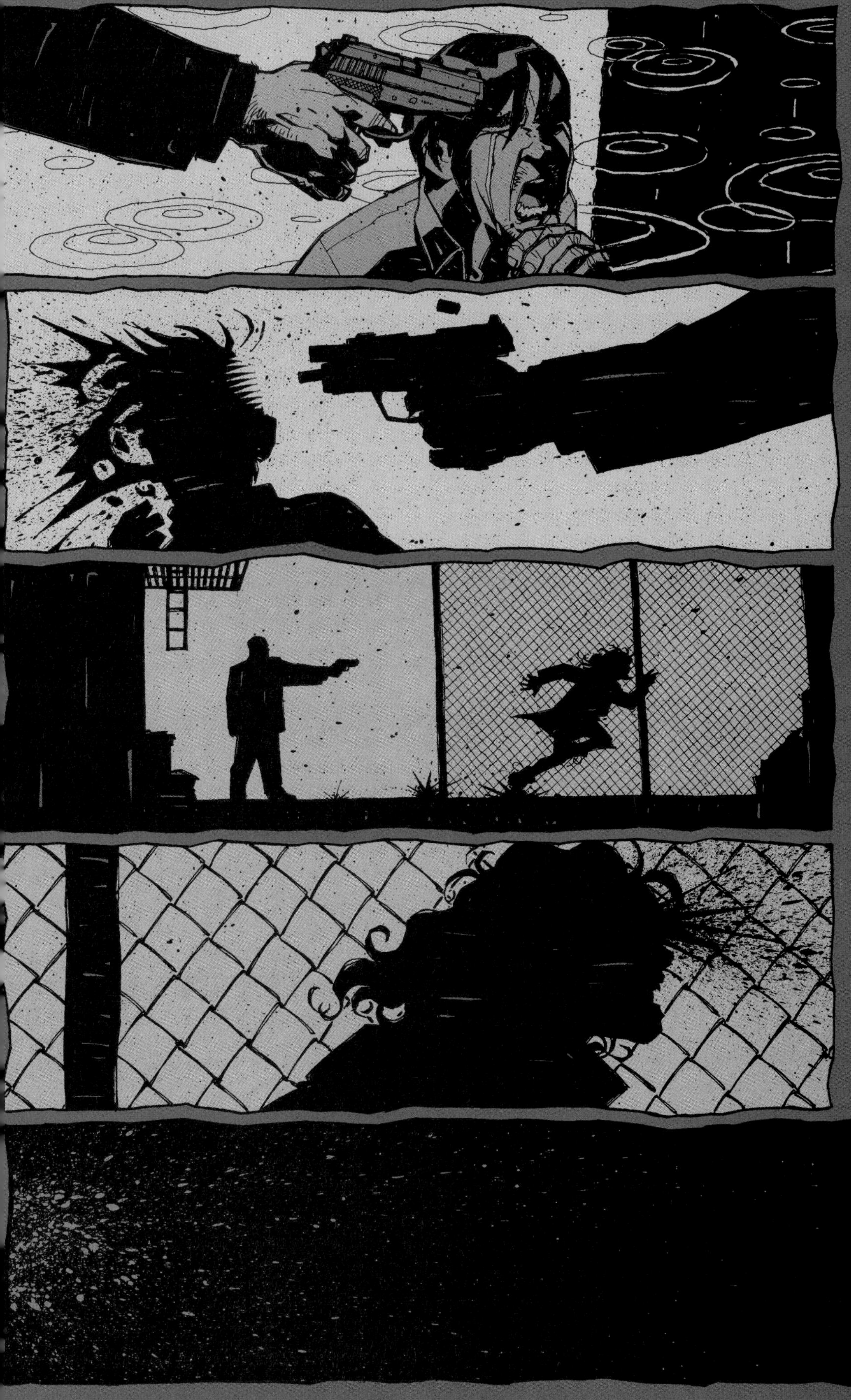

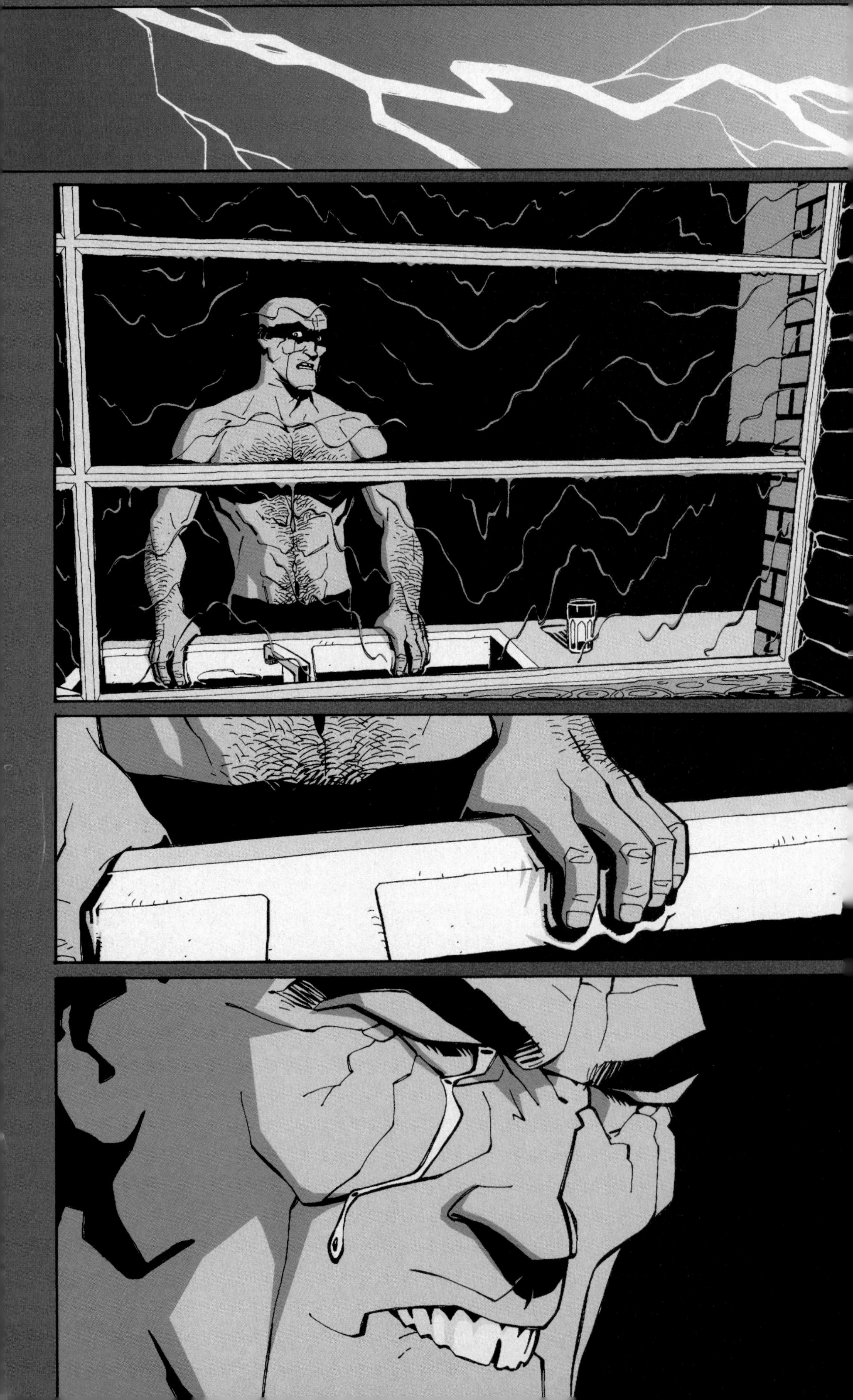

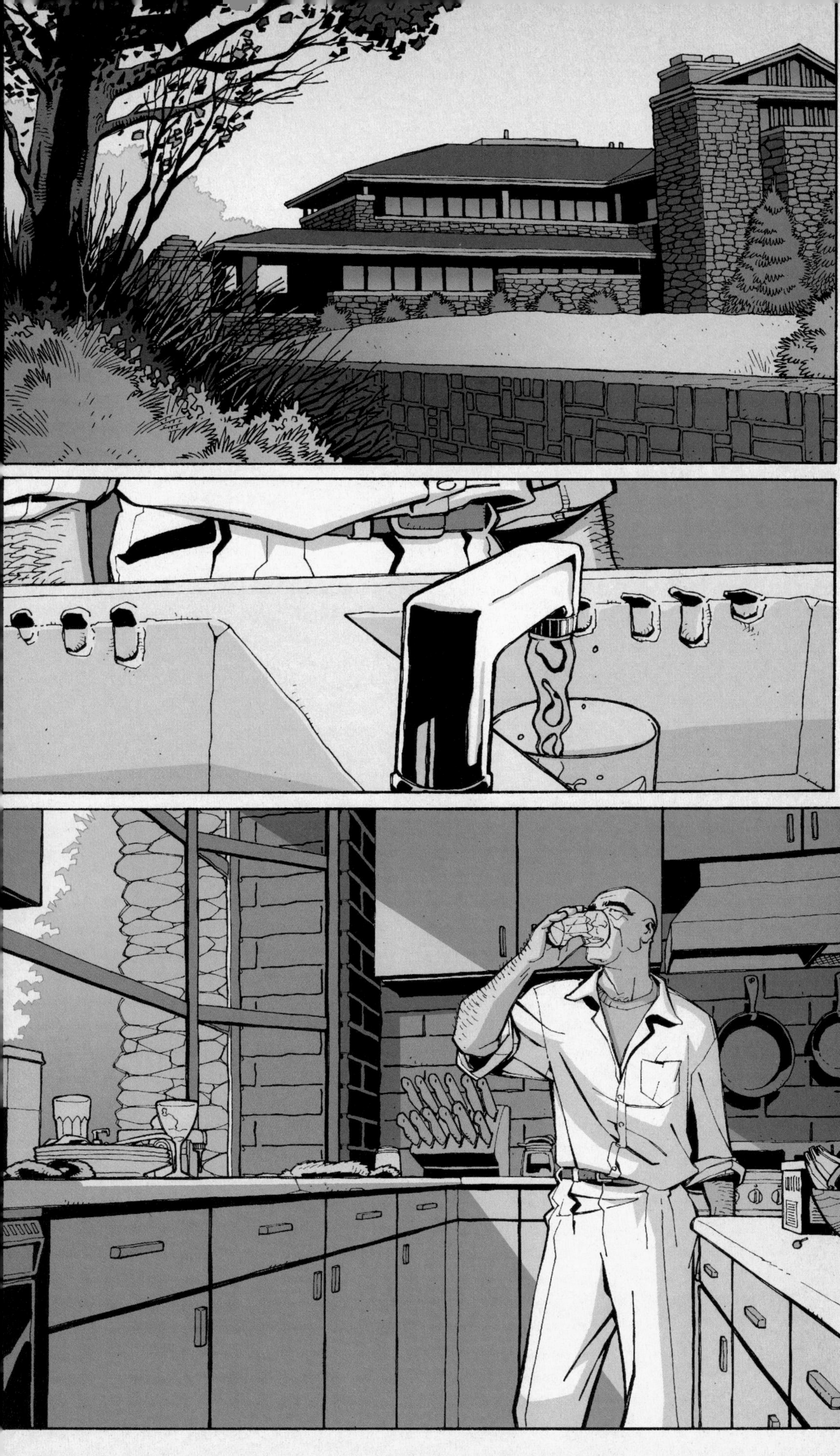

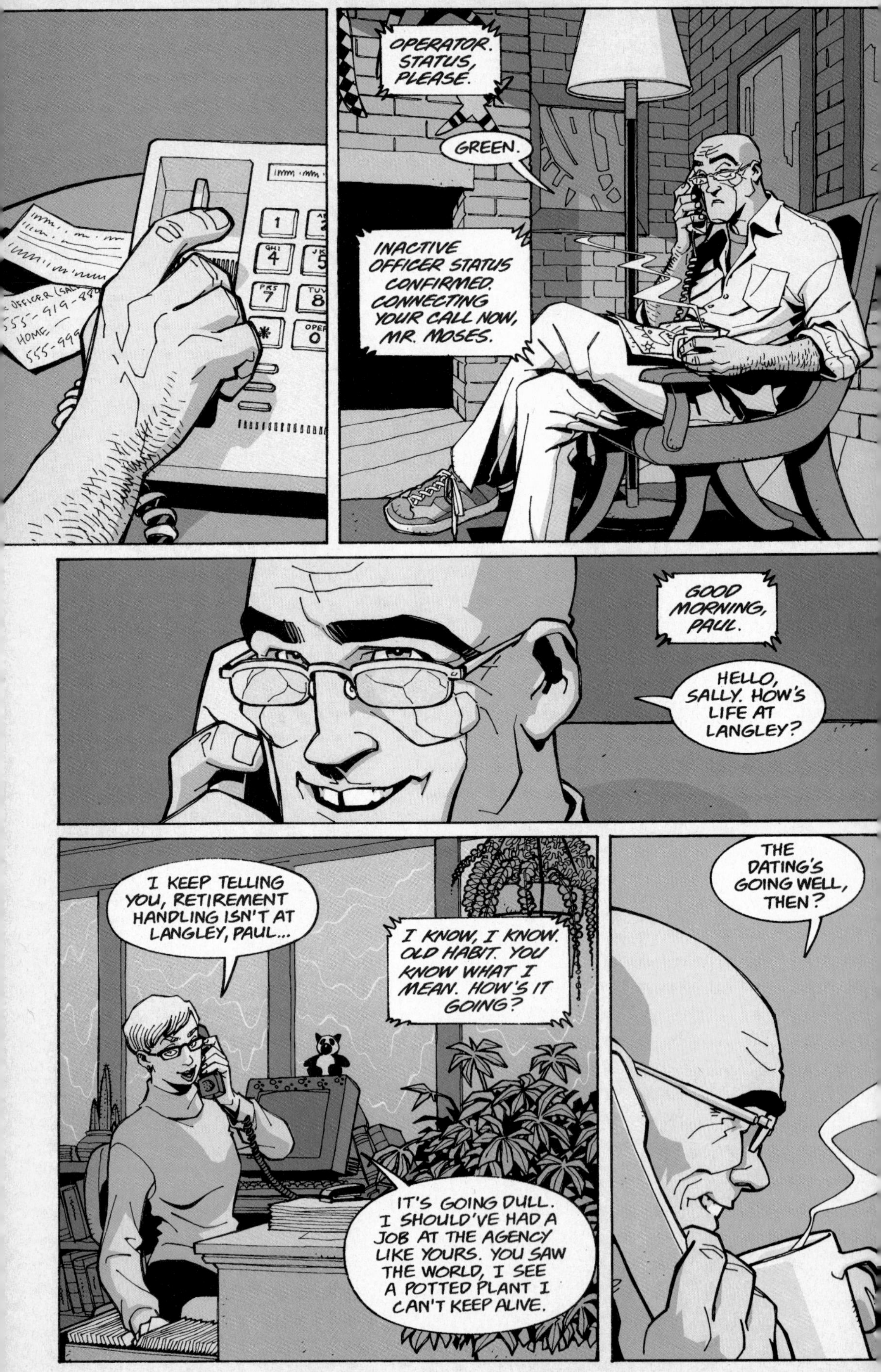
OPERATOR. STATUS, PLEASE.
GREEN.
INACTIVE OFFICER STATUS CONFIRMED. CONNECTING YOUR CALL NOW, MR. MOSES.
GOOD MORNING, PAUL.
HELLO, SALLY. HOW'S LIFE AT LANGLEY?
I KEEP TELLING YOU, RETIREMENT HANDLING ISN'T AT LANGLEY, PAUL...
I KNOW, I KNOW. OLD HABIT. YOU KNOW WHAT I MEAN. HOW'S IT GOING?
IT'S GOING DULL. I SHOULD'VE HAD A JOB AT THE AGENCY LIKE YOURS. YOU SAW THE WORLD, I SEE A POTTED PLANT I CAN'T KEEP ALIVE.
THE DATING'S GOING WELL, THEN?

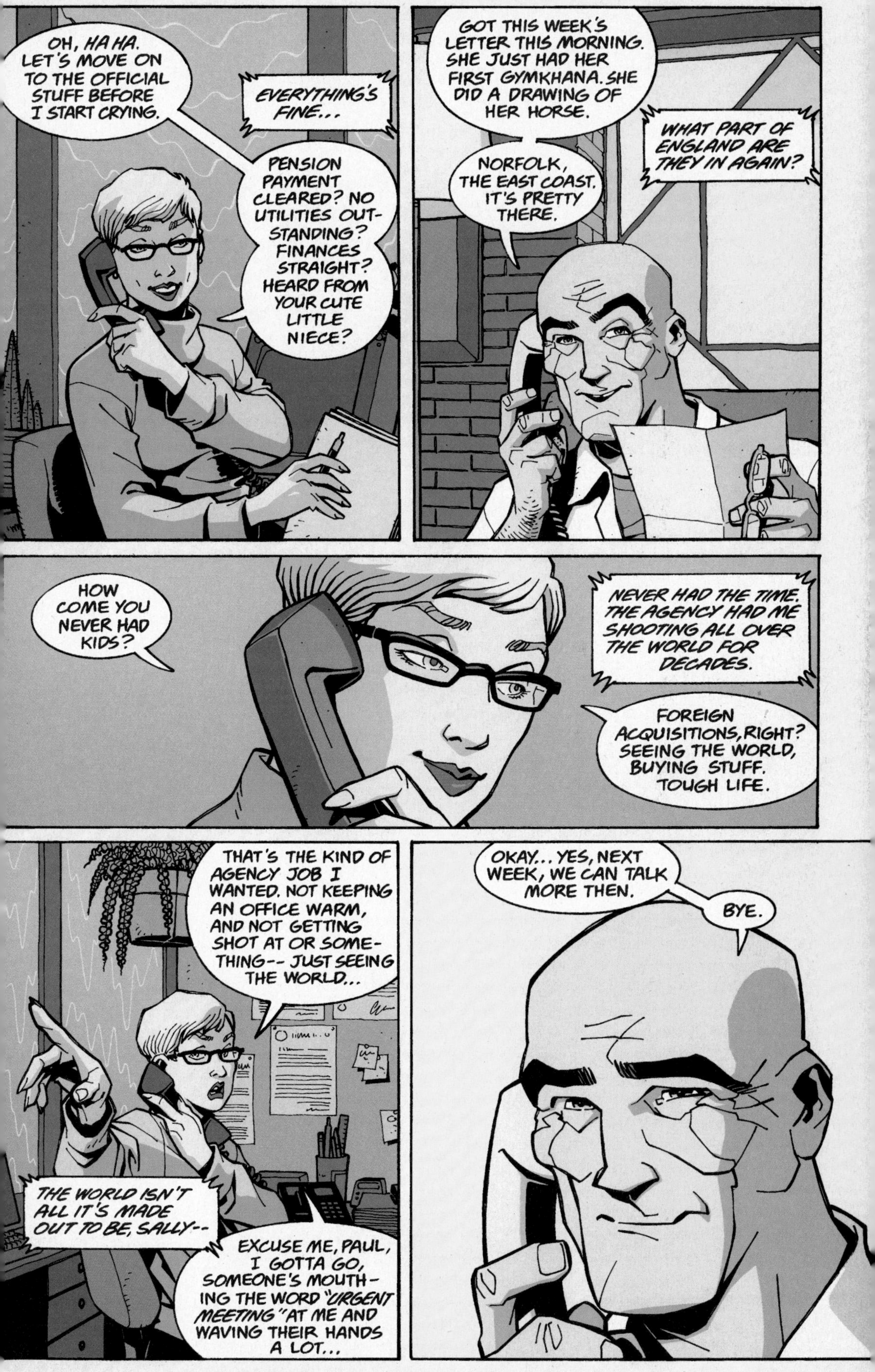
OH, HA HA. LET'S MOVE ON TO THE OFFICIAL STUFF BEFORE I START CRYING.
EVERYTHING'S FINE...
PENSION PAYMENT CLEARED? NO UTILITIES OUT-STANDING? FINANCES STRAIGHT? HEARD FROM YOUR CUTE LITTLE NIECE?
GOT THIS WEEK'S LETTER THIS MORNING. SHE JUST HAD HER FIRST GYMKHANA. SHE DID A DRAWING OF HER HORSE.
WHAT PART OF ENGLAND ARE THEY IN AGAIN?
NORFOLK, THE EAST COAST. IT'S PRETTY THERE.
HOW COME YOU NEVER HAD KIDS?
NEVER HAD THE TIME. THE AGENCY HAD ME SHOOTING ALL OVER THE WORLD FOR DECADES.
FOREIGN ACQUISITIONS, RIGHT? SEEING THE WORLD, BUYING STUFF. TOUGH LIFE.
THAT'S THE KIND OF AGENCY JOB I WANTED. NOT KEEPING AN OFFICE WARM, AND NOT GETTING SHOT AT OR SOME-THING-- JUST SEEING THE WORLD...
THE WORLD ISN'T ALL IT'S MADE OUT TO BE, SALLY--
EXCUSE ME, PAUL, I GOTTA GO, SOMEONE'S MOUTH-ING THE WORD "URGENT MEETING" AT ME AND WAVING THEIR HANDS A LOT...
OKAY... YES, NEXT WEEK, WE CAN TALK MORE THEN.
BYE.

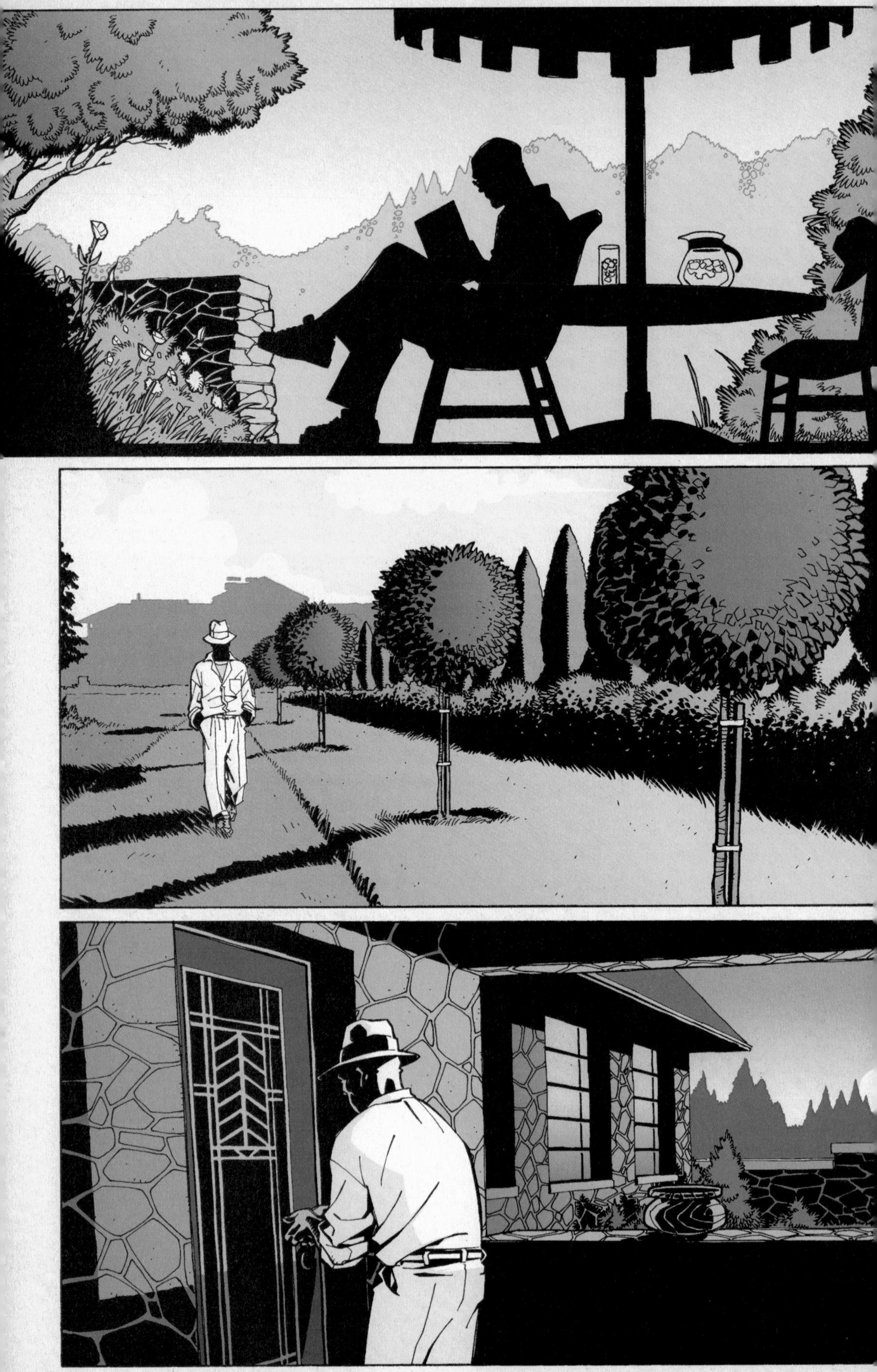

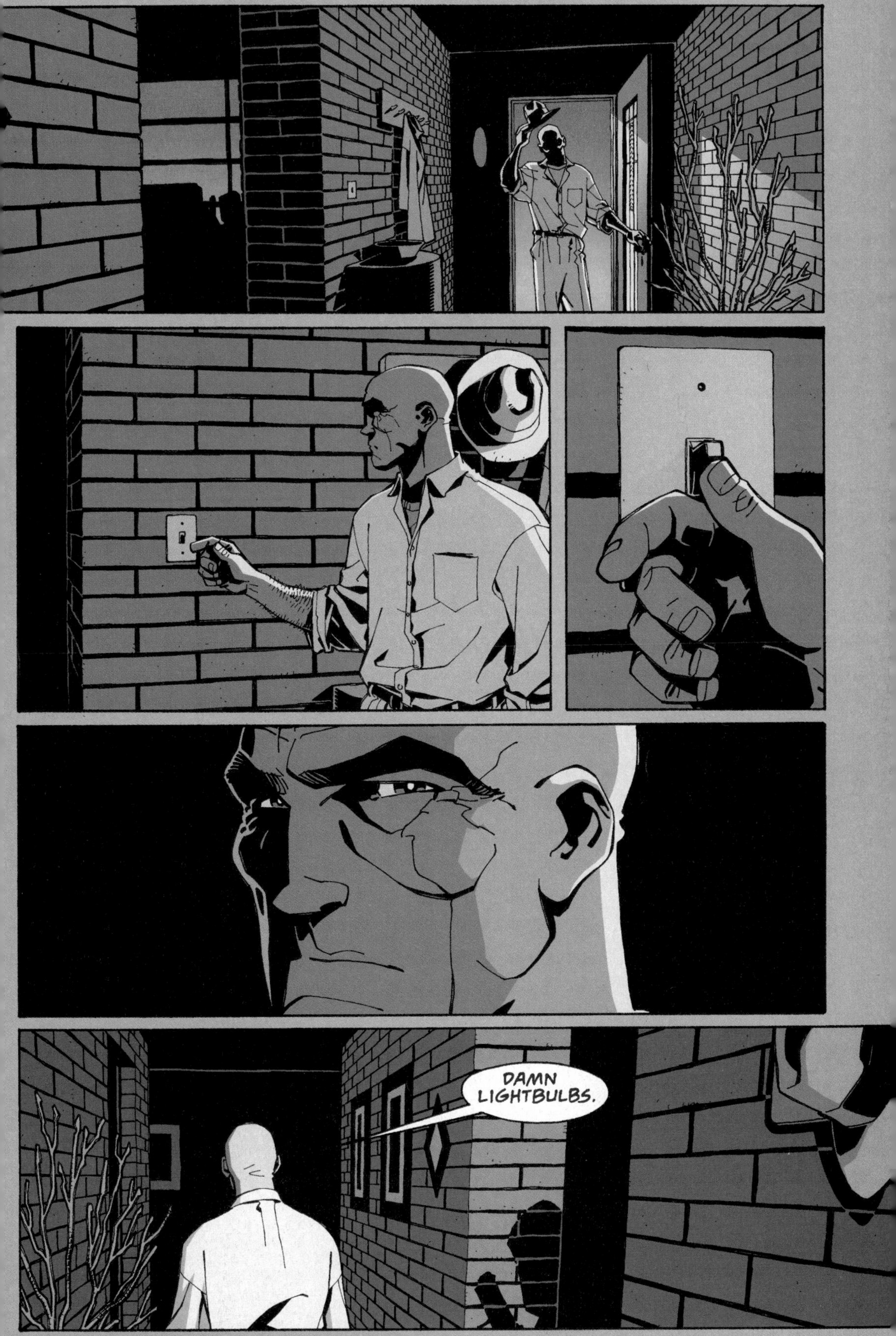
DAMN LIGHTBULBS.

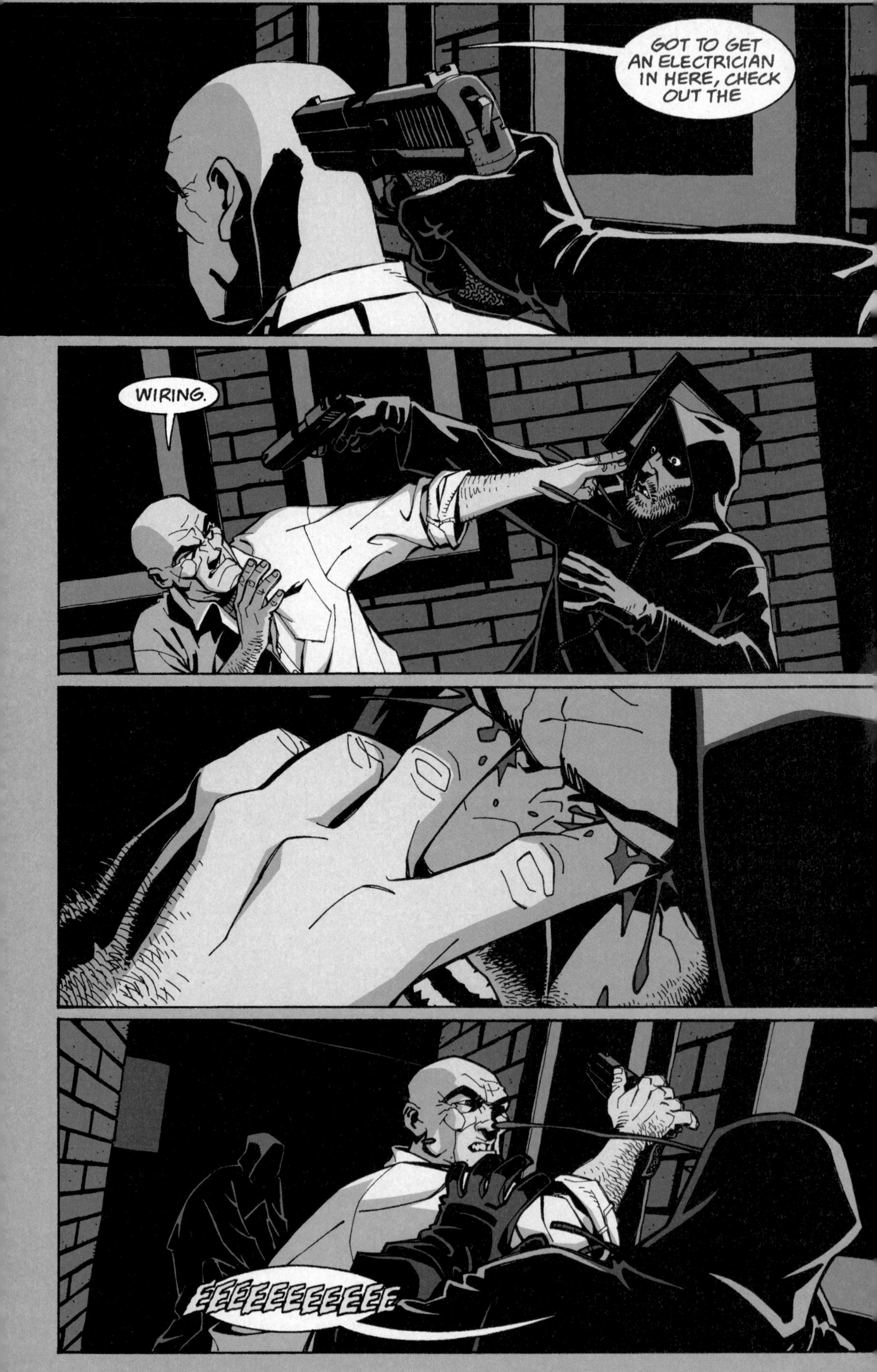
GOT TO GET AN ELECTRICIAN IN HERE, CHECK OUT THE
WIRING.
EEEEEEEEEEEE

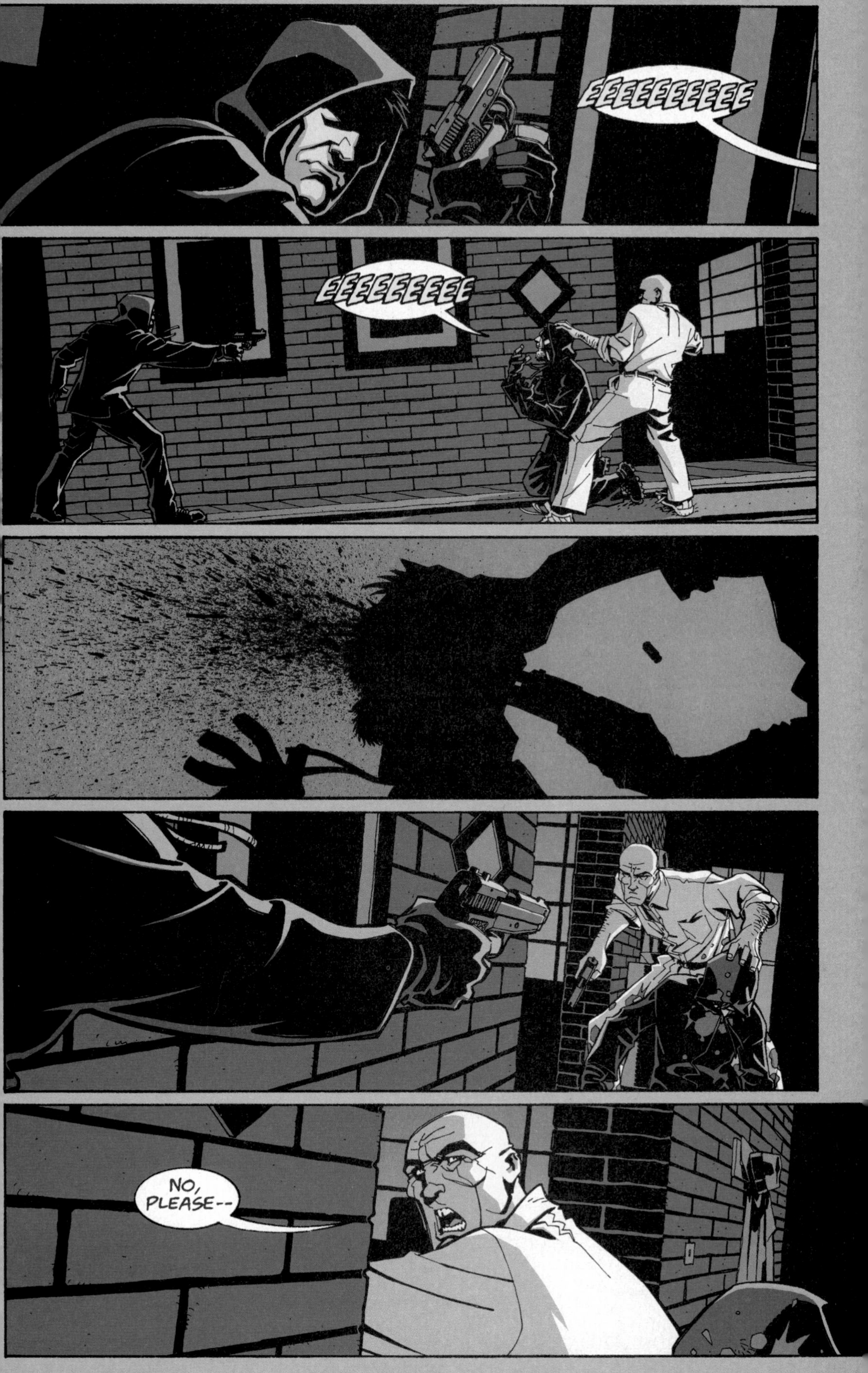
EEEEEEEEEEE
EEEEEEEEEE
NO, PLEASE--

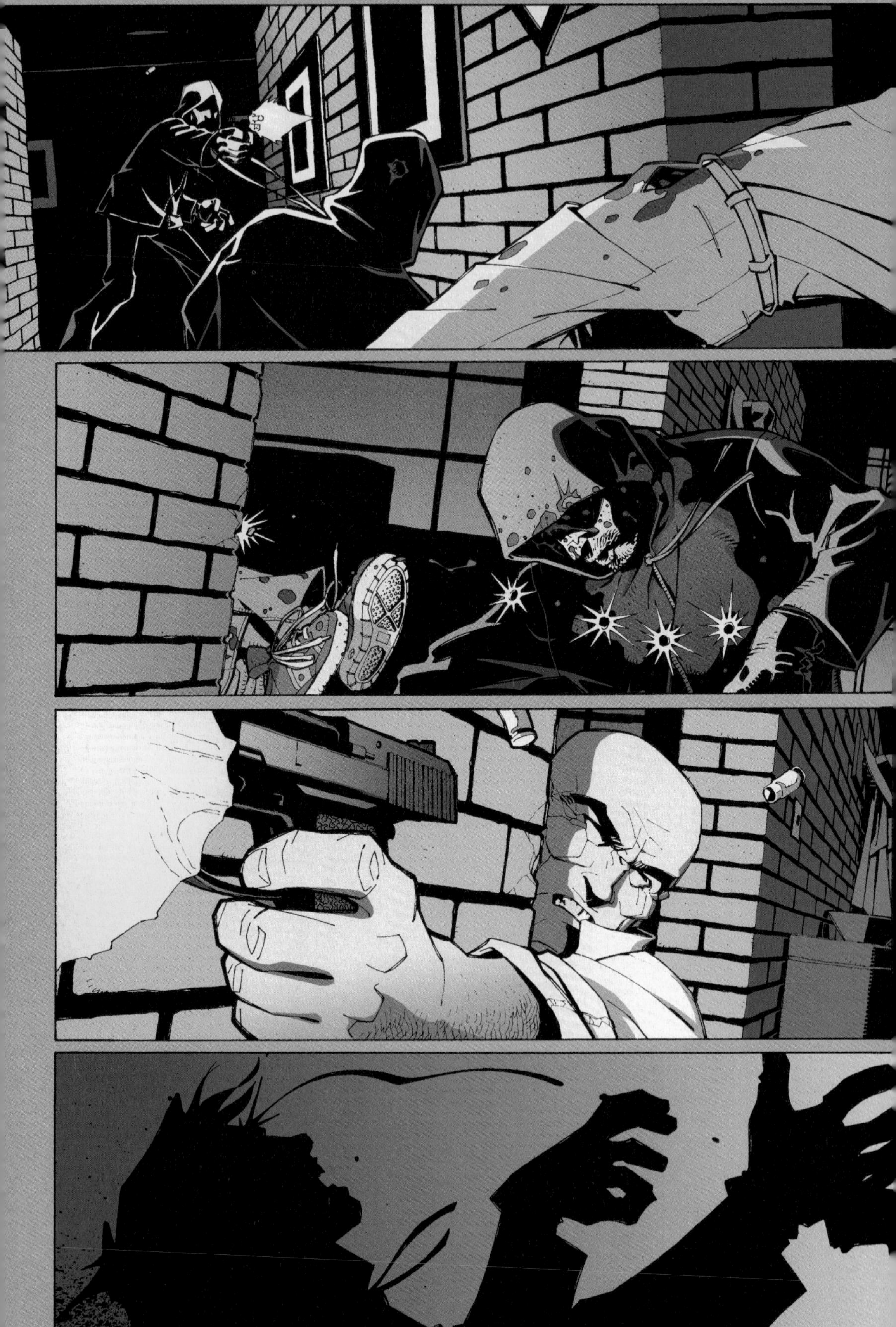

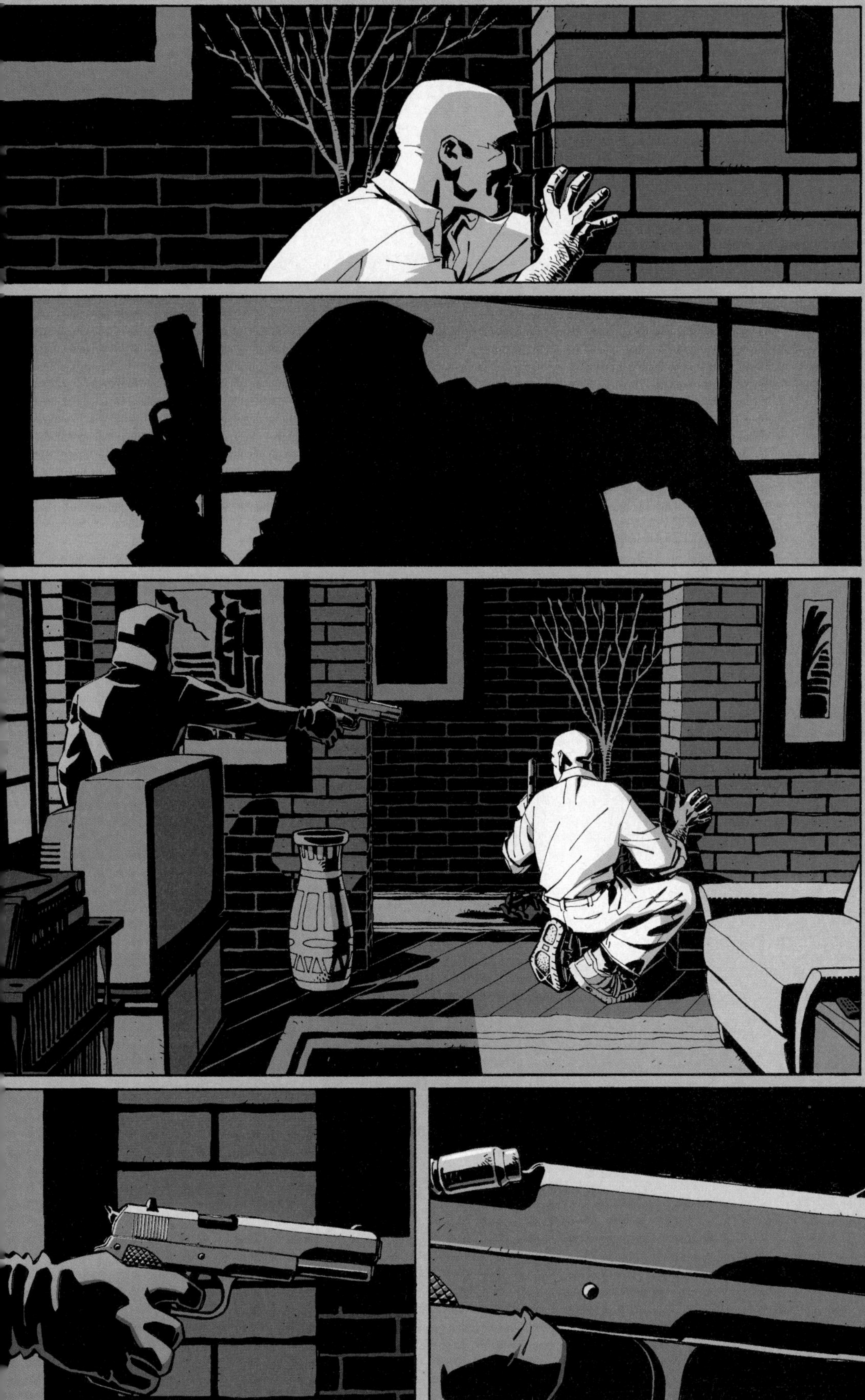

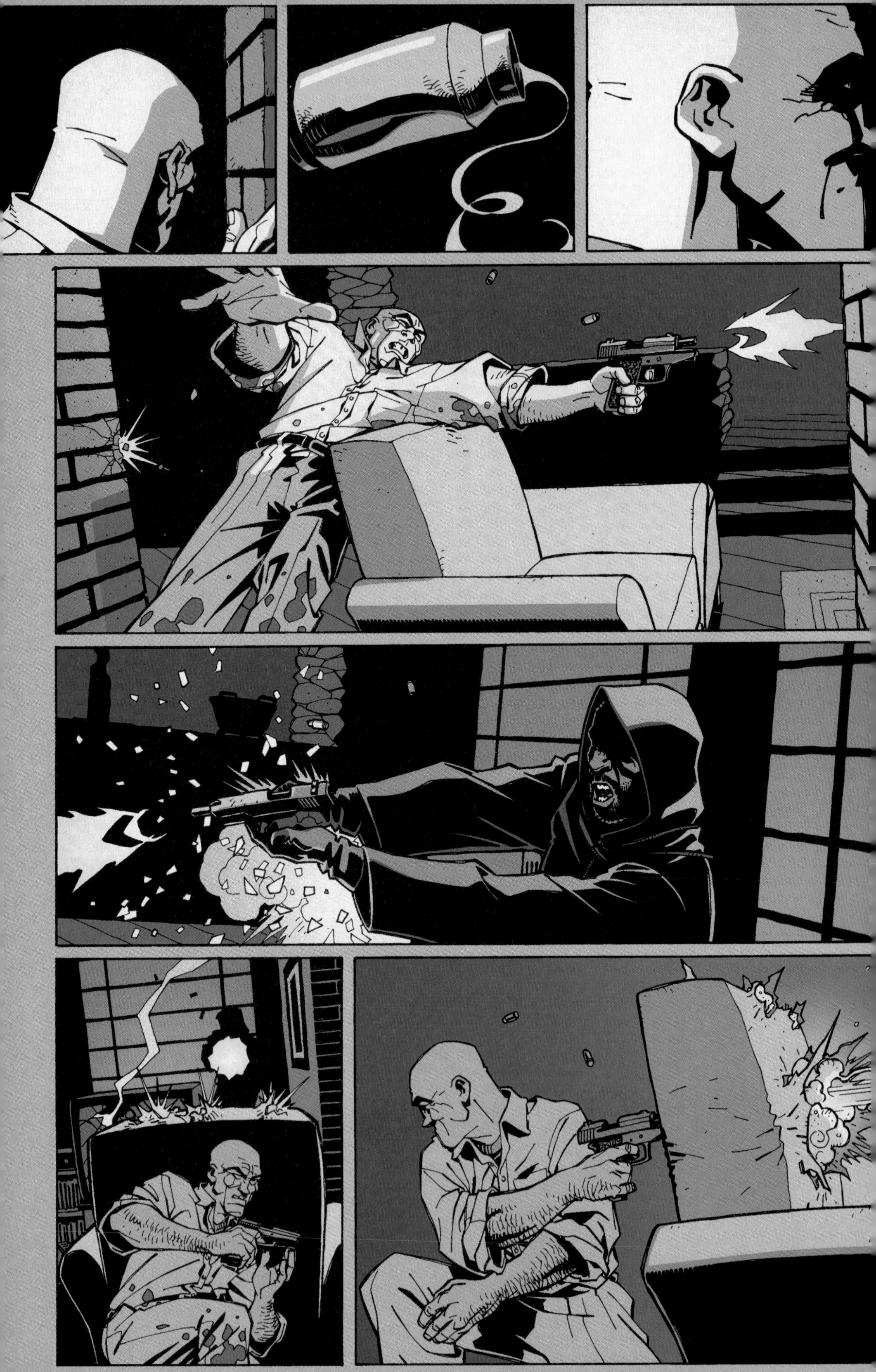

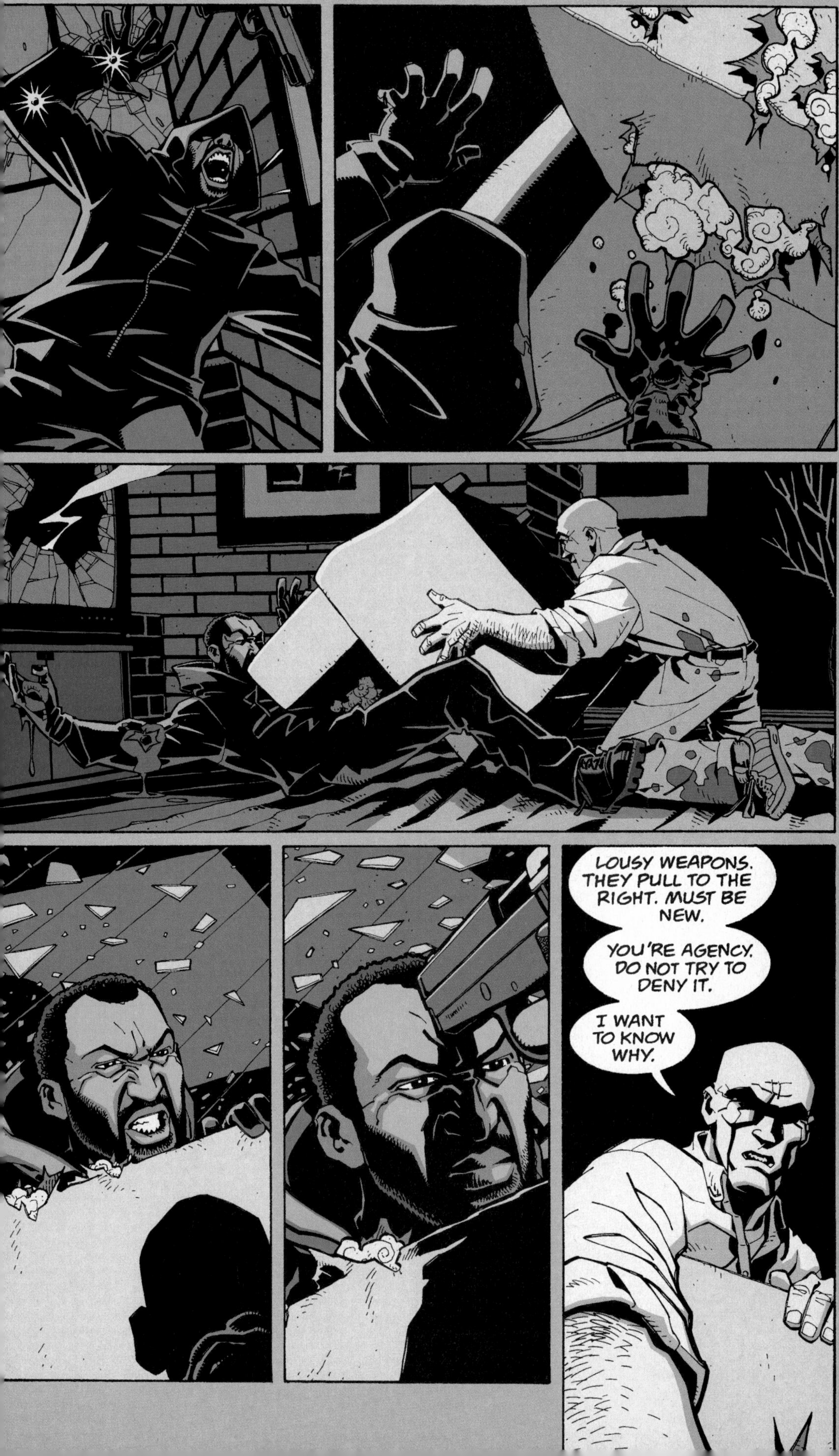
LOUSY WEAPONS. THEY PULL TO THE RIGHT. MUST BE NEW.
YOU'RE AGENCY. DO NOT TRY TO DENY IT.
I WANT TO KNOW WHY.

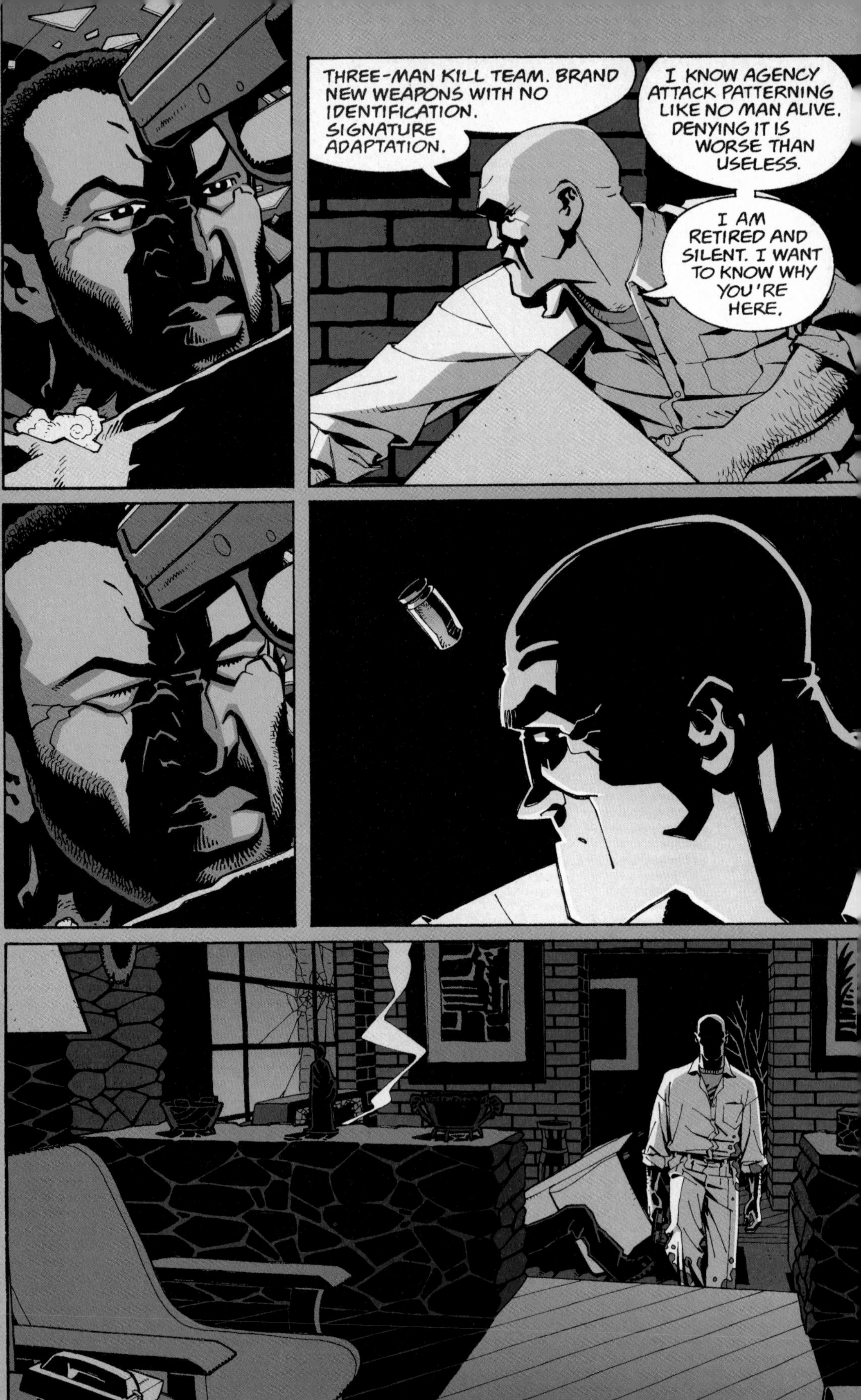
THREE-MAN KILL TEAM. BRAND NEW WEAPONS WITH NO IDENTIFICATION. SIGNATURE ADAPTATION.
I KNOW AGENCY ATTACK PATTERNING LIKE NO MAN ALIVE. DENYING IT IS WORSE THAN USELESS.
I AM RETIRED AND SILENT. I WANT TO KNOW WHY YOU'RE HERE.

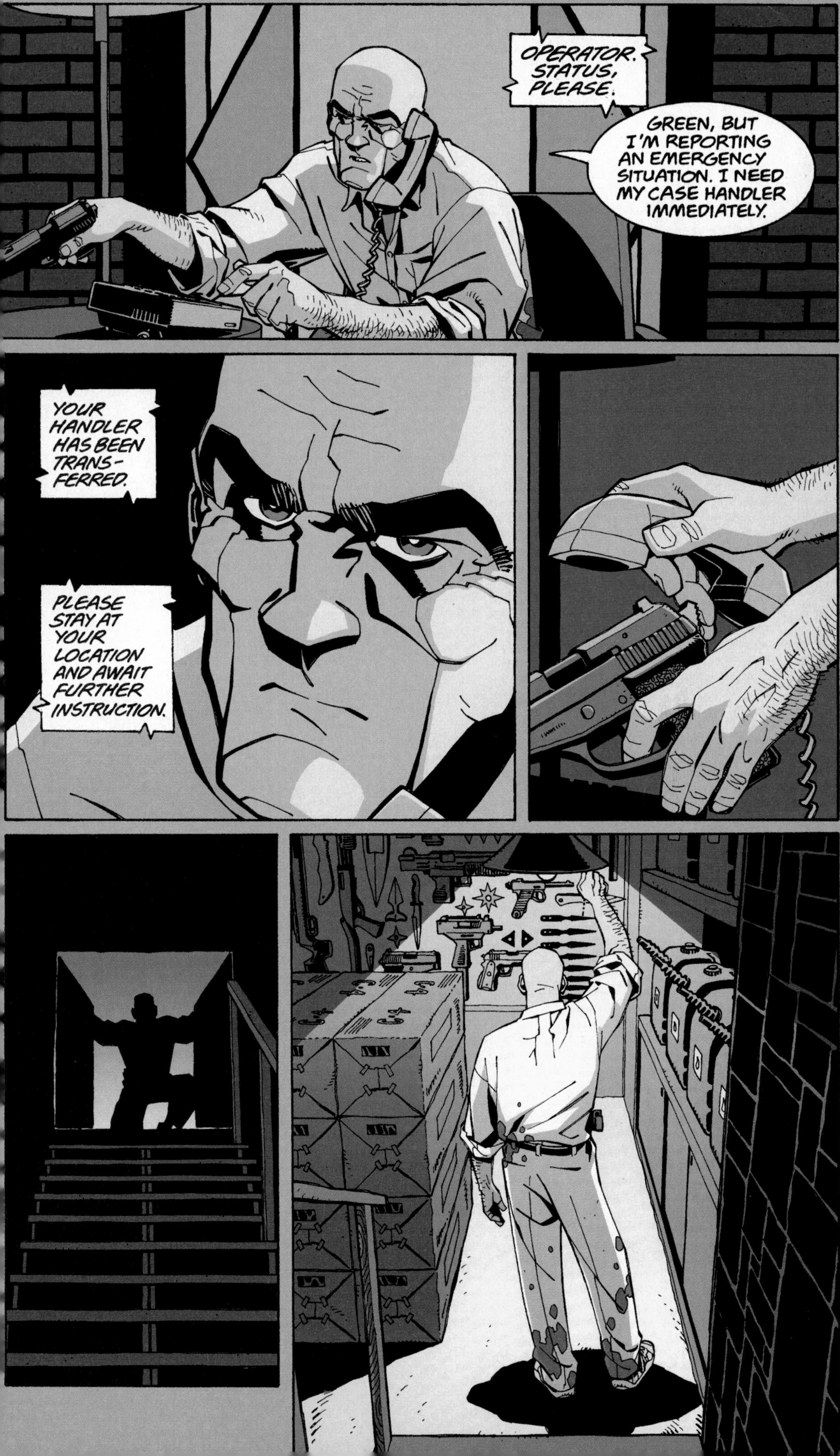
OPERATOR. STATUS, PLEASE.
GREEN, BUT I'M REPORTING AN EMERGENCY SITUATION. I NEED MY CASE HANDLER IMMEDIATELY.
YOUR HANDLER HAS BEEN TRANS-FERRED.
PLEASE STAY AT YOUR LOCATION AND AWAIT FURTHER INSTRUCTION.

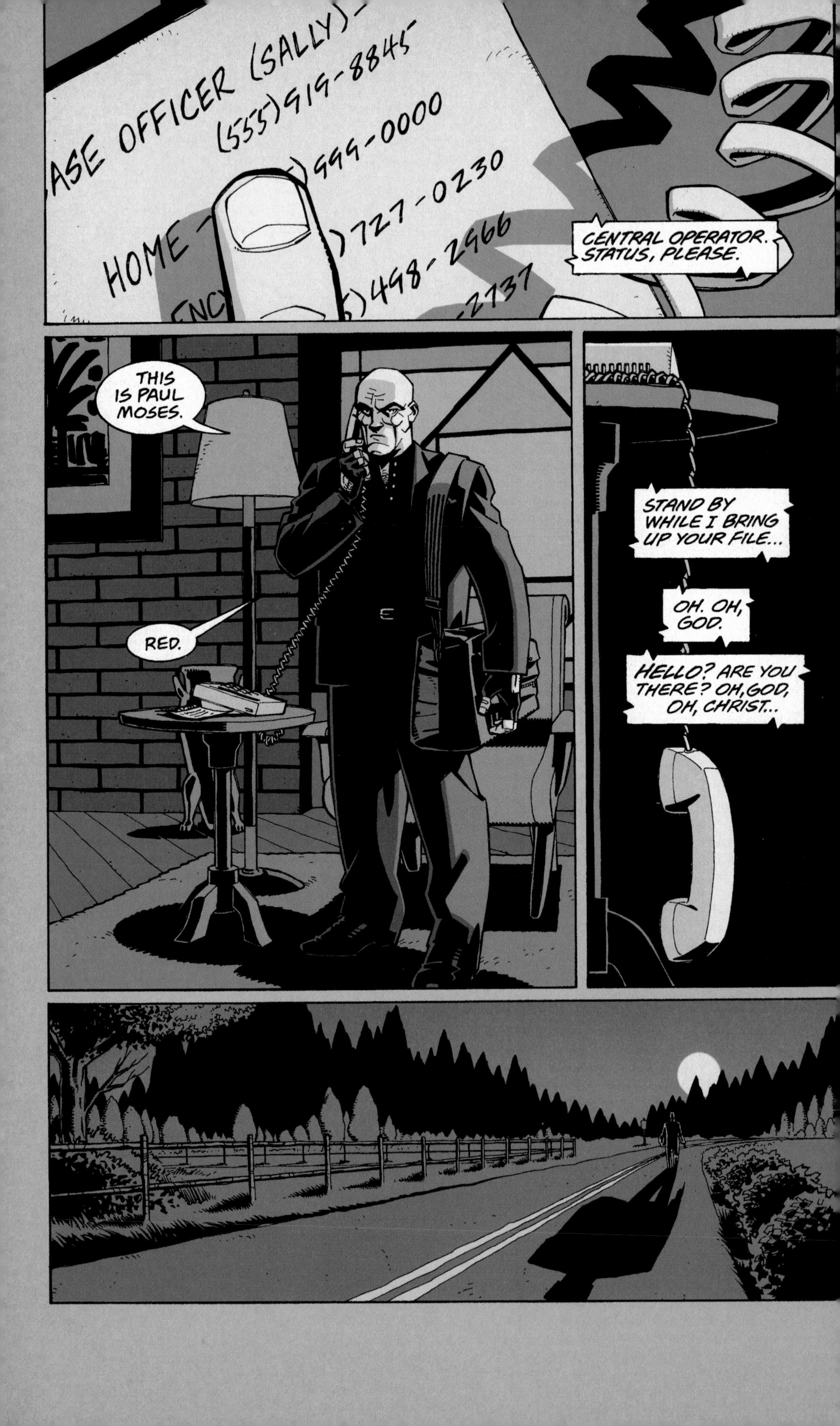
ASE OFFICER (SALLY)-
(555)919-8845
999-0000
HOME
727-0230
498-2966
2737
CENTRAL OPERATOR. STATUS, PLEASE.
THIS IS PAUL MOSES.
RED.
STAND BY WHILE I BRING UP YOUR FILE...
OH. OH, GOD.
HELLO? ARE YOU THERE? OH,GOD, OH, CHRIST...

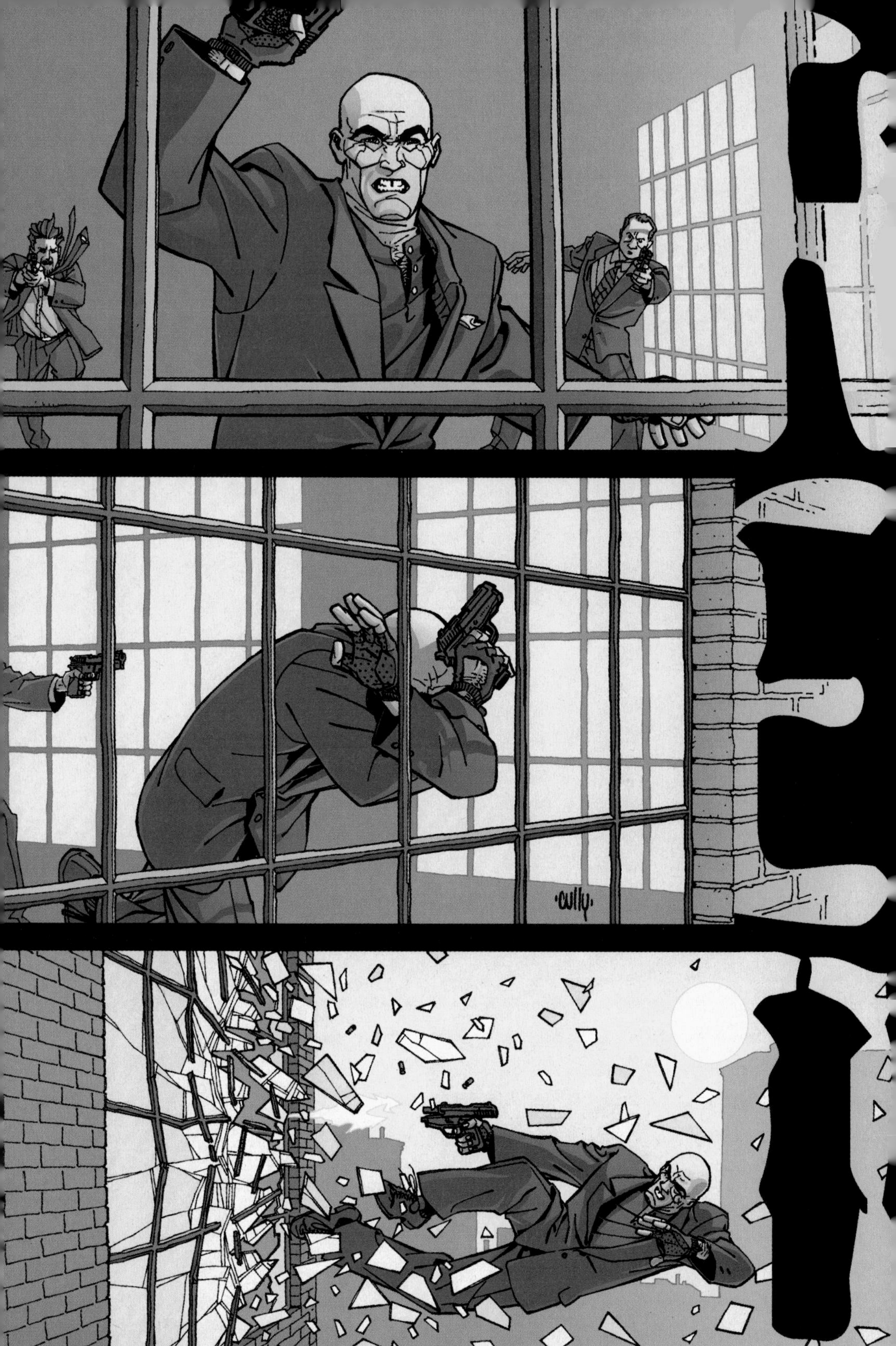
cully

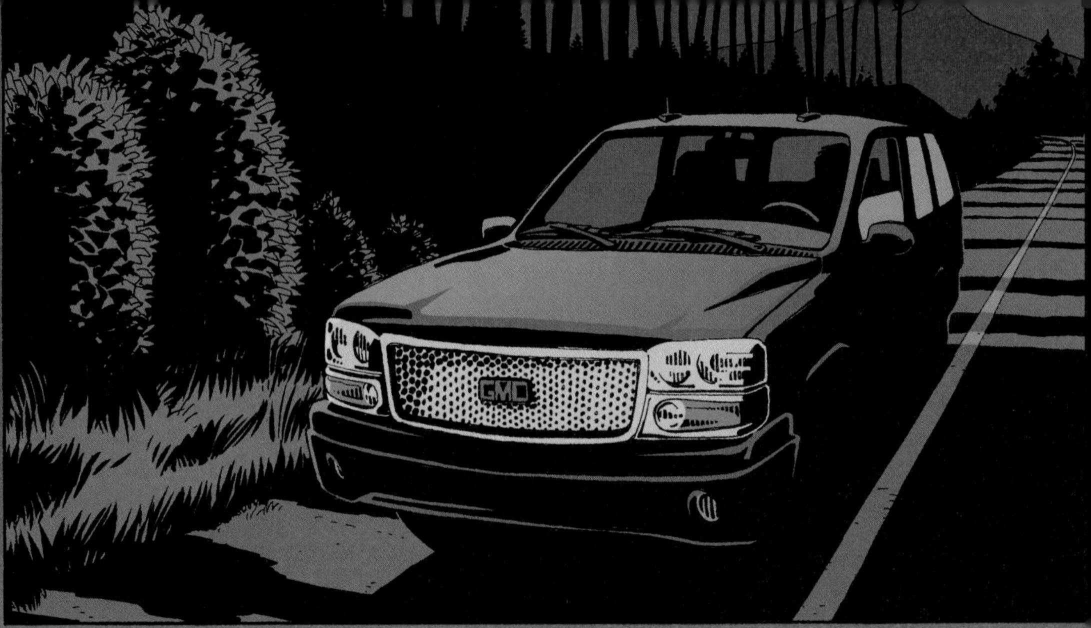

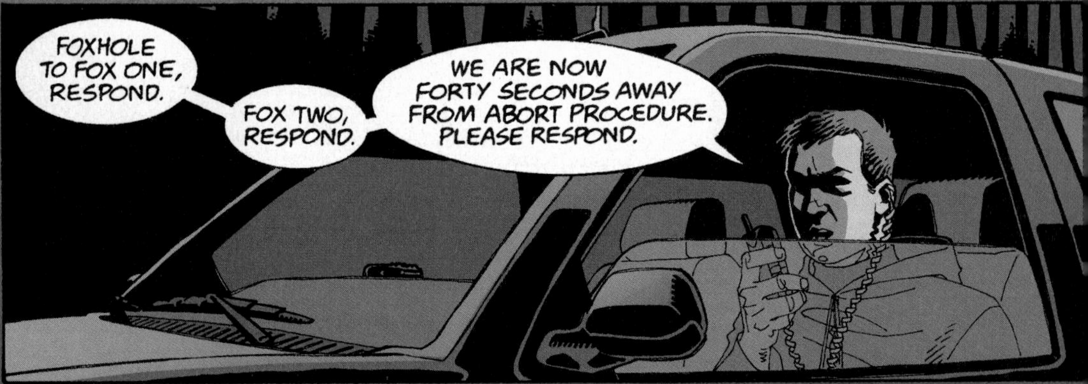
FOXHOLE TO FOX ONE, RESPOND.
FOX TWO, RESPOND.
WE ARE NOW FORTY SECONDS AWAY FROM ABORT PROCEDURE. PLEASE RESPOND.

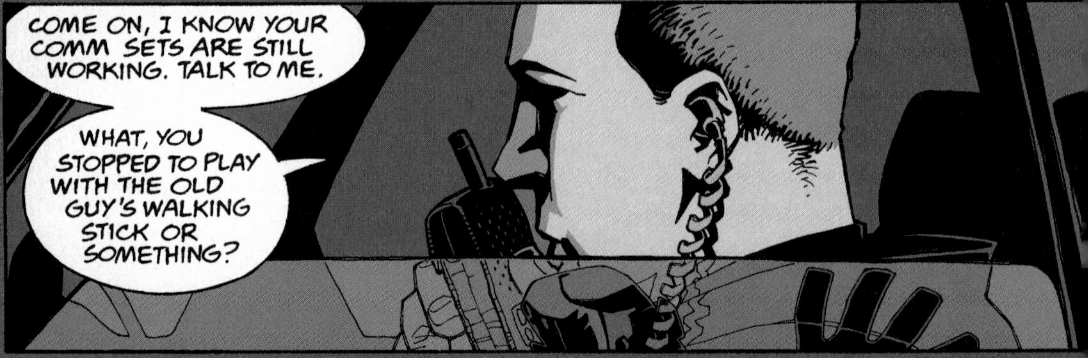
COME ON, I KNOW YOUR COMM SETS ARE STILL WORKING. TALK TO ME.
WHAT, YOU STOPPED TO PLAY WITH THE OLD GUY'S WALKING STICK OR SOMETHING?

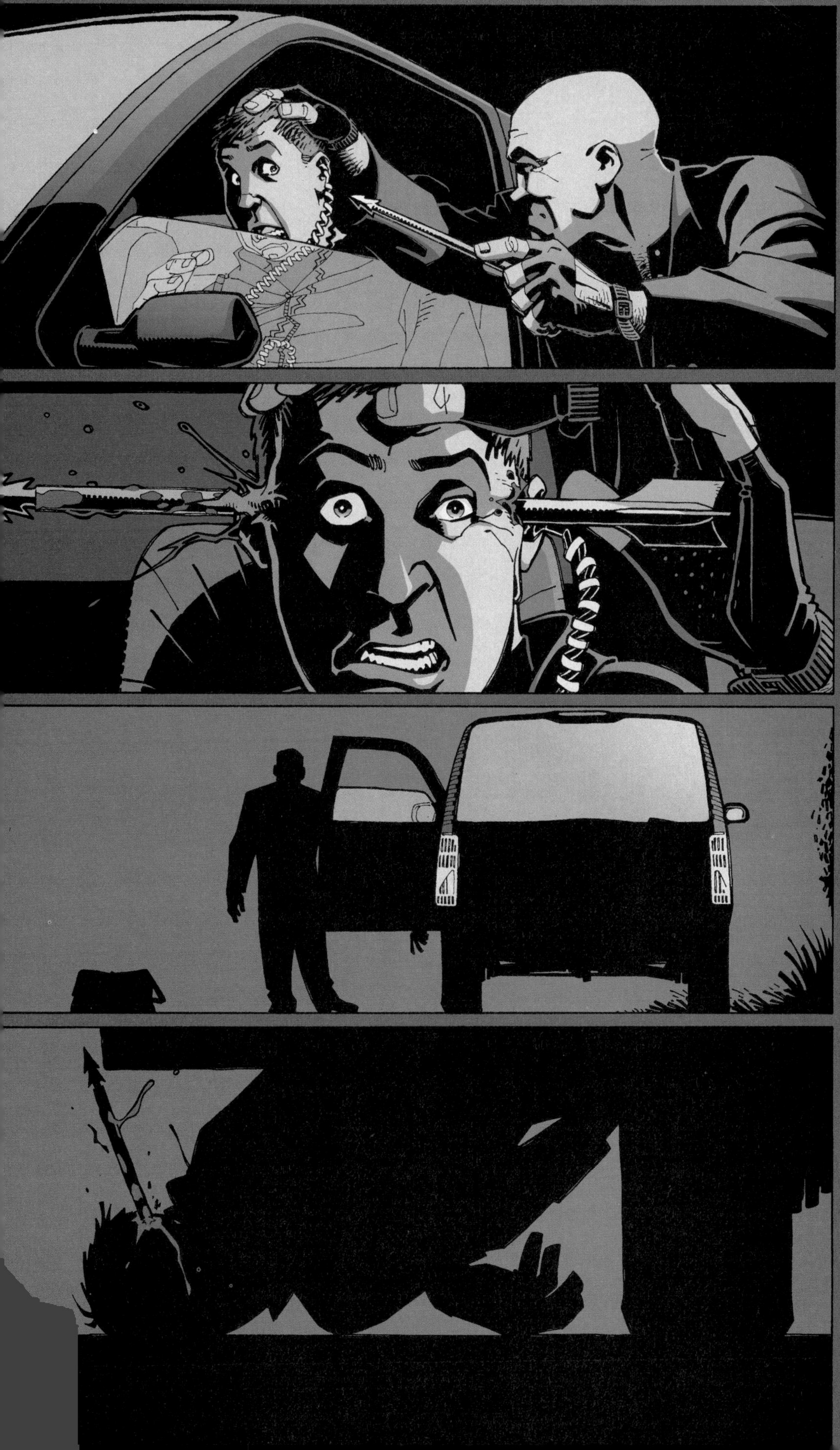

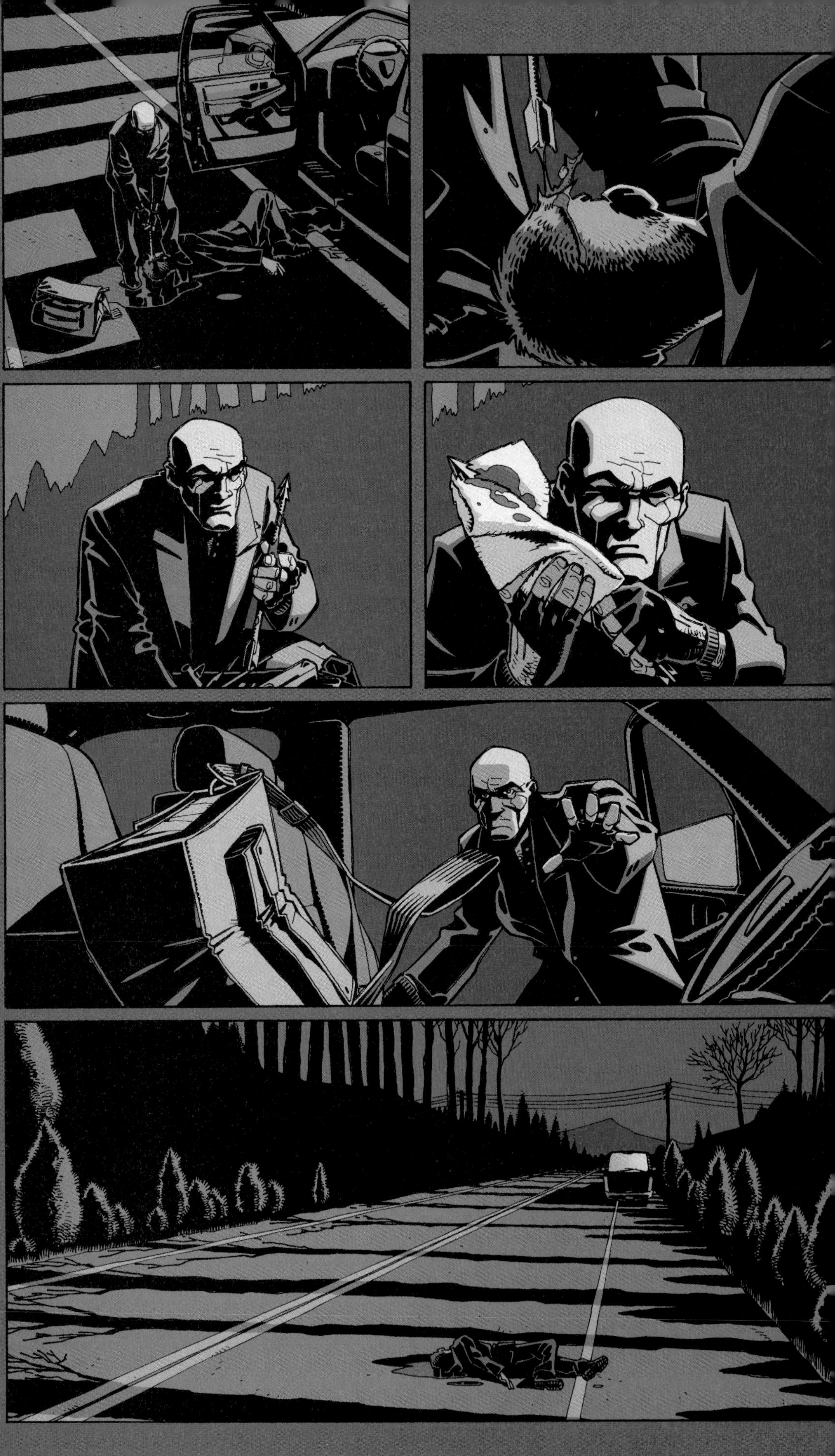

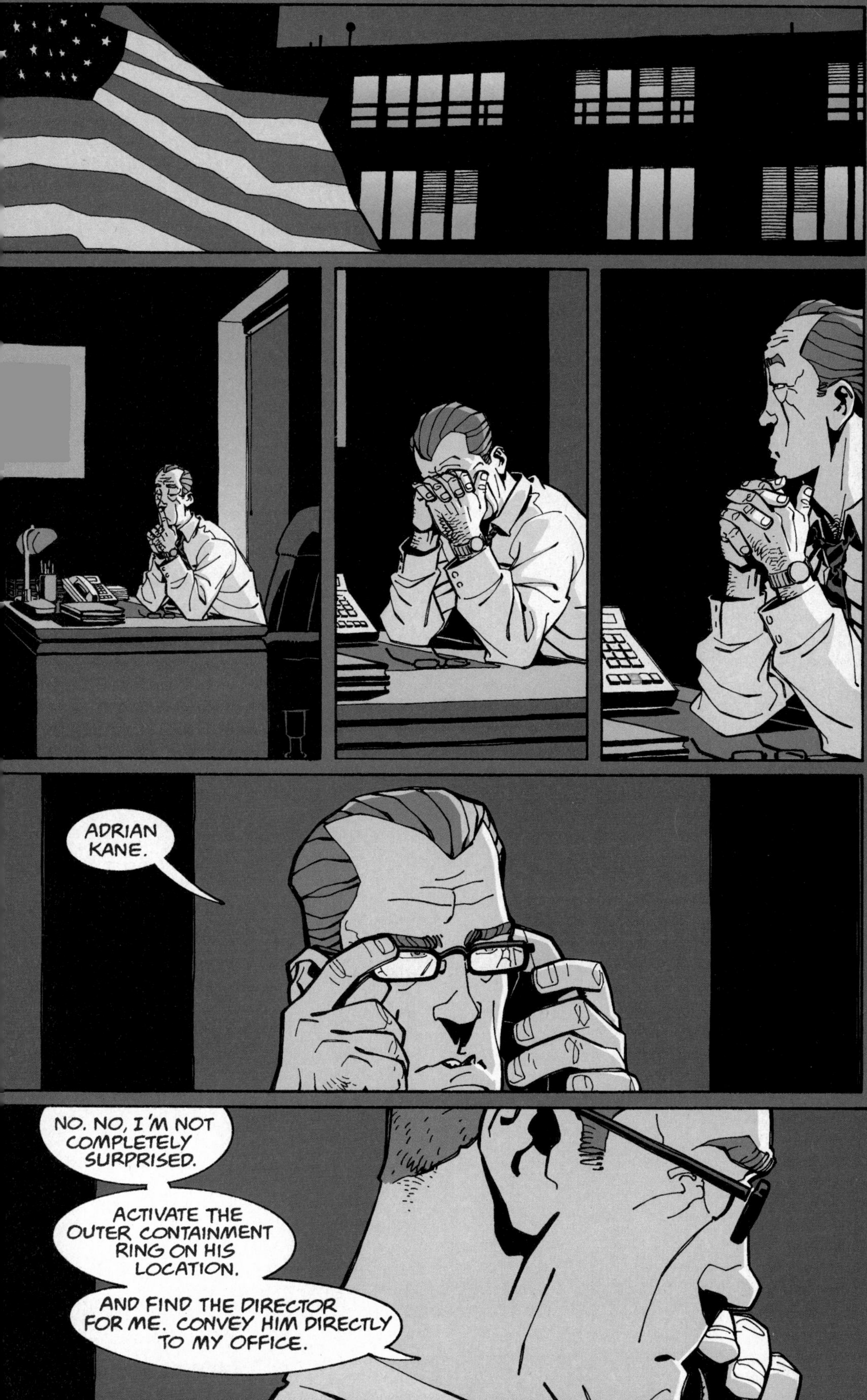
ADRIAN KANE.
NO. NO, I'M NOT COMPLETELY SURPRISED.
ACTIVATE THE OUTER CONTAINMENT RING ON HIS LOCATION.
AND FIND THE DIRECTOR FOR ME. CONVEY HIM DIRECTLY TO MY OFFICE.

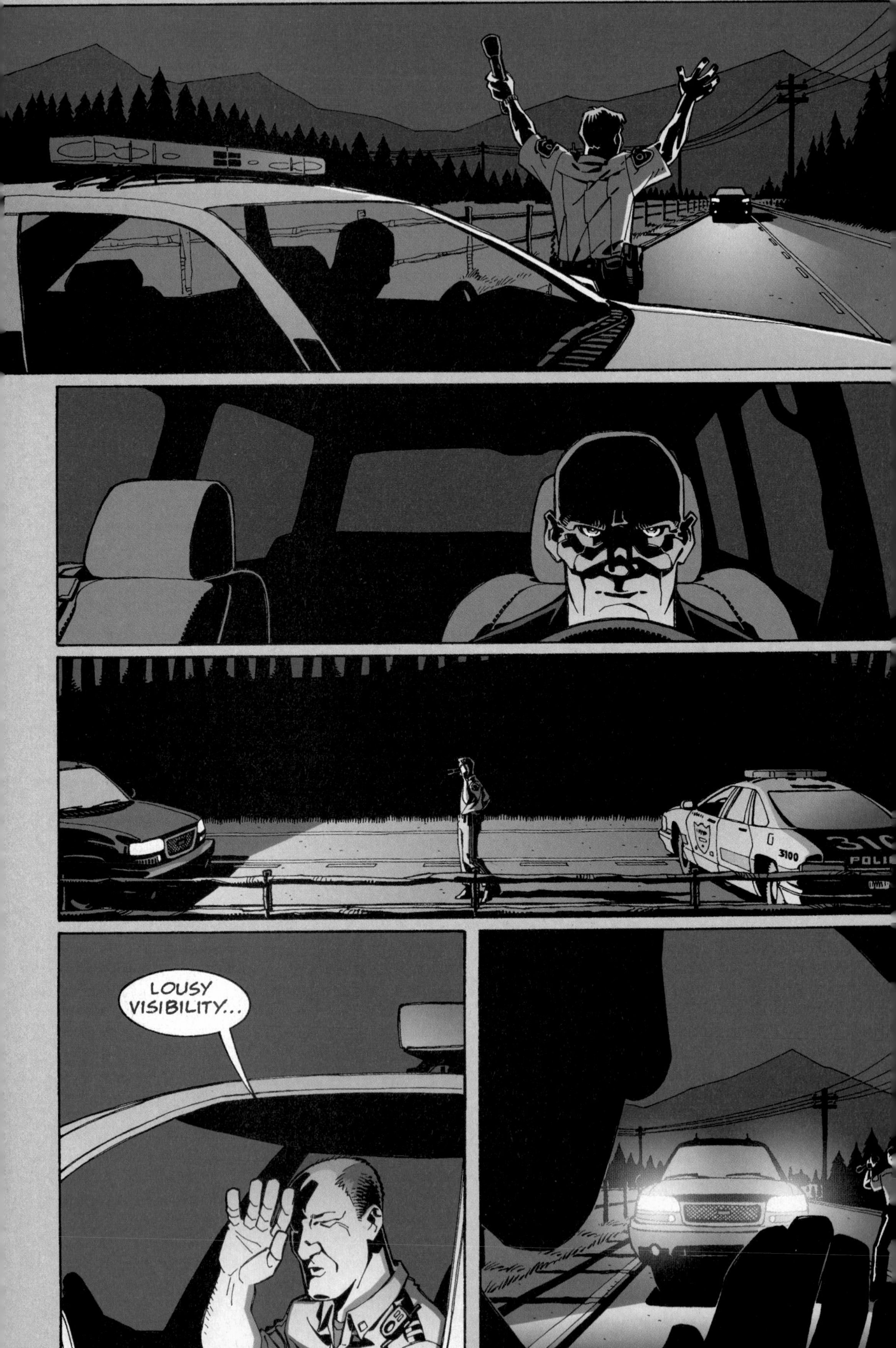
LOUSY VISIBILITY...

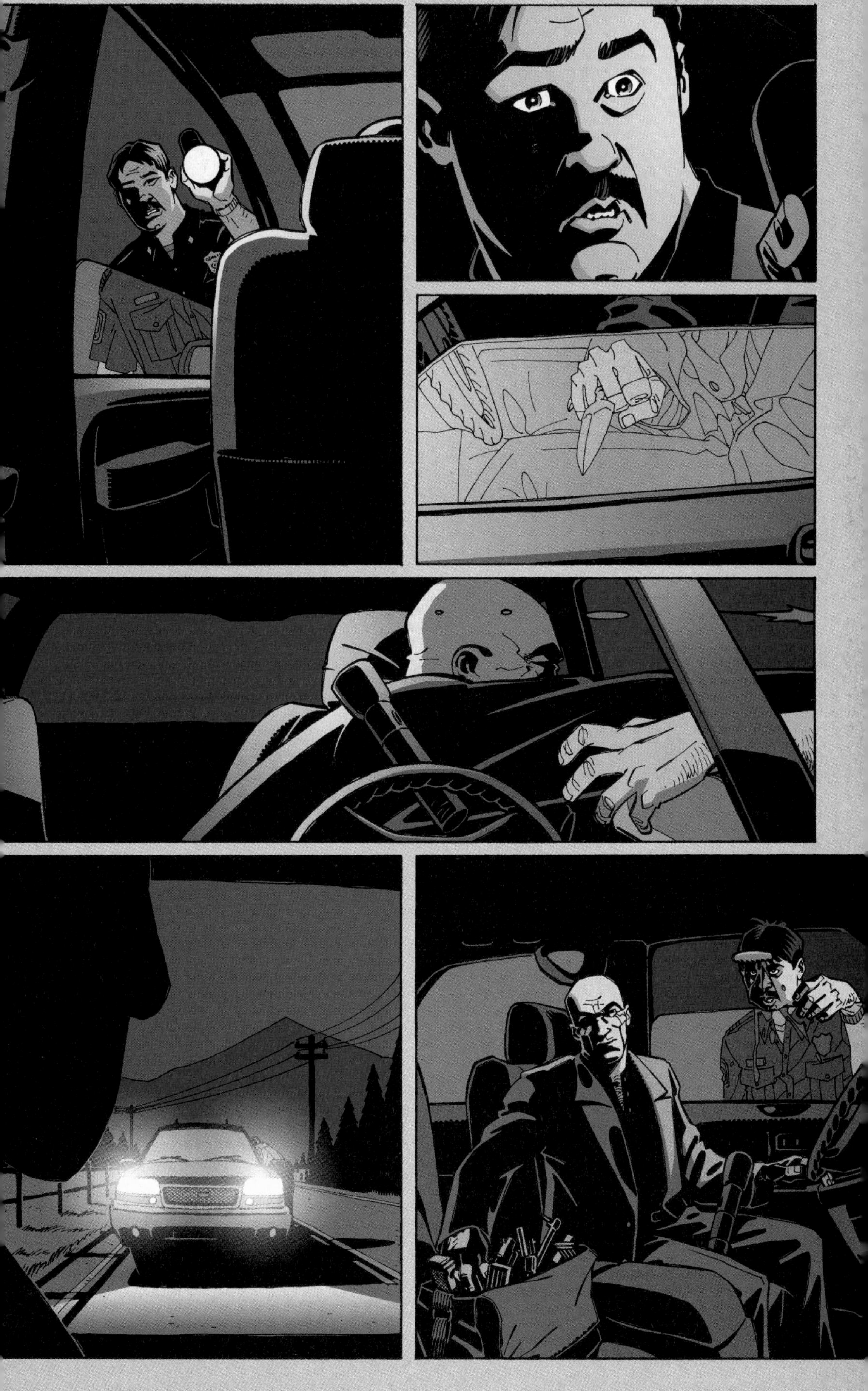

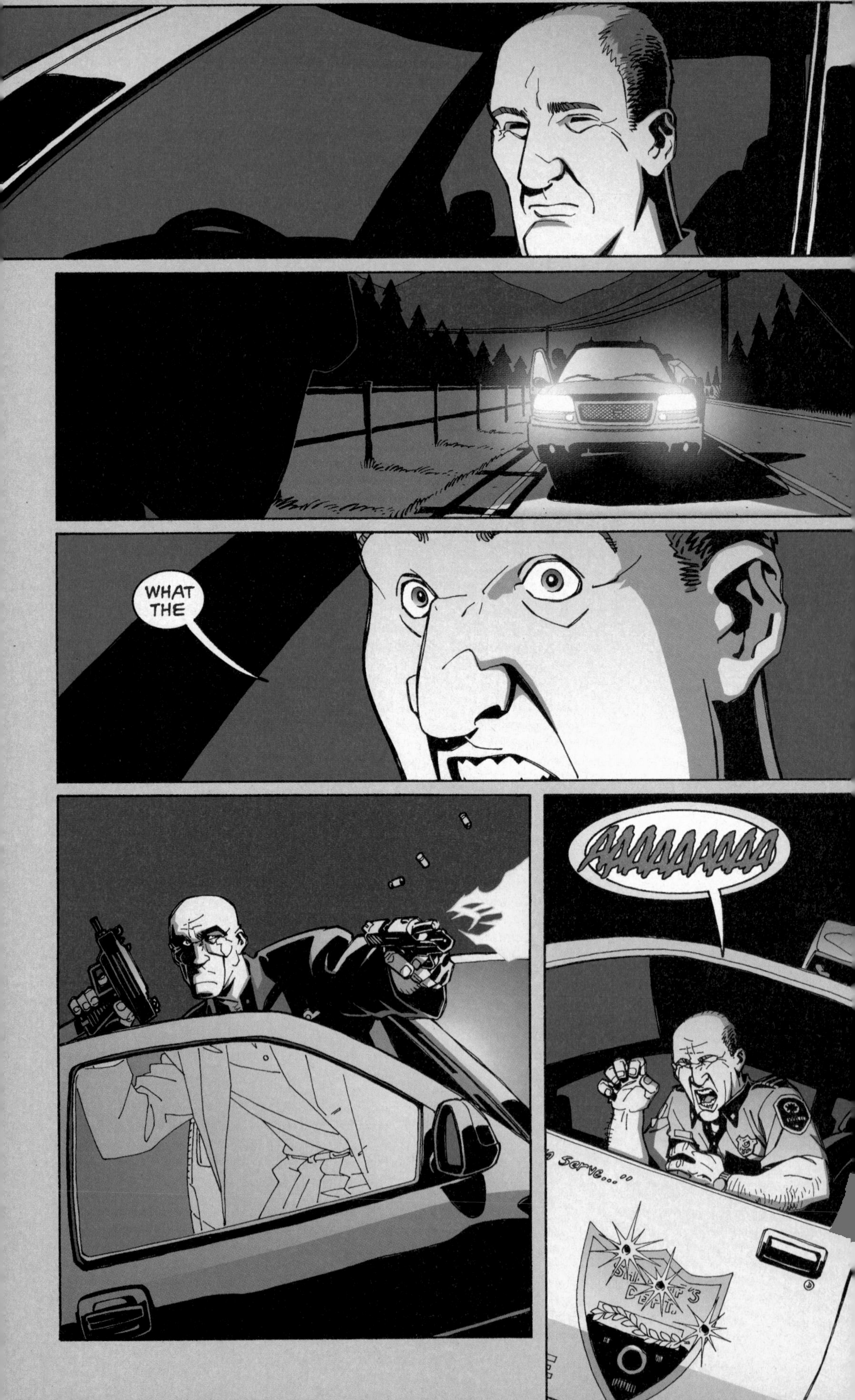
WHAT THE
AAAAAAAAAA

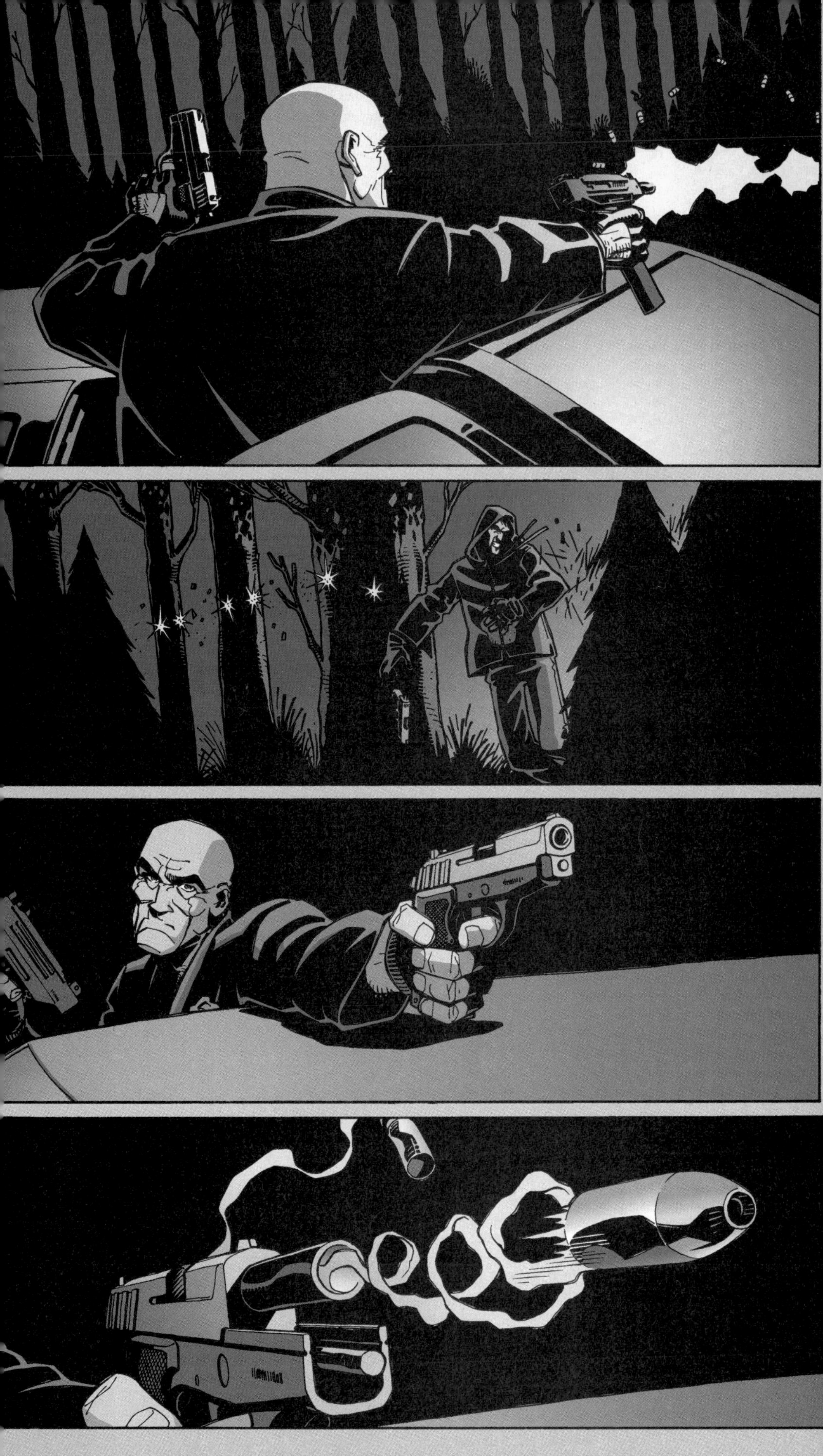

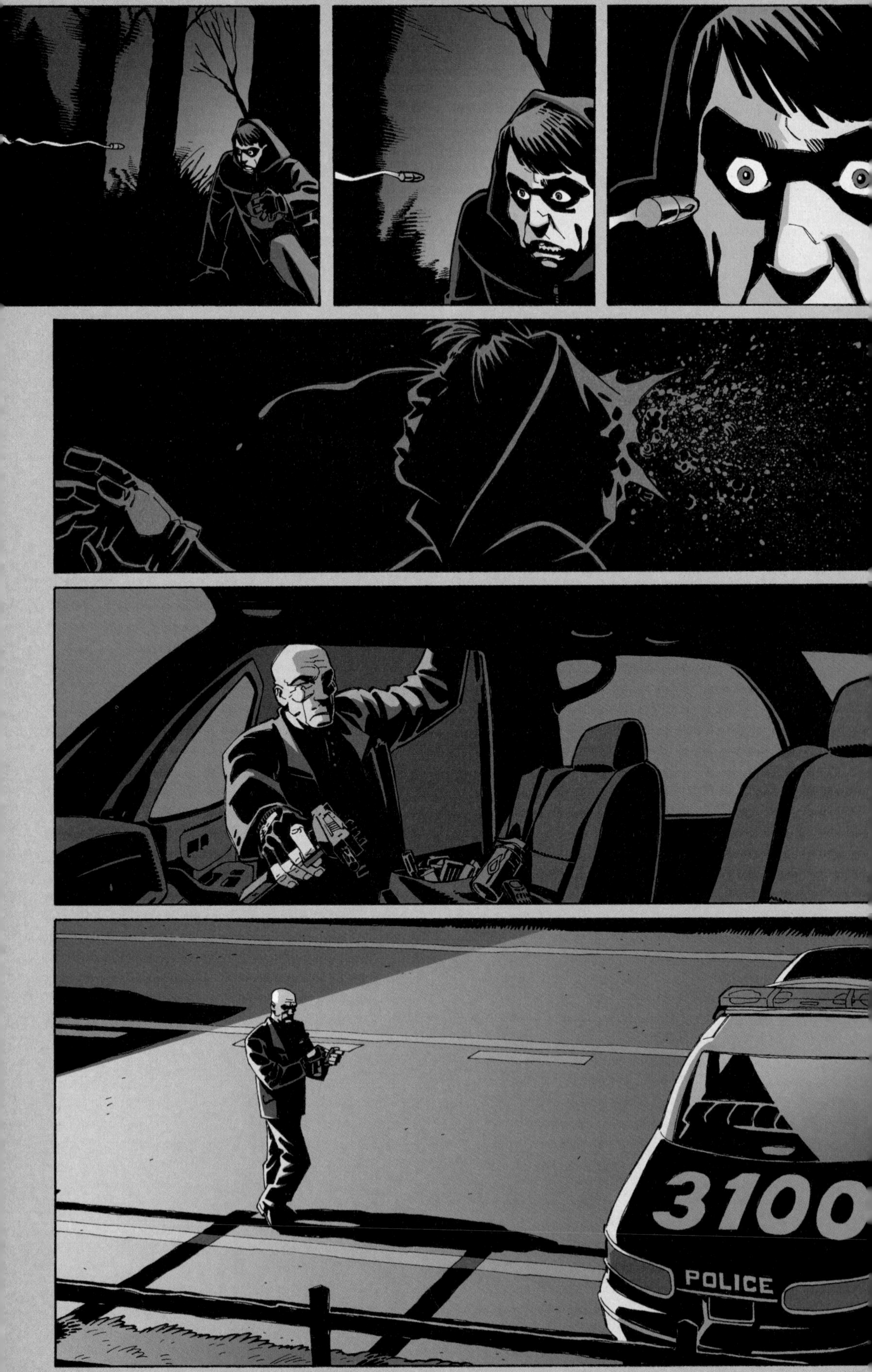
3100
POLICE

THIS IS INSANE.

HOW CAN HE NOT BE DEAD? YOU SENT THREE PEOPLE IN, AND, AND, HE'S AN OLD MAN, AND THIS IS JUST GODDAMN STUPID--

I TRIED TO EXPLAIN TO YOU--

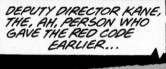

DEPUTY DIRECTOR KANE, THE, AH, PERSON WHO GAVE THE RED CODE EARLIER...

HE'S ON THE LINE AGAIN. AND HE WANTS TO TALK TO YOU.

PUT THE TRACER TEAM ON IT AND PATCH HIM THROUGH, THANK YOU.

HELLO.

MY NAME IS PAUL MOSES.

WHOM AM I ADDRESS-ING?

I'M ADRIAN KANE, THE CURRENT DEPUTY DIRECTOR/ OPERATIONS. THAT WOULD MAKE ME YOUR DIRECT SUPERIOR--

--AND I'M MICHAEL BEESLEY, THE DIRECTOR OF THE CIA, YOU GODDAMN MONSTER!

I'VE BEEN IN ROOM R! I KNOW WHAT YOU ARE!

THEN IT WILL HAVE BEEN THE PAIR OF YOU WHO ORDERED MY DEATH. THANK YOU FOR YOUR NAMES.

MR BEESLEY: WHAT-EVER I AM, I BECAME AT THE BEHEST OF THIS COUNTRY AND THE CIA.

IF I AM A MONSTER-- AND I WAS A VERY QUIET, LOYAL MONSTER--THEN I AM QUITE DEFINITELY YOUR MONSTER.

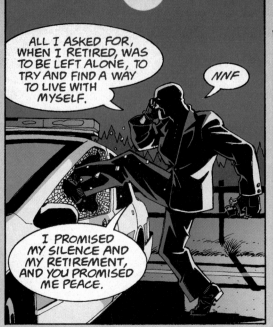

ALL I ASKED FOR, WHEN I RETIRED, WAS TO BE LEFT ALONE, TO TRY AND FIND A WAY TO LIVE WITH MYSELF.

NNF

I PROMISED MY SILENCE AND MY RETIREMENT, AND YOU PROMISED ME PEACE.

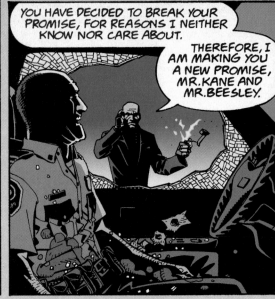

YOU HAVE DECIDED TO BREAK YOUR PROMISE, FOR REASONS I NEITHER KNOW NOR CARE ABOUT.

THEREFORE, I AM MAKING YOU A NEW PROMISE, MR. KANE AND MR. BEESLEY.

I PROMISE YOU THAT EVERYONE AT THE CIA WHO KNOWS MY NAME IS GOING TO DIE.

NOW.

THE NEXT VOICE YOU WILL HEAR IS THE SOLE SURVIVOR OF YOUR OUTER CONTAINMENT TEAM.

EEEEAAAAAA

AAAAEEE-EEEEEE

PLEEEEEASE

OH GOD AAAIIIII-IIII

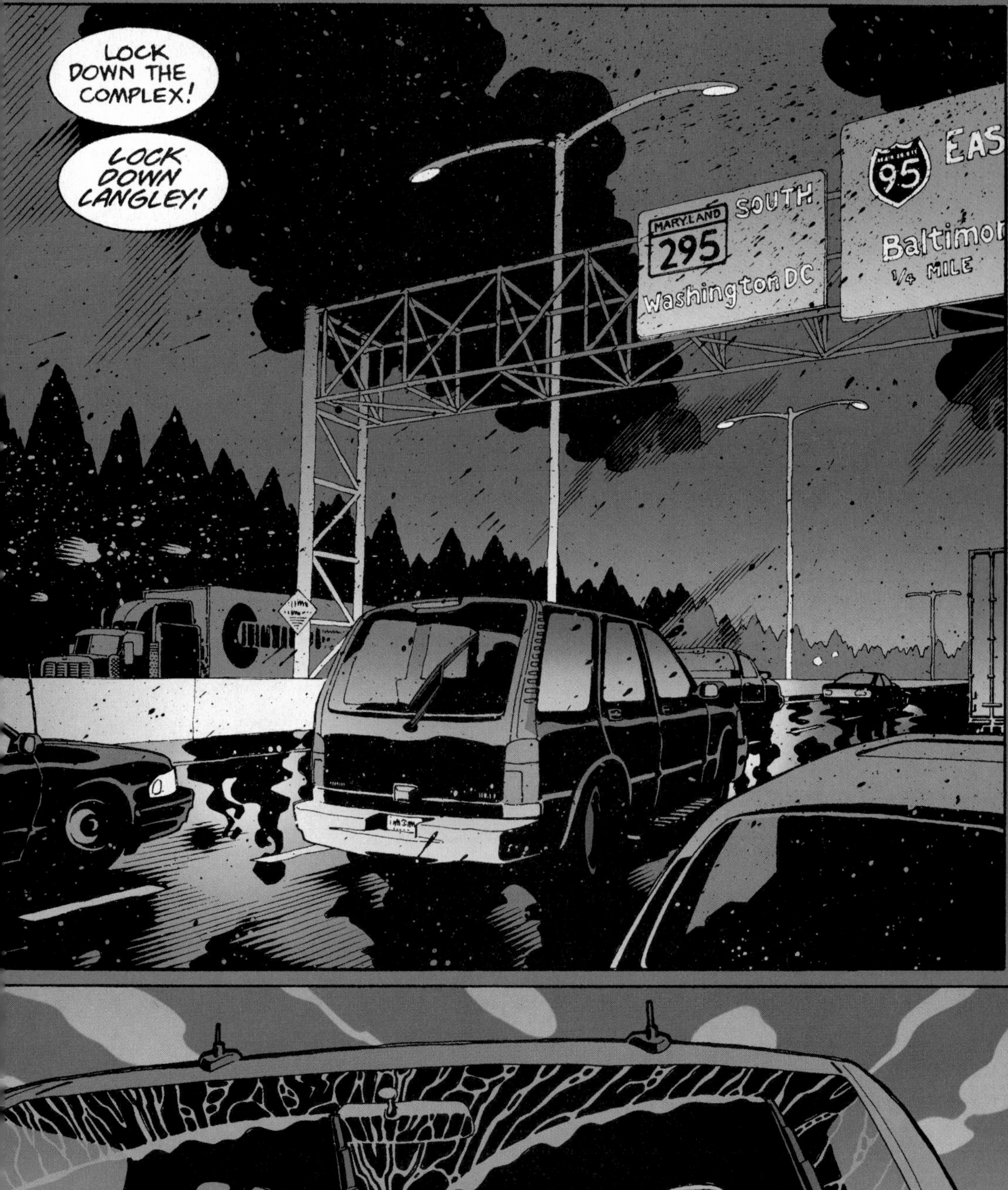
LOCK DOWN THE COMPLEX!
LOCK DOWN LANGLEY!
MARYLAND
295
SOUTH
Washington DC
95
EAS
Baltimor
1/4 MILE

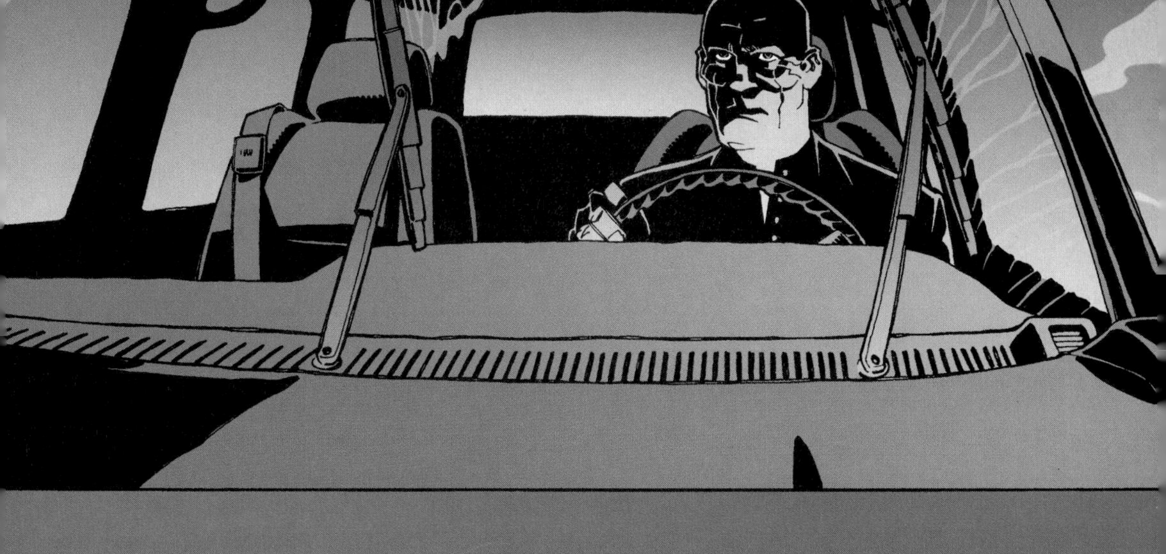

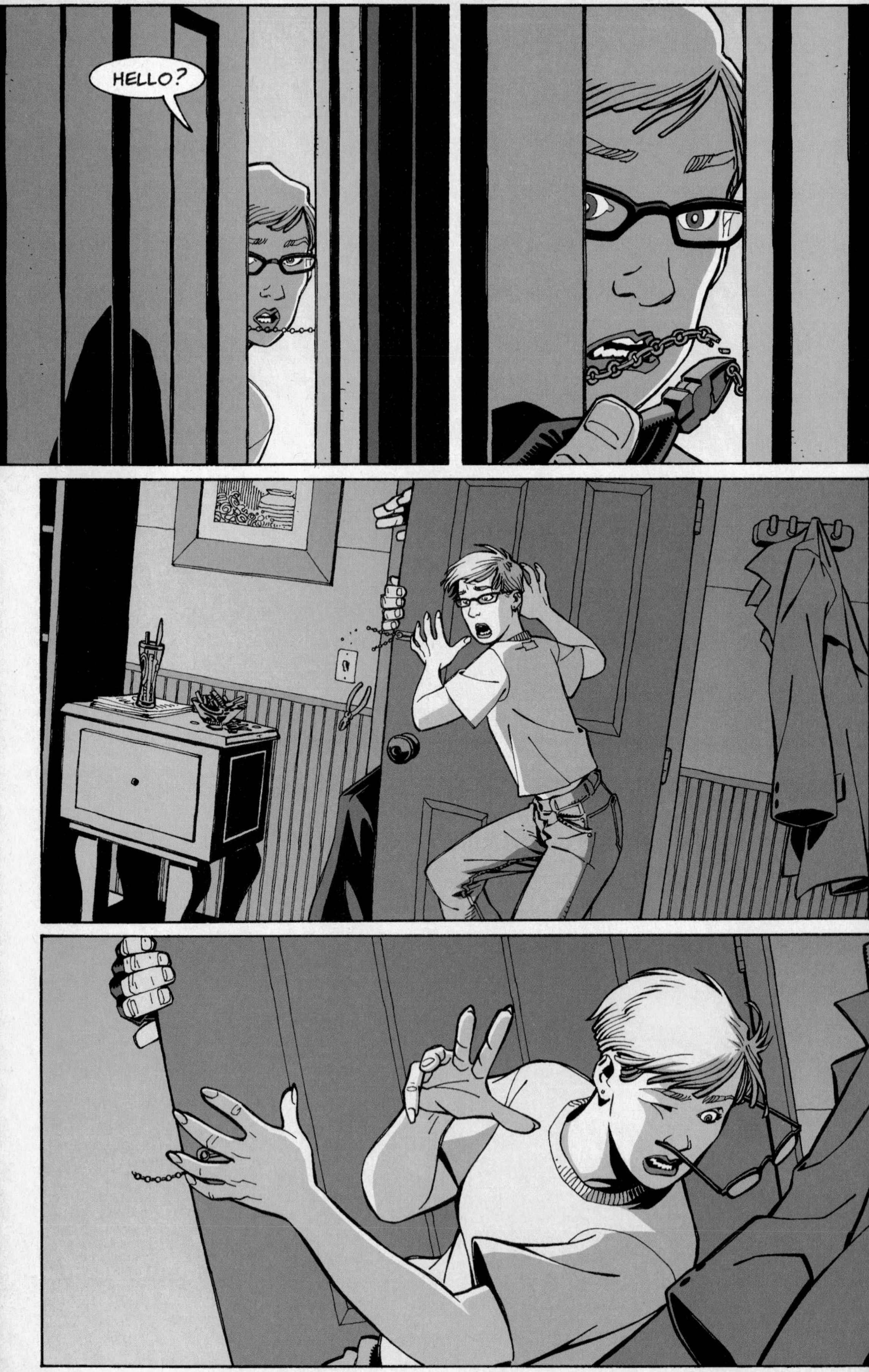
HELLO?

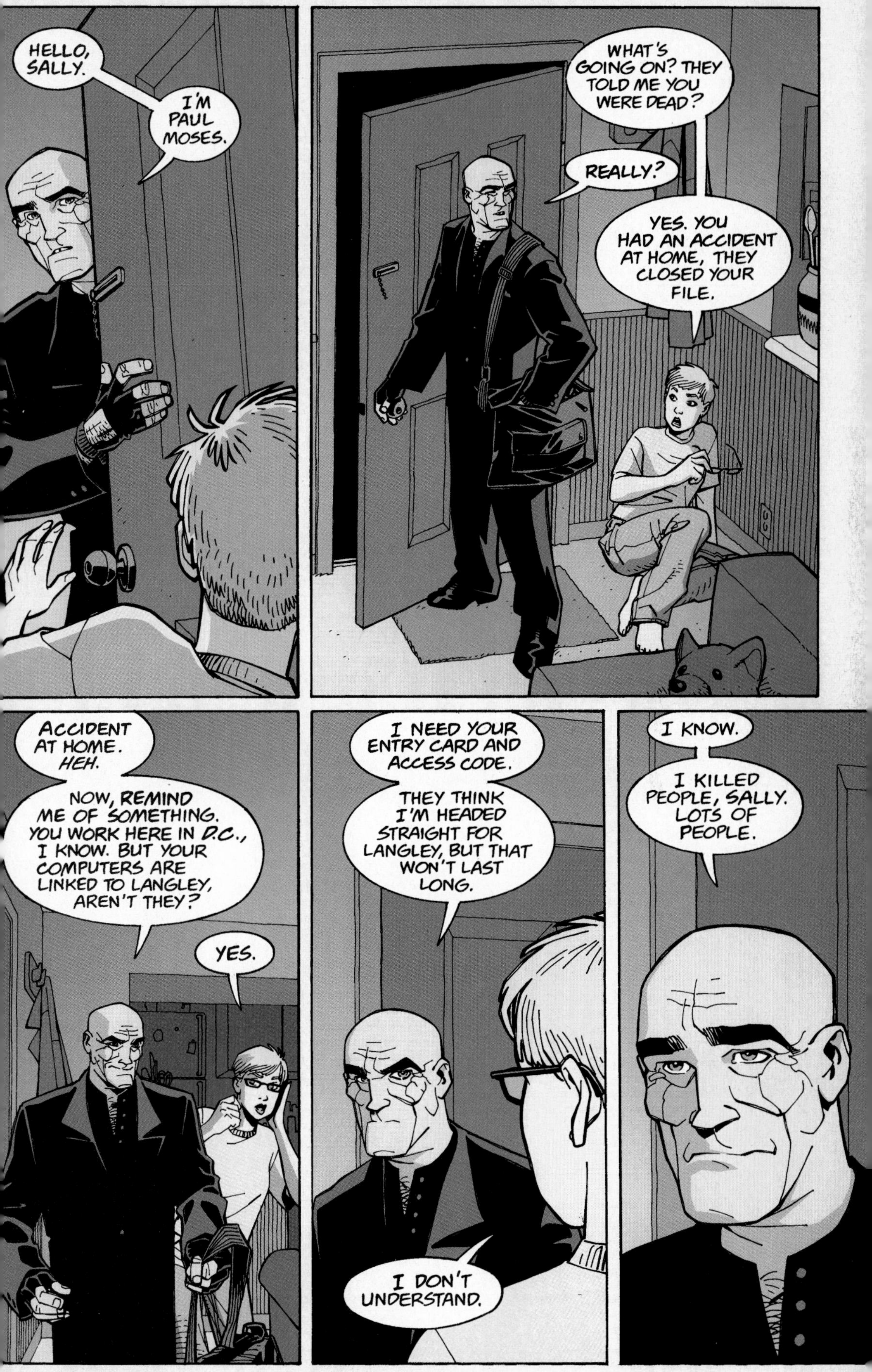
HELLO, SALLY.
I'M PAUL MOSES.
WHAT'S GOING ON? THEY TOLD ME YOU WERE DEAD?
REALLY?
YES. YOU HAD AN ACCIDENT AT HOME, THEY CLOSED YOUR FILE.
ACCIDENT AT HOME. HEH.
NOW, REMIND ME OF SOMETHING. YOU WORK HERE IN D.C., I KNOW. BUT YOUR COMPUTERS ARE LINKED TO LANGLEY, AREN'T THEY?
YES.
I NEED YOUR ENTRY CARD AND ACCESS CODE.
THEY THINK I'M HEADED STRAIGHT FOR LANGLEY, BUT THAT WON'T LAST LONG.
I DON'T UNDERSTAND.
I KNOW.
I KILLED PEOPLE, SALLY. LOTS OF PEOPLE.

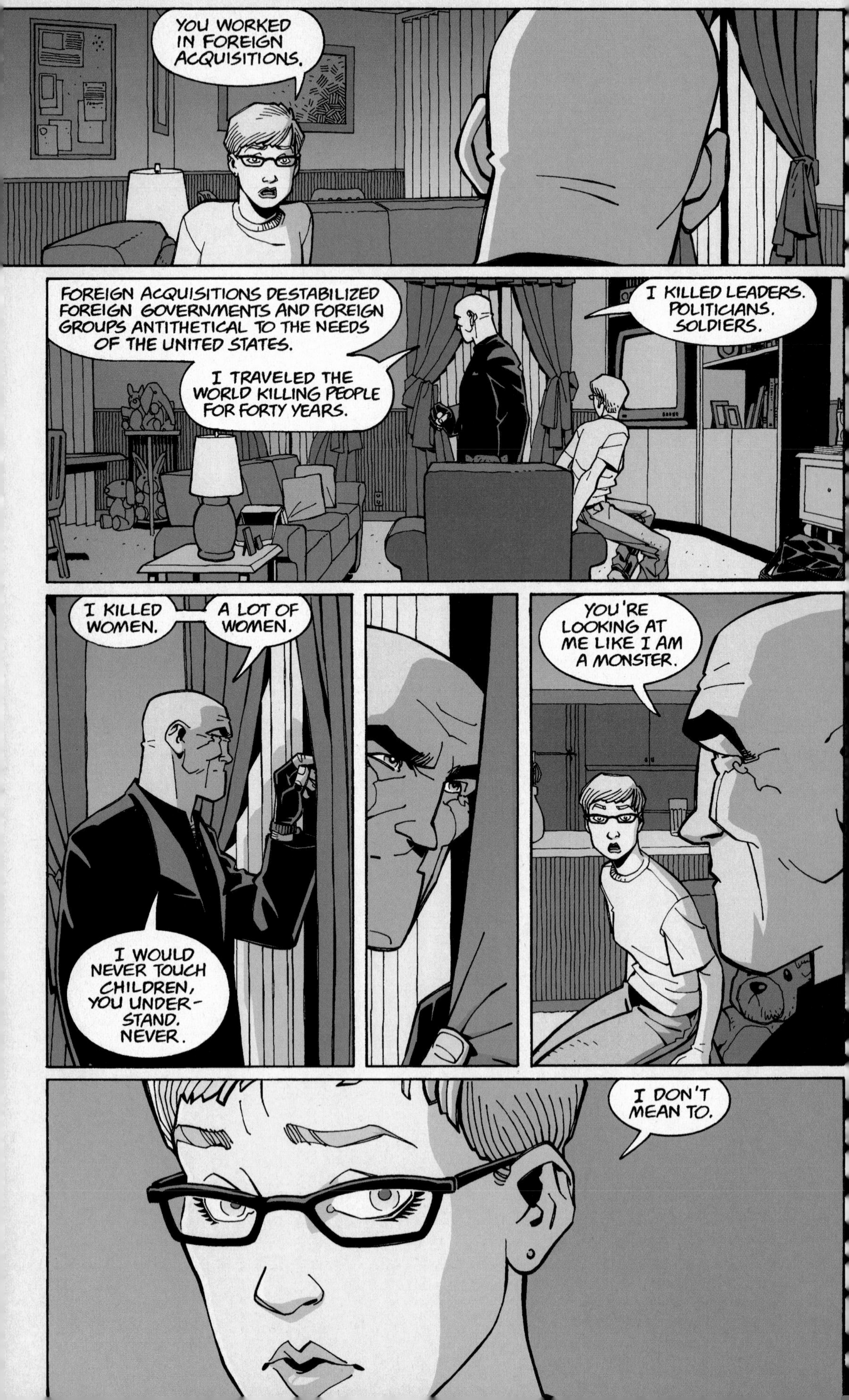
YOU WORKED IN FOREIGN ACQUISITIONS.
FOREIGN ACQUISITIONS DESTABILIZED FOREIGN GOVERNMENTS AND FOREIGN GROUPS ANTITHETICAL TO THE NEEDS OF THE UNITED STATES.
I TRAVELED THE WORLD KILLING PEOPLE FOR FORTY YEARS.
I KILLED LEADERS. POLITICIANS. SOLDIERS.
I KILLED WOMEN.
A LOT OF WOMEN.
I WOULD NEVER TOUCH CHILDREN, YOU UNDER-STAND. NEVER.
YOU'RE LOOKING AT ME LIKE I AM A MONSTER.
I DON'T MEAN TO.

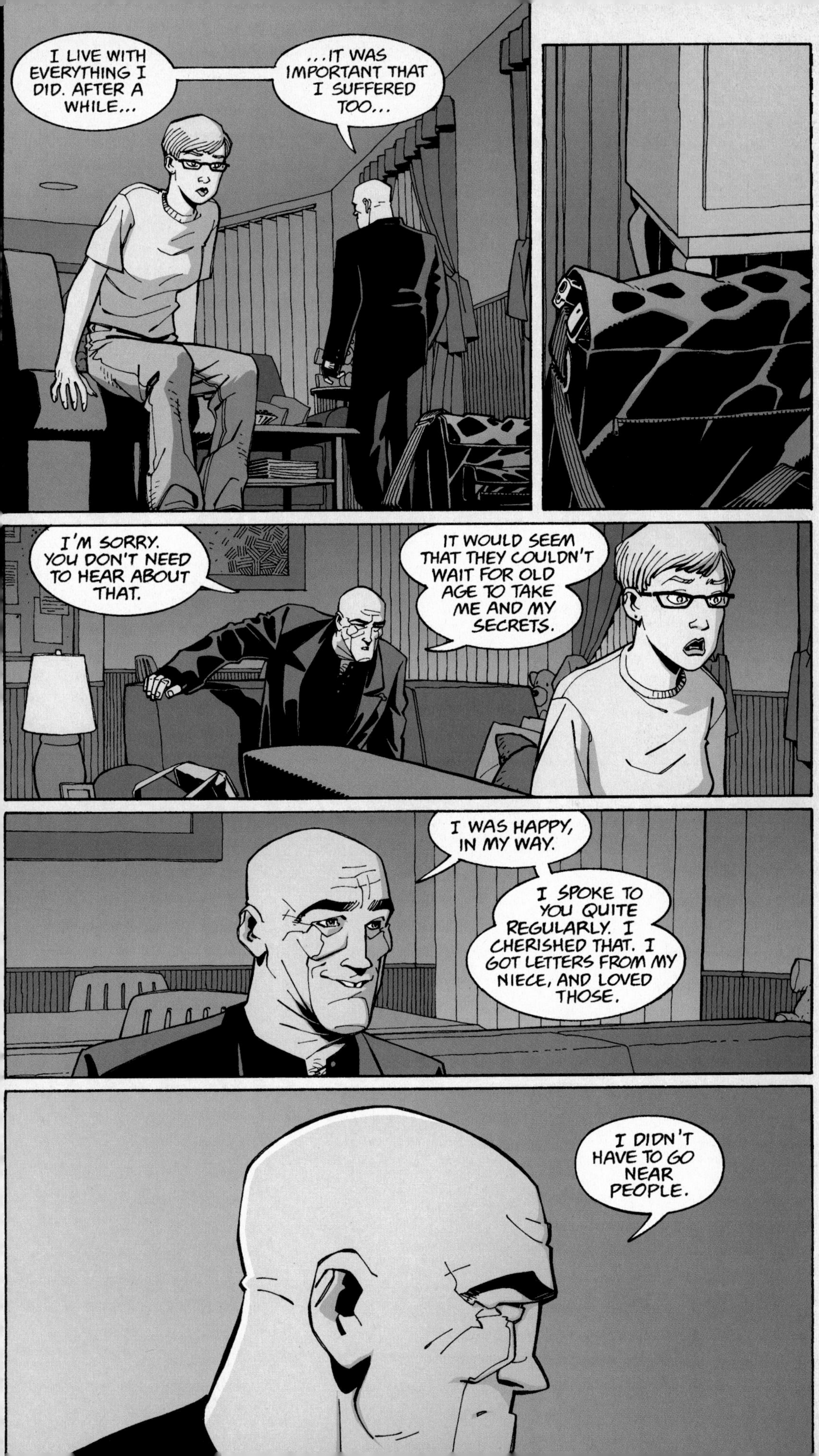
I LIVE WITH EVERYTHING I DID. AFTER A WHILE...
...IT WAS IMPORTANT THAT I SUFFERED TOO...
I'M SORRY. YOU DON'T NEED TO HEAR ABOUT THAT.
IT WOULD SEEM THAT THEY COULDN'T WAIT FOR OLD AGE TO TAKE ME AND MY SECRETS.
I WAS HAPPY, IN MY WAY.
I SPOKE TO YOU QUITE REGULARLY. I CHERISHED THAT. I GOT LETTERS FROM MY NIECE, AND LOVED THOSE.
I DIDN'T HAVE TO GO NEAR PEOPLE.

I WASN'T GOING TO TELL ANYONE. I CAN BARELY STAND KNOWING IT MYSELF.

BUT THE WORLD CHANGED AROUND ME. MEN AREN'T MEN ANY MORE.

FRIGHTENED BOYS IN SUITS, AFRAID OF OLD PEOPLE AND HISTORY.

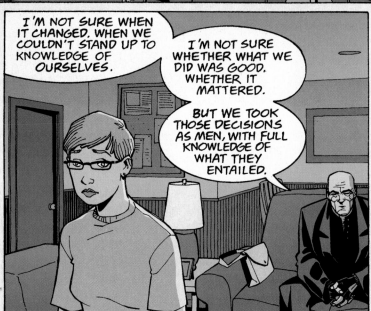

I'M NOT SURE WHEN IT CHANGED. WHEN WE COULDN'T STAND UP TO KNOWLEDGE OF OURSELVES.

I'M NOT SURE WHETHER WHAT WE DID WAS GOOD. WHETHER IT MATTERED.

BUT WE TOOK THOSE DECISIONS AS MEN, WITH FULL KNOWLEDGE OF WHAT THEY ENTAILED.

WE NEVER EXPECTED CHILDREN TO KNOW.

I IMAGINE WE WERE QUITE SHORT-SIGHTED, IN THAT RESPECT.

WHAT ARE YOU GOING TO DO?

I NEED THE CARD AND CODE NOW, PLEASE.

IT'S.

IT'S IN THERE.

SORRY.

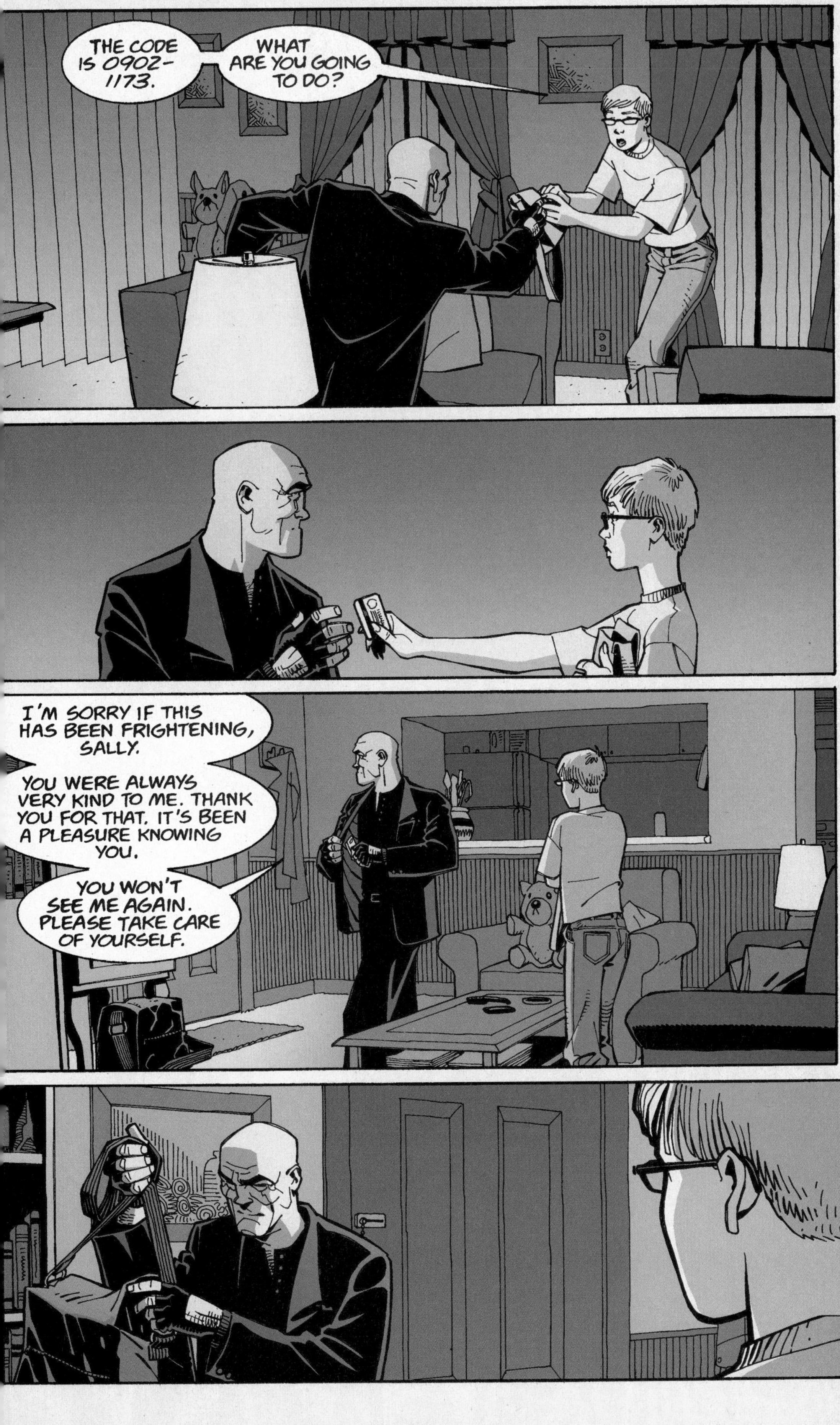
THE CODE IS 0902-1173.
WHAT ARE YOU GOING TO DO?
I'M SORRY IF THIS HAS BEEN FRIGHTENING, SALLY.
YOU WERE ALWAYS VERY KIND TO ME. THANK YOU FOR THAT. IT'S BEEN A PLEASURE KNOWING YOU.
YOU WON'T SEE ME AGAIN. PLEASE TAKE CARE OF YOURSELF.

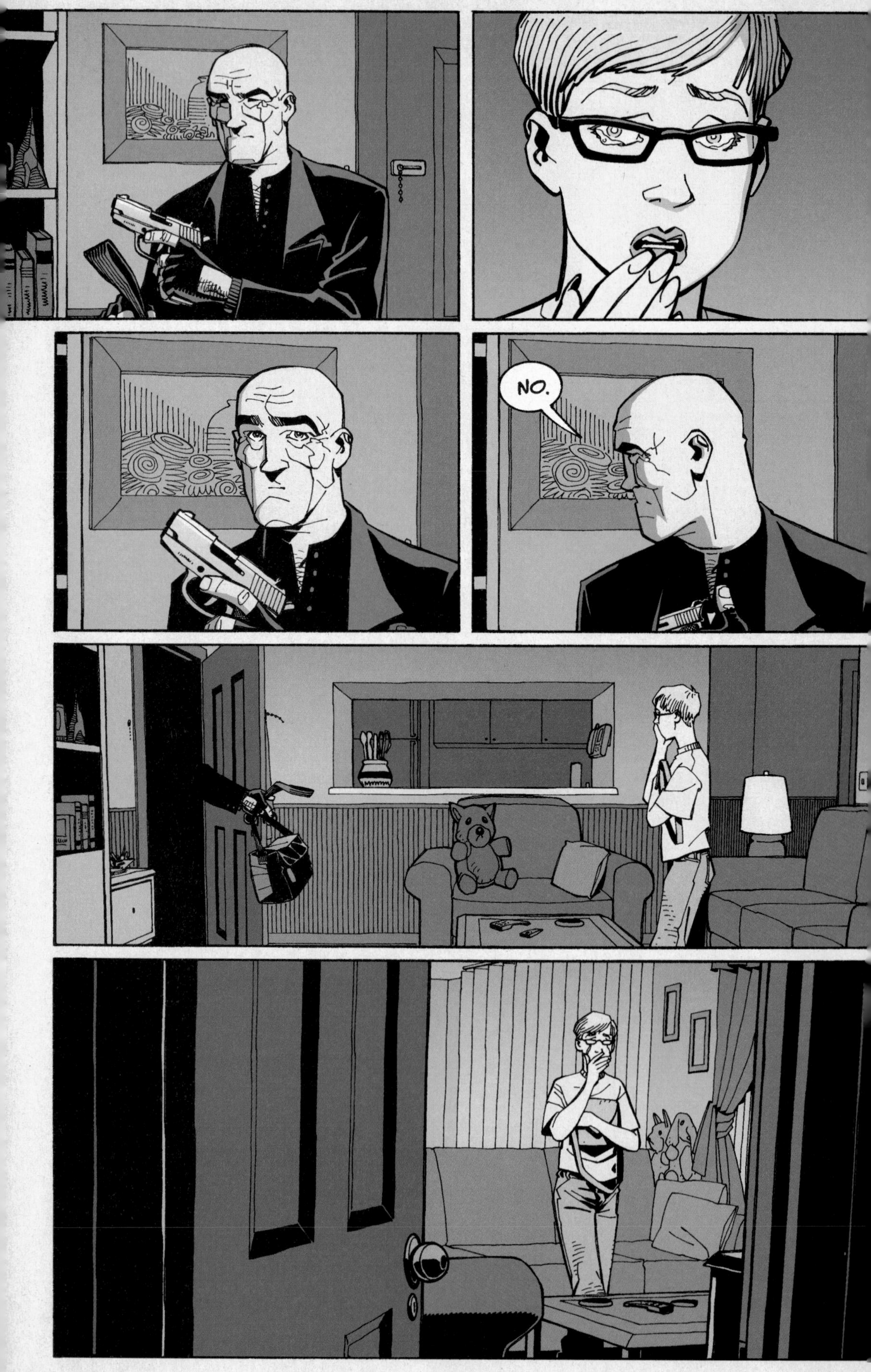
NO.

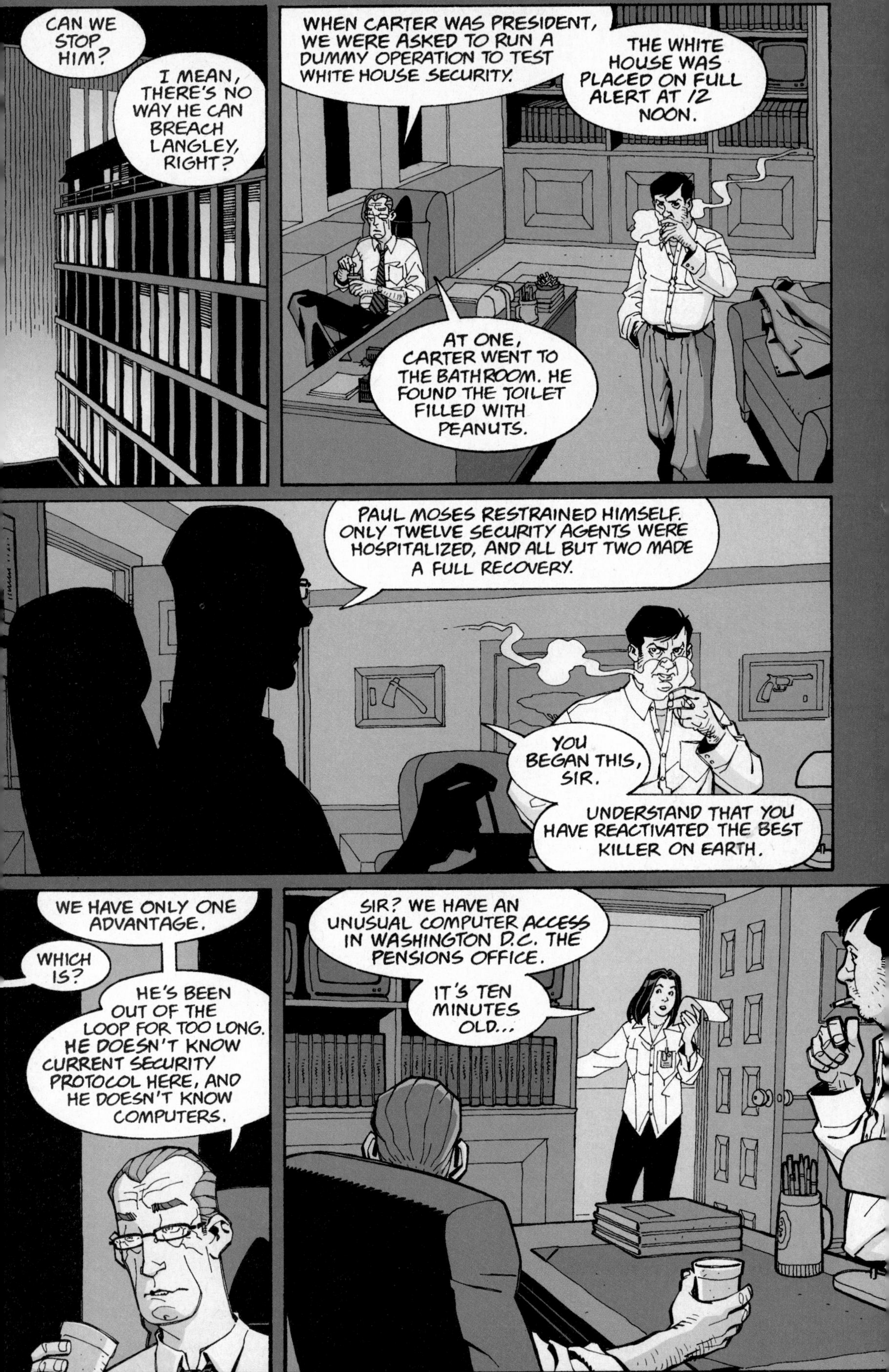
CAN WE STOP HIM?
I MEAN, THERE'S NO WAY HE CAN BREACH LANGLEY, RIGHT?
WHEN CARTER WAS PRESIDENT, WE WERE ASKED TO RUN A DUMMY OPERATION TO TEST WHITE HOUSE SECURITY.
THE WHITE HOUSE WAS PLACED ON FULL ALERT AT 12 NOON.
AT ONE, CARTER WENT TO THE BATHROOM. HE FOUND THE TOILET FILLED WITH PEANUTS.
PAUL MOSES RESTRAINED HIMSELF. ONLY TWELVE SECURITY AGENTS WERE HOSPITALIZED, AND ALL BUT TWO MADE A FULL RECOVERY.
YOU BEGAN THIS, SIR.
UNDERSTAND THAT YOU HAVE REACTIVATED THE BEST KILLER ON EARTH.
WE HAVE ONLY ONE ADVANTAGE.
WHICH IS?
HE'S BEEN OUT OF THE LOOP FOR TOO LONG. HE DOESN'T KNOW CURRENT SECURITY PROTOCOL HERE, AND HE DOESN'T KNOW COMPUTERS.
SIR? WE HAVE AN UNUSUAL COMPUTER ACCESS IN WASHINGTON D.C. THE PENSIONS OFFICE.
IT'S TEN MINUTES OLD...

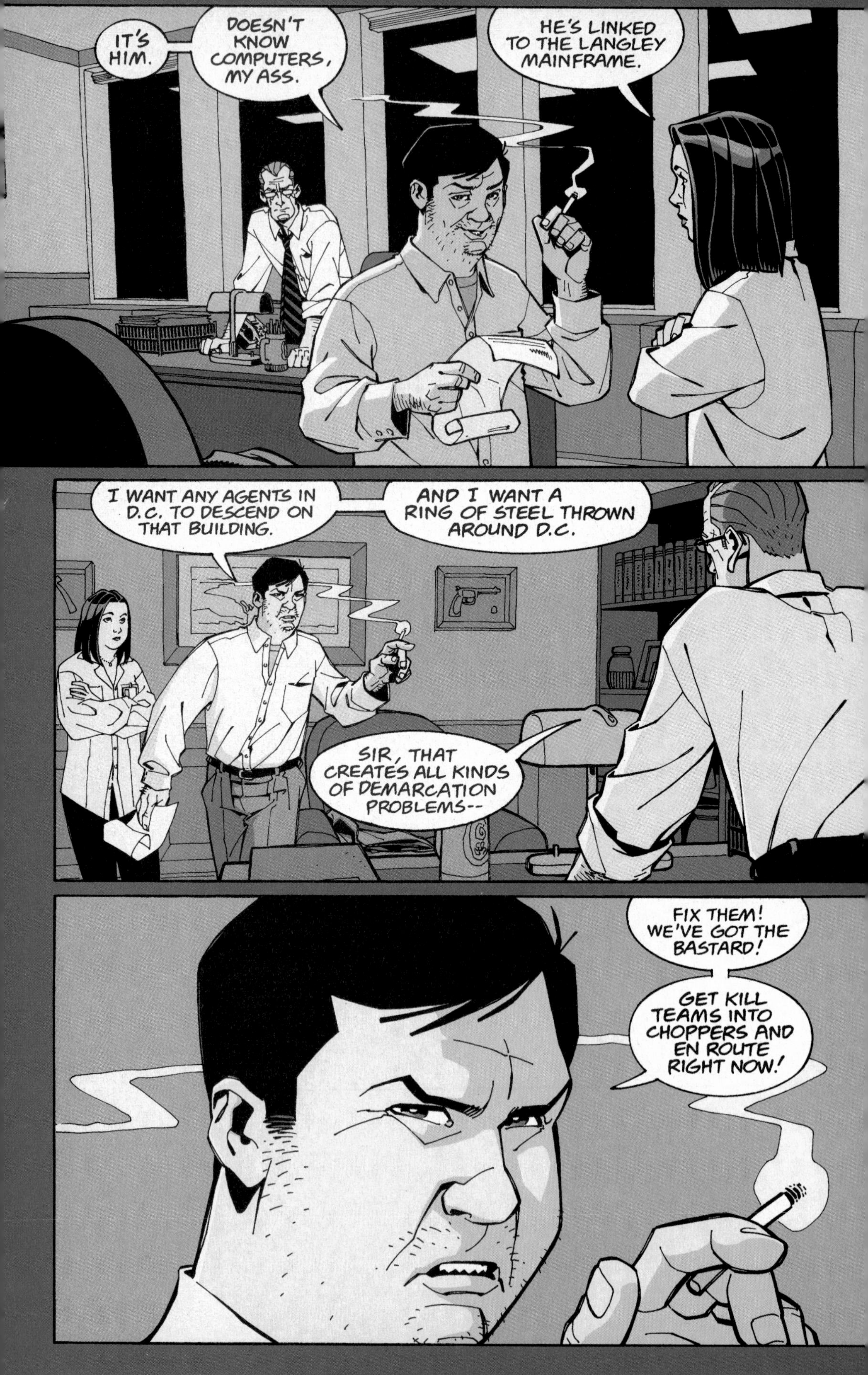
IT'S HIM.
DOESN'T KNOW COMPUTERS, MY ASS.
HE'S LINKED TO THE LANGLEY MAINFRAME.
I WANT ANY AGENTS IN D.C. TO DESCEND ON THAT BUILDING.
AND I WANT A RING OF STEEL THROWN AROUND D.C.
SIR, THAT CREATES ALL KINDS OF DEMARCATION PROBLEMS--
FIX THEM! WE'VE GOT THE BASTARD!
GET KILL TEAMS INTO CHOPPERS AND EN ROUTE RIGHT NOW!

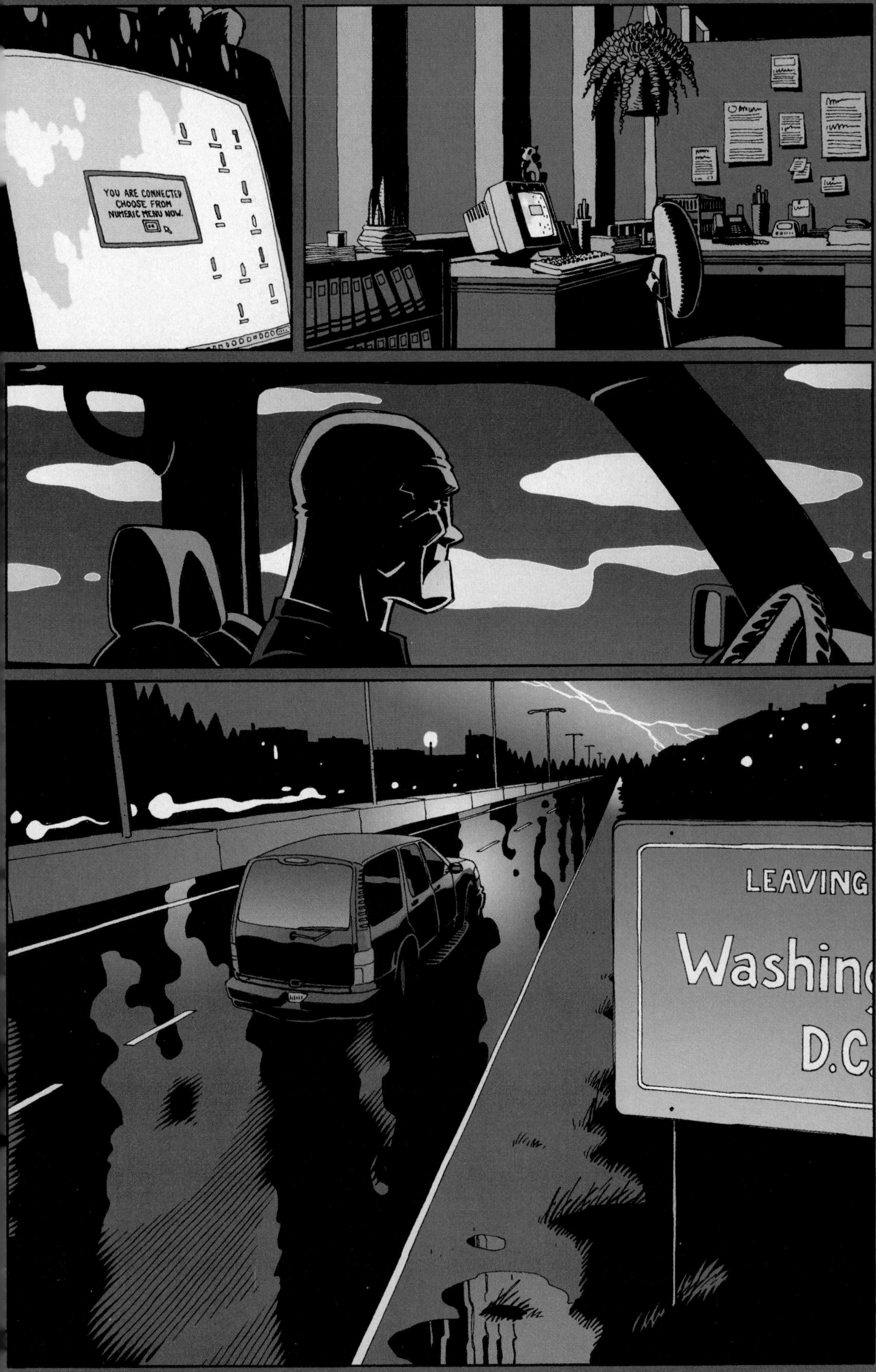

YOU ARE CONNECTED
CHOOSE FROM
NUMERIC MENU NOW.
LEAVING
Washing
D.C.

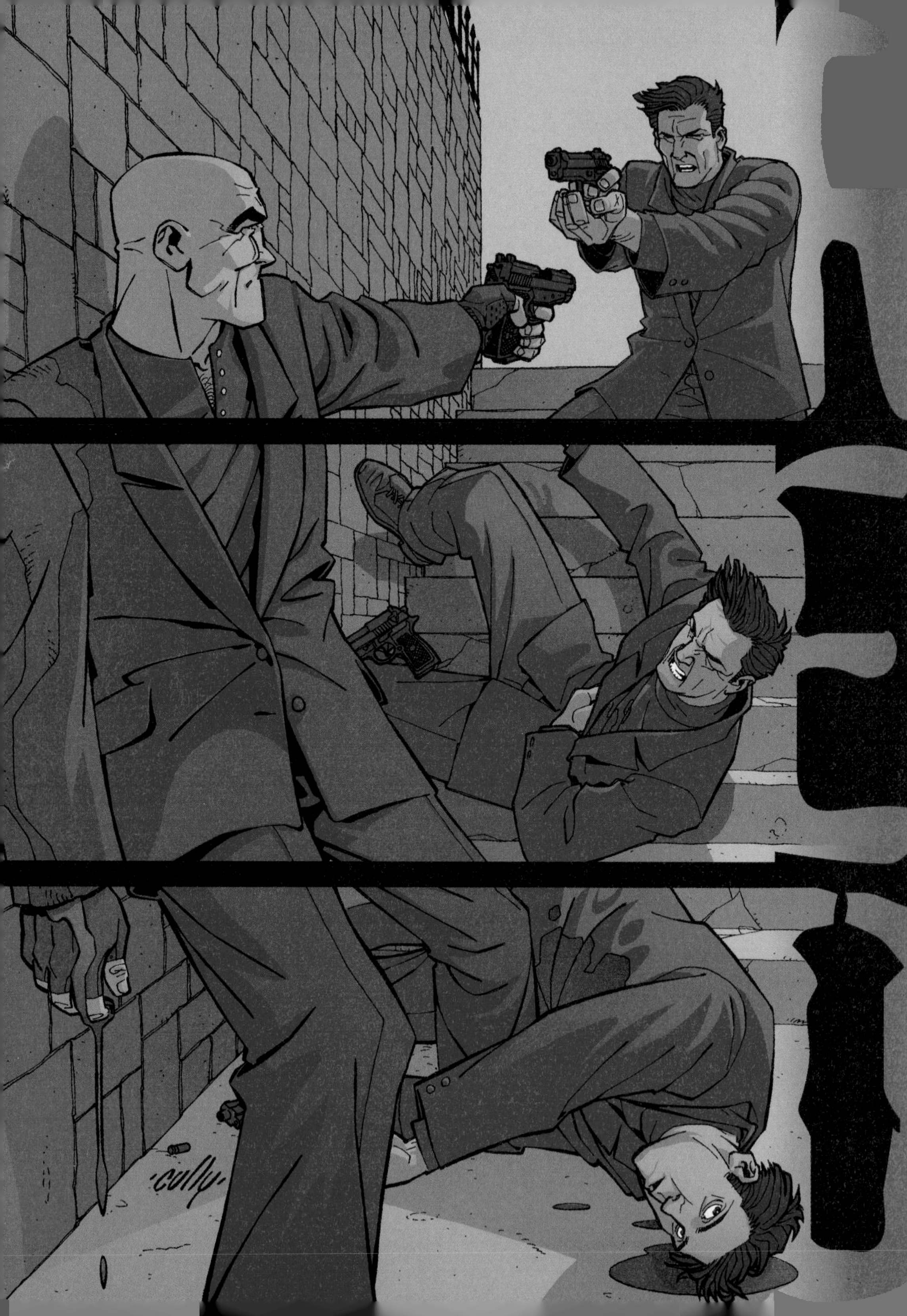
cully

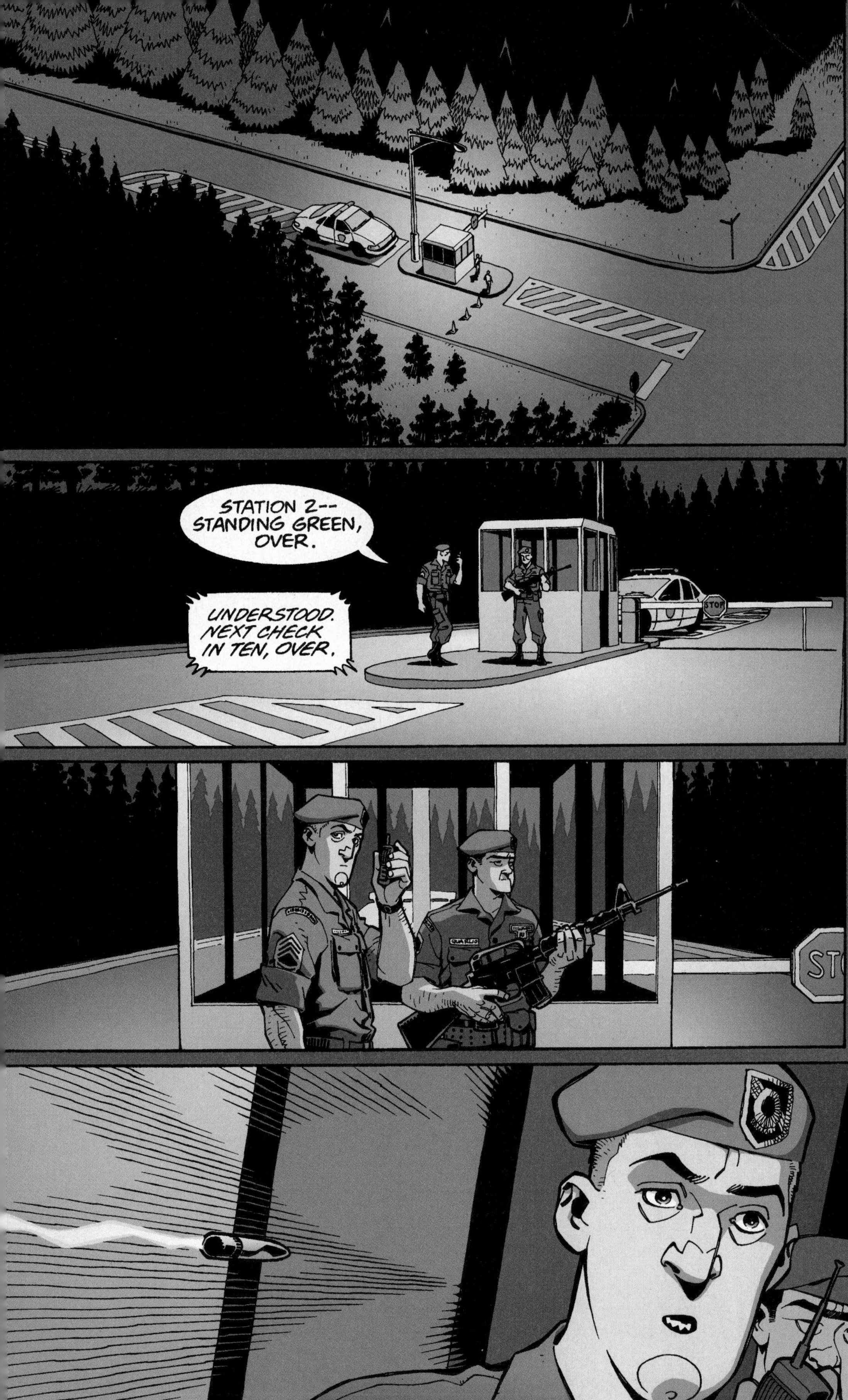
STATION 2--
STANDING GREEN,
OVER.
UNDERSTOOD.
NEXT CHECK
IN TEN, OVER.
STOP

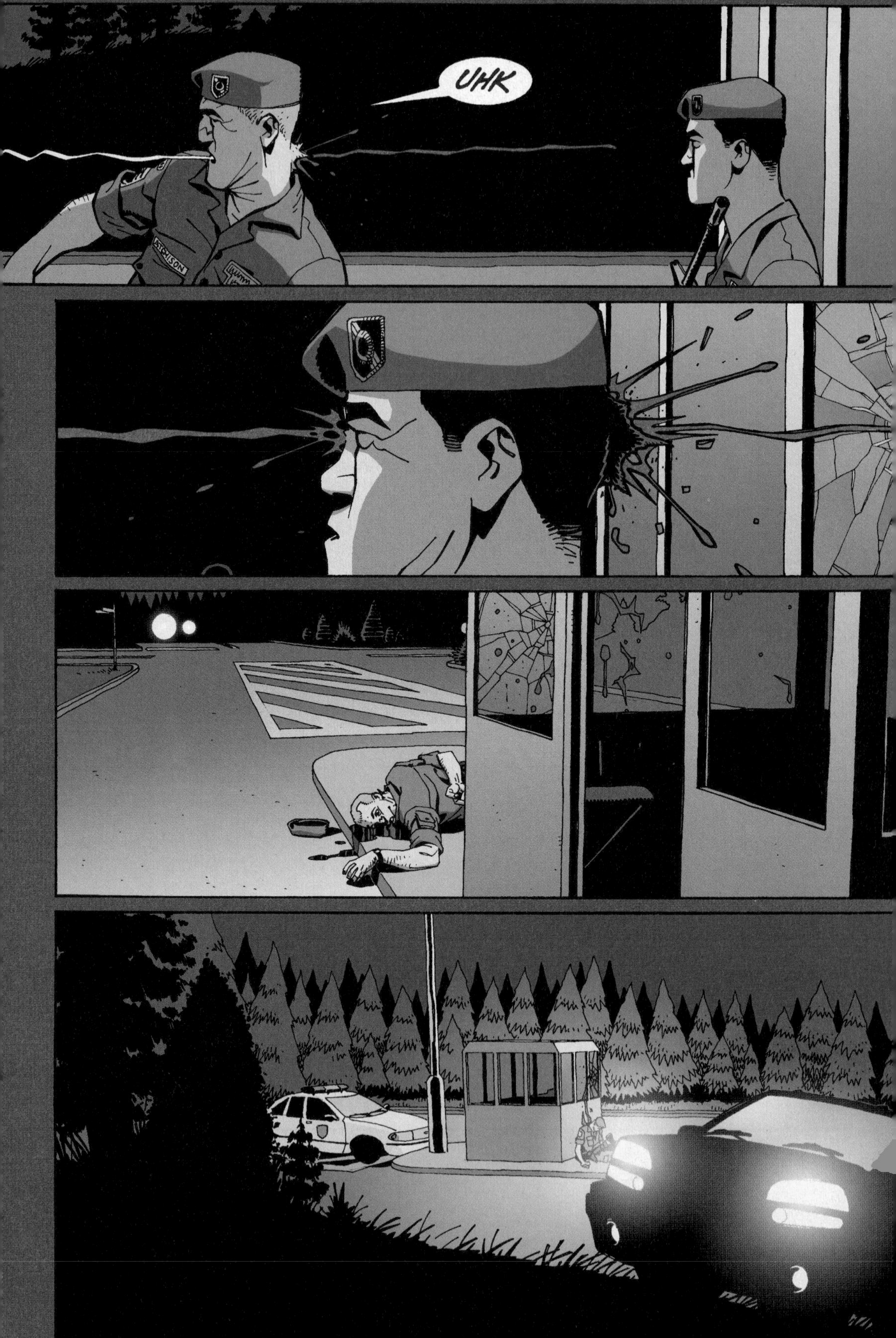
UHK

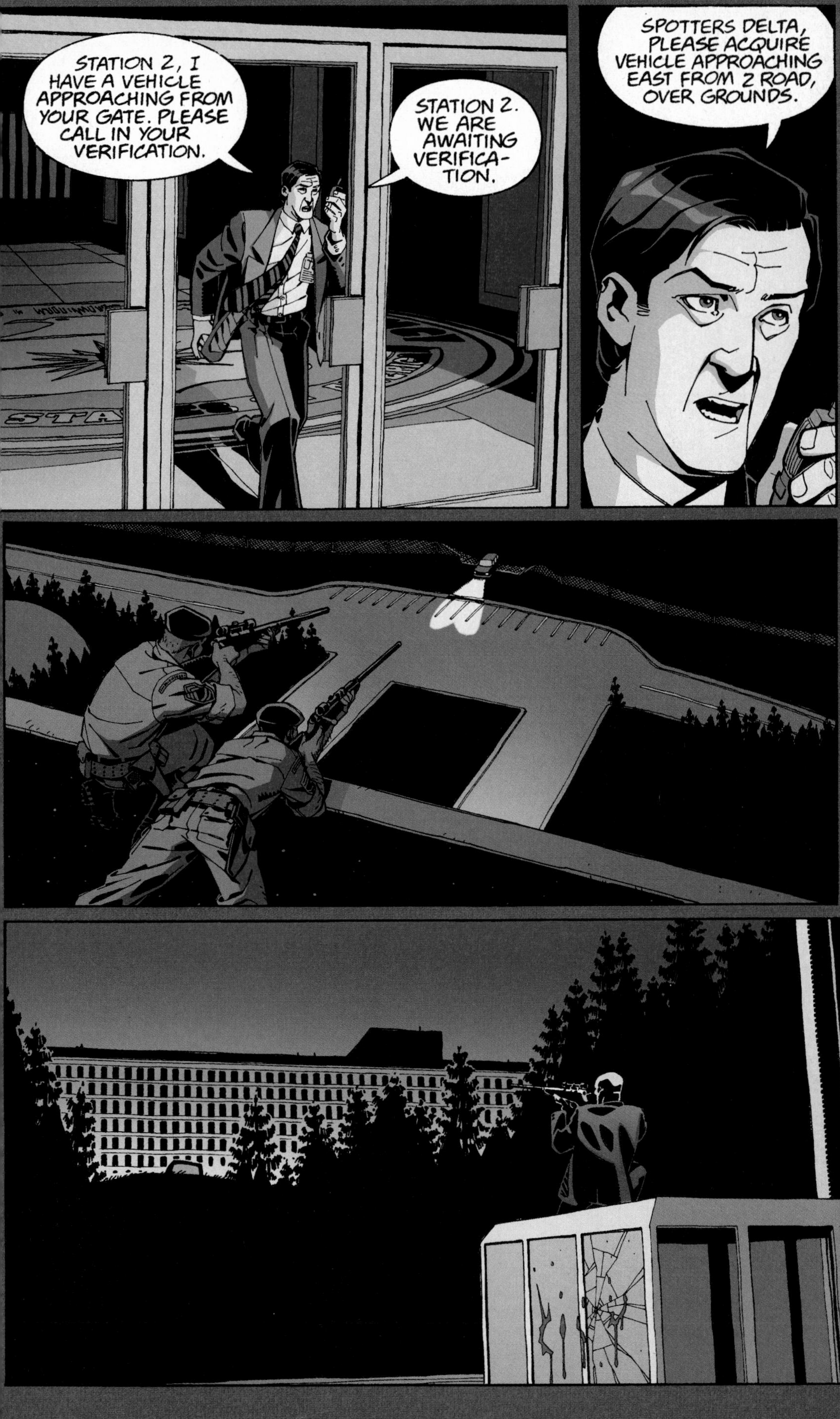
STATION 2, I HAVE A VEHICLE APPROACHING FROM YOUR GATE. PLEASE CALL IN YOUR VERIFICATION.
STATION 2. WE ARE AWAITING VERIFICA- TION.
SPOTTERS DELTA, PLEASE ACQUIRE VEHICLE APPROACHING EAST FROM 2 ROAD, OVER GROUNDS.

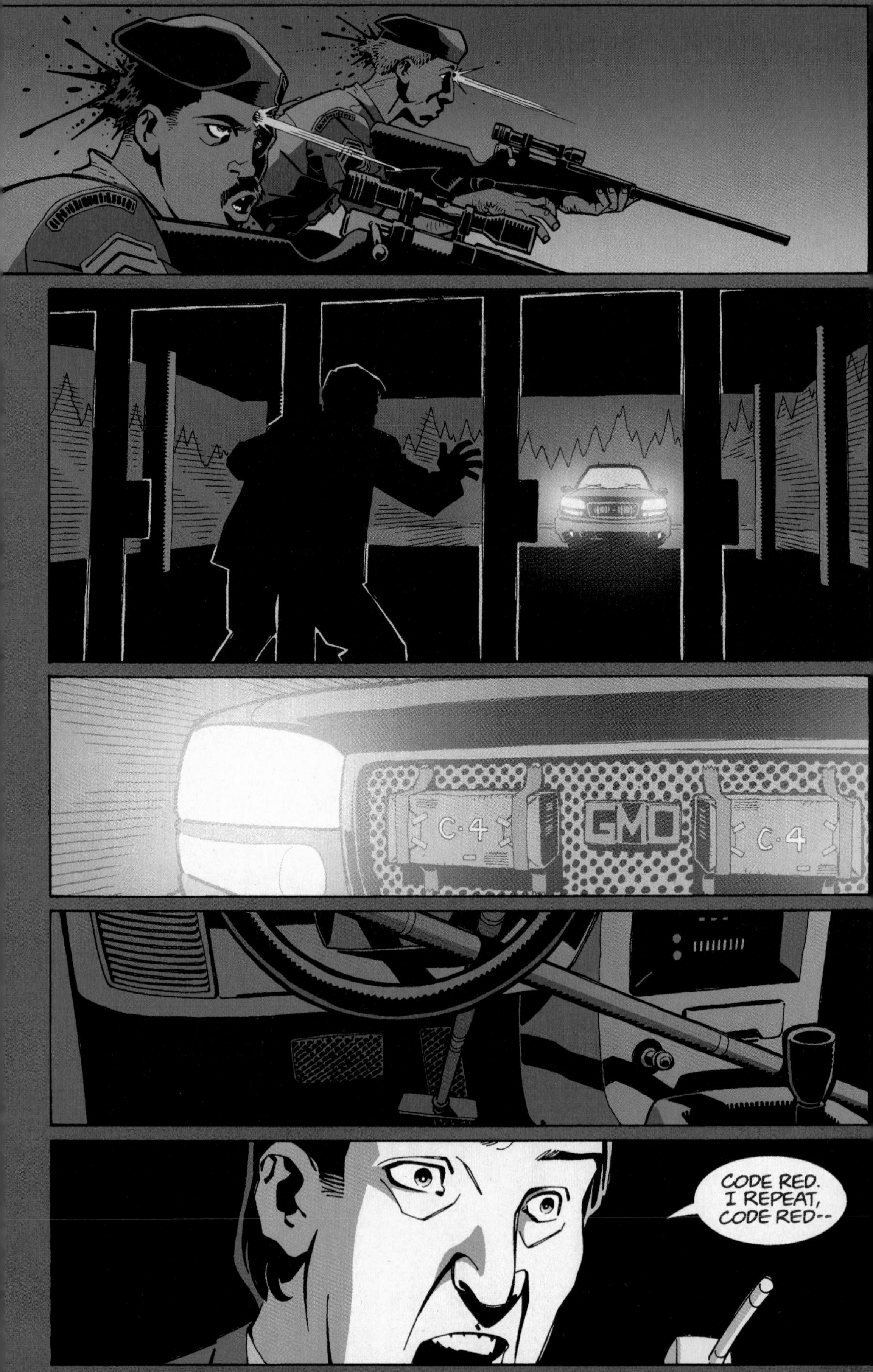
C·4
GMO
C·4
CODE RED. I REPEAT, CODE RED--

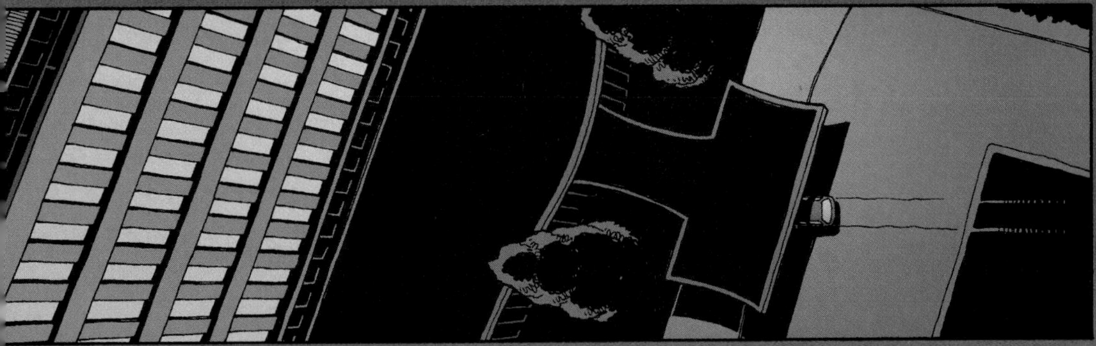

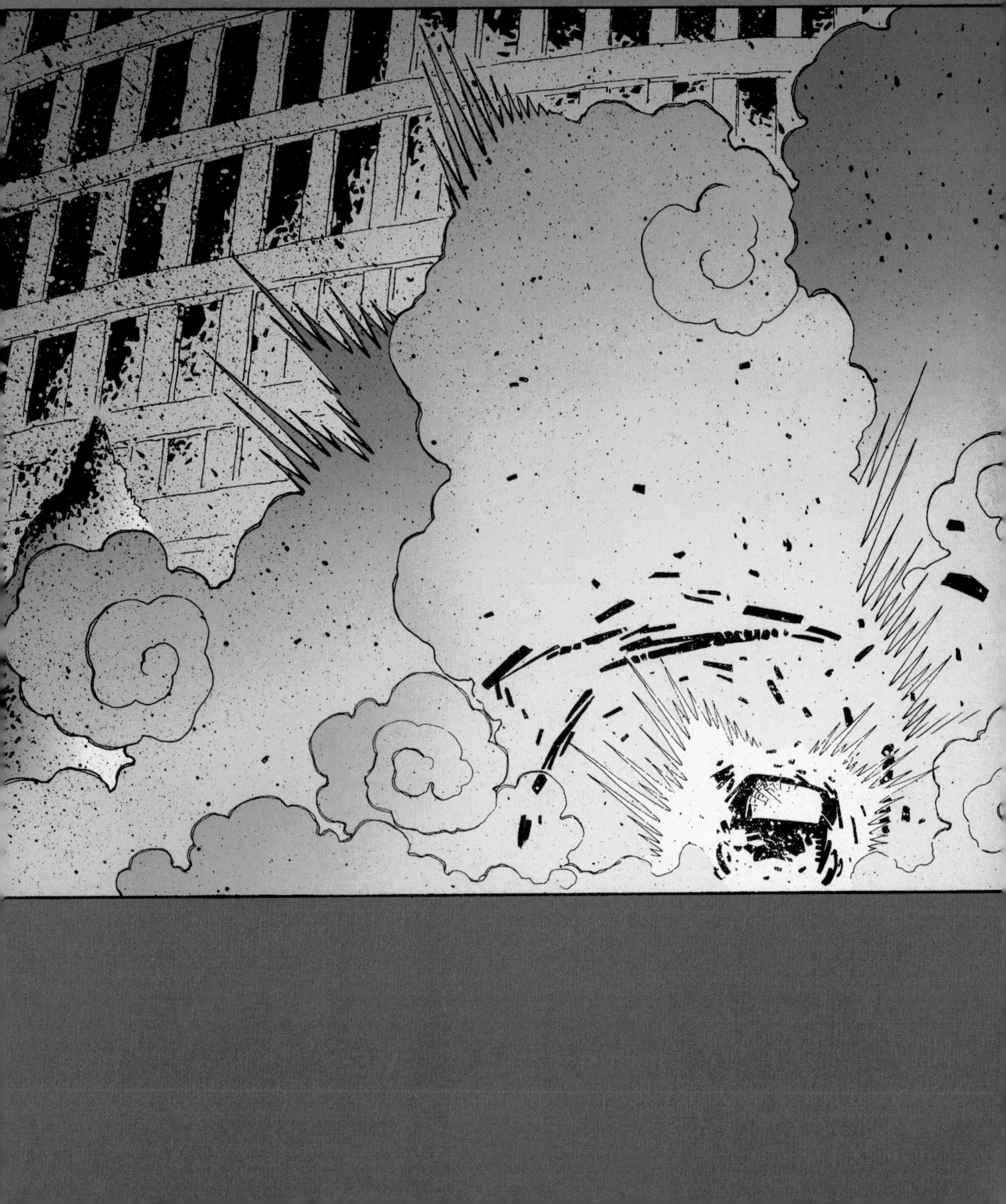

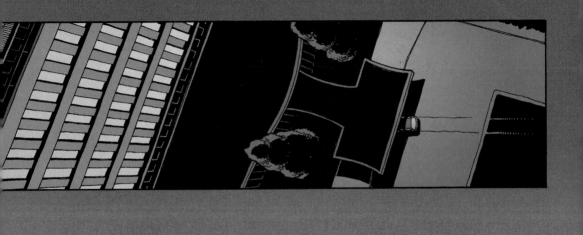

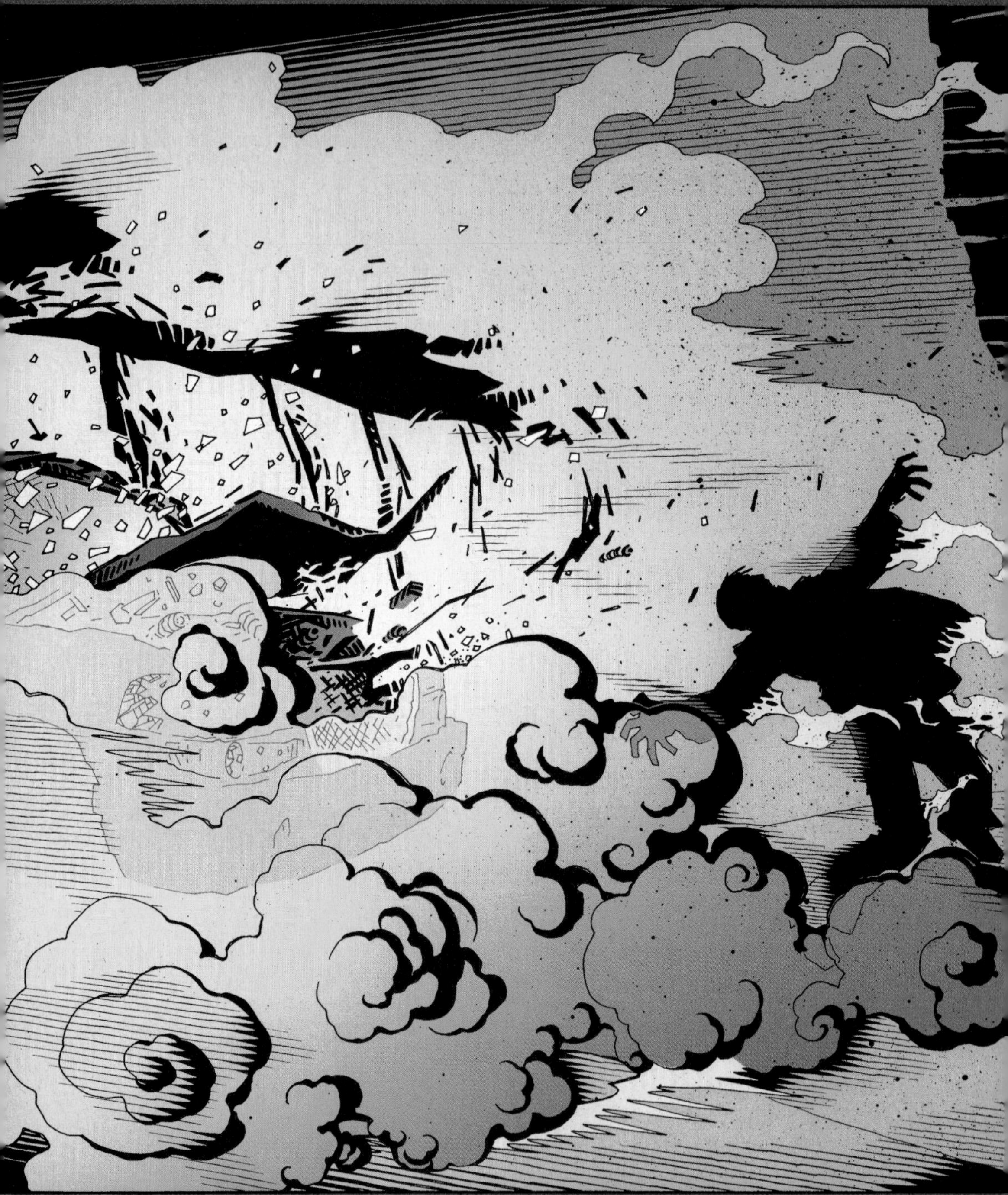

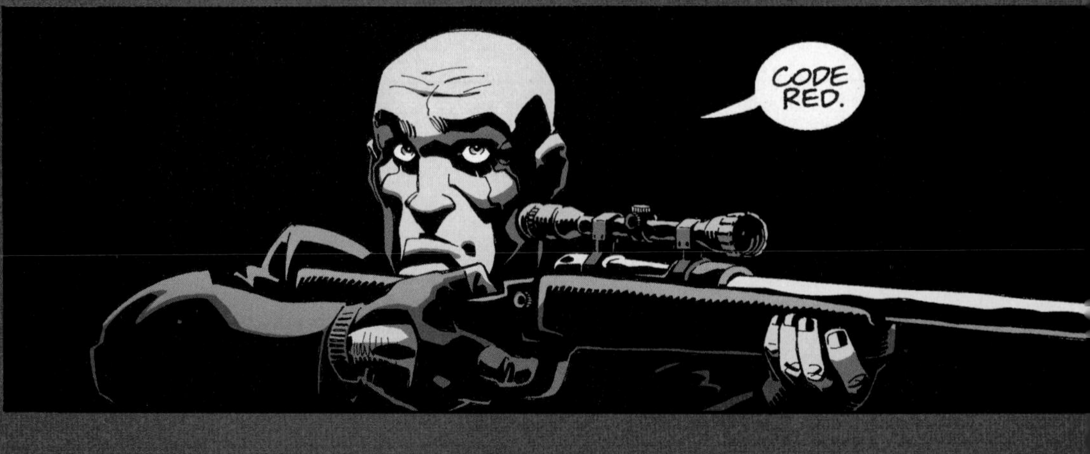
CODE RED.

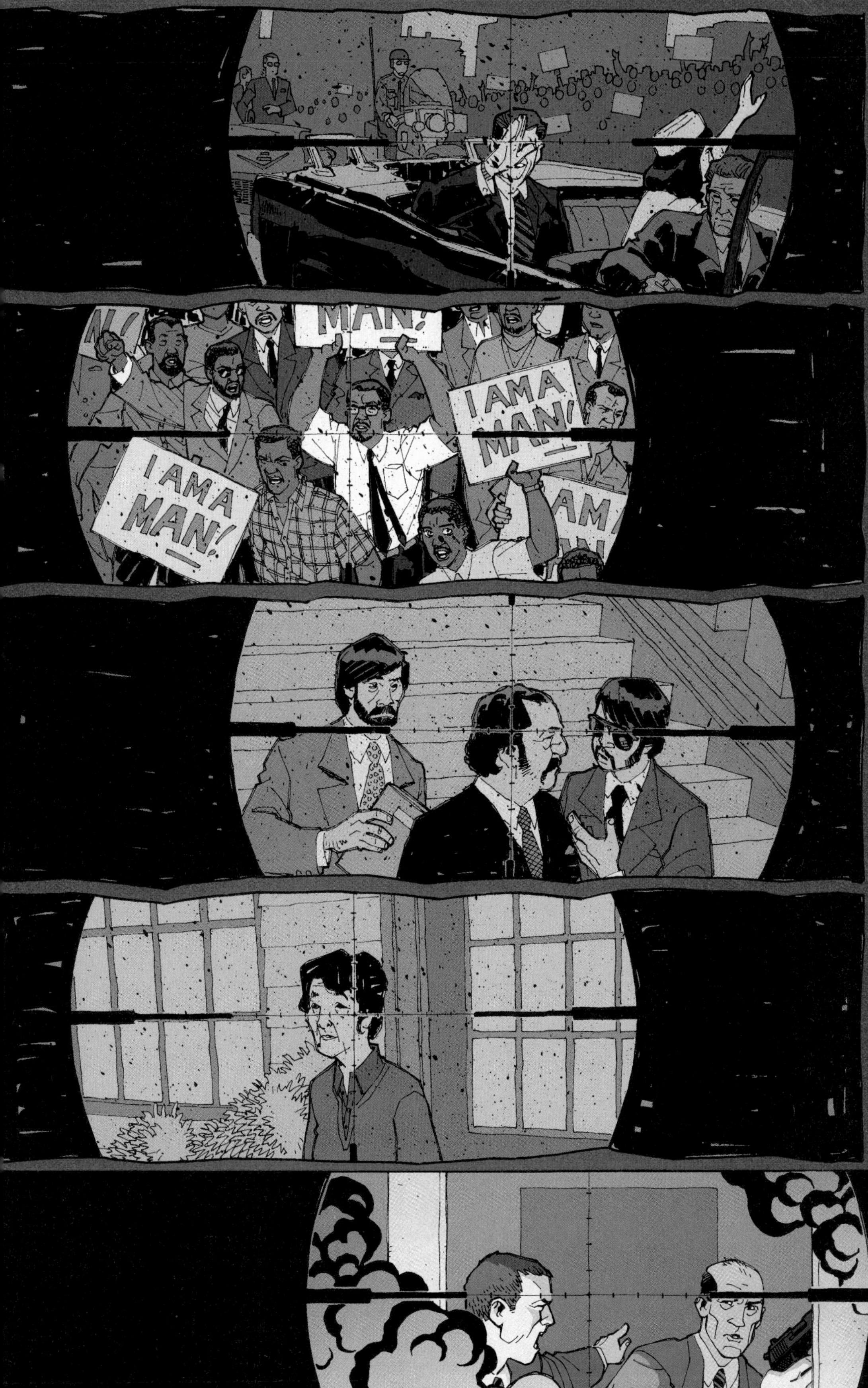
MAN!
I AM A MAN!
I AM A MAN!

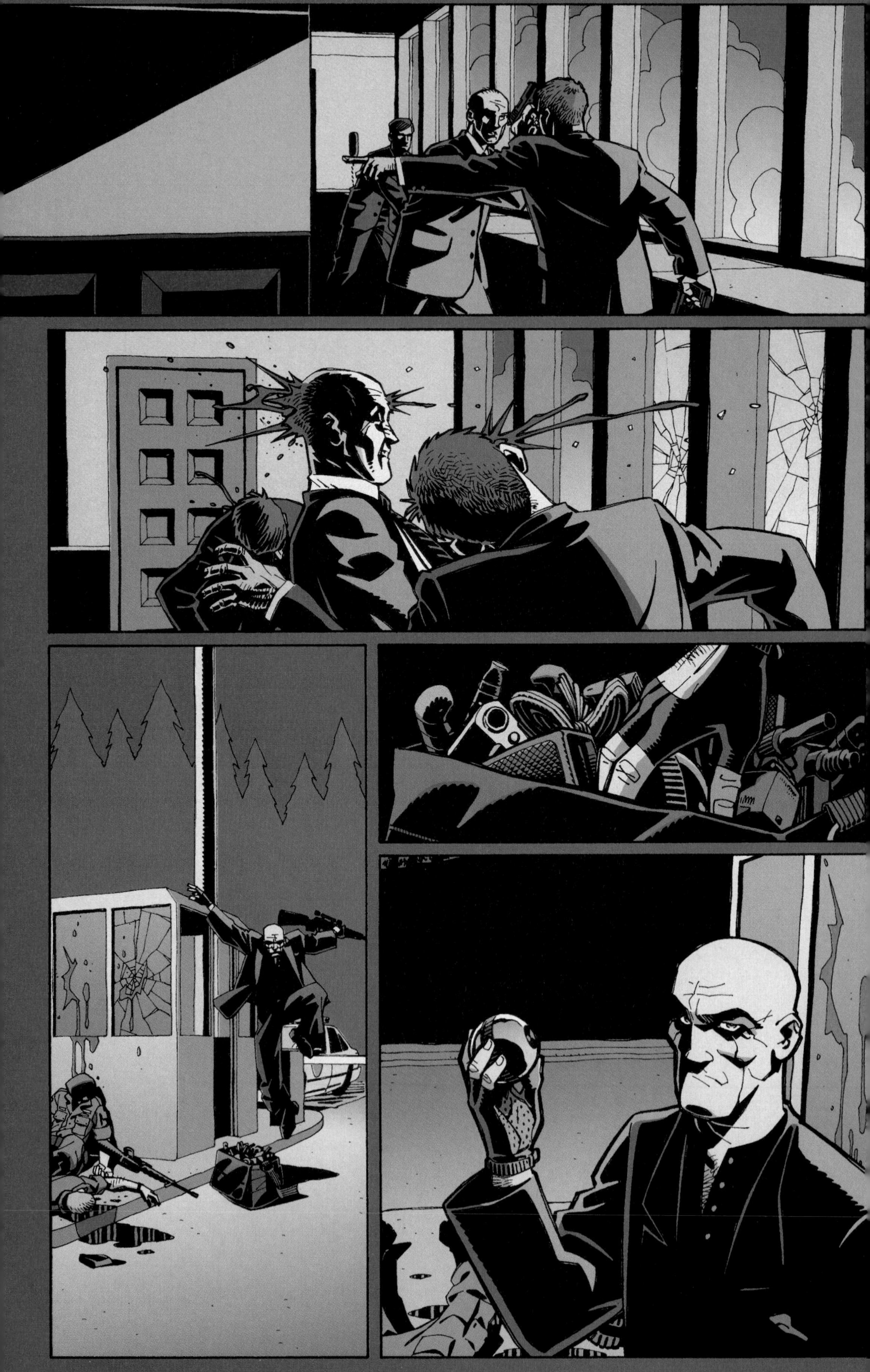

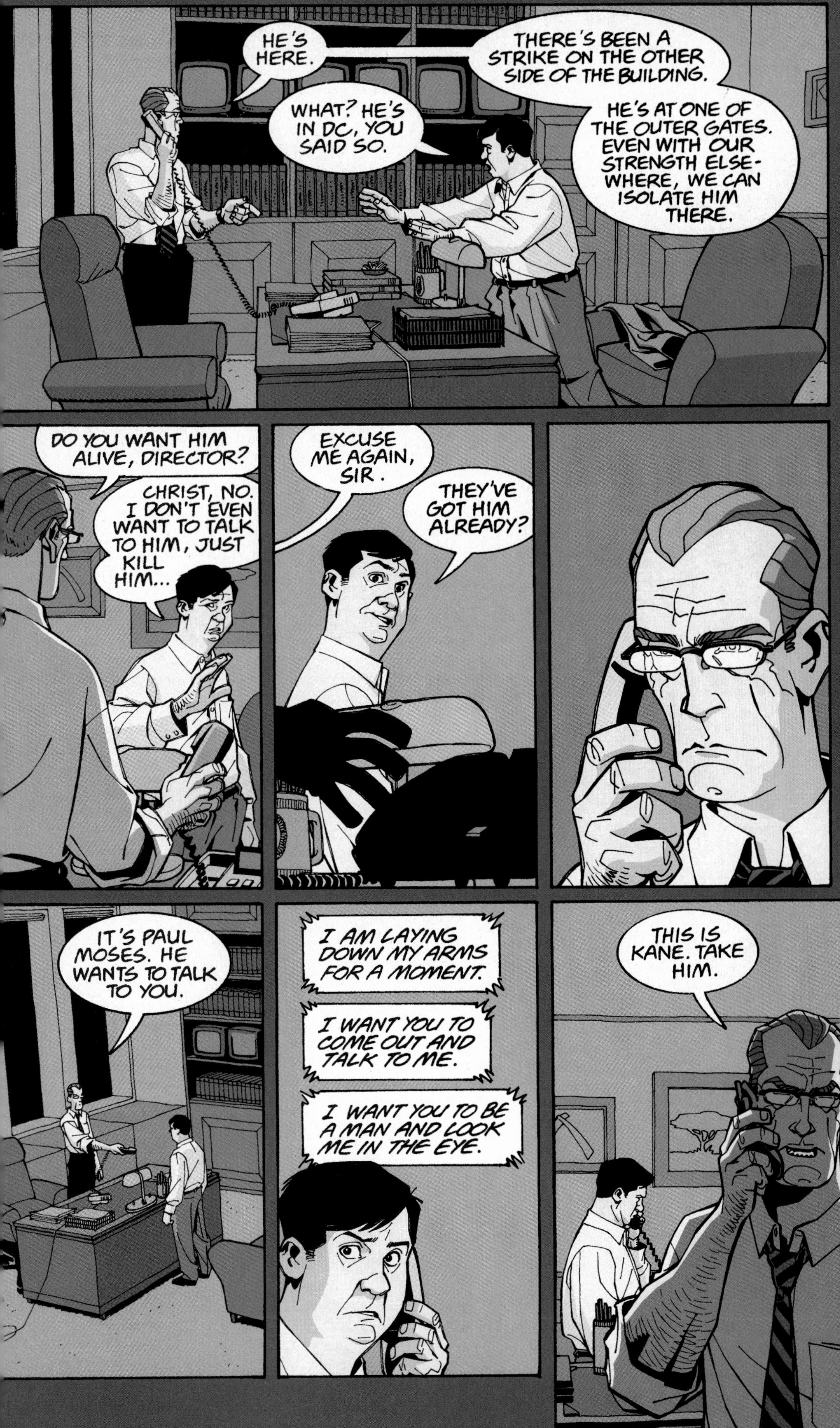
HE'S HERE.
THERE'S BEEN A STRIKE ON THE OTHER SIDE OF THE BUILDING.
WHAT? HE'S IN DC, YOU SAID SO.
HE'S AT ONE OF THE OUTER GATES. EVEN WITH OUR STRENGTH ELSE-WHERE, WE CAN ISOLATE HIM THERE.
DO YOU WANT HIM ALIVE, DIRECTOR?
CHRIST, NO. I DON'T EVEN WANT TO TALK TO HIM, JUST KILL HIM...
EXCUSE ME AGAIN, SIR.
THEY'VE GOT HIM ALREADY?
IT'S PAUL MOSES. HE WANTS TO TALK TO YOU.
I AM LAYING DOWN MY ARMS FOR A MOMENT.
I WANT YOU TO COME OUT AND TALK TO ME.
I WANT YOU TO BE A MAN AND LOOK ME IN THE EYE.
THIS IS KANE. TAKE HIM.

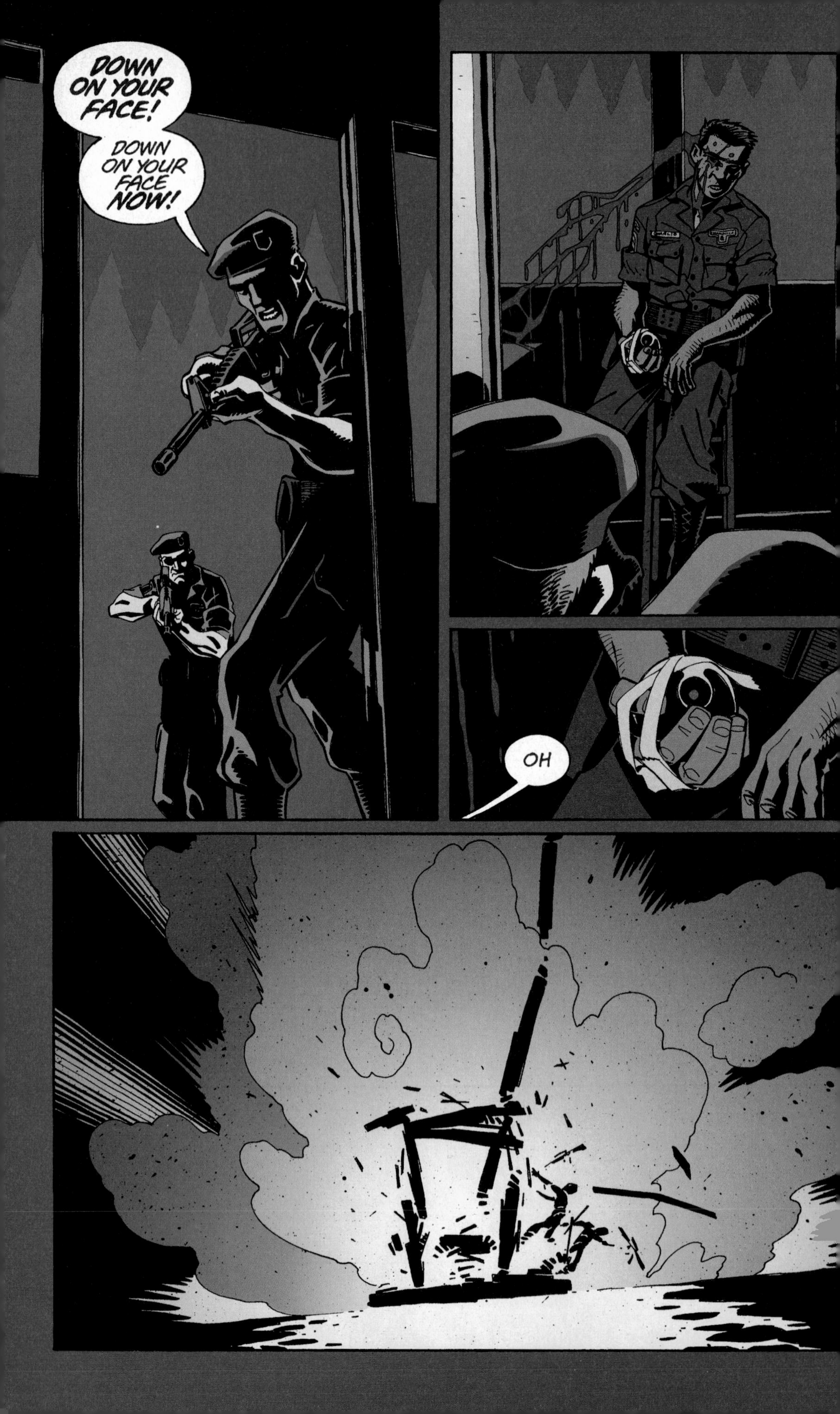
DOWN ON YOUR FACE!
DOWN ON YOUR FACE NOW!
OH

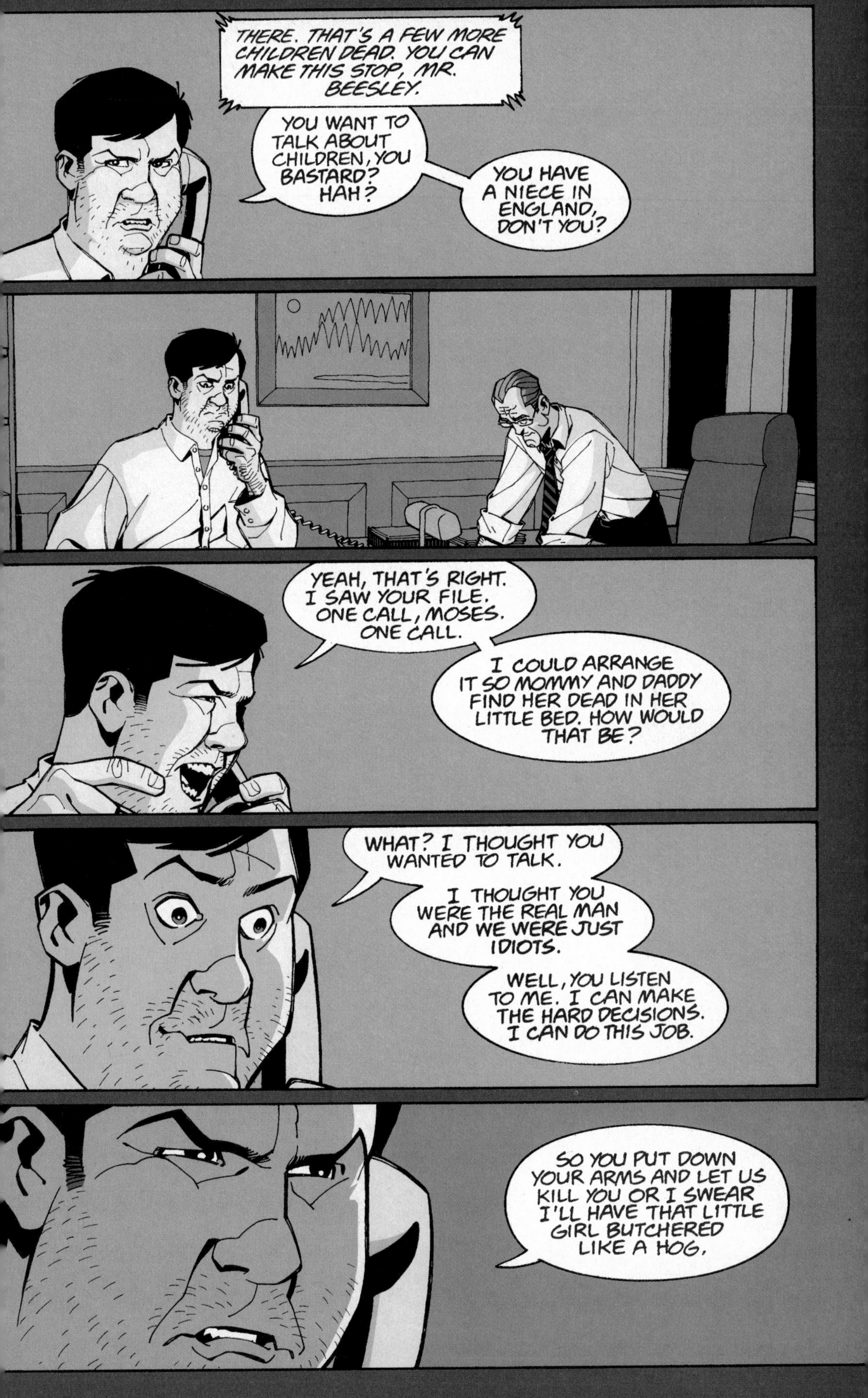
THERE. THAT'S A FEW MORE CHILDREN DEAD. YOU CAN MAKE THIS STOP, MR. BEESLEY.
YOU WANT TO TALK ABOUT CHILDREN, YOU BASTARD? HAH?
YOU HAVE A NIECE IN ENGLAND, DON'T YOU?
YEAH, THAT'S RIGHT. I SAW YOUR FILE. ONE CALL, MOSES. ONE CALL.
I COULD ARRANGE IT SO MOMMY AND DADDY FIND HER DEAD IN HER LITTLE BED. HOW WOULD THAT BE?
WHAT? I THOUGHT YOU WANTED TO TALK.
I THOUGHT YOU WERE THE REAL MAN AND WE WERE JUST IDIOTS.
WELL, YOU LISTEN TO ME. I CAN MAKE THE HARD DECISIONS. I CAN DO THIS JOB.
SO YOU PUT DOWN YOUR ARMS AND LET US KILL YOU OR I SWEAR I'LL HAVE THAT LITTLE GIRL BUTCHERED LIKE A HOG.

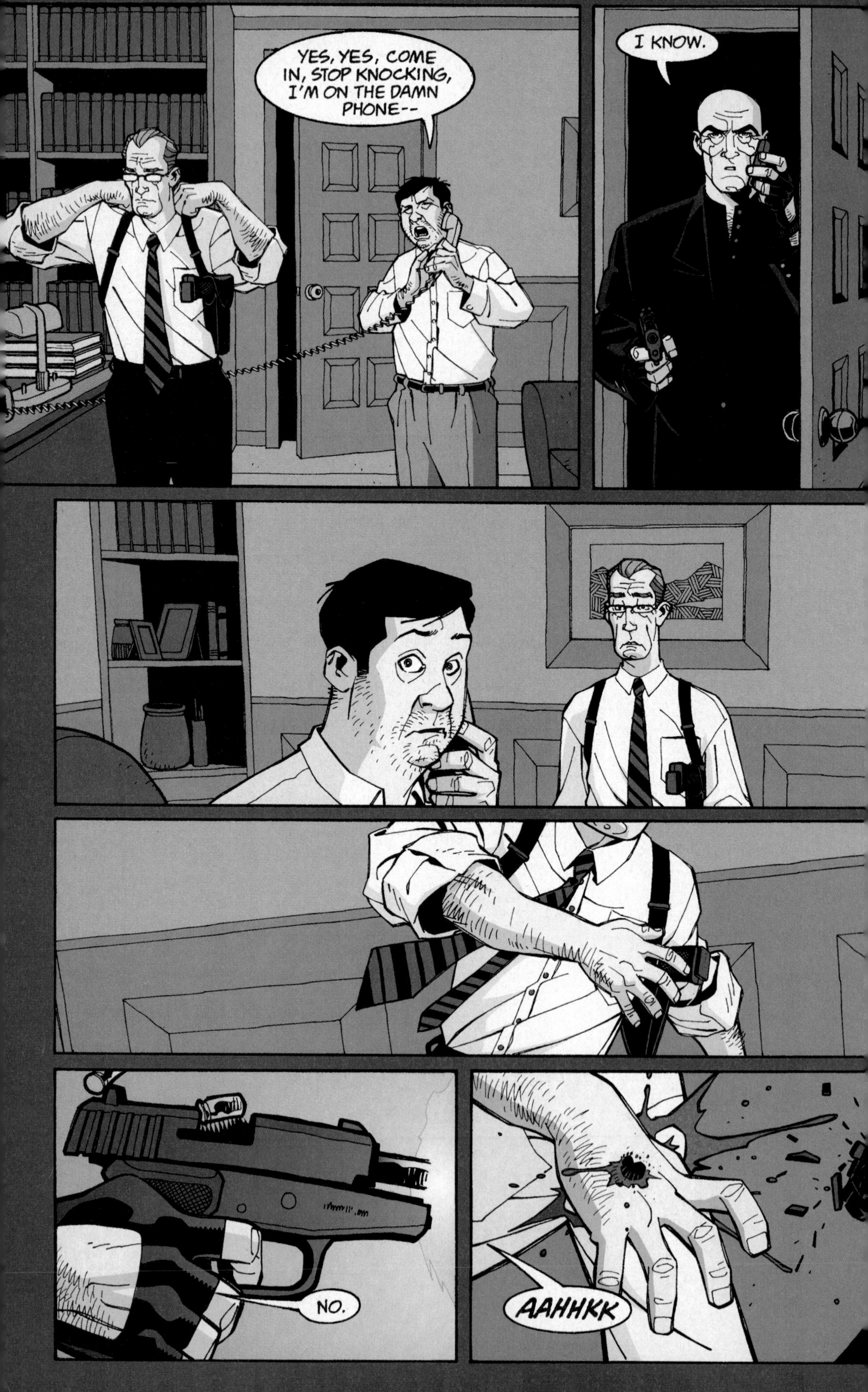
YES, YES, COME IN, STOP KNOCKING, I'M ON THE DAMN PHONE--
I KNOW.
NO.
AAHHKK

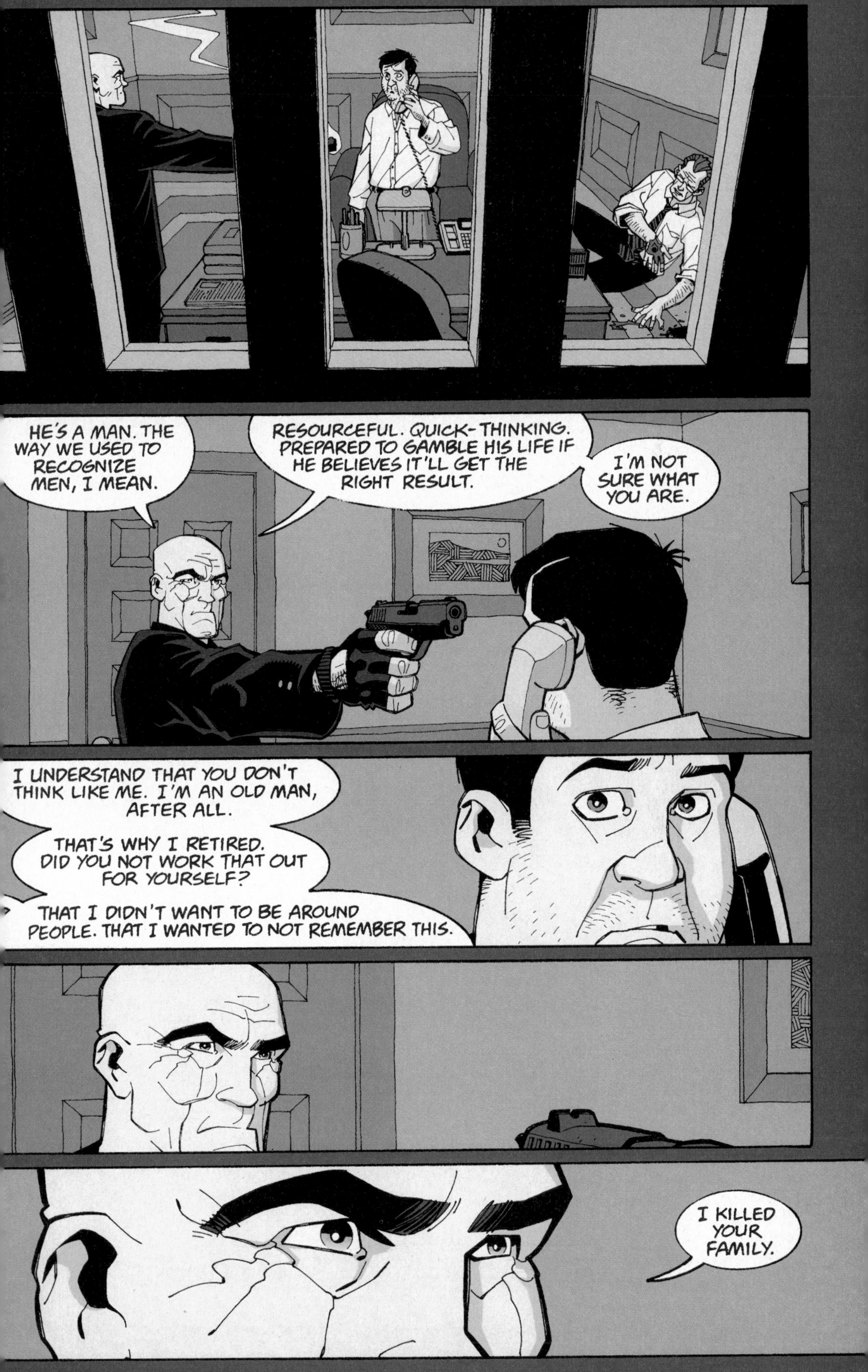
HE'S A MAN. THE WAY WE USED TO RECOGNIZE MEN, I MEAN.
RESOURCEFUL. QUICK-THINKING. PREPARED TO GAMBLE HIS LIFE IF HE BELIEVES IT'LL GET THE RIGHT RESULT.
I'M NOT SURE WHAT YOU ARE.
I UNDERSTAND THAT YOU DON'T THINK LIKE ME. I'M AN OLD MAN, AFTER ALL.
THAT'S WHY I RETIRED. DID YOU NOT WORK THAT OUT FOR YOURSELF?
THAT I DIDN'T WANT TO BE AROUND PEOPLE. THAT I WANTED TO NOT REMEMBER THIS.
I KILLED YOUR FAMILY.

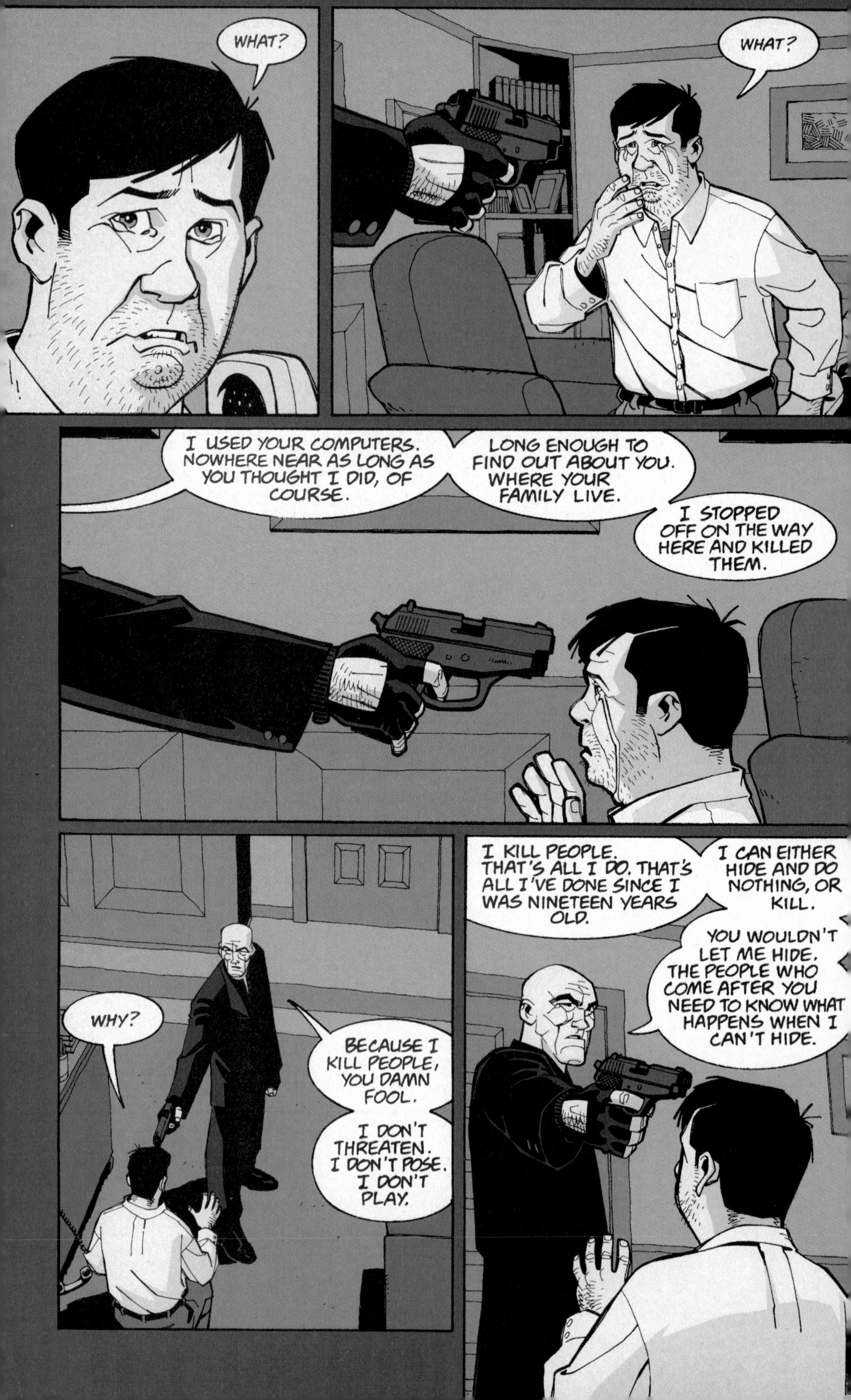
WHAT?
WHAT?
I USED YOUR COMPUTERS. NOWHERE NEAR AS LONG AS YOU THOUGHT I DID, OF COURSE.
LONG ENOUGH TO FIND OUT ABOUT YOU. WHERE YOUR FAMILY LIVE.
I STOPPED OFF ON THE WAY HERE AND KILLED THEM.
WHY?
BECAUSE I KILL PEOPLE, YOU DAMN FOOL.
I DON'T THREATEN. I DON'T POSE. I DON'T PLAY.
I KILL PEOPLE. THAT'S ALL I DO. THAT'S ALL I'VE DONE SINCE I WAS NINETEEN YEARS OLD.
I CAN EITHER HIDE AND DO NOTHING, OR KILL.
YOU WOULDN'T LET ME HIDE. THE PEOPLE WHO COME AFTER YOU NEED TO KNOW WHAT HAPPENS WHEN I CAN'T HIDE.

YOU ON THE FLOOR. YOU SHOWED HIM MY FILE?

I HAVE TO. IT'S MY JOB. INDOCTRINATING A NEW DIRECTOR.

HE SAW IT ALL, THEN.

THEY HAVE TO. THEY HAVE TO UNDERSTAND THE BREADTH OF WHAT WE DO.

HE'S A POLITICAL APPOINTEE. CIA DOESN'T TAKE DIRECTORS FROM WITHIN, OR FROM MILITARY INTEL, ANYMORE.

LIKE DISTRICT ATTORNEYS ARE ELECTED, RATHER THAN APPOINTED. LIKE WE ELECT EVERYTHING. WE DON'T JUST --HA-- TAKE THE PERSON WHO'S BEST FOR THE TOP JOB AND PUT THEM THERE.

GNNF. COMPETENCE ISN'T NECESSARY. JUST BEING IN THE RIGHT PLACE AT THE RIGHT TIME.

YOU'RE GOING TO HAVE TO KILL ME, MOSES.

BECAUSE YOU WILL CHANGE ALL THAT.

YOU'RE GOING TO BE TREATED LIKE SOMEONE WHO FLEW A PLANE INTO A BUILDING.

WE TRIED TO KILL YOU BECAUSE YOU'RE A MONSTER. WE FAILED TO DO IT RIGHT, AND YOU CAME BACK TO PUNISH US FOR OUR INCOMPETENCE.

YOU WILL HAVE TO KILL ME, AND EVERYONE IN THIS BUILDING, BECAUSE WE WILL RAISE AN ARMY UP AGAINST YOU.

HAVE YOU GOT THE STOMACH FOR THAT?

DO YOU UNDERSTAND THAT YOU CAN NOW ONLY FIND THE PEACE YOU WANT BY DYING?

I'M SORRY YOU WERE CHEATED OUT OF YOUR RETIREMENT. BUT IT'S DONE. AND NOW NOTHING CAN BE THE SAME.

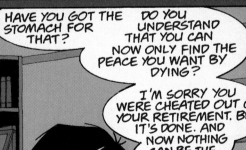

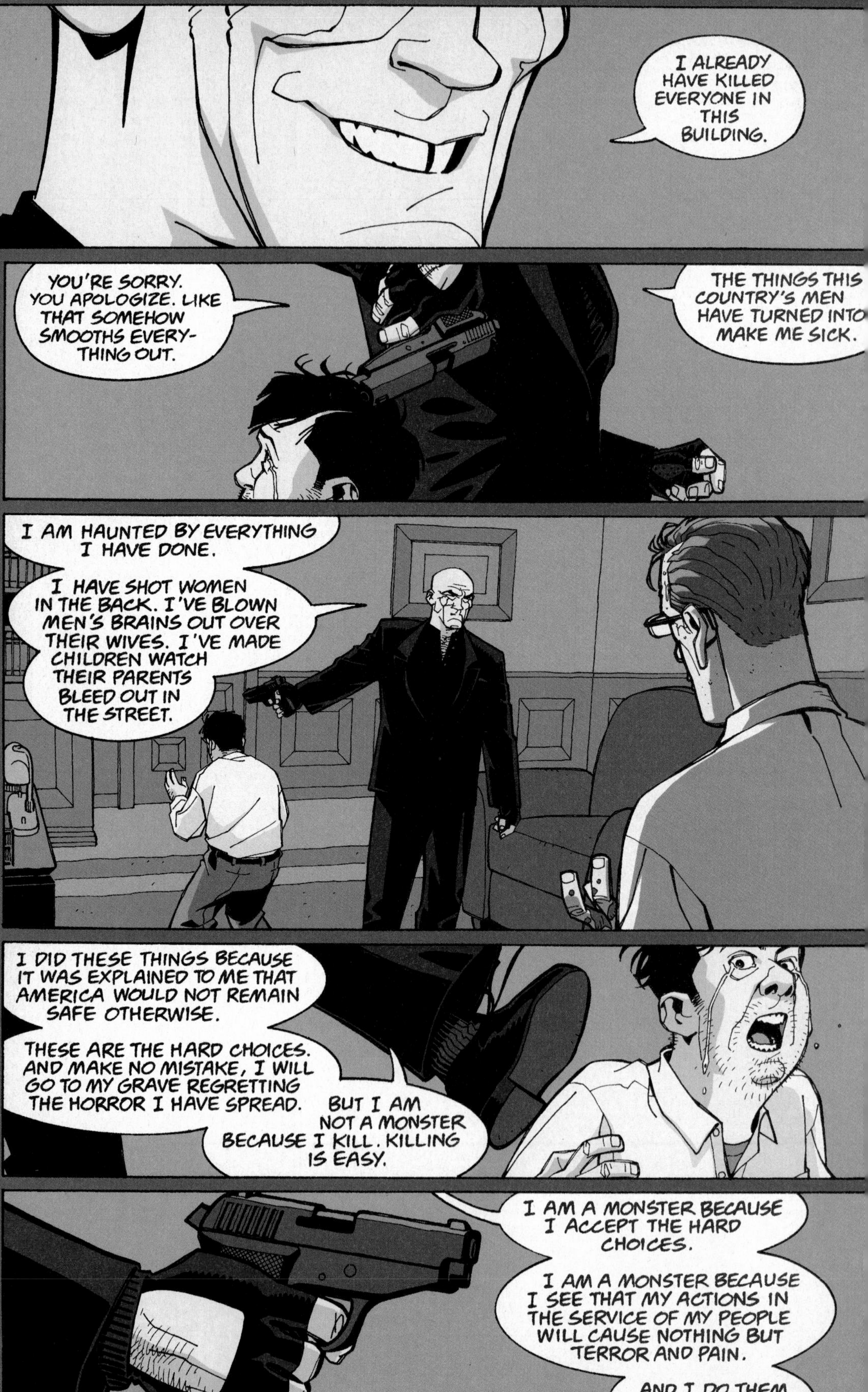
I ALREADY HAVE KILLED EVERYONE IN THIS BUILDING.
YOU'RE SORRY. YOU APOLOGIZE. LIKE THAT SOMEHOW SMOOTHS EVERY-THING OUT.
THE THINGS THIS COUNTRY'S MEN HAVE TURNED INTO MAKE ME SICK.
I AM HAUNTED BY EVERYTHING I HAVE DONE.
I HAVE SHOT WOMEN IN THE BACK. I'VE BLOWN MEN'S BRAINS OUT OVER THEIR WIVES. I'VE MADE CHILDREN WATCH THEIR PARENTS BLEED OUT IN THE STREET.
I DID THESE THINGS BECAUSE IT WAS EXPLAINED TO ME THAT AMERICA WOULD NOT REMAIN SAFE OTHERWISE.
THESE ARE THE HARD CHOICES. AND MAKE NO MISTAKE, I WILL GO TO MY GRAVE REGRETTING THE HORROR I HAVE SPREAD.
BUT I AM NOT A MONSTER BECAUSE I KILL. KILLING IS EASY.
I AM A MONSTER BECAUSE I ACCEPT THE HARD CHOICES.
I AM A MONSTER BECAUSE I SEE THAT MY ACTIONS IN THE SERVICE OF MY PEOPLE WILL CAUSE NOTHING BUT TERROR AND PAIN.
AND I DO THEM ANYWAY.

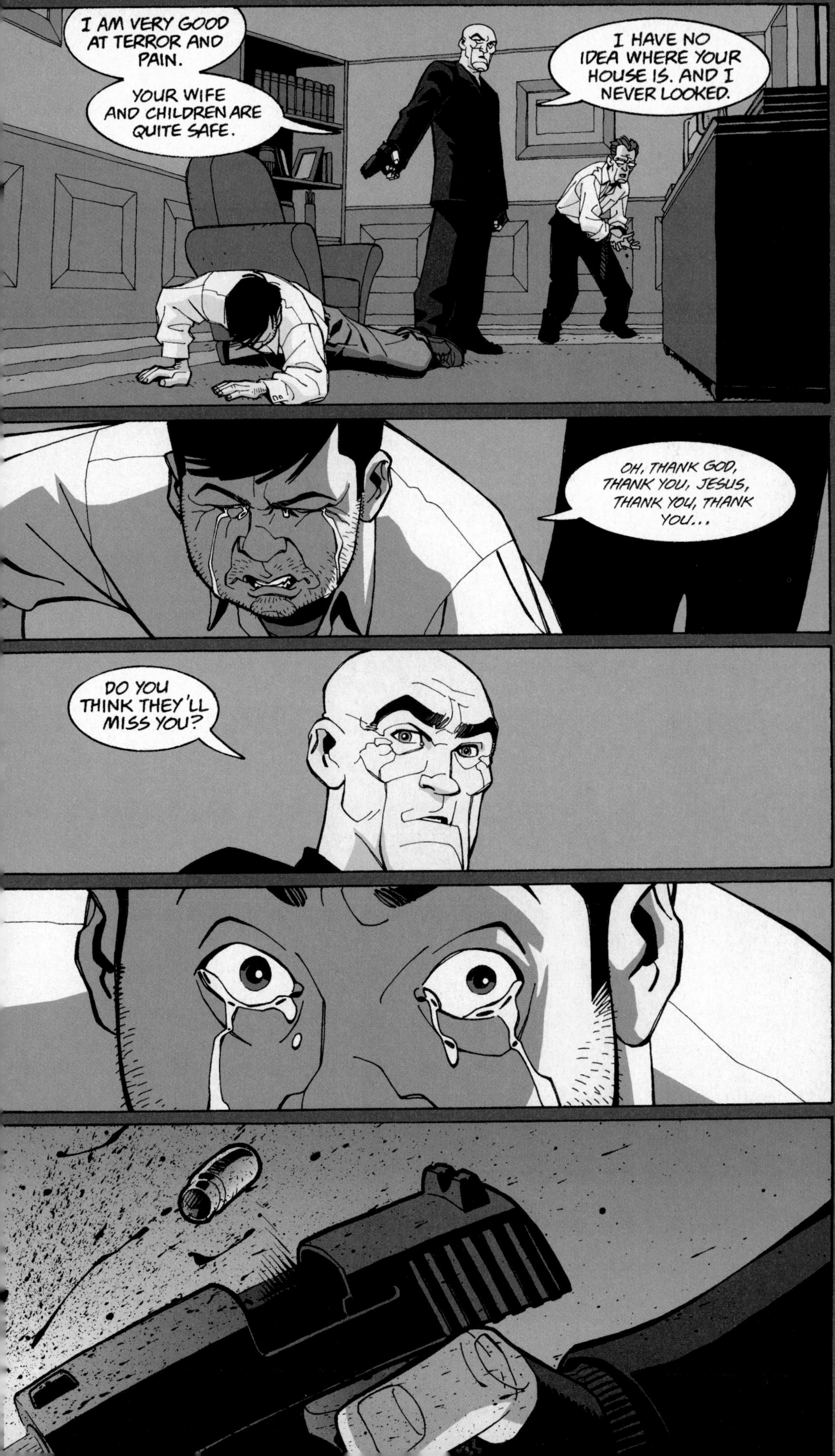
I AM VERY GOOD AT TERROR AND PAIN.
YOUR WIFE AND CHILDREN ARE QUITE SAFE.
I HAVE NO IDEA WHERE YOUR HOUSE IS. AND I NEVER LOOKED.
OH, THANK GOD, THANK YOU, JESUS, THANK YOU, THANK YOU...
DO YOU THINK THEY'LL MISS YOU?

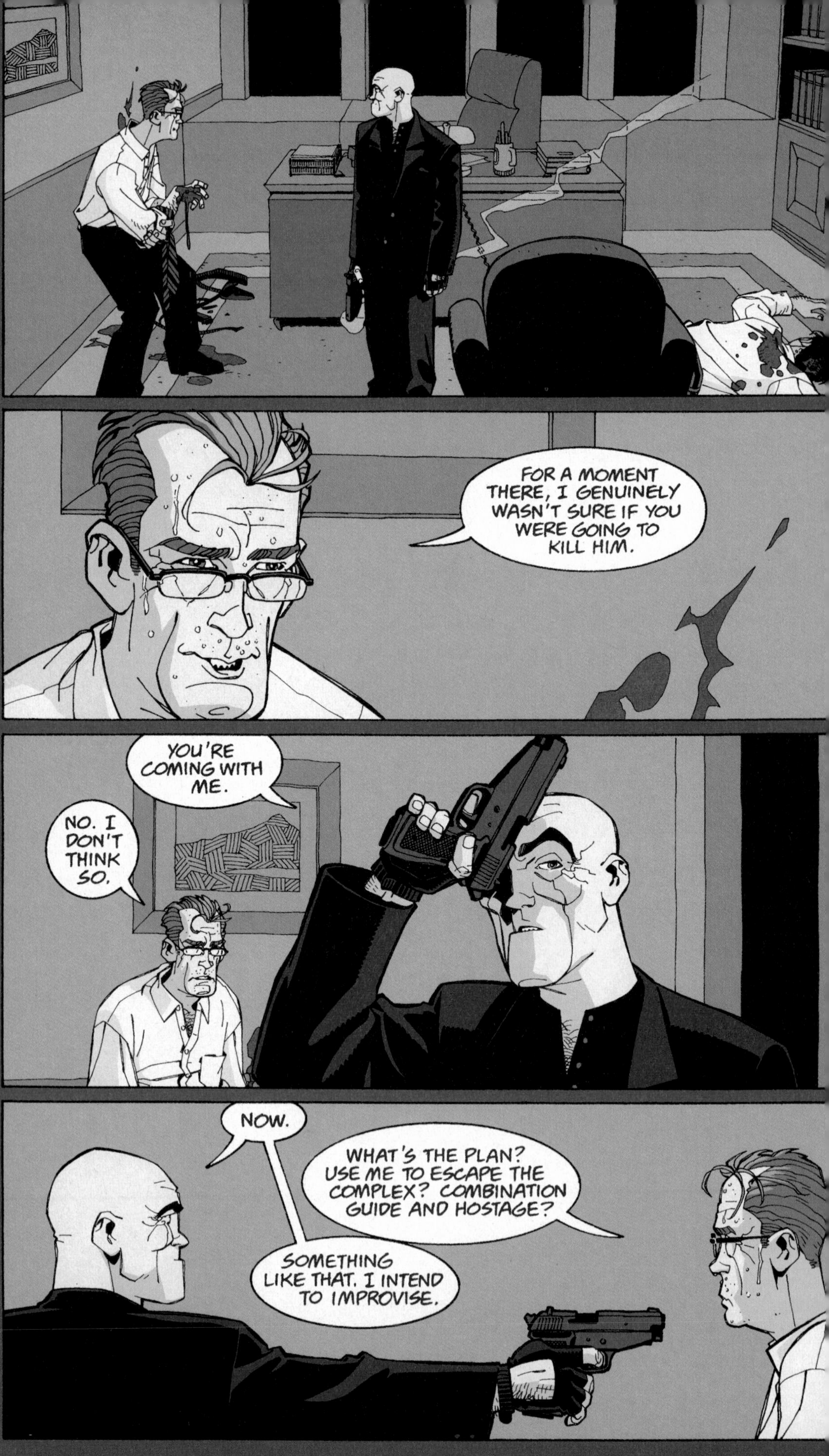
FOR A MOMENT THERE, I GENUINELY WASN'T SURE IF YOU WERE GOING TO KILL HIM.
YOU'RE COMING WITH ME.
NO. I DON'T THINK SO.
NOW.
WHAT'S THE PLAN? USE ME TO ESCAPE THE COMPLEX? COMBINATION GUIDE AND HOSTAGE?
SOMETHING LIKE THAT. I INTEND TO IMPROVISE.

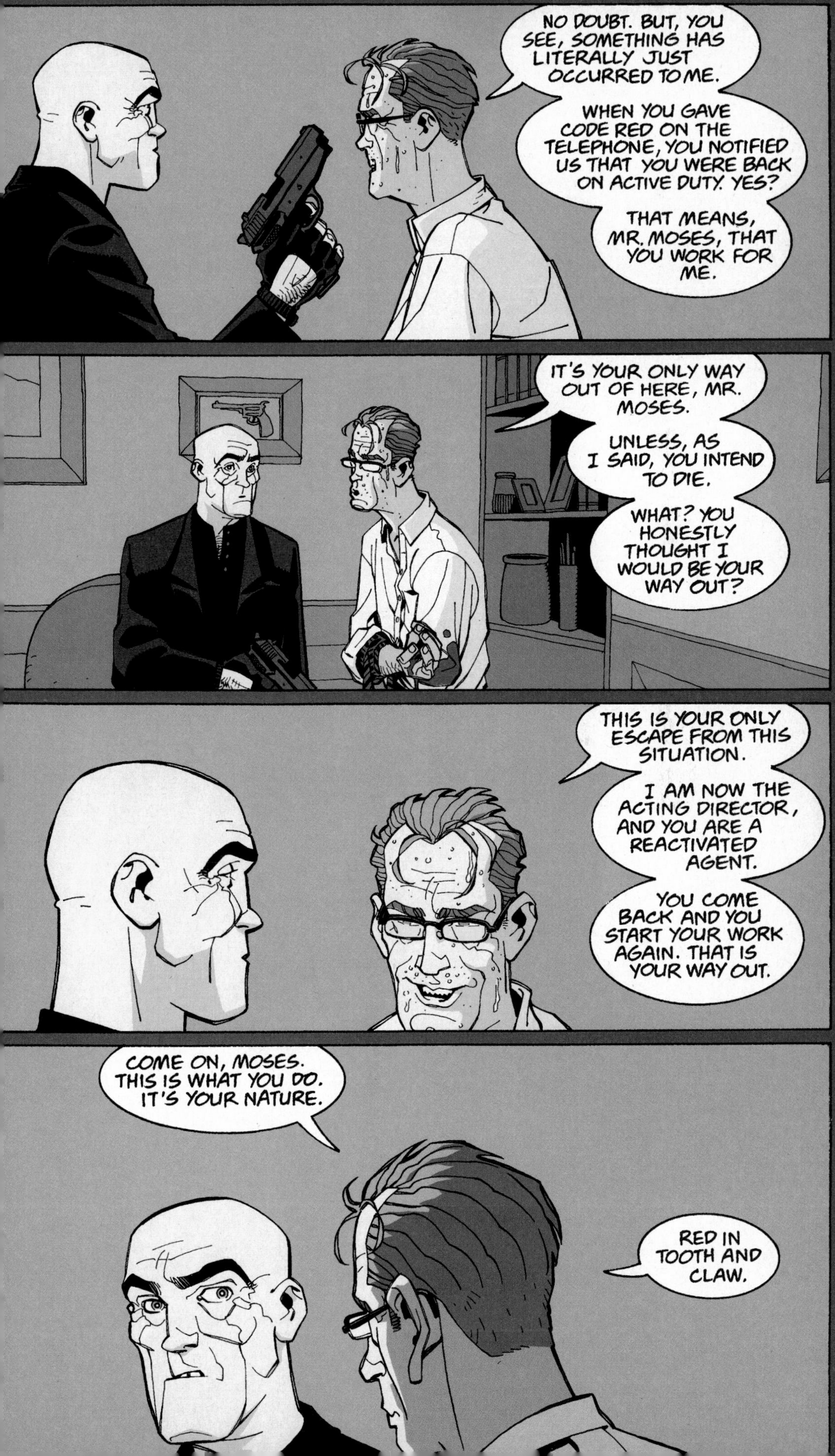
NO DOUBT. BUT, YOU SEE, SOMETHING HAS LITERALLY JUST OCCURRED TO ME.
WHEN YOU GAVE CODE RED ON THE TELEPHONE, YOU NOTIFIED US THAT YOU WERE BACK ON ACTIVE DUTY. YES?
THAT MEANS, MR. MOSES, THAT YOU WORK FOR ME.
IT'S YOUR ONLY WAY OUT OF HERE, MR. MOSES.
UNLESS, AS I SAID, YOU INTEND TO DIE.
WHAT? YOU HONESTLY THOUGHT I WOULD BE YOUR WAY OUT?
THIS IS YOUR ONLY ESCAPE FROM THIS SITUATION.
I AM NOW THE ACTING DIRECTOR, AND YOU ARE A REACTIVATED AGENT.
YOU COME BACK AND YOU START YOUR WORK AGAIN. THAT IS YOUR WAY OUT.
COME ON, MOSES. THIS IS WHAT YOU DO. IT'S YOUR NATURE.
RED IN TOOTH AND CLAW.

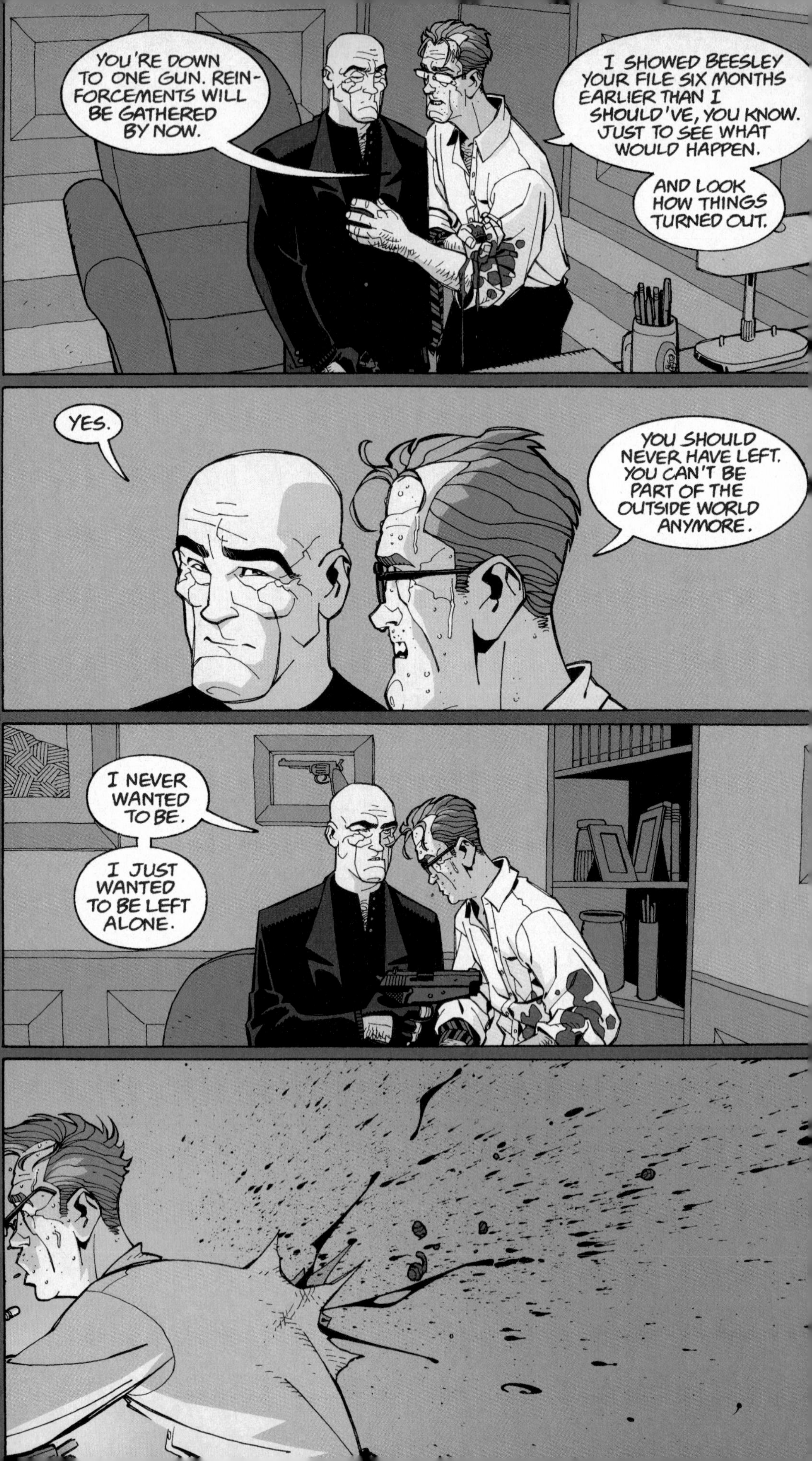
YOU'RE DOWN TO ONE GUN. REIN-FORCEMENTS WILL BE GATHERED BY NOW.
I SHOWED BEESLEY YOUR FILE SIX MONTHS EARLIER THAN I SHOULD'VE, YOU KNOW. JUST TO SEE WHAT WOULD HAPPEN.
AND LOOK HOW THINGS TURNED OUT.
YES.
YOU SHOULD NEVER HAVE LEFT. YOU CAN'T BE PART OF THE OUTSIDE WORLD ANYMORE.
I NEVER WANTED TO BE.
I JUST WANTED TO BE LEFT ALONE.

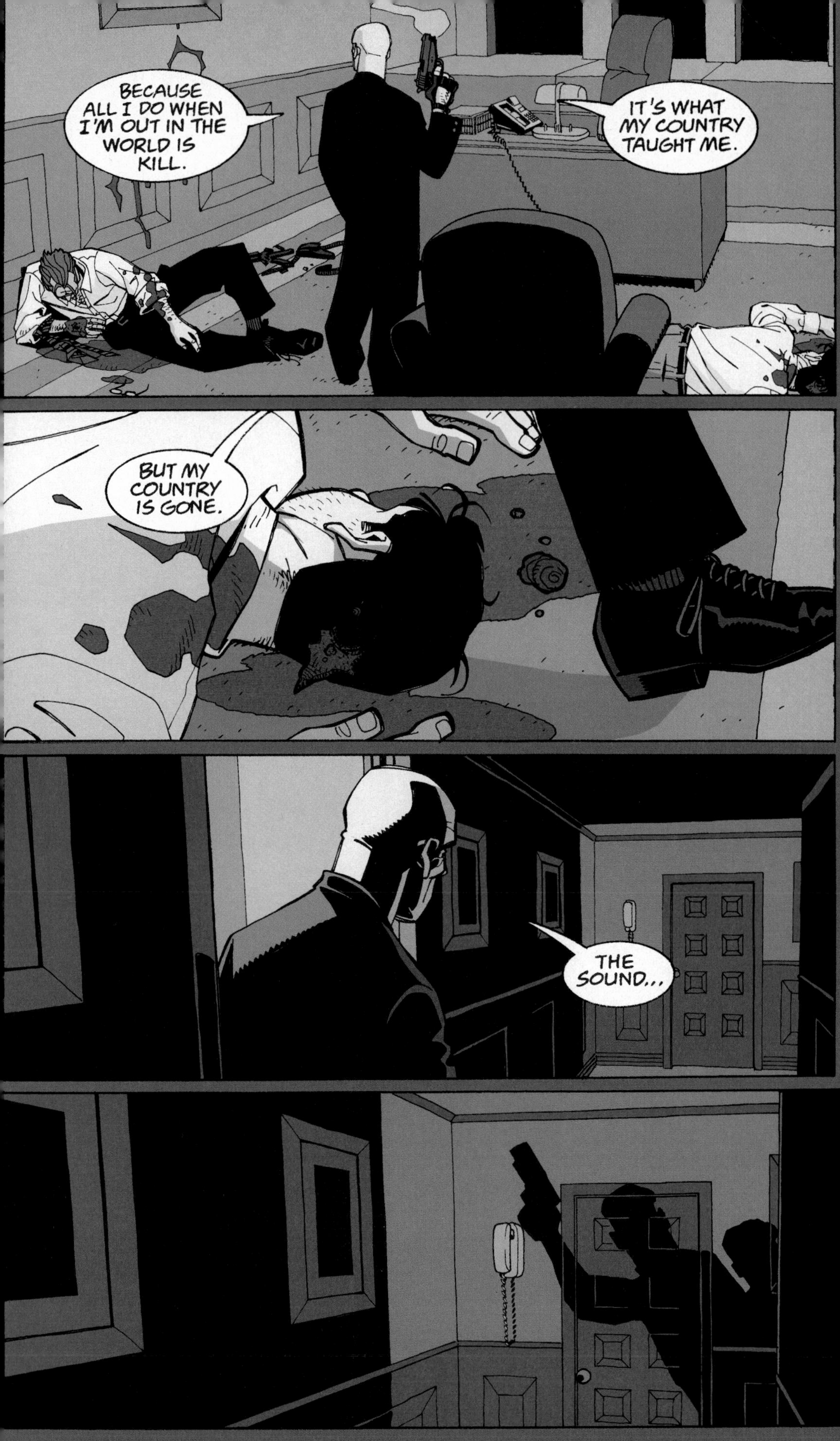
BECAUSE ALL I DO WHEN I'M OUT IN THE WORLD IS KILL.
IT'S WHAT MY COUNTRY TAUGHT ME.
BUT MY COUNTRY IS GONE.
THE SOUND...

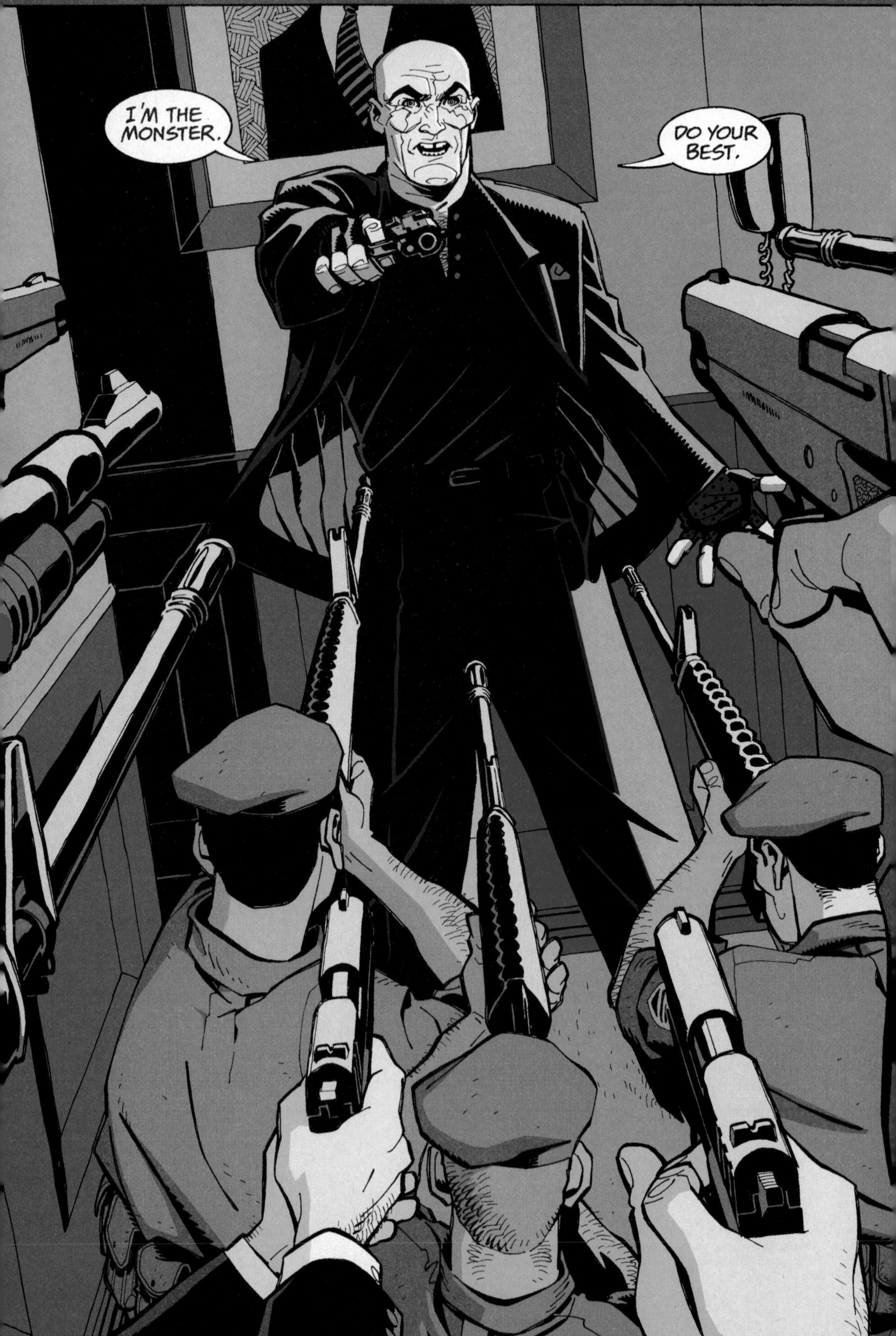
I'M THE MONSTER.
DO YOUR BEST.

end

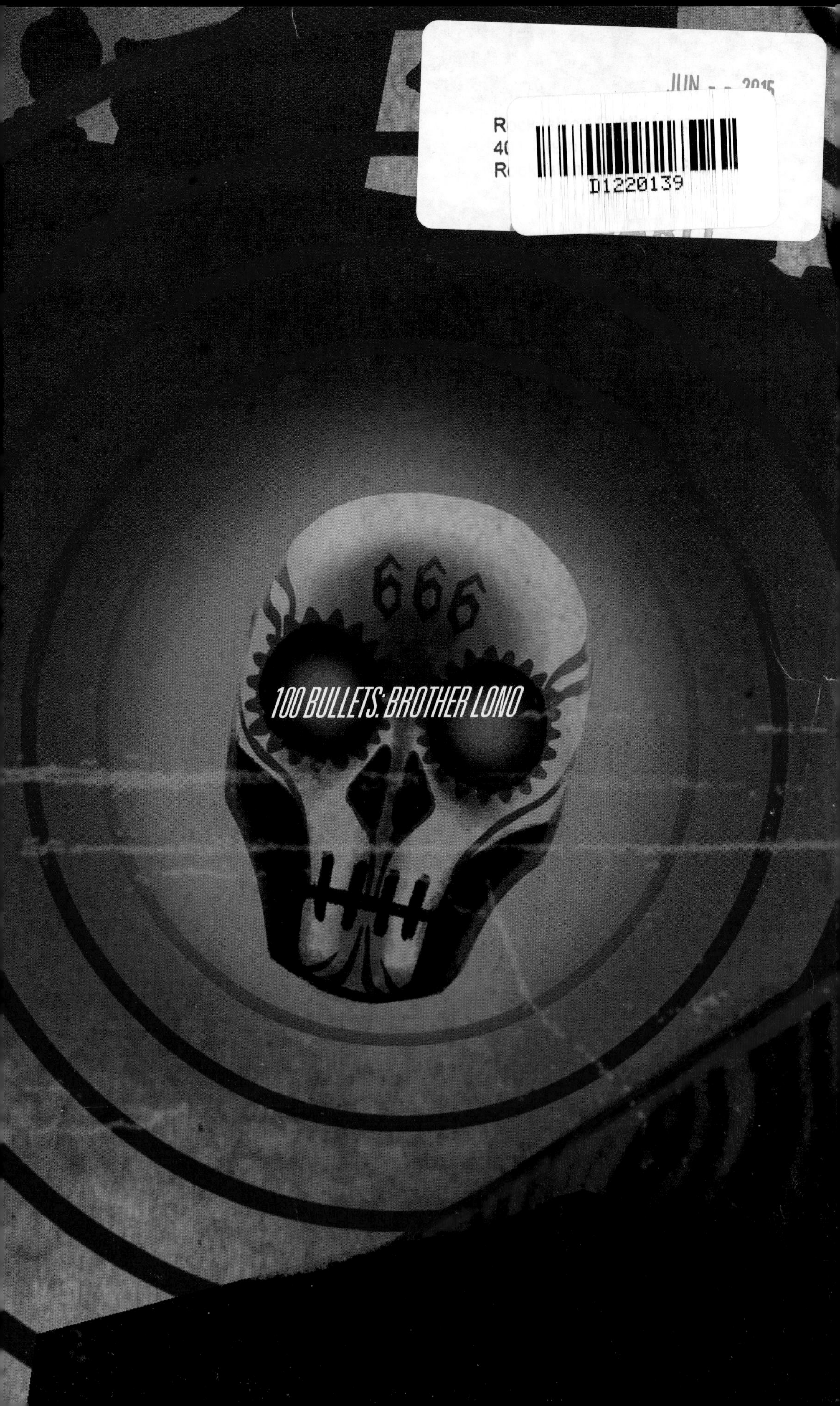
100 BULLETS: BROTHER LONO

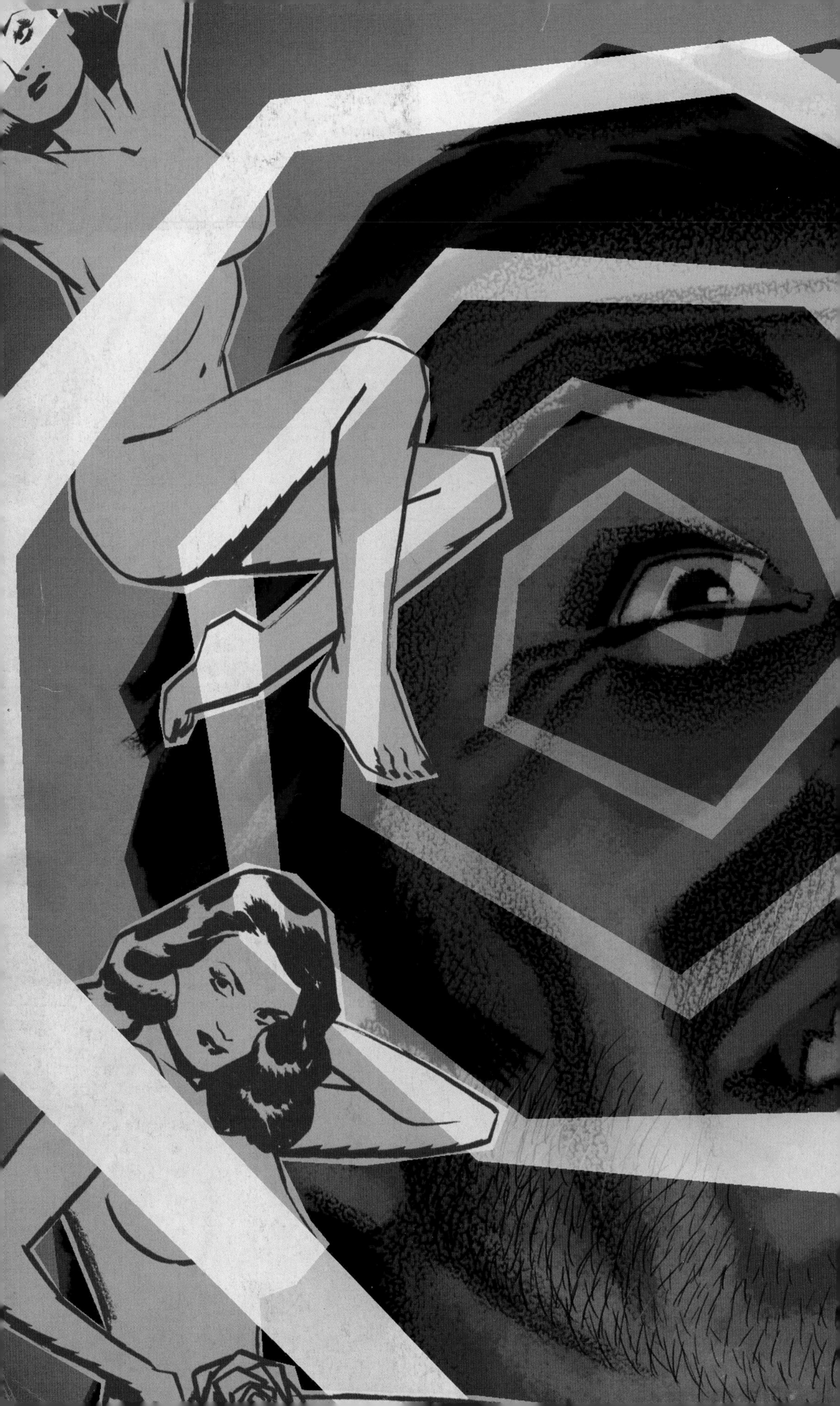

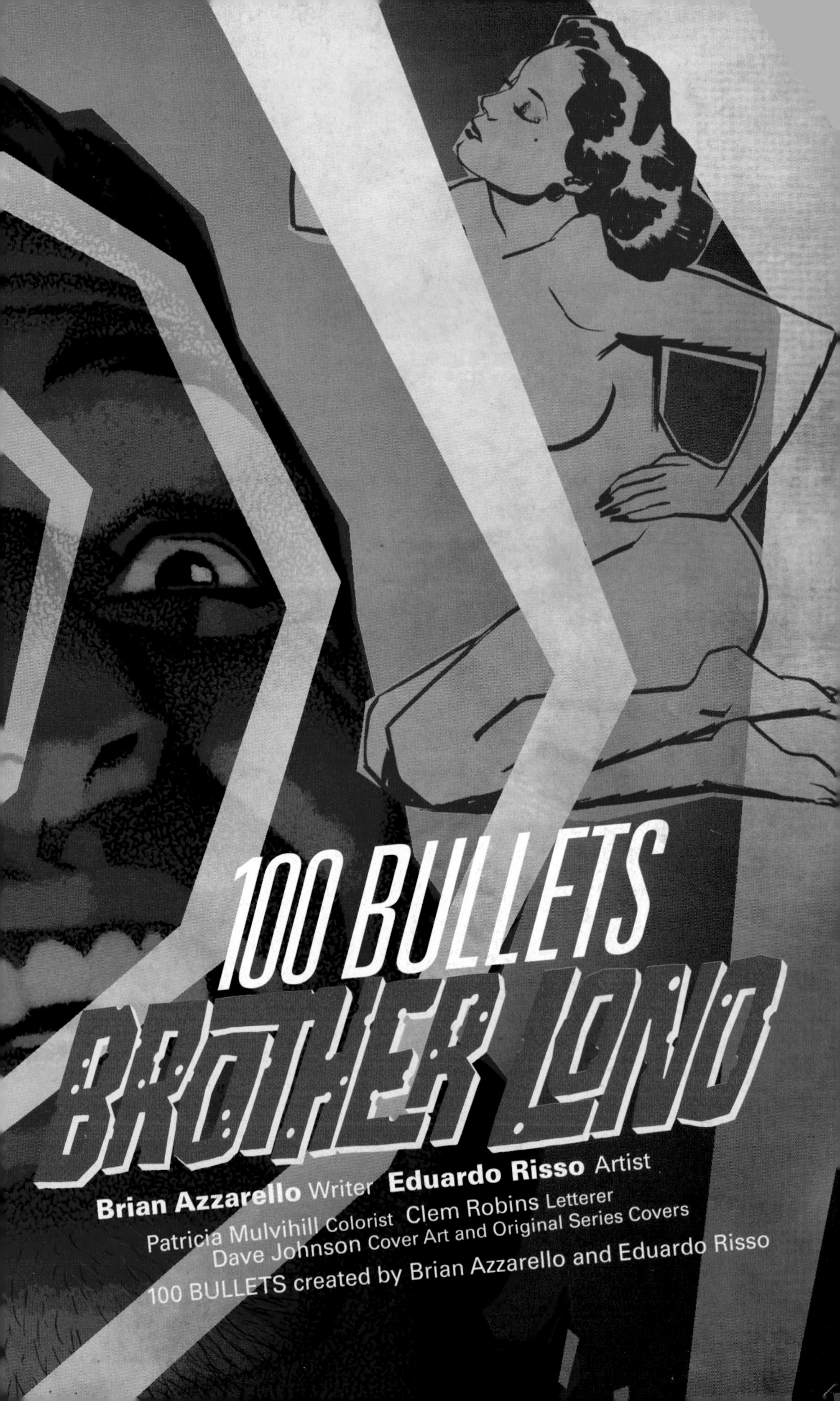
100 BULLETS
BROTHER LONO
Brian Azzarello Writer Eduardo Risso Artist
Patricia Mulvihill Colorist Clem Robins Letterer
Dave Johnson Cover Art and Original Series Covers
100 BULLETS created by Brian Azzarello and Eduardo Risso

Will Dennis Editor – Original Series
Sara Miller Gregory Lockard Assistant Editors – Original Series
Scott Nybakken Editor
Robbin Brosterman Design Director – Books
Louis Prandi Publication Design

Shelly Bond Executive Editor – Vertigo
Hank Kanalz Senior VP – Vertigo & Integrated Publishing

Diane Nelson President
Dan DiDio and **Jim Lee** Co-Publishers
Geoff Johns Chief Creative Officer
John Rood Executive VP – Sales, Marketing & Business Development

Amy Genkins Senior VP – Business & Legal Affairs
Nairi Gardiner Senior VP – Finance
Jeff Boison VP – Publishing Planning
Mark Chiarello VP – Art Direction & Design
John Cunningham VP – Marketing
Terri Cunningham VP – Editorial Administration
Alison Gill Senior VP – Manufacturing & Operations
Jay Kogan VP – Business & Legal Affairs, Publishing
Jack Mahan VP – Business Affairs, Talent
Nick Napolitano VP – Manufacturing Administration
Sue Pohja VP – Book Sales
Courtney Simmons Senior VP – Publicity
Bob Wayne Senior VP – Sales

SUSTAINABLE
FORESTRY
INITIATIVE

Certified Chain of Custody
At Least 20% Certified Forest Content
www.sfiprogram.org
SFI-01042
APPLIES TO TEXT STOCK ONLY

Library of Congress Cataloging-in-Publication Data

Azzarello, Brian, author.
  100 Bullets : Brother Lono / Brian Azzarello ; [illustrated by] Eduardo
Risso.
    pages cm
  Summary: "The Eisner Award-winning team behind 100 BULLETS
— writer Brian Azzarello and artist Eduardo Risso — reunites to tell
the story of the baddest Minuteman of all. When last we saw Lono in
100 BULLETS, Dizzy Cordova had shot him through the chest... but
Lono always was too tough to die. Now, after the final events of 100
BULLETS, Lono finds himself in Mexico working on the side of the
angels. Collects the entire eight-issue run of this limited series." —
Provided by publisher.
  ISBN 978-1-4012-4506-1 (paperback)
  1. Graphic novels. I. Risso, Eduardo, illustrator. II. Title. III. Title:
Brother Lono.
  PN6728.A14A9925 2014
  741.5'973—dc23

                              2013049628

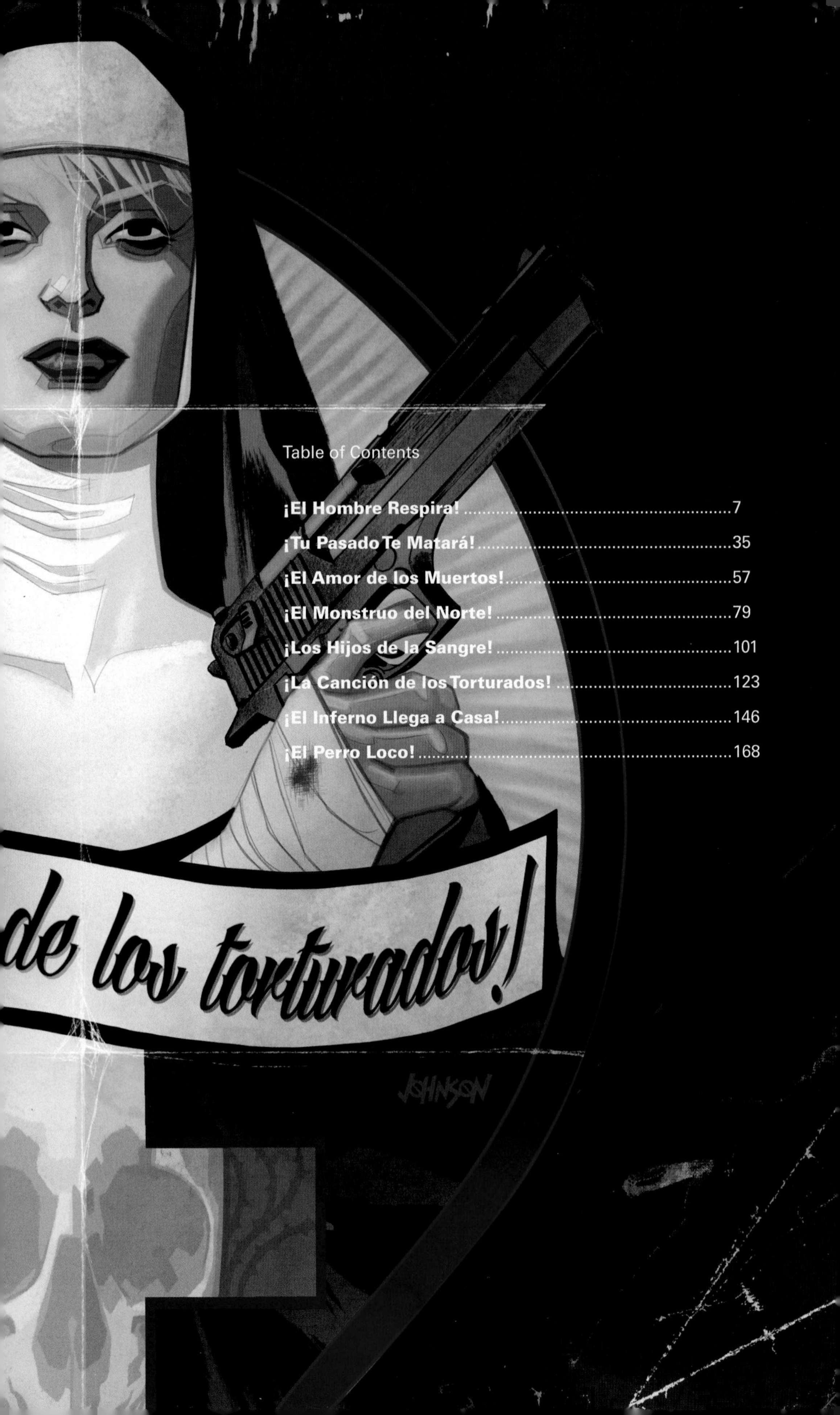
de los torturados!
JOHNSON

Table of Contents

BROTHER LONO

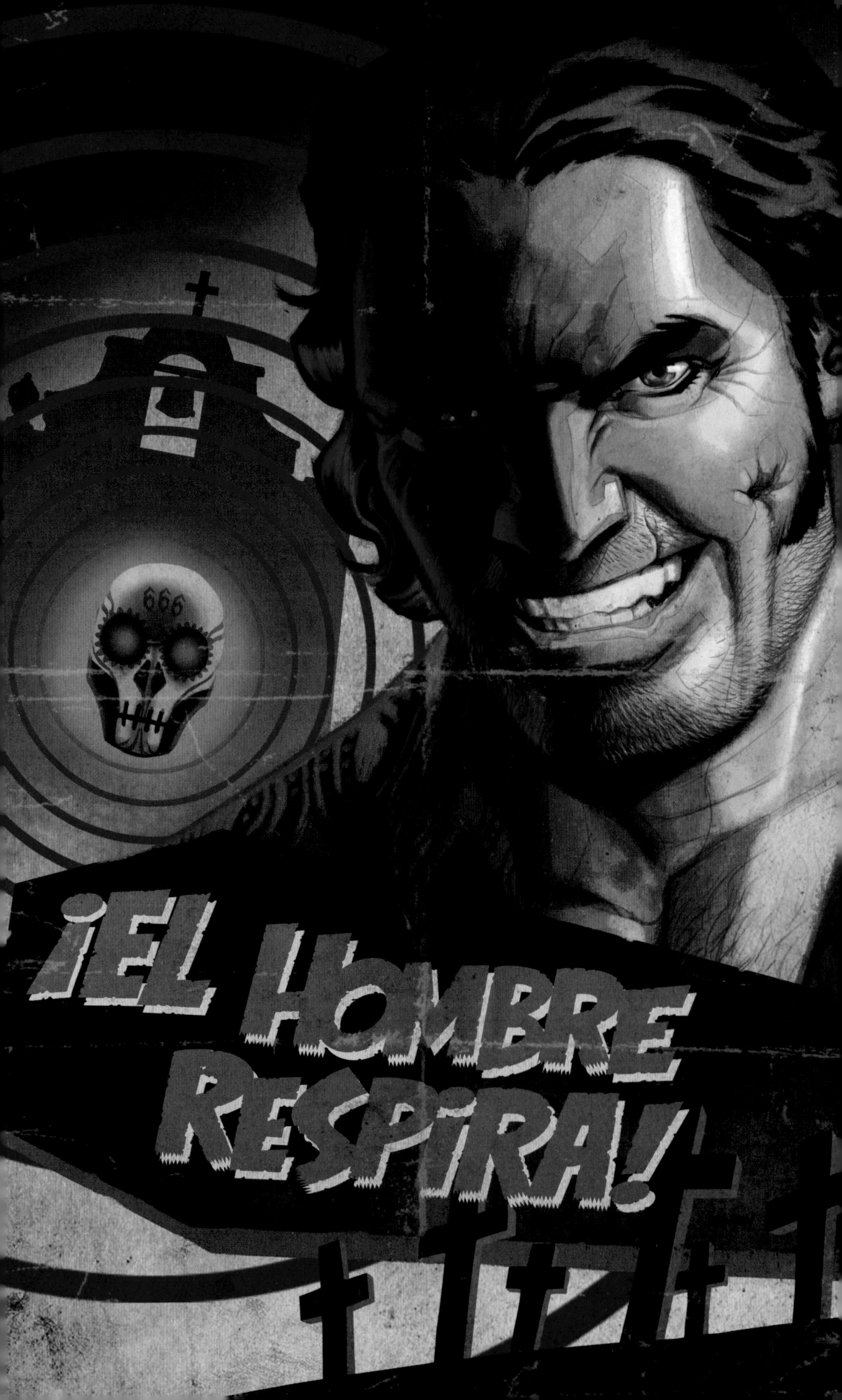
¡EL HOMBRE RESPIRA!
666

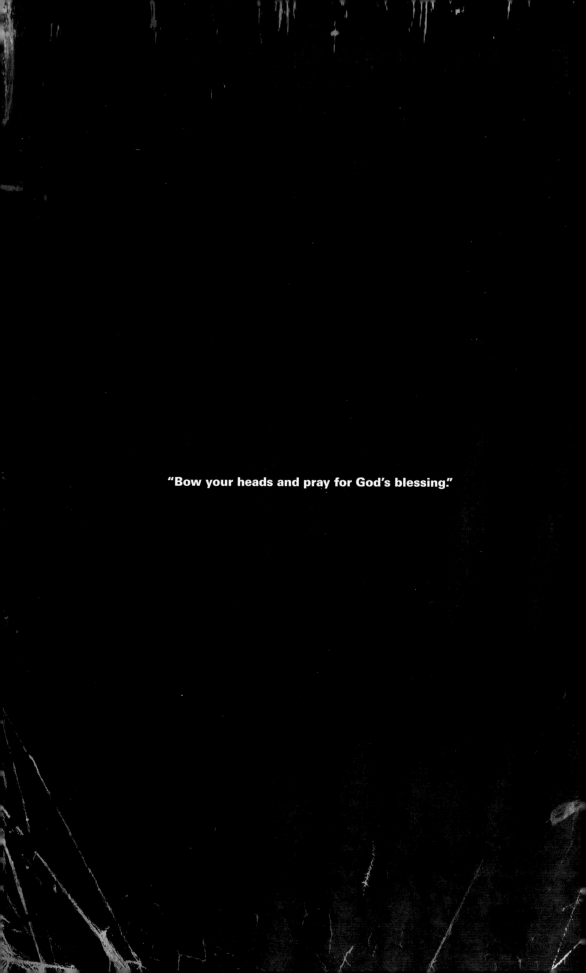

"Bow your heads and pray for God's blessing."

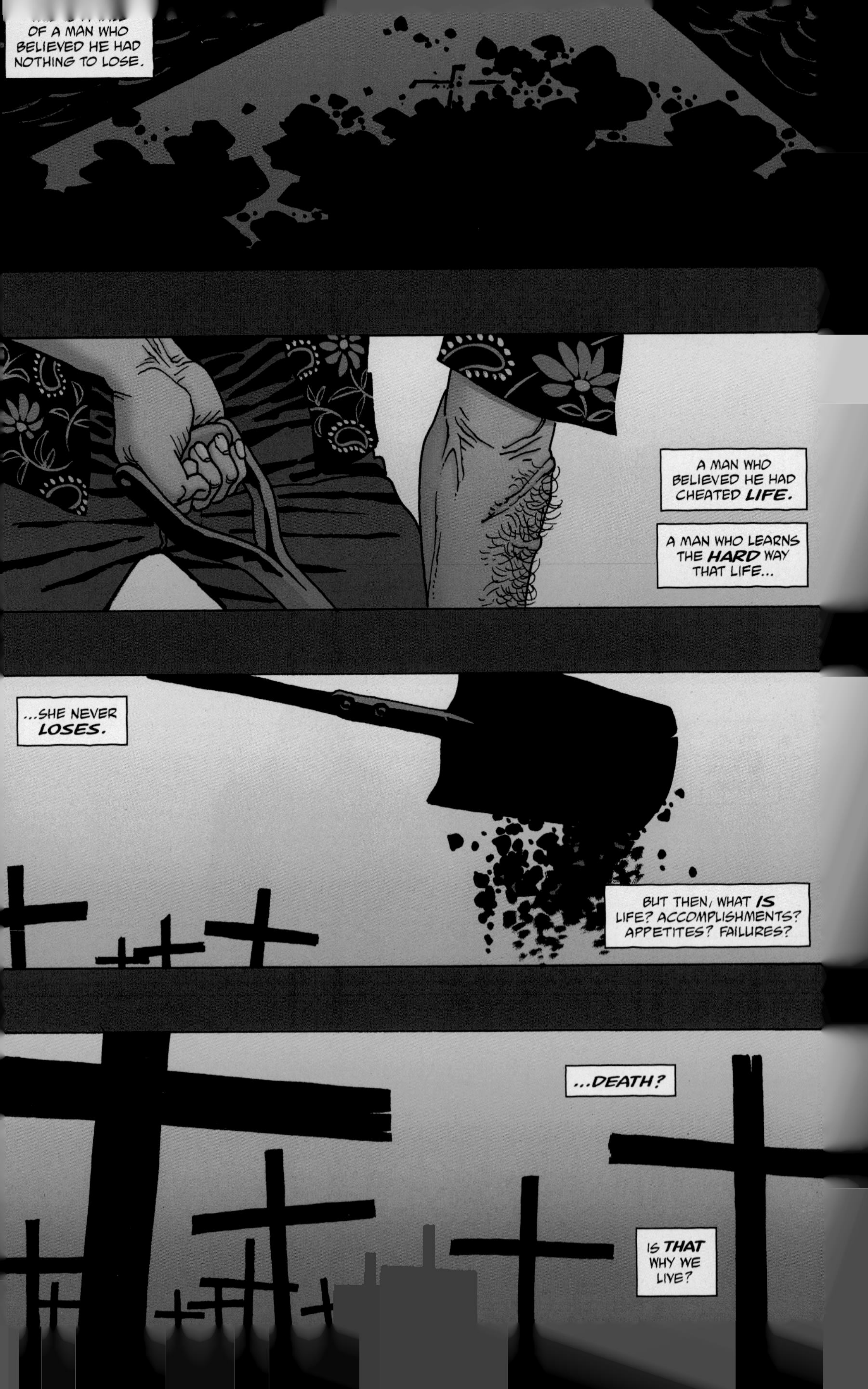
OF A MAN WHO BELIEVED HE HAD NOTHING TO LOSE.
A MAN WHO BELIEVED HE HAD CHEATED LIFE.
A MAN WHO LEARNS THE HARD WAY THAT LIFE...
...SHE NEVER LOSES.
BUT THEN, WHAT IS LIFE? ACCOMPLISHMENTS? APPETITES? FAILURES?
...DEATH?
IS THAT WHY WE LIVE?

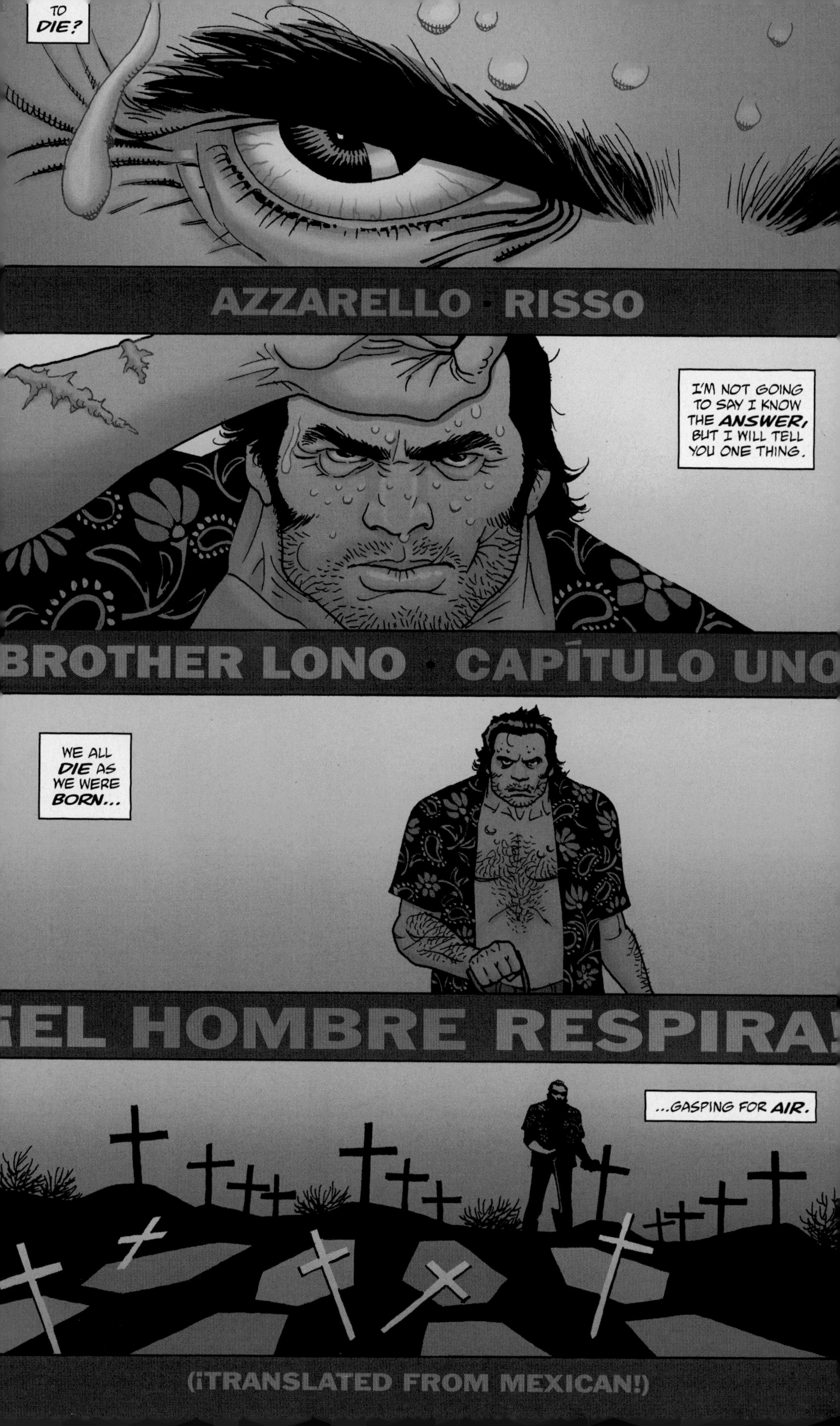

TO DIE?
AZZARELLO · RISSO
I'M NOT GOING TO SAY I KNOW THE ANSWER, BUT I WILL TELL YOU ONE THING.
BROTHER LONO · CAPÍTULO UNO
WE ALL DIE AS WE WERE BORN...
¡EL HOMBRE RESPIRA!
...GASPING FOR AIR.
(¡TRANSLATED FROM MEXICAN!)

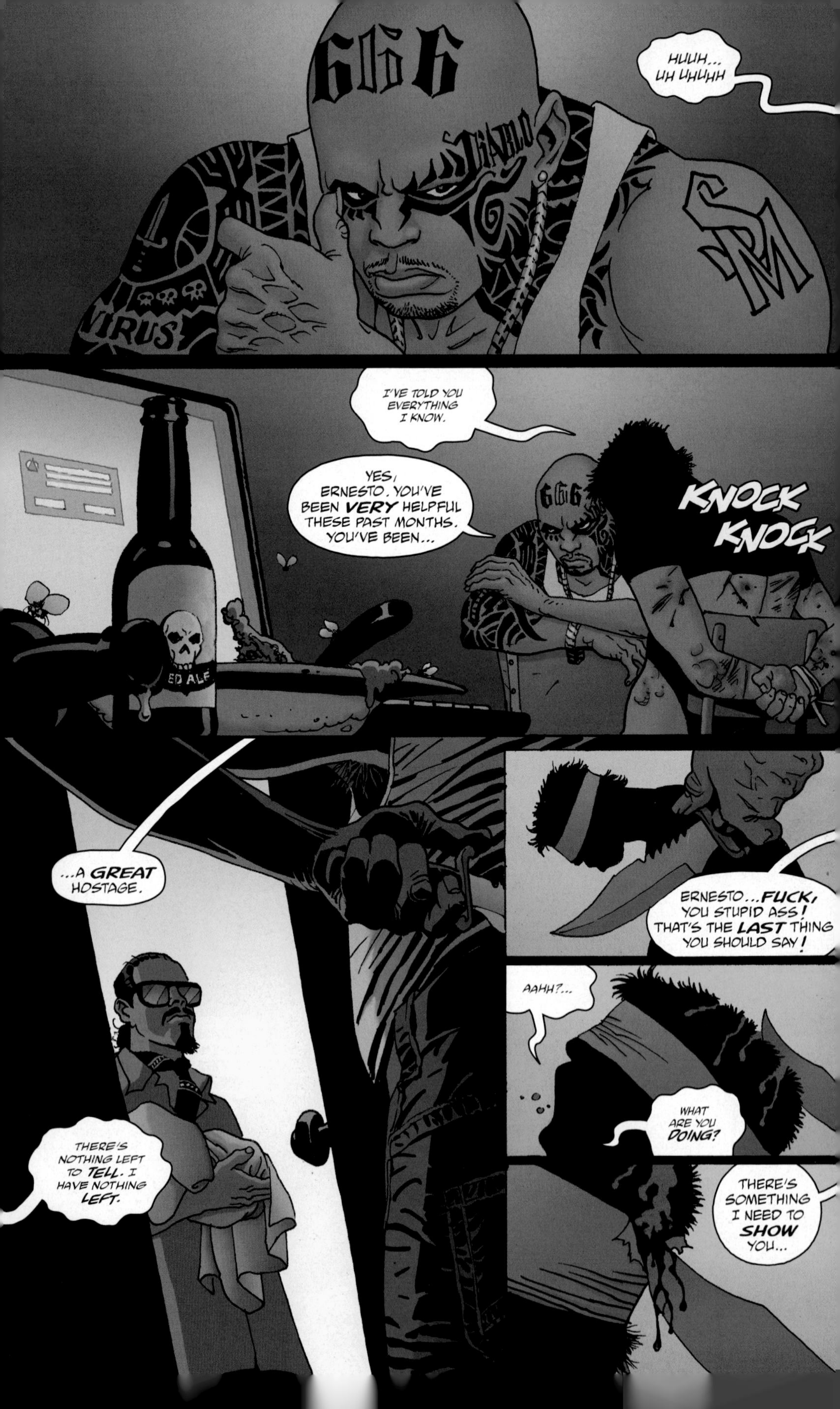

HUUH... UH UHUHH
I'VE TOLD YOU EVERYTHING I KNOW.
YES, ERNESTO. YOU'VE BEEN VERY HELPFUL THESE PAST MONTHS. YOU'VE BEEN...
KNOCK KNOCK
...A GREAT HOSTAGE.
ERNESTO...FUCK, YOU STUPID ASS! THAT'S THE LAST THING YOU SHOULD SAY!
THERE'S NOTHING LEFT TO TELL. I HAVE NOTHING LEFT.
AAHH?...
WHAT ARE YOU DOING?
THERE'S SOMETHING I NEED TO SHOW YOU...

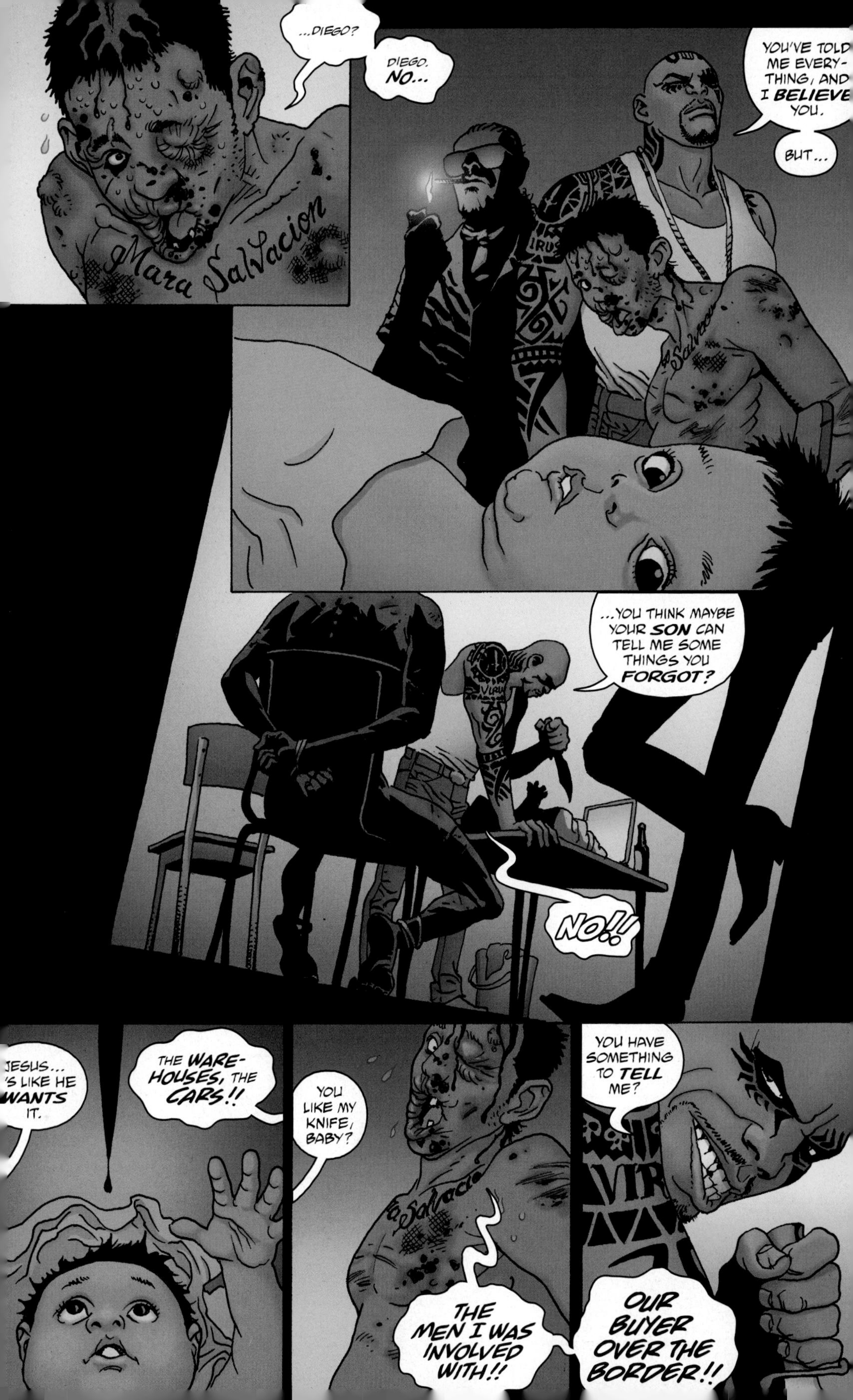
Mara Salvacion
...DIEGO?
DIEGO. NO...
YOU'VE TOLD ME EVERY-THING, AND I BELIEVE YOU.
BUT...
...YOU THINK MAYBE YOUR SON CAN TELL ME SOME THINGS YOU FORGOT?
NO!!
JESUS... 'S LIKE HE WANTS IT.
THE WARE-HOUSES, THE CARS!!
YOU LIKE MY KNIFE, BABY?
THE MEN I WAS INVOLVED WITH!!
YOU HAVE SOMETHING TO TELL ME?
OUR BUYER OVER THE BORDER!!

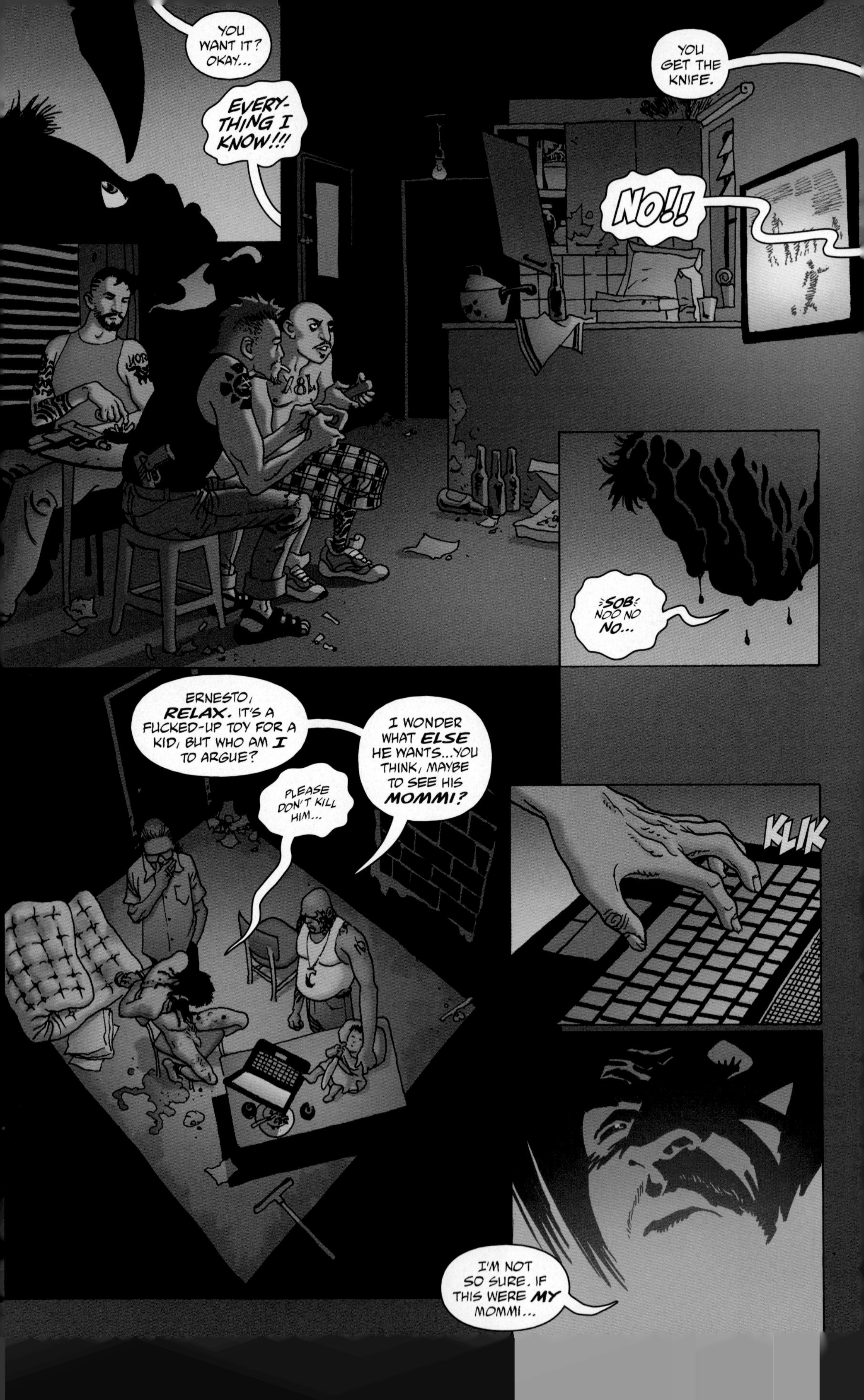
YOU WANT IT? OKAY...
EVERY-THING I KNOW!!!
YOU GET THE KNIFE.
NO!!
SOB NOO NO NO...
ERNESTO, RELAX. IT'S A FUCKED-UP TOY FOR A KID, BUT WHO AM I TO ARGUE?
I WONDER WHAT ELSE HE WANTS...YOU THINK, MAYBE TO SEE HIS MOMMI?
PLEASE DON'T KILL HIM...
KLIK
I'M NOT SO SURE. IF THIS WERE MY MOMMI...

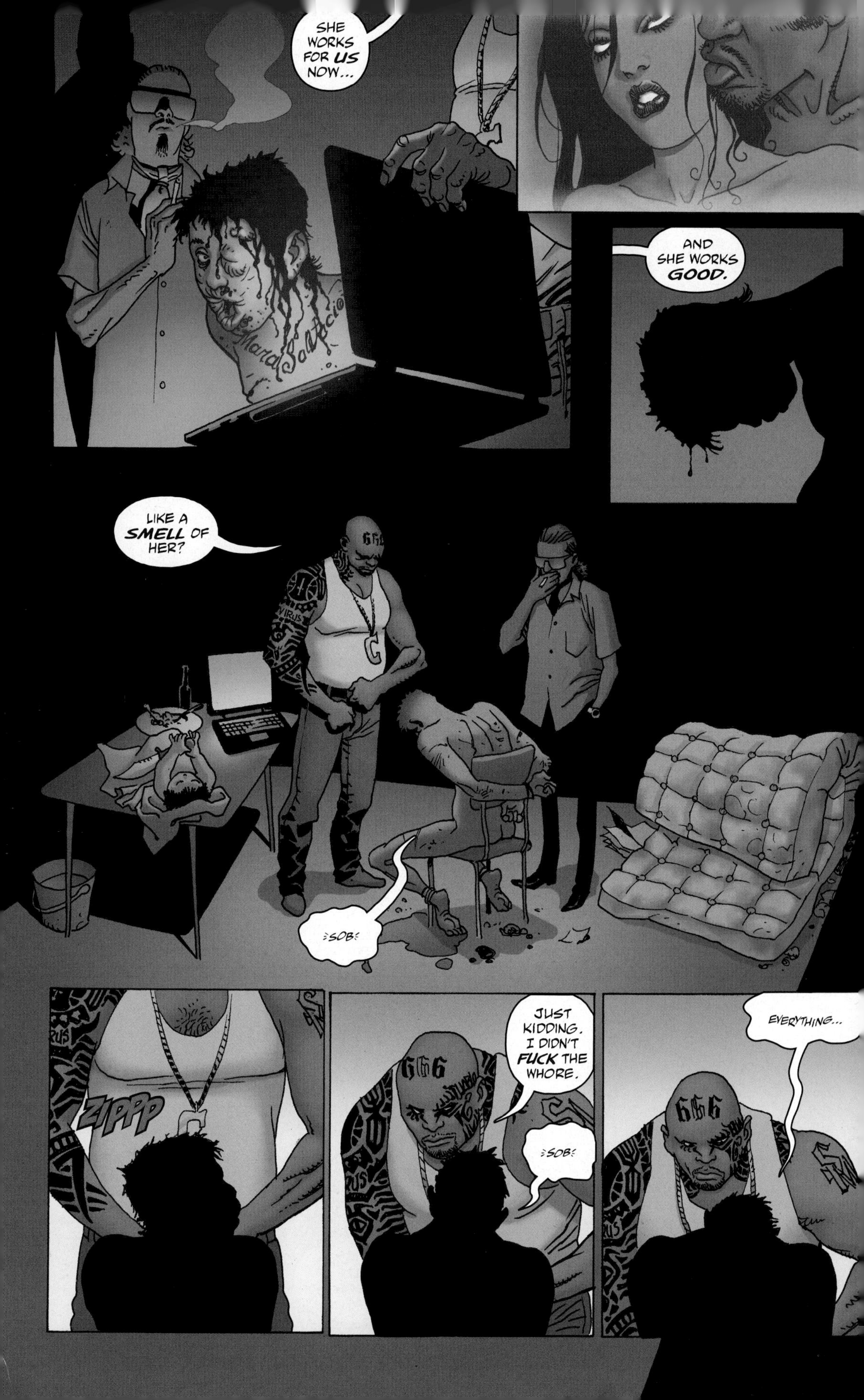
SHE WORKS FOR US NOW...
AND SHE WORKS GOOD.
LIKE A SMELL OF HER?
SOB
ZIPPP
JUST KIDDING. I DIDN'T FUCK THE WHORE.
SOB
EVERYTHING...

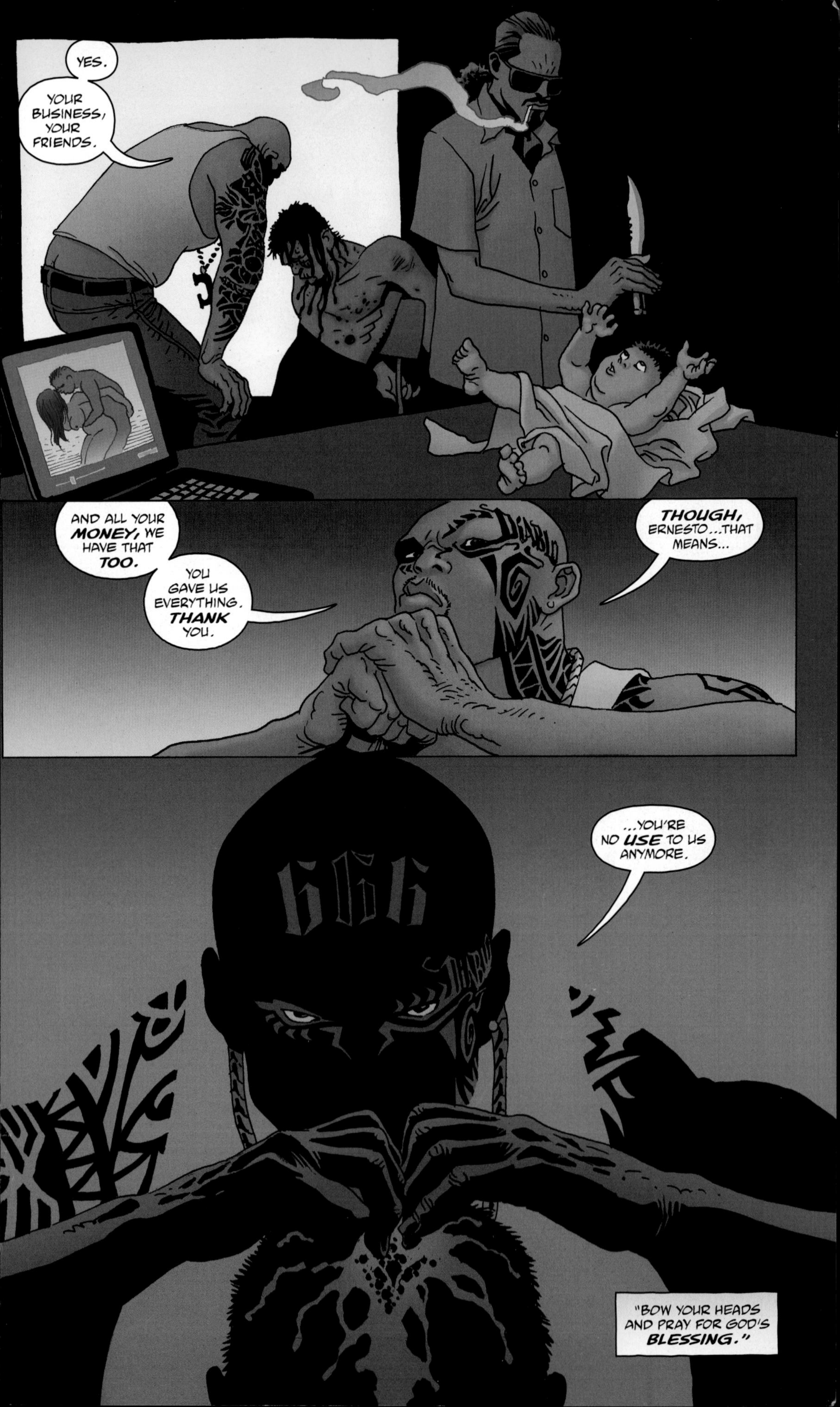

YES.
YOUR BUSINESS, YOUR FRIENDS.
AND ALL YOUR MONEY, WE HAVE THAT TOO.
YOU GAVE US EVERYTHING. THANK YOU.
THOUGH, ERNESTO...THAT MEANS...
...YOU'RE NO USE TO US ANYMORE.
"BOW YOUR HEADS AND PRAY FOR GOD'S BLESSING."

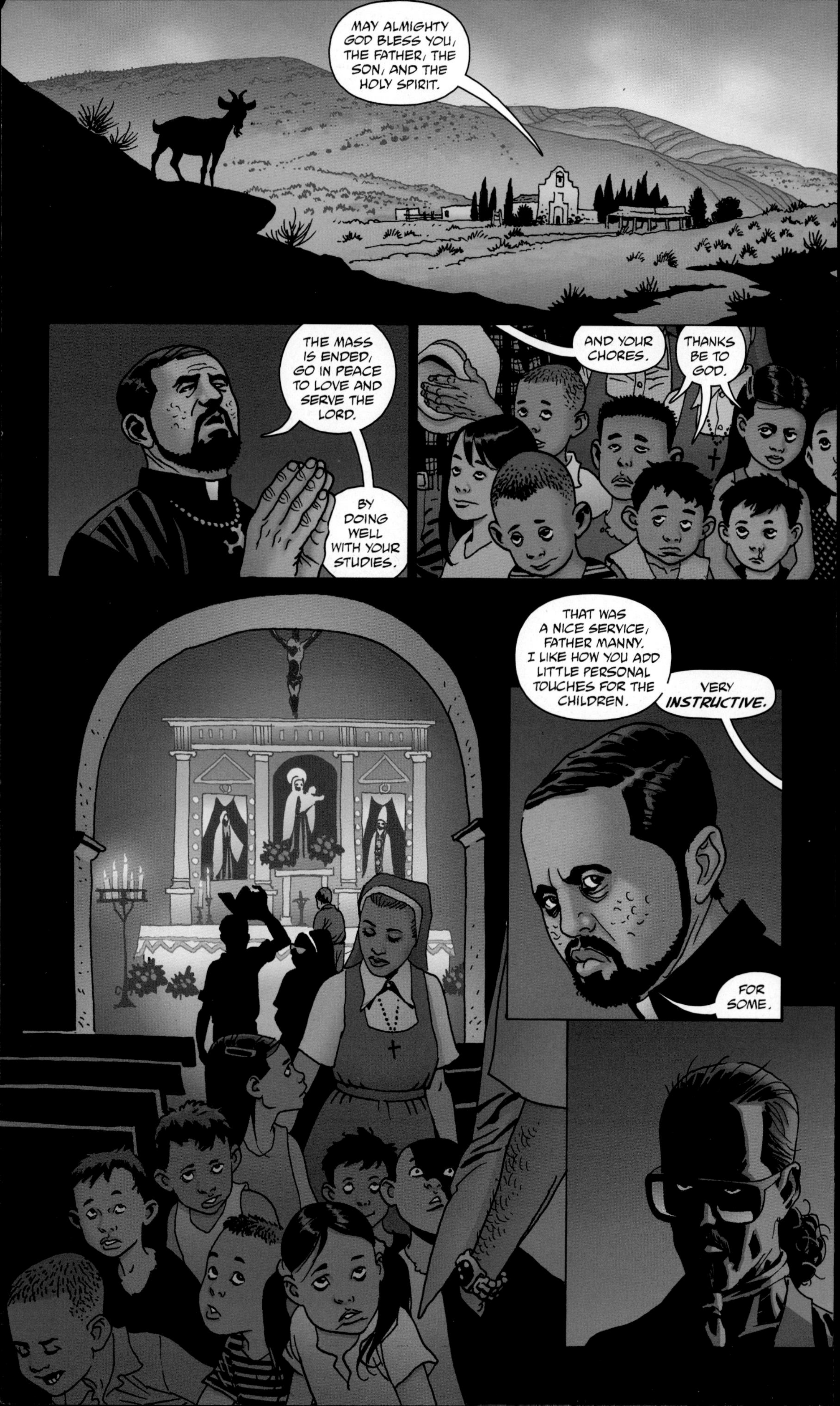
MAY ALMIGHTY GOD BLESS YOU, THE FATHER, THE SON, AND THE HOLY SPIRIT.
THE MASS IS ENDED, GO IN PEACE TO LOVE AND SERVE THE LORD.
BY DOING WELL WITH YOUR STUDIES.
AND YOUR CHORES.
THANKS BE TO GOD.
THAT WAS A NICE SERVICE, FATHER MANNY. I LIKE HOW YOU ADD LITTLE PERSONAL TOUCHES FOR THE CHILDREN.
VERY *INSTRUCTIVE*.
FOR SOME.

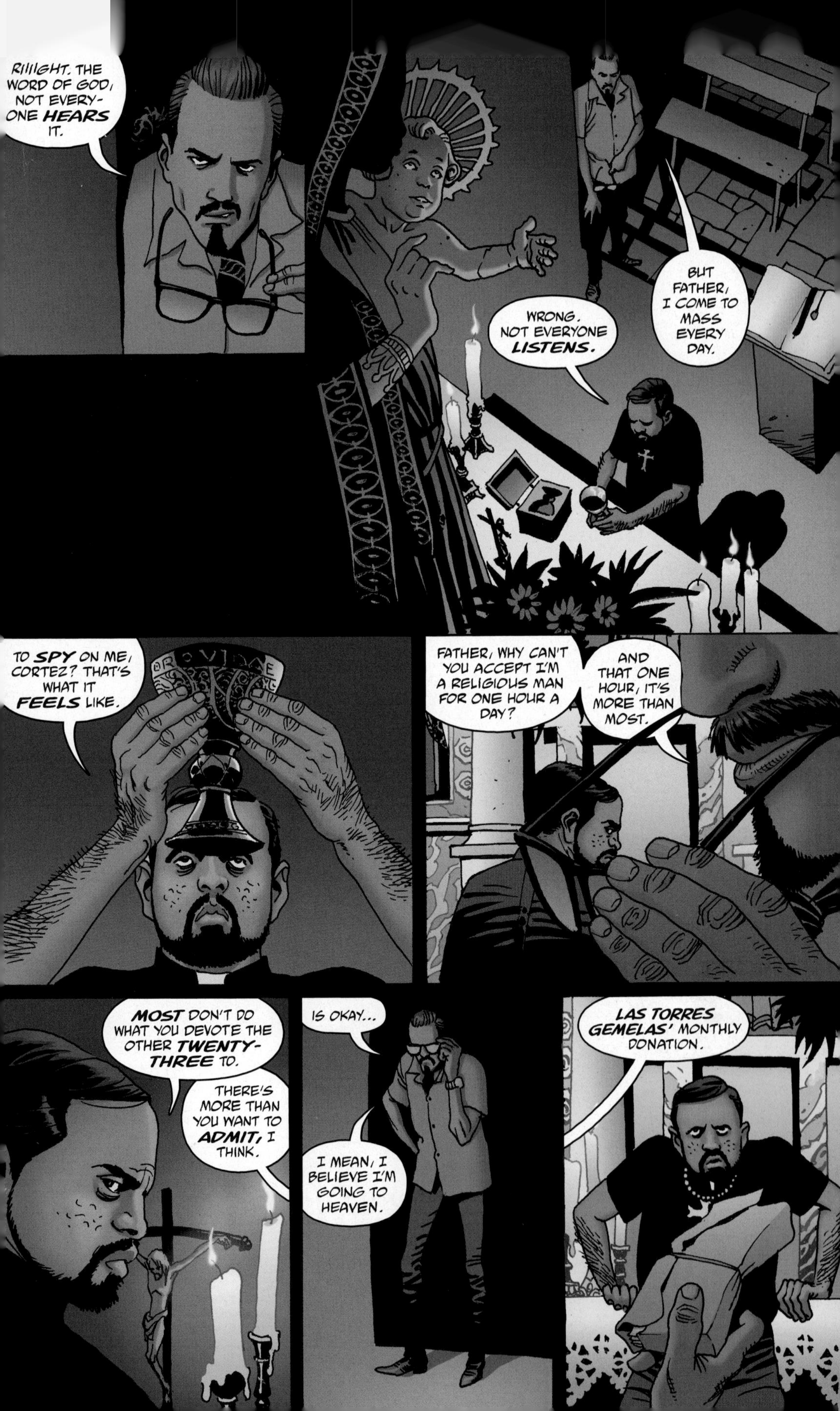
RIIIGHT. THE WORD OF GOD, NOT EVERY-ONE HEARS IT.
WRONG. NOT EVERYONE LISTENS.
BUT FATHER, I COME TO MASS EVERY DAY.
TO SPY ON ME, CORTEZ? THAT'S WHAT IT FEELS LIKE.
FATHER, WHY CAN'T YOU ACCEPT I'M A RELIGIOUS MAN FOR ONE HOUR A DAY?
AND THAT ONE HOUR, IT'S MORE THAN MOST.
MOST DON'T DO WHAT YOU DEVOTE THE OTHER TWENTY-THREE TO.
THERE'S MORE THAN YOU WANT TO ADMIT, I THINK.
IS OKAY...
I MEAN, I BELIEVE I'M GOING TO HEAVEN.
LAS TORRES GEMELAS' MONTHLY DONATION.

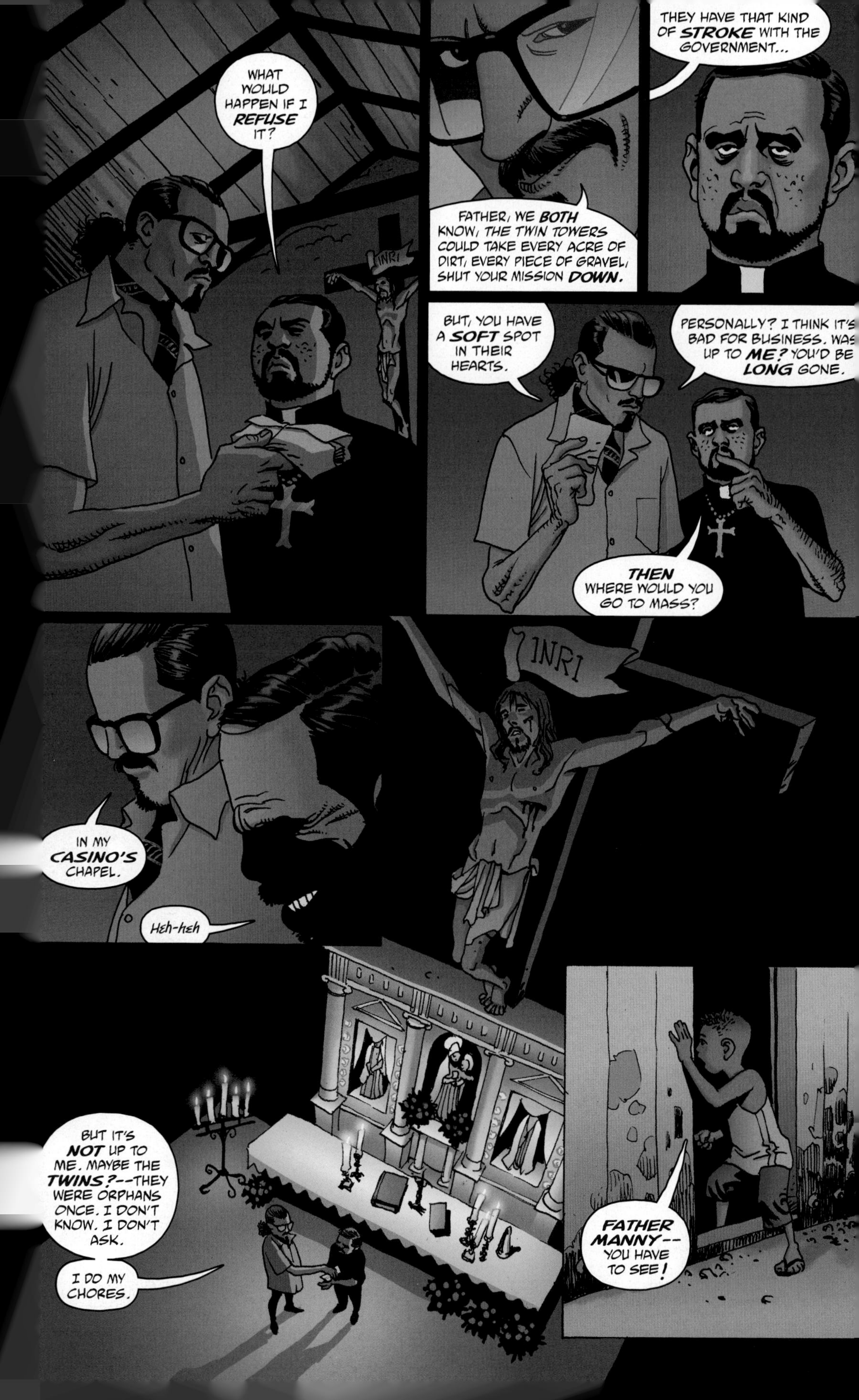
WHAT WOULD HAPPEN IF I REFUSE IT?
FATHER, WE BOTH KNOW, THE TWIN TOWERS COULD TAKE EVERY ACRE OF DIRT, EVERY PIECE OF GRAVEL, SHUT YOUR MISSION DOWN.
THEY HAVE THAT KIND OF STROKE WITH THE GOVERNMENT...
BUT, YOU HAVE A SOFT SPOT IN THEIR HEARTS.
PERSONALLY? I THINK IT'S BAD FOR BUSINESS. WAS UP TO ME? YOU'D BE LONG GONE.
THEN WHERE WOULD YOU GO TO MASS?
IN MY CASINO'S CHAPEL.
Heh-heh
INRI
BUT IT'S NOT UP TO ME. MAYBE THE TWINS?--THEY WERE ORPHANS ONCE. I DON'T KNOW. I DON'T ASK.
I DO MY CHORES.
FATHER MANNY-- YOU HAVE TO SEE!

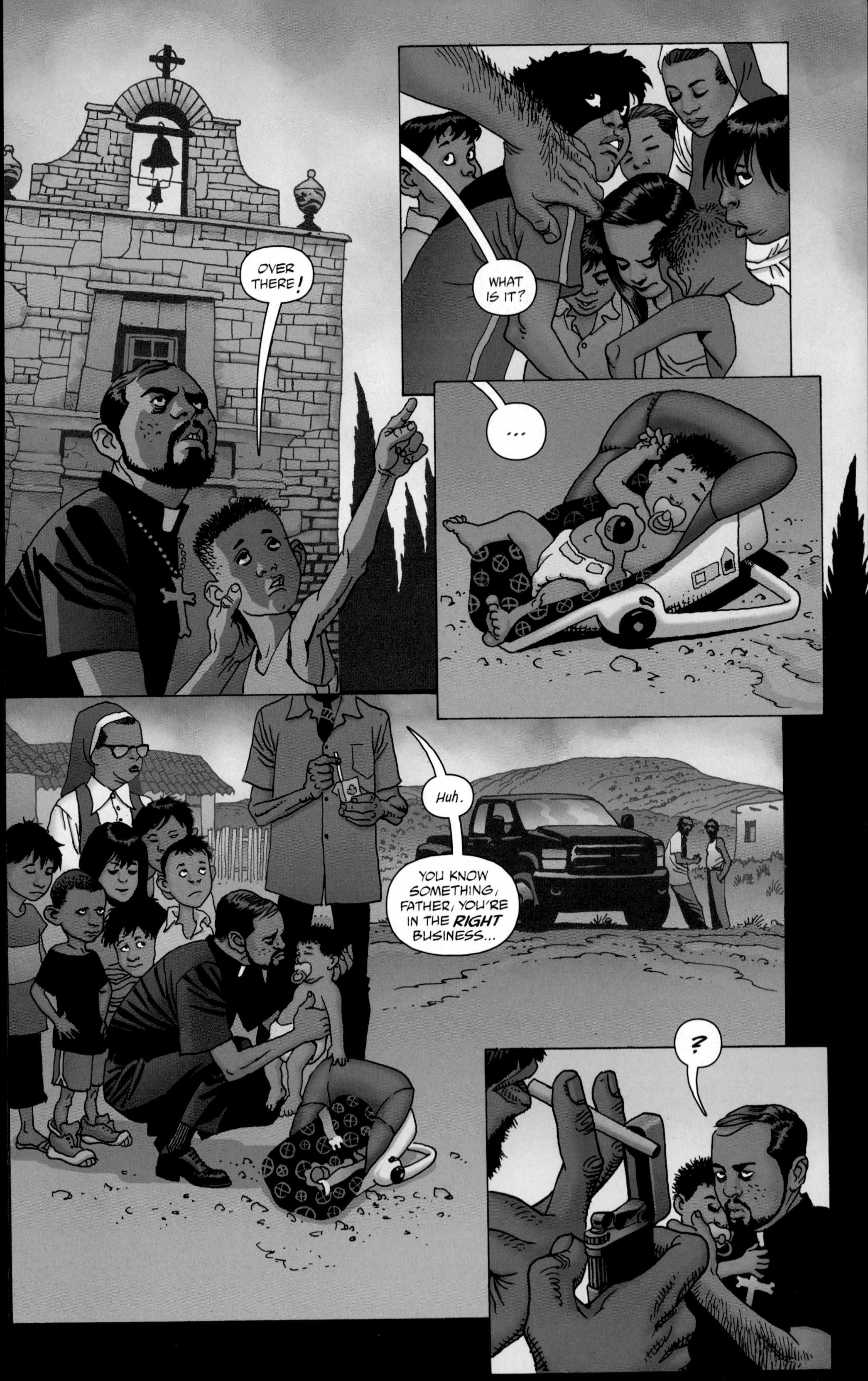
OVER THERE!
WHAT IS IT?
...
Huh.
YOU KNOW SOMETHING, FATHER, YOU'RE IN THE *RIGHT* BUSINESS...
?

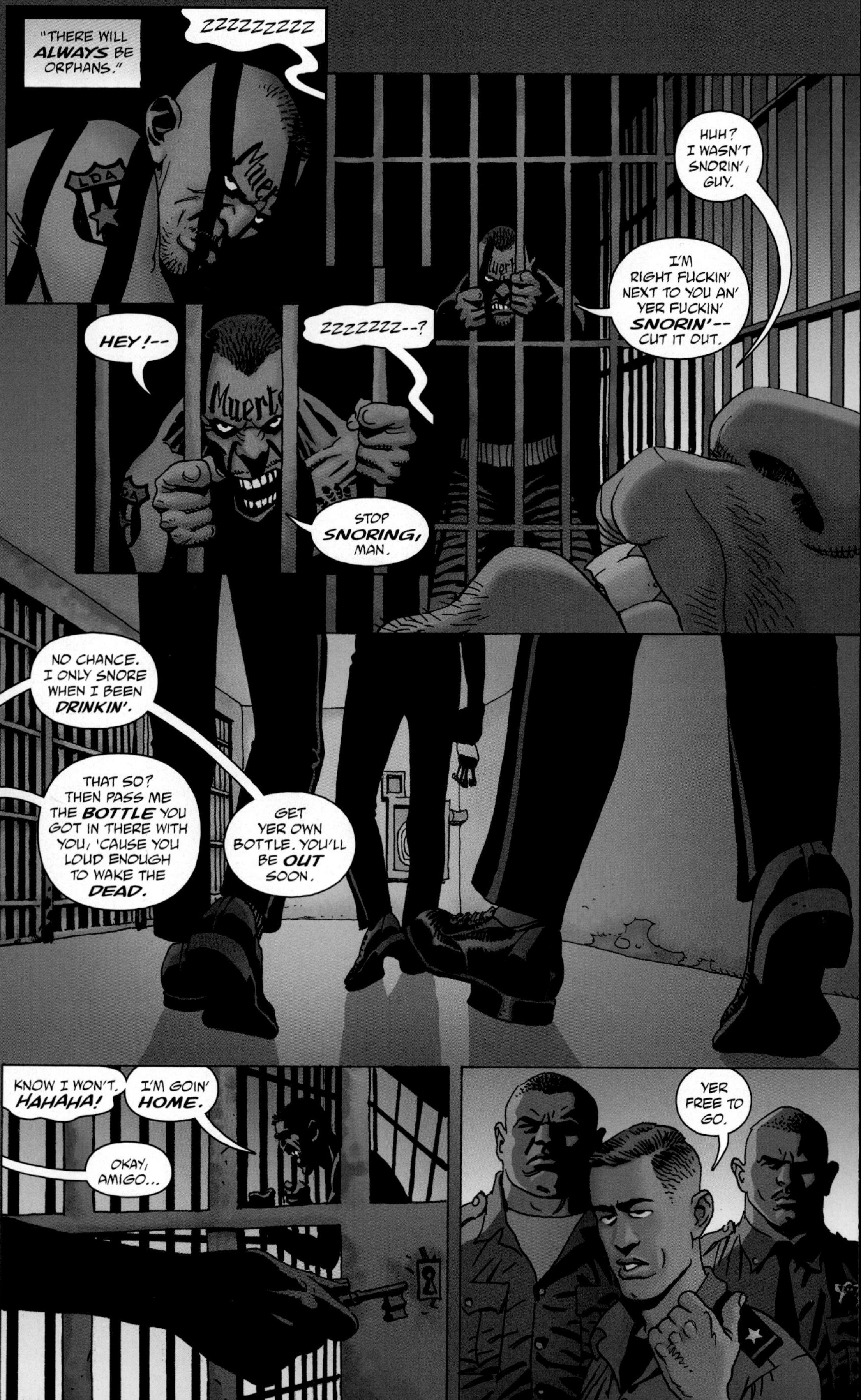
"THERE WILL ALWAYS BE ORPHANS."
ZZZZZZZZZ
HEY!--
ZZZZZZZ--?
STOP SNORING, MAN.
HUH? I WASN'T SNORIN', GUY.
I'M RIGHT FUCKIN' NEXT TO YOU AN' YER FUCKIN' SNORIN'-- CUT IT OUT.
NO CHANCE. I ONLY SNORE WHEN I BEEN DRINKIN'.
THAT SO? THEN PASS ME THE BOTTLE YOU GOT IN THERE WITH YOU, 'CAUSE YOU LOUD ENOUGH TO WAKE THE DEAD.
GET YER OWN BOTTLE. YOU'LL BE OUT SOON.
KNOW I WON'T. HAHAHA!
I'M GOIN' HOME.
OKAY, AMIGO...
YER FREE TO GO.

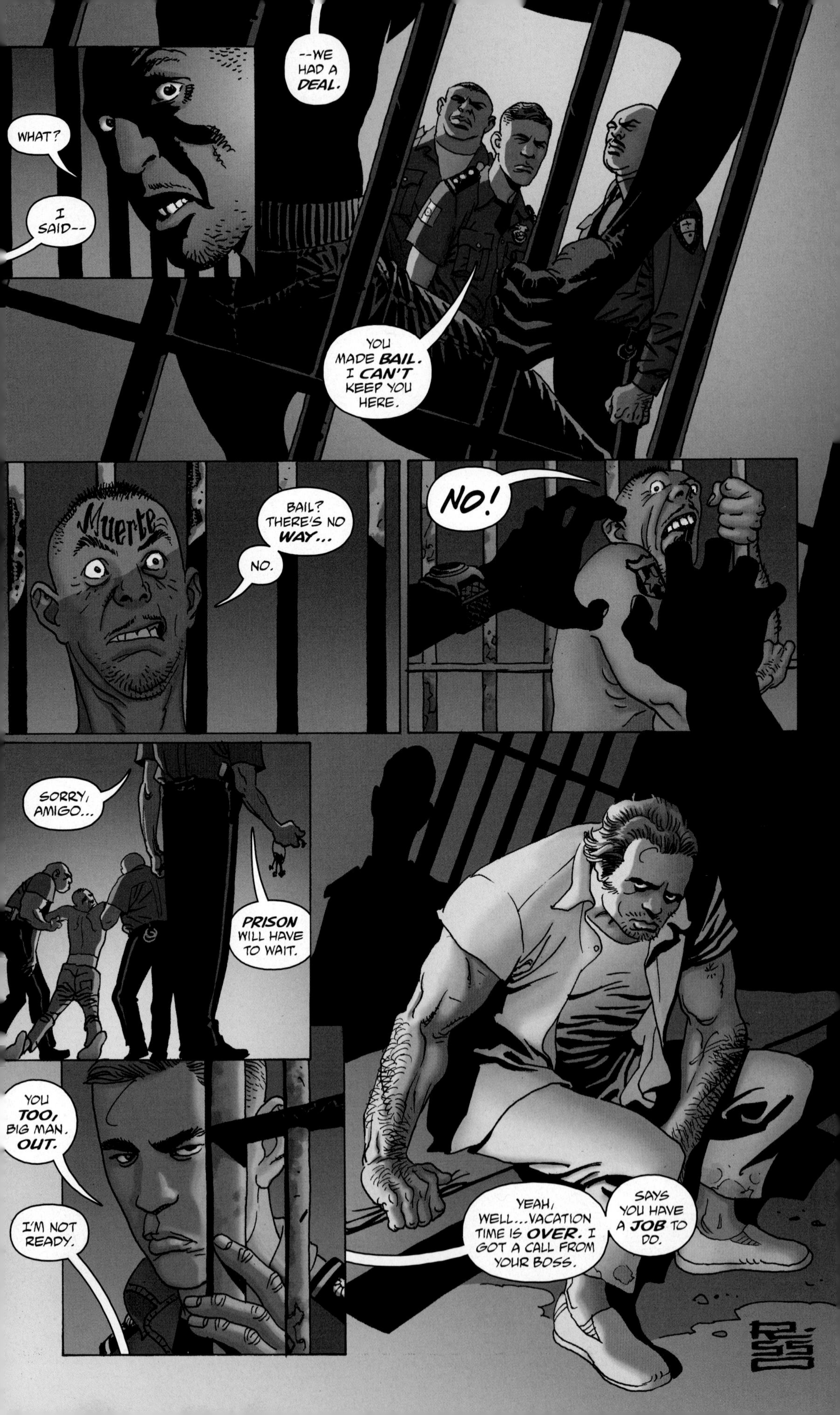
--WE HAD A **DEAL**.
WHAT?
I SAID--
YOU MADE **BAIL**. I **CAN'T** KEEP YOU HERE.
BAIL? THERE'S NO **WAY**...
NO.
Muerte
NO!
SORRY, AMIGO...
PRISON WILL HAVE TO WAIT.
YOU **TOO,** BIG MAN. **OUT.**
I'M NOT READY.
YEAH, WELL...VACATION TIME IS **OVER**. I GOT A CALL FROM YOUR BOSS.
SAYS YOU HAVE A **JOB** TO DO.

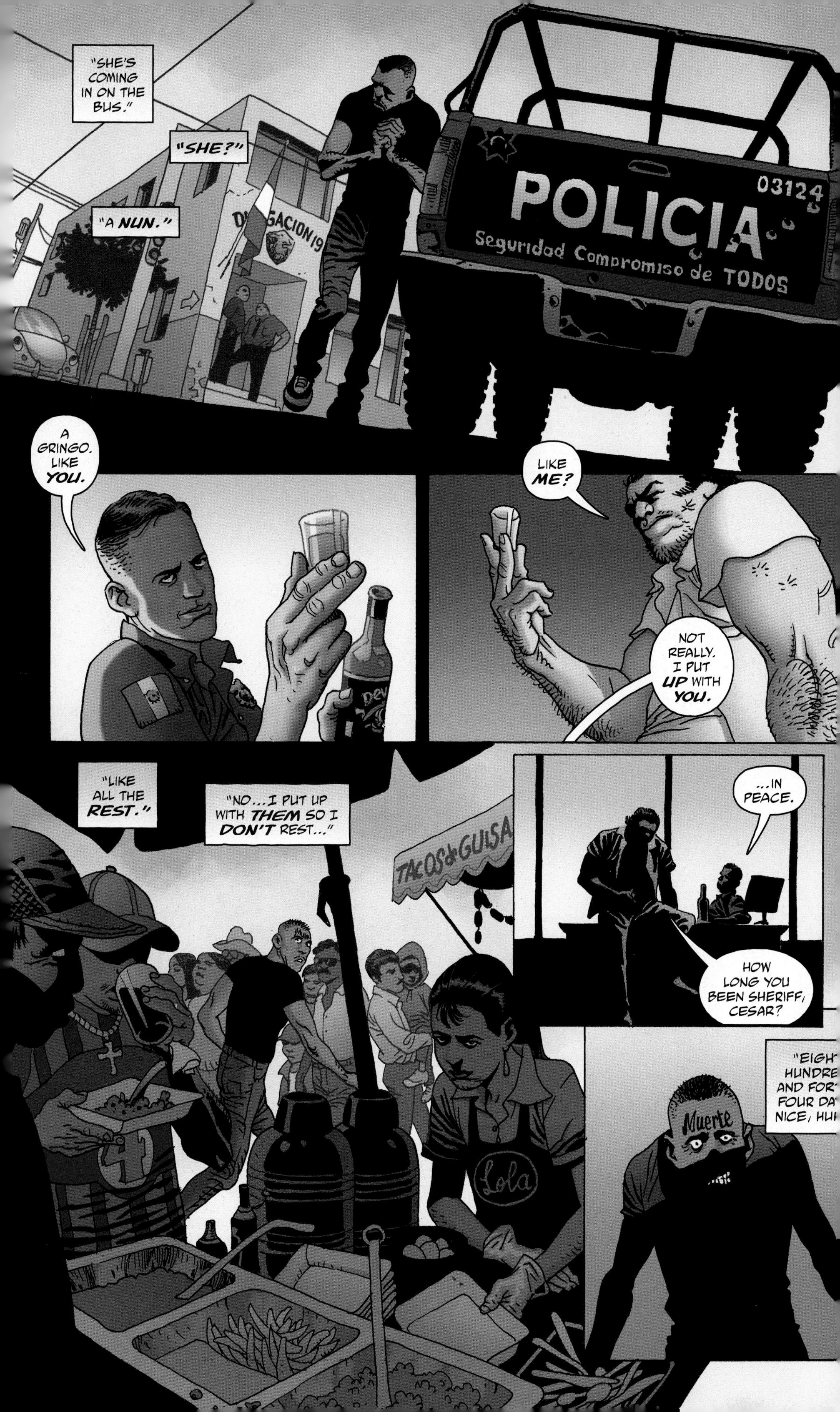

"SHE'S COMING IN ON THE BUS."
"SHE?"
"A NUN."
POLICIA
03124
Seguridad Compromiso de TODOS
A GRINGO. LIKE YOU.
LIKE ME?
NOT REALLY. I PUT UP WITH YOU.
"LIKE ALL THE REST."
"NO...I PUT UP WITH THEM SO I DON'T REST..."
TACOS de GUISA
...IN PEACE.
HOW LONG YOU BEEN SHERIFF, CESAR?
Lola
Muerte

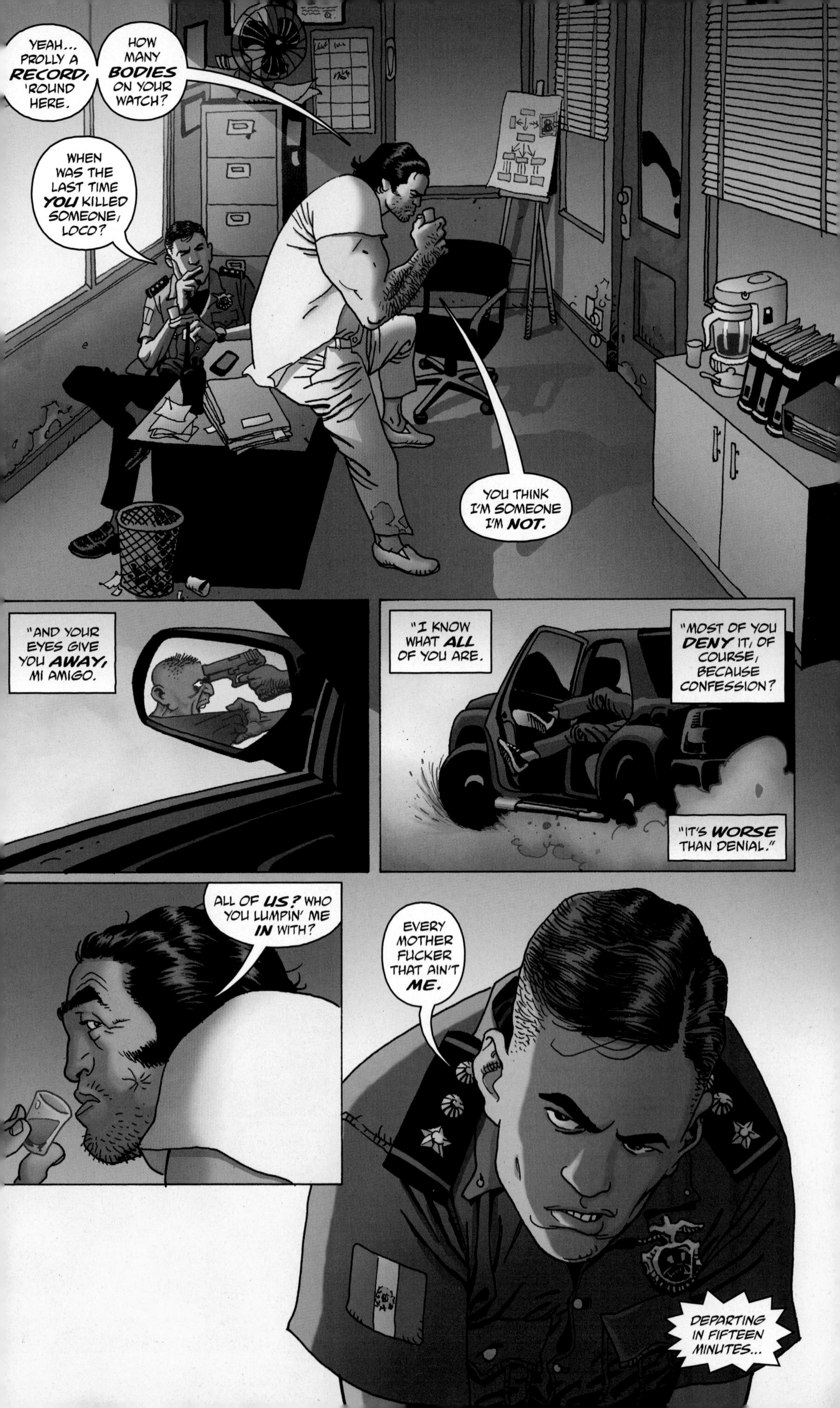
YEAH... PROLLY A RECORD, 'ROUND HERE.
HOW MANY BODIES ON YOUR WATCH?
WHEN WAS THE LAST TIME YOU KILLED SOMEONE, LOCO?
YOU THINK I'M SOMEONE I'M NOT.
"AND YOUR EYES GIVE YOU AWAY, MI AMIGO.
"I KNOW WHAT ALL OF YOU ARE.
"MOST OF YOU DENY IT, OF COURSE, BECAUSE CONFESSION?
"IT'S WORSE THAN DENIAL."
ALL OF US? WHO YOU LUMPIN' ME IN WITH?
EVERY MOTHER FUCKER THAT AIN'T ME.
DEPARTING IN FIFTEEN MINUTES...

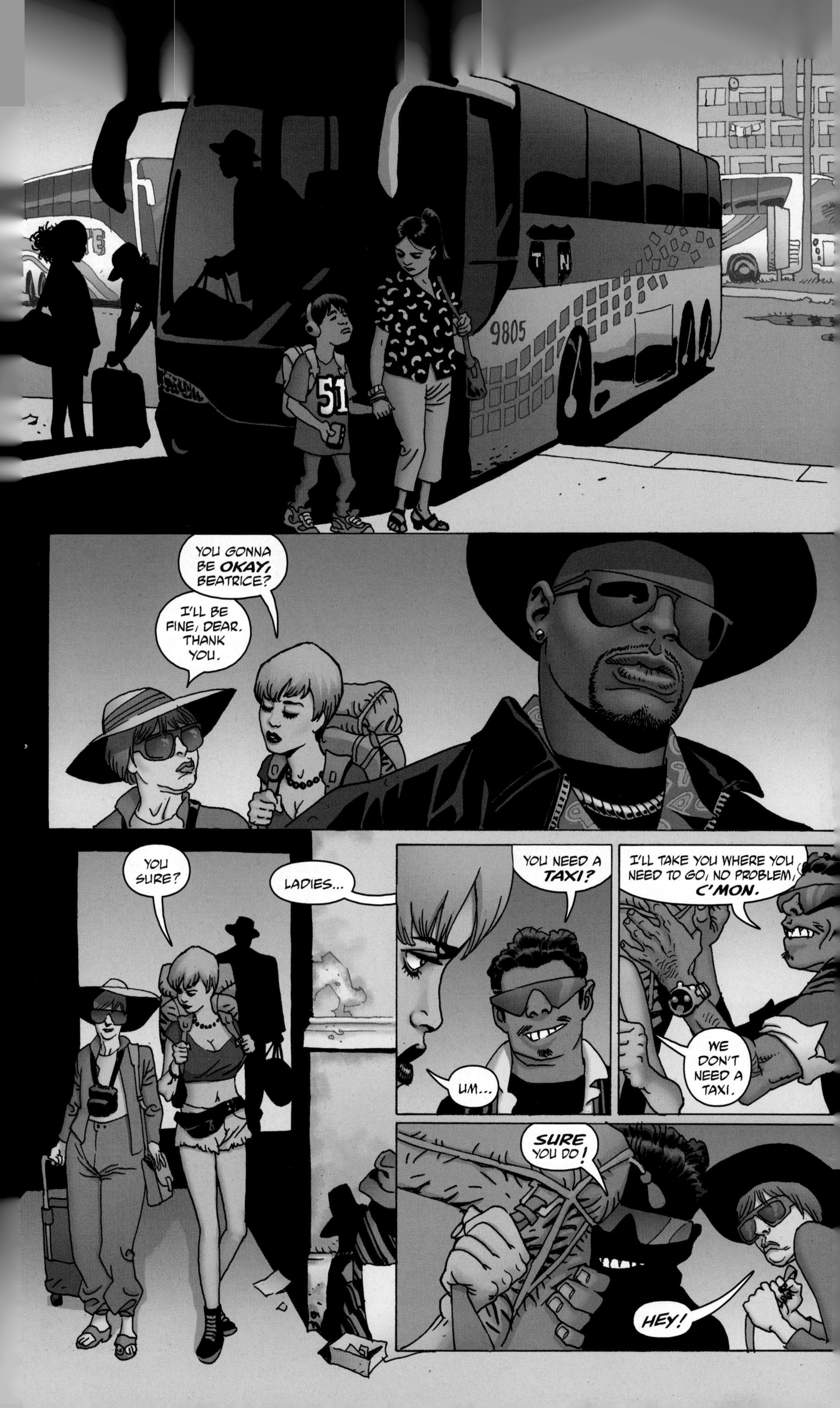
9805
51
YOU GONNA BE OKAY, BEATRICE?
I'LL BE FINE, DEAR. THANK YOU.
YOU SURE?
LADIES...
YOU NEED A TAXI?
UM...
I'LL TAKE YOU WHERE YOU NEED TO GO, NO PROBLEM, C'MON.
WE DON'T NEED A TAXI.
SURE YOU DO!
HEY!

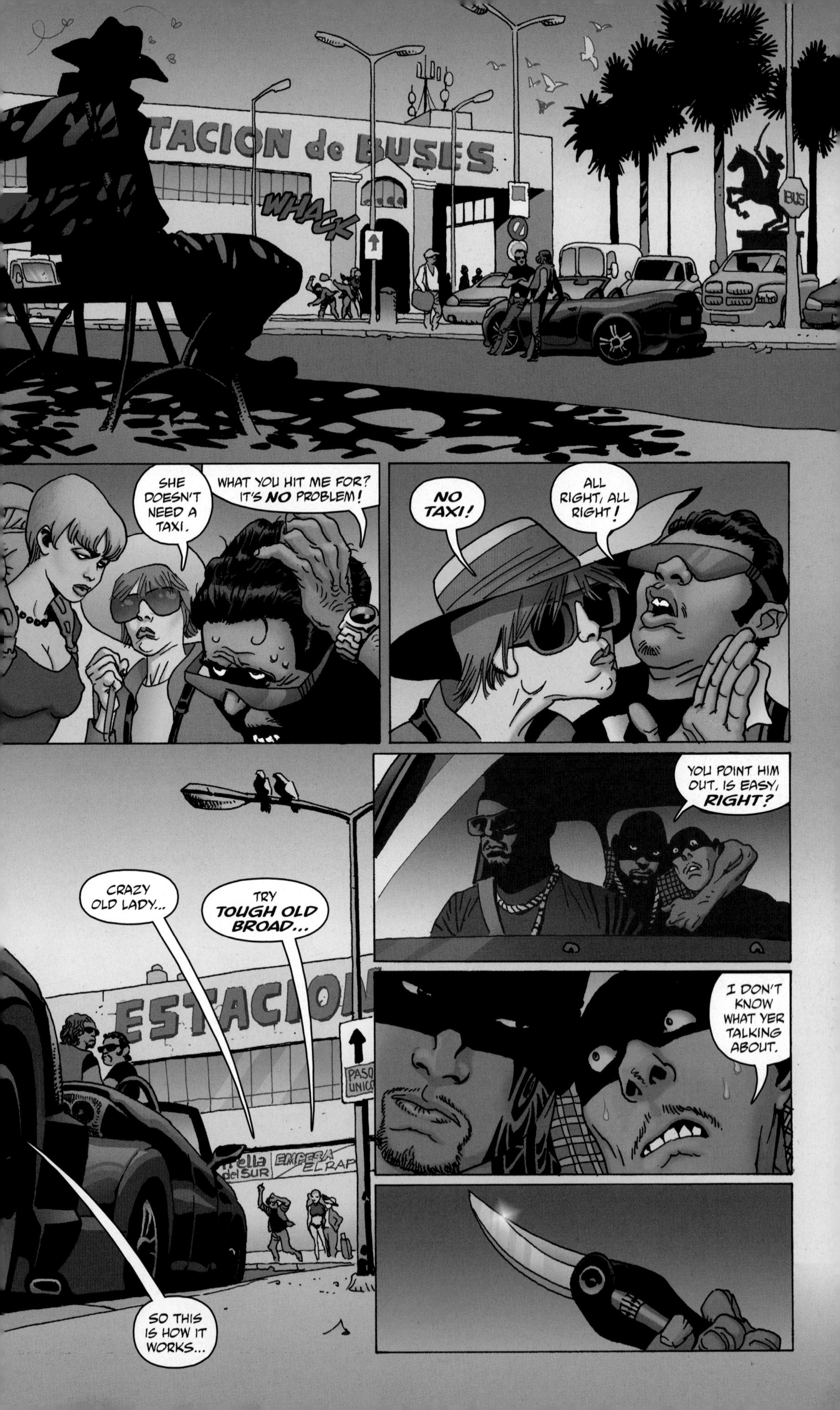
TACION de BUSES
WHACK
BUS
SHE DOESN'T NEED A TAXI.
WHAT YOU HIT ME FOR? IT'S NO PROBLEM!
NO TAXI!
ALL RIGHT, ALL RIGHT!
CRAZY OLD LADY...
TRY TOUGH OLD BROAD...
ESTACION
PASO UNICO
EMPRESA EL RAP
del SUR
SO THIS IS HOW IT WORKS...
YOU POINT HIM OUT. IS EASY, RIGHT?
I DON'T KNOW WHAT YER TALKING ABOUT.

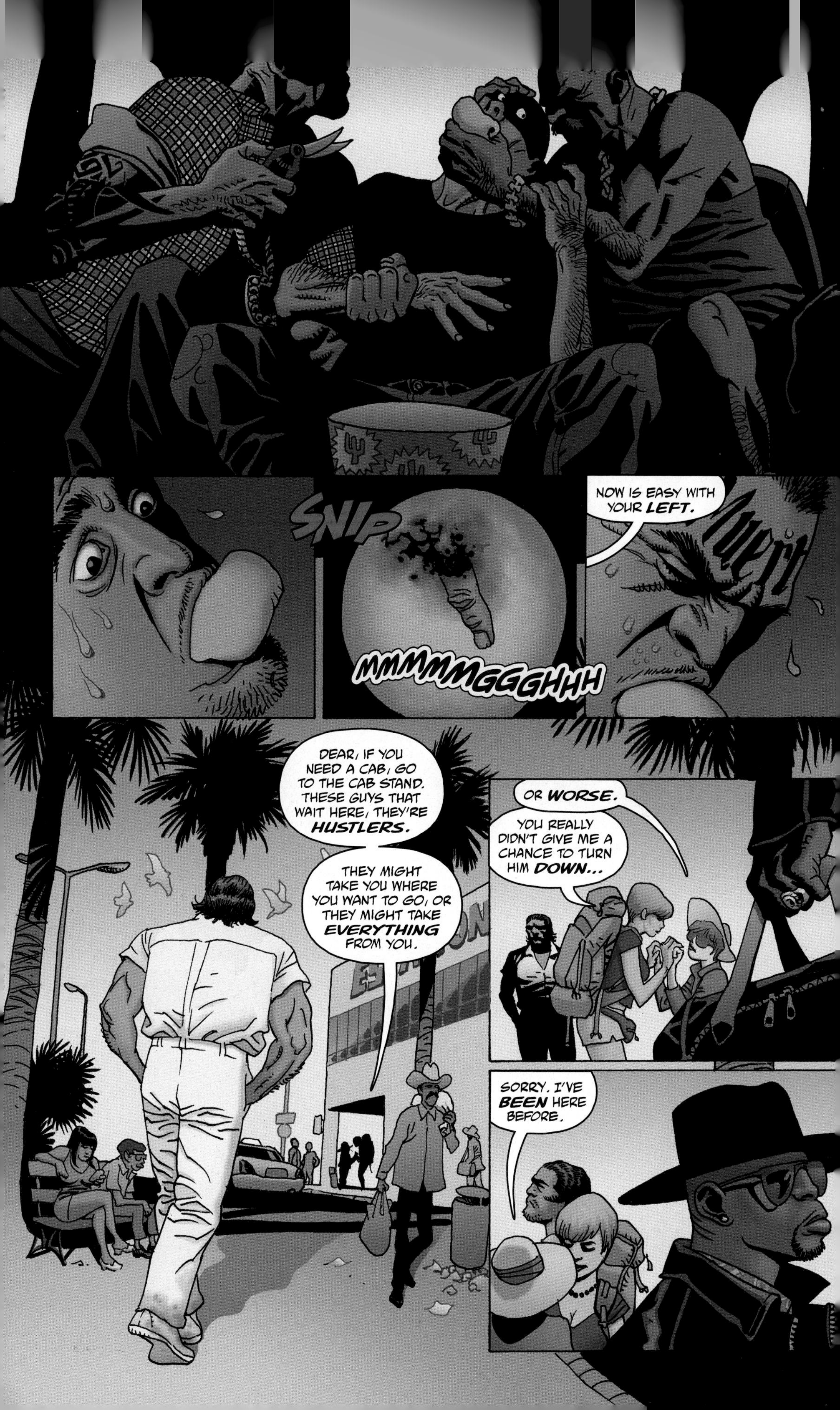
SNIP
NOW IS EASY WITH YOUR LEFT.
MMMMMGGGHHH
DEAR, IF YOU NEED A CAB, GO TO THE CAB STAND. THESE GUYS THAT WAIT HERE, THEY'RE HUSTLERS.
THEY MIGHT TAKE YOU WHERE YOU WANT TO GO, OR THEY MIGHT TAKE EVERYTHING FROM YOU.
OR WORSE.
YOU REALLY DIDN'T GIVE ME A CHANCE TO TURN HIM DOWN...
SORRY. I'VE BEEN HERE BEFORE.

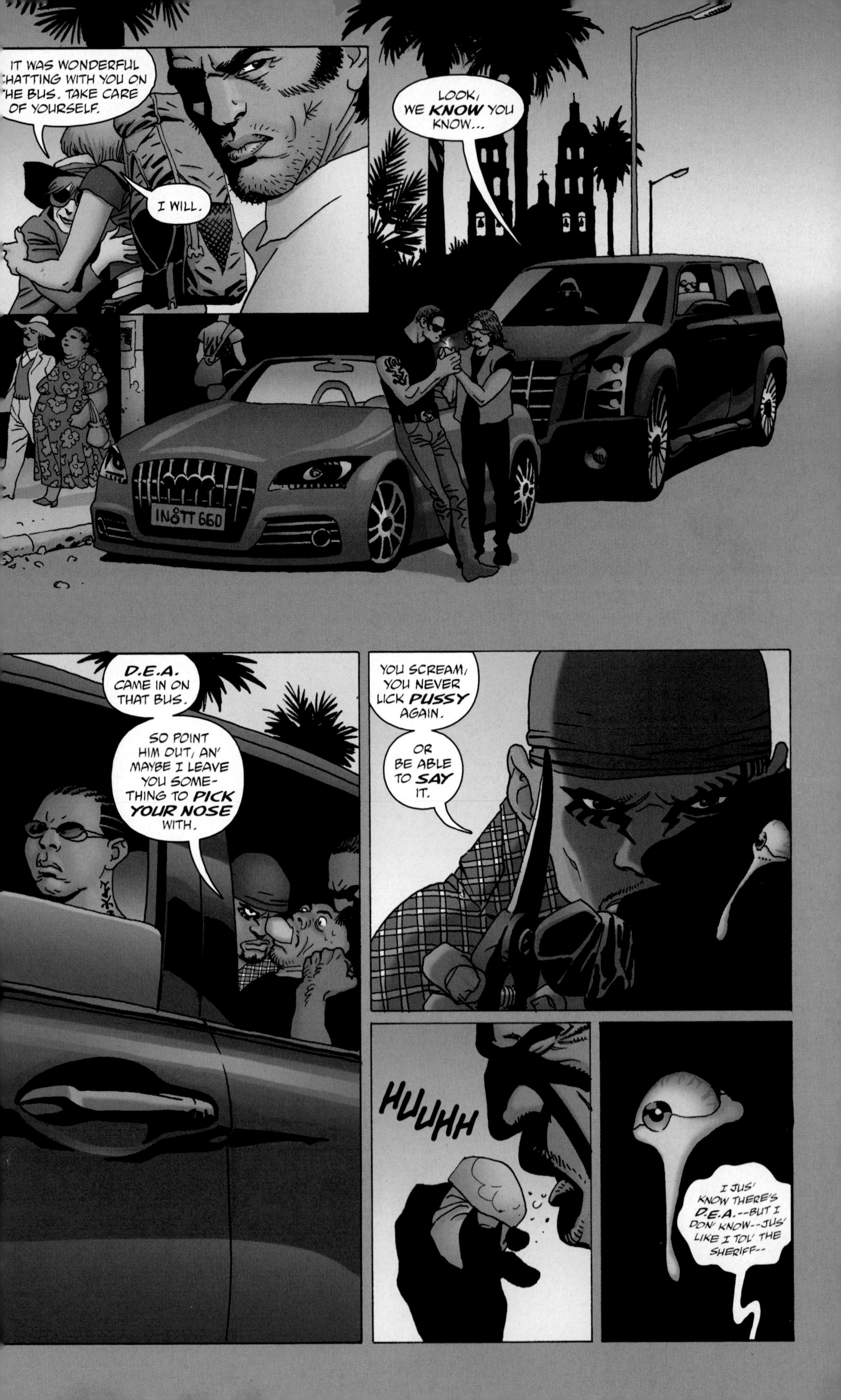
IT WAS WONDERFUL CHATTING WITH YOU ON THE BUS. TAKE CARE OF YOURSELF.
I WILL.
LOOK, WE KNOW YOU KNOW...
IN◎TT 660
D.E.A. CAME IN ON THAT BUS.
SO POINT HIM OUT, AN' MAYBE I LEAVE YOU SOME-THING TO PICK YOUR NOSE WITH.
YOU SCREAM, YOU NEVER LICK PUSSY AGAIN.
OR BE ABLE TO SAY IT.
HUUHH
I JUS' KNOW THERE'S D.E.A.--BUT I DON' KNOW--JUS' LIKE I TOL' THE SHERIFF--

MMGGGG

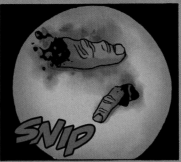

SNIP

I'M NO SHERIFF.

I'M *LAW.*

NOW, ONE MORE TIME...

HIM?

"HUH."

SNIP

SNIP

SNIP

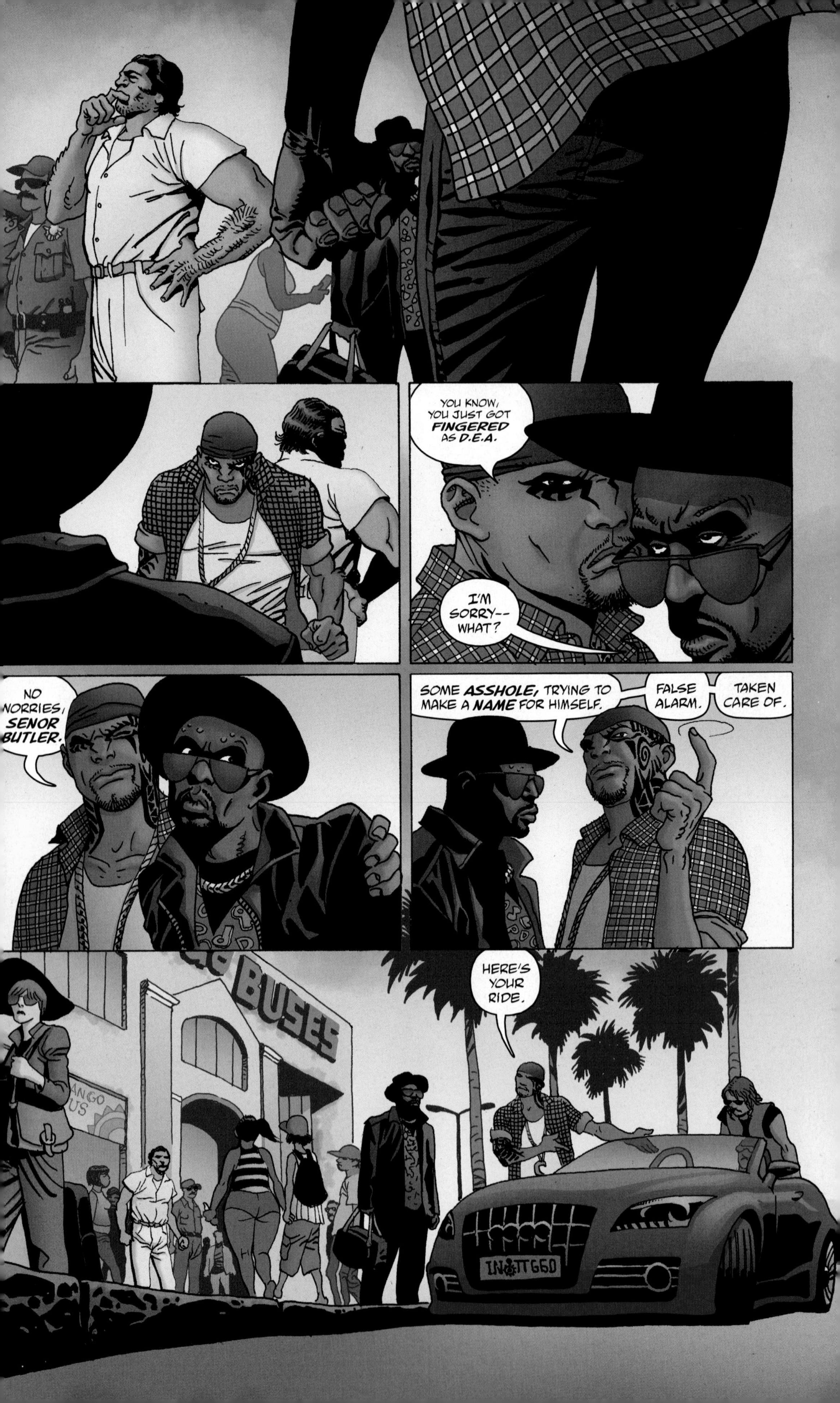
YOU KNOW, YOU JUST GOT FINGERED AS D.E.A.
I'M SORRY-- WHAT?
NO WORRIES, SENOR BUTLER.
SOME ASSHOLE, TRYING TO MAKE A NAME FOR HIMSELF.
FALSE ALARM.
TAKEN CARE OF.
BUSES
HERE'S YOUR RIDE.

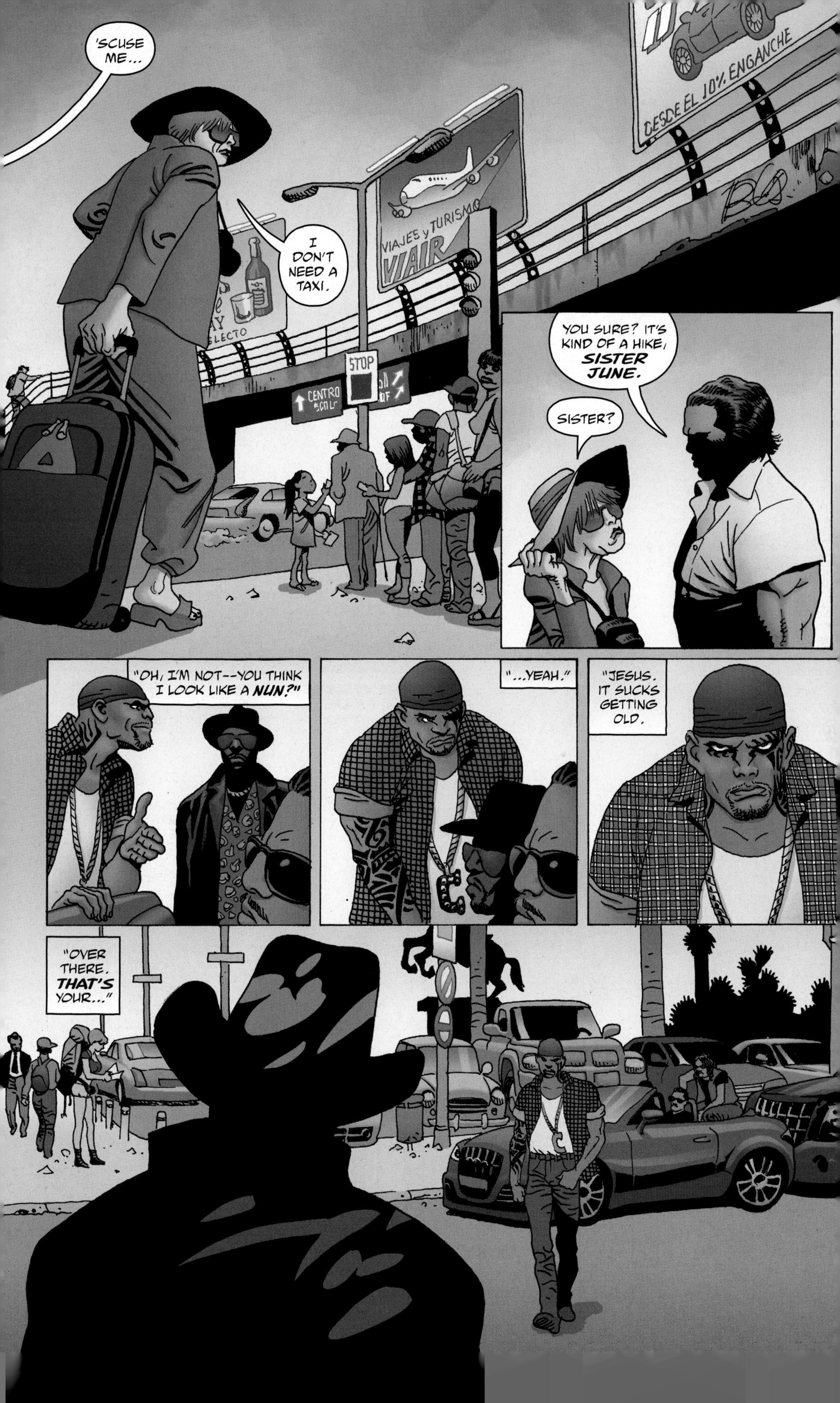
DESDE EL 10% ENGANCHE
'SCUSE ME...
VIAJES y TURISMO
VIAIR
I DON'T NEED A TAXI.
STOP
CENTRO
YOU SURE? IT'S KIND OF A HIKE, **SISTER JUNE.**
SISTER?
"OH, I'M NOT--YOU THINK I LOOK LIKE A ***NUN?***"
"...YEAH."
"JESUS. IT SUCKS GETTING OLD.
"OVER THERE. ***THAT'S*** YOUR..."

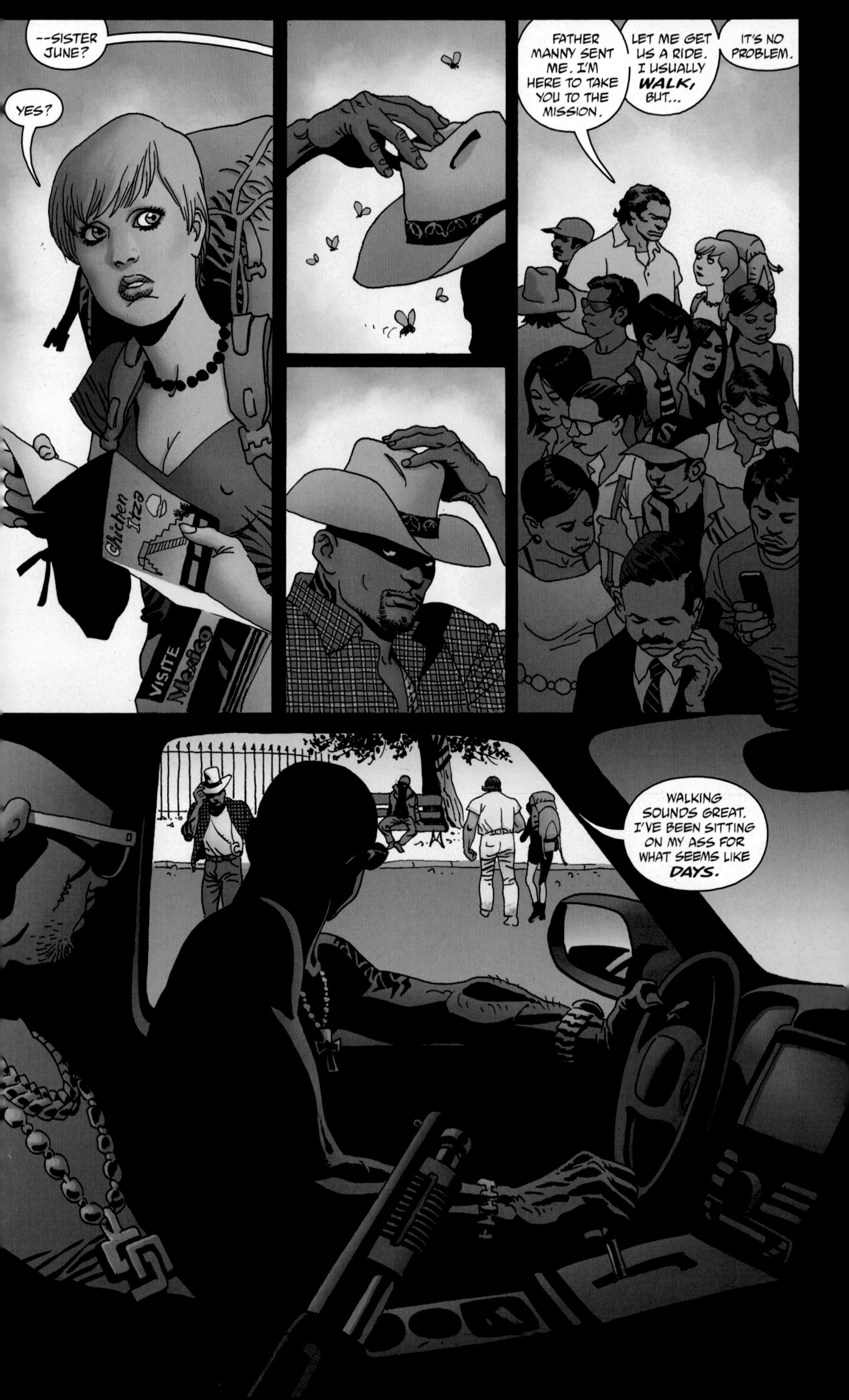
--SISTER JUNE?
YES?
Chichen Itza
VISITE Mexico
FATHER MANNY SENT ME. I'M HERE TO TAKE YOU TO THE MISSION.
LET ME GET US A RIDE. I USUALLY **WALK,** BUT...
IT'S NO PROBLEM.
WALKING SOUNDS GREAT. I'VE BEEN SITTING ON MY ASS FOR WHAT SEEMS LIKE **DAYS.**

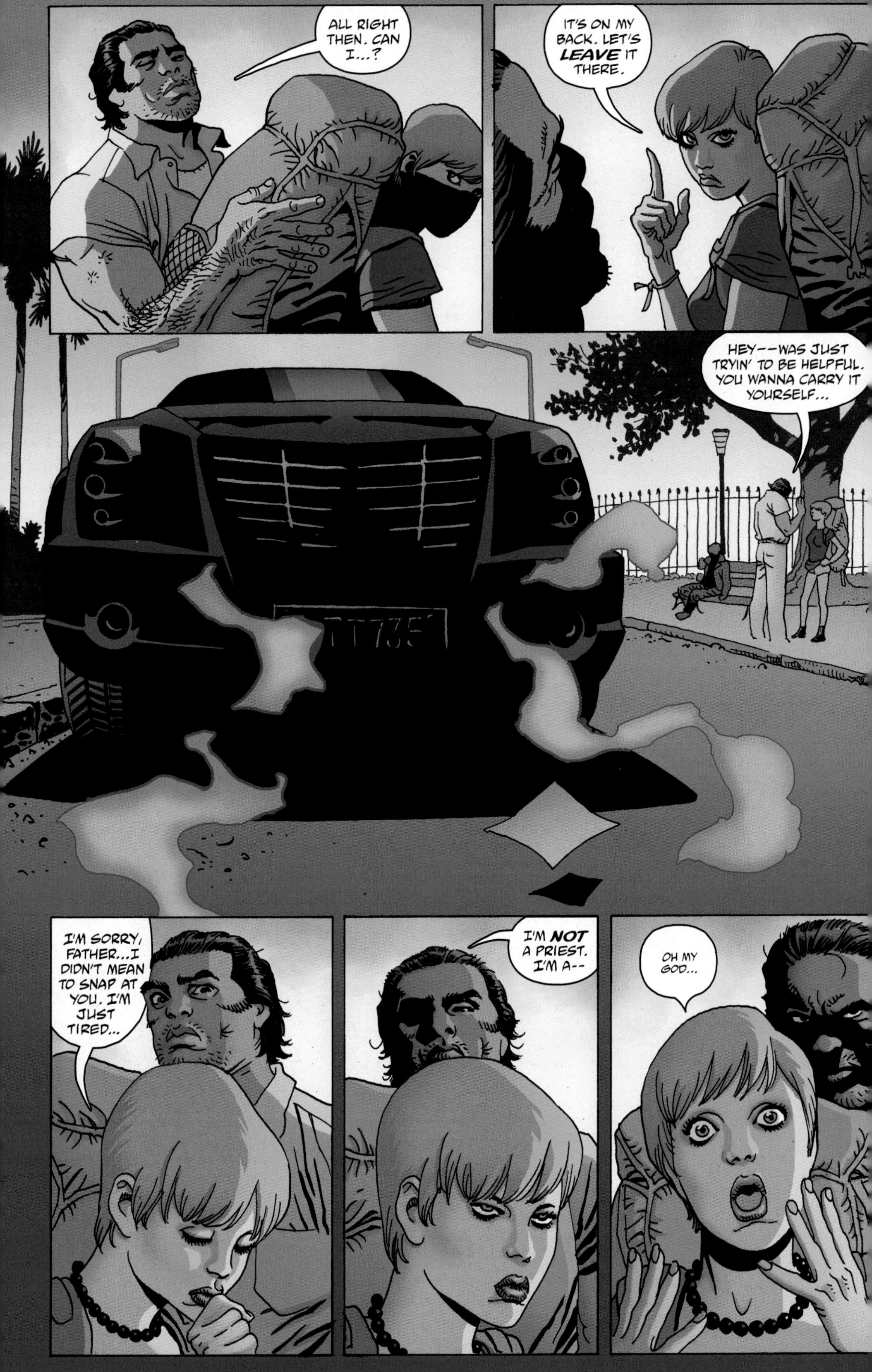
ALL RIGHT THEN. CAN I...?
IT'S ON MY BACK. LET'S LEAVE IT THERE.
HEY--WAS JUST TRYIN' TO BE HELPFUL. YOU WANNA CARRY IT YOURSELF...
I'M SORRY, FATHER...I DIDN'T MEAN TO SNAP AT YOU. I'M JUST TIRED...
I'M NOT A PRIEST. I'M A--
OH MY GOD...

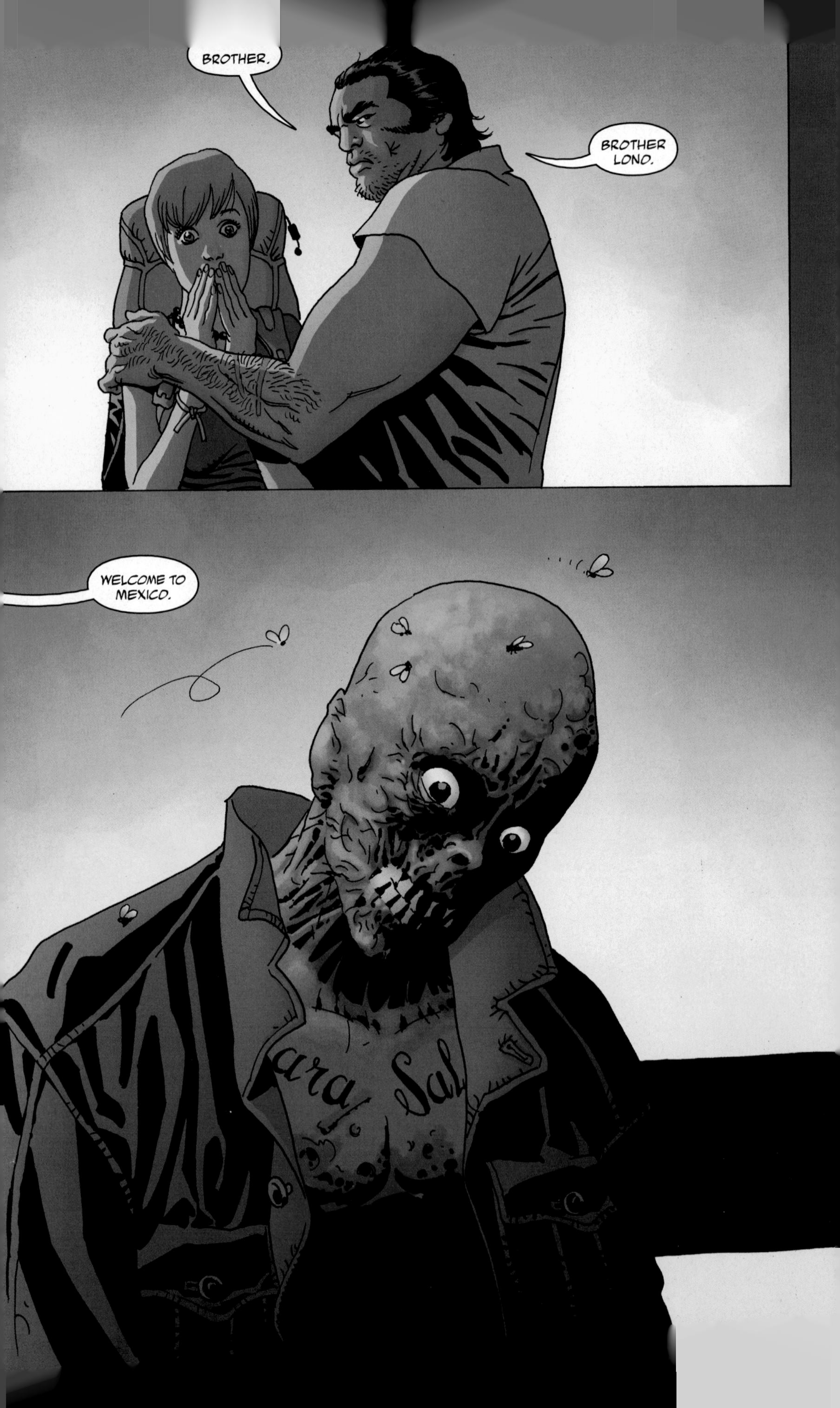
BROTHER.
BROTHER LONO.
WELCOME TO MEXICO.
ara Sal

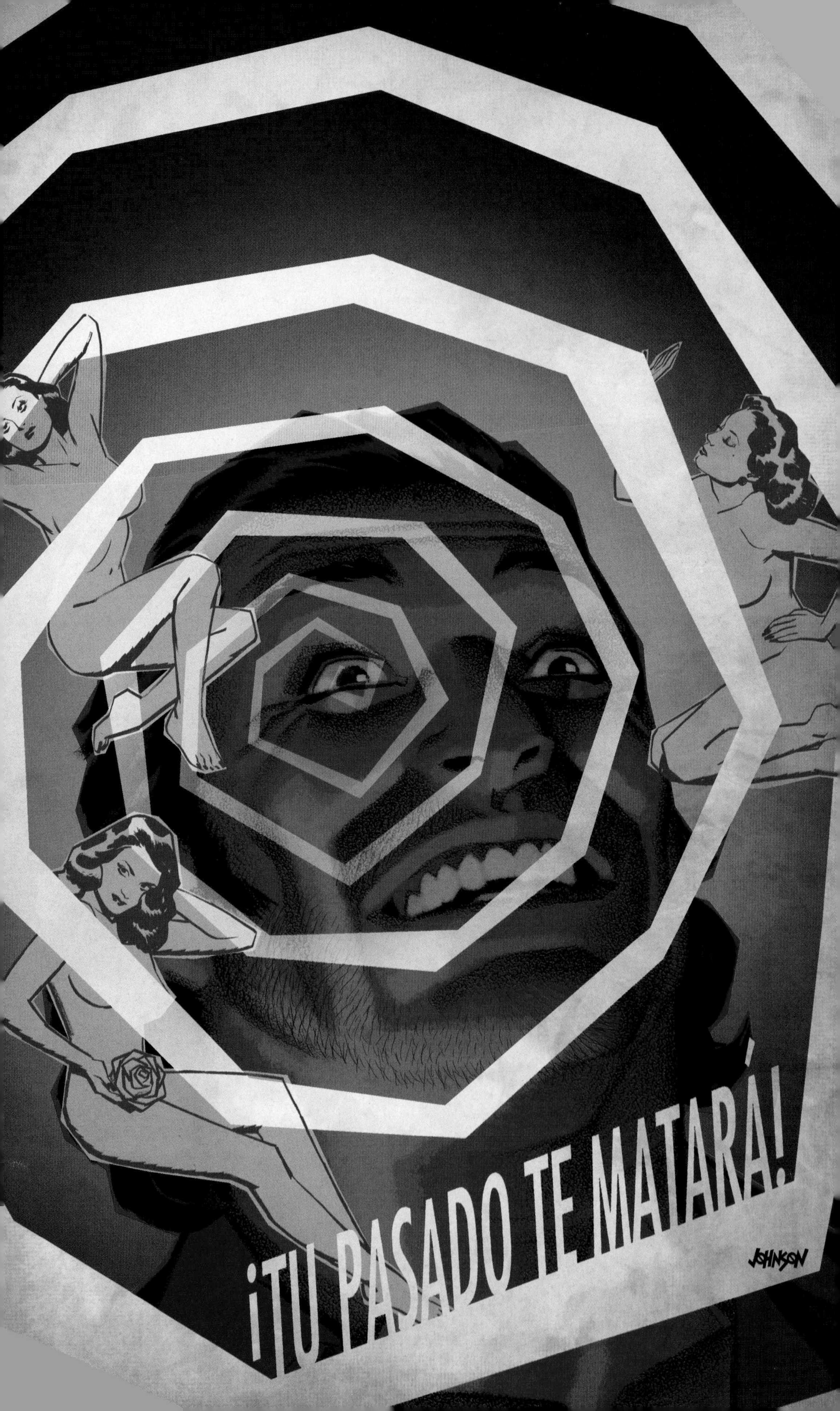
¡TU PASADO TE MATARÁ!
JOHNSON

"What makes you believe that you can be any different?"

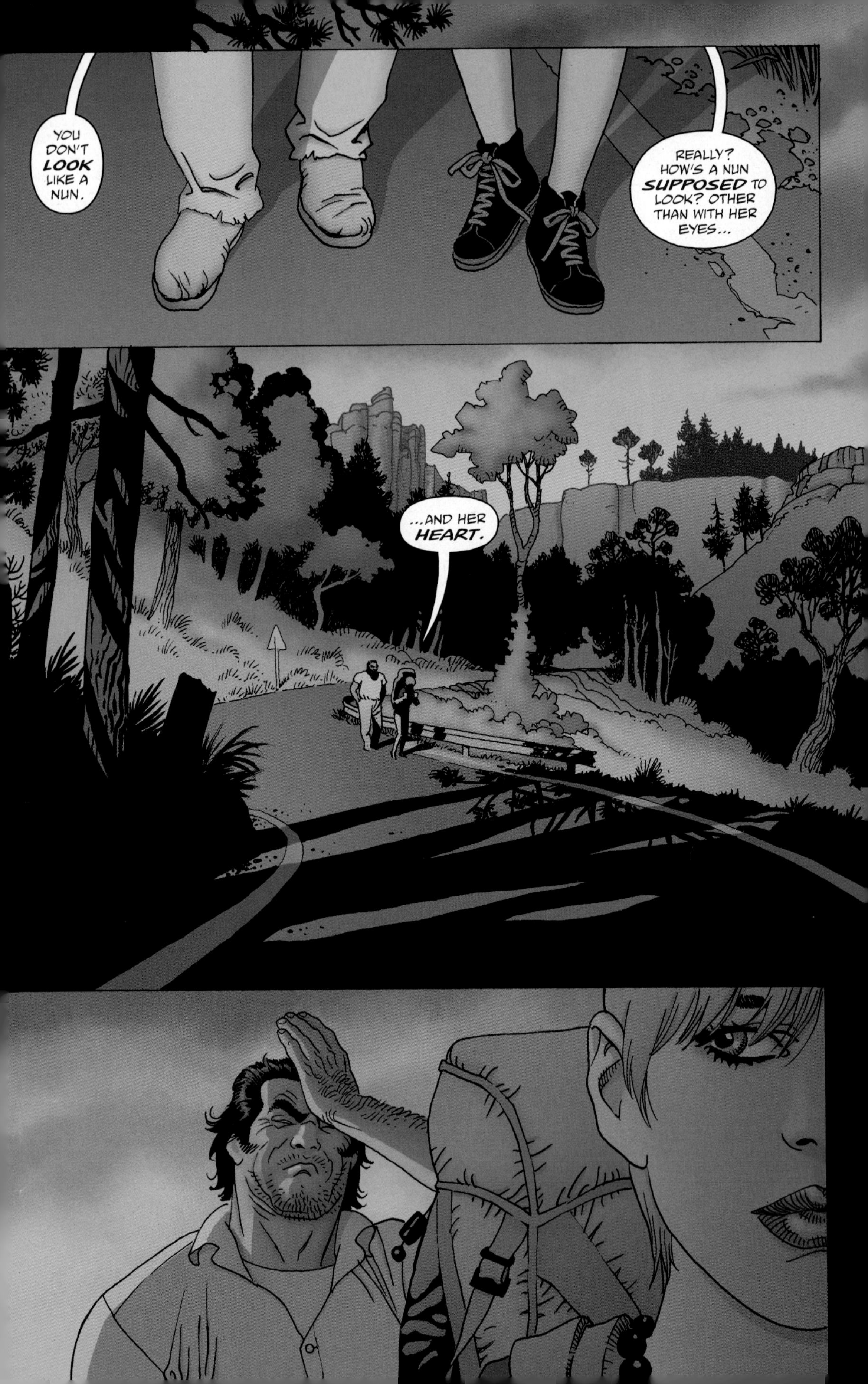
YOU DON'T LOOK LIKE A NUN.
REALLY? HOW'S A NUN SUPPOSED TO LOOK? OTHER THAN WITH HER EYES...
...AND HER HEART.

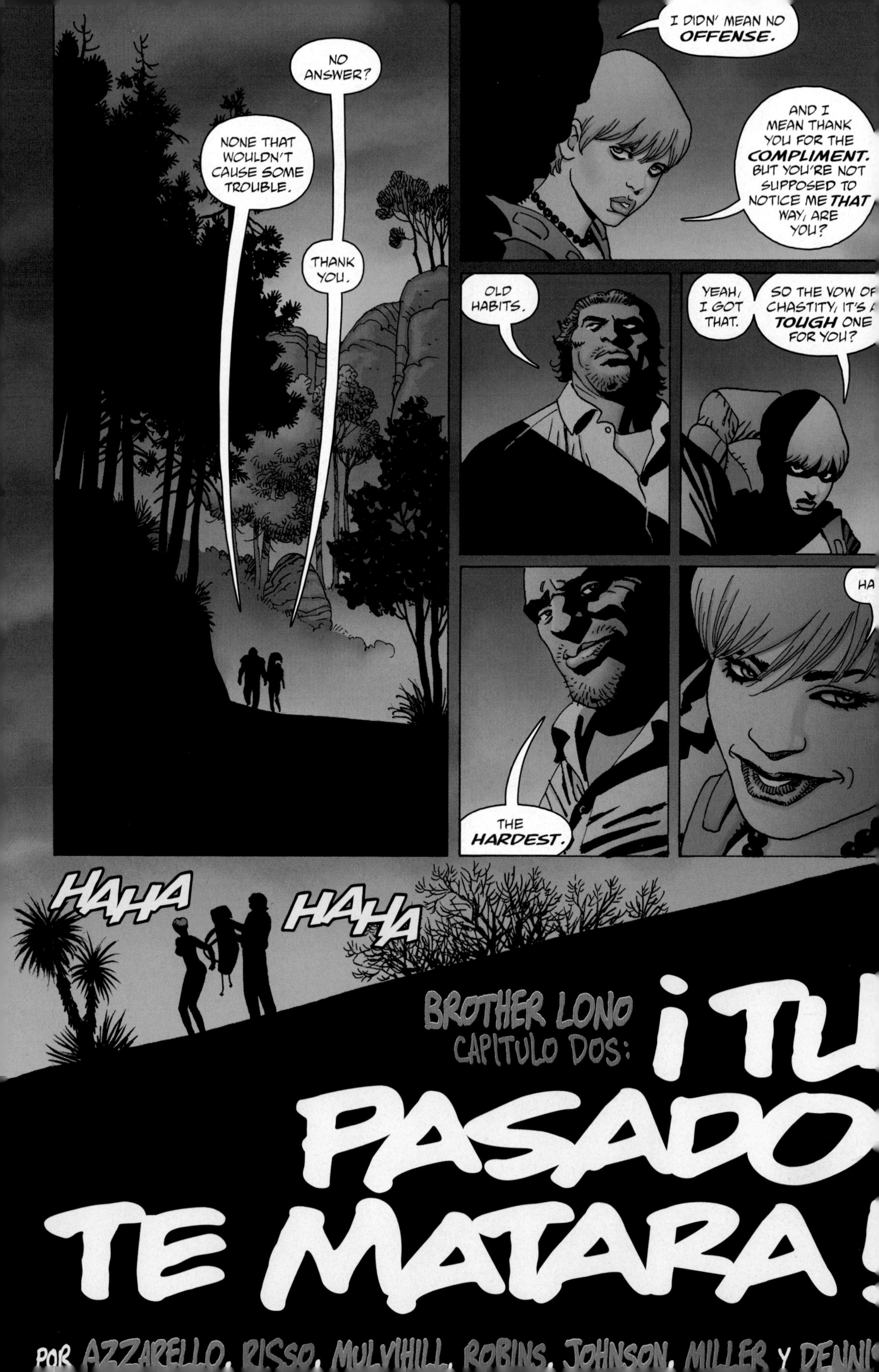
NO ANSWER?
NONE THAT WOULDN'T CAUSE SOME TROUBLE.
THANK YOU.
I DIDN' MEAN NO OFFENSE.
AND I MEAN THANK YOU FOR THE COMPLIMENT. BUT YOU'RE NOT SUPPOSED TO NOTICE ME THAT WAY, ARE YOU?
OLD HABITS.
YEAH, I GOT THAT.
SO THE VOW OF CHASTITY, IT'S A TOUGH ONE FOR YOU?
THE HARDEST.
HA
HAHA
HAHA
BROTHER LONO CAPITULO DOS:
¡TU PASADO TE MATARA!
POR AZZARELLO, RISSO, MULVIHILL, ROBINS, JOHNSON, MILLER Y DENNI

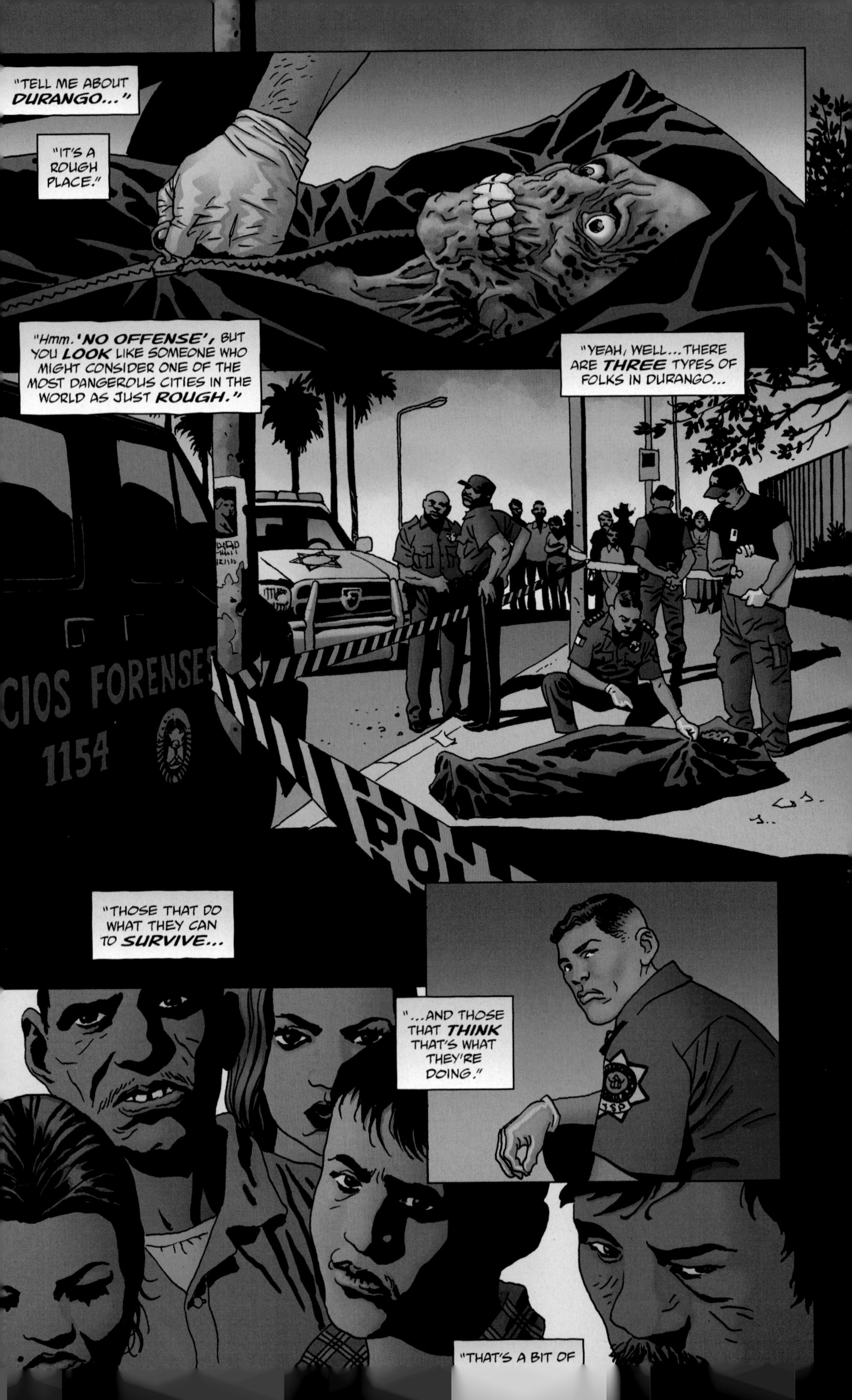
"TELL ME ABOUT DURANGO..."
"IT'S A ROUGH PLACE."
"Hmm. 'NO OFFENSE', BUT YOU LOOK LIKE SOMEONE WHO MIGHT CONSIDER ONE OF THE MOST DANGEROUS CITIES IN THE WORLD AS JUST ROUGH."
"YEAH, WELL... THERE ARE THREE TYPES OF FOLKS IN DURANGO...
CIOS FORENSES
1154
"THOSE THAT DO WHAT THEY CAN TO SURVIVE...
"...AND THOSE THAT THINK THAT'S WHAT THEY'RE DOING."
"THAT'S A BIT OF

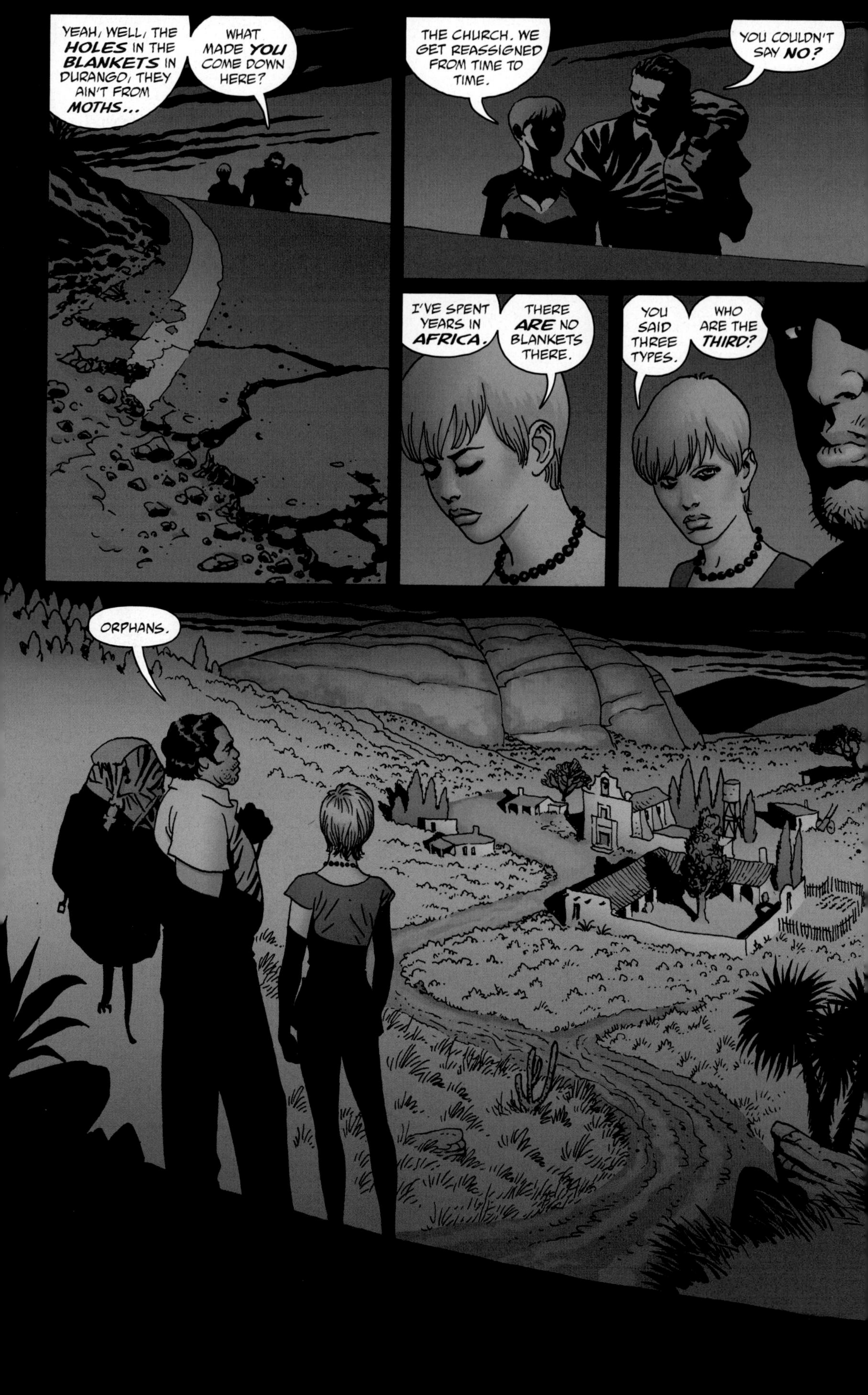
YEAH, WELL, THE HOLES IN THE BLANKETS IN DURANGO, THEY AIN'T FROM MOTHS...
WHAT MADE YOU COME DOWN HERE?
THE CHURCH. WE GET REASSIGNED FROM TIME TO TIME.
YOU COULDN'T SAY NO?
I'VE SPENT YEARS IN AFRICA.
THERE ARE NO BLANKETS THERE.
YOU SAID THREE TYPES.
WHO ARE THE THIRD?
ORPHANS.

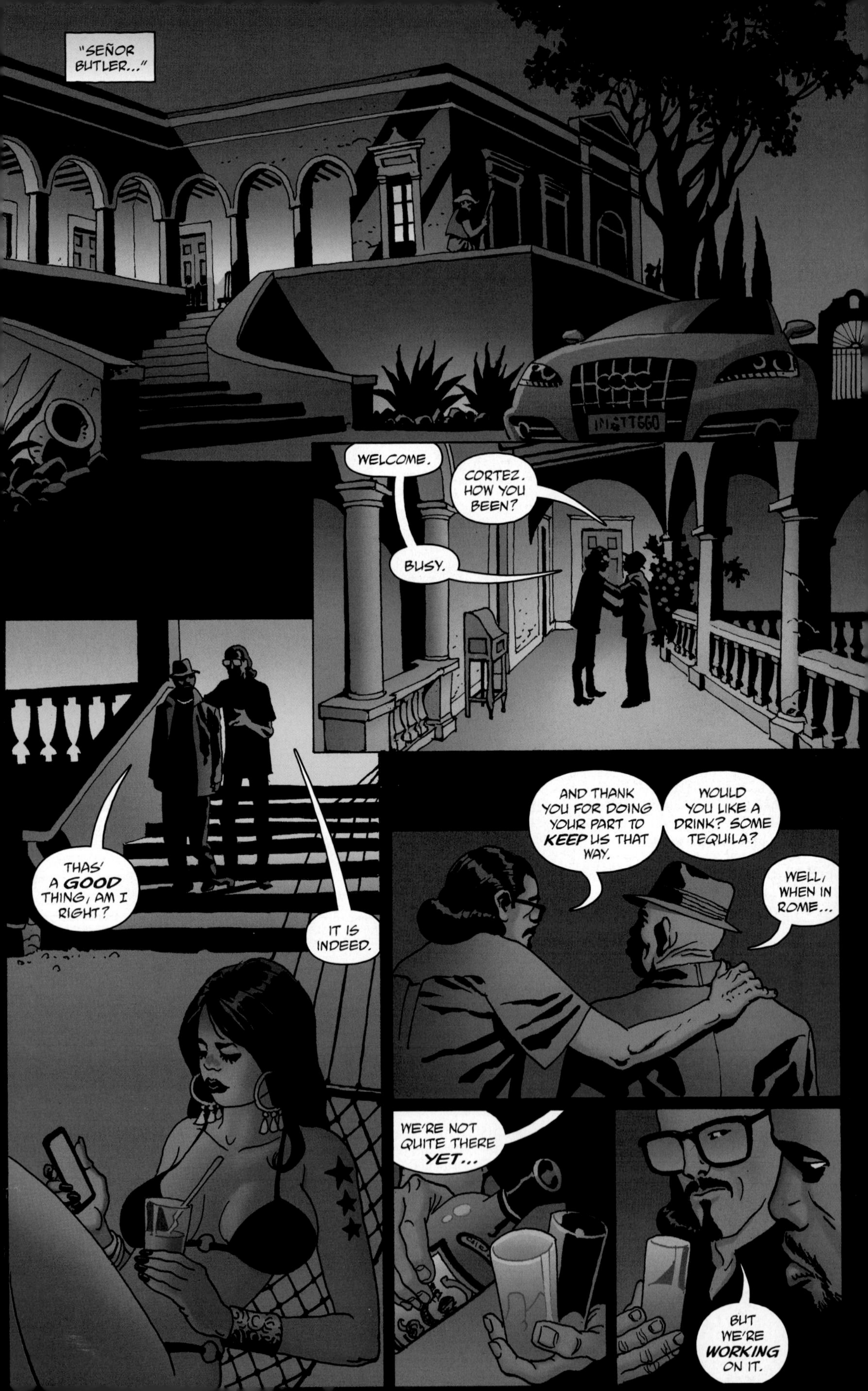
"SEÑOR BUTLER..."
WELCOME.
CORTEZ. HOW YOU BEEN?
BUSY.
THAS' A GOOD THING, AM I RIGHT?
IT IS INDEED.
AND THANK YOU FOR DOING YOUR PART TO KEEP US THAT WAY.
WOULD YOU LIKE A DRINK? SOME TEQUILA?
WELL, WHEN IN ROME...
WE'RE NOT QUITE THERE YET...
BUT WE'RE WORKING ON IT.

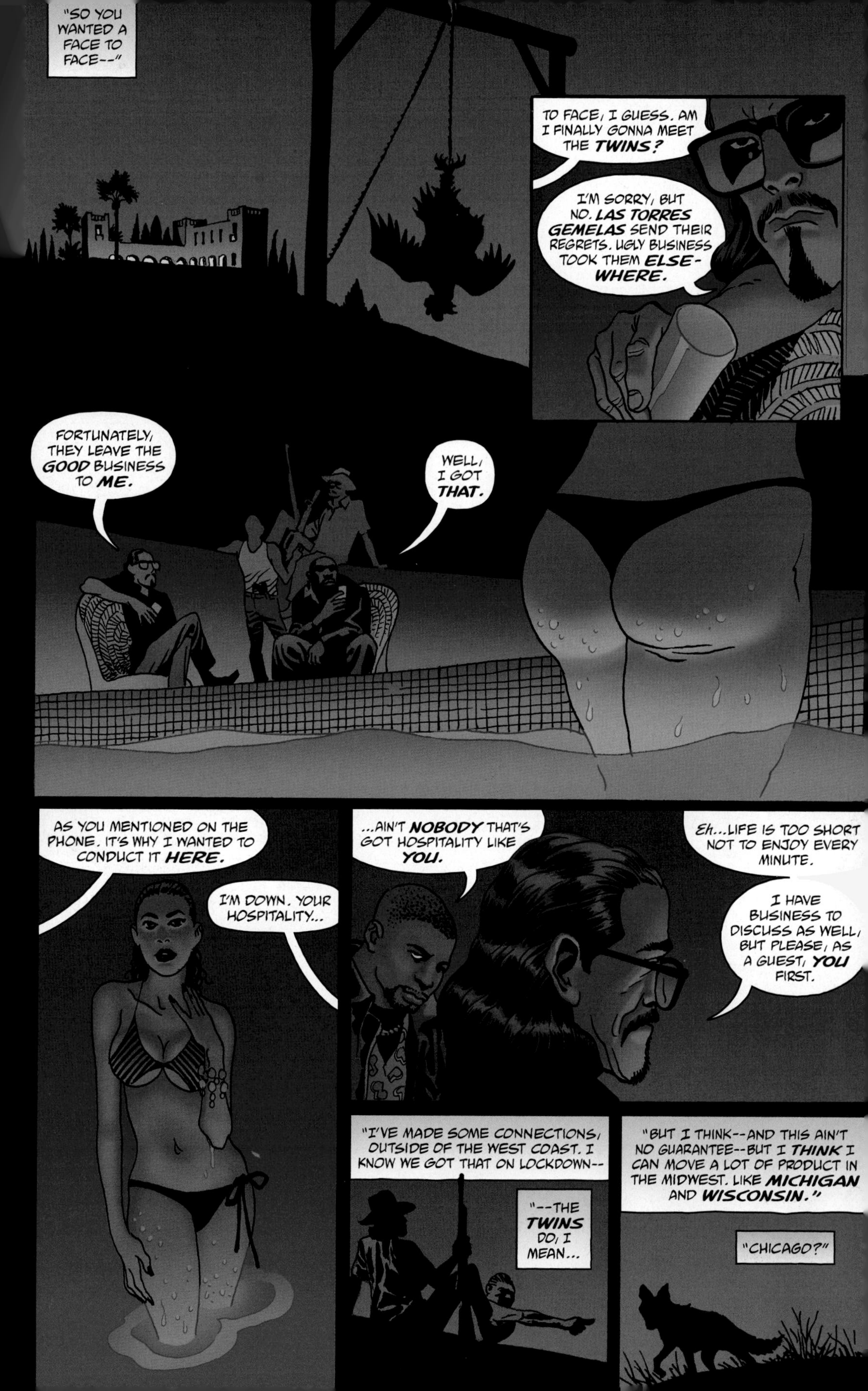
"SO YOU WANTED A FACE TO FACE--"
TO FACE, I GUESS. AM I FINALLY GONNA MEET THE TWINS?
I'M SORRY, BUT NO. LAS TORRES GEMELAS SEND THEIR REGRETS. UGLY BUSINESS TOOK THEM ELSE-WHERE.
FORTUNATELY, THEY LEAVE THE GOOD BUSINESS TO ME.
WELL, I GOT THAT.
AS YOU MENTIONED ON THE PHONE. IT'S WHY I WANTED TO CONDUCT IT HERE.
I'M DOWN. YOUR HOSPITALITY...
...AIN'T NOBODY THAT'S GOT HOSPITALITY LIKE YOU.
Eh...LIFE IS TOO SHORT NOT TO ENJOY EVERY MINUTE.
I HAVE BUSINESS TO DISCUSS AS WELL, BUT PLEASE, AS A GUEST, YOU FIRST.
"I'VE MADE SOME CONNECTIONS, OUTSIDE OF THE WEST COAST. I KNOW WE GOT THAT ON LOCKDOWN--
"--THE TWINS DO, I MEAN...
"BUT I THINK--AND THIS AIN'T NO GUARANTEE--BUT I THINK I CAN MOVE A LOT OF PRODUCT IN THE MIDWEST. LIKE MICHIGAN AND WISCONSIN."
"CHICAGO?"

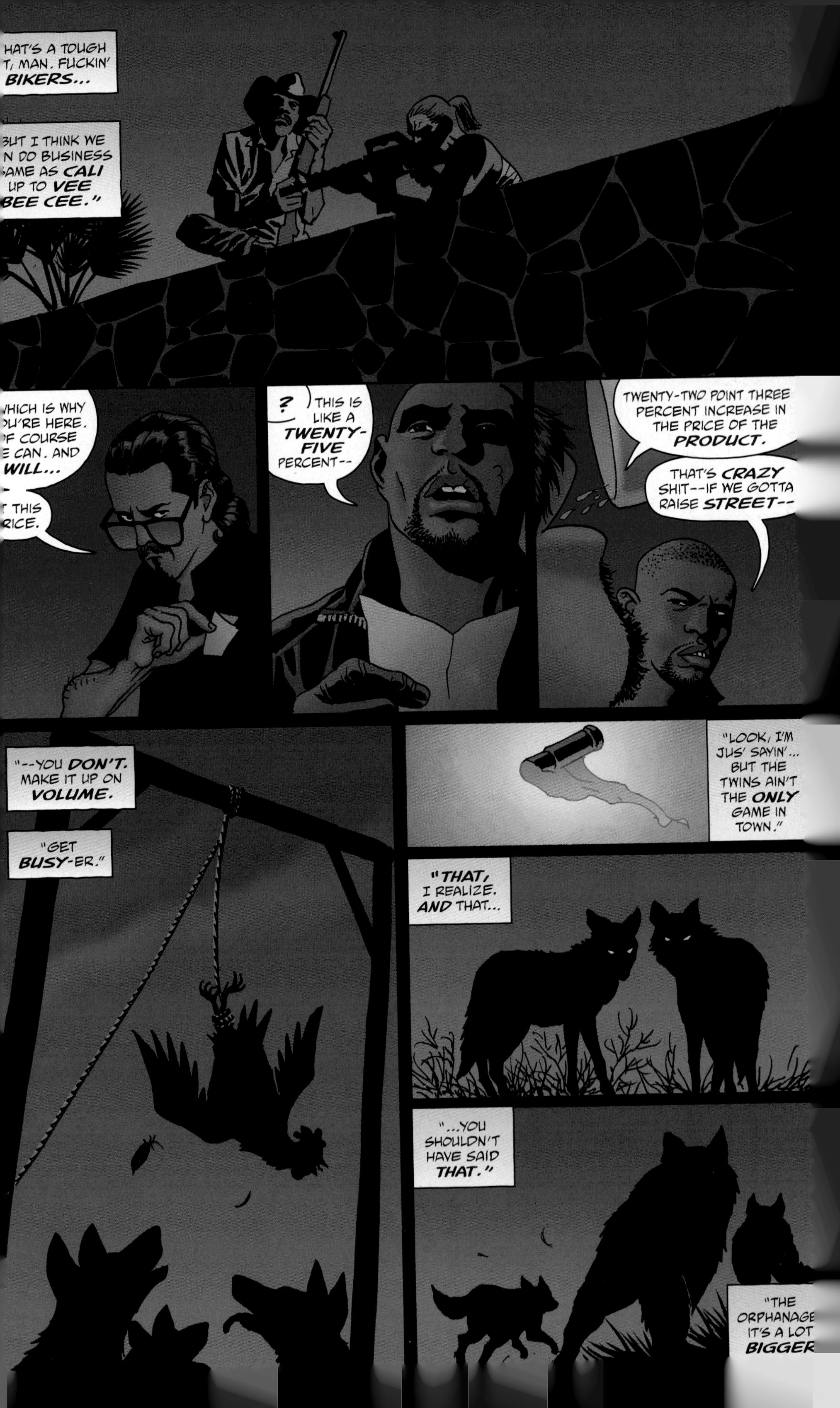

HAT'S A TOUGH
T, MAN. FUCKIN'
BIKERS...
BUT I THINK WE
N DO BUSINESS
SAME AS CALI
UP TO VEE
BEE CEE."
WHICH IS WHY
OU'RE HERE.
OF COURSE
E CAN. AND
WILL...
T THIS
RICE.
? THIS IS LIKE A TWENTY-FIVE PERCENT--
TWENTY-TWO POINT THREE PERCENT INCREASE IN THE PRICE OF THE PRODUCT.
THAT'S CRAZY SHIT--IF WE GOTTA RAISE STREET--
"--YOU DON'T. MAKE IT UP ON VOLUME.
"GET BUSY-ER."
"LOOK, I'M JUS' SAYIN'... BUT THE TWINS AIN'T THE ONLY GAME IN TOWN."
"THAT, I REALIZE. AND THAT...
"...YOU SHOULDN'T HAVE SAID THAT."
"THE ORPHANAGE IT'S A LOT BIGGER

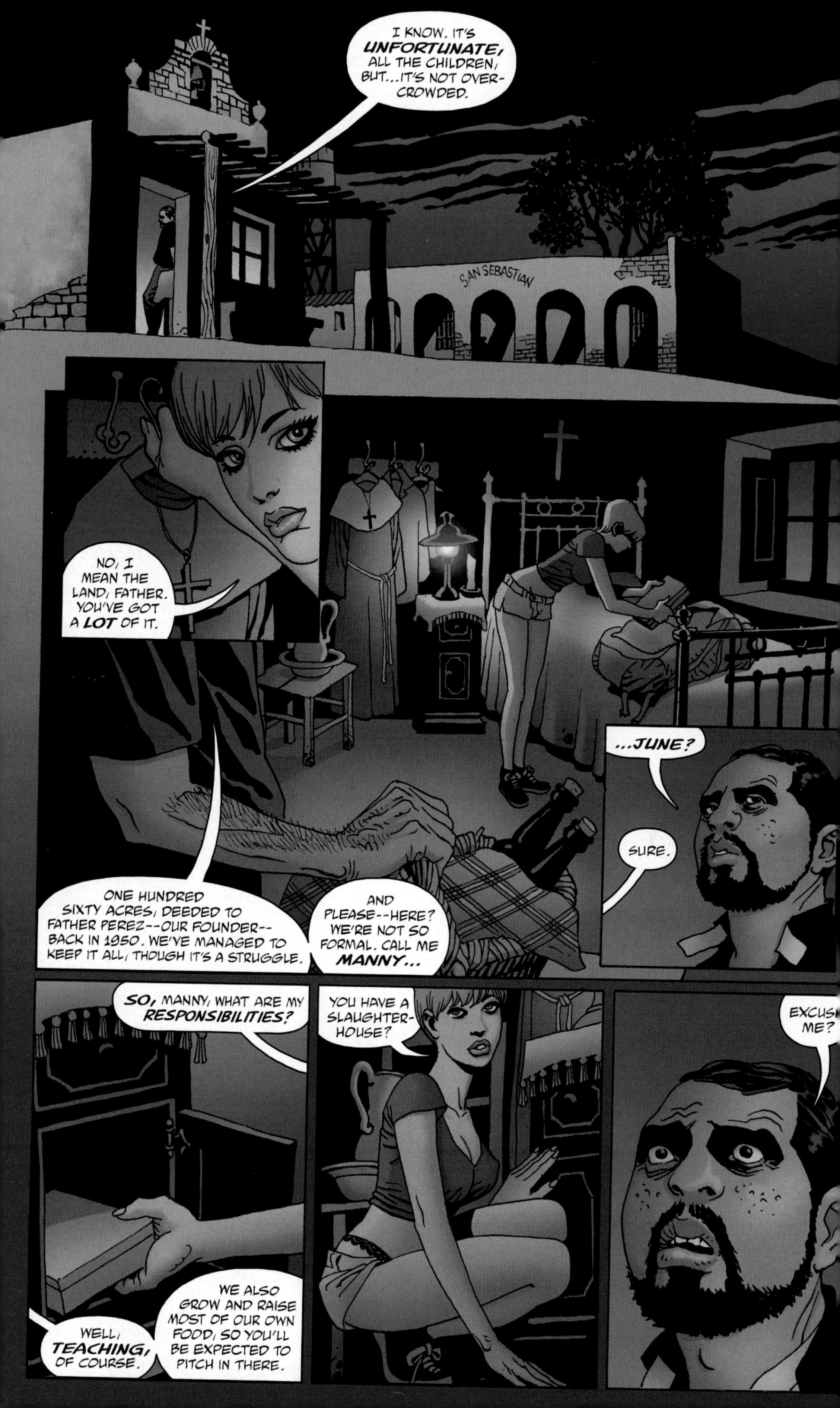
I KNOW. IT'S UNFORTUNATE, ALL THE CHILDREN, BUT...IT'S NOT OVER-CROWDED.
SAN SEBASTIAN
NO, I MEAN THE LAND, FATHER. YOU'VE GOT A LOT OF IT.
ONE HUNDRED SIXTY ACRES, DEEDED TO FATHER PEREZ--OUR FOUNDER--BACK IN 1950. WE'VE MANAGED TO KEEP IT ALL, THOUGH IT'S A STRUGGLE.
AND PLEASE--HERE? WE'RE NOT SO FORMAL. CALL ME MANNY...
...JUNE?
SURE.
SO, MANNY, WHAT ARE MY RESPONSIBILITIES?
WELL, TEACHING, OF COURSE.
WE ALSO GROW AND RAISE MOST OF OUR OWN FOOD, SO YOU'LL BE EXPECTED TO PITCH IN THERE.
YOU HAVE A SLAUGHTER-HOUSE?
EXCUS ME?

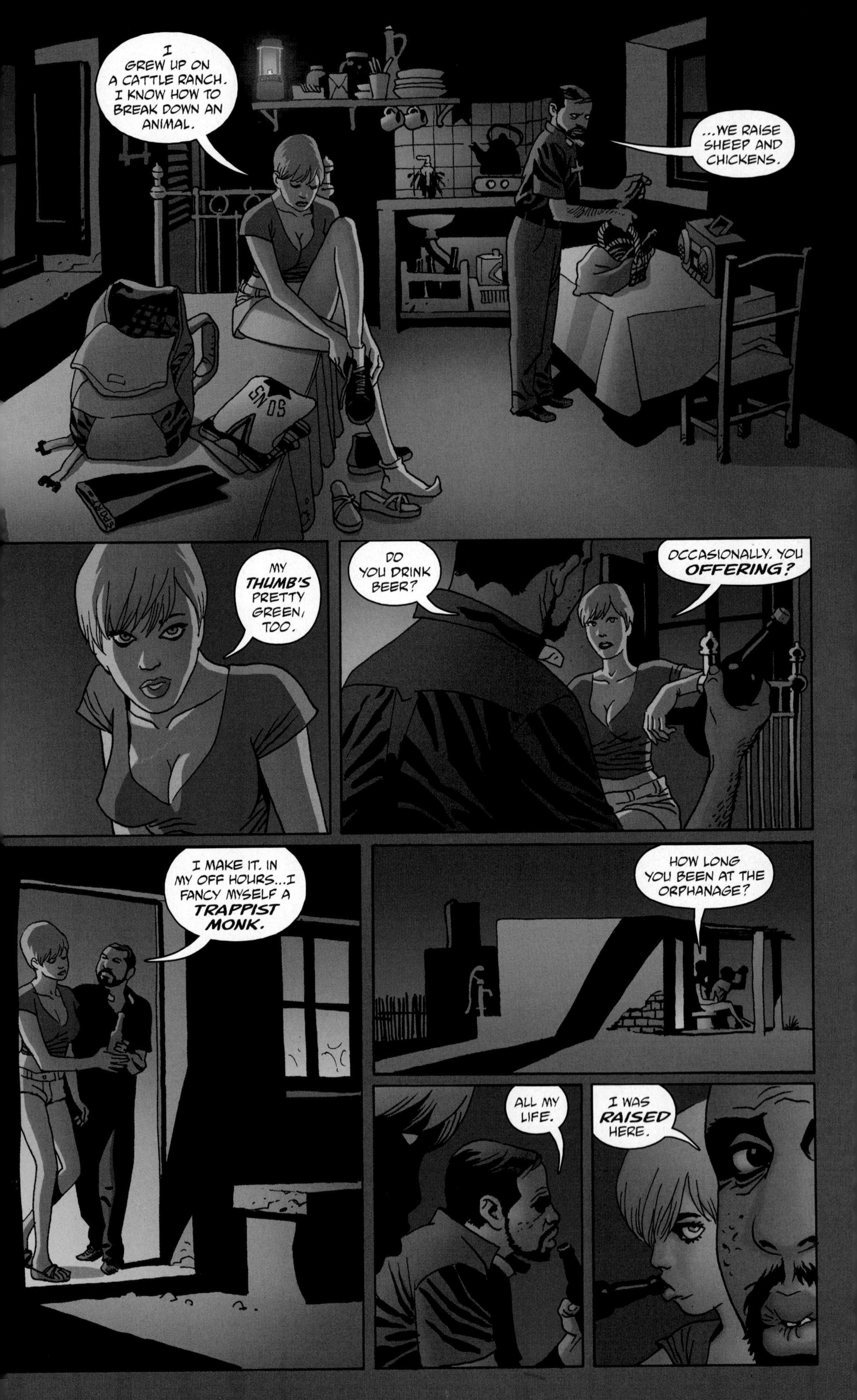
I GREW UP ON A CATTLE RANCH. I KNOW HOW TO BREAK DOWN AN ANIMAL.
...WE RAISE SHEEP AND CHICKENS.
MY THUMB'S PRETTY GREEN, TOO.
DO YOU DRINK BEER?
OCCASIONALLY. YOU OFFERING?
I MAKE IT. IN MY OFF HOURS...I FANCY MYSELF A TRAPPIST MONK.
HOW LONG YOU BEEN AT THE ORPHANAGE?
ALL MY LIFE.
I WAS RAISED HERE.

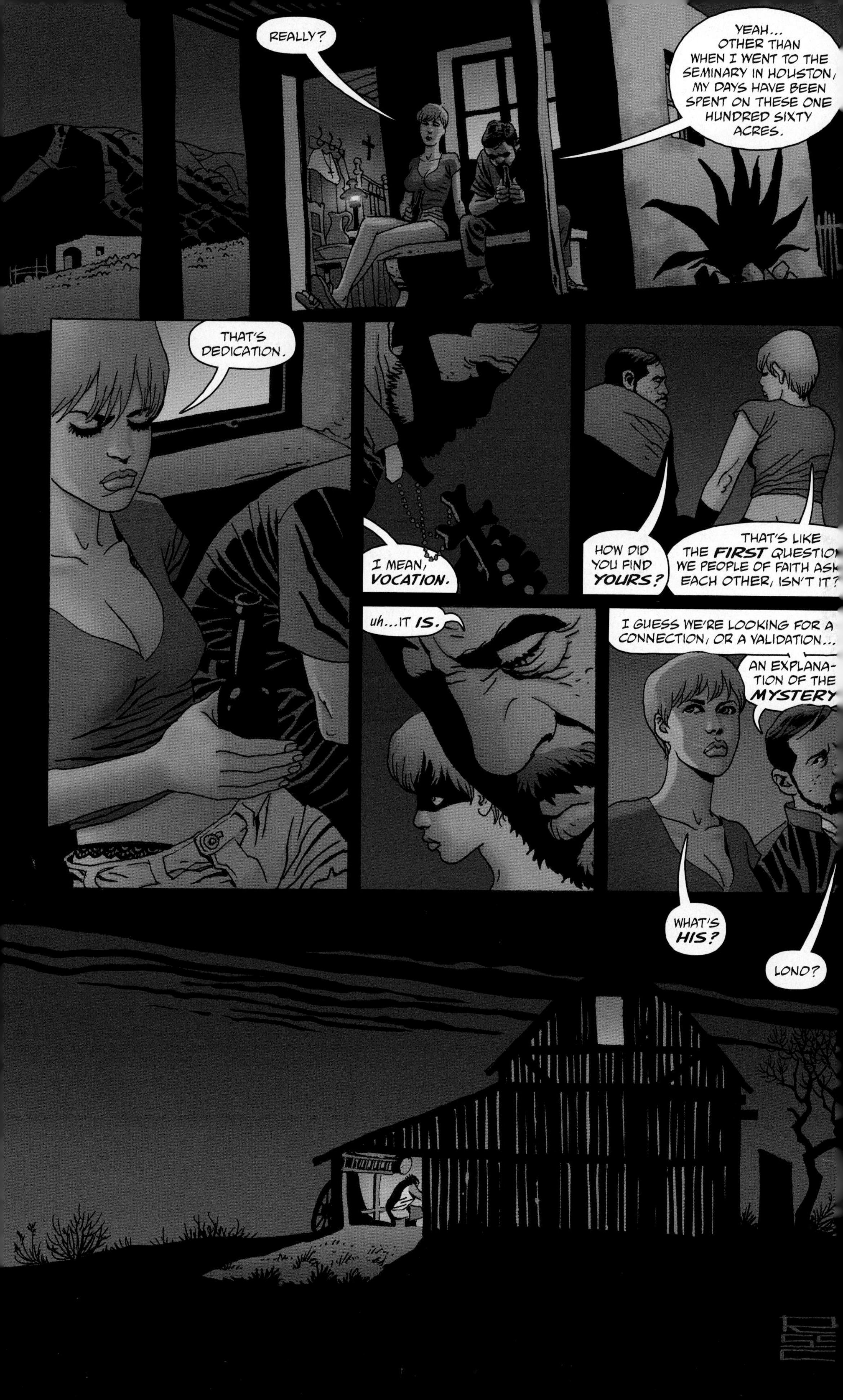
REALLY?
YEAH... OTHER THAN WHEN I WENT TO THE SEMINARY IN HOUSTON, MY DAYS HAVE BEEN SPENT ON THESE ONE HUNDRED SIXTY ACRES.
THAT'S DEDICATION.
I MEAN, VOCATION.
HOW DID YOU FIND YOURS?
THAT'S LIKE THE FIRST QUESTIO WE PEOPLE OF FAITH ASK EACH OTHER, ISN'T IT?
uh...IT IS.
I GUESS WE'RE LOOKING FOR A CONNECTION, OR A VALIDATION...
AN EXPLANATION OF THE MYSTERY
WHAT'S HIS?
LONO?

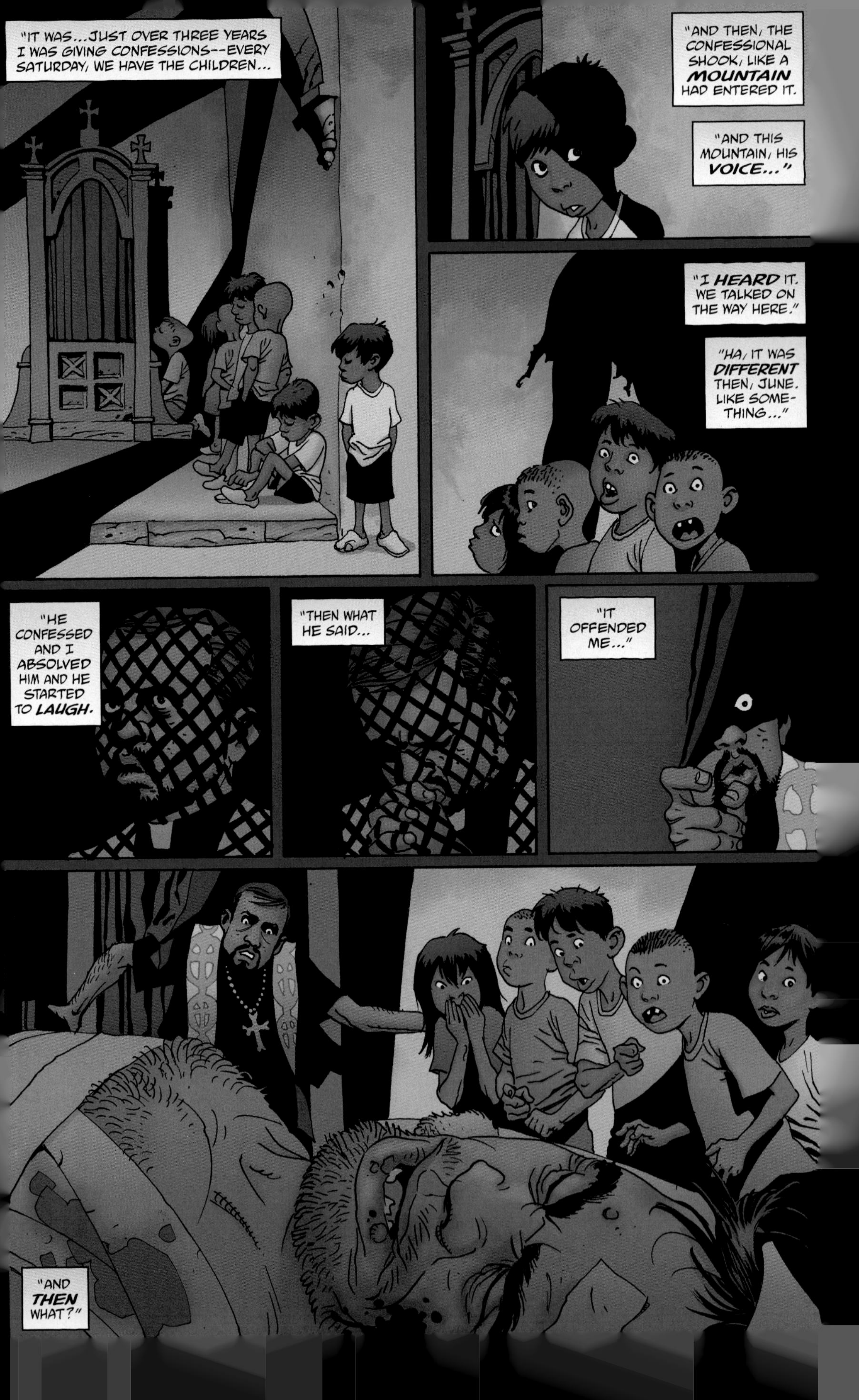
"IT WAS...JUST OVER THREE YEARS I WAS GIVING CONFESSIONS--EVERY SATURDAY, WE HAVE THE CHILDREN...
"AND THEN, THE CONFESSIONAL SHOOK, LIKE A MOUNTAIN HAD ENTERED IT.
"AND THIS MOUNTAIN, HIS VOICE..."
"I HEARD IT. WE TALKED ON THE WAY HERE."
"HA, IT WAS DIFFERENT THEN, JUNE. LIKE SOME-THING..."
"HE CONFESSED AND I ABSOLVED HIM AND HE STARTED TO LAUGH.
"THEN WHAT HE SAID...
"IT OFFENDED ME..."
"AND THEN WHAT?"

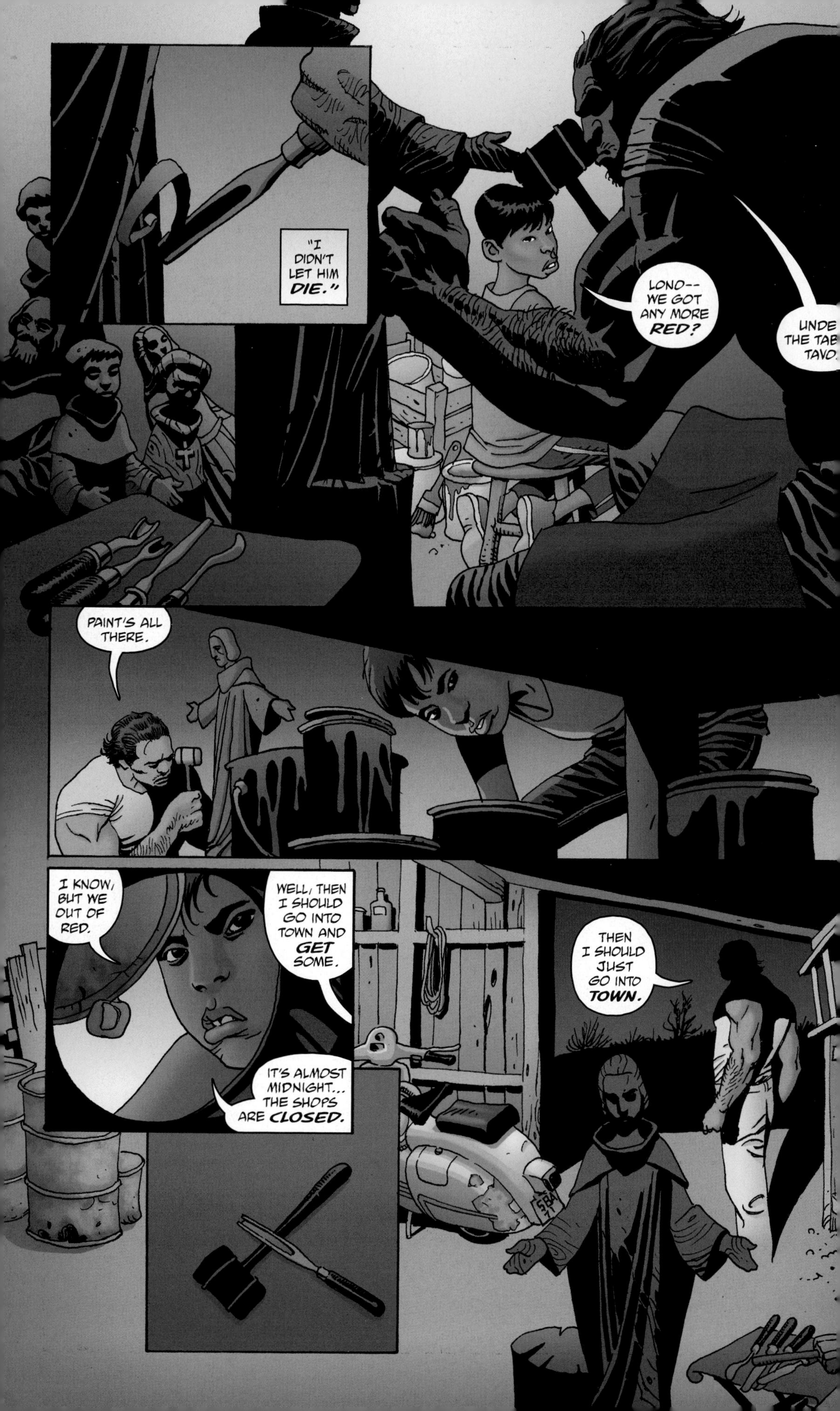
"I DIDN'T LET HIM DIE."
LONO-- WE GOT ANY MORE RED?
UNDE THE TAB TAVO.
PAINT'S ALL THERE.
I KNOW, BUT WE OUT OF RED.
WELL, THEN I SHOULD GO INTO TOWN AND GET SOME.
IT'S ALMOST MIDNIGHT... THE SHOPS ARE CLOSED.
THEN I SHOULD JUST GO INTO TOWN.

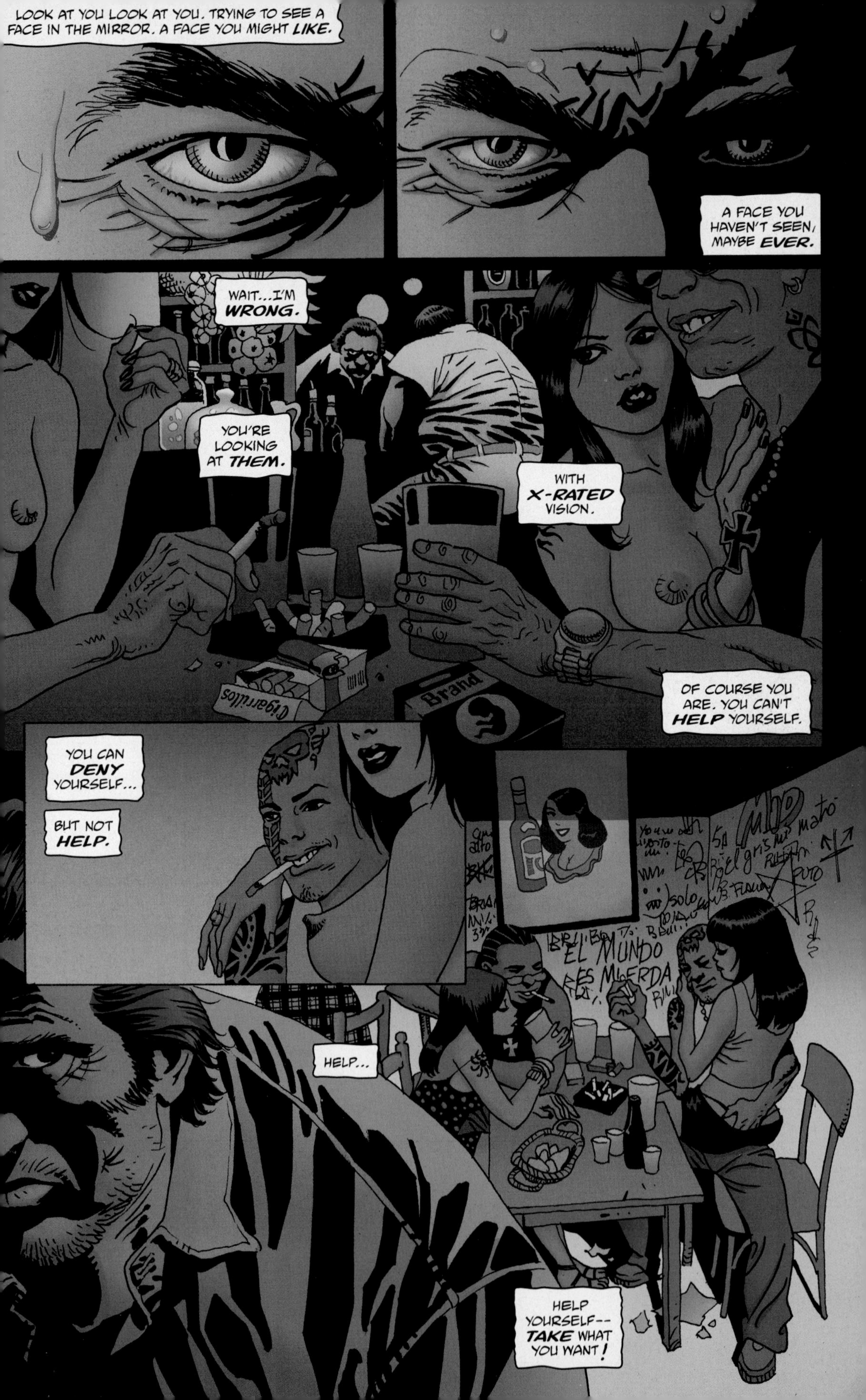

LOOK AT YOU LOOK AT YOU. TRYING TO SEE A FACE IN THE MIRROR. A FACE YOU MIGHT LIKE.
A FACE YOU HAVEN'T SEEN, MAYBE EVER.
WAIT...I'M WRONG.
YOU'RE LOOKING AT THEM.
WITH X-RATED VISION.
Brand
OF COURSE YOU ARE. YOU CAN'T HELP YOURSELF.
YOU CAN DENY YOURSELF...
BUT NOT HELP.
EL MUNDO
HELP...
HELP YOURSELF--TAKE WHAT YOU WANT!

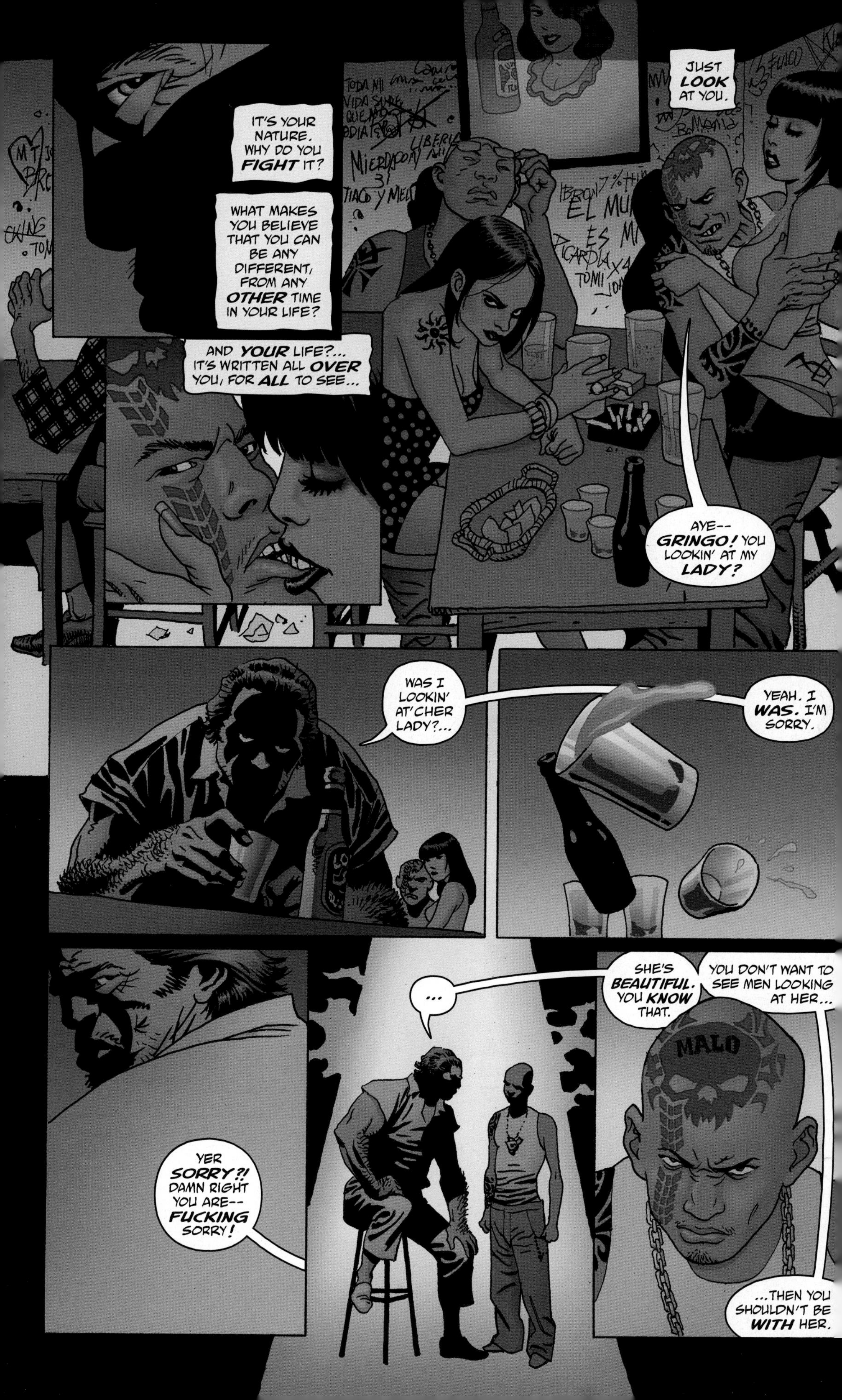
IT'S YOUR NATURE. WHY DO YOU FIGHT IT?
WHAT MAKES YOU BELIEVE THAT YOU CAN BE ANY DIFFERENT, FROM ANY OTHER TIME IN YOUR LIFE?
JUST LOOK AT YOU.
AND YOUR LIFE?... IT'S WRITTEN ALL OVER YOU, FOR ALL TO SEE...
AYE-- GRINGO! YOU LOOKIN' AT MY LADY?
WAS I LOOKIN' AT'CHER LADY?...
YEAH. I WAS. I'M SORRY.
YER SORRY?! DAMN RIGHT YOU ARE-- FUCKING SORRY!
...
SHE'S BEAUTIFUL. YOU KNOW THAT.
YOU DON'T WANT TO SEE MEN LOOKING AT HER...
...THEN YOU SHOULDN'T BE WITH HER.
MALO

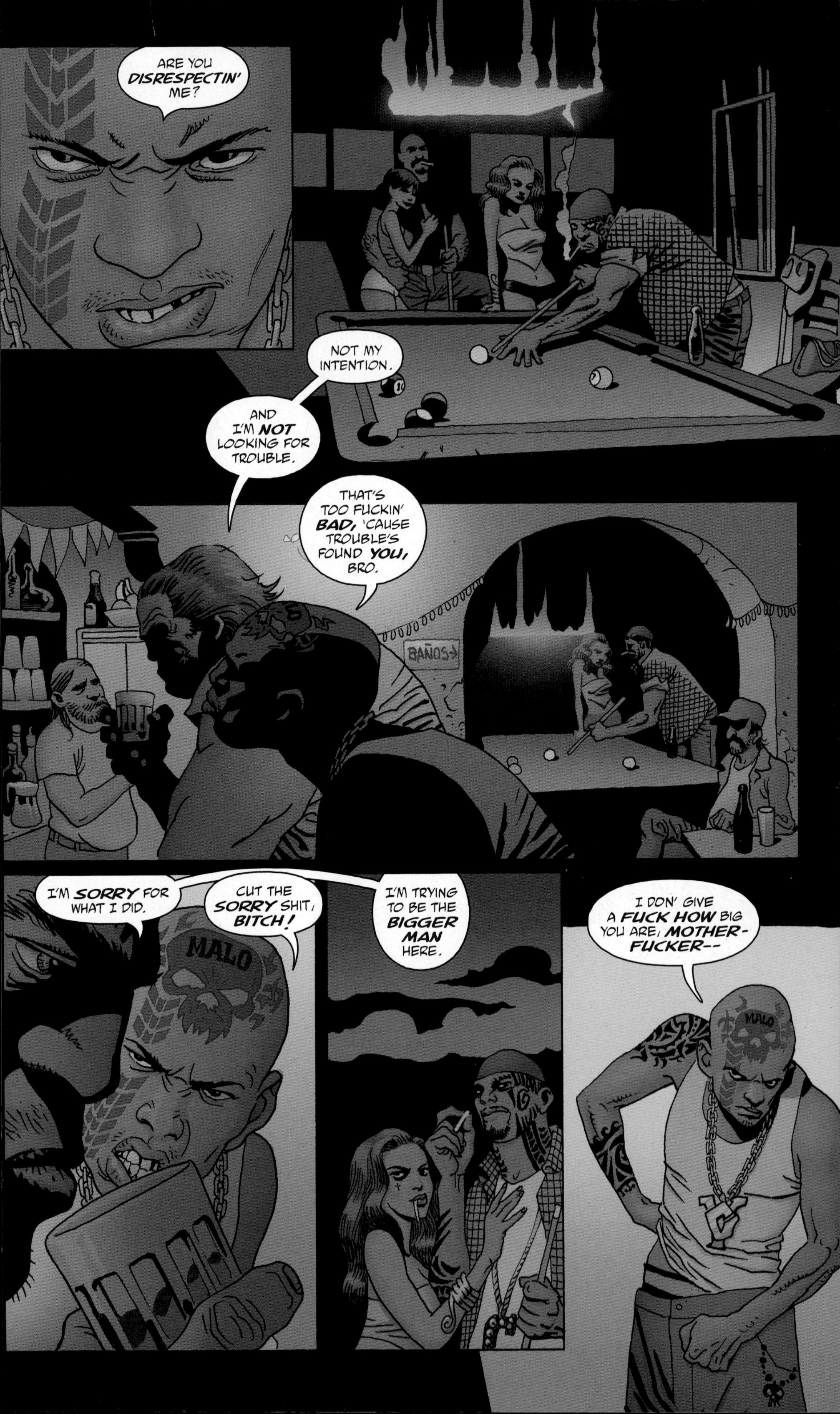
ARE YOU DISRESPECTIN' ME?
NOT MY INTENTION.
AND I'M NOT LOOKING FOR TROUBLE.
THAT'S TOO FUCKIN' BAD, 'CAUSE TROUBLE'S FOUND YOU, BRO.
BAÑOS→
I'M SORRY FOR WHAT I DID.
CUT THE SORRY SHIT, BITCH!
I'M TRYING TO BE THE BIGGER MAN HERE.
MALO
I DON' GIVE A FUCK HOW BIG YOU ARE, MOTHER-FUCKER--
MALO

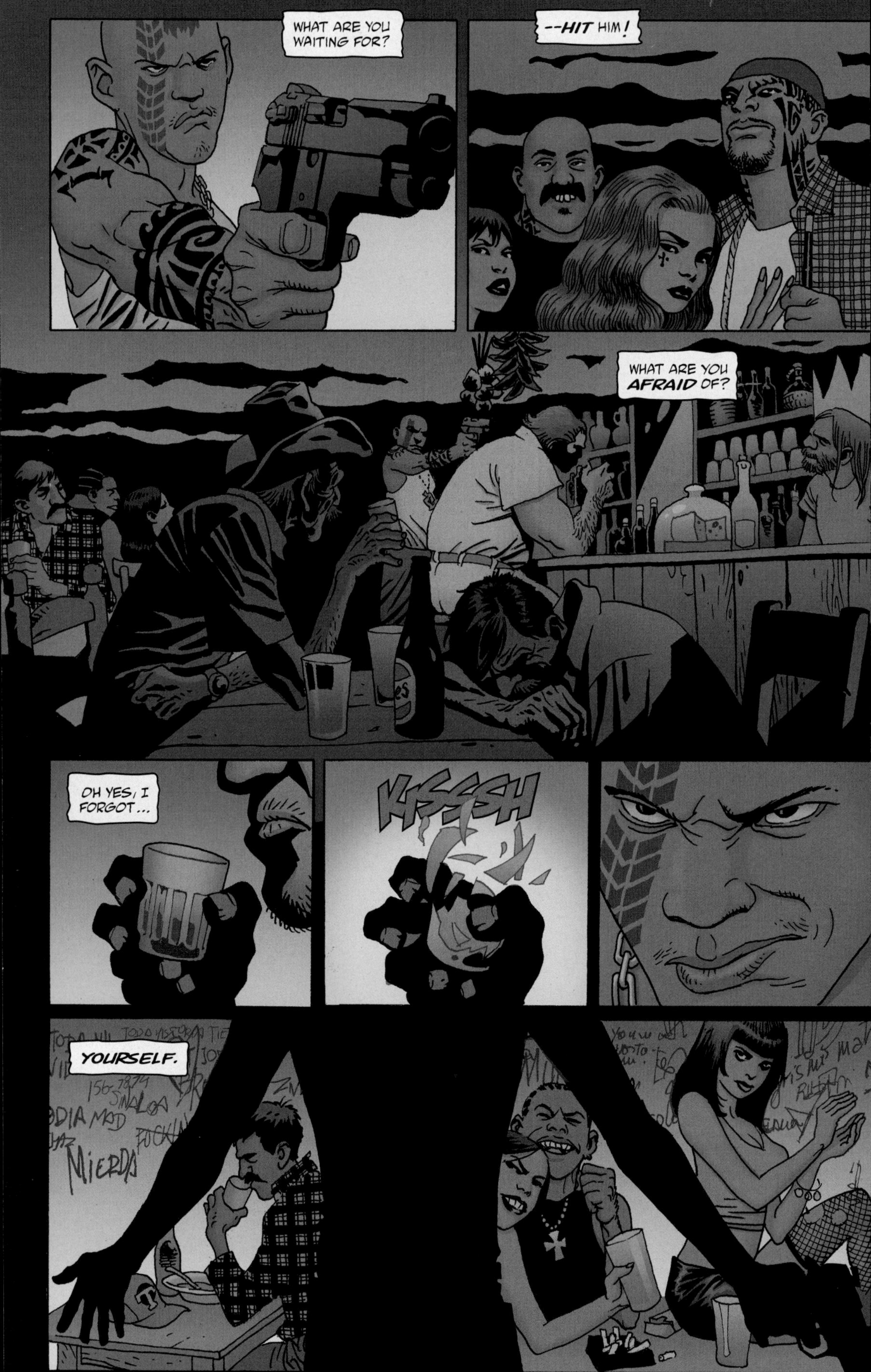
WHAT ARE YOU WAITING FOR?
--HIT HIM!
WHAT ARE YOU AFRAID OF?
OH YES, I FORGOT...
KSSSH
YOURSELF.
SINALOA
MIERDA

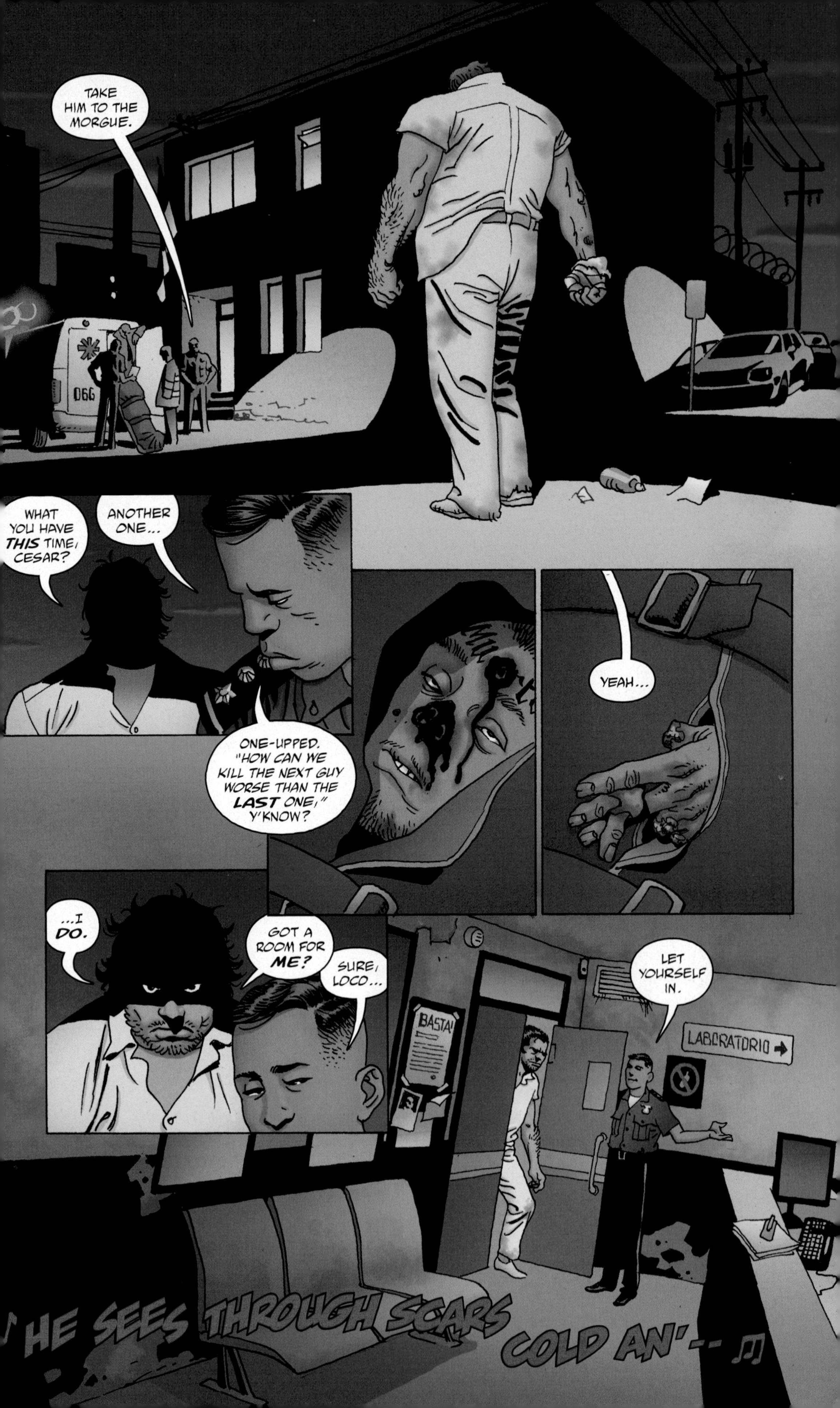
TAKE HIM TO THE MORGUE.
06G
WHAT YOU HAVE THIS TIME, CESAR?
ANOTHER ONE...
ONE-UPPED. "HOW CAN WE KILL THE NEXT GUY WORSE THAN THE LAST ONE," Y'KNOW?
YEAH...
...I DO.
GOT A ROOM FOR ME?
SURE, LOCO...
LET YOURSELF IN.
BASTA!
LABORATORIO
♪ HE SEES THROUGH SCARS COLD AN'-- ♫

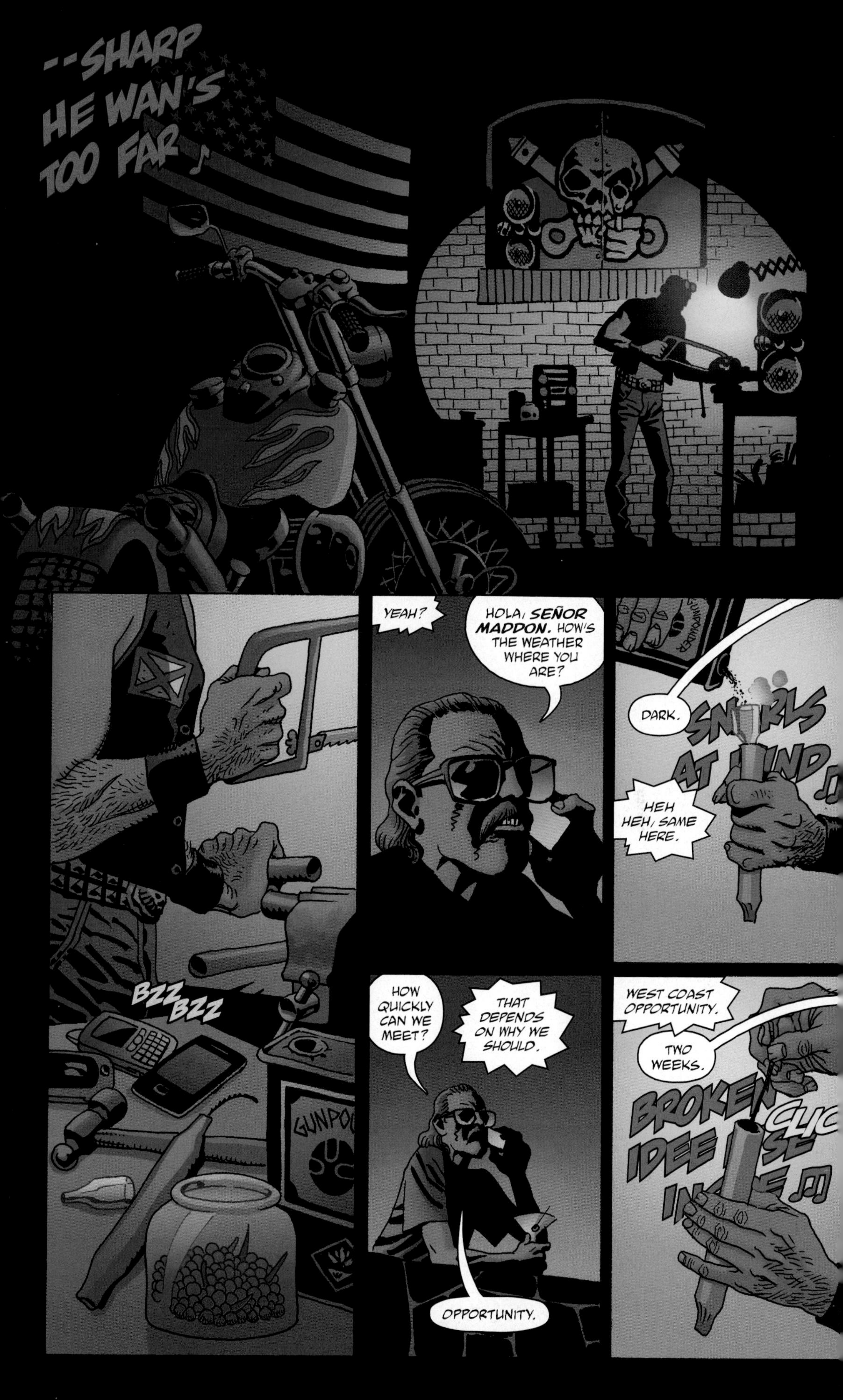
--SHARP HE WAN'S TOO FAR ♪
YEAH?
HOLA, SEÑOR MADDON. HOW'S THE WEATHER WHERE YOU ARE?
DARK.
HEH HEH, SAME HERE.
BZZ BZZ
GUNPOU
HOW QUICKLY CAN WE MEET?
THAT DEPENDS ON WHY WE SHOULD.
OPPORTUNITY.
WEST COAST OPPORTUNITY.
TWO WEEKS.

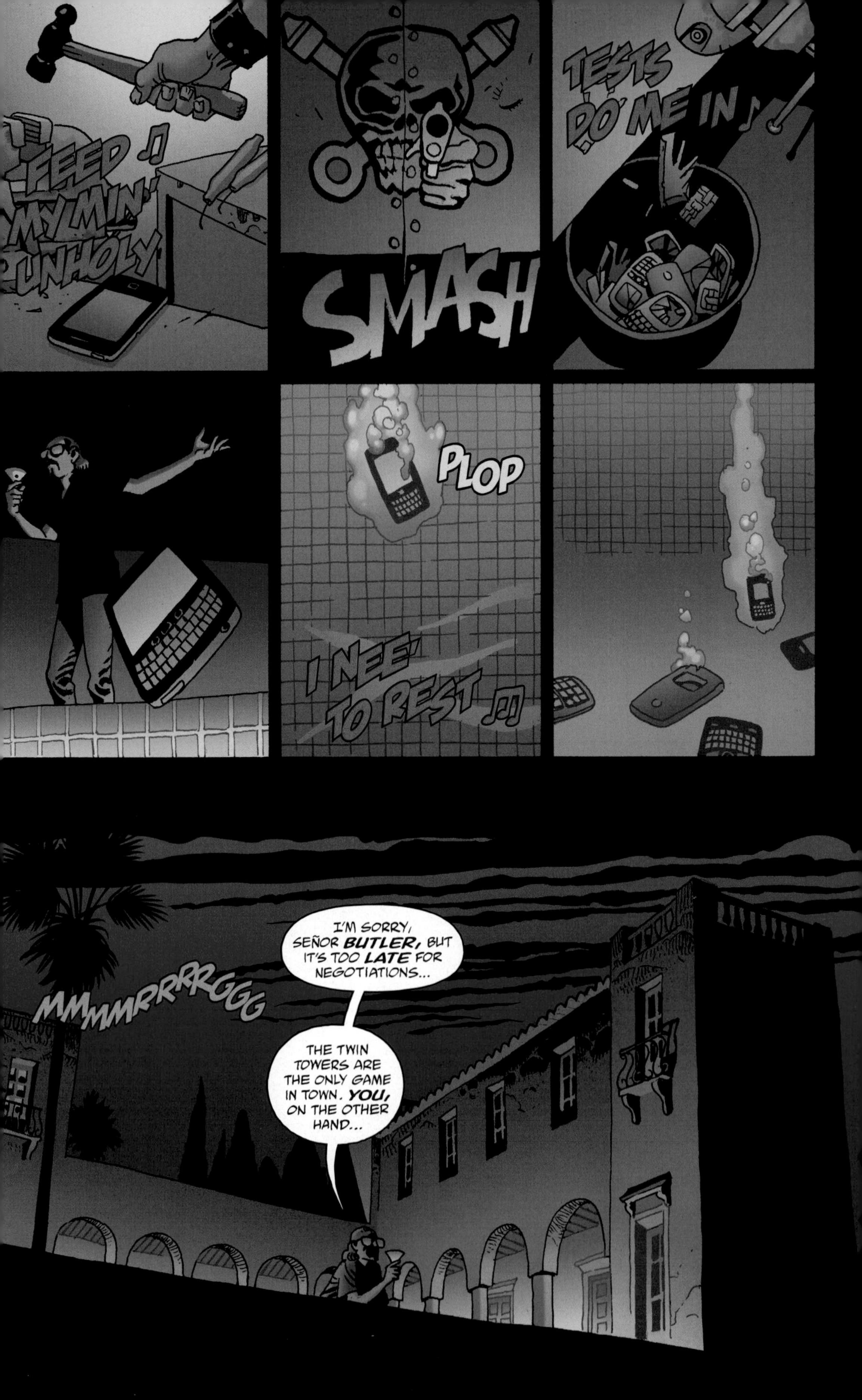
FEED MY LMIN' UNHOLY ♫
SMASH
TESTS DO ME IN ♪
PLOP
I NEE' TO REST ♫
MMMMRRRRGGG
I'M SORRY, SEÑOR **BUTLER,** BUT IT'S TOO **LATE** FOR NEGOTIATIONS...
THE TWIN TOWERS ARE THE ONLY GAME IN TOWN. **YOU,** ON THE OTHER HAND...

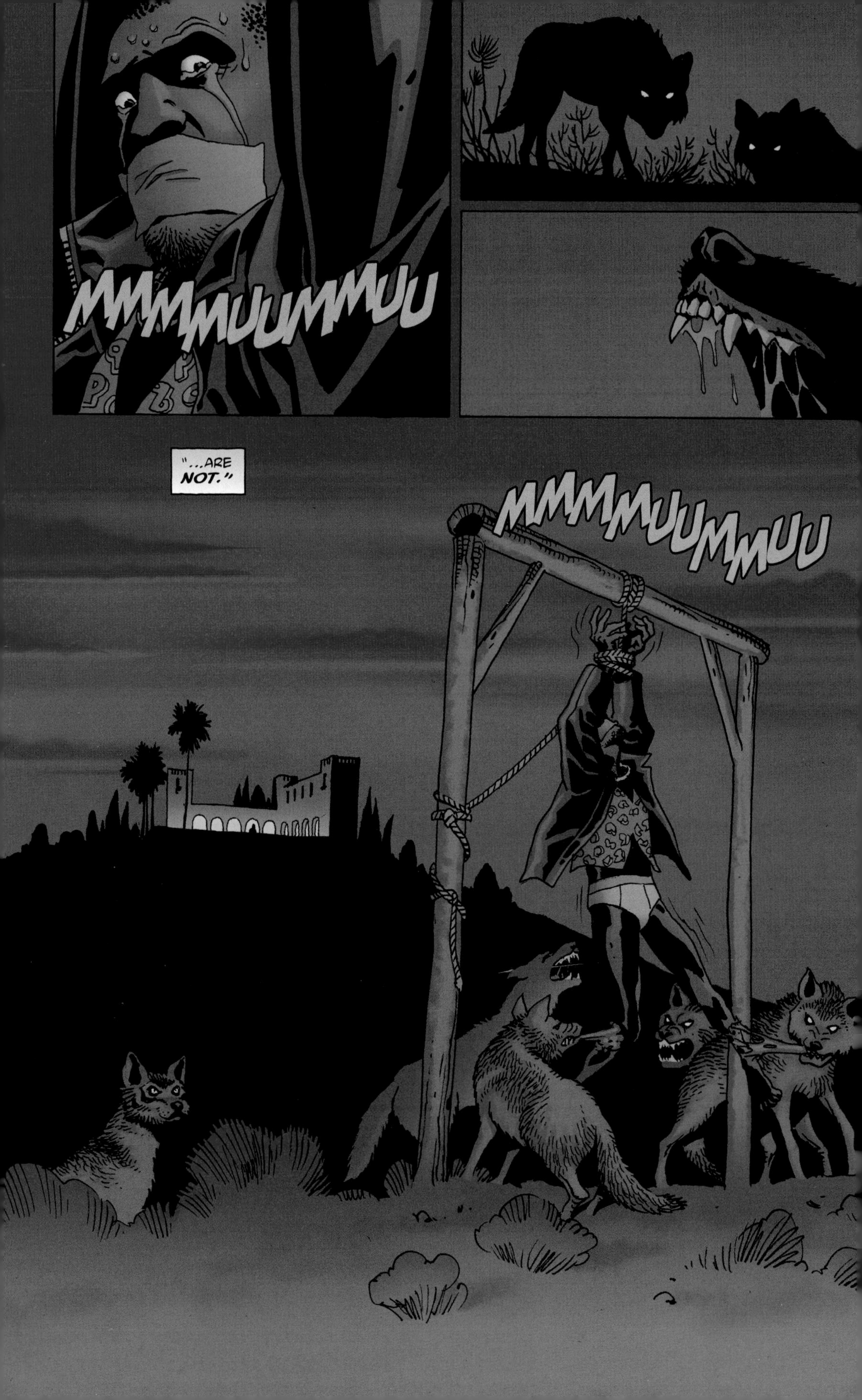
MMMMUUMMUU
"...ARE NOT."
MMMMUUMMUU

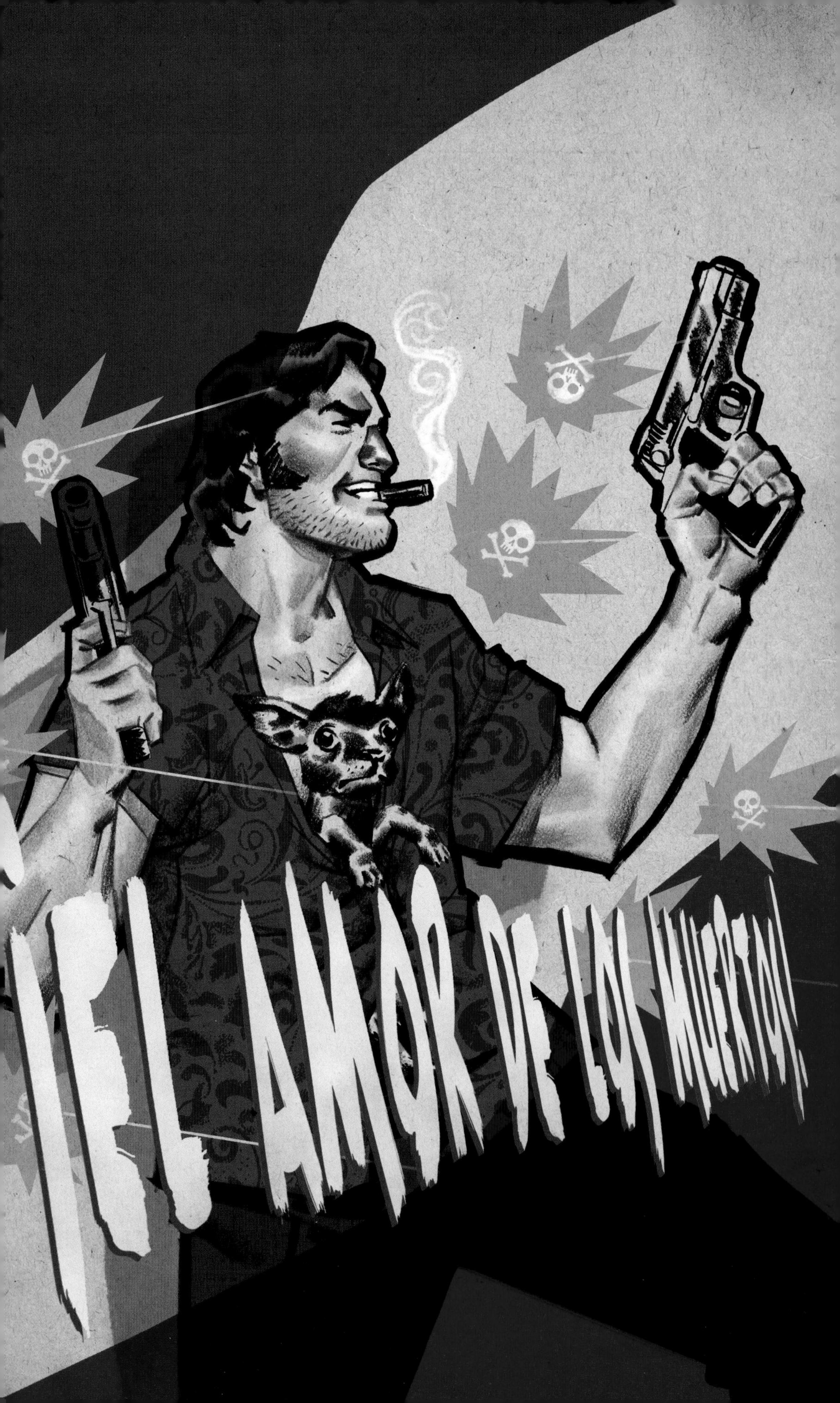
¡EL AMOR DE LOS MUERTOS!

"There's nothing on you that hasn't touched death."

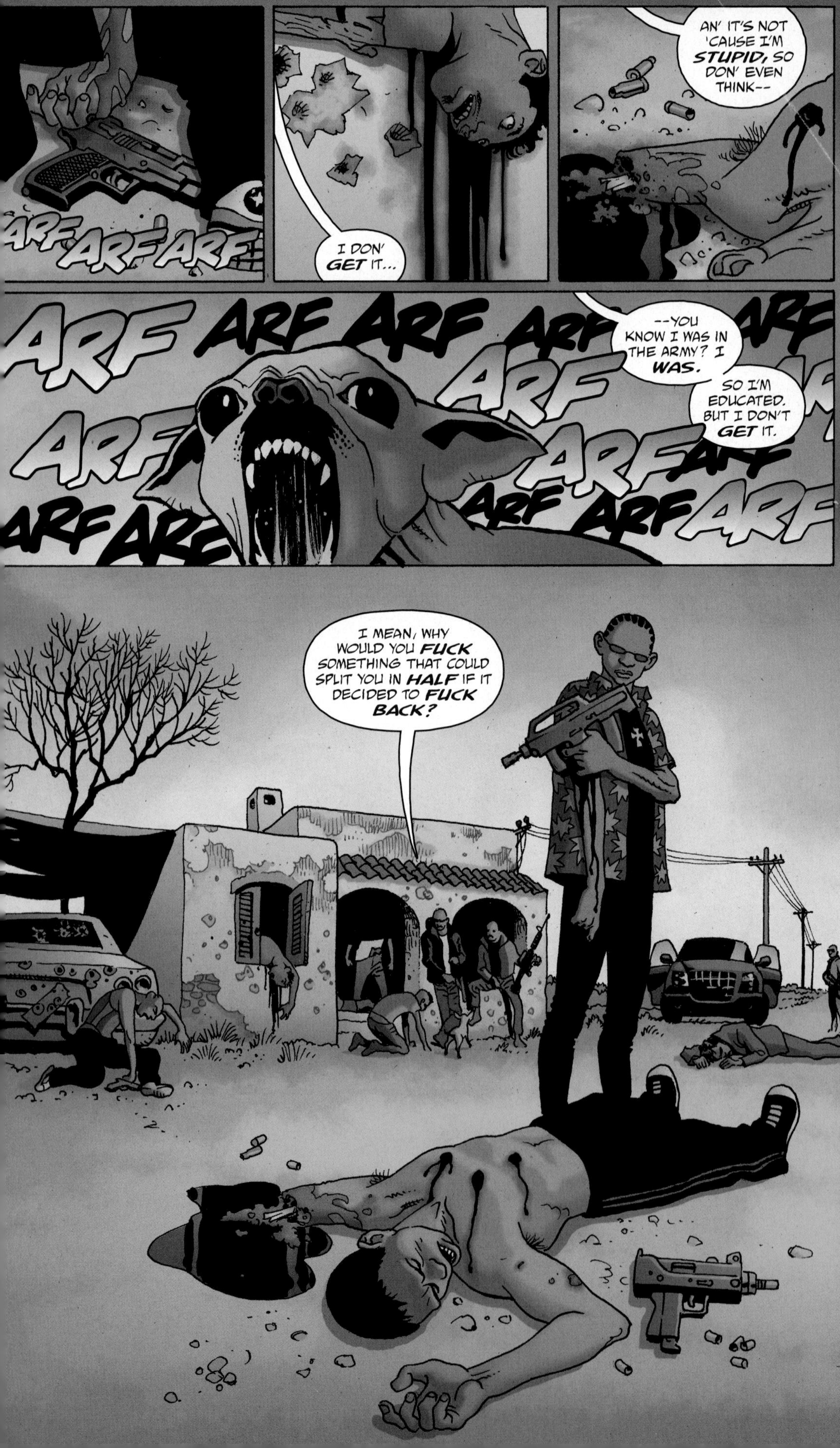
ARF ARF ARF
I DON' GET IT...
AN' IT'S NOT 'CAUSE I'M STUPID, SO DON' EVEN THINK--
ARF ARF ARF
--YOU KNOW I WAS IN THE ARMY? I WAS.
SO I'M EDUCATED. BUT I DON'T GET IT.
ARF ARF ARF ARF ARF ARF
I MEAN, WHY WOULD YOU FUCK SOMETHING THAT COULD SPLIT YOU IN HALF IF IT DECIDED TO FUCK BACK?

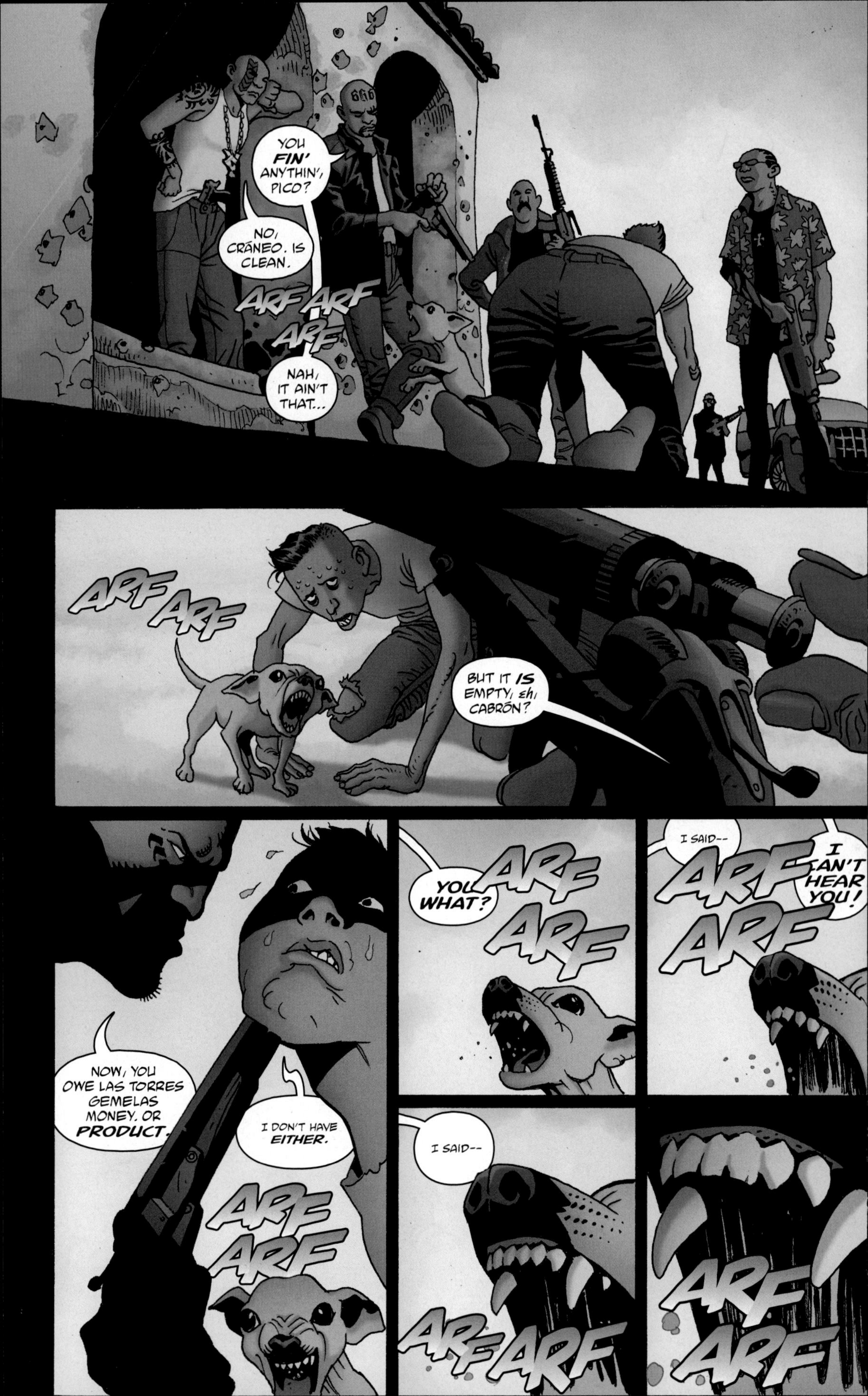
YOU FIN' ANYTHIN', PICO?
NO, CRÁNEO. IS CLEAN.
ARF ARF ARF
NAH, IT AIN'T THAT...
ARF ARF
BUT IT IS EMPTY, EH, CABRÓN?
NOW, YOU OWE LAS TORRES GEMELAS MONEY. OR PRODUCT.
I DON'T HAVE EITHER.
ARF ARF
YOU WHAT?
ARF ARF
I SAID--
I CAN'T HEAR YOU!
ARF ARF
I SAID--
ARF ARF
ARF ARF

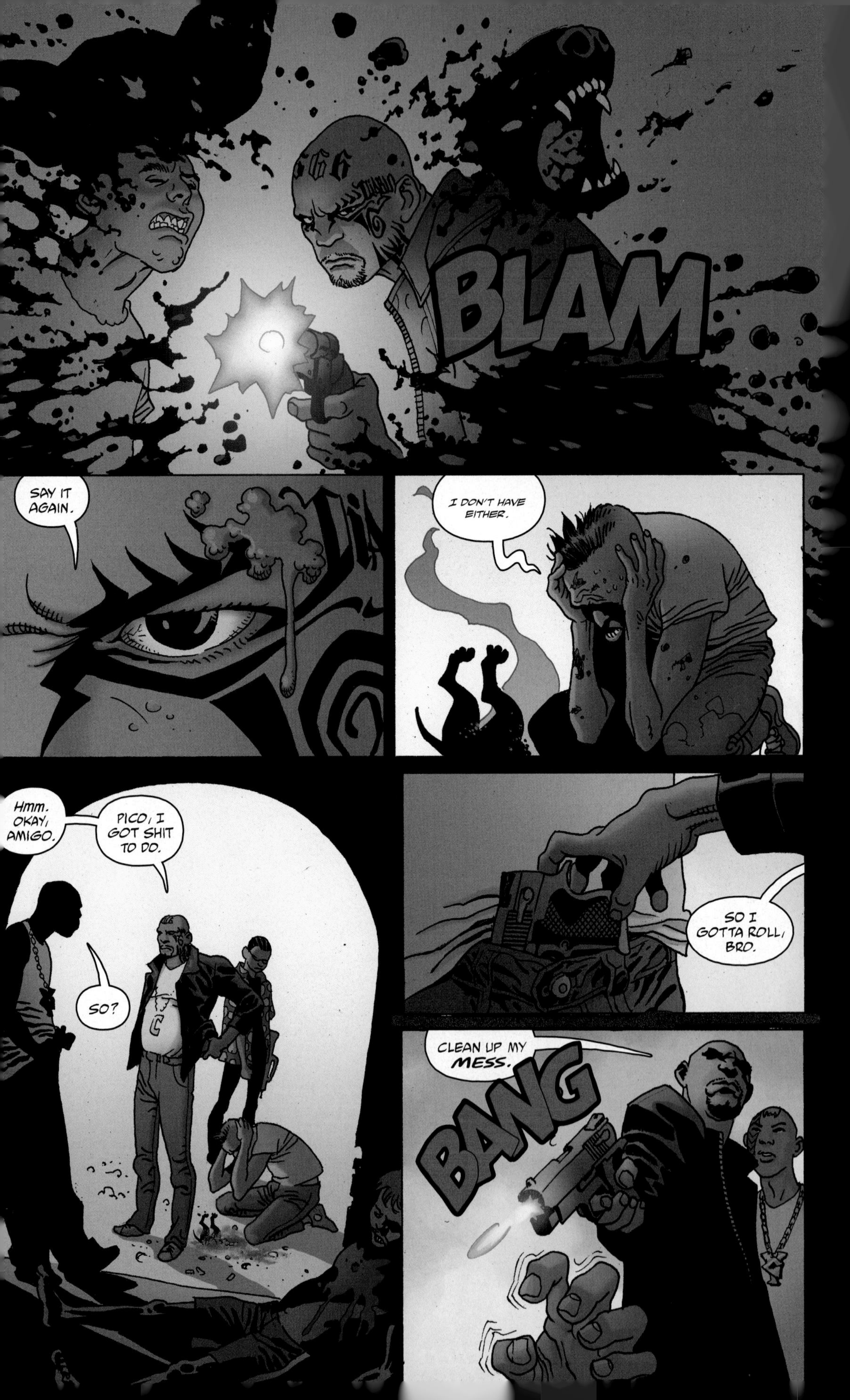
BLAM
SAY IT AGAIN.
I DON'T HAVE EITHER.
Hmm. OKAY, AMIGO.
PICO, I GOT SHIT TO DO.
SO?
SO I GOTTA ROLL, BRO.
CLEAN UP MY MESS.
BANG

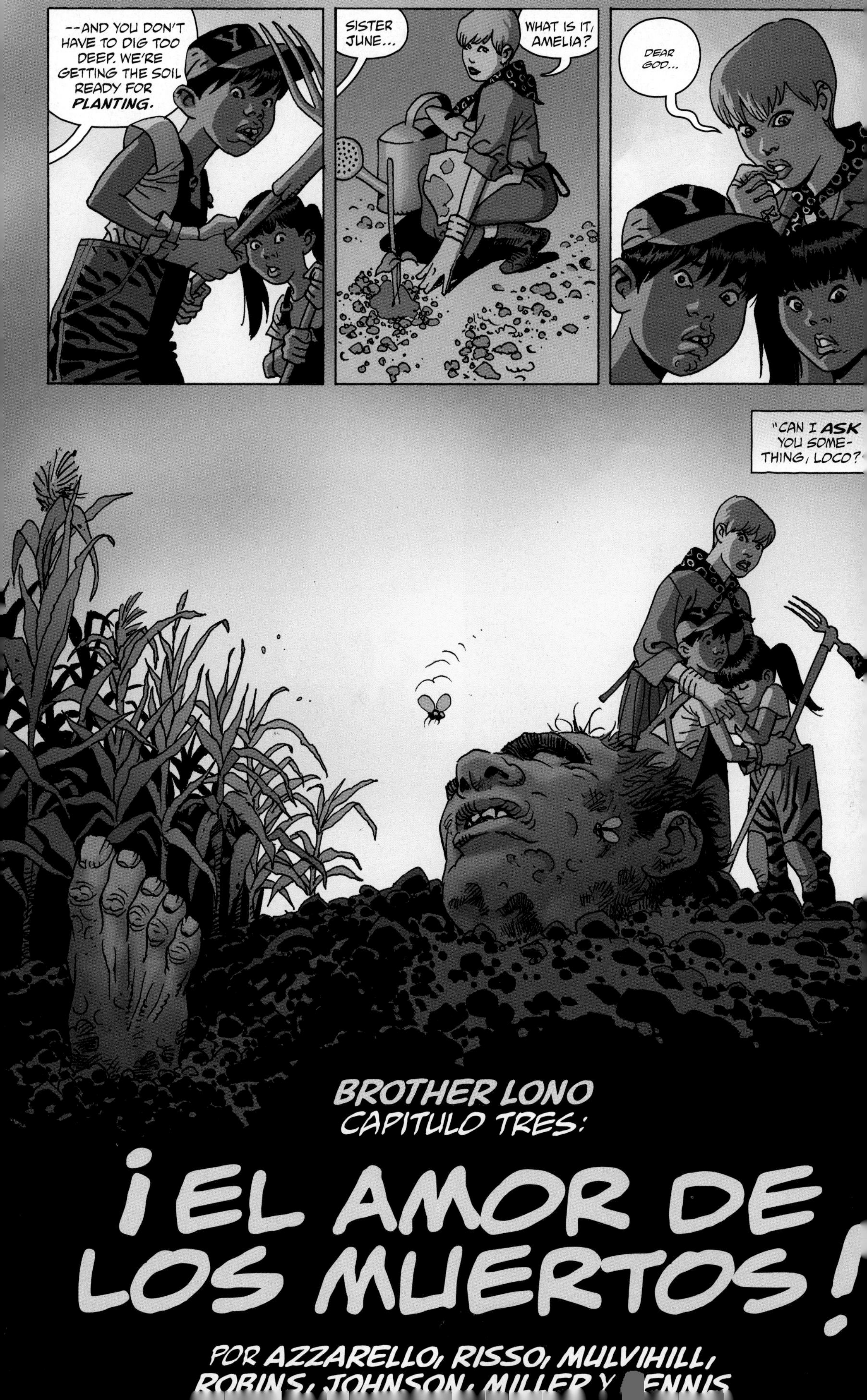
--AND YOU DON'T HAVE TO DIG TOO DEEP. WE'RE GETTING THE SOIL READY FOR PLANTING.
SISTER JUNE...
WHAT IS IT, AMELIA?
DEAR GOD...
"CAN I ASK YOU SOME-THING, LOCO?
BROTHER LONO
CAPITULO TRES:
¡EL AMOR DE LOS MUERTOS!
POR AZZARELLO, RISSO, MULVIHILL,
ROBINS, JOHNSON, MILLER Y ENNIS

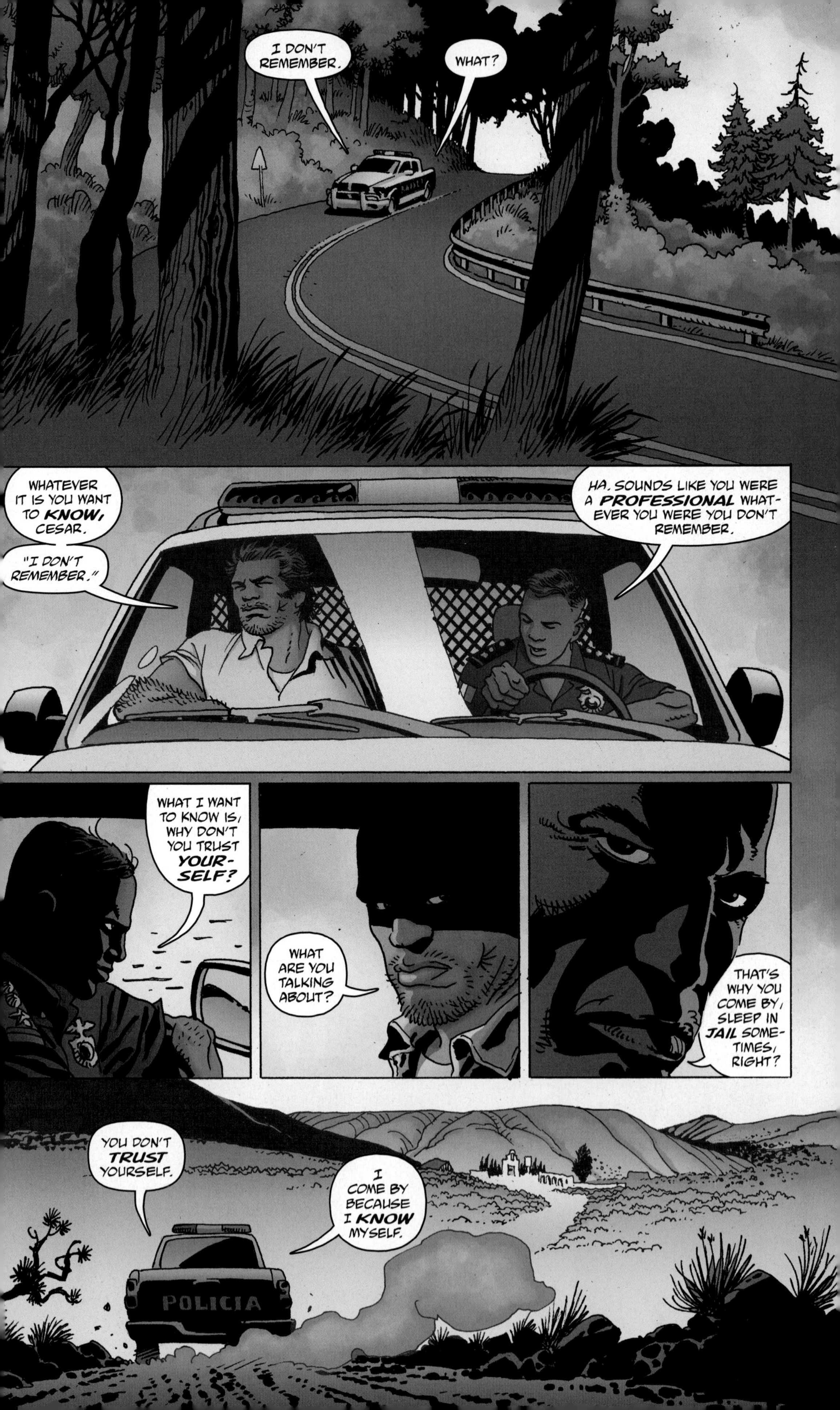

I DON'T REMEMBER.
WHAT?
WHATEVER IT IS YOU WANT TO KNOW, CESAR.
"I DON'T REMEMBER."
HA. SOUNDS LIKE YOU WERE A PROFESSIONAL WHATEVER YOU WERE YOU DON'T REMEMBER.
WHAT I WANT TO KNOW IS, WHY DON'T YOU TRUST YOURSELF?
WHAT ARE YOU TALKING ABOUT?
THAT'S WHY YOU COME BY, SLEEP IN JAIL SOMETIMES, RIGHT?
YOU DON'T TRUST YOURSELF.
I COME BY BECAUSE I KNOW MYSELF.
POLICIA

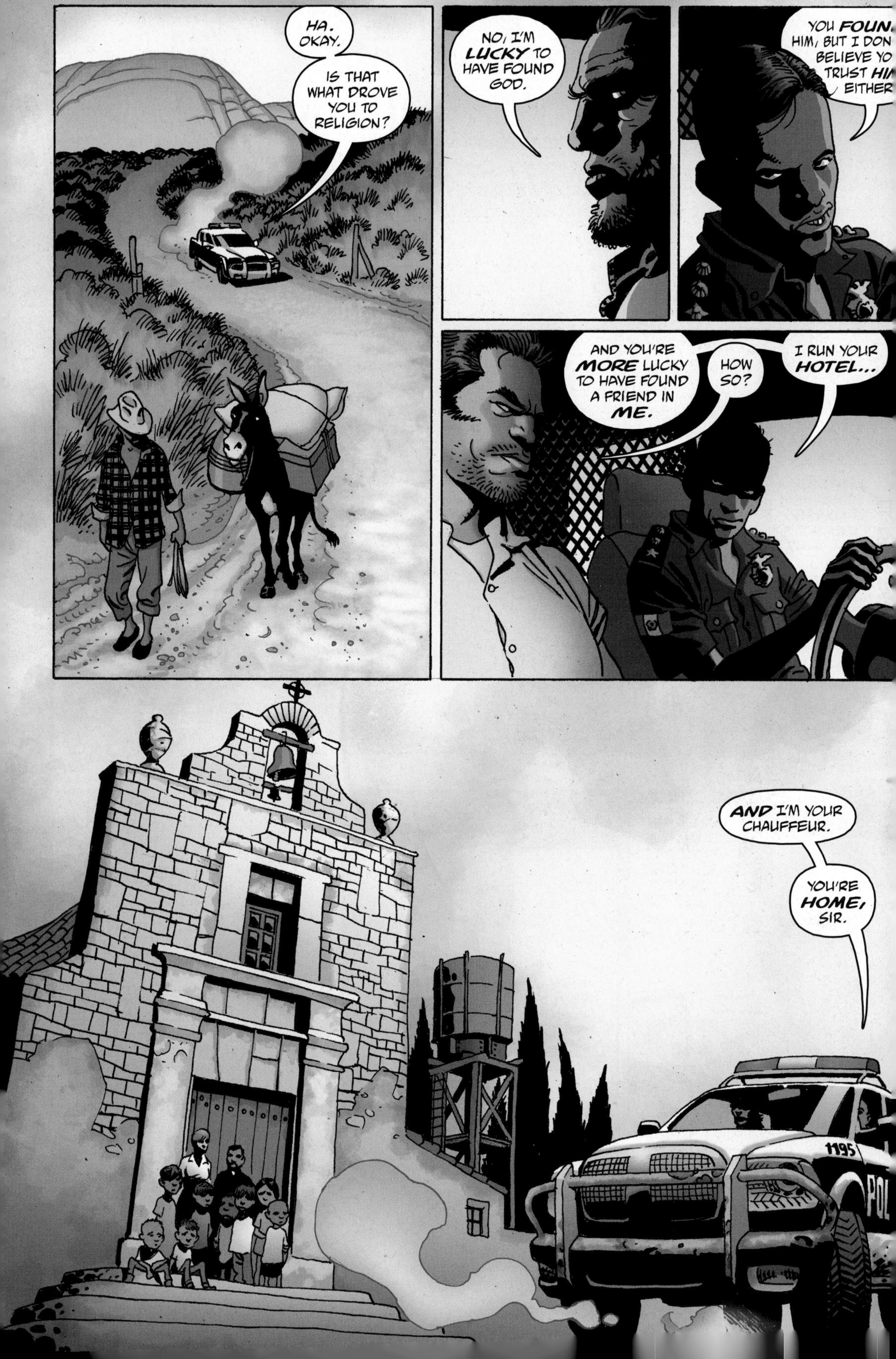

HA. OKAY.
IS THAT WHAT DROVE YOU TO RELIGION?
NO, I'M LUCKY TO HAVE FOUND GOD.
YOU FOUN HIM, BUT I DON BELIEVE YO TRUST HI EITHER
AND YOU'RE MORE LUCKY TO HAVE FOUND A FRIEND IN ME.
HOW SO?
I RUN YOUR HOTEL...
AND I'M YOUR CHAUFFEUR.
YOU'RE HOME, SIR.
1195

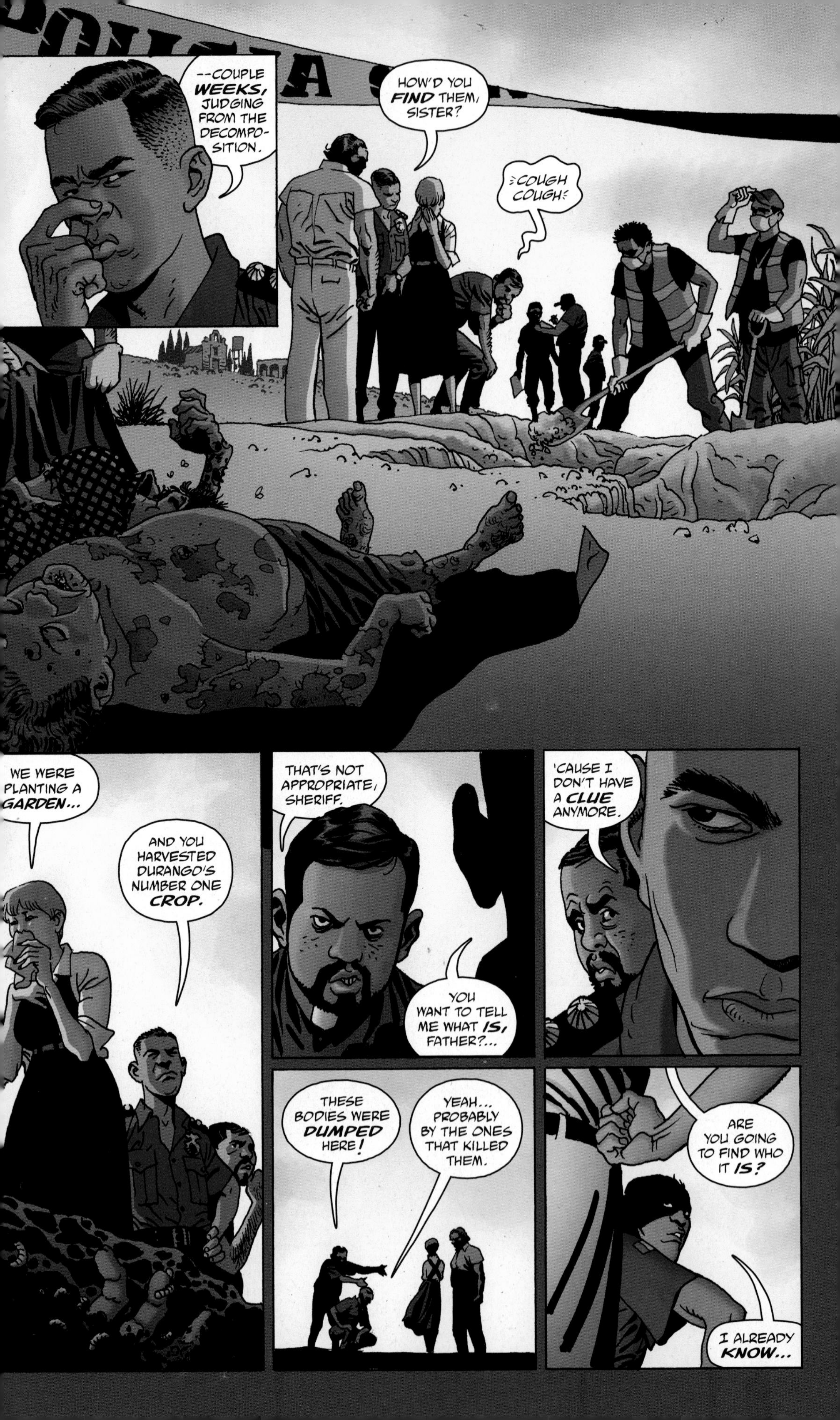
--COUPLE WEEKS, JUDGING FROM THE DECOMPOSITION.
HOW'D YOU FIND THEM, SISTER?
COUGH COUGH
WE WERE PLANTING A GARDEN...
AND YOU HARVESTED DURANGO'S NUMBER ONE CROP.
THAT'S NOT APPROPRIATE, SHERIFF.
YOU WANT TO TELL ME WHAT IS, FATHER?...
'CAUSE I DON'T HAVE A CLUE ANYMORE.
THESE BODIES WERE DUMPED HERE!
YEAH... PROBABLY BY THE ONES THAT KILLED THEM.
ARE YOU GOING TO FIND WHO IT IS?
I ALREADY KNOW...

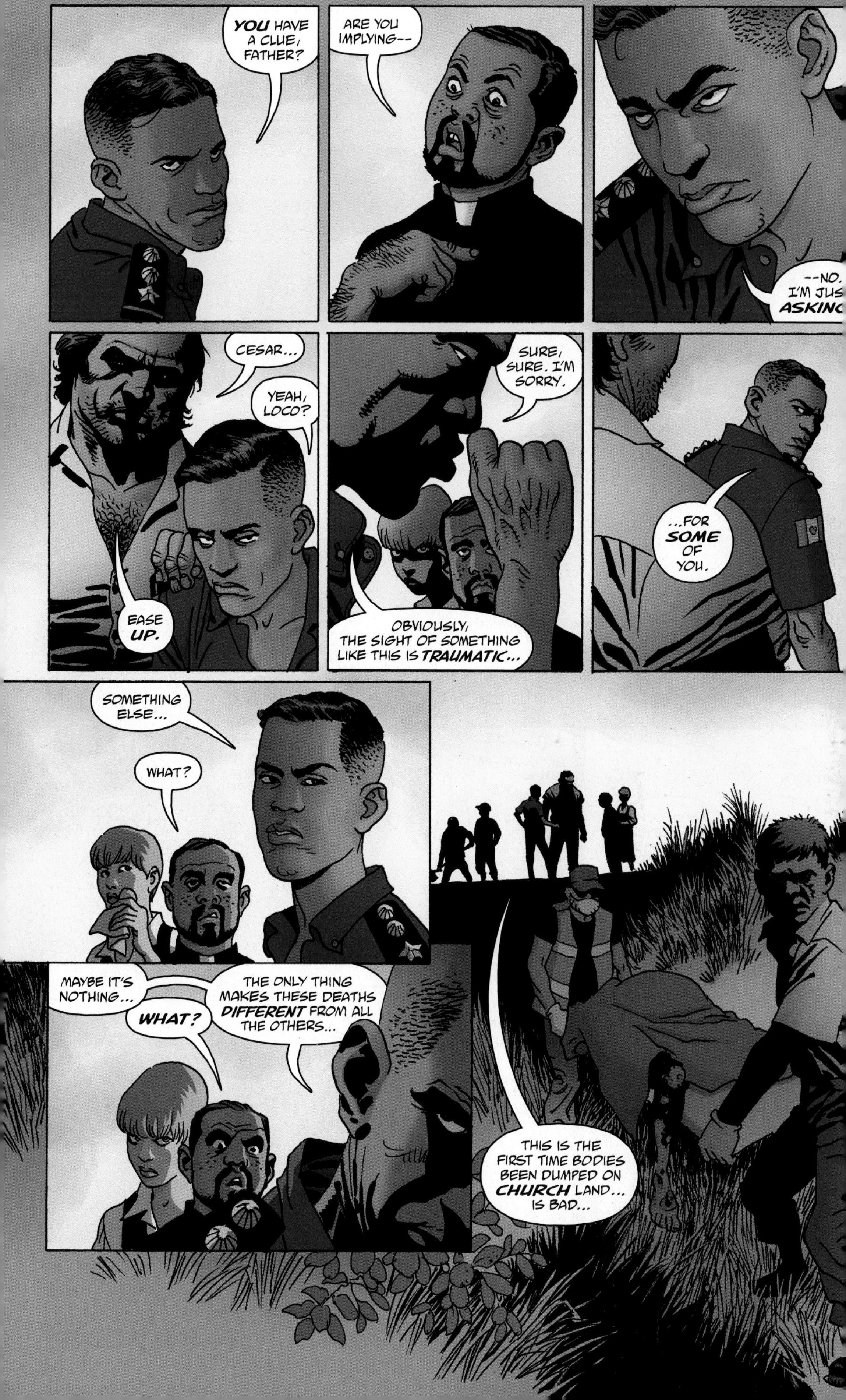

YOU HAVE A CLUE, FATHER?
ARE YOU IMPLYING--
--NO. I'M JUS ASKING
CESAR...
YEAH, LOCO?
EASE UP.
SURE, SURE. I'M SORRY.
OBVIOUSLY, THE SIGHT OF SOMETHING LIKE THIS IS TRAUMATIC...
...FOR SOME OF YOU.
SOMETHING ELSE...
WHAT?
MAYBE IT'S NOTHING...
WHAT?
THE ONLY THING MAKES THESE DEATHS DIFFERENT FROM ALL THE OTHERS...
THIS IS THE FIRST TIME BODIES BEEN DUMPED ON CHURCH LAND... IS BAD...

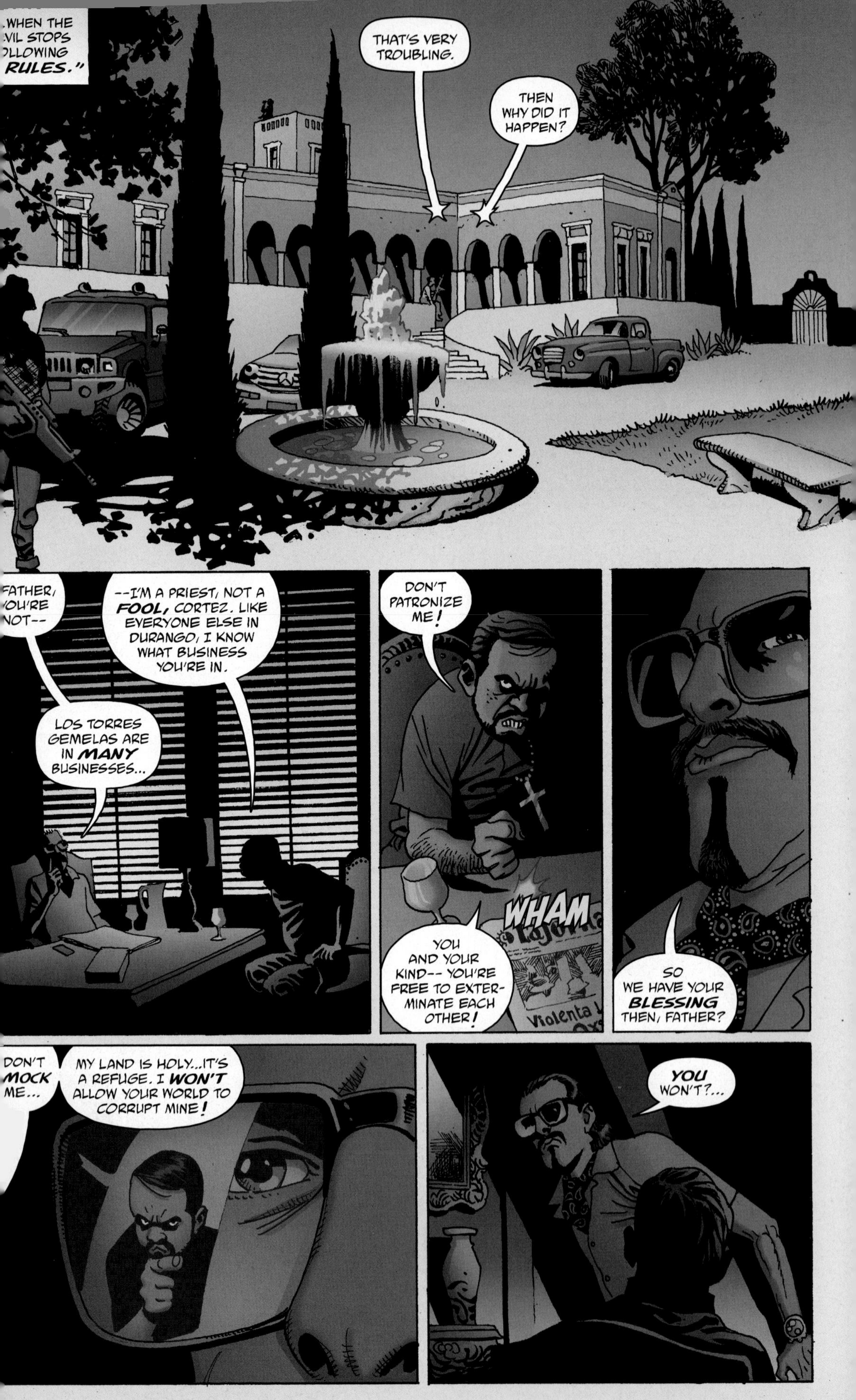
..WHEN THE
..VIL STOPS
..OLLOWING
RULES."
THAT'S VERY TROUBLING.
THEN WHY DID IT HAPPEN?
..FATHER, ..OU'RE ..NOT--
--I'M A PRIEST, NOT A FOOL, CORTEZ. LIKE EVERYONE ELSE IN DURANGO, I KNOW WHAT BUSINESS YOU'RE IN.
LOS TORRES GEMELAS ARE IN MANY BUSINESSES...
DON'T PATRONIZE ME!
WHAM
YOU AND YOUR KIND-- YOU'RE FREE TO EXTERMINATE EACH OTHER!
Violenta
SO WE HAVE YOUR BLESSING THEN, FATHER?
DON'T MOCK ME...
MY LAND IS HOLY...IT'S A REFUGE. I WON'T ALLOW YOUR WORLD TO CORRUPT MINE!
YOU WON'T?...

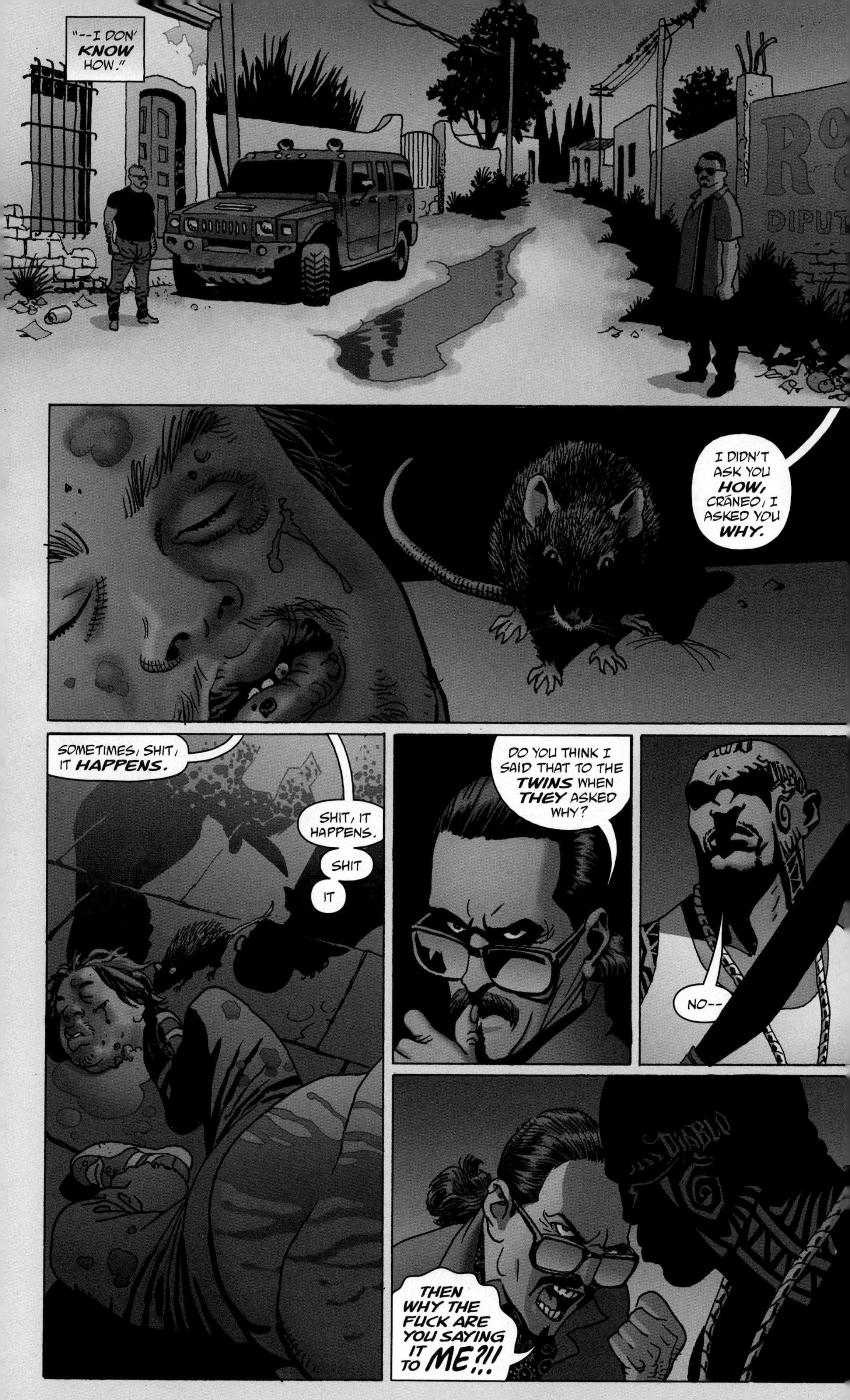

"--I DON' KNOW HOW."
I DIDN'T ASK YOU HOW, CRANEO, I ASKED YOU WHY.
SOMETIMES, SHIT, IT HAPPENS.
SHIT, IT HAPPENS.
SHIT
IT
DO YOU THINK I SAID THAT TO THE TWINS WHEN THEY ASKED WHY?
NO--
THEN WHY THE FUCK ARE YOU SAYING IT TO ME?!!

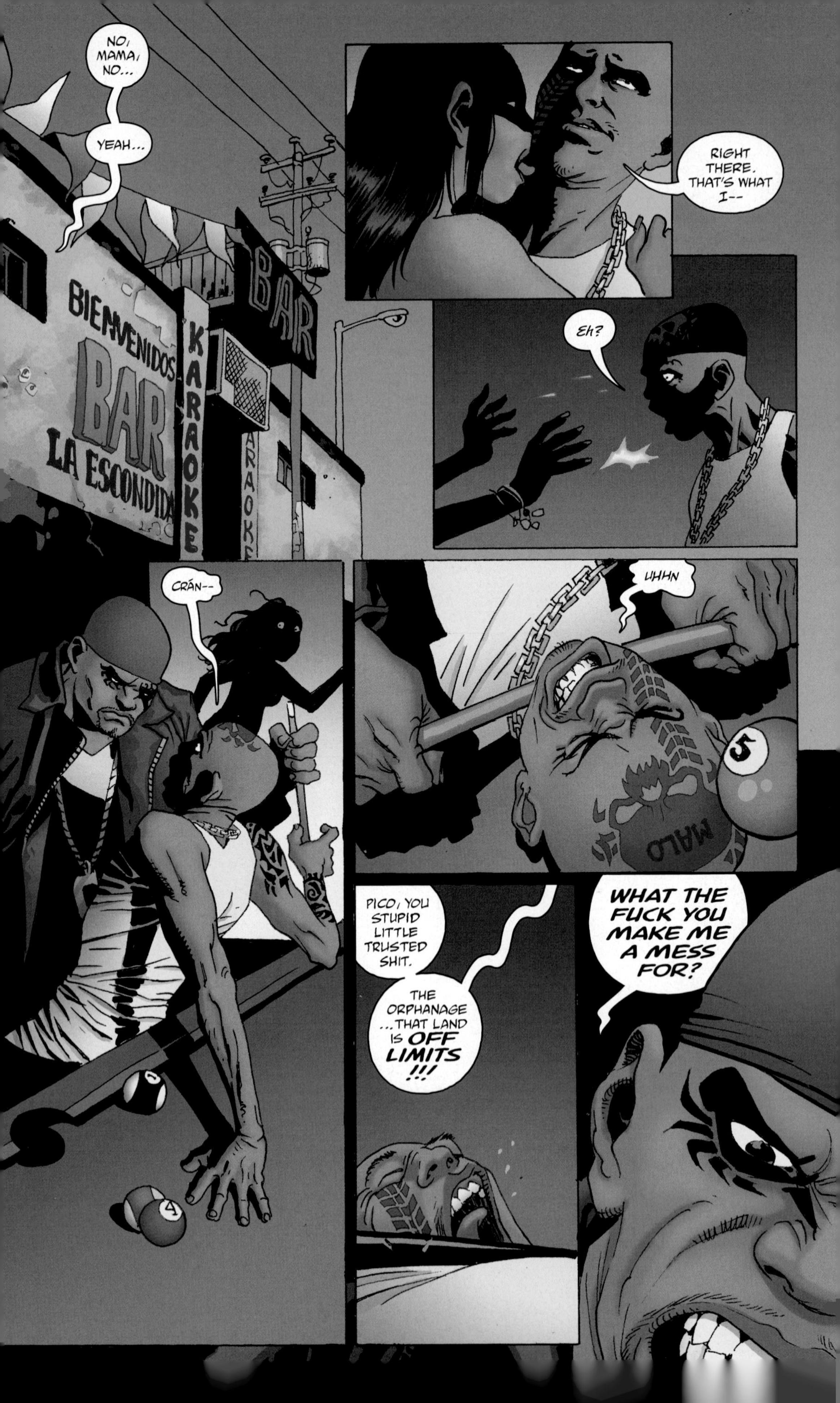
NO, MAMA, NO...
YEAH...
BIENVENIDOS BAR LA ESCONDIDA
KARAOKE
BAR
RIGHT THERE. THAT'S WHAT I--
Eh?
CRÁN--
UHHN
MALO
PICO, YOU STUPID LITTLE TRUSTED SHIT.
THE ORPHANAGE ...THAT LAND IS OFF LIMITS !!!
WHAT THE FUCK YOU MAKE ME A MESS FOR?

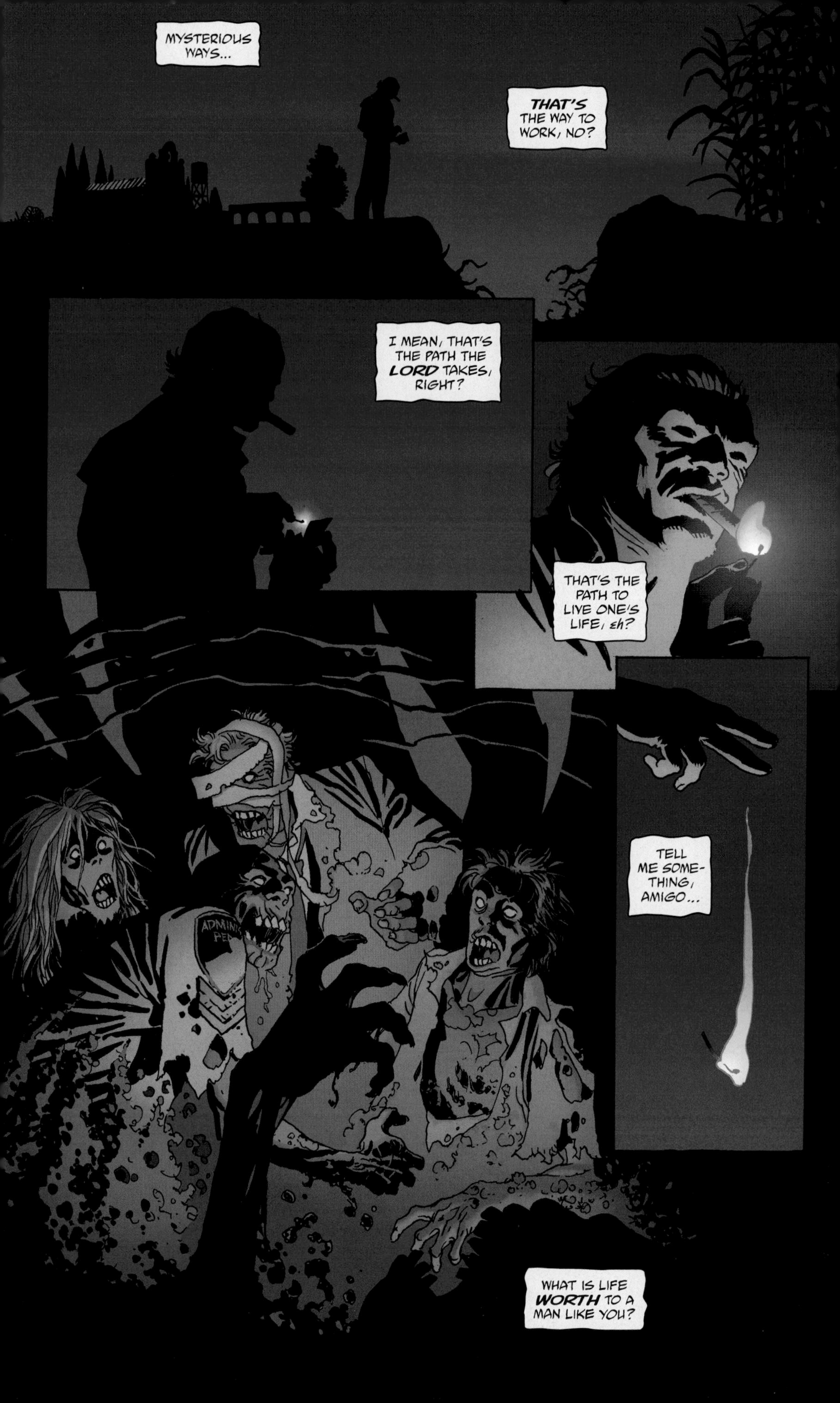
MYSTERIOUS WAYS...
THAT'S THE WAY TO WORK, NO?
I MEAN, THAT'S THE PATH THE LORD TAKES, RIGHT?
THAT'S THE PATH TO LIVE ONE'S LIFE, eh?
TELL ME SOME-THING, AMIGO...
WHAT IS LIFE WORTH TO A MAN LIKE YOU?

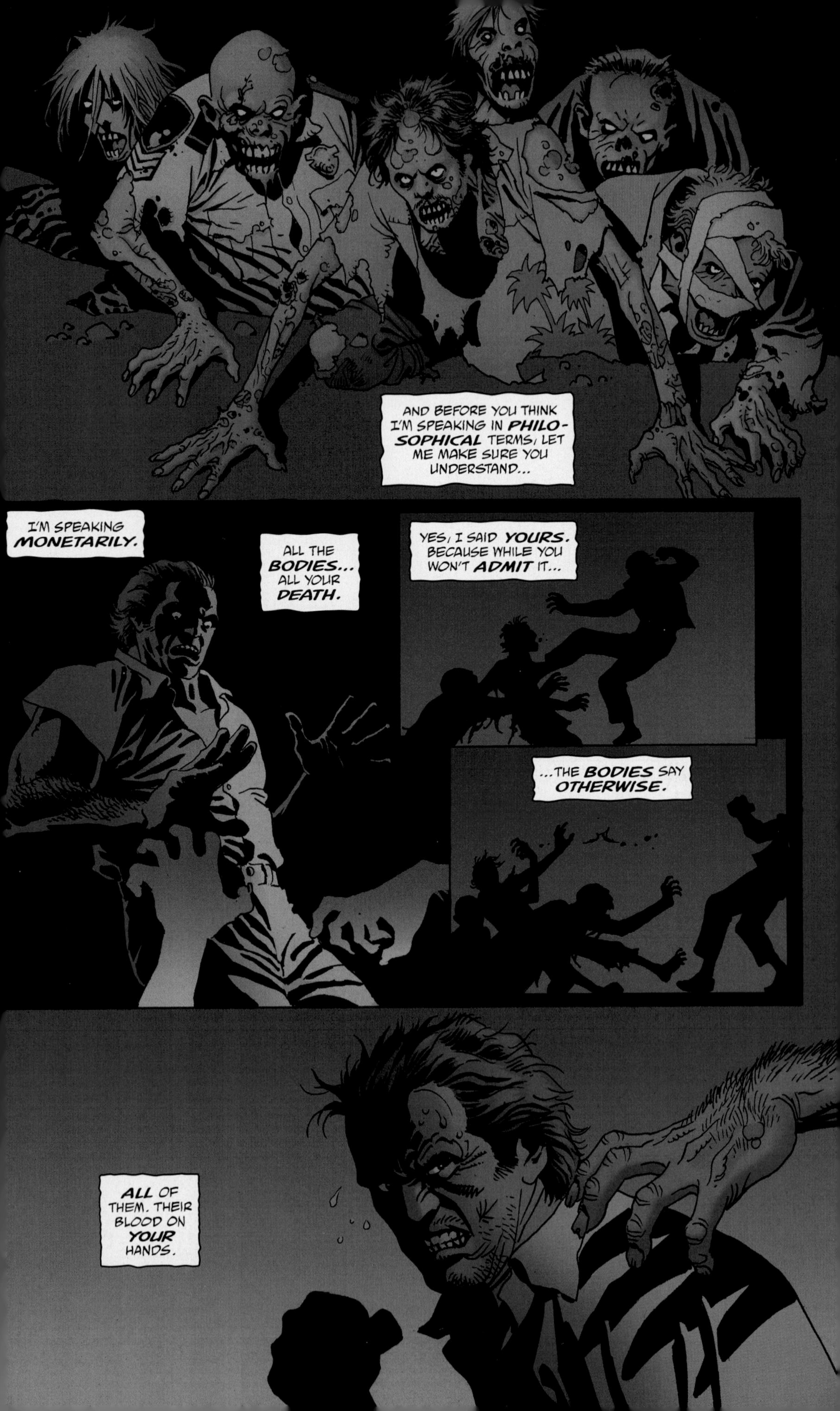
AND BEFORE YOU THINK I'M SPEAKING IN PHILOSOPHICAL TERMS, LET ME MAKE SURE YOU UNDERSTAND...
I'M SPEAKING MONETARILY.
ALL THE BODIES... ALL YOUR DEATH.
YES, I SAID YOURS. BECAUSE WHILE YOU WON'T ADMIT IT...
...THE BODIES SAY OTHERWISE.
ALL OF THEM. THEIR BLOOD ON YOUR HANDS.

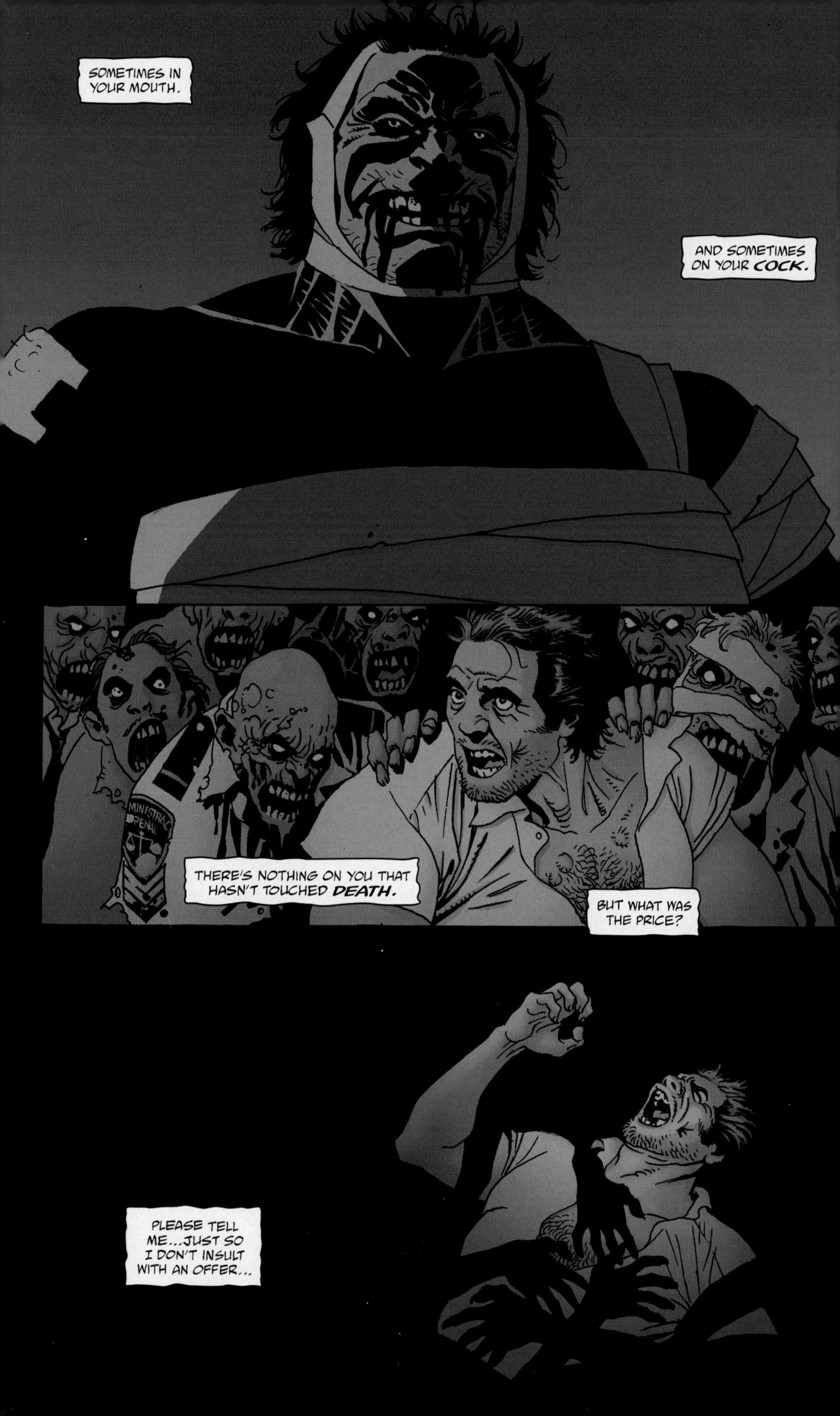
SOMETIMES IN YOUR MOUTH.
AND SOMETIMES ON YOUR COCK.
MINISTRAC PENAL
THERE'S NOTHING ON YOU THAT HASN'T TOUCHED DEATH.
BUT WHAT WAS THE PRICE?
PLEASE TELL ME...JUST SO I DON'T INSULT WITH AN OFFER...

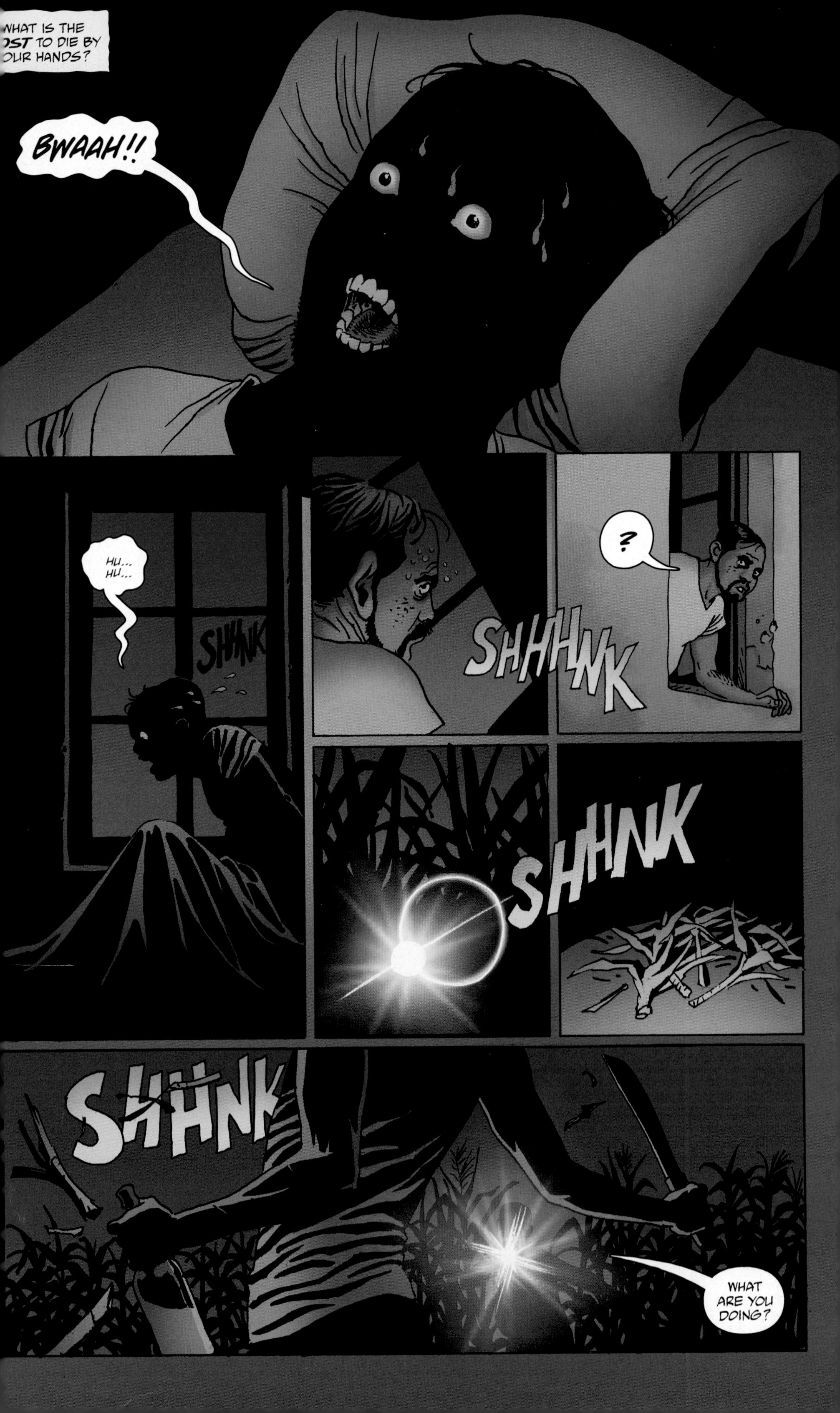
WHAT IS THE OST TO DIE BY OUR HANDS?
BWAAH!!
HU... HU...
SHHNK
SHHHNK
?
SHHNK
SHHNK
WHAT ARE YOU DOING?

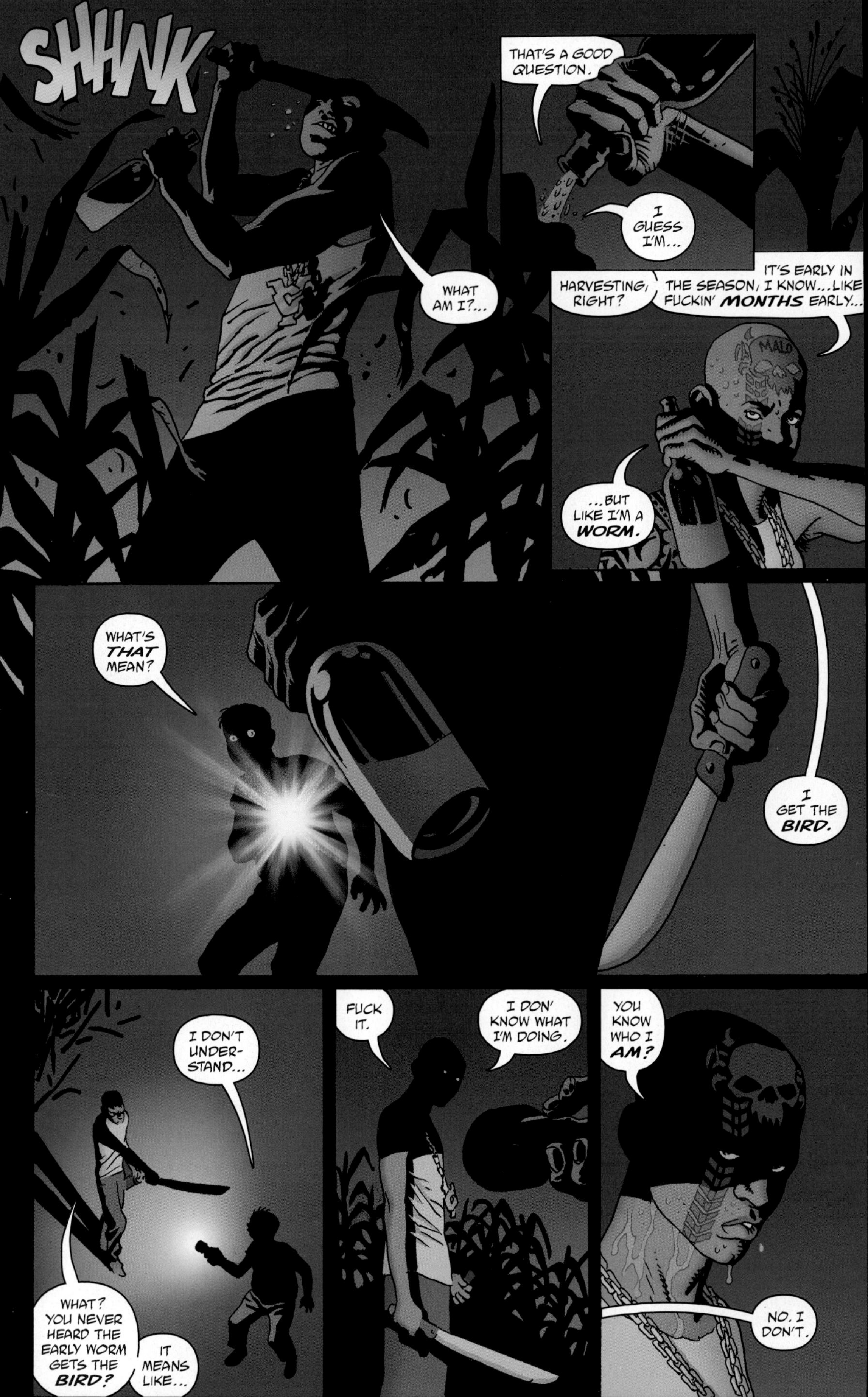
SHHNK
WHAT AM I?...
THAT'S A GOOD QUESTION.
I GUESS I'M...
HARVESTING, RIGHT?
IT'S EARLY IN THE SEASON, I KNOW... LIKE FUCKIN' MONTHS EARLY...
...BUT LIKE I'M A WORM.
WHAT'S THAT MEAN?
I GET THE BIRD.
I DON'T UNDER-STAND...
WHAT? YOU NEVER HEARD THE EARLY WORM GETS THE BIRD?
IT MEANS LIKE...
FUCK IT.
I DON' KNOW WHAT I'M DOING.
YOU KNOW WHO I AM?
NO. I DON'T.

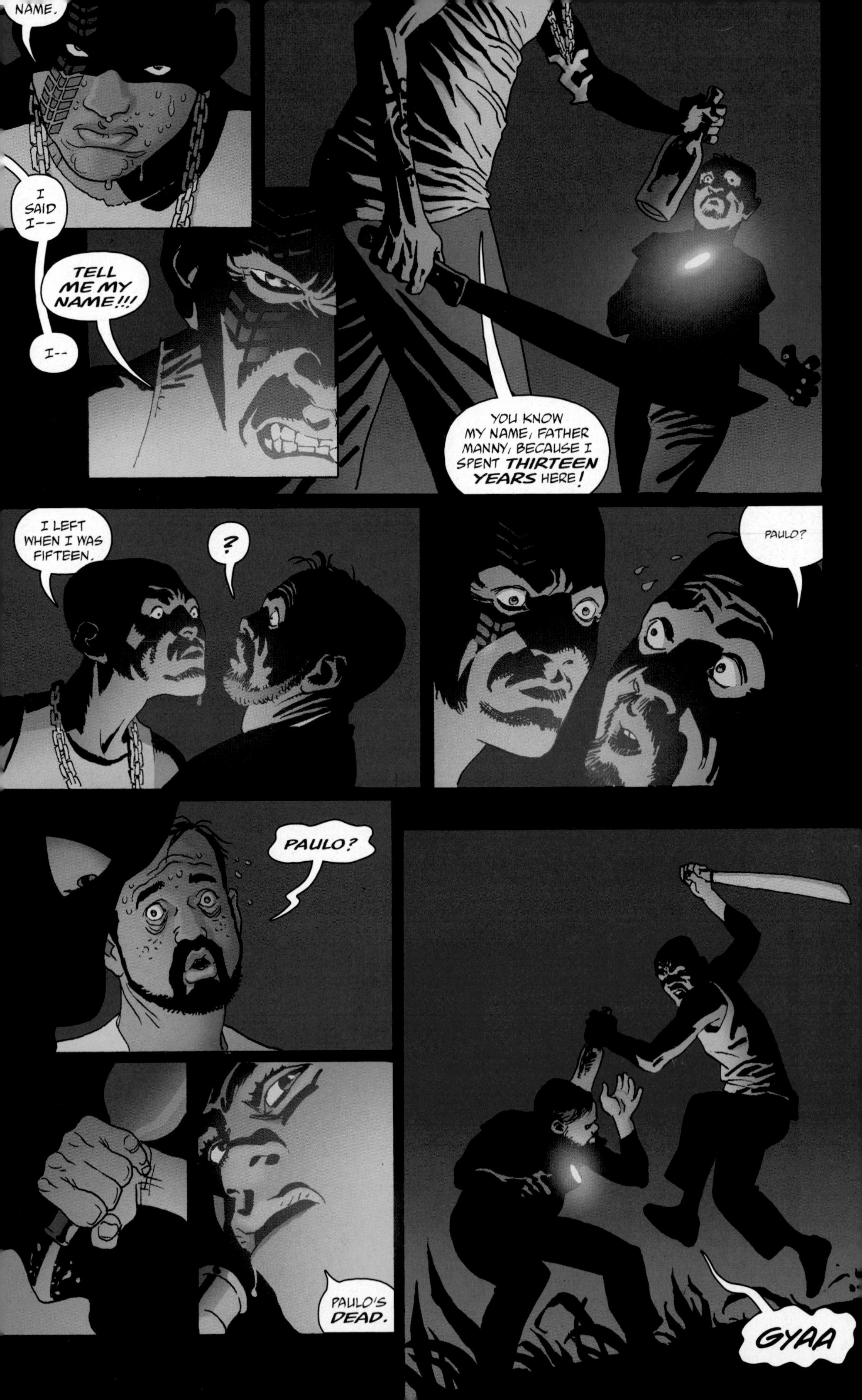
NAME.
I SAID I--
TELL ME MY NAME!!!
I--
YOU KNOW MY NAME, FATHER MANNY, BECAUSE I SPENT THIRTEEN YEARS HERE!
I LEFT WHEN I WAS FIFTEEN.
?
PAULO?
PAULO?
PAULO'S DEAD.
GYAA

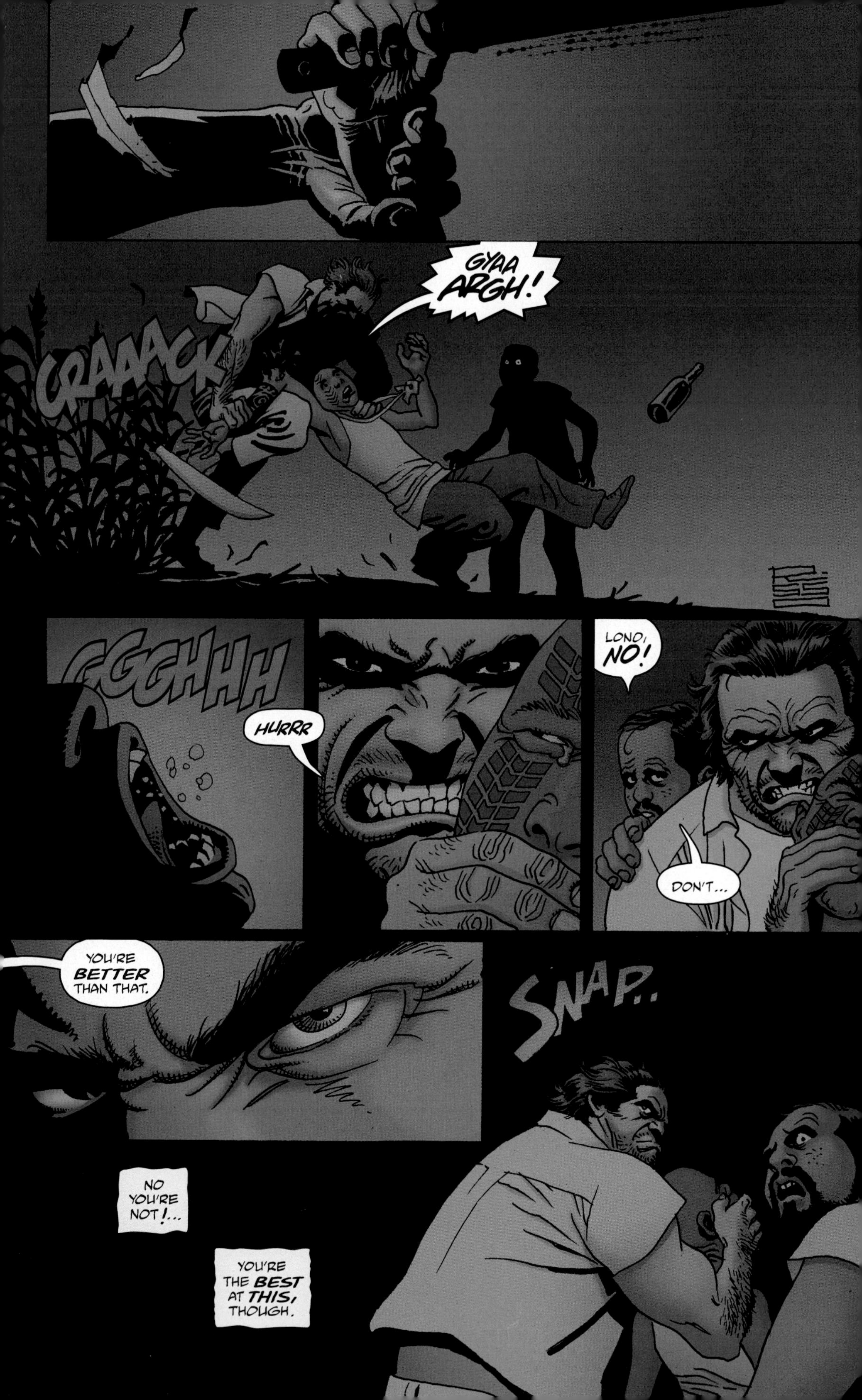
GYAA ARGH!
CRAAACK
GGGHHH
HURRR
LONO, NO!
DON'T...
YOU'RE BETTER THAN THAT.
SNAP..
NO YOU'RE NOT!...
YOU'RE THE BEST AT THIS, THOUGH.

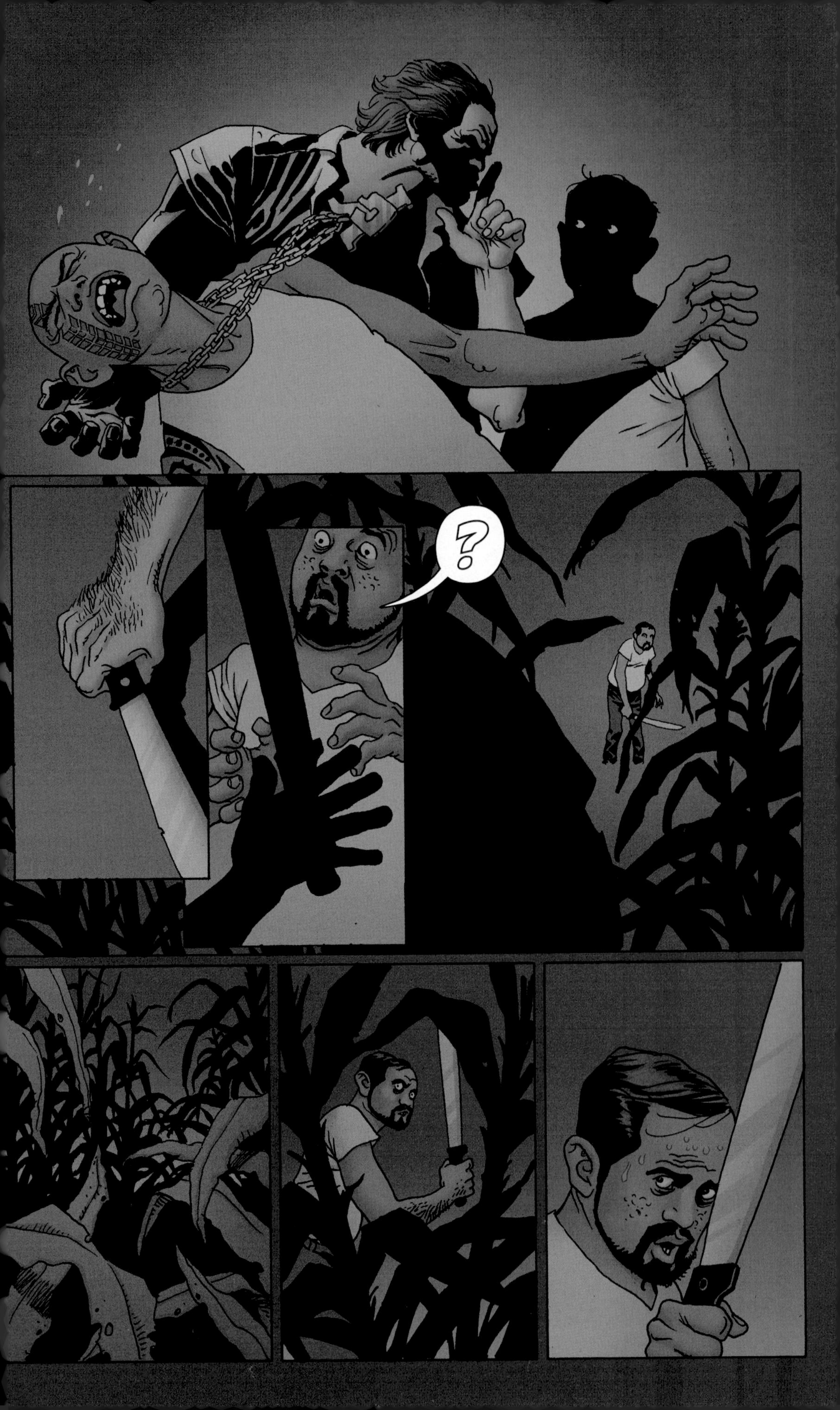
?

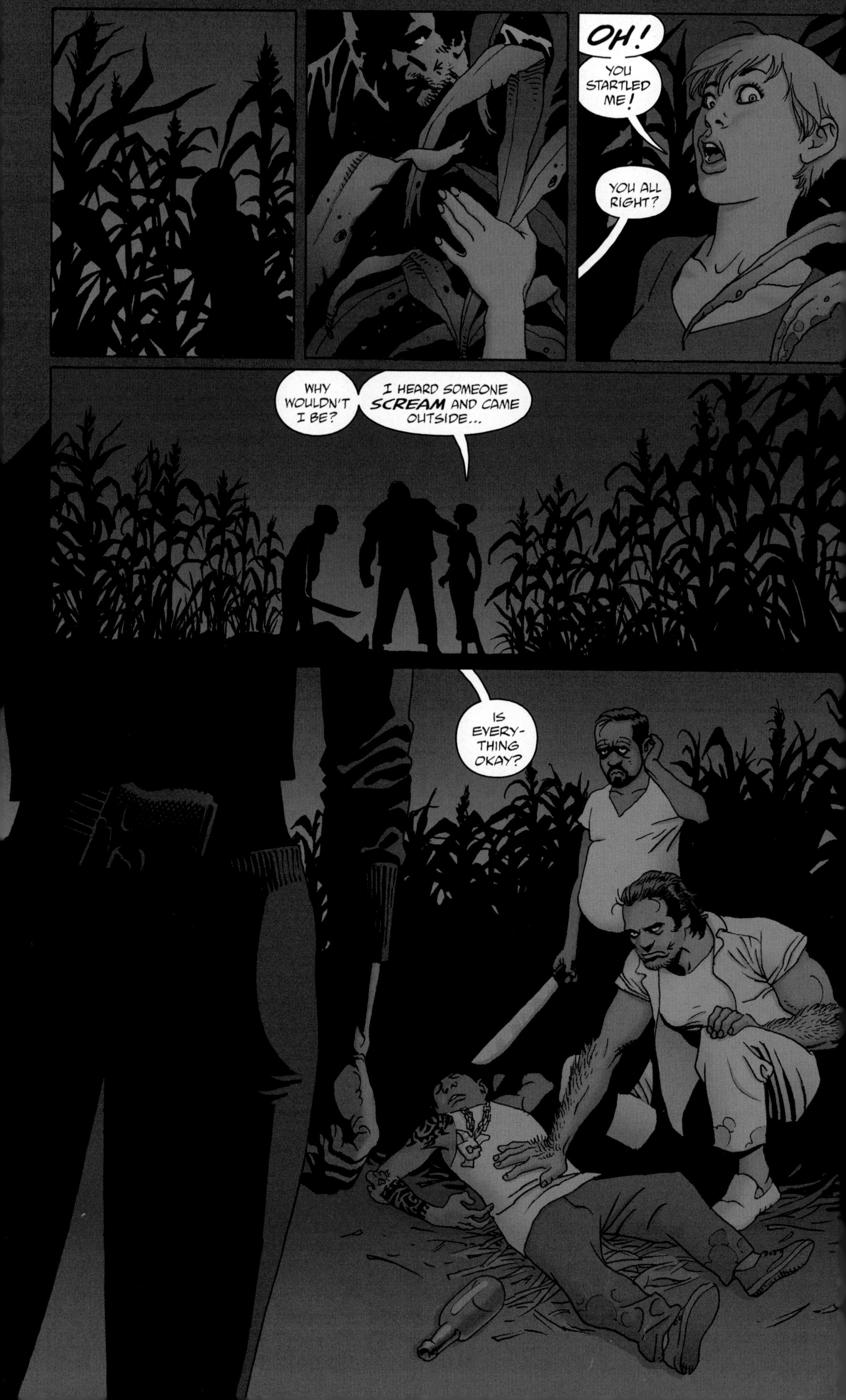
OH!
YOU STARTLED ME!
YOU ALL RIGHT?
WHY WOULDN'T I BE?
I HEARD SOMEONE SCREAM AND CAME OUTSIDE...
IS EVERYTHING OKAY?

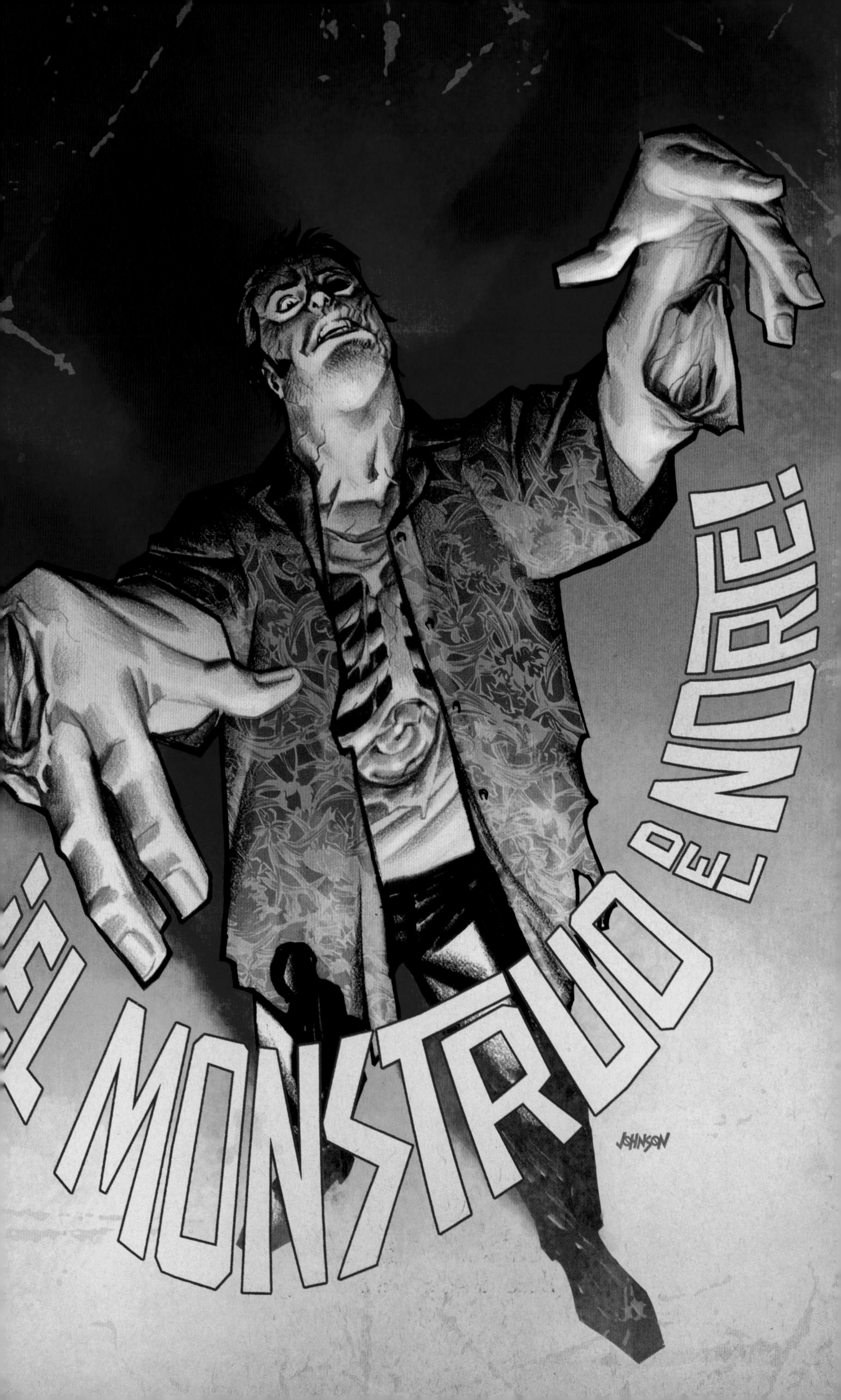
¡EL MONSTRUO DEL NORTE!
JOHNSON

"I've killed more friends than I can count."

HOLA, AMIGO. WELCOME TO DURANGO.

HOW LONG YOU PLAN TO **STAY**?

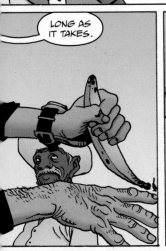

LONG AS IT TAKES.

YER LOOKING TO **DIE** HERE?

THAT'S **NOT** GONNA HAPPEN. I'M A **TOURIST**...

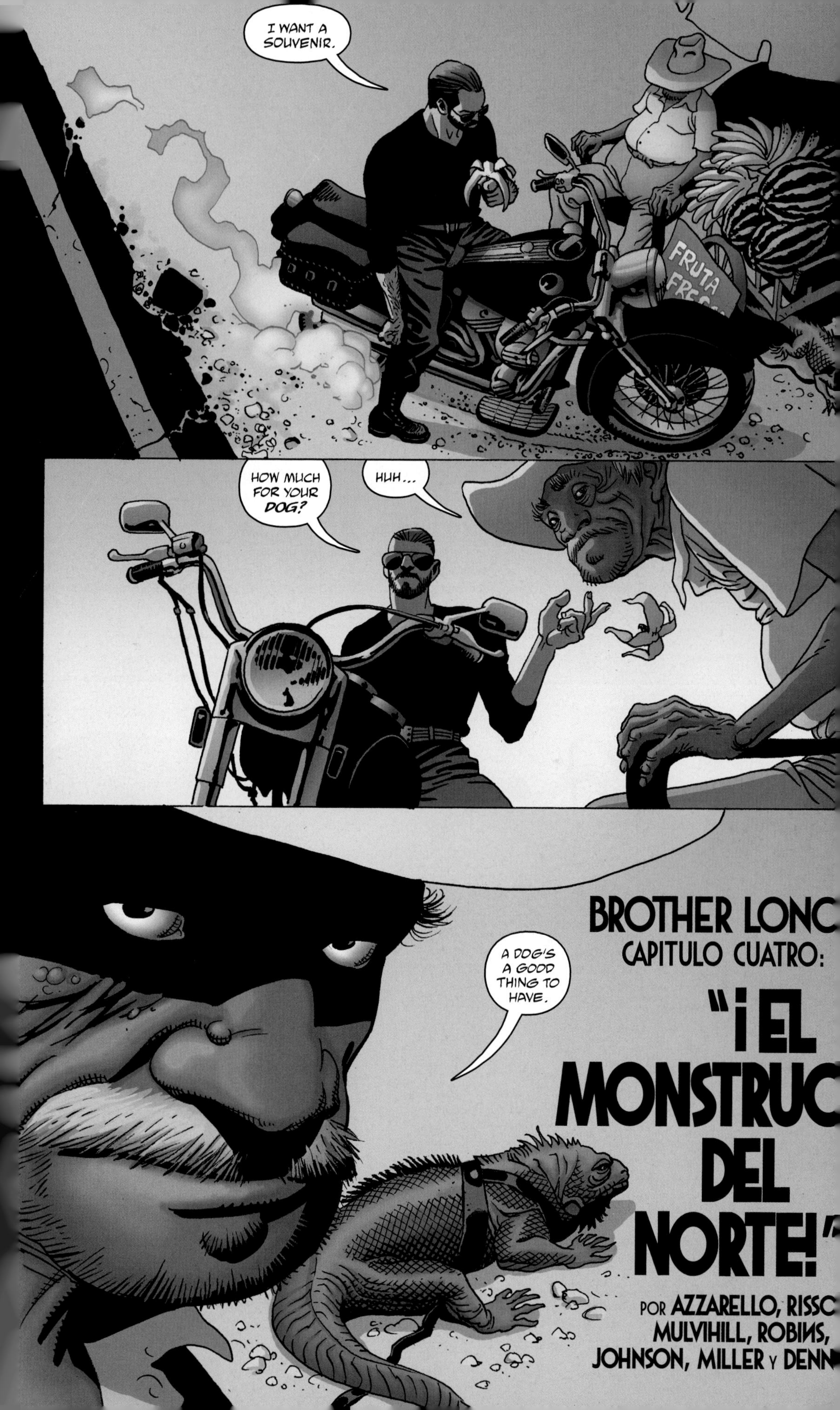
I WANT A SOUVENIR.
FRUTA FRES...
HOW MUCH FOR YOUR DOG?
HUH...
A DOG'S A GOOD THING TO HAVE.
BROTHER LONC
CAPITULO CUATRO:
"¡EL MONSTRUO DEL NORTE!"
POR AZZARELLO, RISSO
MULVIHILL, ROBINS,
JOHNSON, MILLER Y DENN

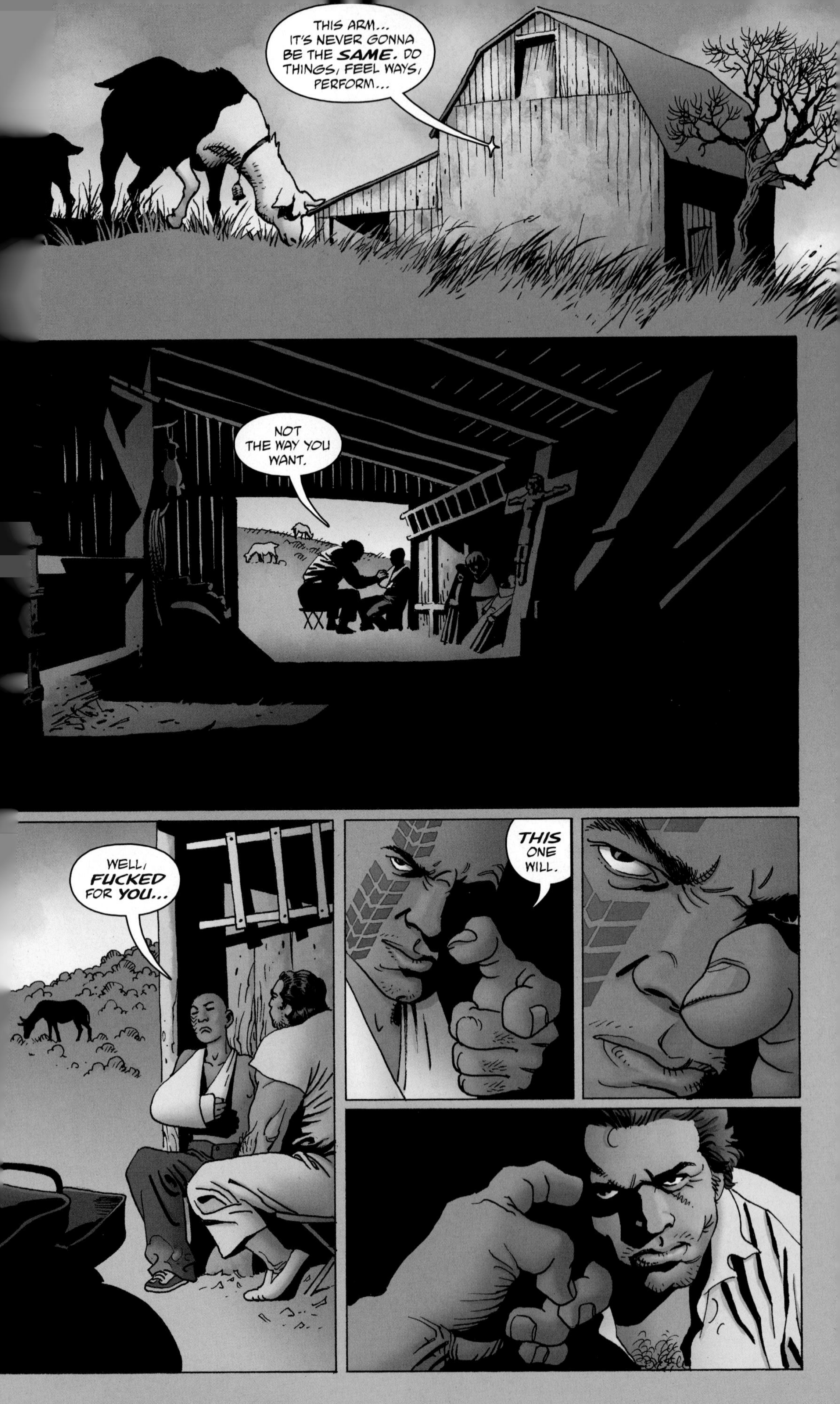
THIS ARM... IT'S NEVER GONNA BE THE SAME. DO THINGS, FEEL WAYS, PERFORM...
NOT THE WAY YOU WANT.
WELL, FUCKED FOR YOU...
THIS ONE WILL.

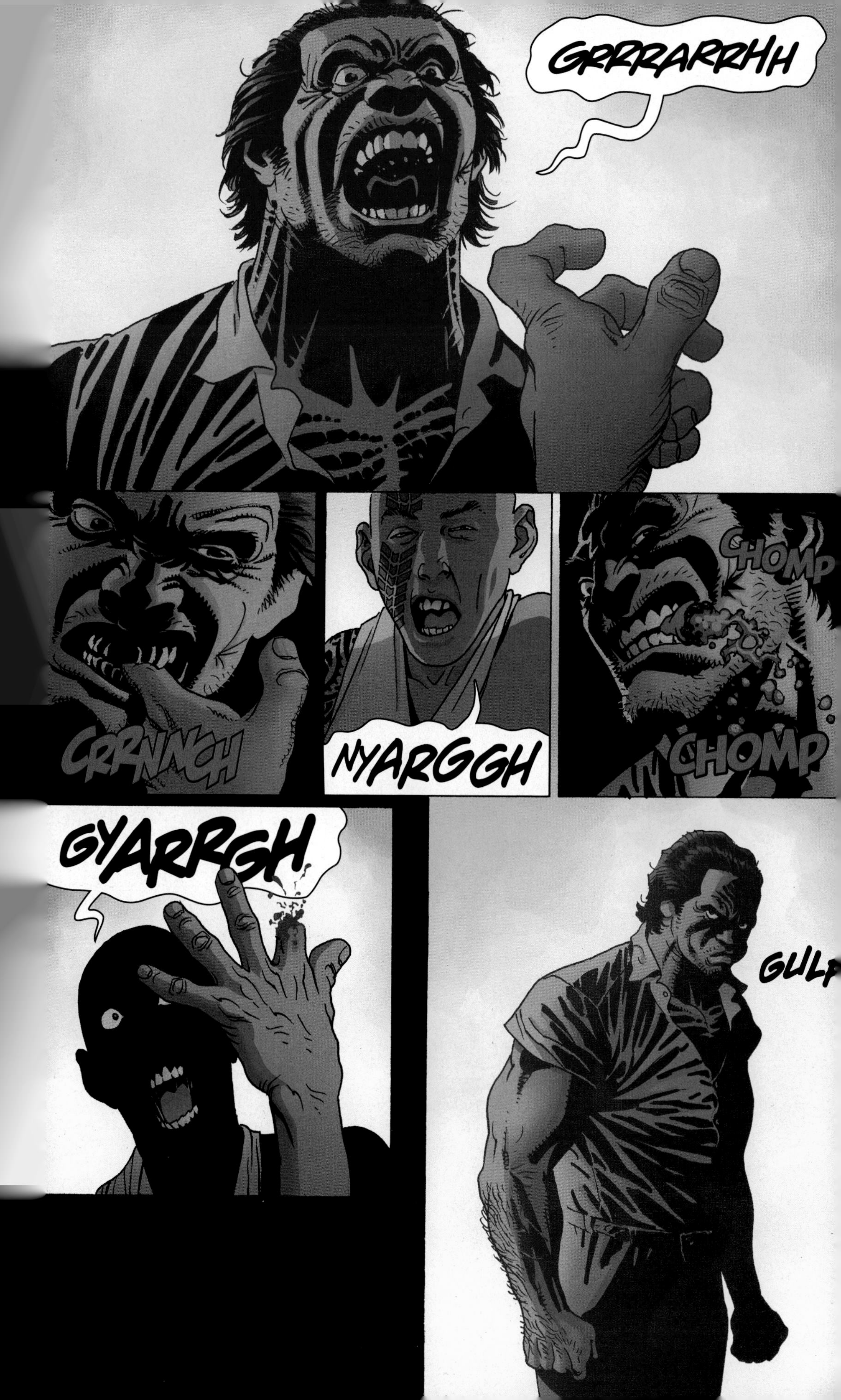
GRRRARRRHH
CRRNNCH
NYARGGH
CHOMP
CHOMP
GYARRGH
GULP

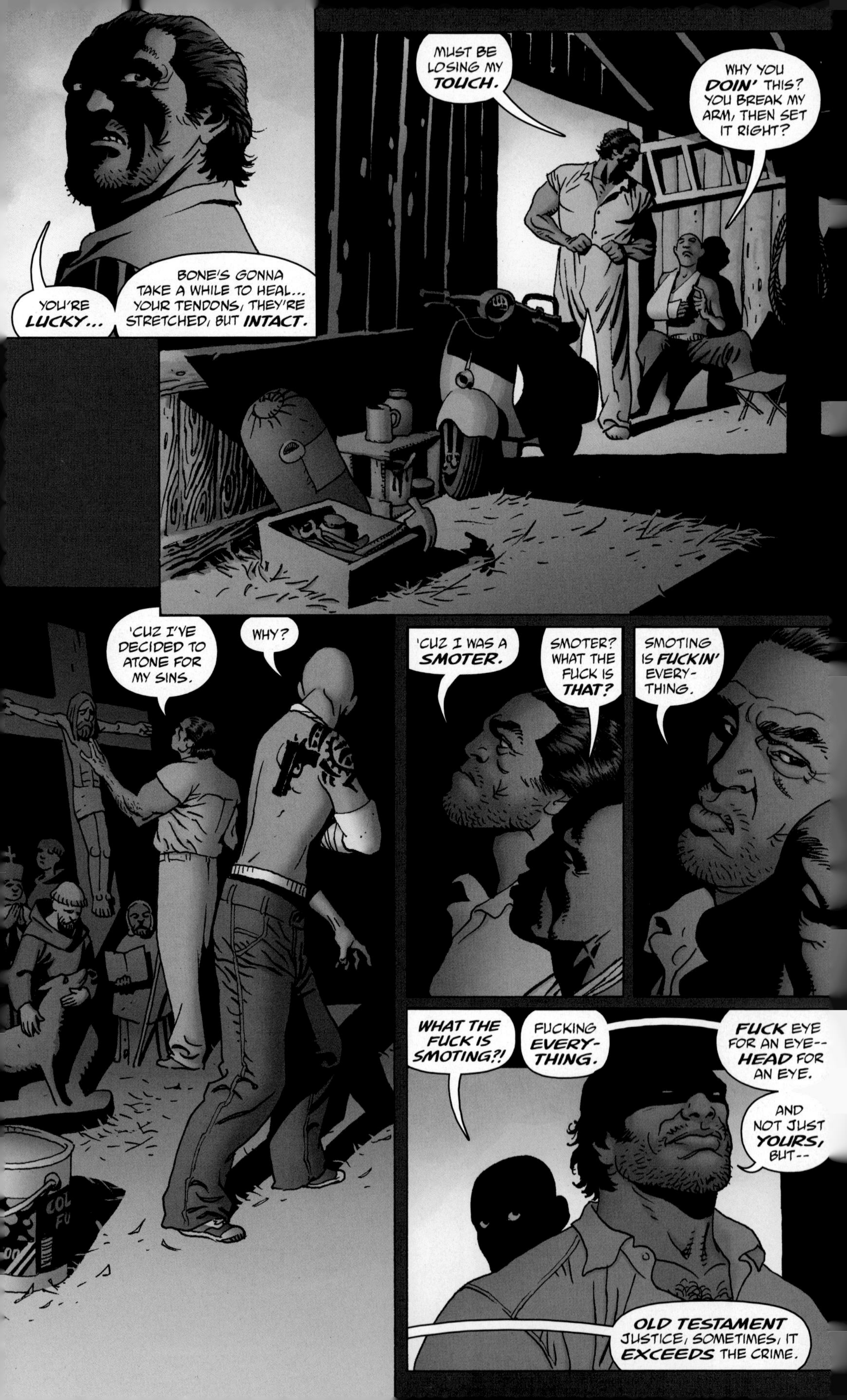

YOU'RE LUCKY...
BONE'S GONNA TAKE A WHILE TO HEAL... YOUR TENDONS, THEY'RE STRETCHED, BUT INTACT.
MUST BE LOSING MY TOUCH.
WHY YOU DOIN' THIS? YOU BREAK MY ARM, THEN SET IT RIGHT?
'CUZ I'VE DECIDED TO ATONE FOR MY SINS.
WHY?
'CUZ I WAS A SMOTER.
SMOTER? WHAT THE FUCK IS THAT?
SMOTING IS FUCKIN' EVERY-THING.
WHAT THE FUCK IS SMOTING?!
FUCKING EVERY-THING.
FUCK EYE FOR AN EYE-- HEAD FOR AN EYE.
AND NOT JUST YOURS, BUT--
OLD TESTAMENT JUSTICE, SOMETIMES, IT EXCEEDS THE CRIME.

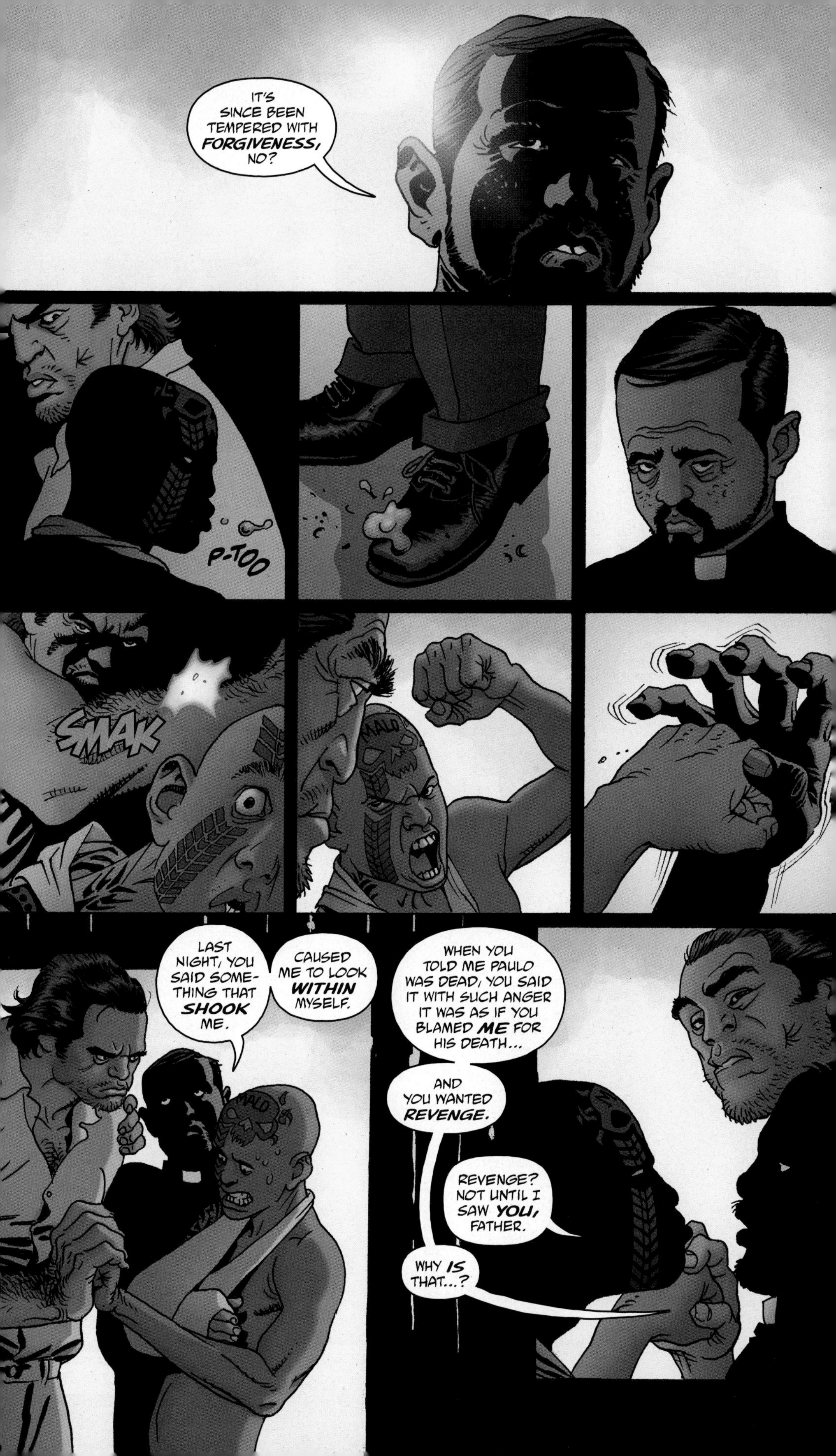
IT'S SINCE BEEN TEMPERED WITH FORGIVENESS, NO?
P-TOO
SMAK
LAST NIGHT, YOU SAID SOME-THING THAT SHOOK ME.
CAUSED ME TO LOOK WITHIN MYSELF.
WHEN YOU TOLD ME PAULO WAS DEAD, YOU SAID IT WITH SUCH ANGER IT WAS AS IF YOU BLAMED ME FOR HIS DEATH...
AND YOU WANTED REVENGE.
REVENGE? NOT UNTIL I SAW YOU, FATHER.
WHY IS THAT...?

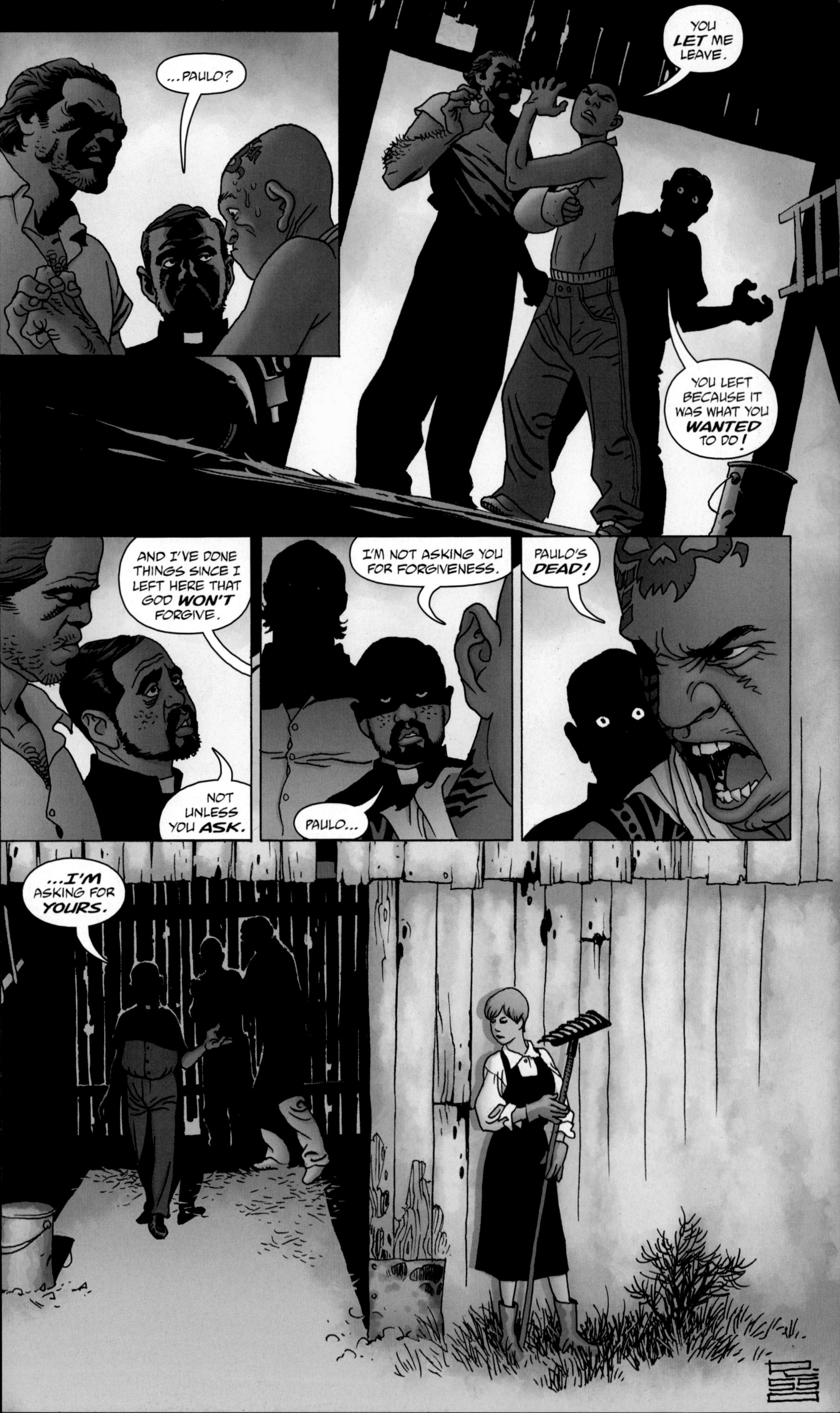
...PAULO?
YOU LET ME LEAVE.
YOU LEFT BECAUSE IT WAS WHAT YOU WANTED TO DO!
AND I'VE DONE THINGS SINCE I LEFT HERE THAT GOD WON'T FORGIVE.
NOT UNLESS YOU ASK.
I'M NOT ASKING YOU FOR FORGIVENESS.
PAULO...
PAULO'S DEAD!
...I'M ASKING FOR YOURS.

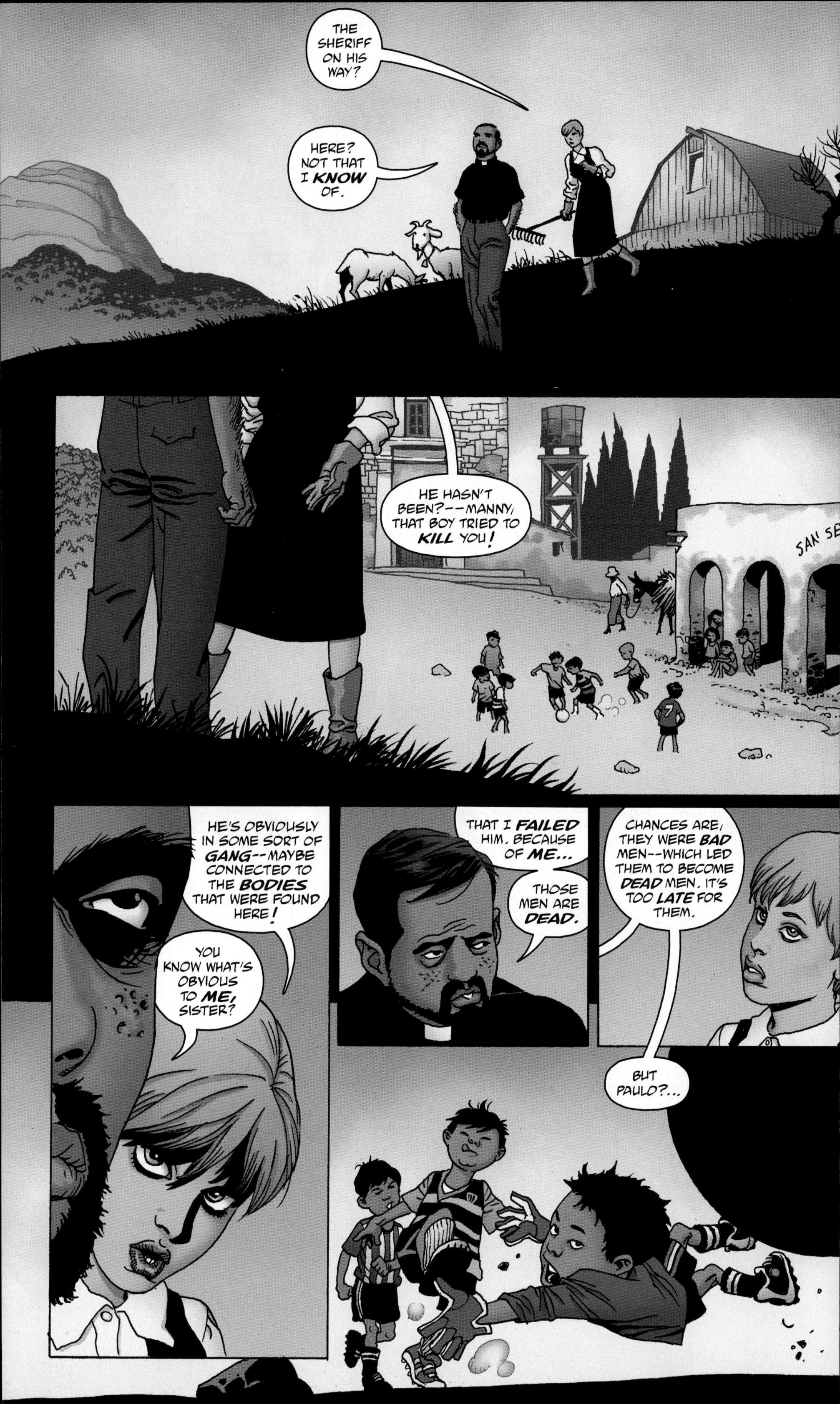

THE SHERIFF ON HIS WAY?
HERE? NOT THAT I KNOW OF.
HE HASN'T BEEN?--MANNY, THAT BOY TRIED TO KILL YOU!
SAN SE
HE'S OBVIOUSLY IN SOME SORT OF GANG--MAYBE CONNECTED TO THE BODIES THAT WERE FOUND HERE!
YOU KNOW WHAT'S OBVIOUS TO ME, SISTER?
THAT I FAILED HIM. BECAUSE OF ME...
THOSE MEN ARE DEAD.
CHANCES ARE, THEY WERE BAD MEN--WHICH LED THEM TO BECOME DEAD MEN. IT'S TOO LATE FOR THEM.
BUT PAULO?...

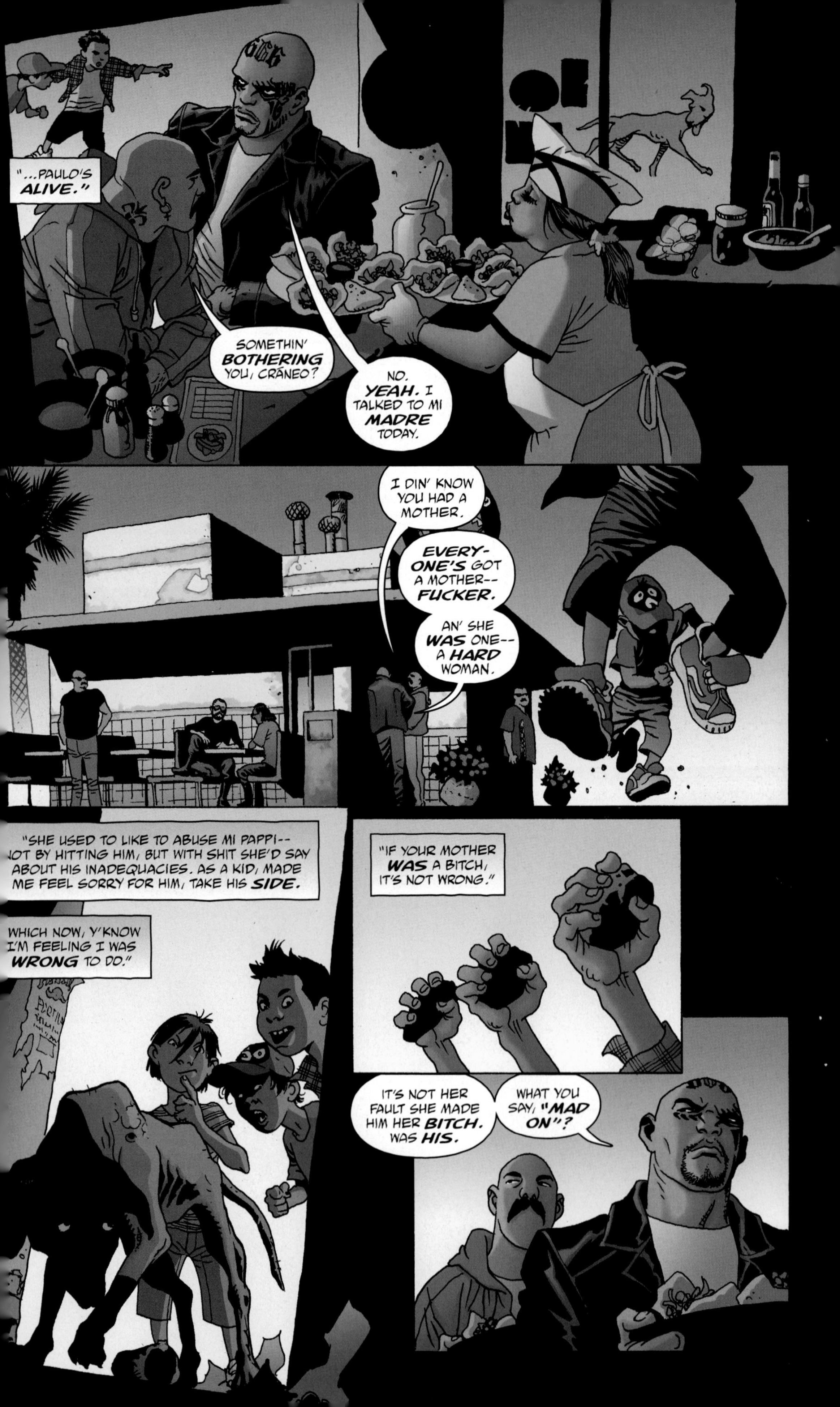
"...PAULO'S ALIVE."
SOMETHIN' BOTHERING YOU, CRÁNEO?
NO. YEAH. I TALKED TO MI MADRE TODAY.
I DIN' KNOW YOU HAD A MOTHER.
EVERY-ONE'S GOT A MOTHER--FUCKER.
AN' SHE WAS ONE--A HARD WOMAN.
"SHE USED TO LIKE TO ABUSE MI PAPPI--NOT BY HITTING HIM, BUT WITH SHIT SHE'D SAY ABOUT HIS INADEQUACIES. AS A KID, MADE ME FEEL SORRY FOR HIM, TAKE HIS SIDE.
WHICH NOW, Y'KNOW I'M FEELING I WAS WRONG TO DO."
"IF YOUR MOTHER WAS A BITCH, IT'S NOT WRONG."
IT'S NOT HER FAULT SHE MADE HIM HER BITCH. WAS HIS.
WHAT YOU SAY, "MAD ON"?

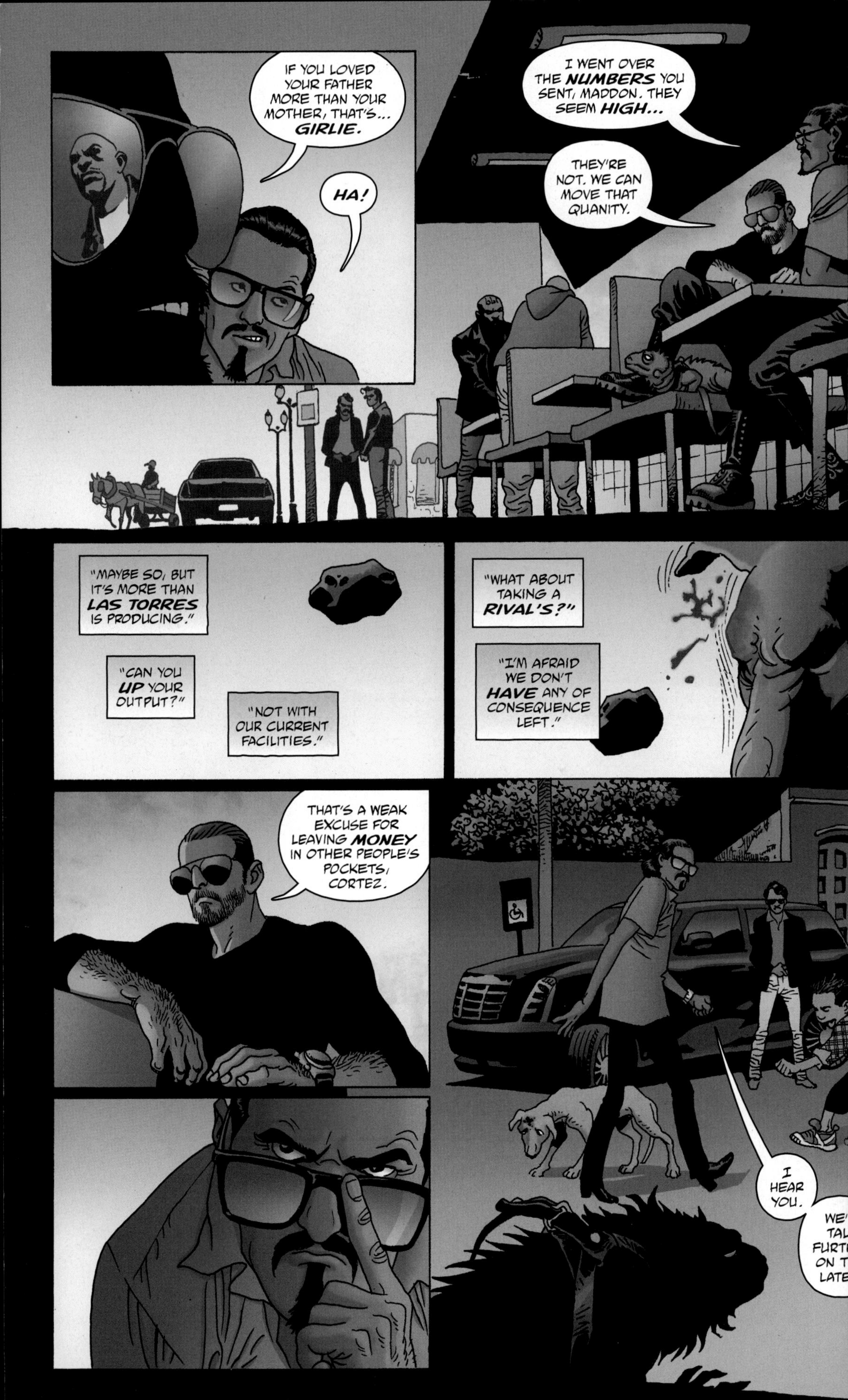

IF YOU LOVED YOUR FATHER MORE THAN YOUR MOTHER, THAT'S... GIRLIE.
HA!
I WENT OVER THE NUMBERS YOU SENT, MADDON. THEY SEEM HIGH...
THEY'RE NOT. WE CAN MOVE THAT QUANITY.
"MAYBE SO, BUT IT'S MORE THAN LAS TORRES IS PRODUCING."
"CAN YOU UP YOUR OUTPUT?"
"NOT WITH OUR CURRENT FACILITIES."
"WHAT ABOUT TAKING A RIVAL'S?"
"I'M AFRAID WE DON'T HAVE ANY OF CONSEQUENCE LEFT."
THAT'S A WEAK EXCUSE FOR LEAVING MONEY IN OTHER PEOPLE'S POCKETS, CORTEZ.
I HEAR YOU.

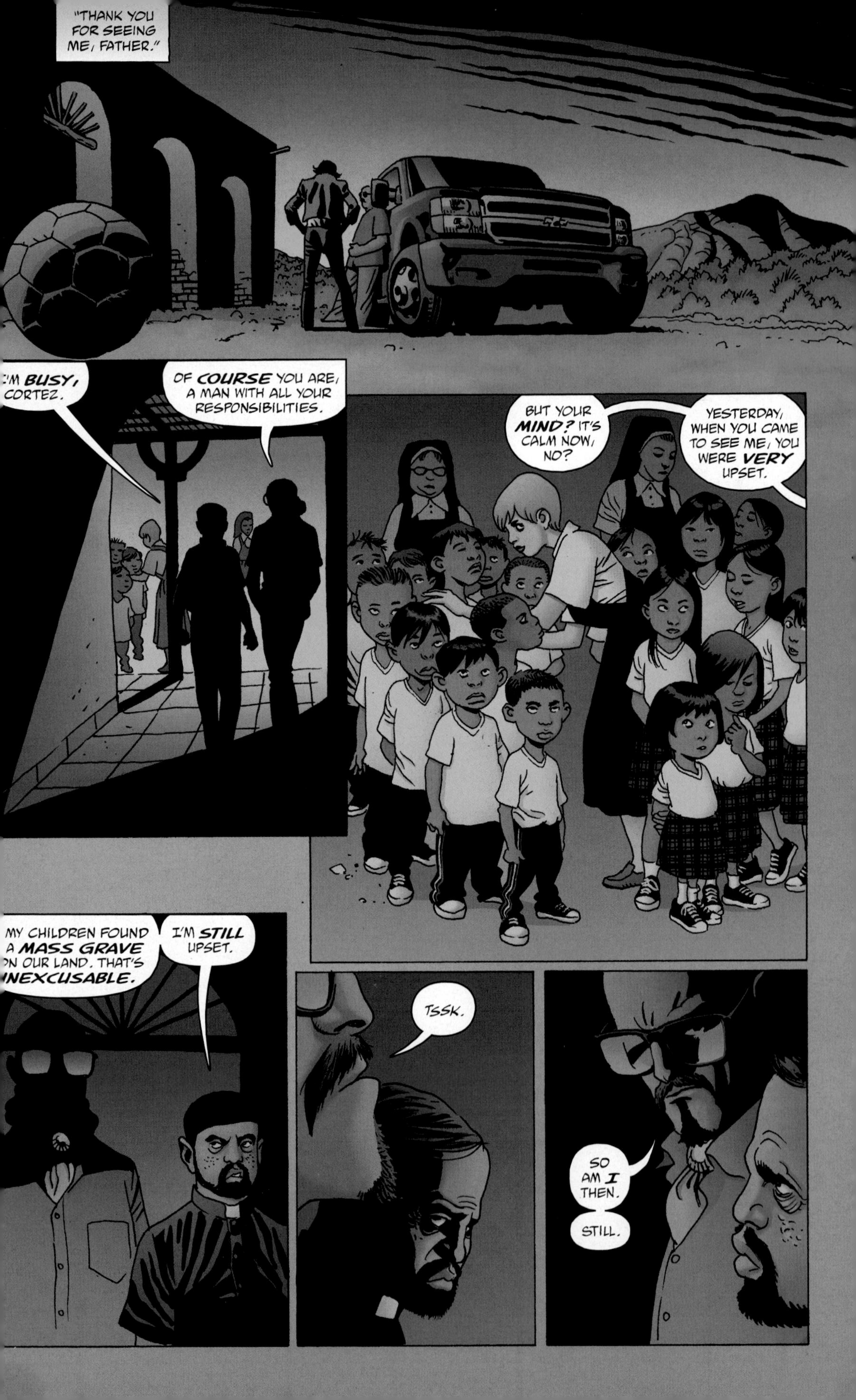
"THANK YOU FOR SEEING ME, FATHER."
I'M BUSY, CORTEZ.
OF COURSE YOU ARE, A MAN WITH ALL YOUR RESPONSIBILITIES.
BUT YOUR MIND? IT'S CALM NOW, NO?
YESTERDAY, WHEN YOU CAME TO SEE ME, YOU WERE VERY UPSET.
MY CHILDREN FOUND A MASS GRAVE ON OUR LAND. THAT'S INEXCUSABLE.
I'M STILL UPSET.
TSSK.
SO AM I THEN.
STILL.

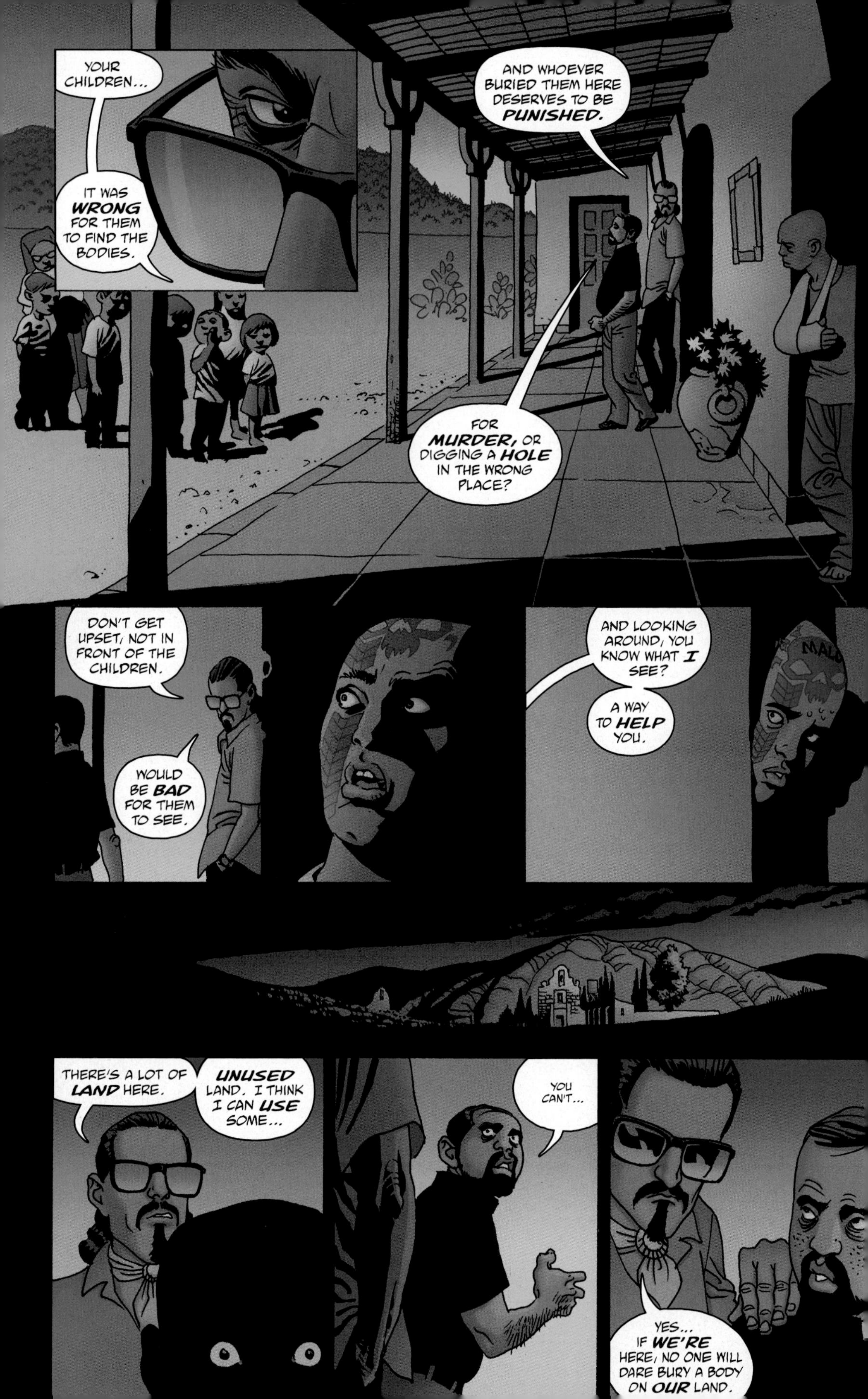
YOUR CHILDREN...
IT WAS WRONG FOR THEM TO FIND THE BODIES.
AND WHOEVER BURIED THEM HERE DESERVES TO BE PUNISHED.
FOR MURDER, OR DIGGING A HOLE IN THE WRONG PLACE?
DON'T GET UPSET, NOT IN FRONT OF THE CHILDREN.
WOULD BE BAD FOR THEM TO SEE.
AND LOOKING AROUND, YOU KNOW WHAT I SEE?
A WAY TO HELP YOU.
THERE'S A LOT OF LAND HERE.
UNUSED LAND. I THINK I CAN USE SOME...
YOU CAN'T...
YES... IF WE'RE HERE, NO ONE WILL DARE BURY A BODY ON OUR LAND.

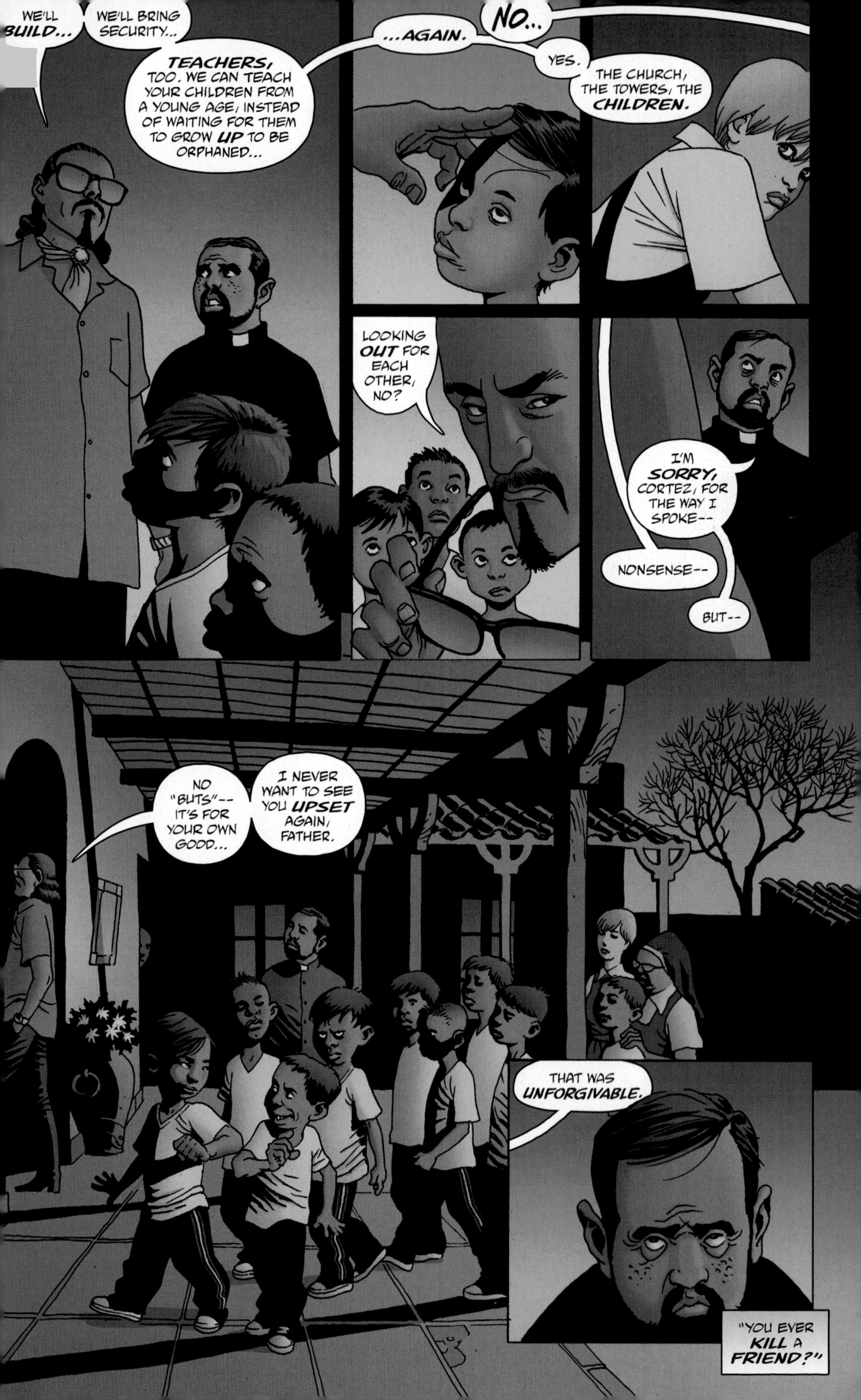
WE'LL BUILD...
WE'LL BRING SECURITY...
TEACHERS, TOO. WE CAN TEACH YOUR CHILDREN FROM A YOUNG AGE, INSTEAD OF WAITING FOR THEM TO GROW UP TO BE ORPHANED...
...AGAIN.
NO...
YES.
THE CHURCH, THE TOWERS, THE CHILDREN.
LOOKING OUT FOR EACH OTHER, NO?
I'M SORRY, CORTEZ, FOR THE WAY I SPOKE--
NONSENSE--
BUT--
NO "BUTS"-- IT'S FOR YOUR OWN GOOD...
I NEVER WANT TO SEE YOU UPSET AGAIN, FATHER.
THAT WAS UNFORGIVABLE.
"YOU EVER KILL A FRIEND?"

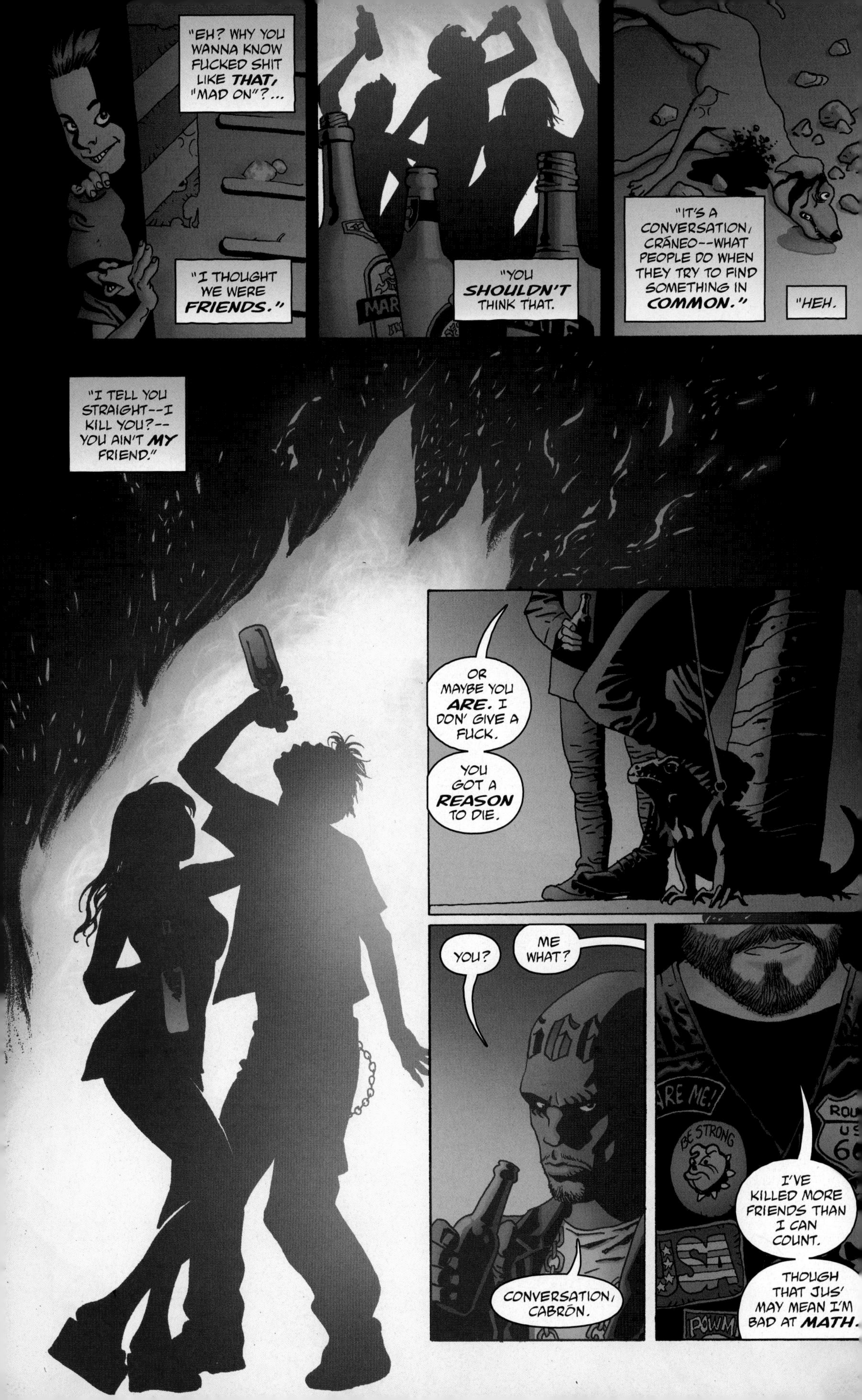
"EH? WHY YOU WANNA KNOW FUCKED SHIT LIKE THAT, "MAD ON"?...
"I THOUGHT WE WERE FRIENDS."
"YOU SHOULDN'T THINK THAT.
"IT'S A CONVERSATION, CRÁNEO--WHAT PEOPLE DO WHEN THEY TRY TO FIND SOMETHING IN COMMON."
"HEH.
"I TELL YOU STRAIGHT--I KILL YOU?--YOU AIN'T MY FRIEND."
OR MAYBE YOU ARE. I DON' GIVE A FUCK.
YOU GOT A REASON TO DIE.
YOU?
ME WHAT?
CONVERSATION, CABRÓN.
I'VE KILLED MORE FRIENDS THAN I CAN COUNT.
THOUGH THAT JUS' MAY MEAN I'M BAD AT MATH.

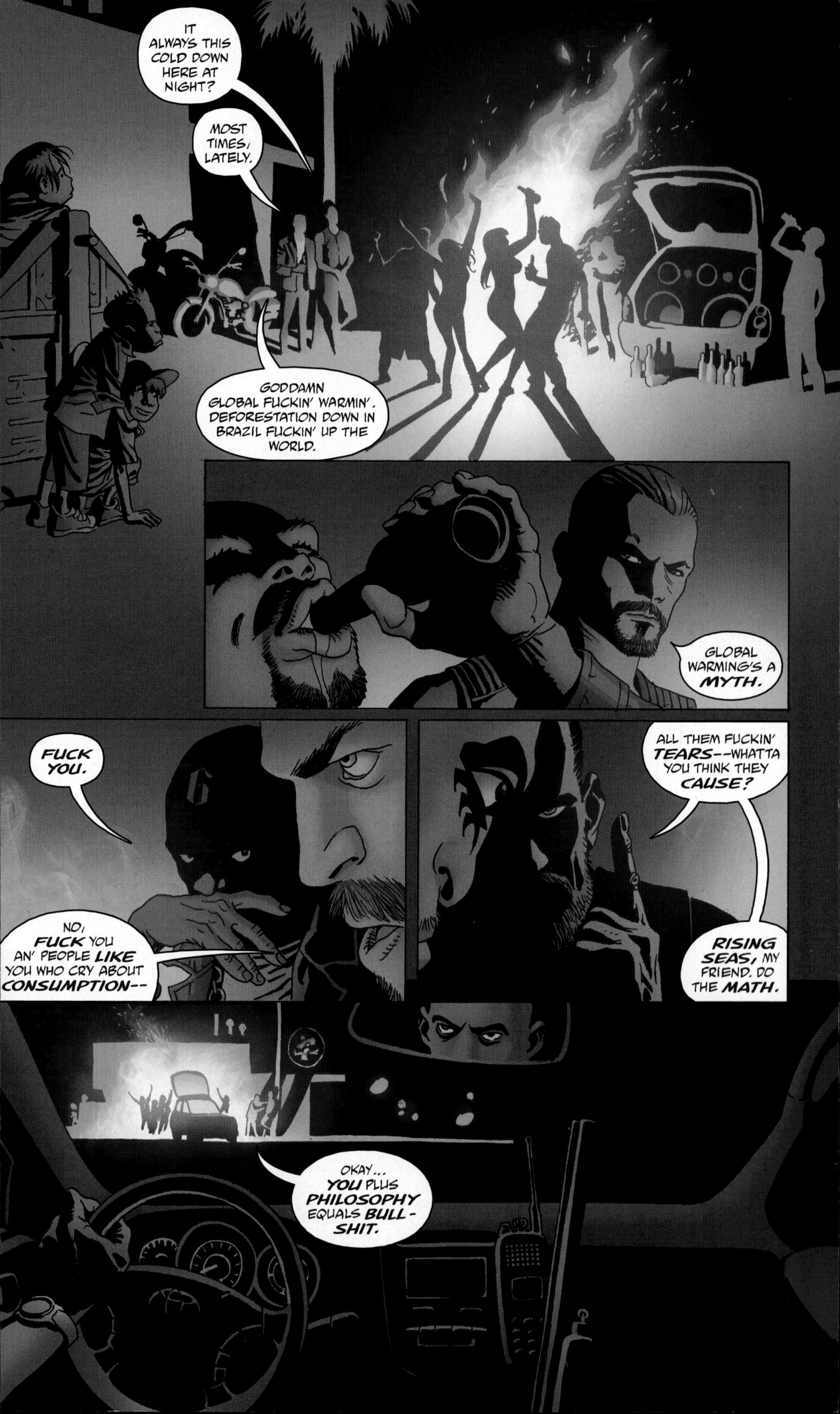
IT ALWAYS THIS COLD DOWN HERE AT NIGHT?
MOST TIMES, LATELY.
GODDAMN GLOBAL FUCKIN' WARMIN'. DEFORESTATION DOWN IN BRAZIL FUCKIN' UP THE WORLD.
GLOBAL WARMING'S A MYTH.
FUCK YOU.
NO, FUCK YOU AN' PEOPLE LIKE YOU WHO CRY ABOUT CONSUMPTION--
ALL THEM FUCKIN' TEARS--WHATTA YOU THINK THEY CAUSE?
RISING SEAS, MY FRIEND. DO THE MATH.
OKAY... YOU PLUS PHILOSOPHY EQUALS BULL-SHIT.

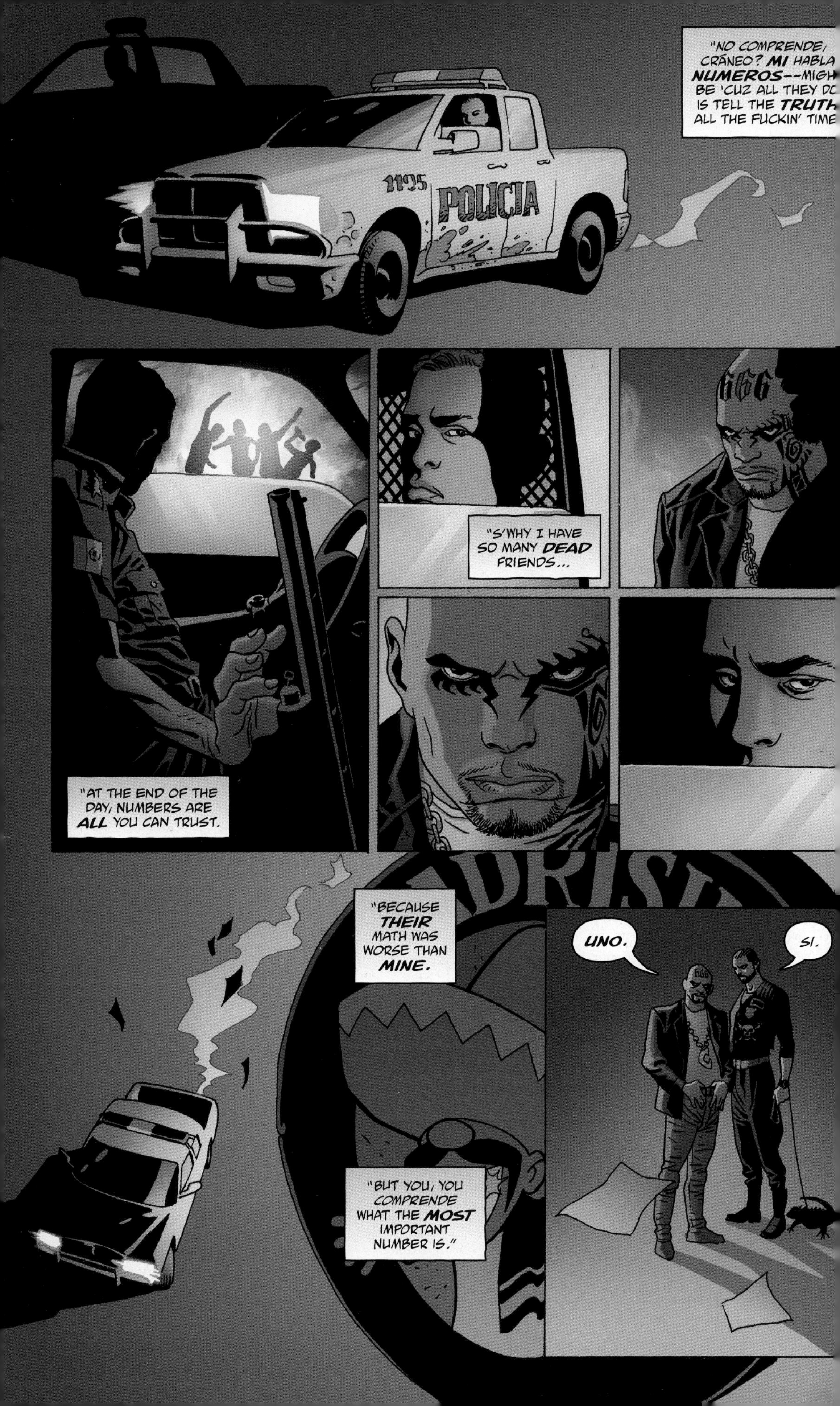

"NO COMPRENDE, CRÁNEO? MI HABLA NUMEROS--MIGH BE 'CUZ ALL THEY DO IS TELL THE TRUTH ALL THE FUCKIN' TIME
1195 POLICIA
"AT THE END OF THE DAY, NUMBERS ARE ALL YOU CAN TRUST.
"S'WHY I HAVE SO MANY DEAD FRIENDS...
666
"BECAUSE THEIR MATH WAS WORSE THAN MINE.
"BUT YOU, YOU COMPRENDE WHAT THE MOST IMPORTANT NUMBER IS."
UNO.
SI.

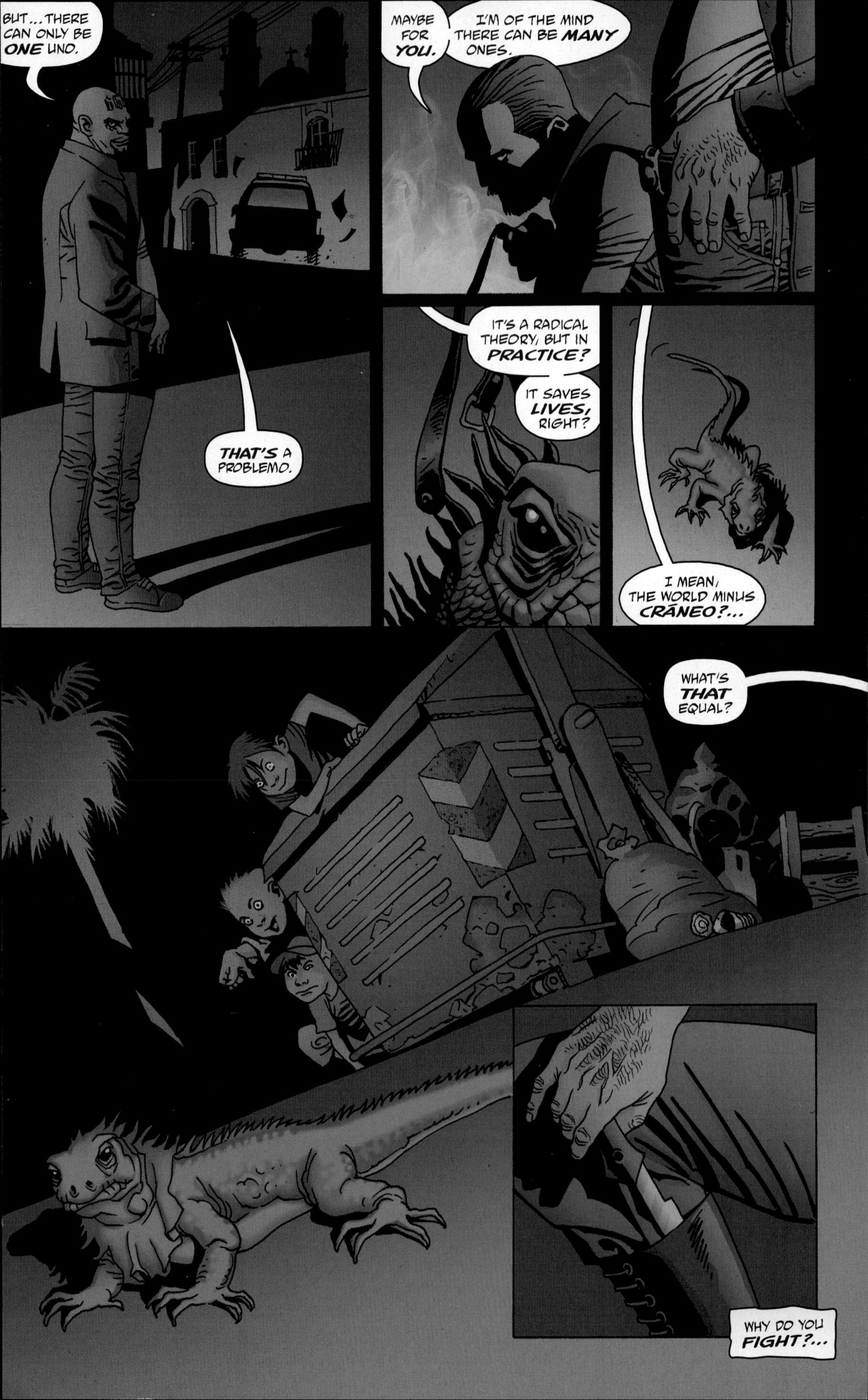
BUT... THERE CAN ONLY BE ONE UNO.
THAT'S A PROBLEMO.
MAYBE FOR YOU.
I'M OF THE MIND THERE CAN BE MANY ONES.
IT'S A RADICAL THEORY, BUT IN PRACTICE?
IT SAVES LIVES, RIGHT?
I MEAN, THE WORLD MINUS CRÁNEO?...
WHAT'S THAT EQUAL?
WHY DO YOU FIGHT?...

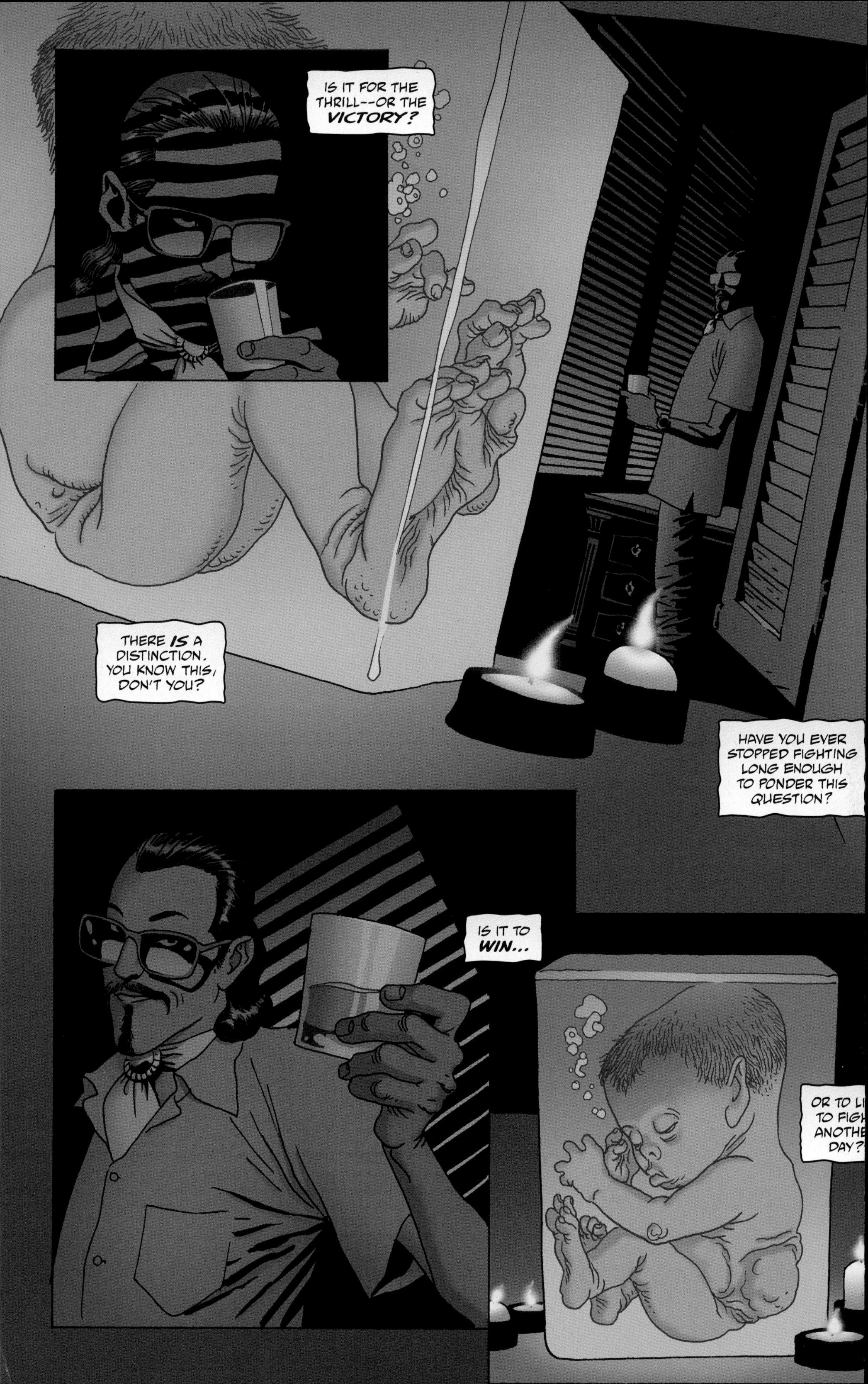
IS IT FOR THE THRILL--OR THE VICTORY?
THERE IS A DISTINCTION. YOU KNOW THIS, DON'T YOU?
HAVE YOU EVER STOPPED FIGHTING LONG ENOUGH TO PONDER THIS QUESTION?
IS IT TO WIN...
OR TO LI TO FIGH ANOTHE DAY?

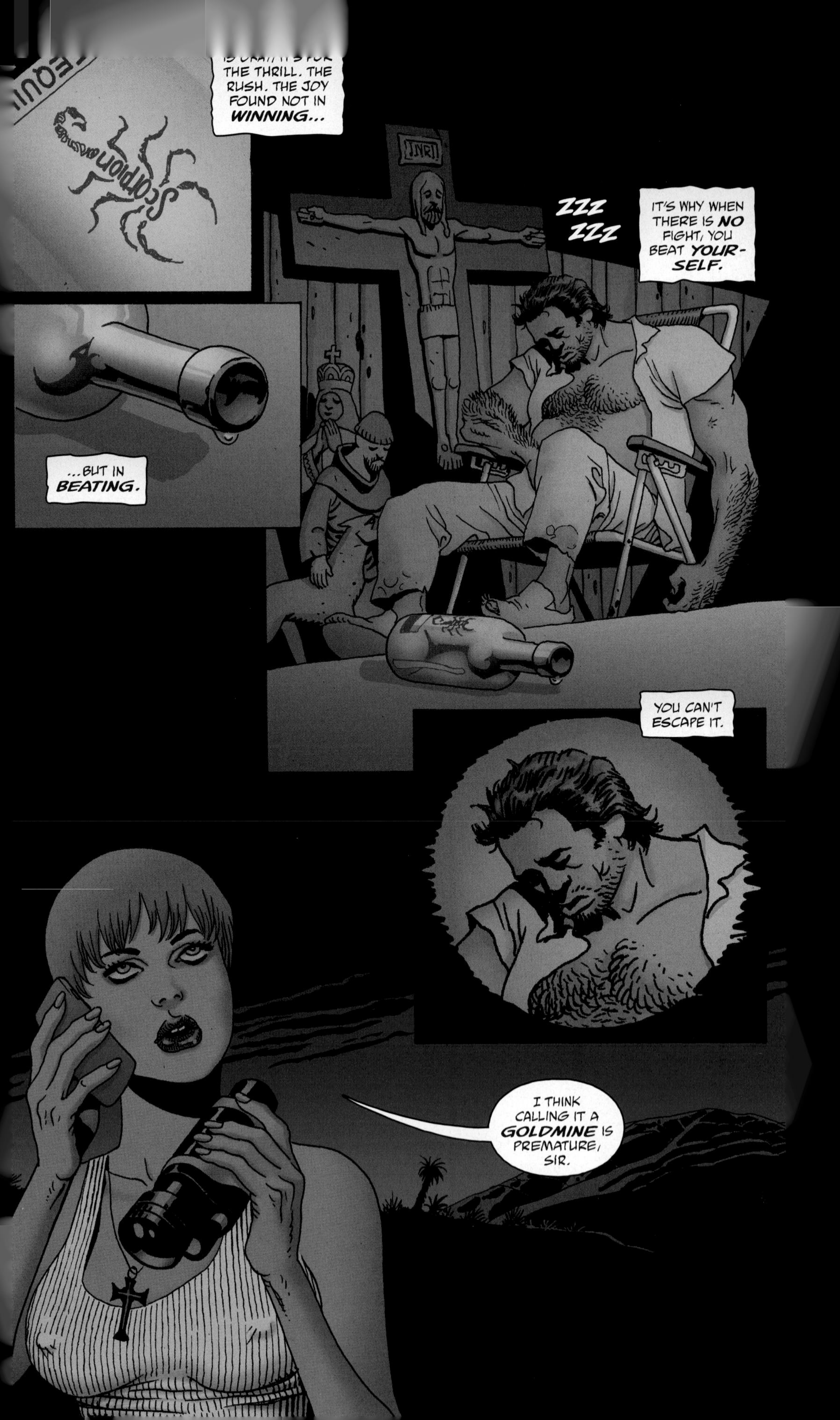
THE THRILL. THE RUSH. THE JOY FOUND NOT IN WINNING...
Scorpion
...BUT IN BEATING.
INRI
ZZZ ZZZ
IT'S WHY WHEN THERE IS NO FIGHT, YOU BEAT YOURSELF.
YOU CAN'T ESCAPE IT.
I THINK CALLING IT A GOLDMINE IS PREMATURE, SIR.

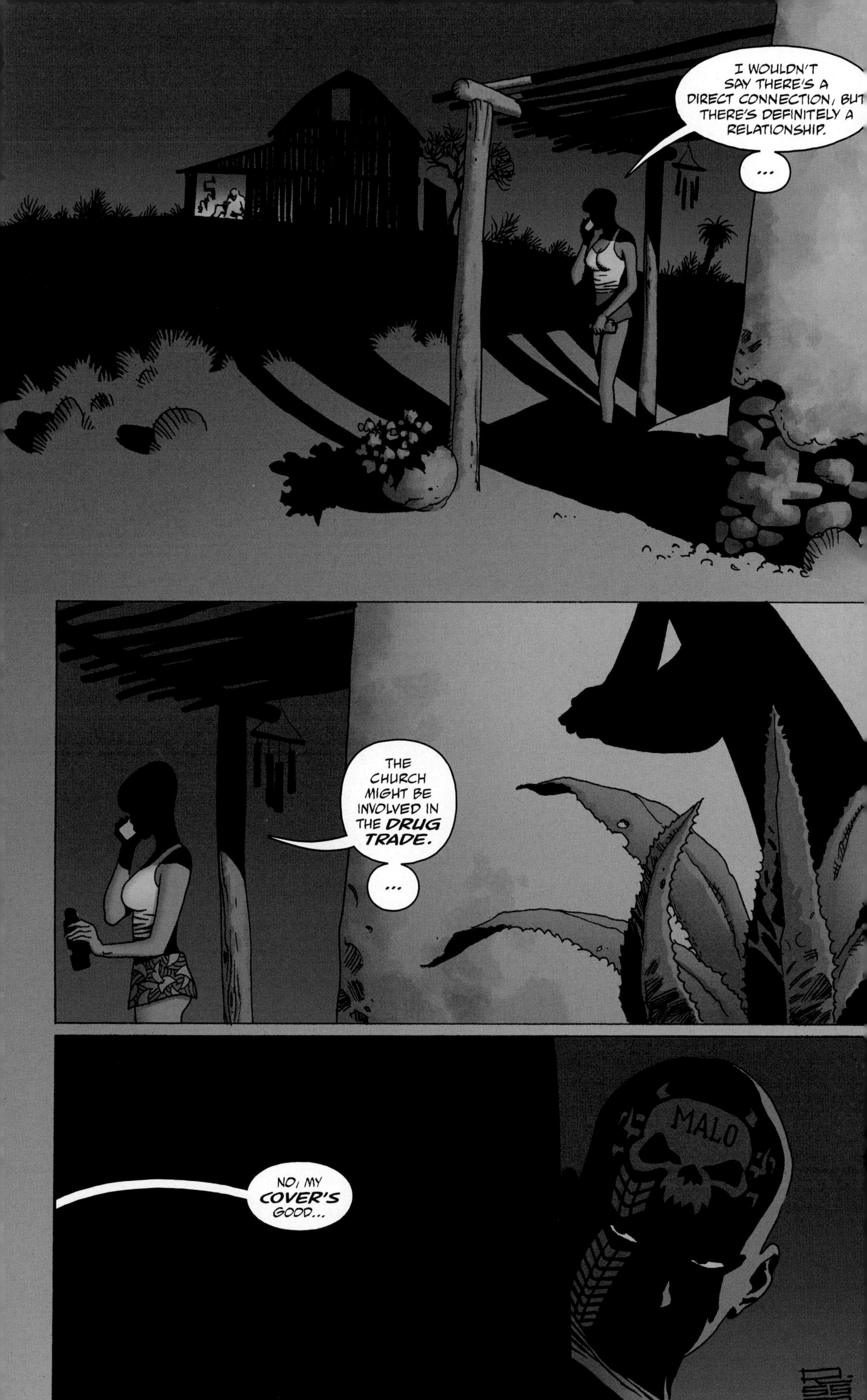
I WOULDN'T SAY THERE'S A DIRECT CONNECTION, BUT THERE'S DEFINITELY A RELATIONSHIP.
...
THE CHURCH MIGHT BE INVOLVED IN THE DRUG TRADE.
...
MALO
NO, MY COVER'S GOOD...

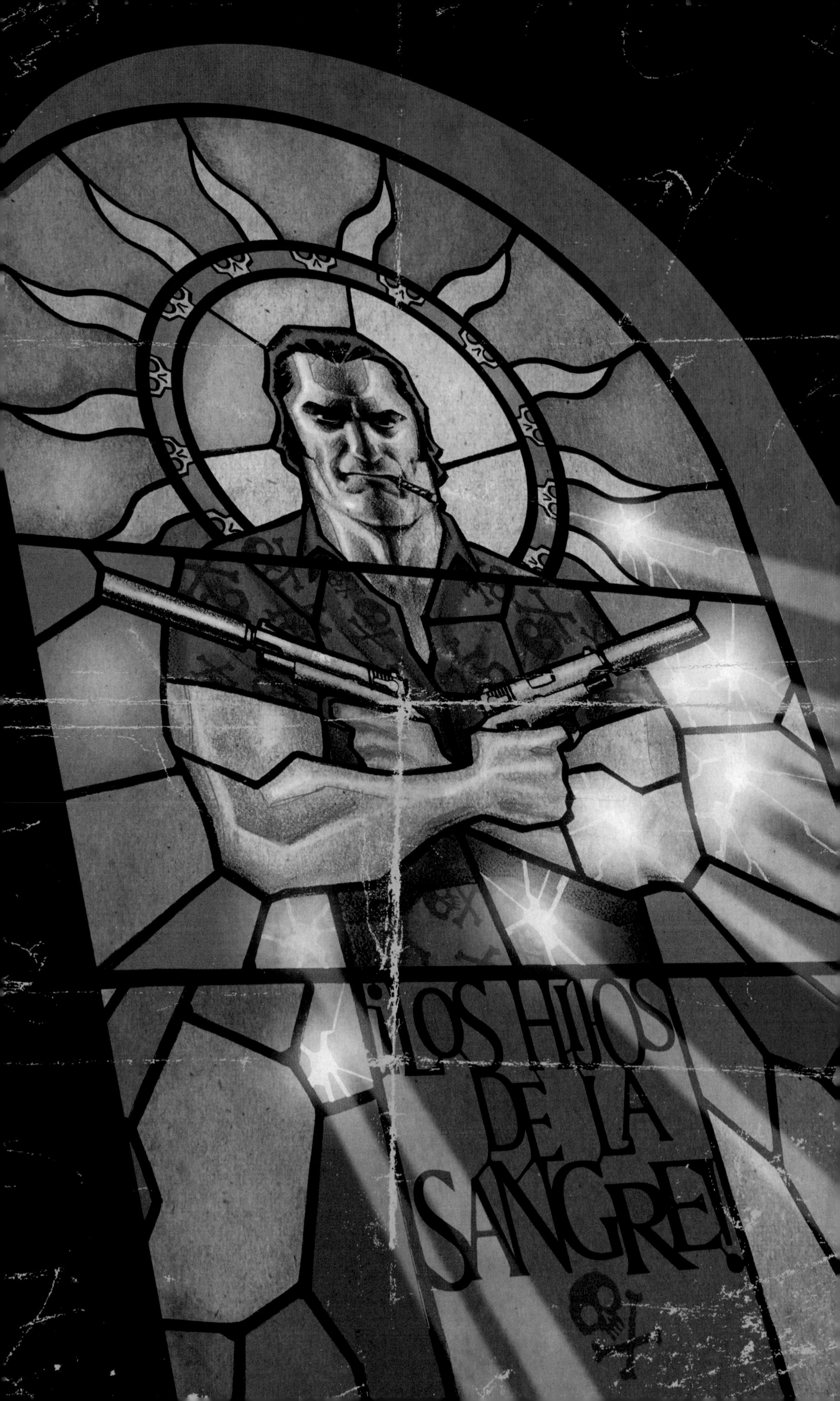
¡LOS HIJOS
DE LA
SANGRE!

"Who wants to make some money?"

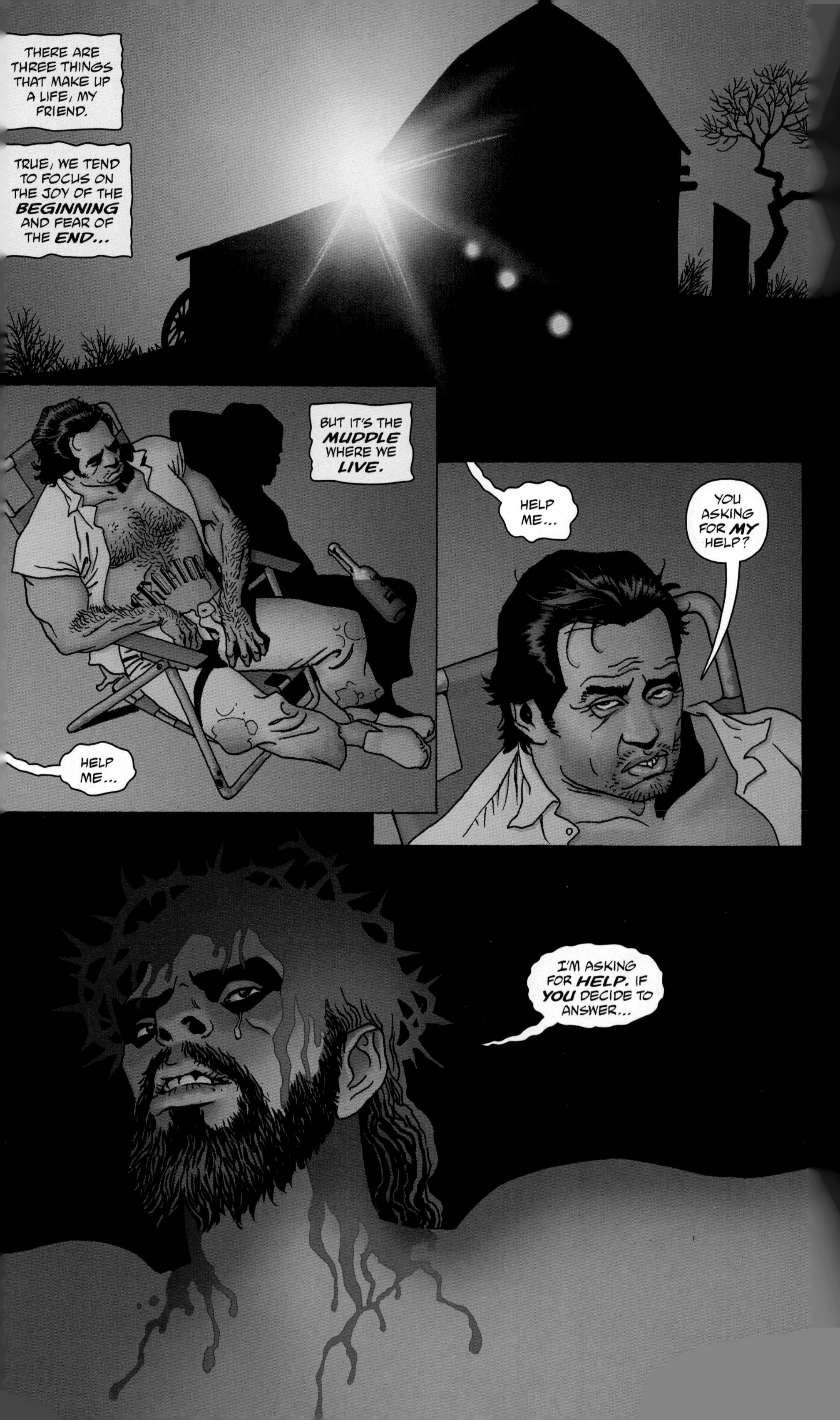
THERE ARE THREE THINGS THAT MAKE UP A LIFE, MY FRIEND.
TRUE, WE TEND TO FOCUS ON THE JOY OF THE BEGINNING AND FEAR OF THE END...
BUT IT'S THE MUDDLE WHERE WE LIVE.
HELP ME...
HELP ME...
YOU ASKING FOR MY HELP?
I'M ASKING FOR HELP. IF YOU DECIDE TO ANSWER...

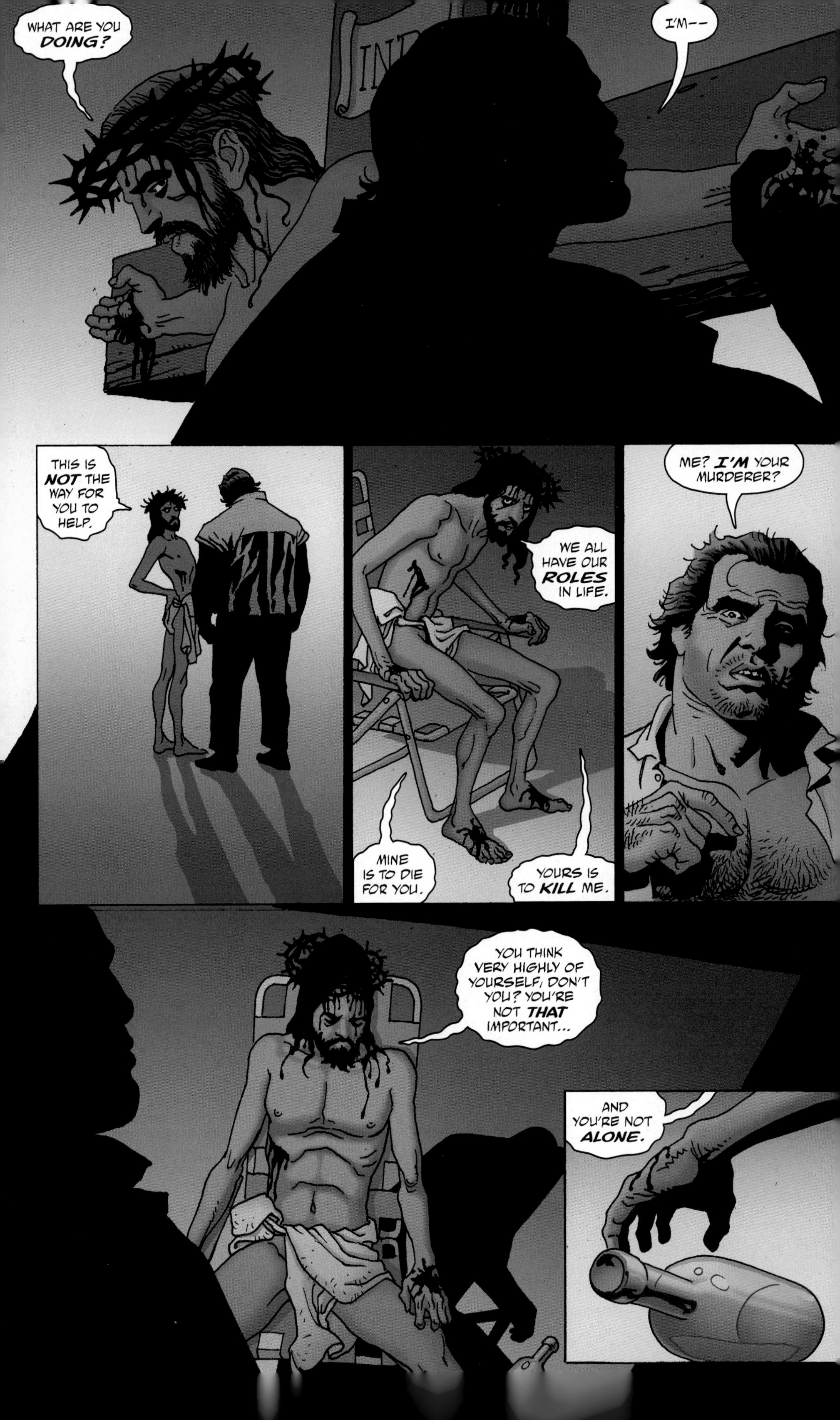
WHAT ARE YOU DOING?
I'M--
THIS IS NOT THE WAY FOR YOU TO HELP.
WE ALL HAVE OUR ROLES IN LIFE.
MINE IS TO DIE FOR YOU.
YOURS IS TO KILL ME.
ME? I'M YOUR MURDERER?
YOU THINK VERY HIGHLY OF YOURSELF, DON'T YOU? YOU'RE NOT THAT IMPORTANT...
AND YOU'RE NOT ALONE.

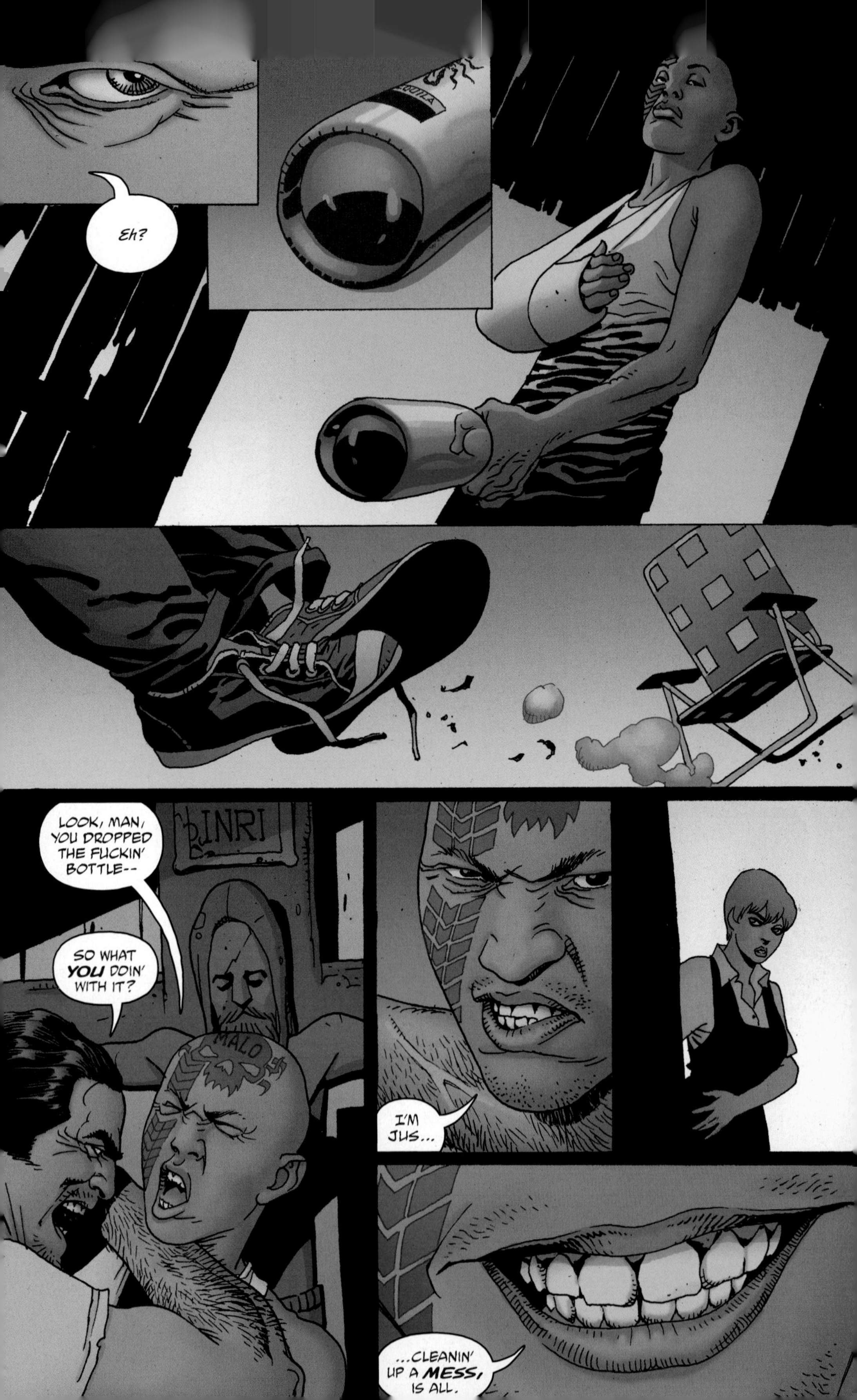
Eh?
LOOK, MAN, YOU DROPPED THE FUCKIN' BOTTLE--
SO WHAT YOU DOIN' WITH IT?
I'M JUS...
...CLEANIN' UP A MESS, IS ALL.

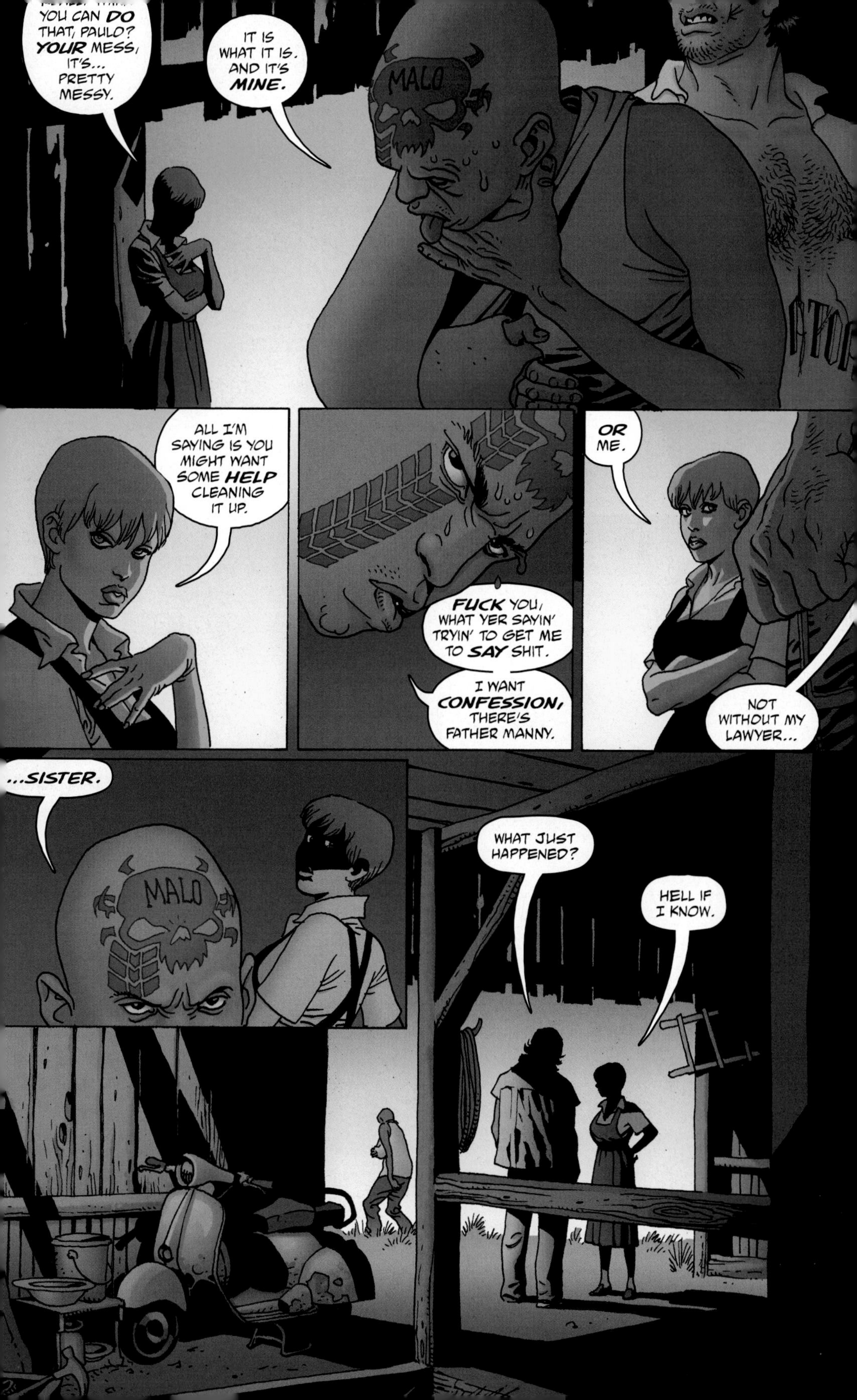
YOU CAN DO THAT, PAULO? YOUR MESS, IT'S... PRETTY MESSY.
IT IS WHAT IT IS. AND IT'S MINE.
ALL I'M SAYING IS YOU MIGHT WANT SOME HELP CLEANING IT UP.
FUCK YOU, WHAT YER SAYIN' TRYIN' TO GET ME TO SAY SHIT.
I WANT CONFESSION, THERE'S FATHER MANNY.
OR ME.
NOT WITHOUT MY LAWYER...
...SISTER.
MALO
WHAT JUST HAPPENED?
HELL IF I KNOW.

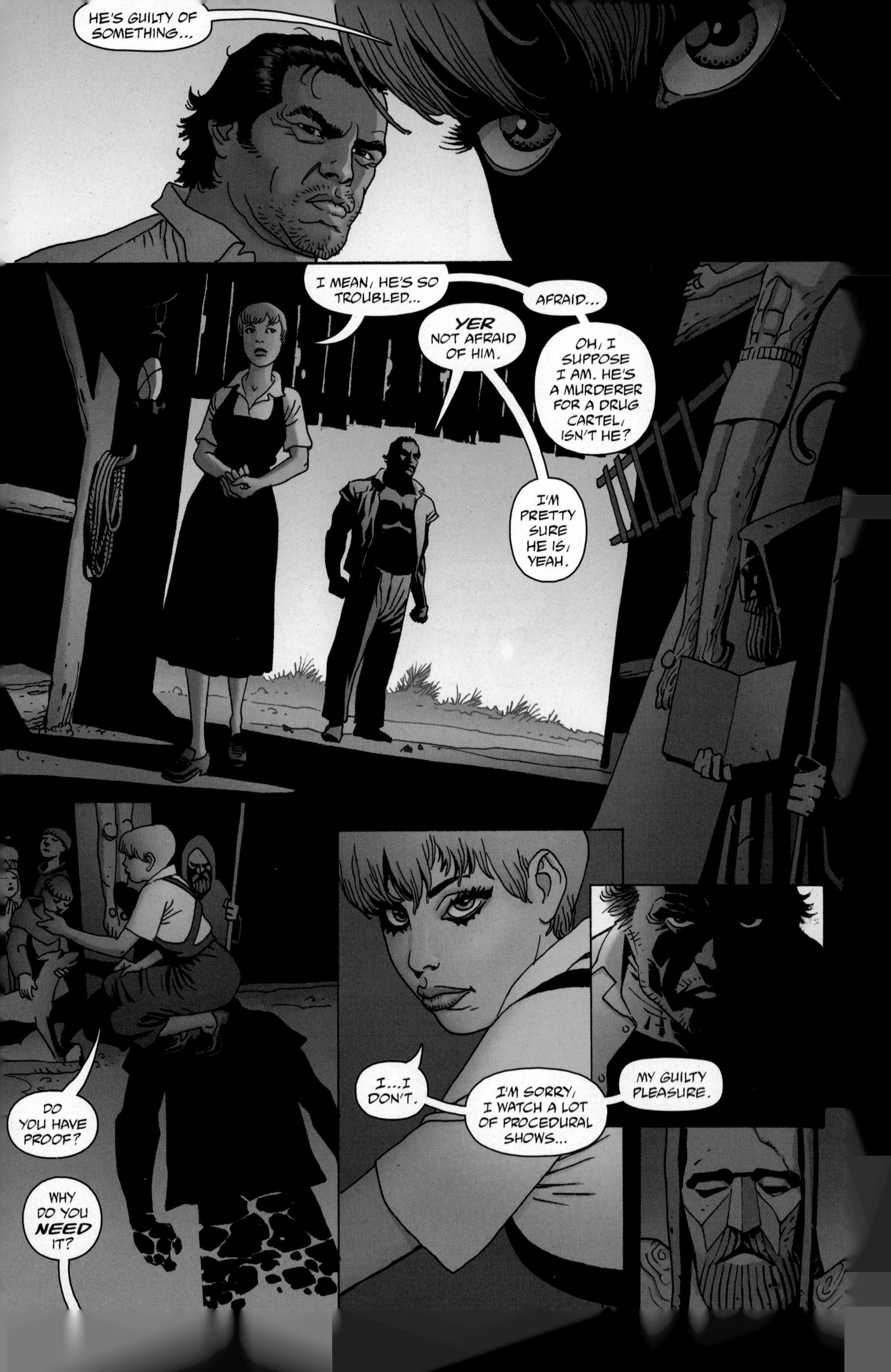

HE'S GUILTY OF SOMETHING...
I MEAN, HE'S SO TROUBLED...
AFRAID...
YER NOT AFRAID OF HIM.
OH, I SUPPOSE I AM. HE'S A MURDERER FOR A DRUG CARTEL, ISN'T HE?
I'M PRETTY SURE HE IS, YEAH.
DO YOU HAVE PROOF?
WHY DO YOU NEED IT?
I...I DON'T.
I'M SORRY, I WATCH A LOT OF PROCEDURAL SHOWS...
MY GUILTY PLEASURE.

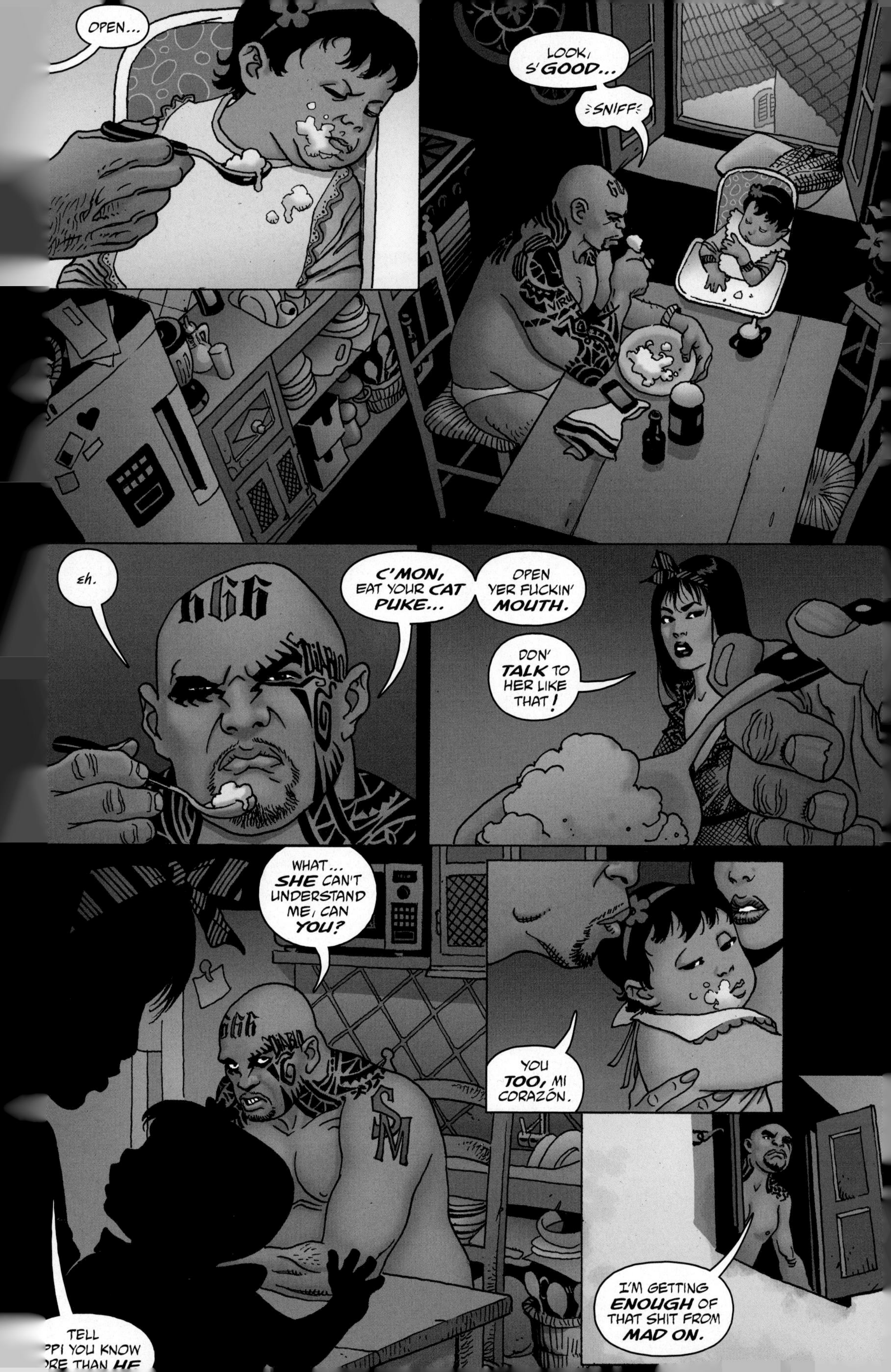
OPEN...
LOOK, S'GOOD...
SNIFF
εh.
C'MON, EAT YOUR CAT PUKE...
OPEN YER FUCKIN' MOUTH.
DON' TALK TO HER LIKE THAT!
WHAT... SHE CAN'T UNDERSTAND ME, CAN YOU?
YOU TOO, MI CORAZÓN.
TELL
PPI YOU KNOW
ORE THAN HE
I'M GETTING ENOUGH OF THAT SHIT FROM MAD ON.

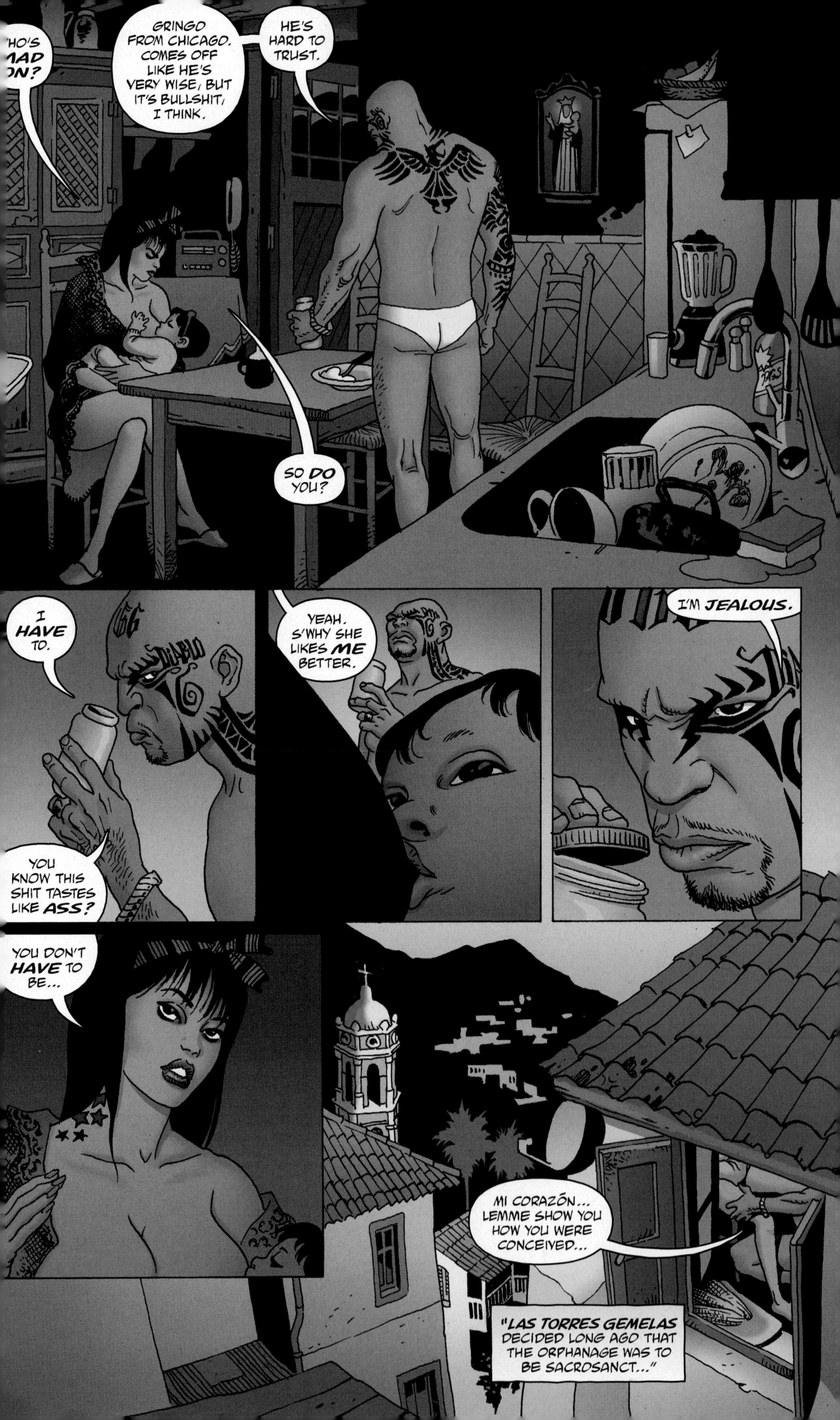

HO'S
MAD
ON?
GRINGO FROM CHICAGO. COMES OFF LIKE HE'S VERY WISE, BUT IT'S BULLSHIT, I THINK.
HE'S HARD TO TRUST.
SO DO YOU?
I HAVE TO.
YOU KNOW THIS SHIT TASTES LIKE ASS?
YEAH. S'WHY SHE LIKES ME BETTER.
I'M JEALOUS.
YOU DON'T HAVE TO BE...
MI CORAZÓN... LEMME SHOW YOU HOW YOU WERE CONCEIVED...
"LAS TORRES GEMELAS DECIDED LONG AGO THAT THE ORPHANAGE WAS TO BE SACROSANCT..."

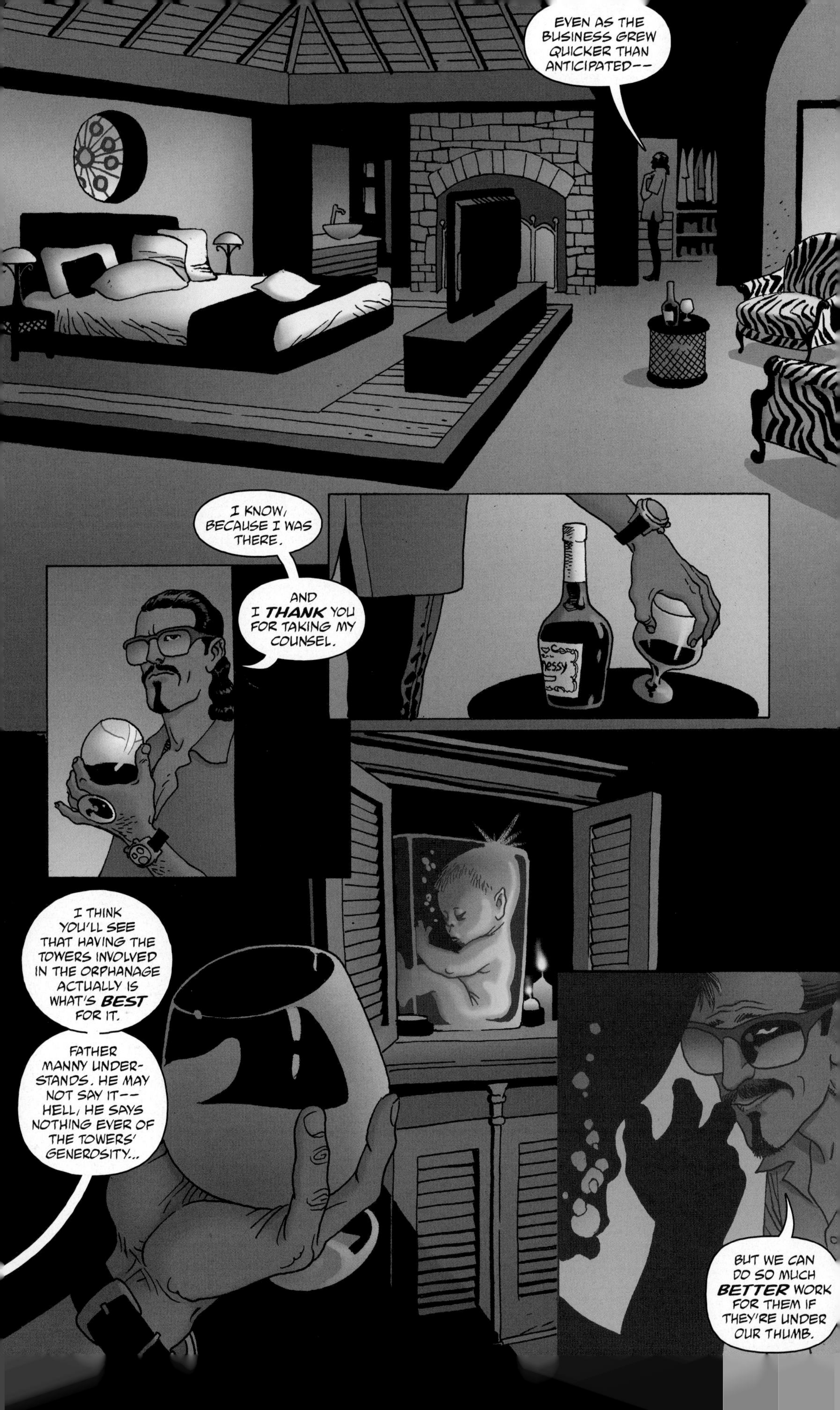
EVEN AS THE BUSINESS GREW QUICKER THAN ANTICIPATED--
I KNOW, BECAUSE I WAS THERE.
AND I **THANK** YOU FOR TAKING MY COUNSEL.
I THINK YOU'LL SEE THAT HAVING THE TOWERS INVOLVED IN THE ORPHANAGE ACTUALLY IS WHAT'S **BEST** FOR IT.
FATHER MANNY UNDERSTANDS. HE MAY NOT SAY IT-- HELL, HE SAYS NOTHING EVER OF THE TOWERS' GENEROSITY...
BUT WE CAN DO SO MUCH **BETTER** WORK FOR THEM IF THEY'RE UNDER OUR THUMB.

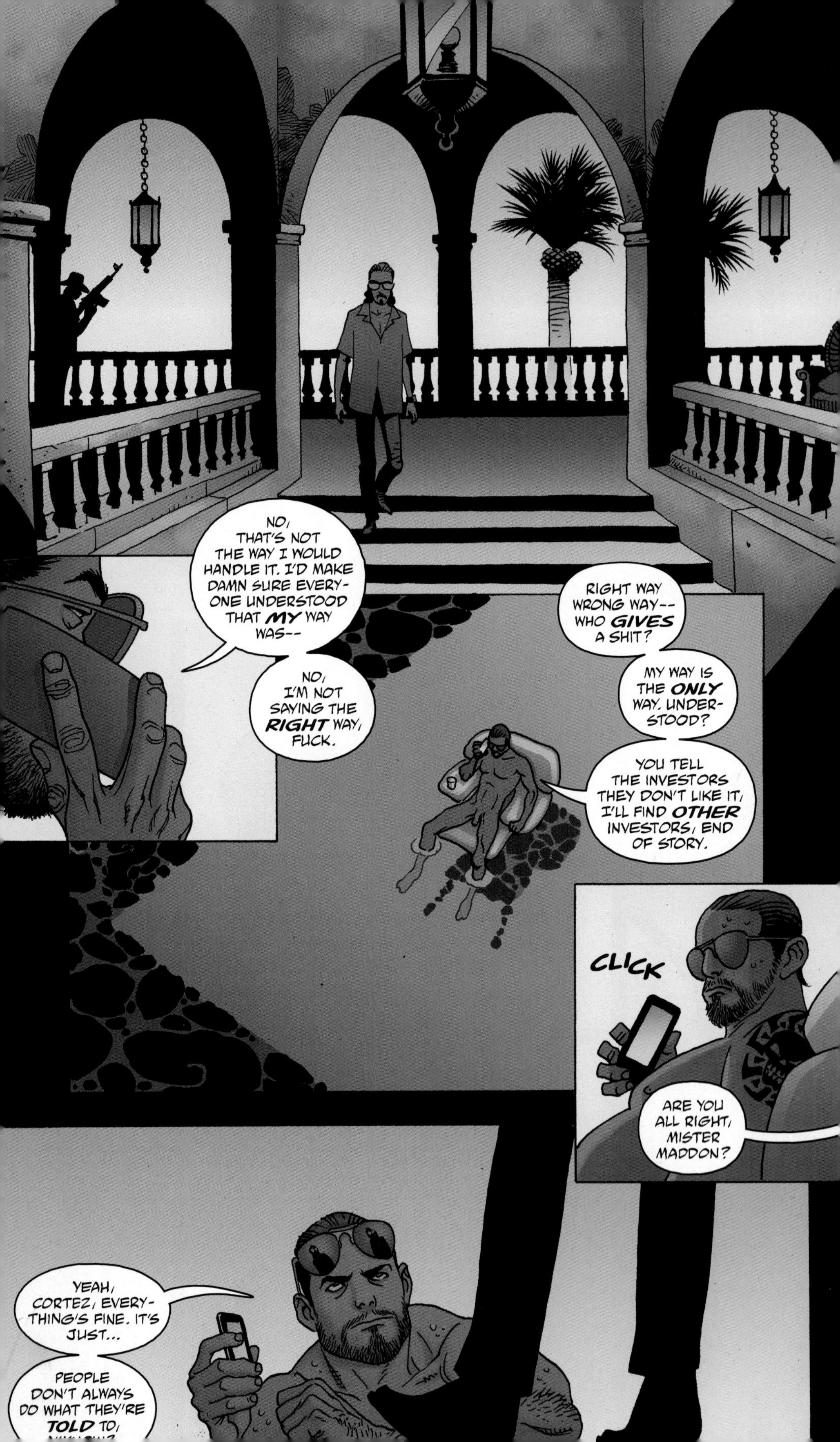
NO, THAT'S NOT THE WAY I WOULD HANDLE IT. I'D MAKE DAMN SURE EVERY-ONE UNDERSTOOD THAT MY WAY WAS--
NO, I'M NOT SAYING THE RIGHT WAY, FUCK.
RIGHT WAY WRONG WAY-- WHO GIVES A SHIT?
MY WAY IS THE ONLY WAY. UNDER-STOOD?
YOU TELL THE INVESTORS THEY DON'T LIKE IT, I'LL FIND OTHER INVESTORS, END OF STORY.
CLICK
ARE YOU ALL RIGHT, MISTER MADDON?
YEAH, CORTEZ, EVERY-THING'S FINE. IT'S JUST...
PEOPLE DON'T ALWAYS DO WHAT THEY'RE TOLD TO,

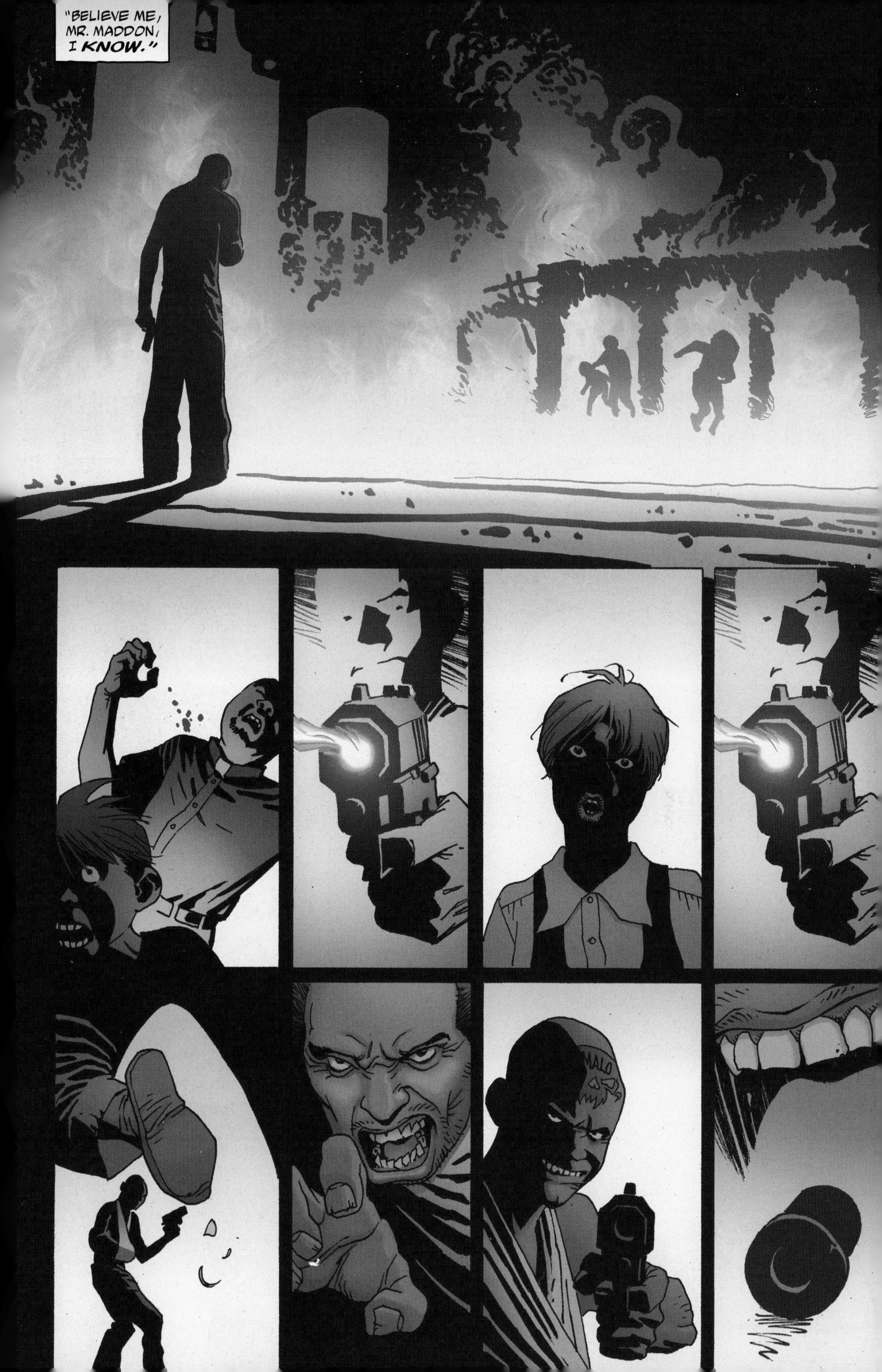
"BELIEVE ME, MR. MADDON, I KNOW."
MALO

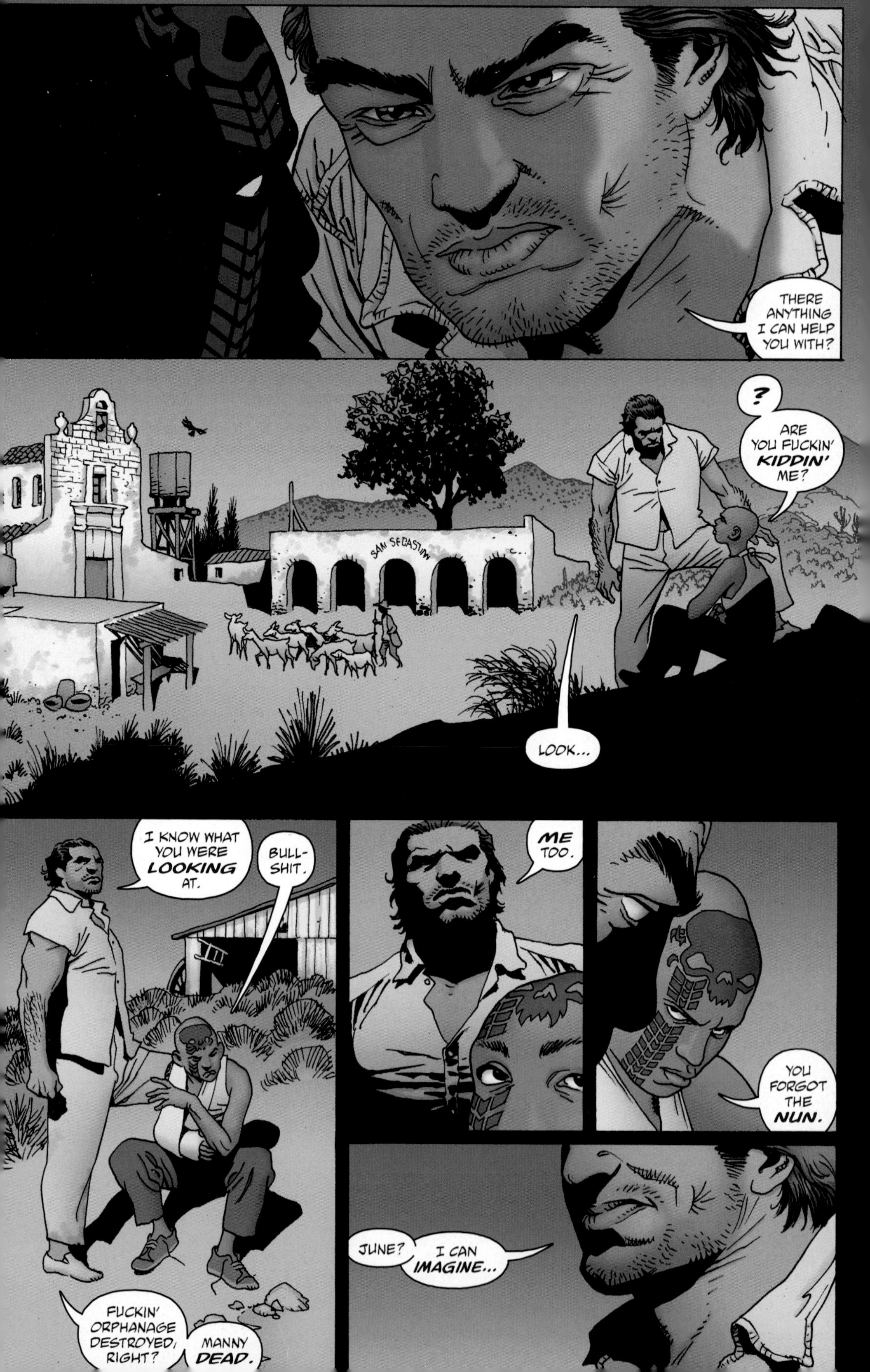

THERE ANYTHING I CAN HELP YOU WITH?
?
ARE YOU FUCKIN' KIDDIN' ME?
LOOK...
I KNOW WHAT YOU WERE LOOKING AT.
BULL-SHIT.
FUCKIN' ORPHANAGE DESTROYED, RIGHT?
MANNY DEAD.
ME TOO.
YOU FORGOT THE NUN.
JUNE?
I CAN IMAGINE...

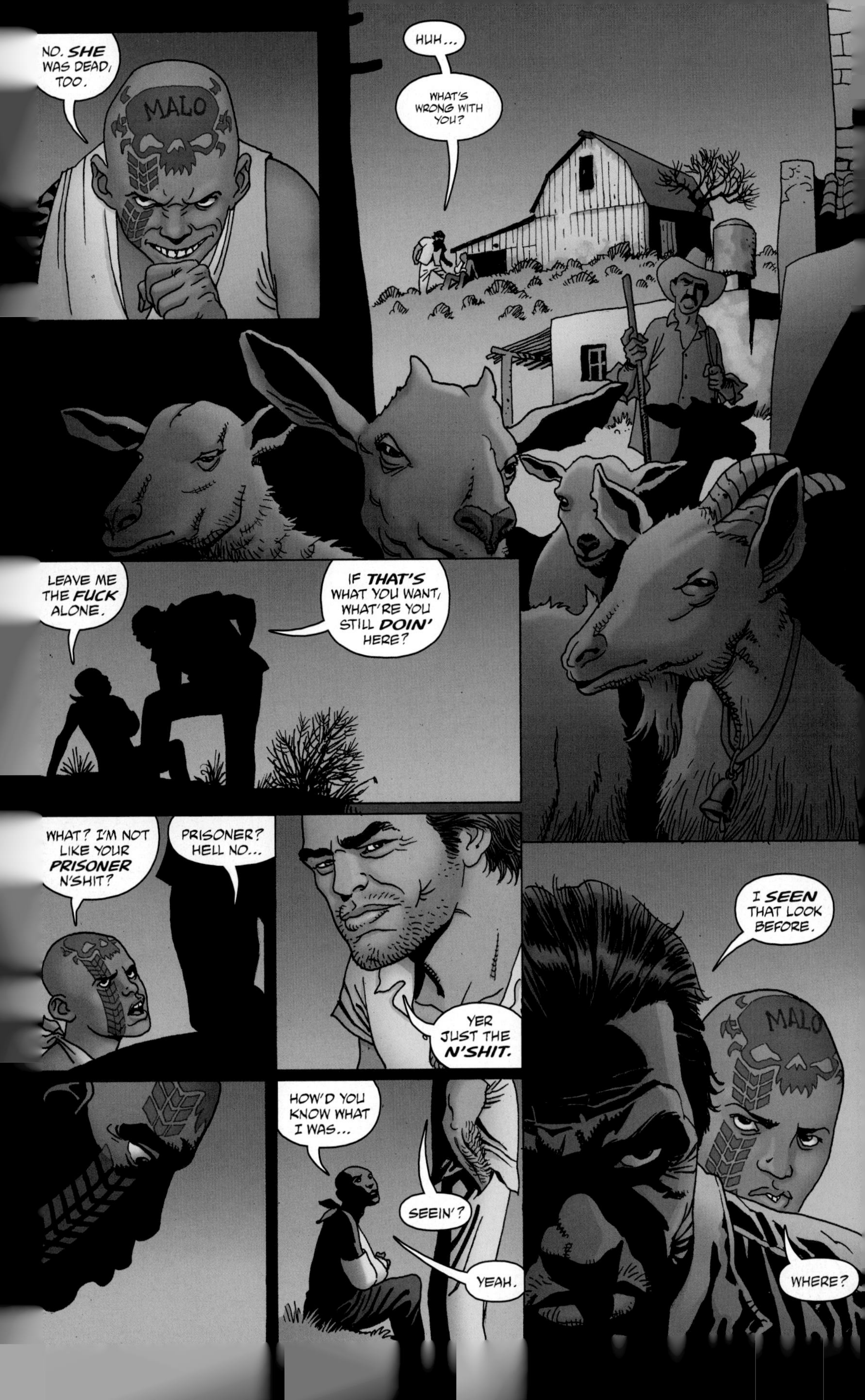
NO. SHE WAS DEAD, TOO.
HUH...
WHAT'S WRONG WITH YOU?
LEAVE ME THE FUCK ALONE.
IF THAT'S WHAT YOU WANT, WHAT'RE YOU STILL DOIN' HERE?
WHAT? I'M NOT LIKE YOUR PRISONER N'SHIT?
PRISONER? HELL NO...
YER JUST THE N'SHIT.
I SEEN THAT LOOK BEFORE.
HOW'D YOU KNOW WHAT I WAS...
SEEIN'?
YEAH.
WHERE?
MALO

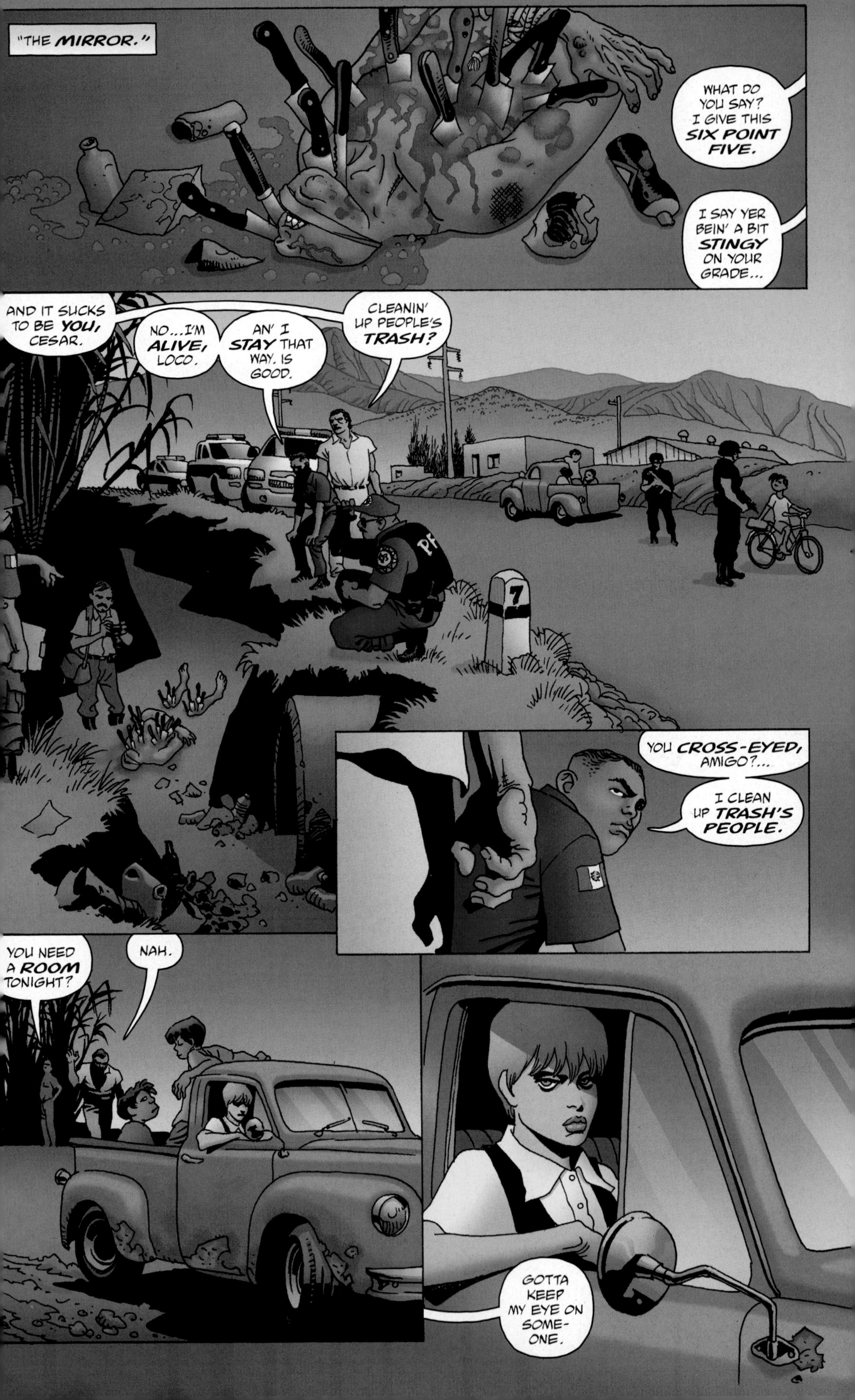
"THE MIRROR."
WHAT DO YOU SAY? I GIVE THIS SIX POINT FIVE.
I SAY YER BEIN' A BIT STINGY ON YOUR GRADE...
AND IT SUCKS TO BE YOU, CESAR.
NO...I'M ALIVE, LOCO.
AN' I STAY THAT WAY. IS GOOD.
CLEANIN' UP PEOPLE'S TRASH?
7
YOU CROSS-EYED, AMIGO?...
I CLEAN UP TRASH'S PEOPLE.
YOU NEED A ROOM TONIGHT?
NAH.
GOTTA KEEP MY EYE ON SOME-ONE.

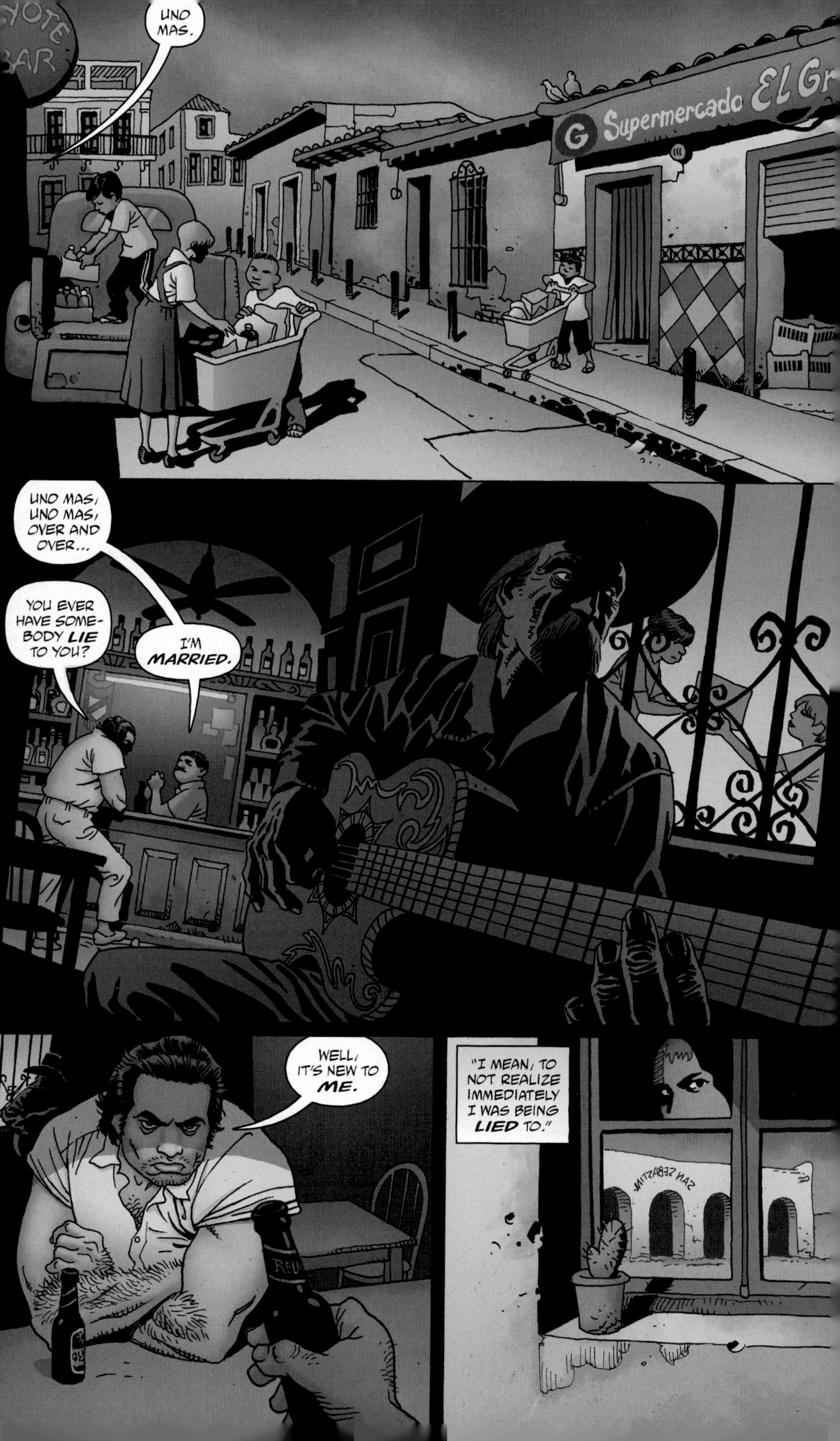
UNO MAS.
Supermercado El Gr
UNO MAS, UNO MAS, OVER AND OVER...
YOU EVER HAVE SOMEBODY LIE TO YOU?
I'M MARRIED.
WELL, IT'S NEW TO ME.
"I MEAN, TO NOT REALIZE IMMEDIATELY I WAS BEING LIED TO."

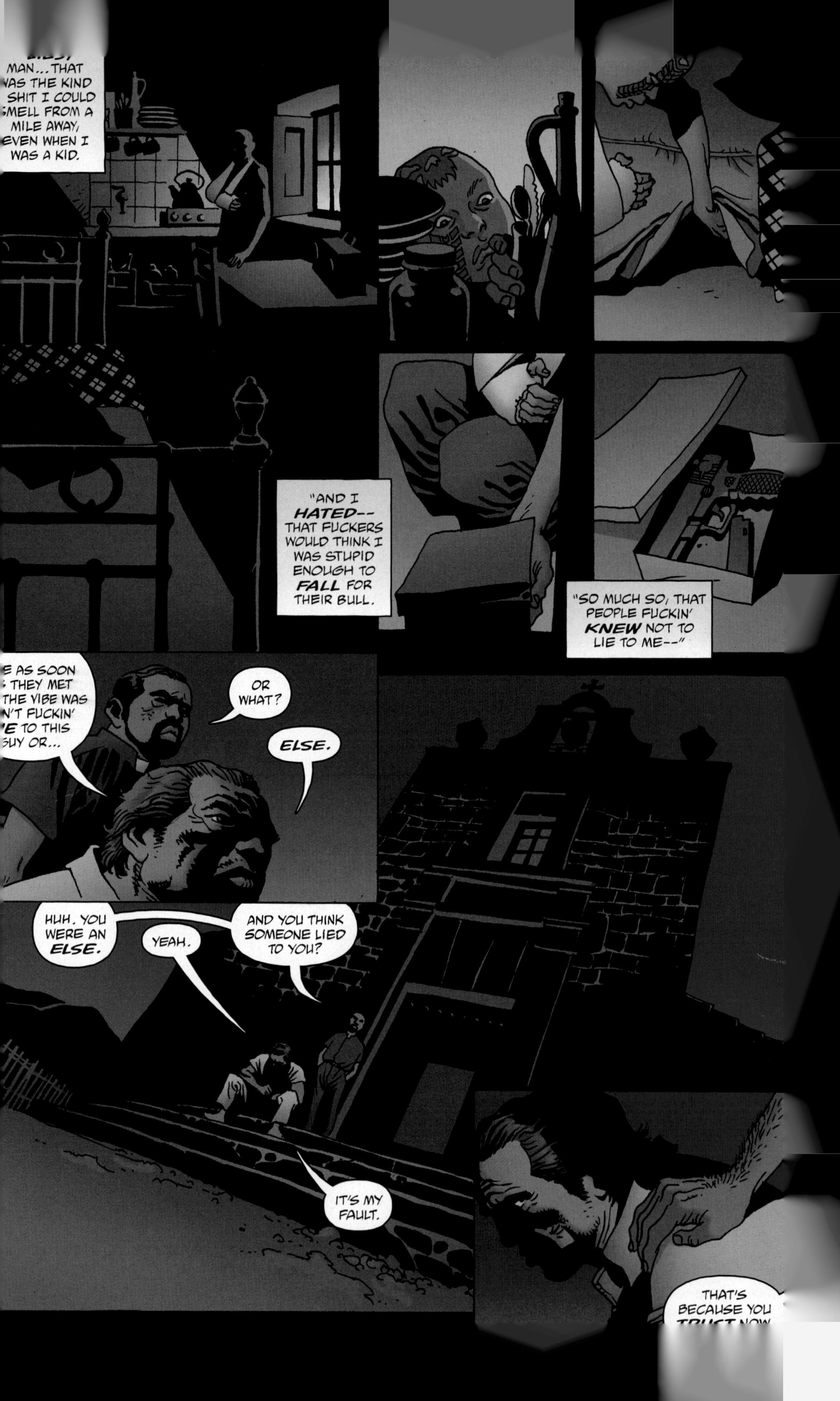

MAN... THAT
WAS THE KIND
SHIT I COULD
SMELL FROM A
MILE AWAY,
EVEN WHEN I
WAS A KID.
"AND I HATED-- THAT FUCKERS WOULD THINK I WAS STUPID ENOUGH TO FALL FOR THEIR BULL.
"SO MUCH SO, THAT PEOPLE FUCKIN' KNEW NOT TO LIE TO ME--"
E AS SOON THEY MET THE VIBE WAS N'T FUCKIN' E TO THIS GUY OR...
OR WHAT?
ELSE.
HUH. YOU WERE AN ELSE.
YEAH.
AND YOU THINK SOMEONE LIED TO YOU?
IT'S MY FAULT.
THAT'S BECAUSE YOU

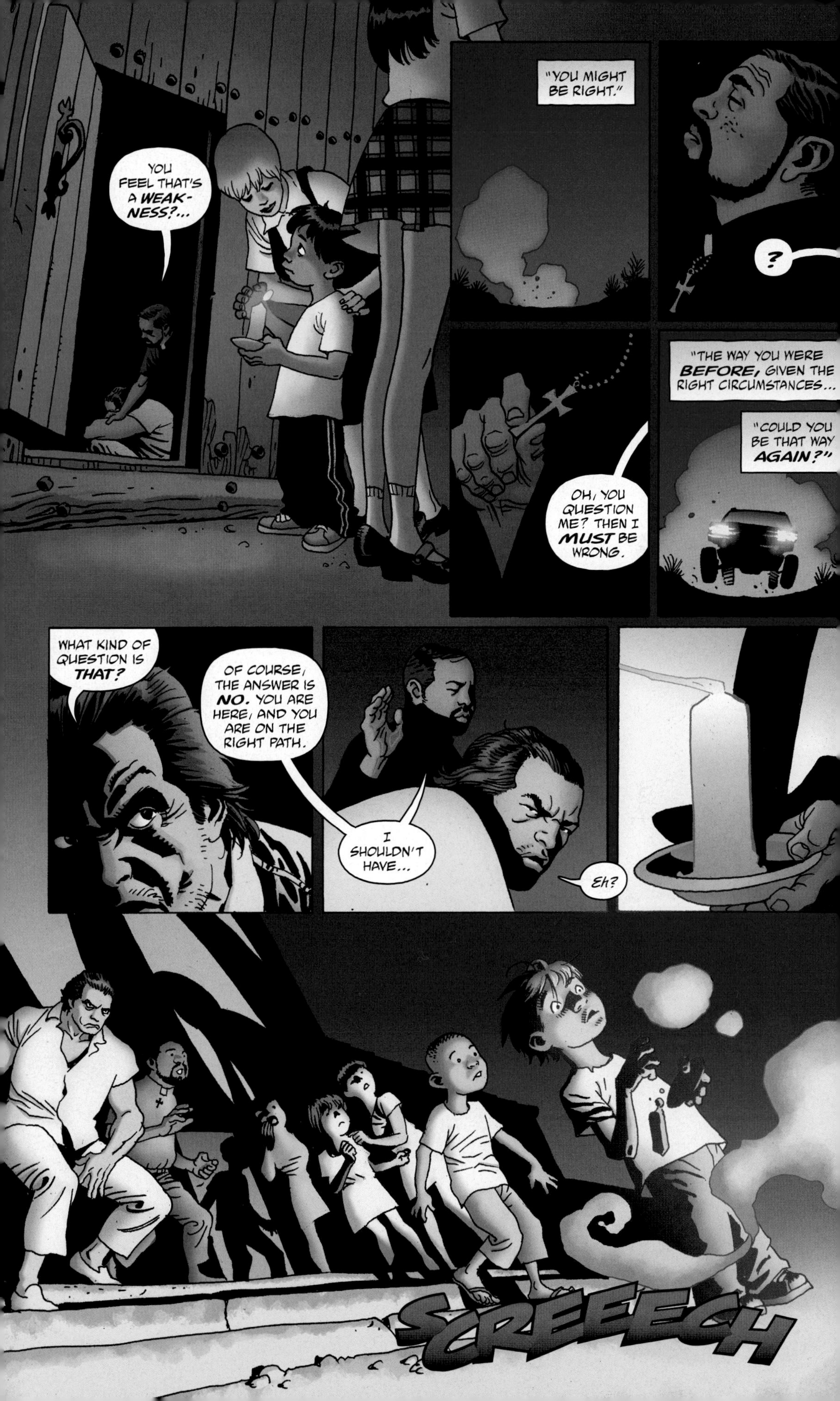

YOU FEEL THAT'S A WEAK-NESS?...
"YOU MIGHT BE RIGHT."
?
"THE WAY YOU WERE BEFORE, GIVEN THE RIGHT CIRCUMSTANCES...
"COULD YOU BE THAT WAY AGAIN?"
OH, YOU QUESTION ME? THEN I MUST BE WRONG.
WHAT KIND OF QUESTION IS THAT?
OF COURSE, THE ANSWER IS NO. YOU ARE HERE, AND YOU ARE ON THE RIGHT PATH.
I SHOULDN'T HAVE...
Eh?
SCREEECH

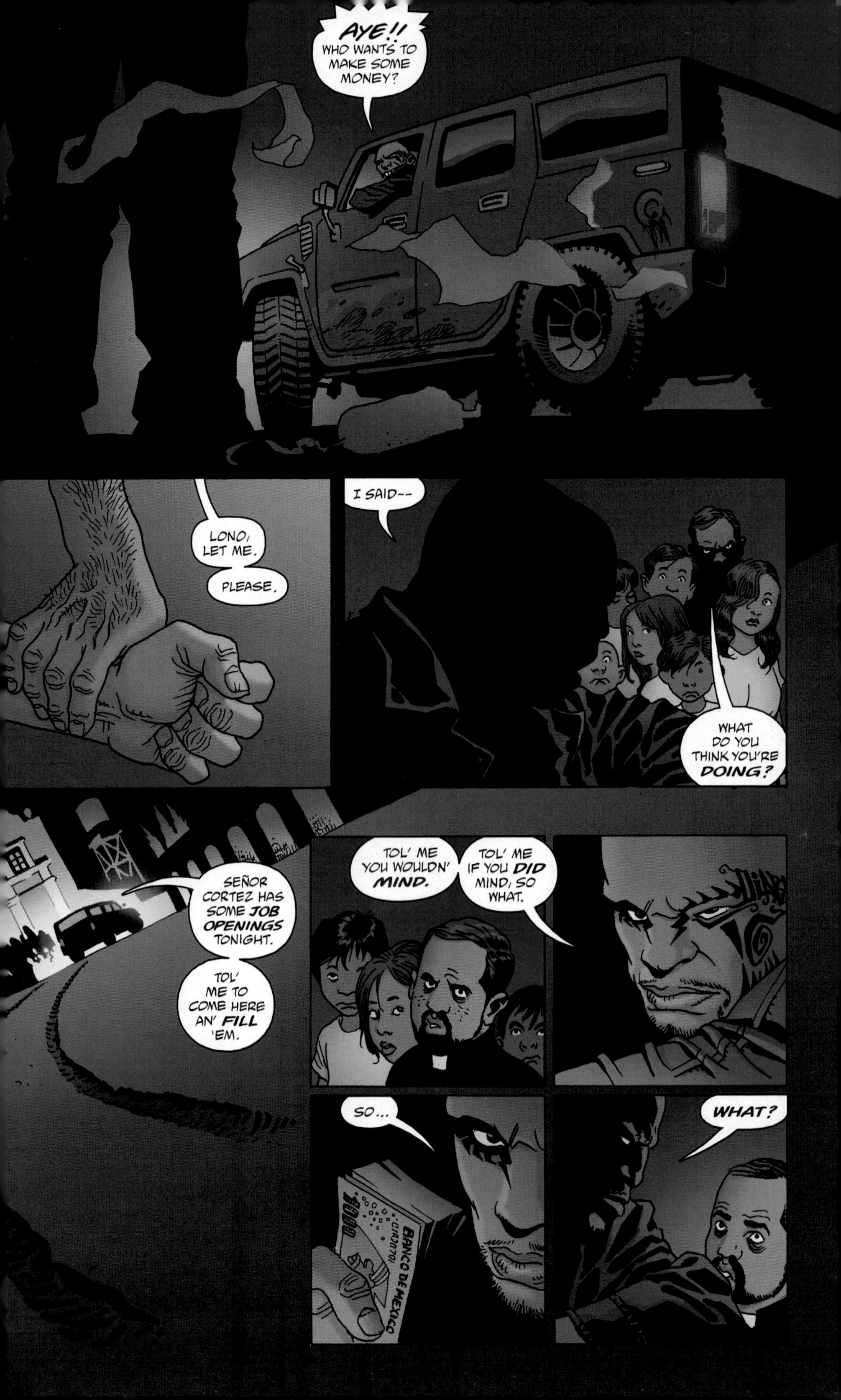
AYE!! WHO WANTS TO MAKE SOME MONEY?
LONO, LET ME.
PLEASE.
I SAID--
WHAT DO YOU THINK YOU'RE DOING?
SEÑOR CORTEZ HAS SOME JOB OPENINGS TONIGHT.
TOL' ME TO COME HERE AN' FILL 'EM.
TOL' ME YOU WOULDN' MIND.
TOL' ME IF YOU DID MIND, SO WHAT.
SO...
WHAT?
BANCO DE MEXICO

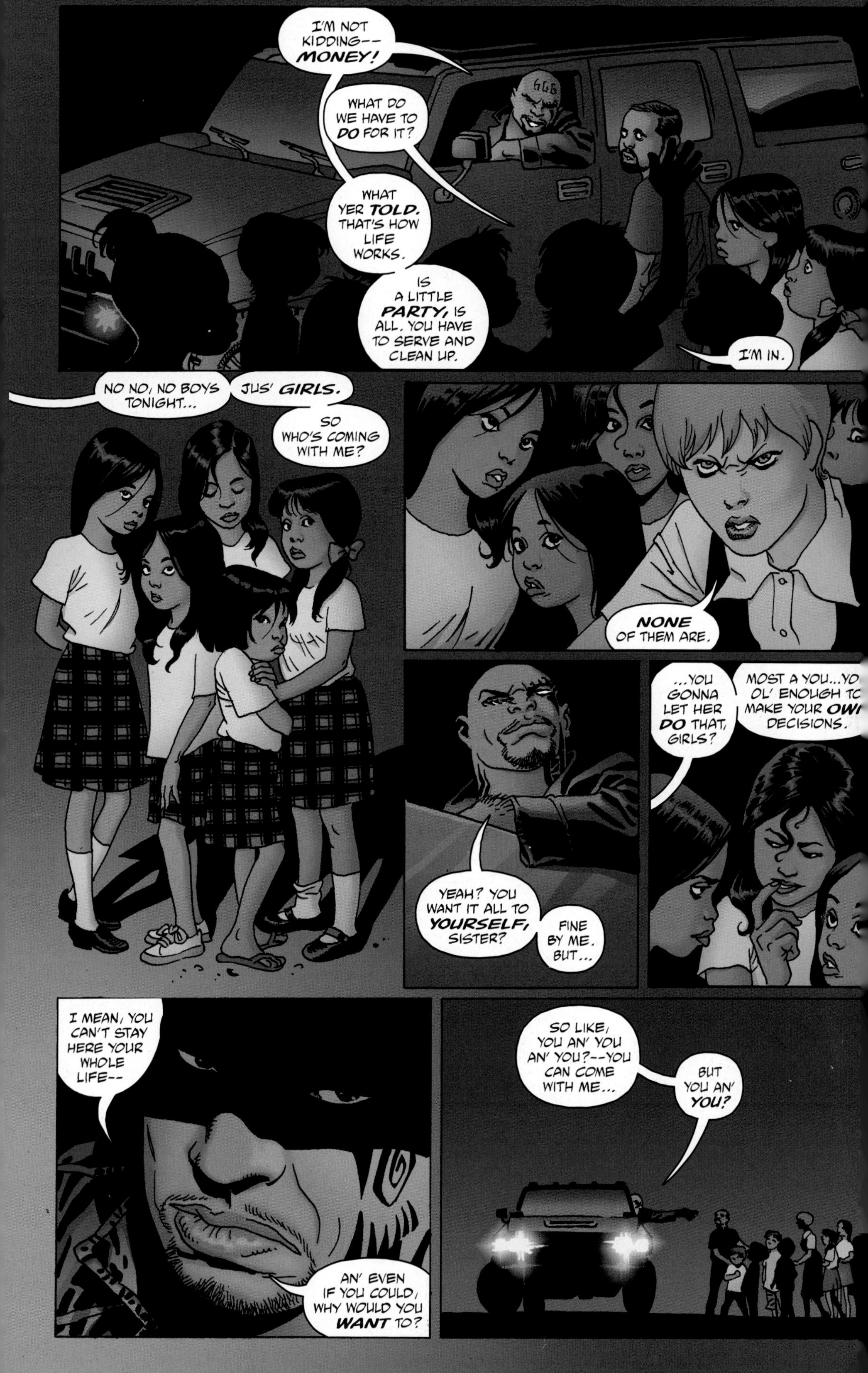
I'M NOT KIDDING-- MONEY!
WHAT DO WE HAVE TO DO FOR IT?
WHAT YER TOLD. THAT'S HOW LIFE WORKS.
IS A LITTLE PARTY, IS ALL. YOU HAVE TO SERVE AND CLEAN UP.
I'M IN.
NO NO, NO BOYS TONIGHT...
JUS' GIRLS.
SO WHO'S COMING WITH ME?
NONE OF THEM ARE.
YEAH? YOU WANT IT ALL TO YOURSELF, SISTER?
FINE BY ME. BUT...
...YOU GONNA LET HER DO THAT, GIRLS?
I MEAN, YOU CAN'T STAY HERE YOUR WHOLE LIFE--
AN' EVEN IF YOU COULD, WHY WOULD YOU WANT TO?
SO LIKE, YOU AN' YOU AN' YOU?--YOU CAN COME WITH ME...
BUT YOU AN' YOU?

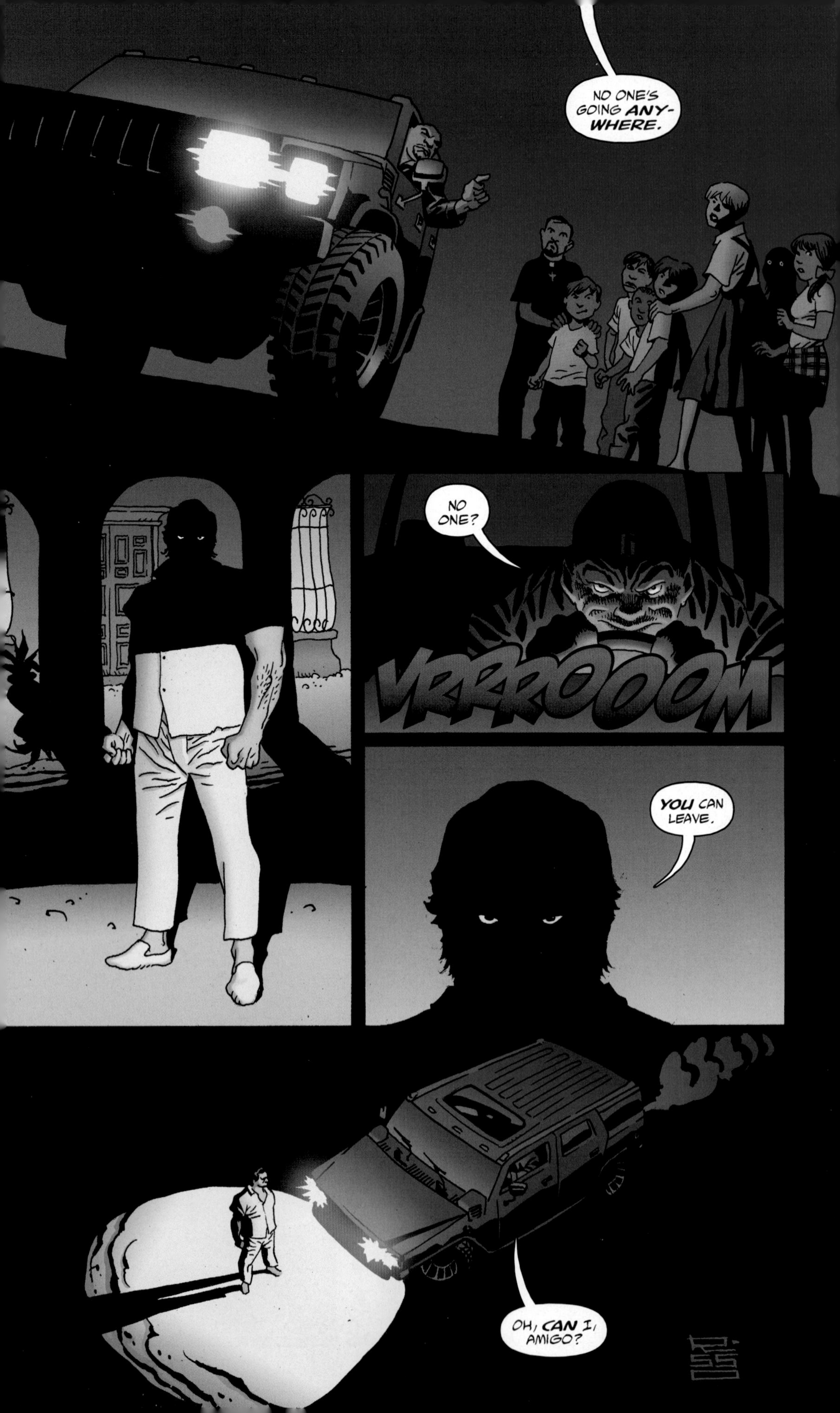
NO ONE'S GOING ANY-WHERE.
NO ONE?
VRRROOOM
YOU CAN LEAVE.
OH, CAN I, AMIGO?

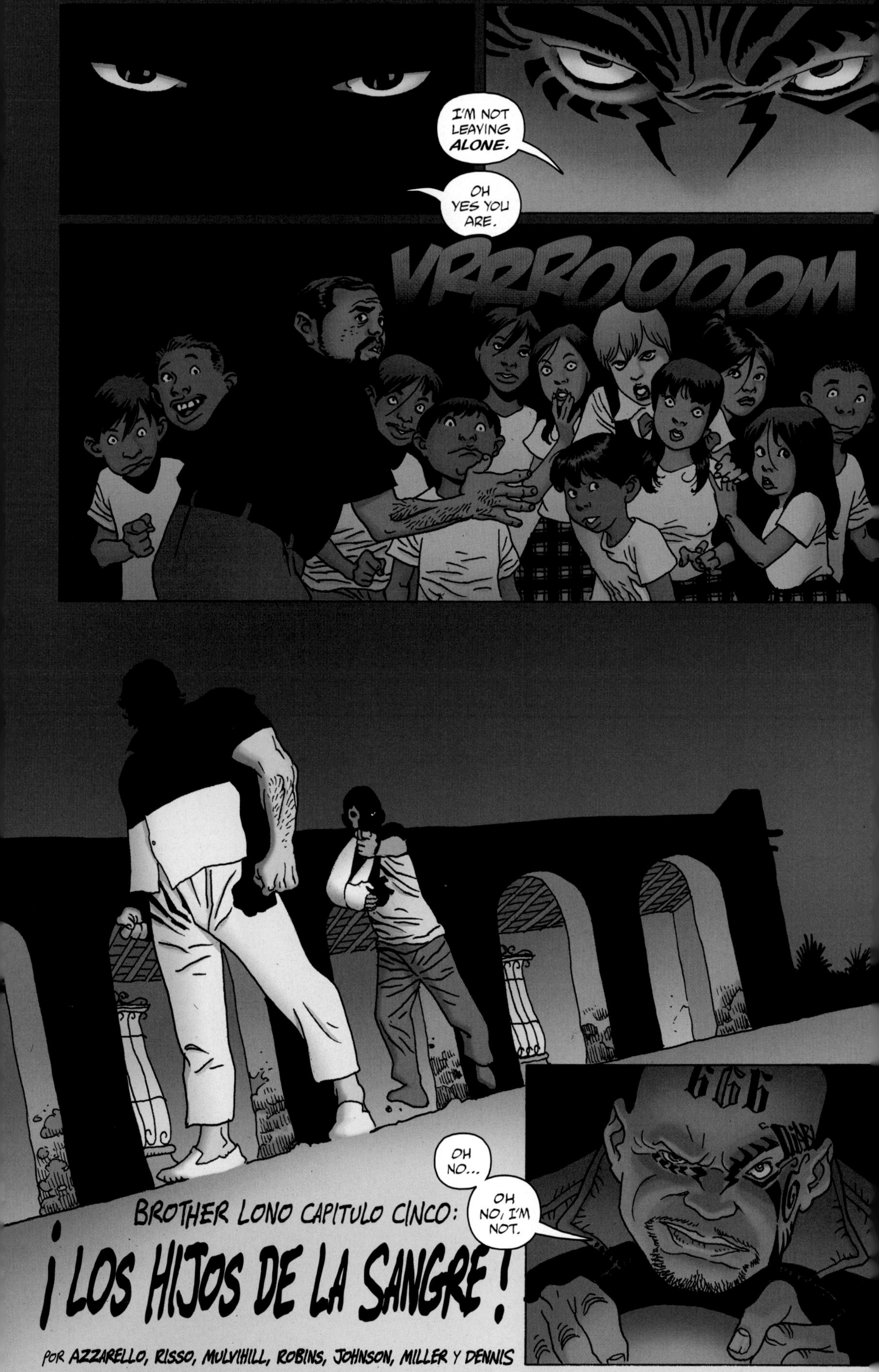
I'M NOT LEAVING ALONE.
OH YES YOU ARE.
VRRROOOOOM
OH NO...
OH NO, I'M NOT.
666
BROTHER LONO CAPITULO CINCO:
¡LOS HIJOS DE LA SANGRE!
POR AZZARELLO, RISSO, MULVIHILL, ROBINS, JOHNSON, MILLER Y DENNIS

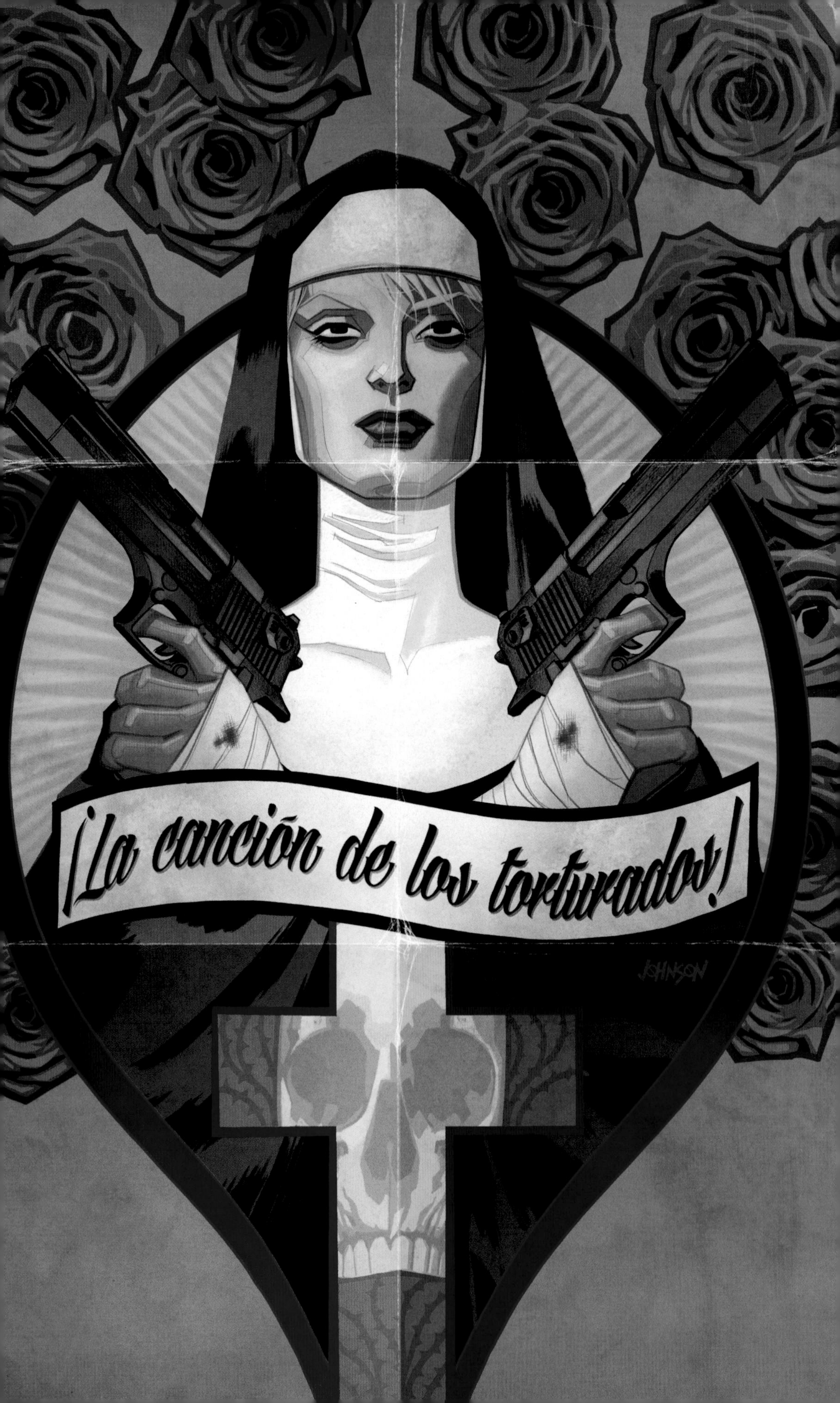
¡La canción de los torturados!
JOHNSON

"A truth, once spoken, is understood 'til death."

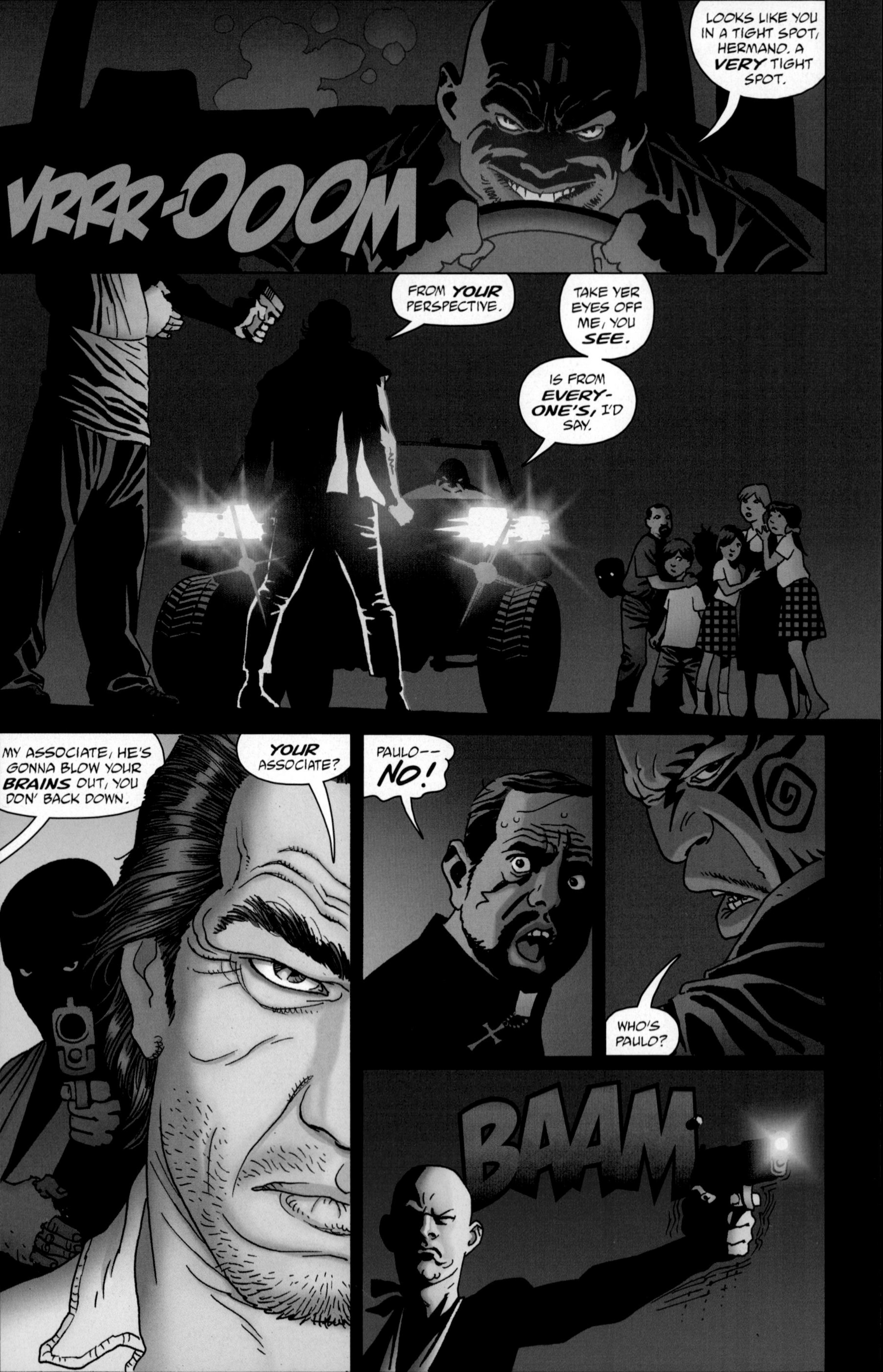
LOOKS LIKE YOU IN A TIGHT SPOT, HERMANO. A VERY TIGHT SPOT.
VRRR-OOOM
FROM YOUR PERSPECTIVE.
TAKE YER EYES OFF ME, YOU SEE.
IS FROM EVERY-ONE'S, I'D SAY.
MY ASSOCIATE, HE'S GONNA BLOW YOUR BRAINS OUT, YOU DON' BACK DOWN.
YOUR ASSOCIATE?
PAULO-- NO!
WHO'S PAULO?
BAAM

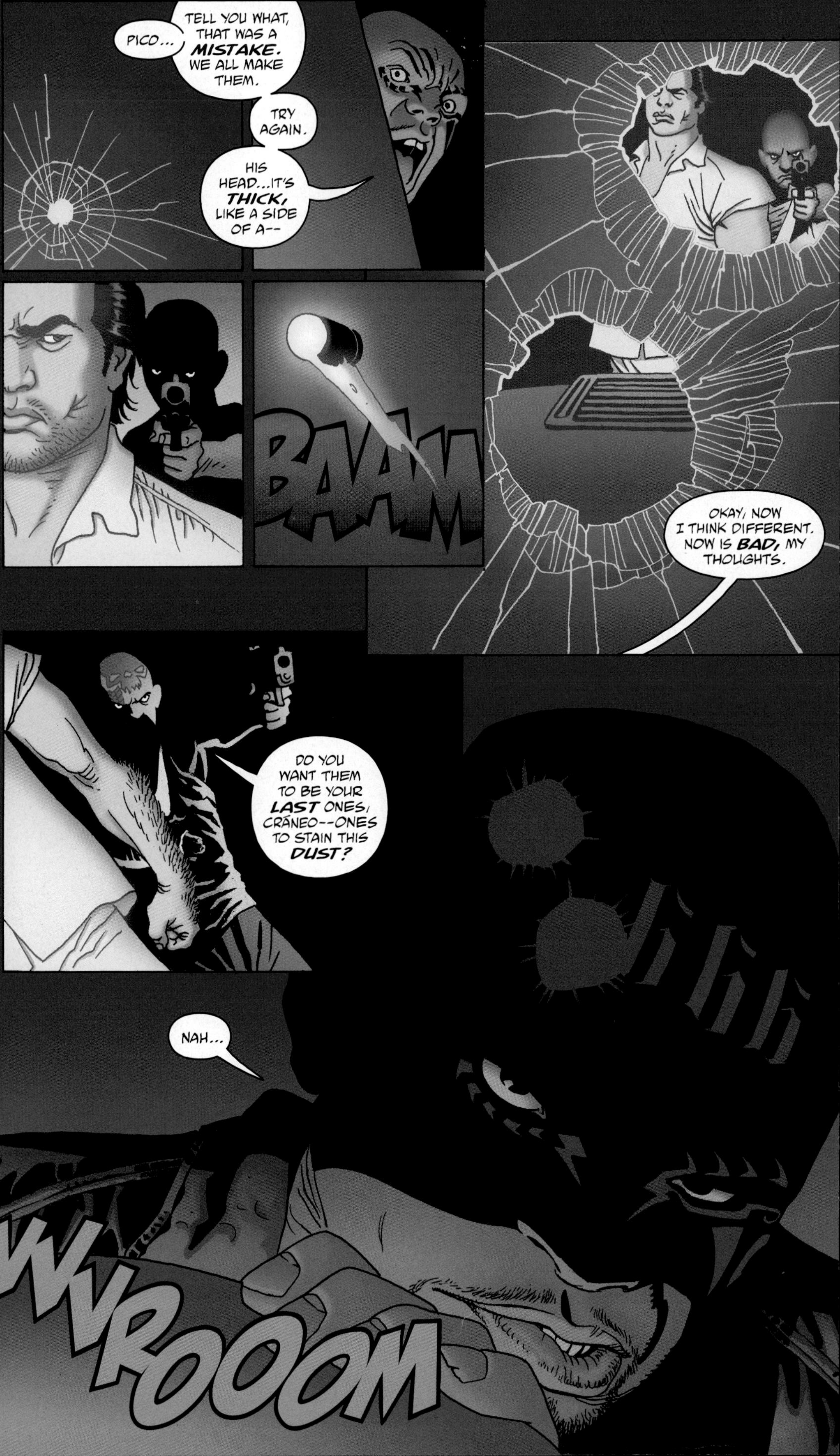
PICO...
TELL YOU WHAT, THAT WAS A MISTAKE. WE ALL MAKE THEM.
TRY AGAIN.
HIS HEAD...IT'S THICK, LIKE A SIDE OF A--
BAAM
OKAY, NOW I THINK DIFFERENT. NOW IS BAD, MY THOUGHTS.
DO YOU WANT THEM TO BE YOUR LAST ONES, CRÁNEO--ONES TO STAIN THIS DUST?
NAH...
WWROOOM

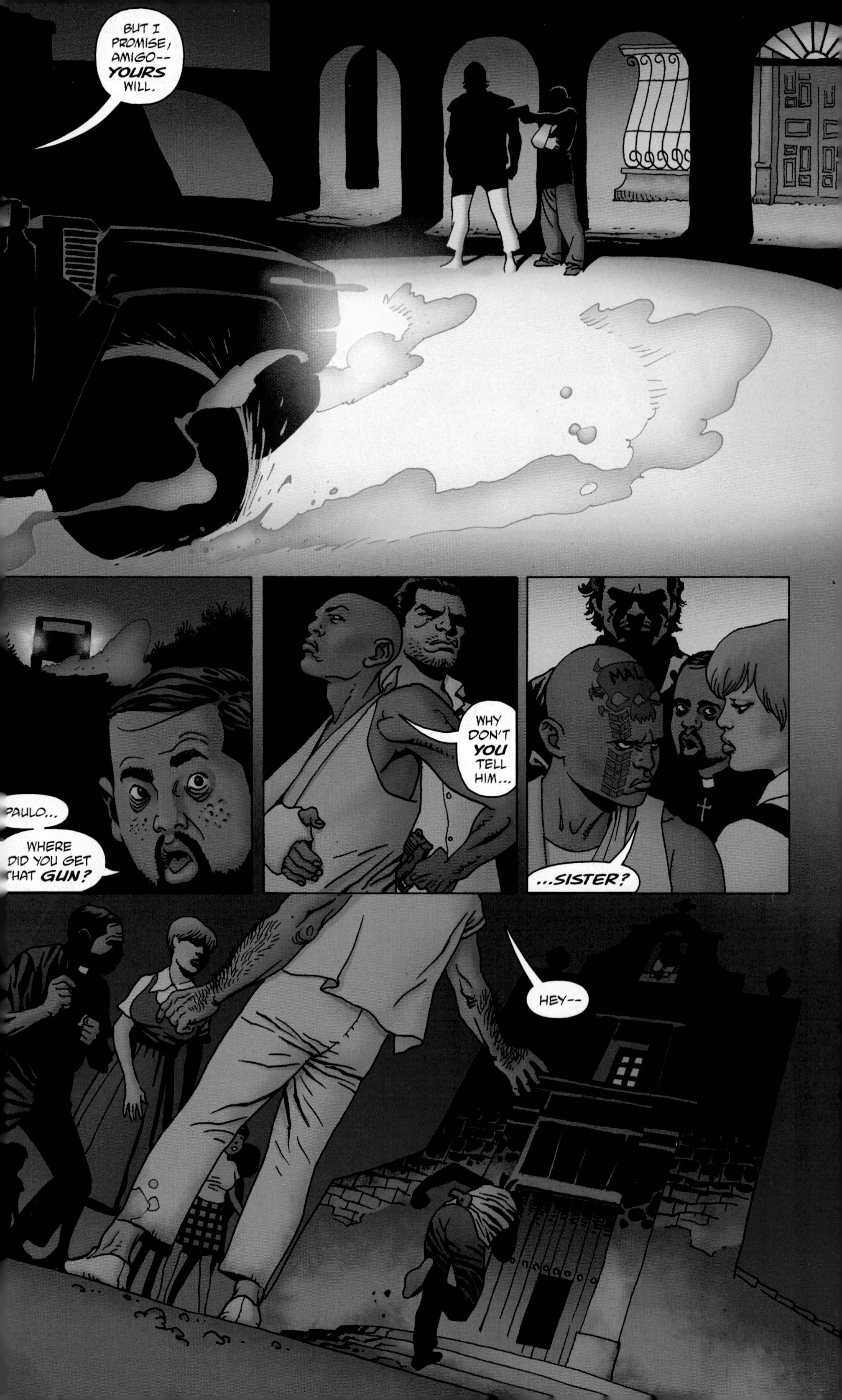
BUT I PROMISE, AMIGO-- YOURS WILL.
PAULO...
WHERE DID YOU GET THAT GUN?
WHY DON'T YOU TELL HIM...
...SISTER?
HEY--

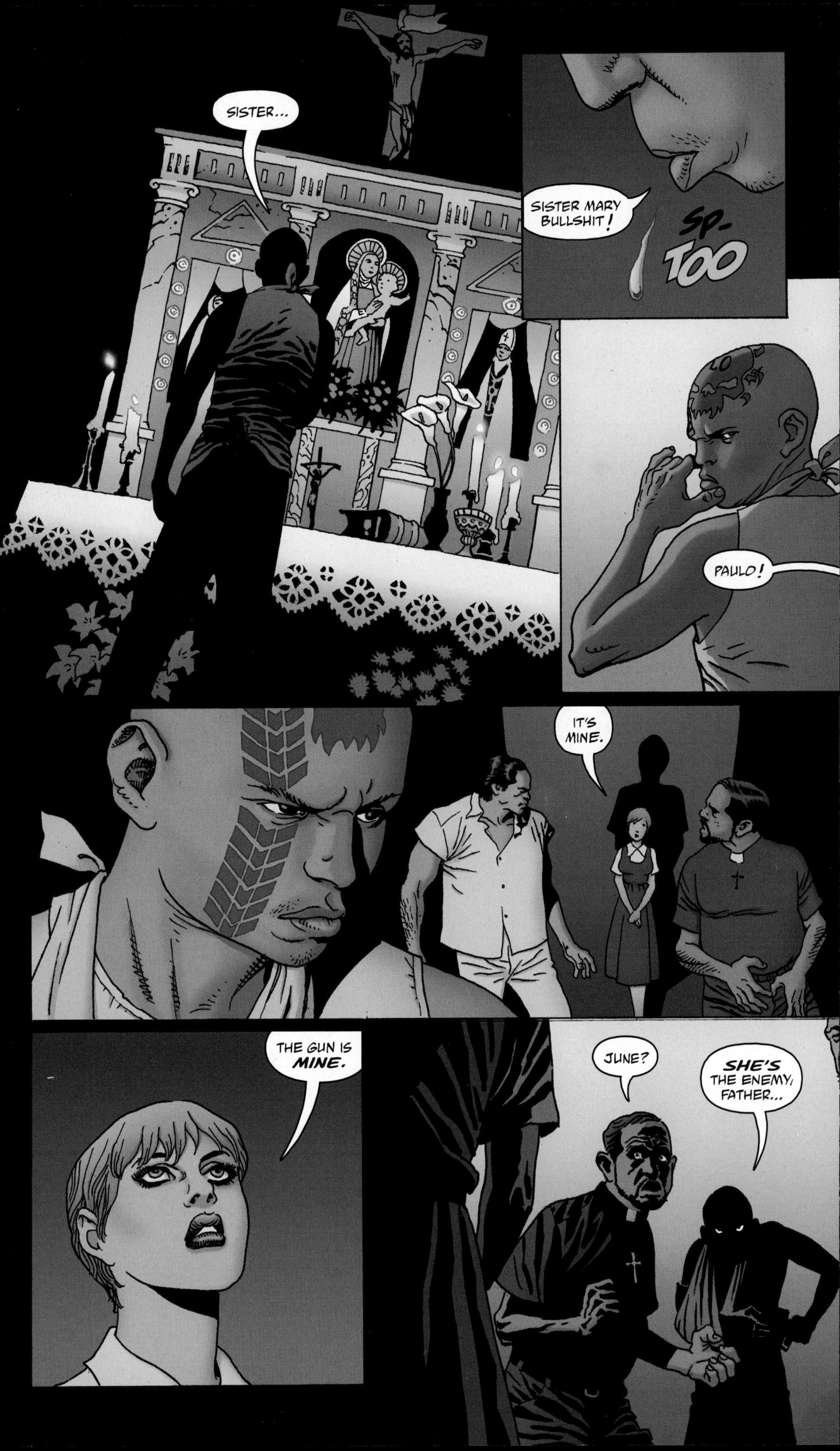
SISTER...
SISTER MARY BULLSHIT!
SP-TOO
PAULO!
IT'S MINE.
THE GUN IS MINE.
JUNE?
SHE'S THE ENEMY, FATHER...

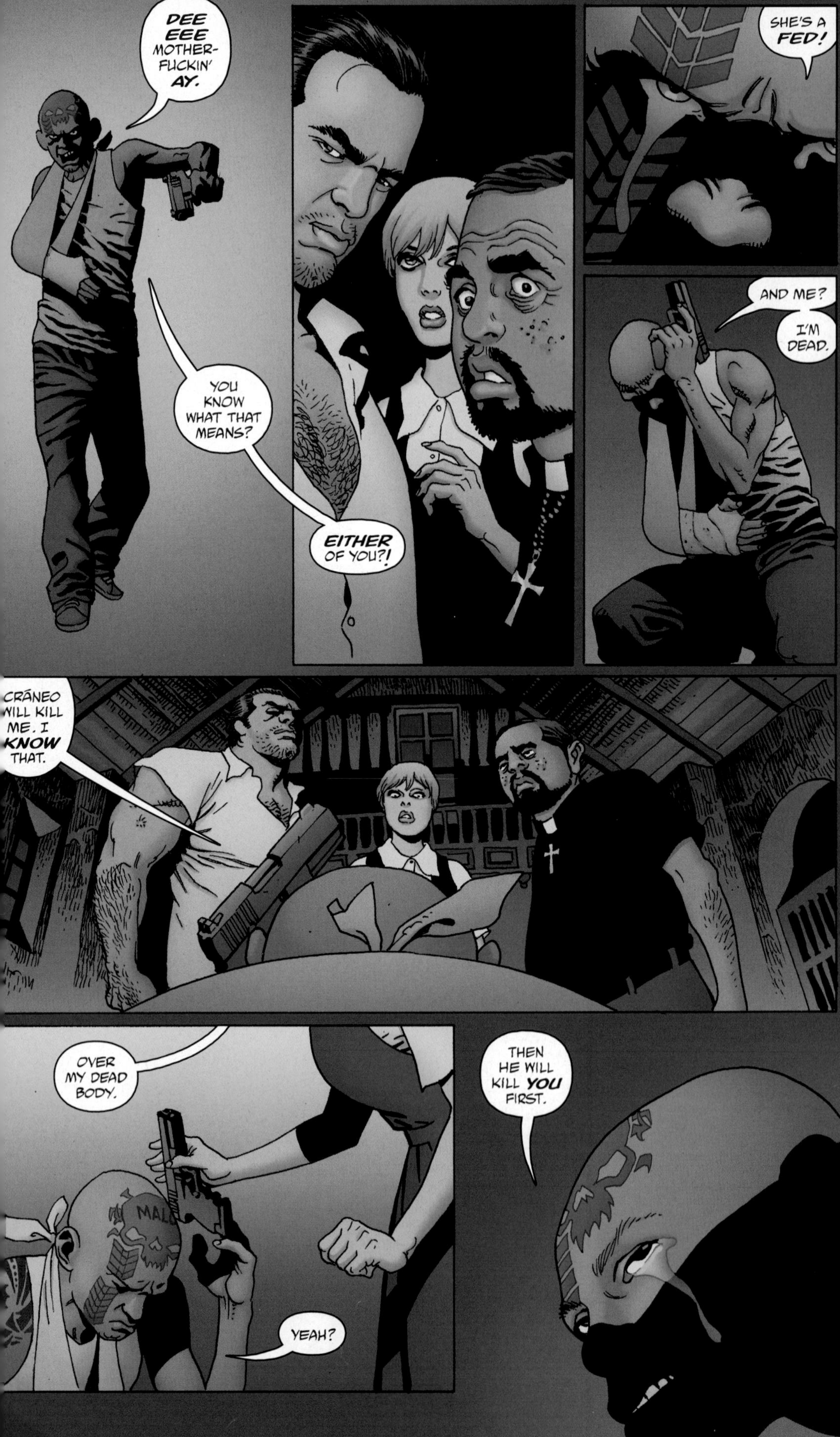
DEE EEE MOTHER-FUCKIN' AY.
YOU KNOW WHAT THAT MEANS?
EITHER OF YOU?!
SHE'S A FED!
AND ME?
I'M DEAD.
CRÁNEO WILL KILL ME. I KNOW THAT.
OVER MY DEAD BODY.
YEAH?
THEN HE WILL KILL YOU FIRST.

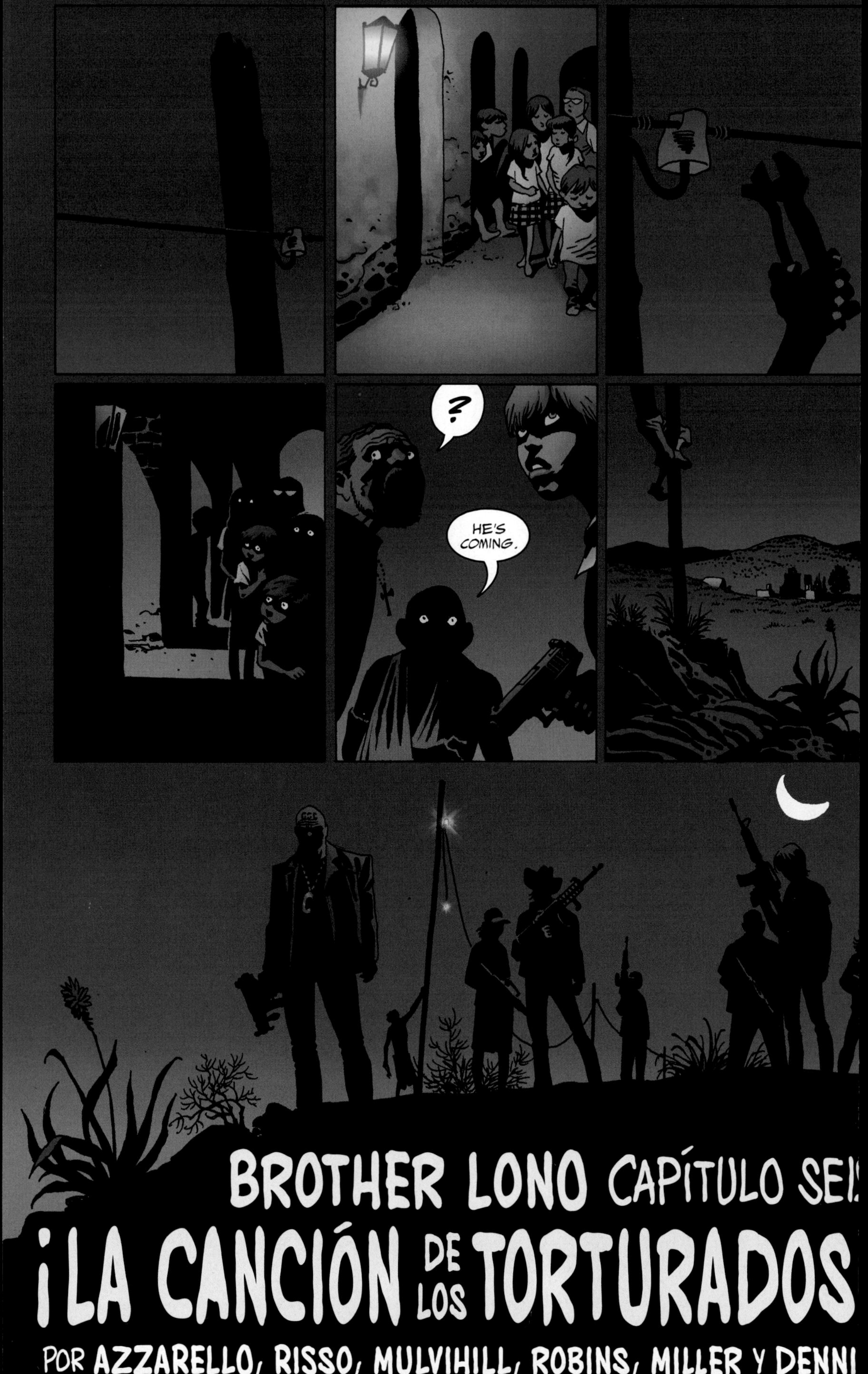
?
HE'S COMING.
BROTHER LONO CAPÍTULO SEI
¡LA CANCIÓN DE LOS TORTURADOS
POR AZZARELLO, RISSO, MULVIHILL, ROBINS, MILLER Y DENNI

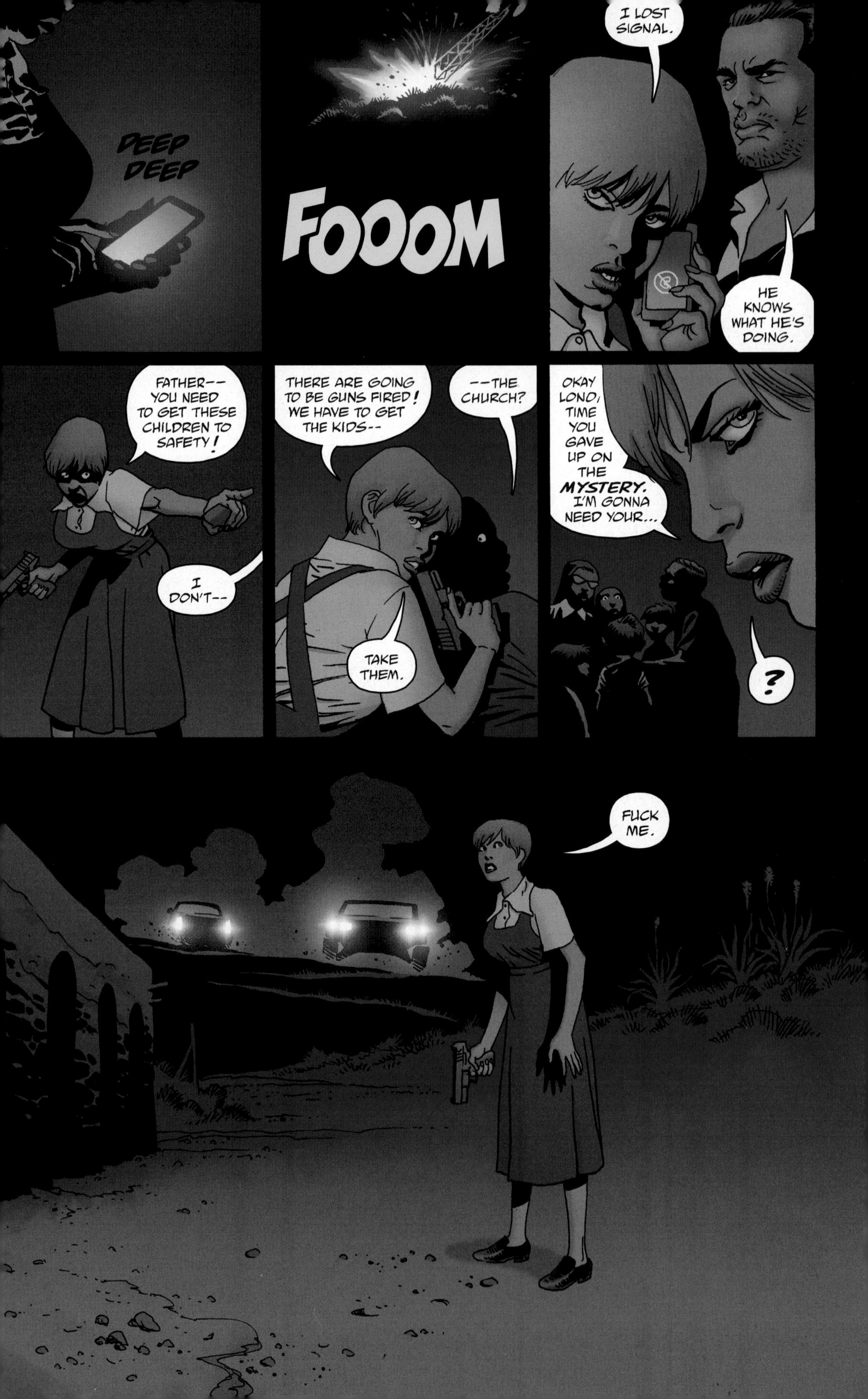
DEEP DEEP
FOOOM
I LOST SIGNAL.
HE KNOWS WHAT HE'S DOING.
FATHER-- YOU NEED TO GET THESE CHILDREN TO SAFETY!
I DON'T--
THERE ARE GOING TO BE GUNS FIRED! WE HAVE TO GET THE KIDS--
--THE CHURCH?
TAKE THEM.
OKAY LONO, TIME YOU GAVE UP ON THE MYSTERY. I'M GONNA NEED YOUR...
?
FUCK ME.

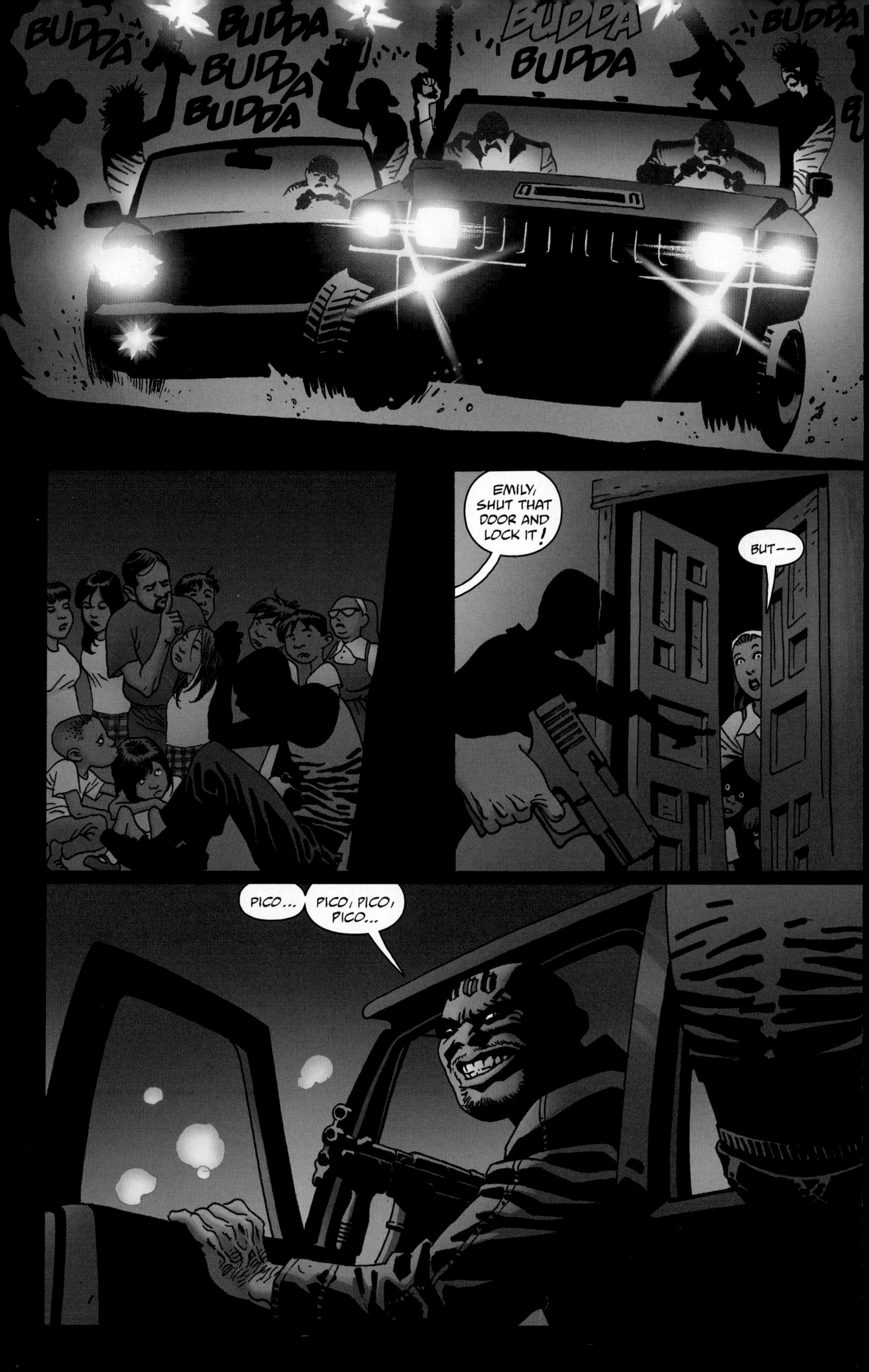
BUDDA
BUDDA BUDDA BUDDA
BUDDA BUDDA
BUDDA
EMILY, SHUT THAT DOOR AND LOCK IT!
BUT--
PICO...
PICO, PICO, PICO...

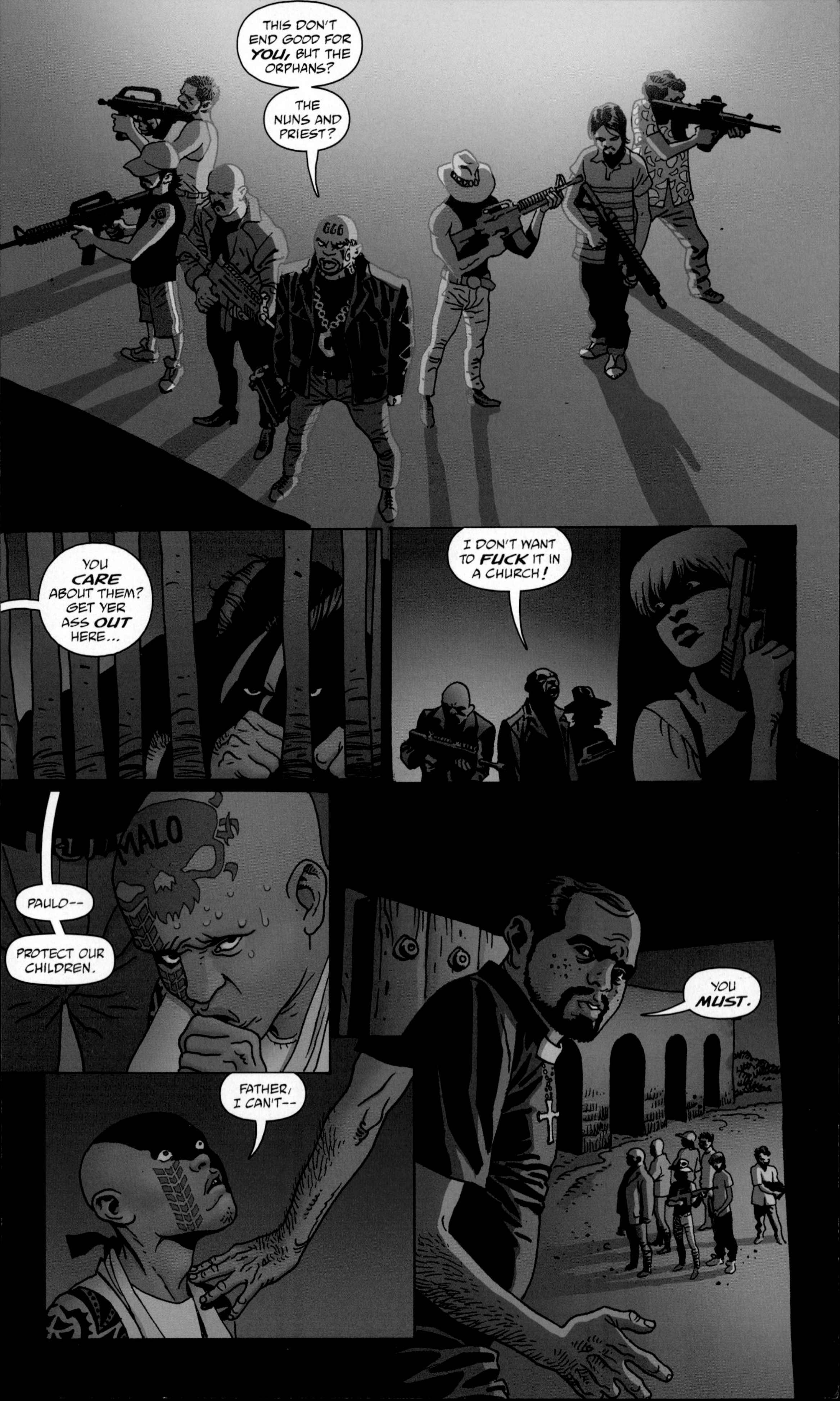
THIS DON'T END GOOD FOR YOU, BUT THE ORPHANS?
THE NUNS AND PRIEST?
YOU CARE ABOUT THEM? GET YER ASS OUT HERE...
I DON'T WANT TO FUCK IT IN A CHURCH!
MALO
PAULO--
PROTECT OUR CHILDREN.
YOU MUST.
FATHER, I CAN'T--

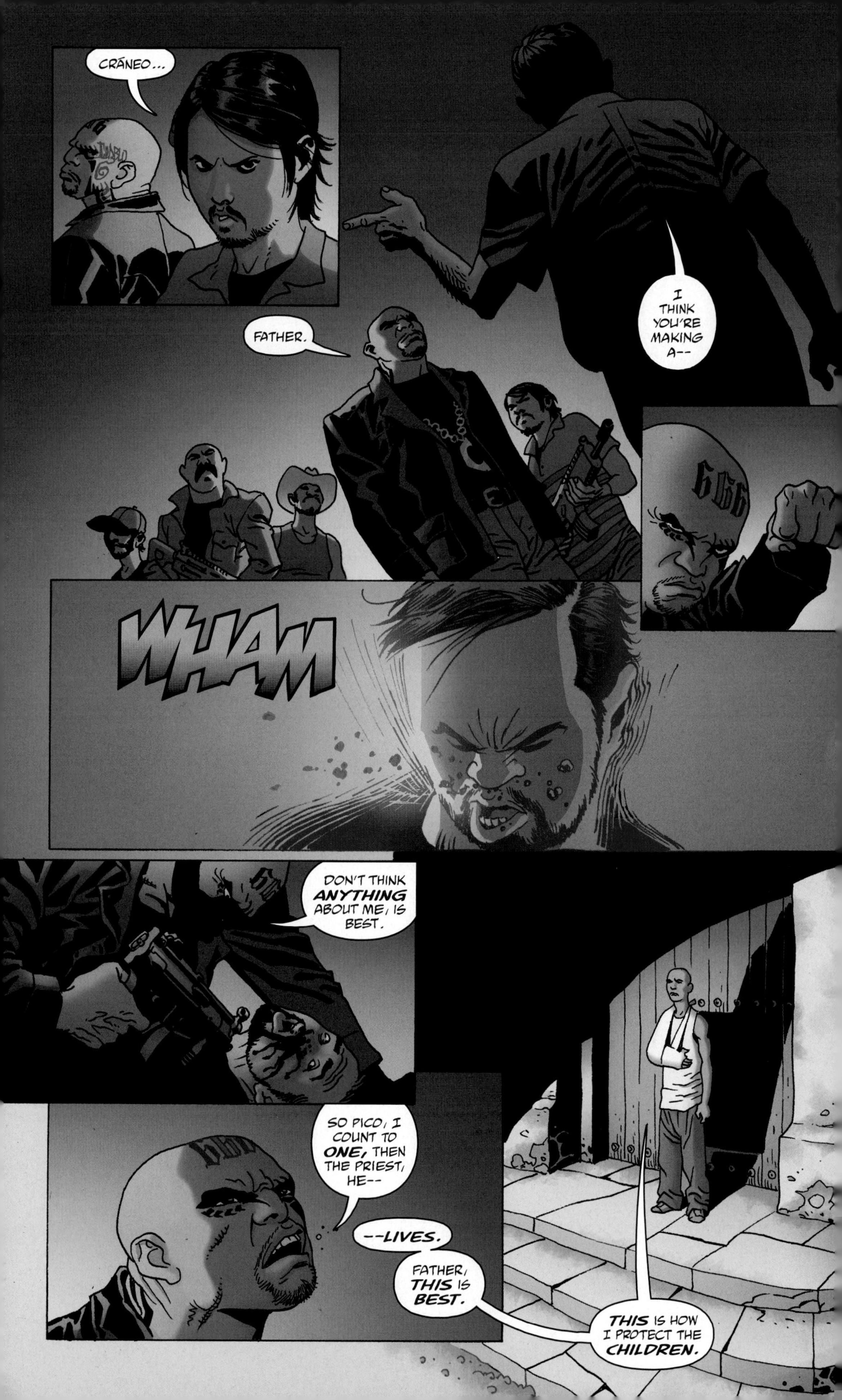
CRÁNEO...
I THINK YOU'RE MAKING A--
FATHER.
WHAM
DON'T THINK ANYTHING ABOUT ME, IS BEST.
SO PICO, I COUNT TO ONE, THEN THE PRIEST, HE--
--LIVES.
FATHER, THIS IS BEST.
THIS IS HOW I PROTECT THE CHILDREN.

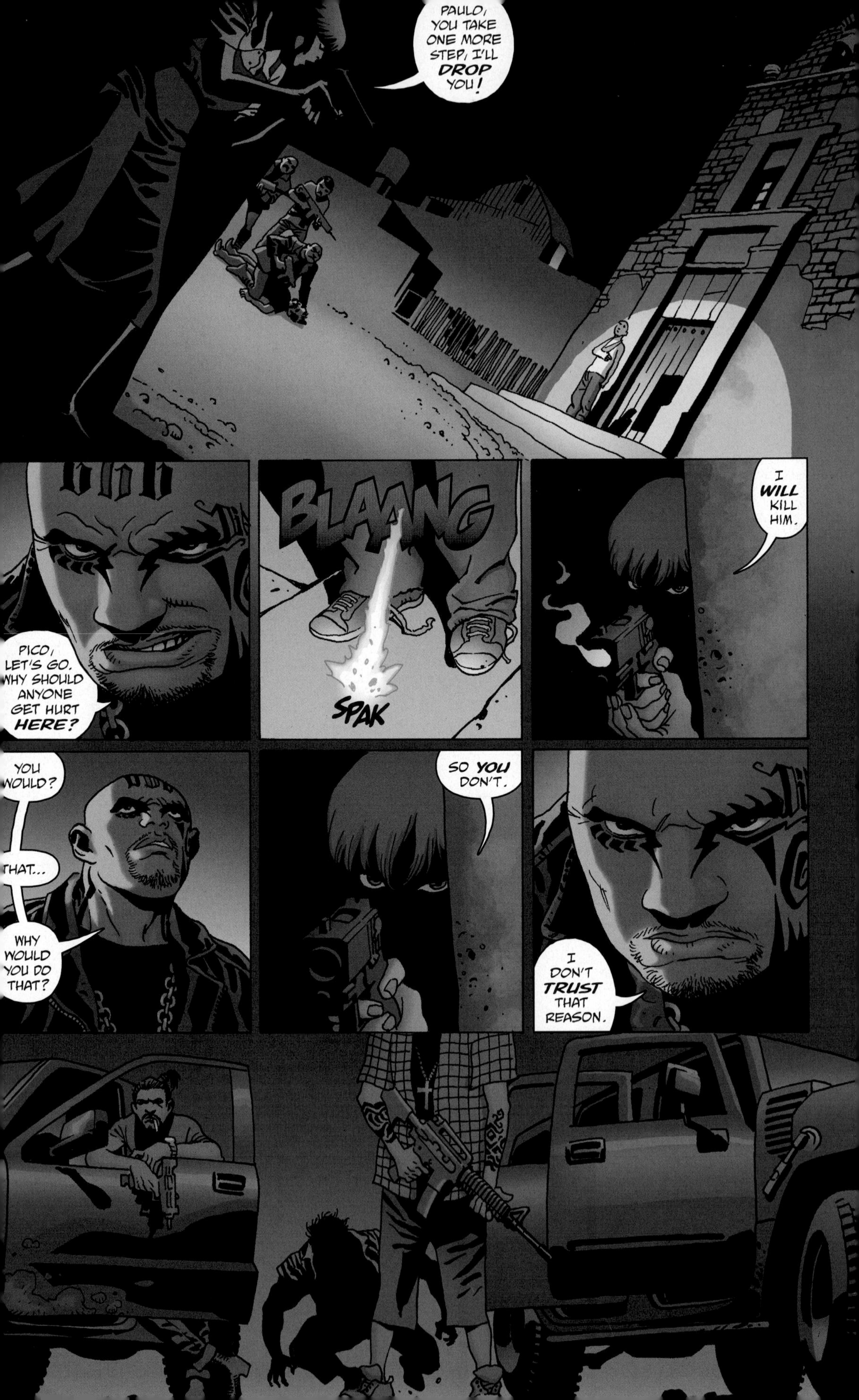
PAULO, YOU TAKE ONE MORE STEP, I'LL **DROP** YOU!
BLAANG
SPAK
I **WILL** KILL HIM.
PICO, LET'S GO. WHY SHOULD ANYONE GET HURT **HERE?**
YOU WOULD?
THAT...
WHY WOULD YOU DO THAT?
SO **YOU** DON'T.
I DON'T **TRUST** THAT REASON.

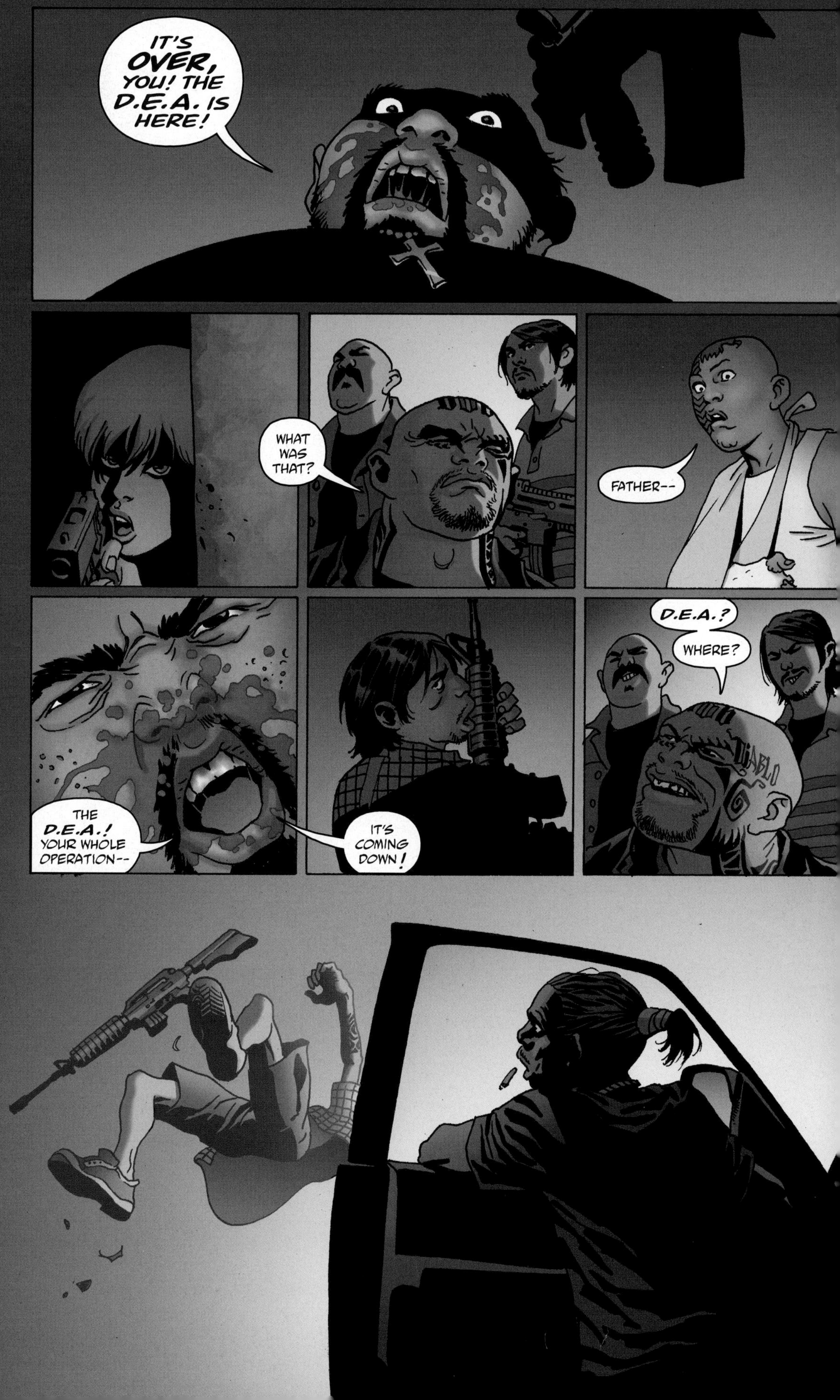
IT'S OVER, YOU! THE D.E.A. IS HERE!
WHAT WAS THAT?
FATHER--
THE D.E.A.! YOUR WHOLE OPERATION--
IT'S COMING DOWN!
D.E.A.?
WHERE?
DIABLO

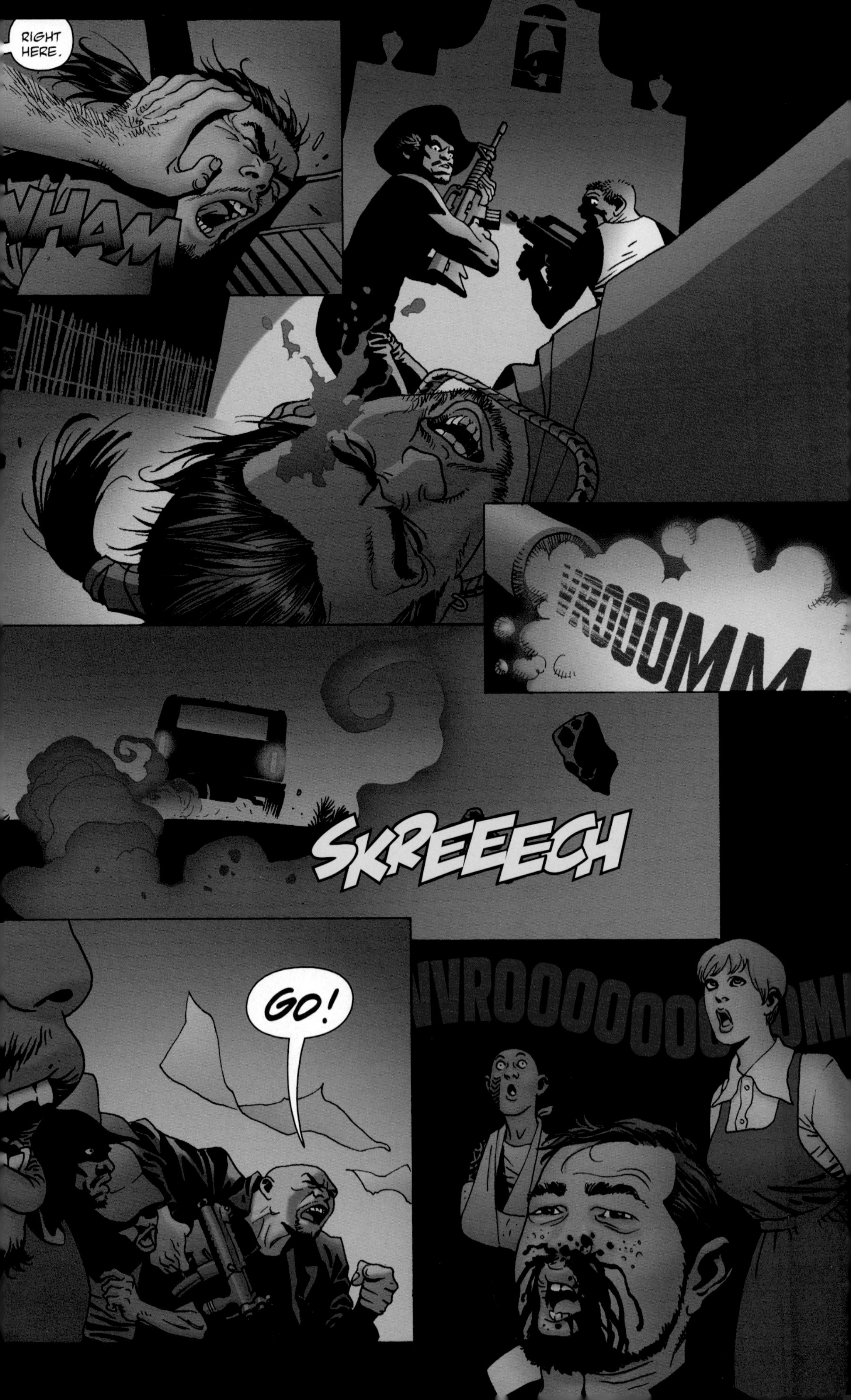
RIGHT HERE.
WHAM
VROOOMM
SKREEECH
GO!
VVROOOOOOOOOM

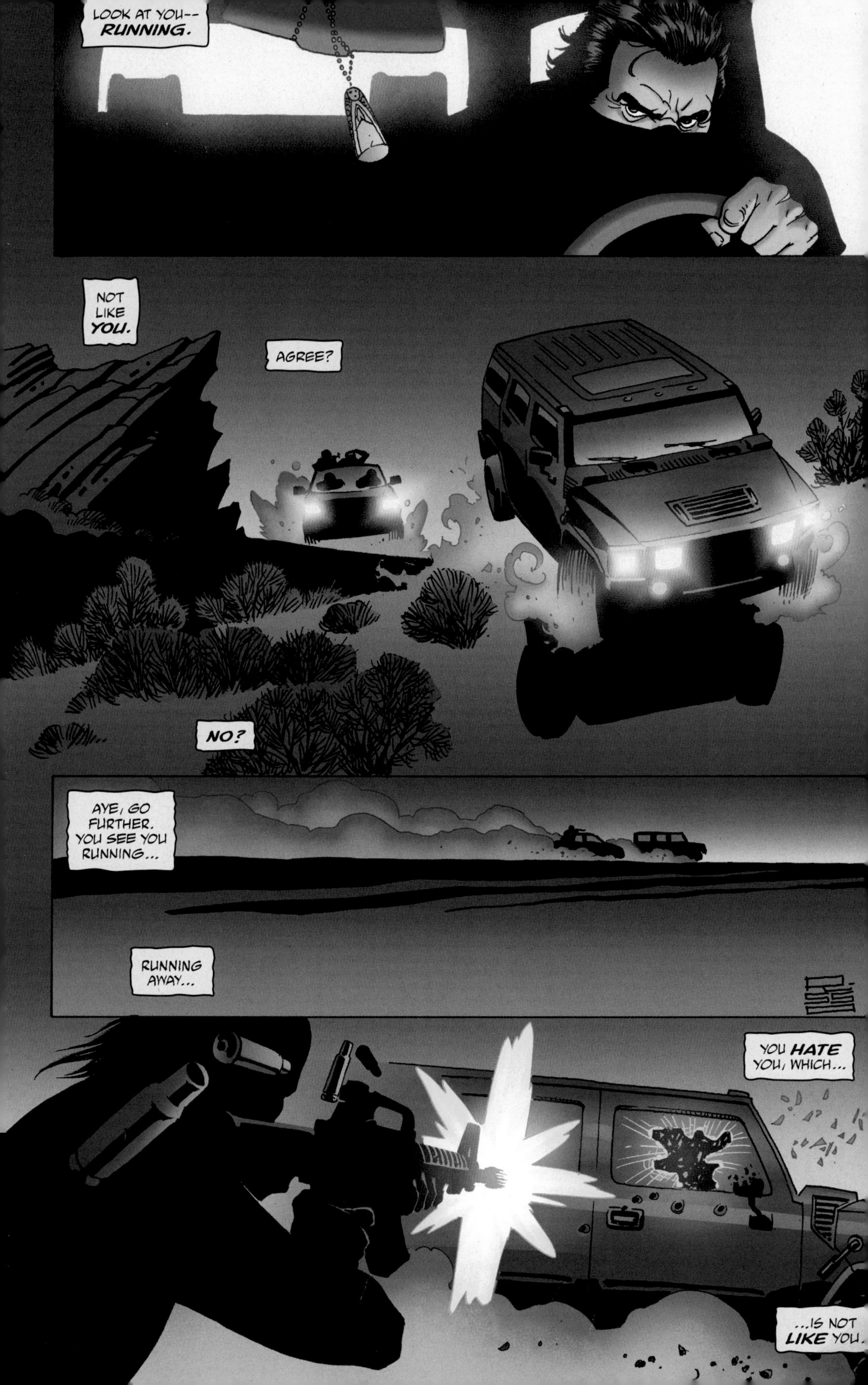
LOOK AT YOU--
RUNNING.
NOT LIKE YOU.
AGREE?
NO?
AYE, GO FURTHER. YOU SEE YOU RUNNING...
RUNNING AWAY...
YOU HATE YOU, WHICH...
...IS NOT LIKE YOU.

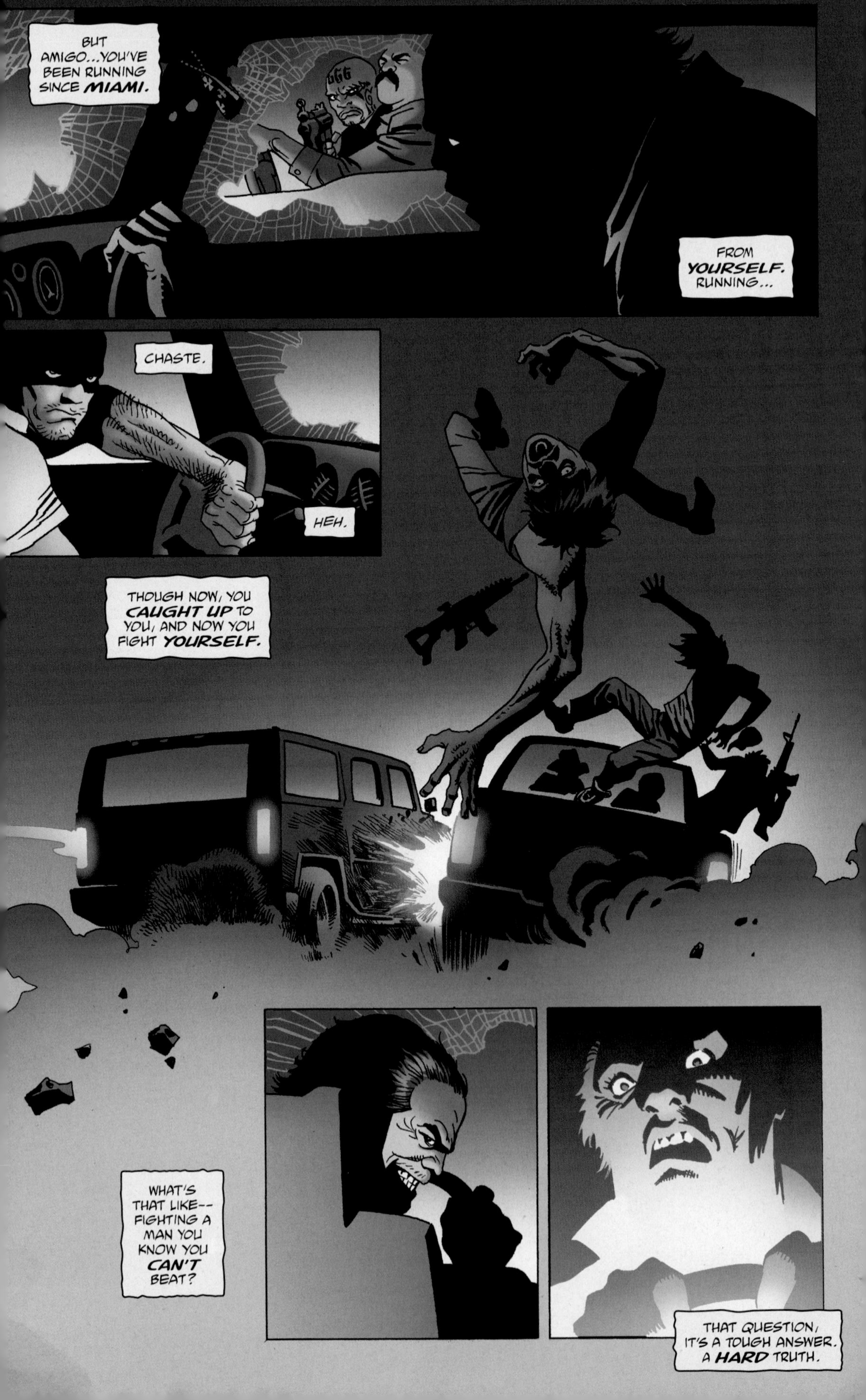
BUT AMIGO...YOU'VE BEEN RUNNING SINCE **MIAMI.**
FROM **YOURSELF.** RUNNING...
CHASTE.
HEH.
THOUGH NOW, YOU **CAUGHT UP** TO YOU, AND NOW YOU FIGHT **YOURSELF.**
WHAT'S THAT LIKE-- FIGHTING A MAN YOU KNOW YOU **CAN'T** BEAT?
THAT QUESTION, IT'S A TOUGH ANSWER. A **HARD** TRUTH.

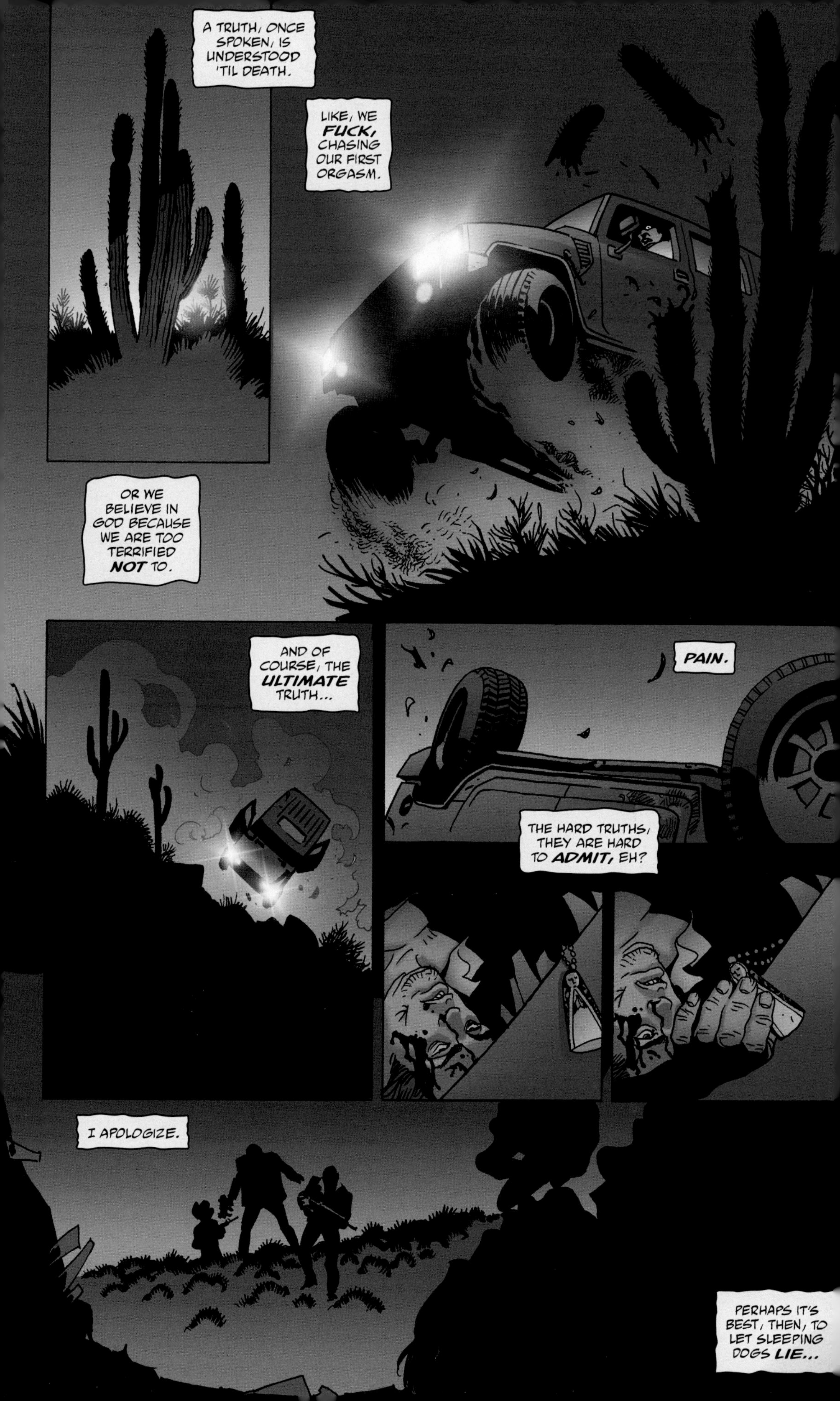
A TRUTH, ONCE SPOKEN, IS UNDERSTOOD 'TIL DEATH.
LIKE, WE **FUCK,** CHASING OUR FIRST ORGASM.
OR WE BELIEVE IN GOD BECAUSE WE ARE TOO TERRIFIED **NOT** TO.
AND OF COURSE, THE ***ULTIMATE*** TRUTH...
PAIN.
THE HARD TRUTHS, THEY ARE HARD TO ***ADMIT,*** EH?
I APOLOGIZE.
PERHAPS IT'S BEST, THEN, TO LET SLEEPING DOGS **LIE...**

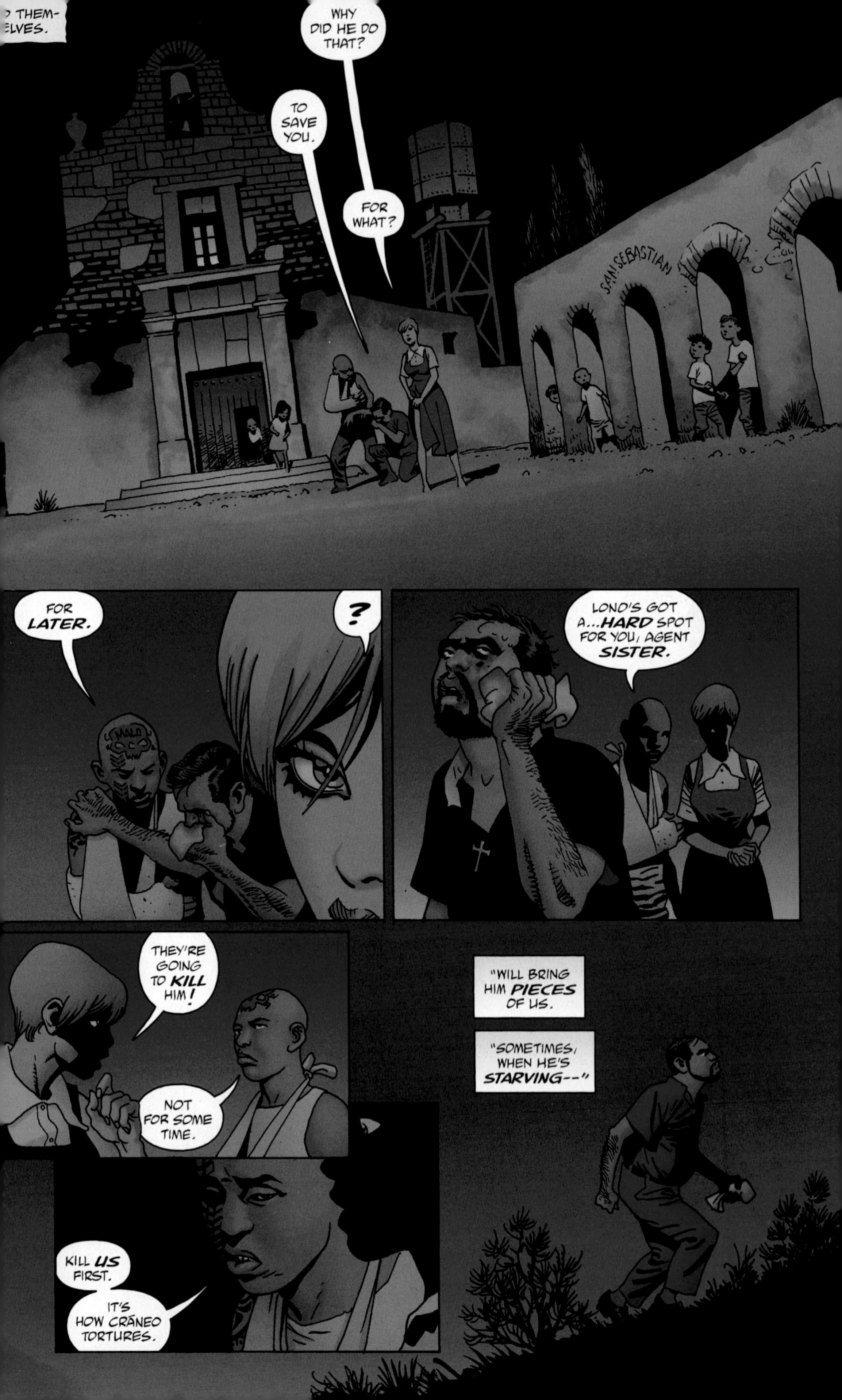

...THEM-
...ELVES.
WHY DID HE DO THAT?
TO SAVE YOU.
FOR WHAT?
SAN SEBASTIAN
FOR LATER.
?
LONO'S GOT A...HARD SPOT FOR YOU, AGENT SISTER.
THEY'RE GOING TO KILL HIM!
NOT FOR SOME TIME.
KILL US FIRST.
IT'S HOW CRÁNEO TORTURES.
"WILL BRING HIM PIECES OF US.
"SOMETIMES, WHEN HE'S STARVING--"

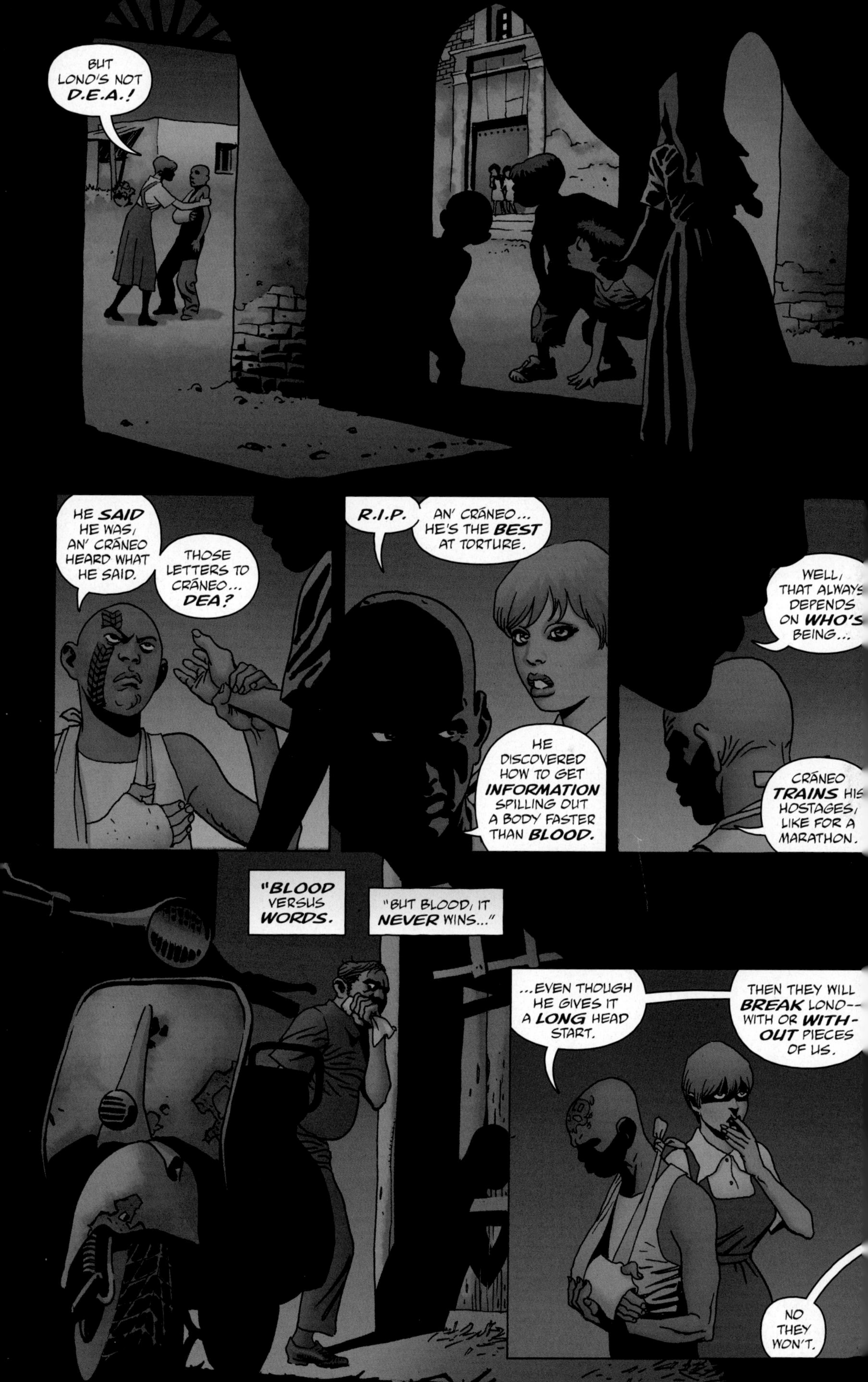
BUT LONO'S NOT D.E.A.!
HE SAID HE WAS, AN' CRÁNEO HEARD WHAT HE SAID.
THOSE LETTERS TO CRÁNEO... DEA?
R.I.P.
AN' CRÁNEO... HE'S THE BEST AT TORTURE.
HE DISCOVERED HOW TO GET INFORMATION SPILLING OUT A BODY FASTER THAN BLOOD.
WELL, THAT ALWAYS DEPENDS ON WHO'S BEING...
CRÁNEO TRAINS HIS HOSTAGES, LIKE FOR A MARATHON.
"BLOOD VERSUS WORDS.
"BUT BLOOD, IT NEVER WINS..."
...EVEN THOUGH HE GIVES IT A LONG HEAD START.
THEN THEY WILL BREAK LONO--WITH OR WITHOUT PIECES OF US.
NO THEY WON'T.

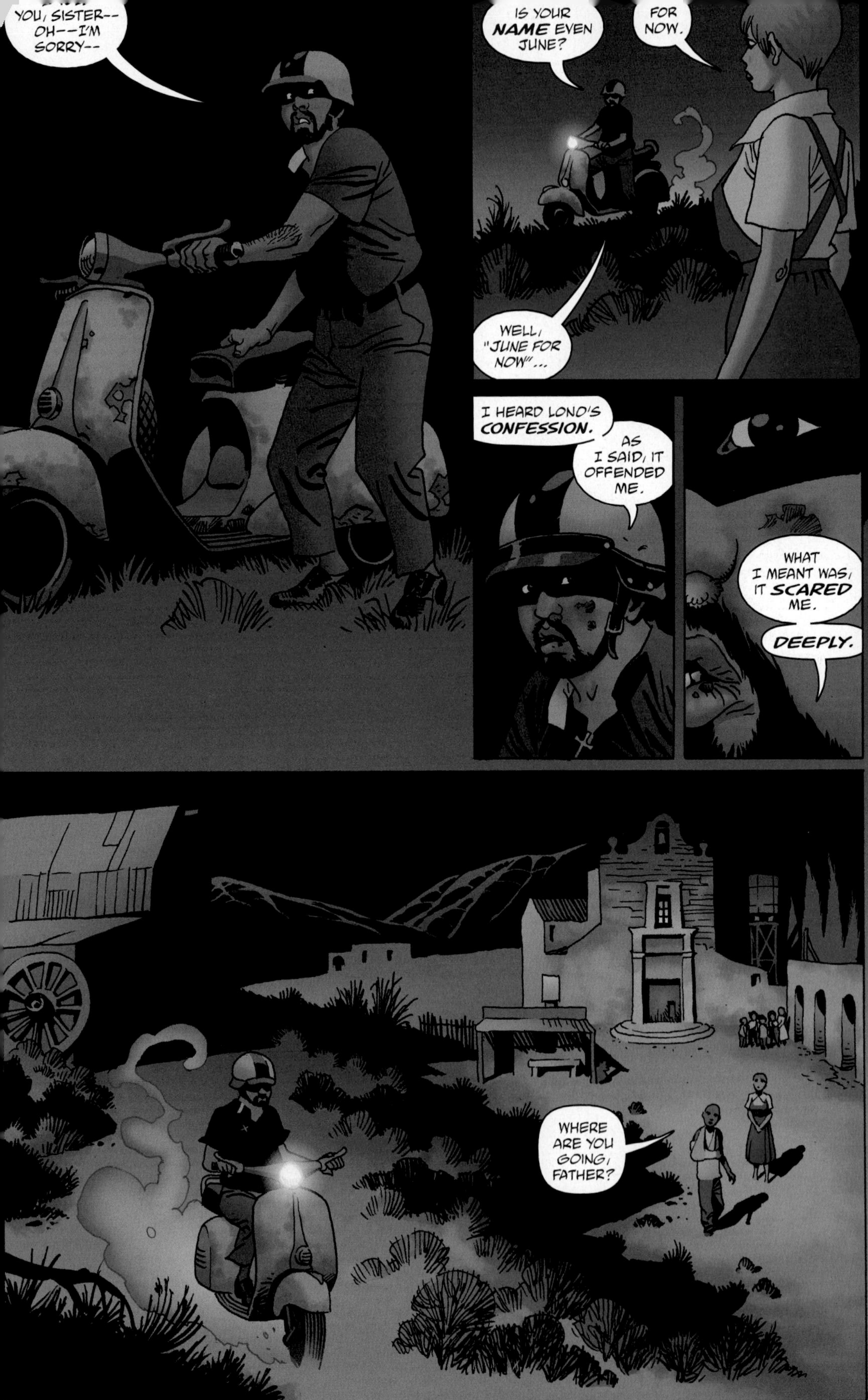
YOU, SISTER-- OH--I'M SORRY--
IS YOUR NAME EVEN JUNE?
FOR NOW.
WELL, "JUNE FOR NOW"...
I HEARD LONO'S CONFESSION.
AS I SAID, IT OFFENDED ME.
WHAT I MEANT WAS, IT SCARED ME.
DEEPLY.
WHERE ARE YOU GOING, FATHER?

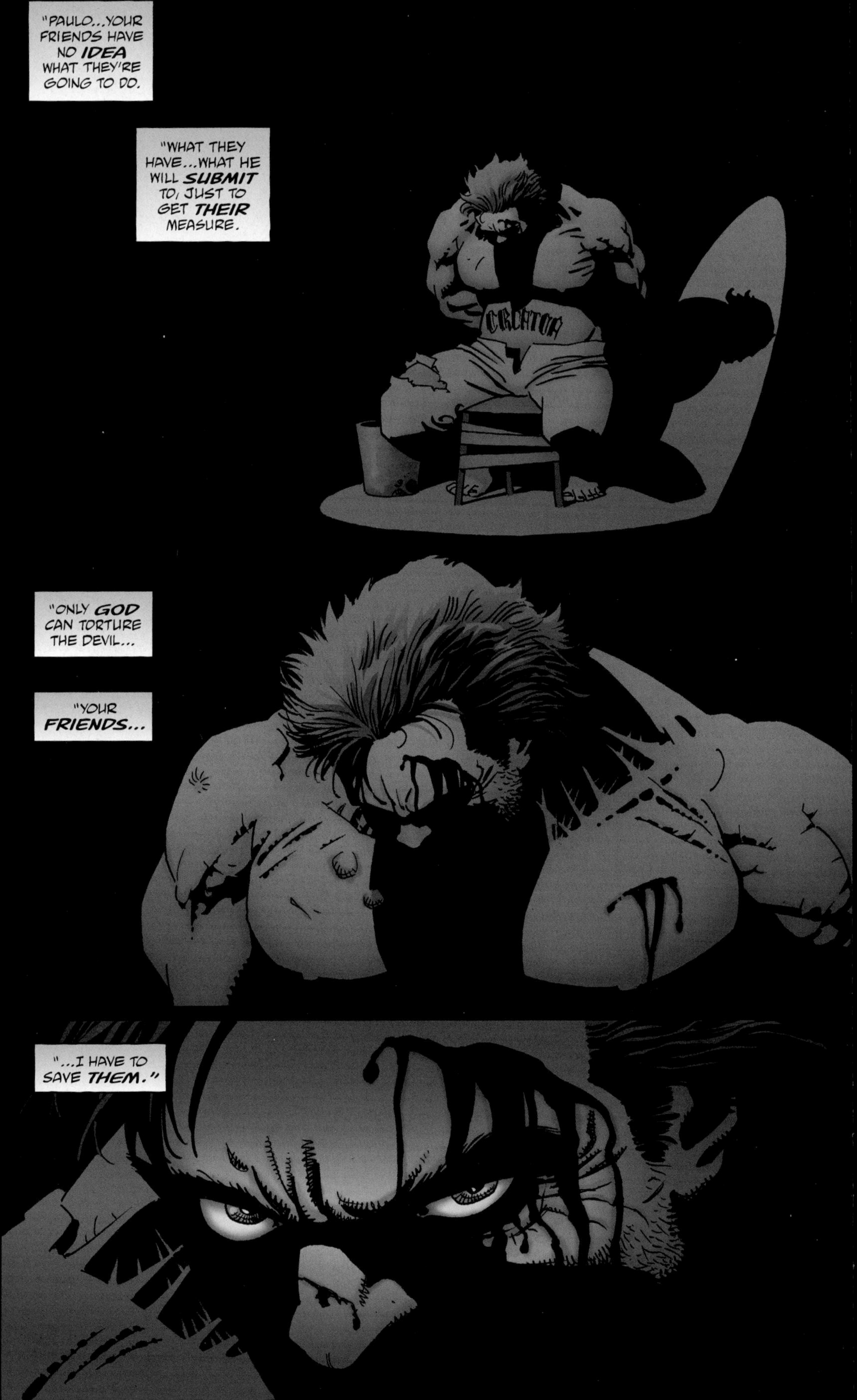
"PAULO...YOUR FRIENDS HAVE NO IDEA WHAT THEY'RE GOING TO DO.
"WHAT THEY HAVE...WHAT HE WILL SUBMIT TO, JUST TO GET THEIR MEASURE.
CREATOR
"ONLY GOD CAN TORTURE THE DEVIL...
"YOUR FRIENDS...
"...I HAVE TO SAVE THEM."

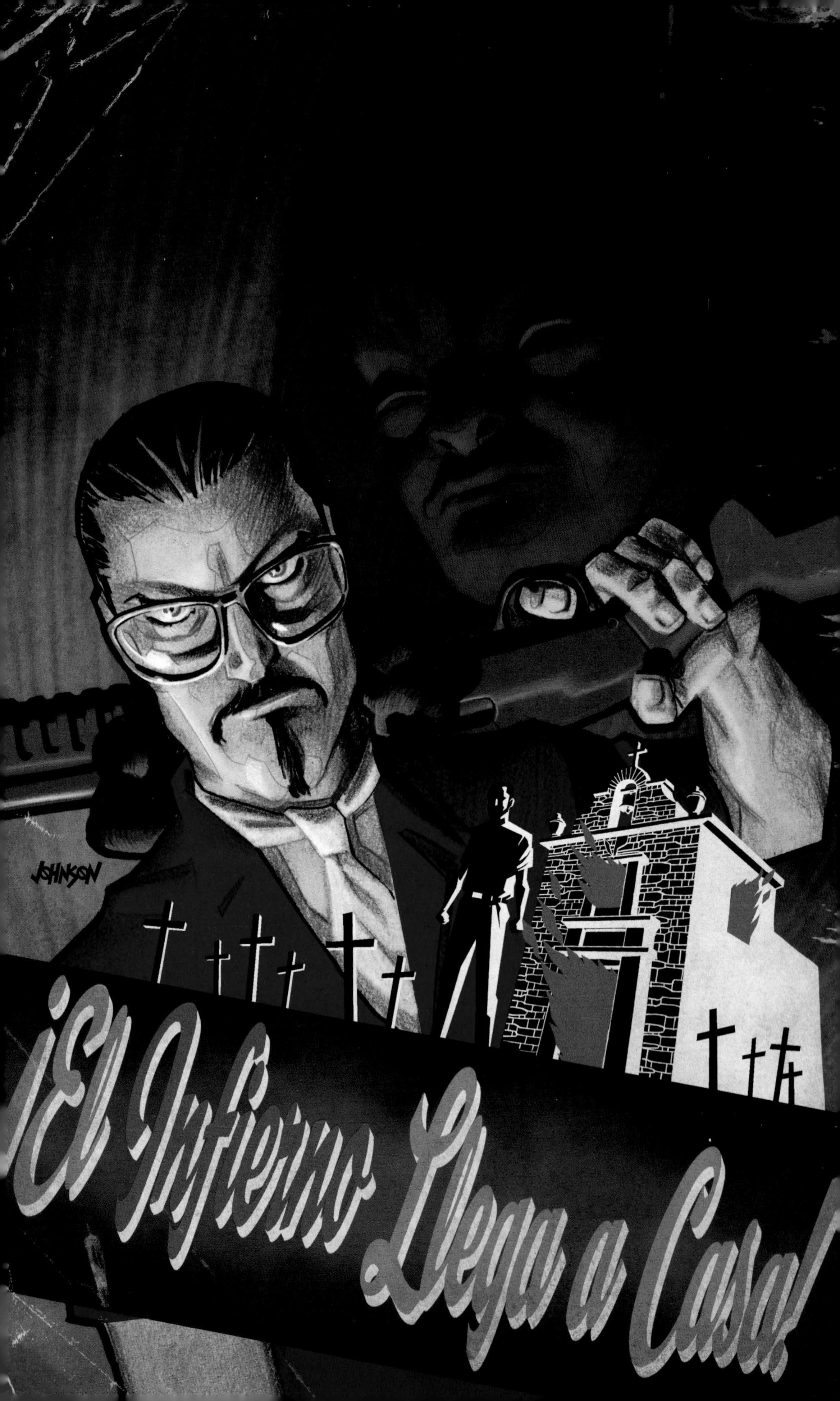
JOHNSON
¡El Infierno Llega a Casa!

"Look what happens when you lie."

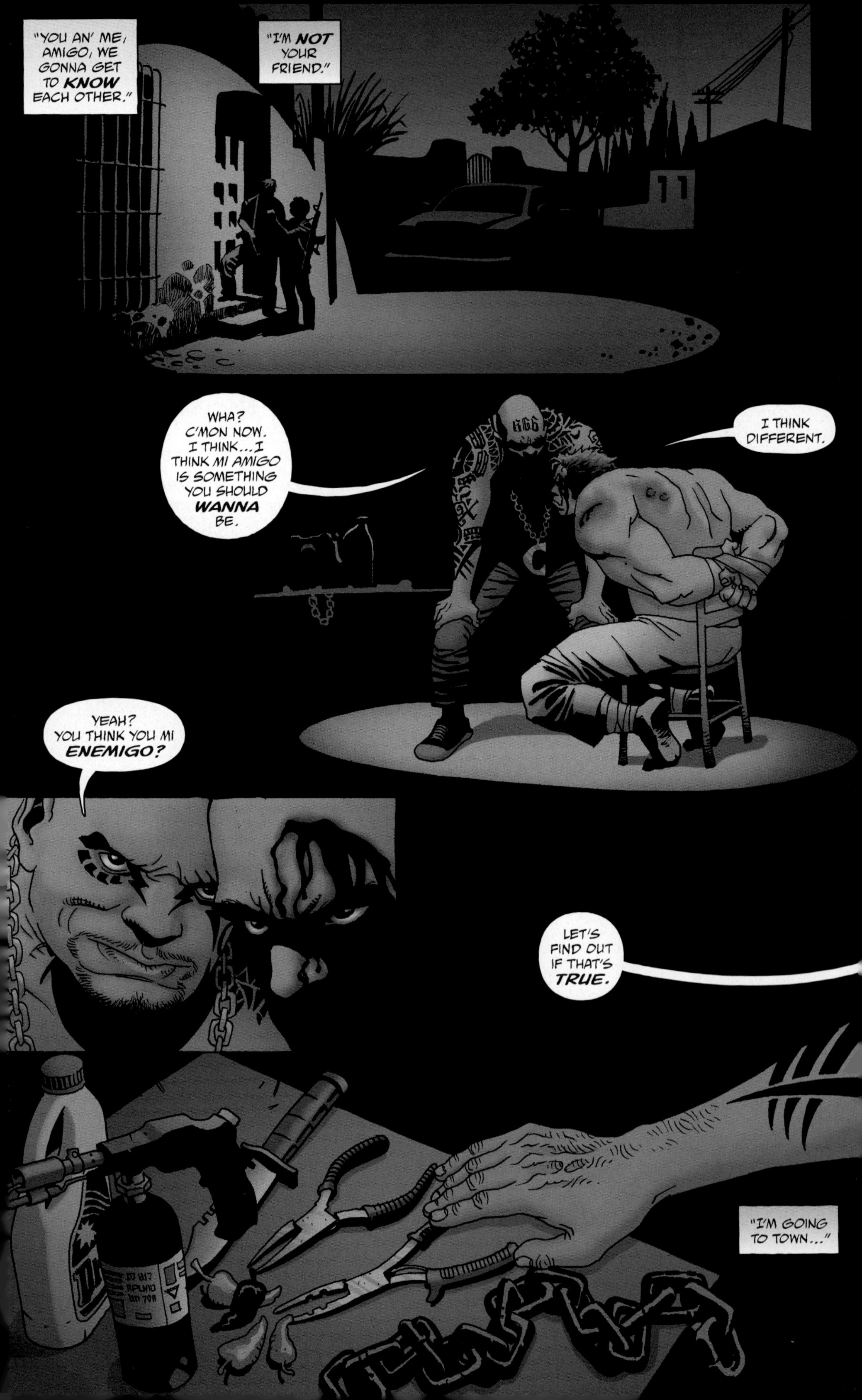
"YOU AN' ME, AMIGO, WE GONNA GET TO **KNOW** EACH OTHER."
"I'M **NOT** YOUR FRIEND."
WHA? C'MON NOW. I THINK...I THINK *MI AMIGO* IS SOMETHING YOU SHOULD **WANNA** BE.
I THINK DIFFERENT.
YEAH? YOU THINK YOU *MI* ***ENEMIGO?***
LET'S FIND OUT IF THAT'S ***TRUE.***
"I'M GOING TO TOWN..."

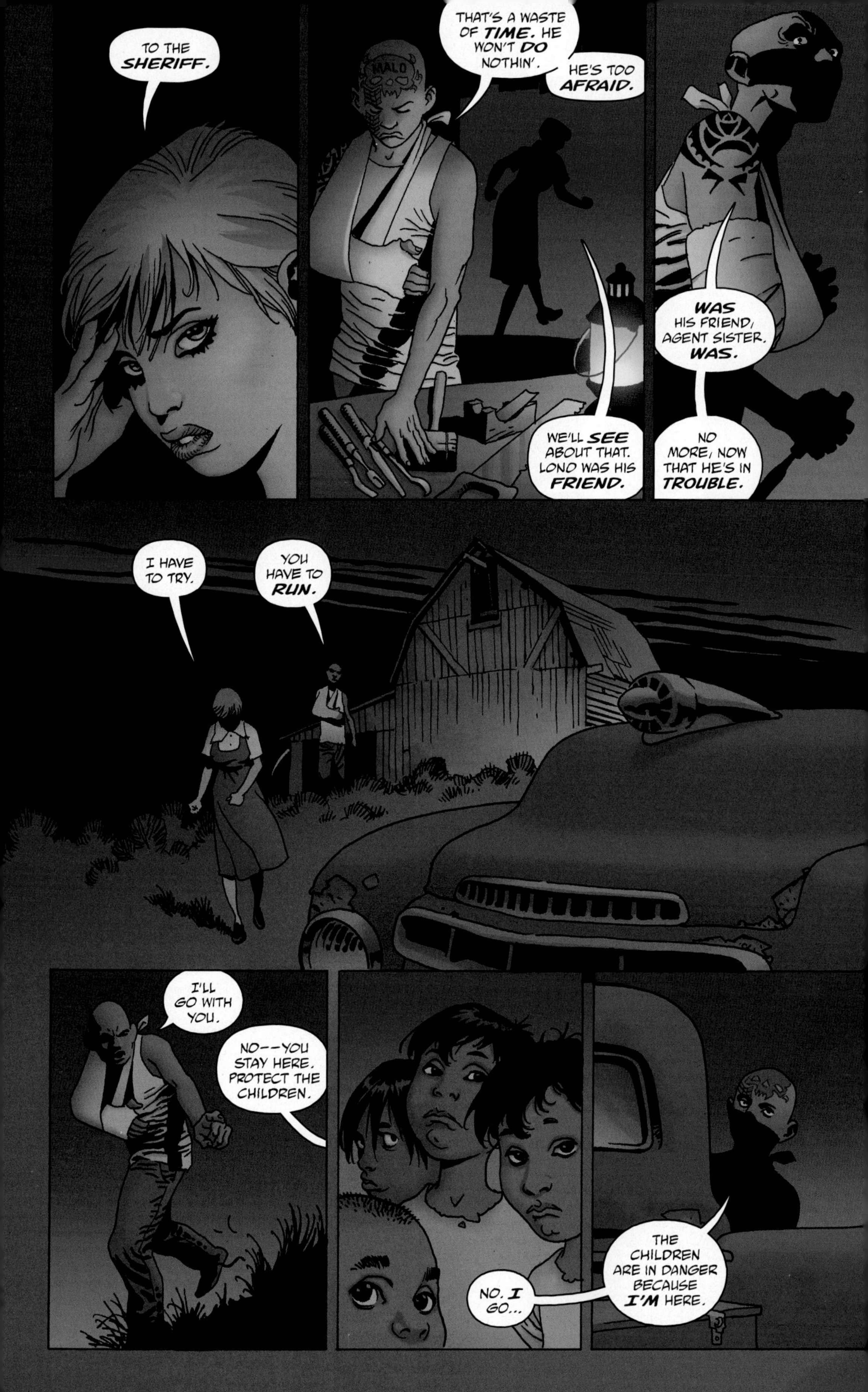
TO THE SHERIFF.
THAT'S A WASTE OF TIME. HE WON'T DO NOTHIN'.
HE'S TOO AFRAID.
WE'LL SEE ABOUT THAT. LONO WAS HIS FRIEND.
WAS HIS FRIEND, AGENT SISTER. WAS.
NO MORE, NOW THAT HE'S IN TROUBLE.
I HAVE TO TRY.
YOU HAVE TO RUN.
I'LL GO WITH YOU.
NO--YOU STAY HERE. PROTECT THE CHILDREN.
NO. I GO...
THE CHILDREN ARE IN DANGER BECAUSE I'M HERE.

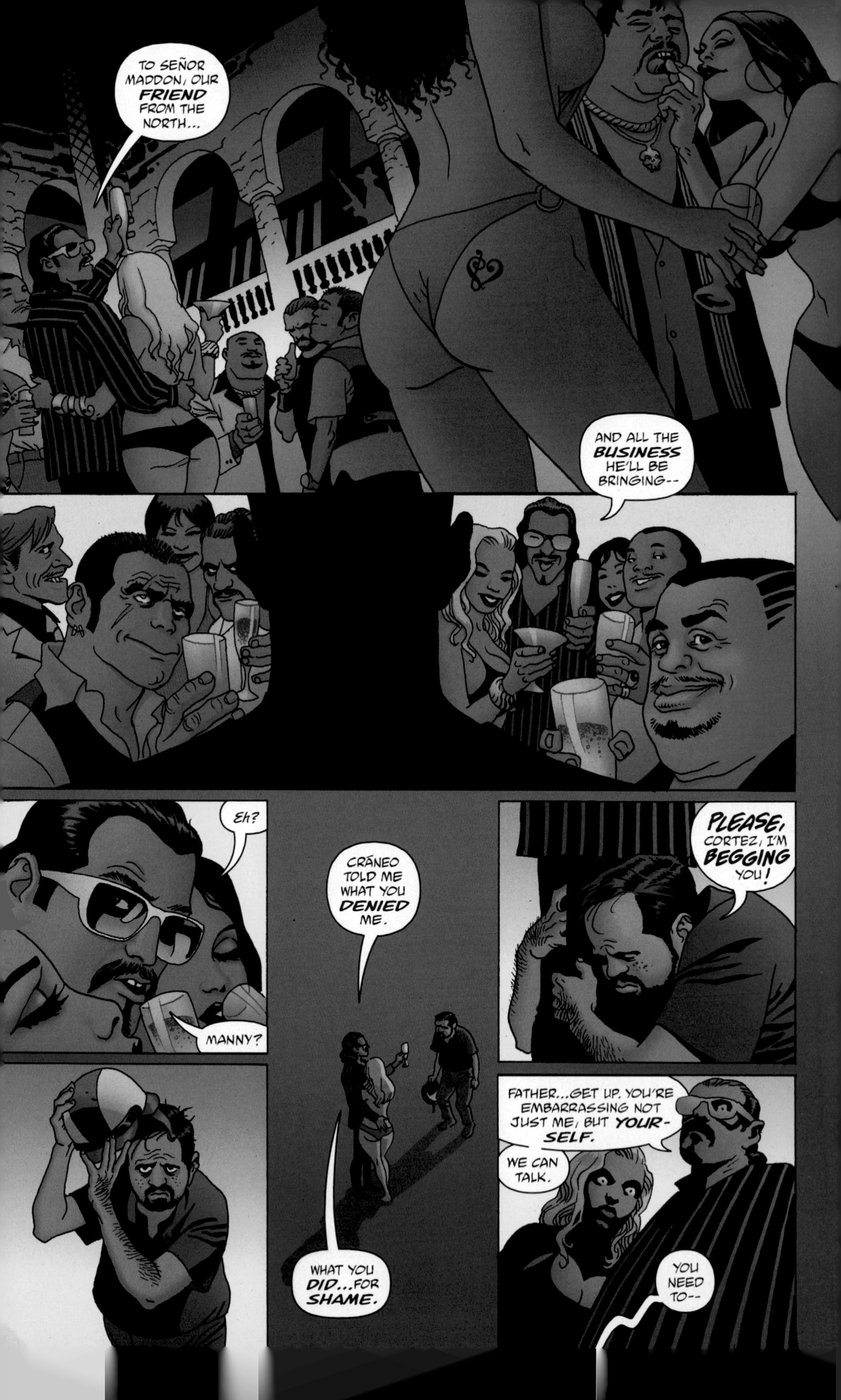
TO SEÑOR MADDON, OUR FRIEND FROM THE NORTH...
AND ALL THE BUSINESS HE'LL BE BRINGING--
Eh?
MANNY?
CRÁNEO TOLD ME WHAT YOU DENIED ME.
PLEASE, CORTEZ, I'M BEGGING YOU!
WHAT YOU DID...FOR SHAME.
FATHER...GET UP. YOU'RE EMBARRASSING NOT JUST ME, BUT YOURSELF.
WE CAN TALK.
YOU NEED TO--

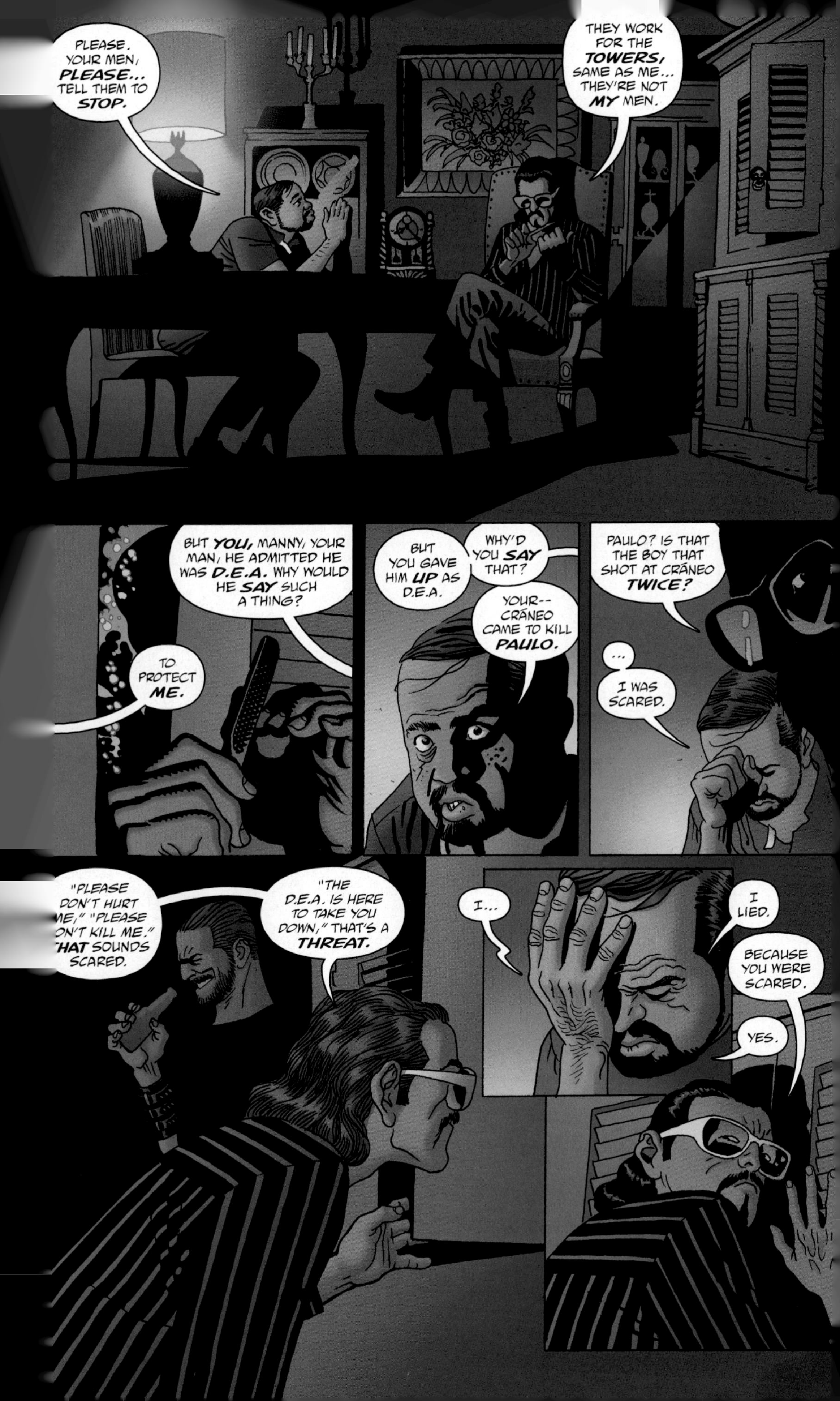
PLEASE. YOUR MEN, PLEASE... TELL THEM TO STOP.
THEY WORK FOR THE TOWERS, SAME AS ME... THEY'RE NOT MY MEN.
BUT YOU, MANNY, YOUR MAN, HE ADMITTED HE WAS D.E.A. WHY WOULD HE SAY SUCH A THING?
TO PROTECT ME.
BUT YOU GAVE HIM UP AS D.E.A.
WHY'D YOU SAY THAT?
YOUR-- CRÁNEO CAME TO KILL PAULO.
PAULO? IS THAT THE BOY THAT SHOT AT CRÁNEO TWICE?
...
I WAS SCARED.
"PLEASE DON'T HURT ME," "PLEASE DON'T KILL ME." THAT SOUNDS SCARED.
"THE D.E.A. IS HERE TO TAKE YOU DOWN," THAT'S A THREAT.
I...
I LIED.
BECAUSE YOU WERE SCARED.
YES.

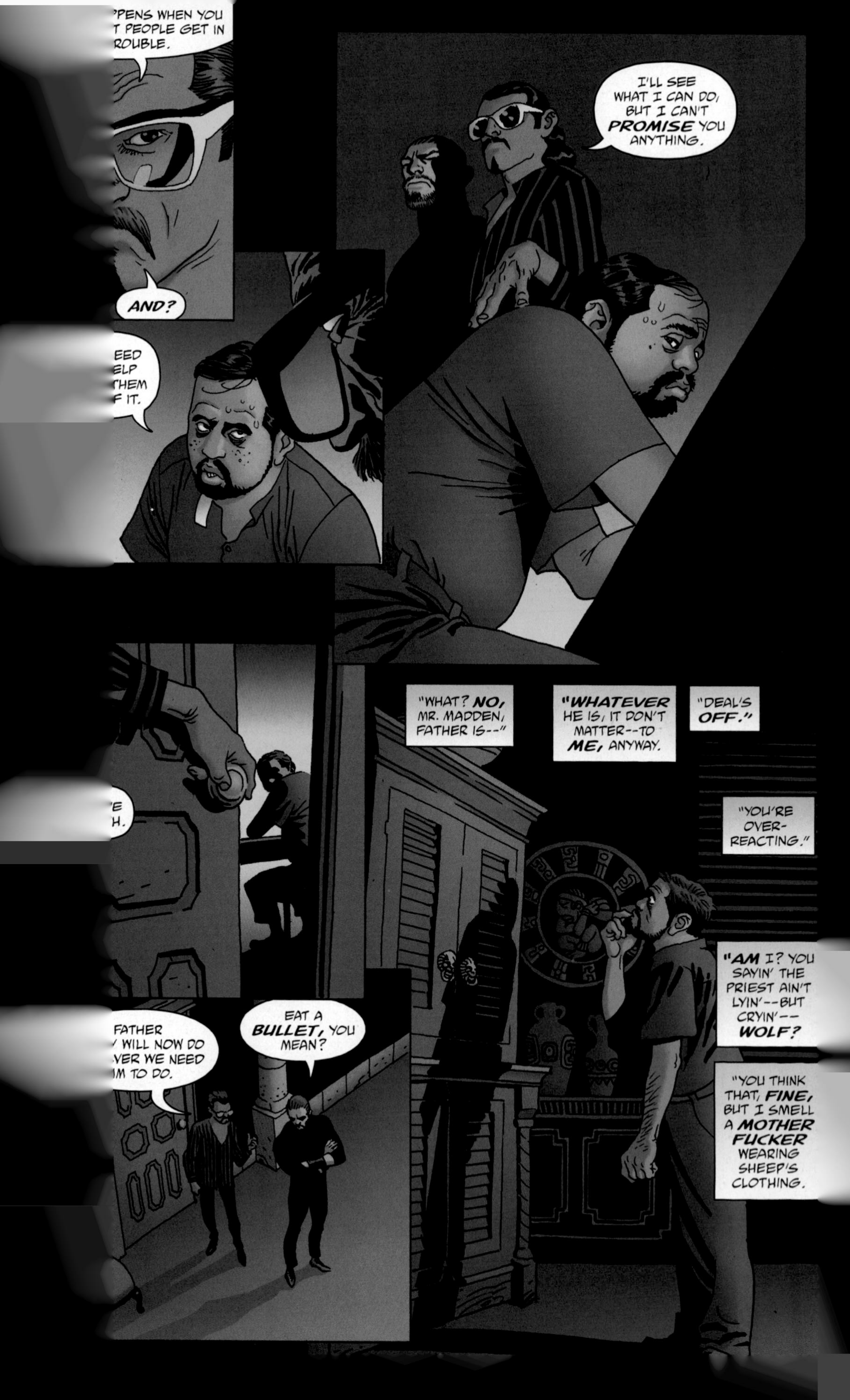
PPENS WHEN YOU T PEOPLE GET IN ROUBLE.
AND?
I'LL SEE WHAT I CAN DO, BUT I CAN'T PROMISE YOU ANYTHING.
EED ELP THEM F IT.
"WHAT? NO, MR. MADDEN, FATHER IS--"
"WHATEVER HE IS, IT DON'T MATTER--TO ME, ANYWAY.
"DEAL'S OFF."
"YOU'RE OVER-REACTING."
"AM I? YOU SAYIN' THE PRIEST AIN'T LYIN'--BUT CRYIN'--WOLF?
"YOU THINK THAT, FINE, BUT I SMELL A MOTHER FUCKER WEARING SHEEP'S CLOTHING.
FATHER Y WILL NOW DO VER WE NEED M TO DO.
EAT A BULLET, YOU MEAN?

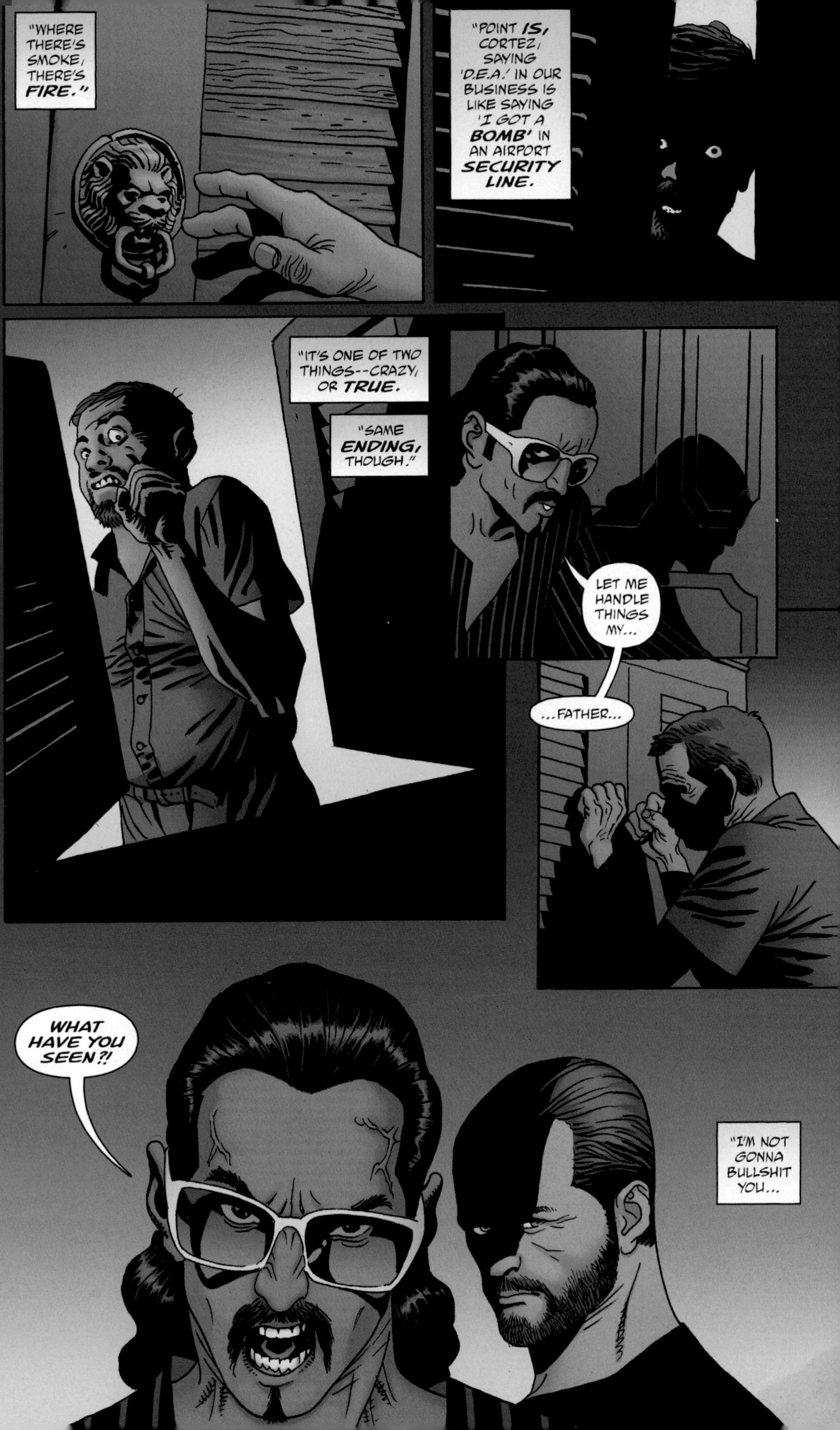
"WHERE THERE'S SMOKE, THERE'S FIRE."
"POINT IS, CORTEZ, SAYING 'D.E.A.' IN OUR BUSINESS IS LIKE SAYING 'I GOT A BOMB' IN AN AIRPORT SECURITY LINE.
"IT'S ONE OF TWO THINGS--CRAZY, OR TRUE.
"SAME ENDING, THOUGH."
LET ME HANDLE THINGS MY...
...FATHER...
WHAT HAVE YOU SEEN?!
"I'M NOT GONNA BULLSHIT YOU...

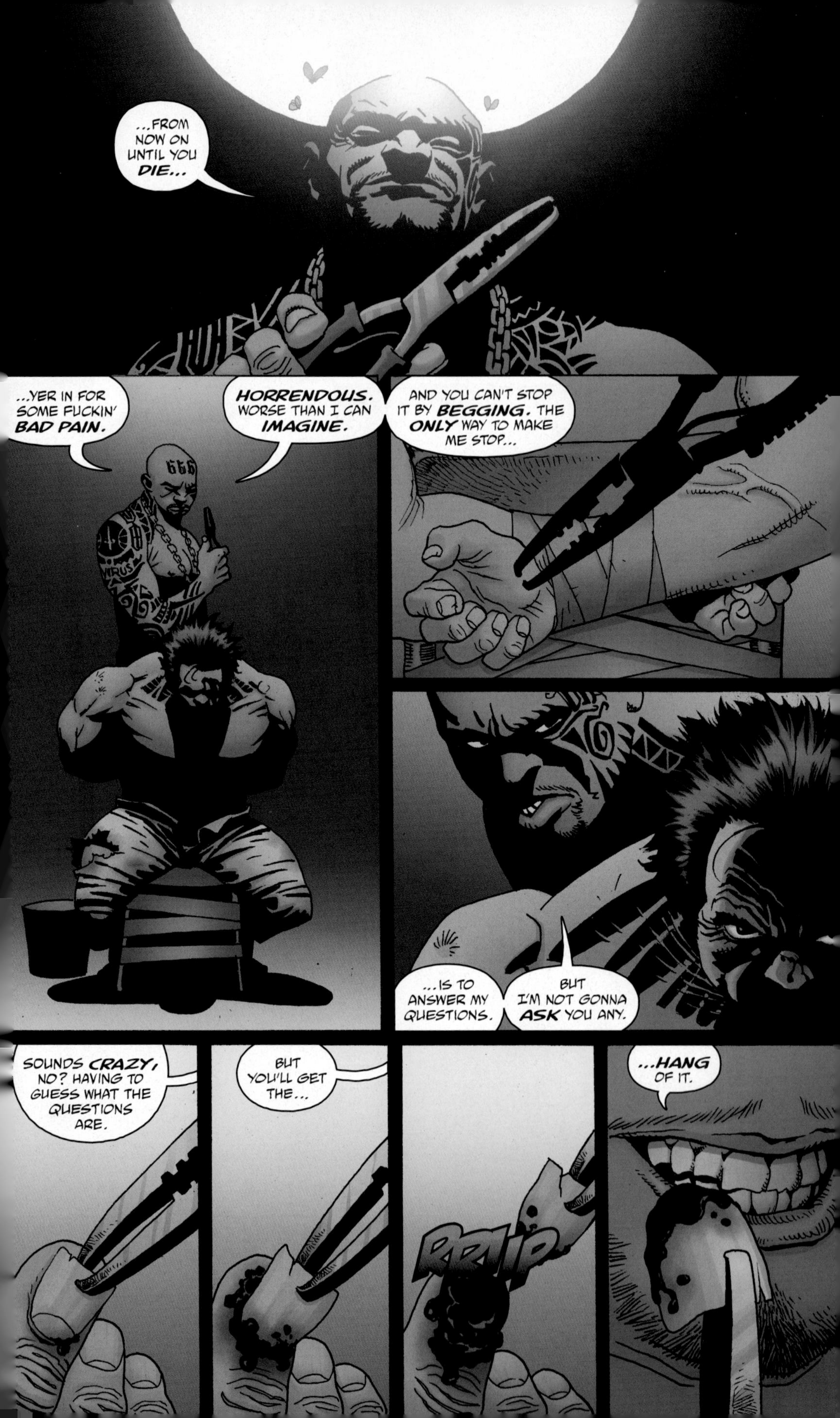
...FROM NOW ON UNTIL YOU DIE...
...YER IN FOR SOME FUCKIN' BAD PAIN.
HORRENDOUS. WORSE THAN I CAN IMAGINE.
AND YOU CAN'T STOP IT BY BEGGING. THE ONLY WAY TO MAKE ME STOP...
...IS TO ANSWER MY QUESTIONS.
BUT I'M NOT GONNA ASK YOU ANY.
SOUNDS CRAZY, NO? HAVING TO GUESS WHAT THE QUESTIONS ARE.
BUT YOU'LL GET THE...
RRIIP
...HANG OF IT.

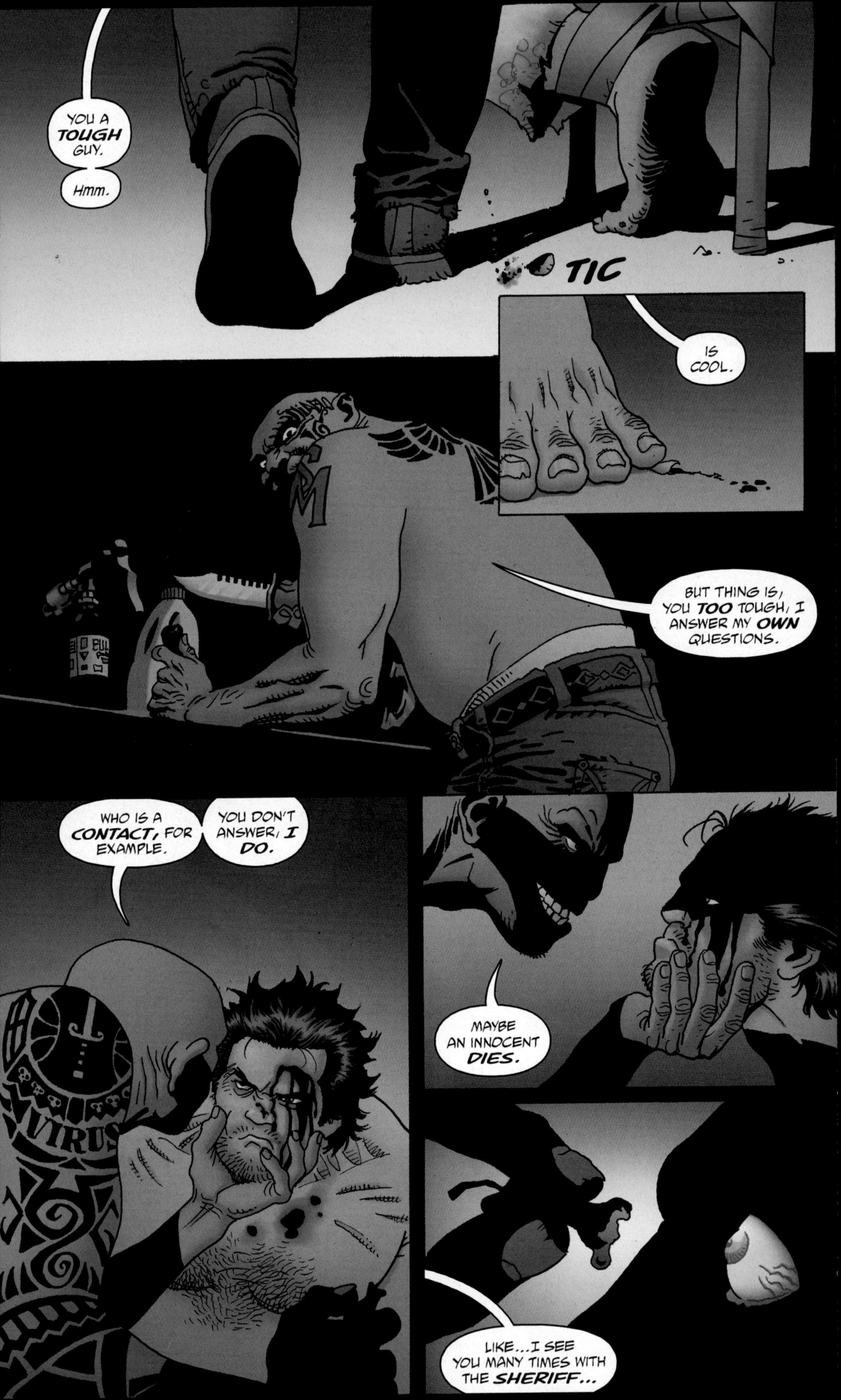
YOU A TOUGH GUY.
Hmm.
TIC
IS COOL.
BUT THING IS, YOU TOO TOUGH, I ANSWER MY OWN QUESTIONS.
WHO IS A CONTACT, FOR EXAMPLE.
YOU DON'T ANSWER, I DO.
MAYBE AN INNOCENT DIES.
LIKE...I SEE YOU MANY TIMES WITH THE SHERIFF...

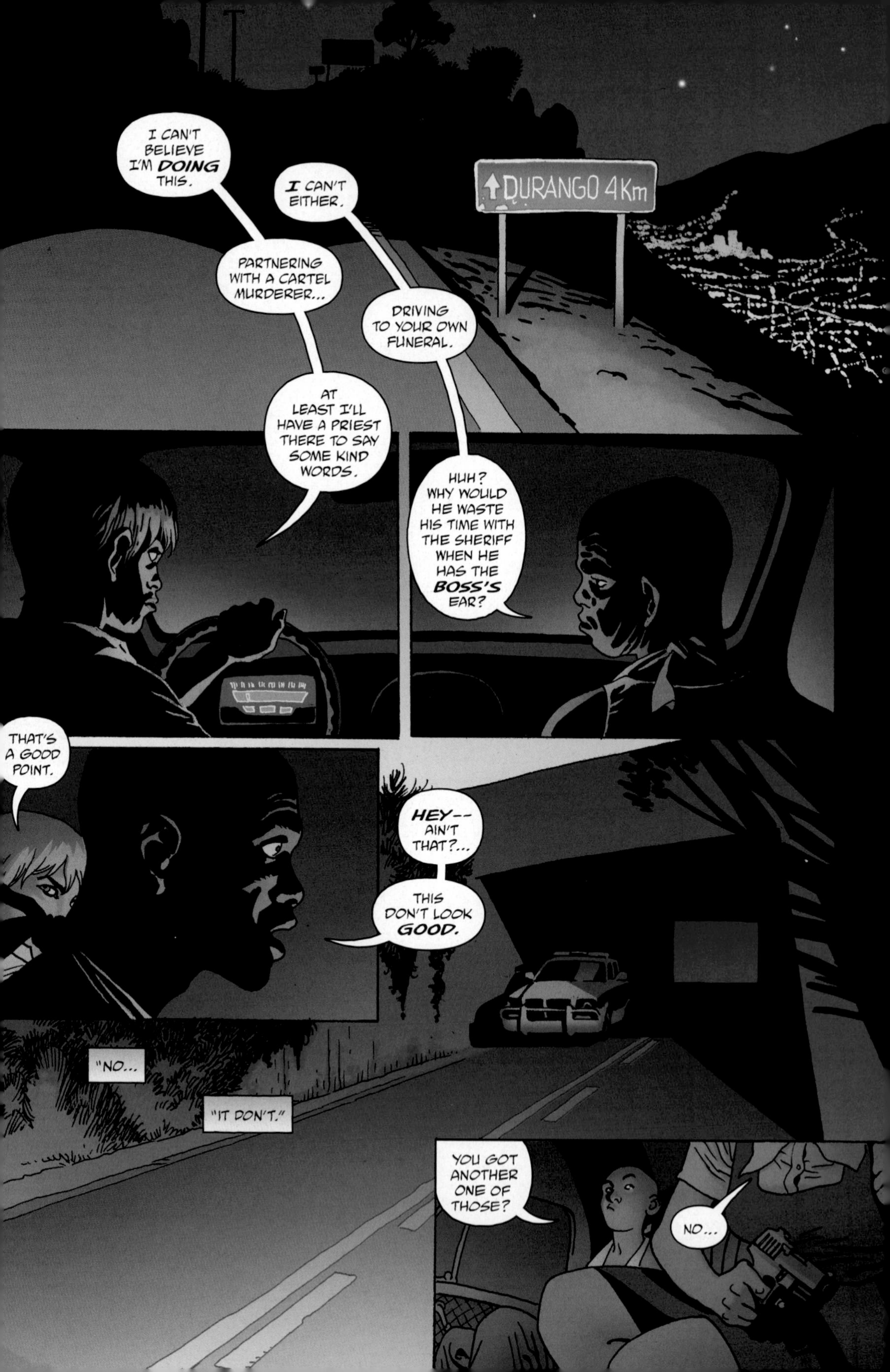
I CAN'T BELIEVE I'M DOING THIS.
I CAN'T EITHER.
DURANGO 4Km
PARTNERING WITH A CARTEL MURDERER...
DRIVING TO YOUR OWN FUNERAL.
AT LEAST I'LL HAVE A PRIEST THERE TO SAY SOME KIND WORDS.
HUH? WHY WOULD HE WASTE HIS TIME WITH THE SHERIFF WHEN HE HAS THE BOSS'S EAR?
THAT'S A GOOD POINT.
HEY-- AIN'T THAT?...
THIS DON'T LOOK GOOD.
"NO...
"IT DON'T."
YOU GOT ANOTHER ONE OF THOSE?
NO...

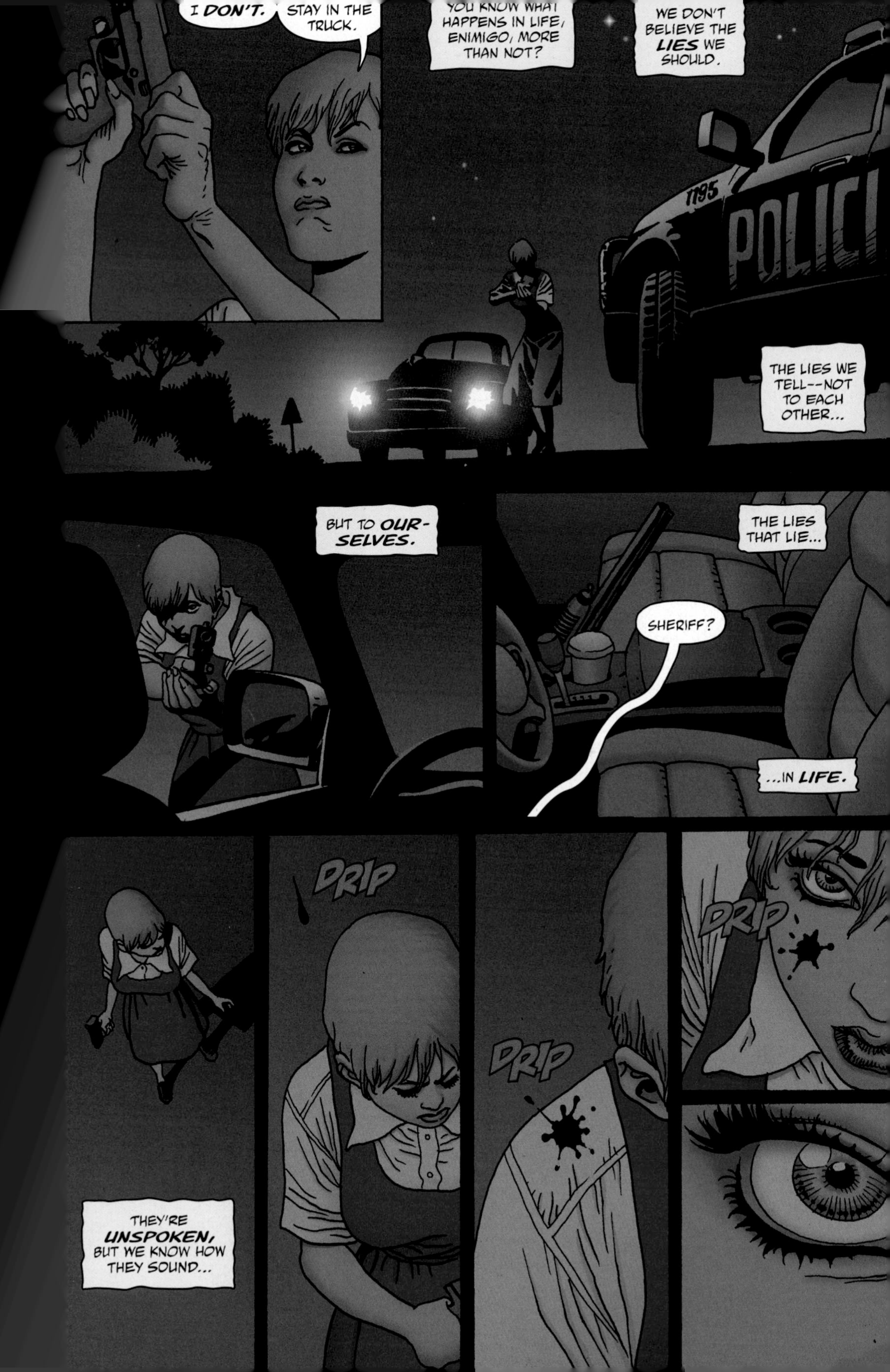
I DON'T.
STAY IN THE TRUCK.
YOU KNOW WHAT HAPPENS IN LIFE, ENIMIGO, MORE THAN NOT?
WE DON'T BELIEVE THE LIES WE SHOULD.
1195
POLIC
THE LIES WE TELL--NOT TO EACH OTHER...
BUT TO OUR-SELVES.
THE LIES THAT LIE...
SHERIFF?
...IN LIFE.
DRIP
DRIP
DRIP
THEY'RE UNSPOKEN, BUT WE KNOW HOW THEY SOUND...

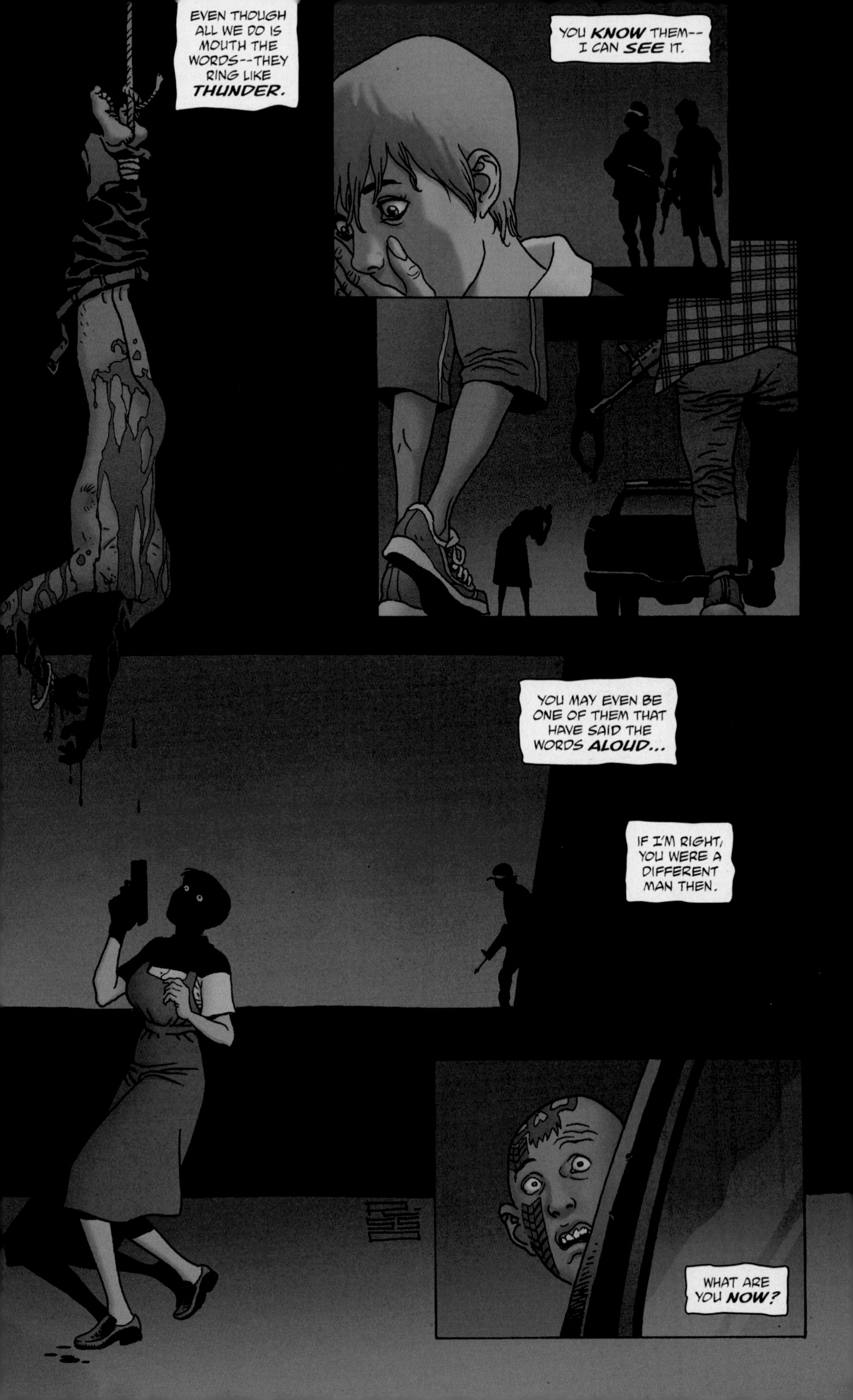
EVEN THOUGH ALL WE DO IS MOUTH THE WORDS--THEY RING LIKE THUNDER.
YOU KNOW THEM-- I CAN SEE IT.
YOU MAY EVEN BE ONE OF THEM THAT HAVE SAID THE WORDS ALOUD...
IF I'M RIGHT, YOU WERE A DIFFERENT MAN THEN.
WHAT ARE YOU NOW?

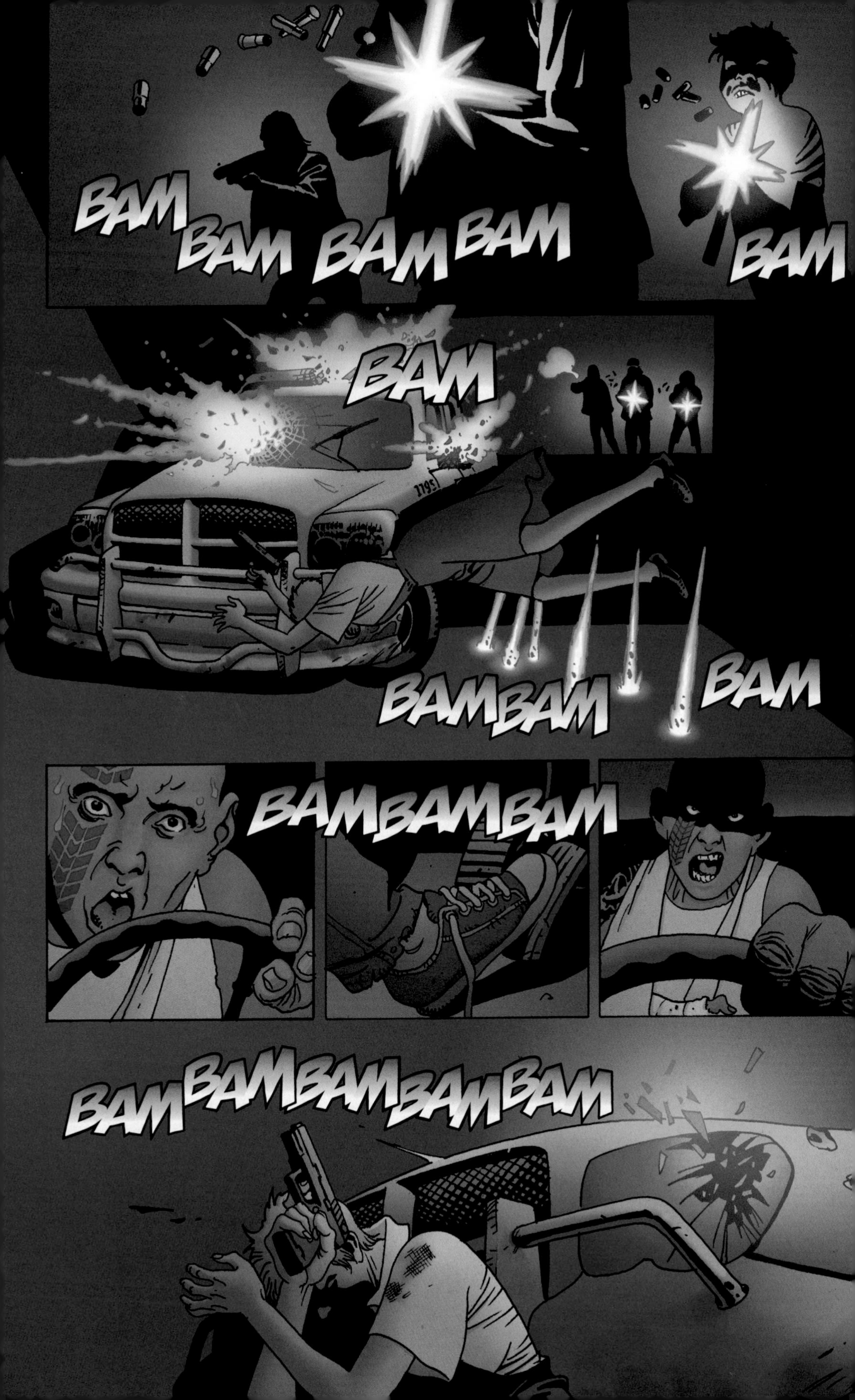
BAM
BAM
BAM
BAM
BAM
BAM
BAMBAM
BAM
BAMBAMBAM
BAMBAMBAMBAMBAM

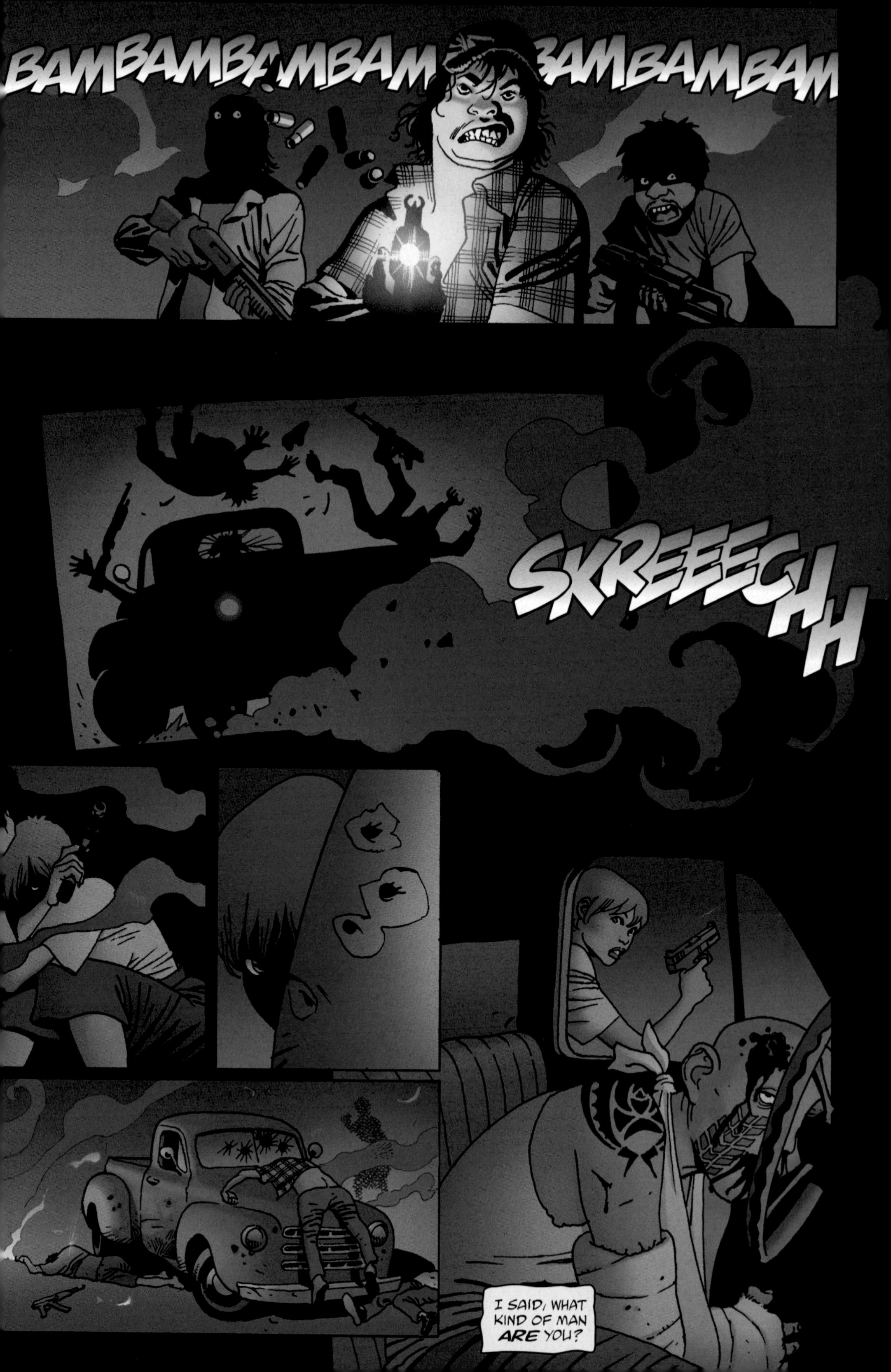
BAMBAMBAMBAMBAMBAMBAMBAMBAM
SKREEECHH
I SAID, WHAT KIND OF MAN *ARE* YOU?

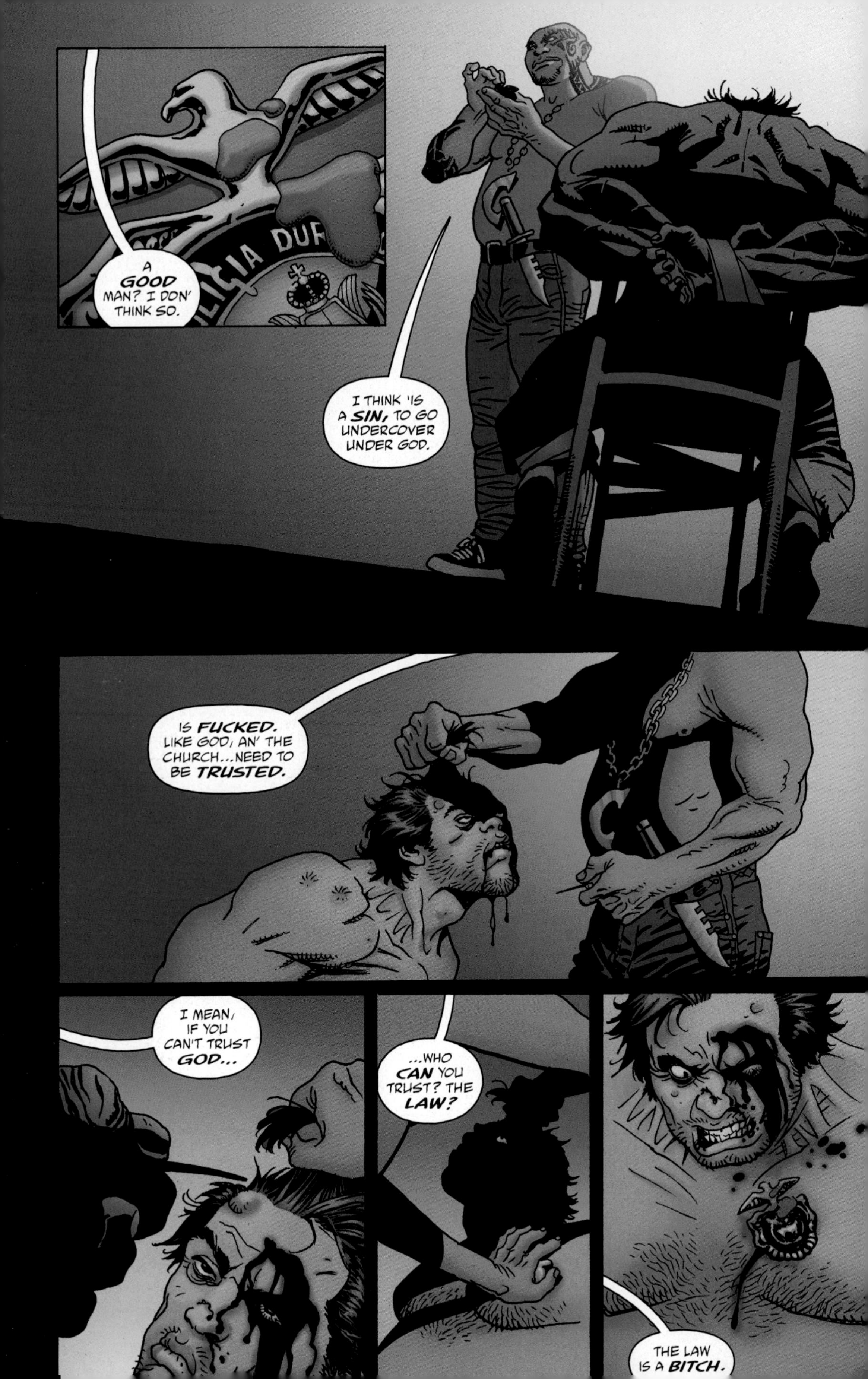

ICIA DUR
A GOOD MAN? I DON' THINK SO.
I THINK 'IS A SIN, TO GO UNDERCOVER UNDER GOD.
IS FUCKED. LIKE GOD, AN' THE CHURCH...NEED TO BE TRUSTED.
I MEAN, IF YOU CAN'T TRUST GOD...
...WHO CAN YOU TRUST? THE LAW?
THE LAW IS A BITCH.

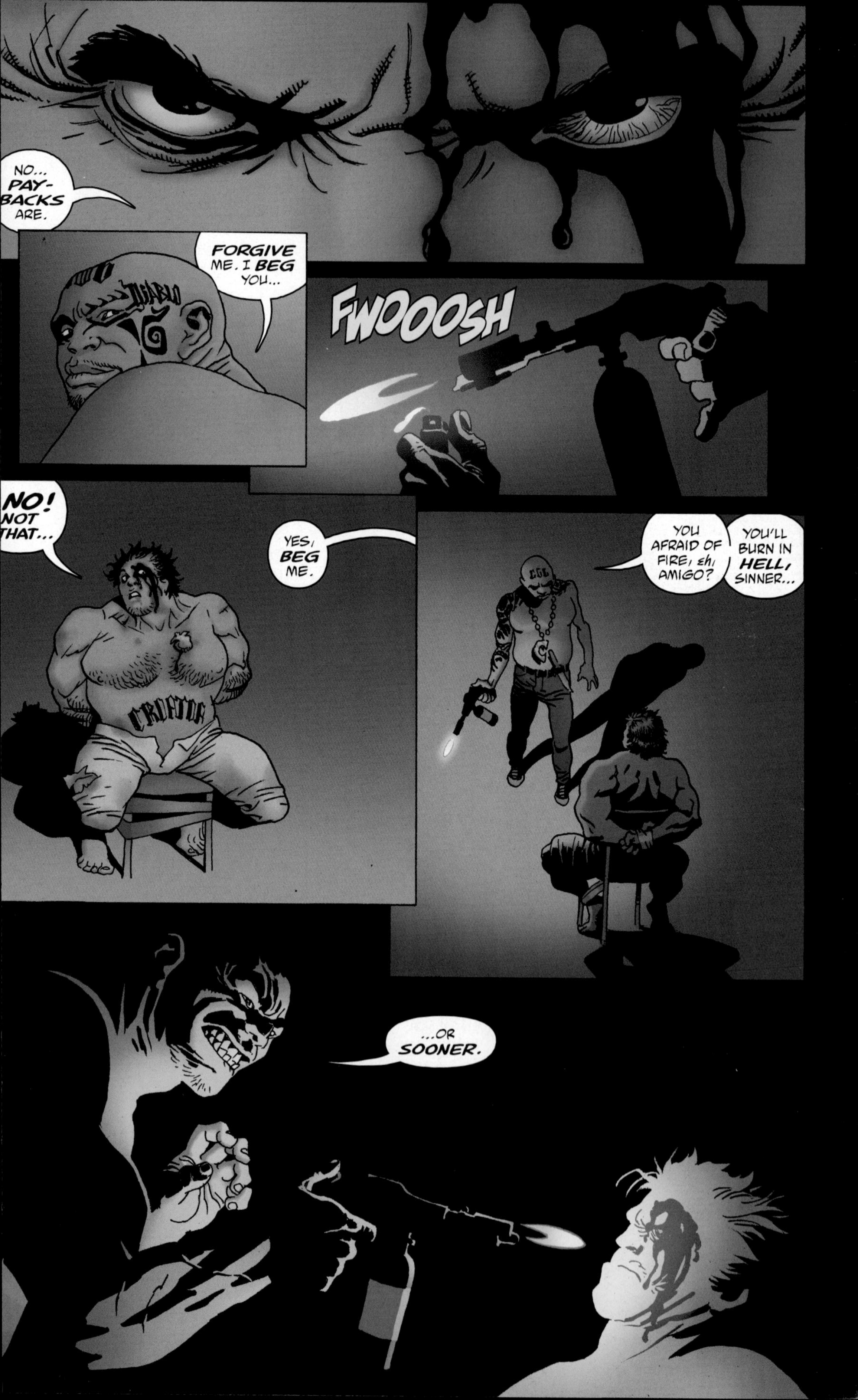
NO... PAY-BACKS ARE.
FORGIVE ME. I BEG YOU...
FWOOOSH
NO! NOT THAT...
YES, BEG ME.
YOU AFRAID OF FIRE, EH, AMIGO?
YOU'LL BURN IN HELL, SINNER...
...OR SOONER.

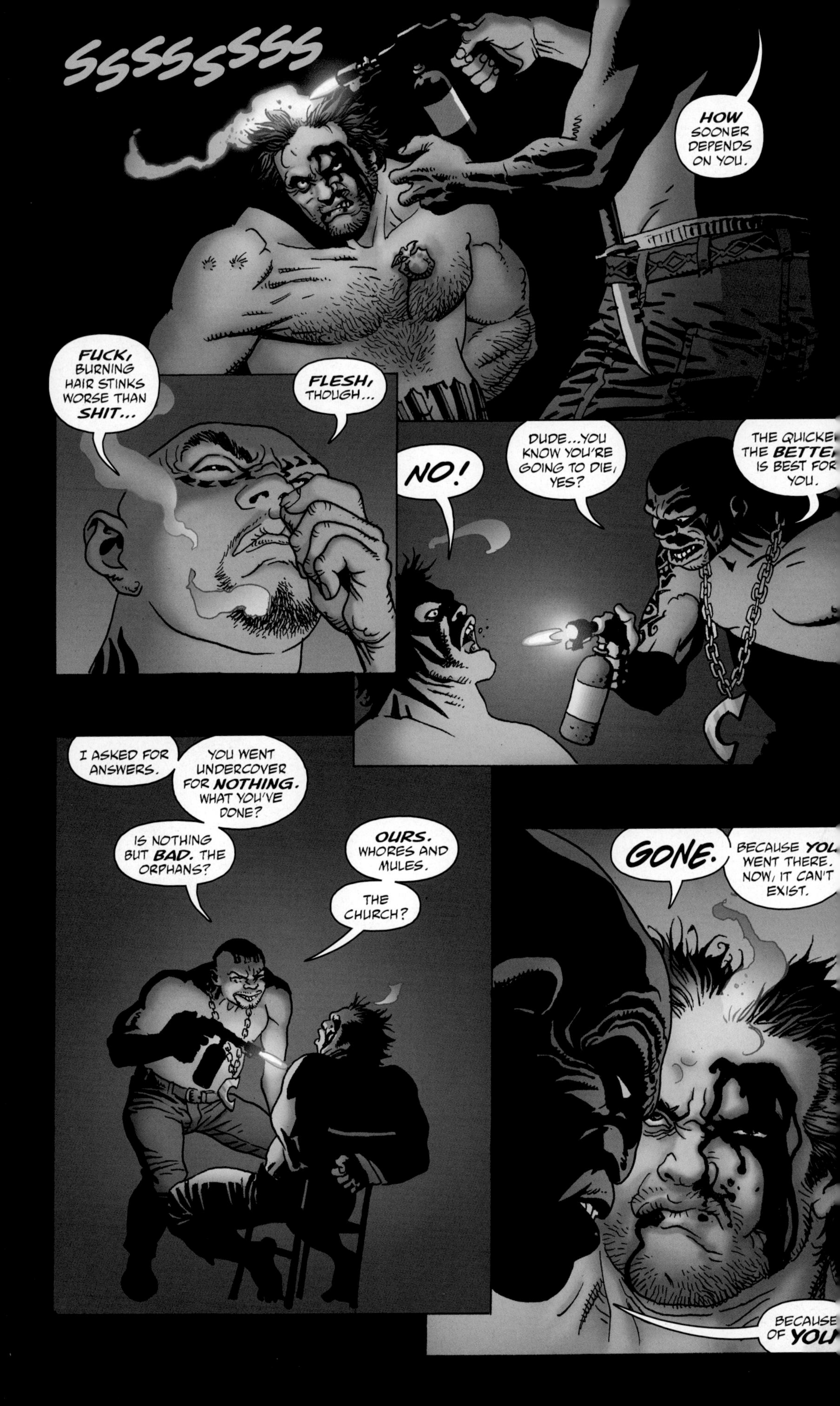

SSSSSSSS
HOW SOONER DEPENDS ON YOU.
FUCK, BURNING HAIR STINKS WORSE THAN SHIT...
FLESH, THOUGH...
NO!
DUDE...YOU KNOW YOU'RE GOING TO DIE, YES?
I ASKED FOR ANSWERS.
YOU WENT UNDERCOVER FOR NOTHING. WHAT YOU'VE DONE?
IS NOTHING BUT BAD. THE ORPHANS?
OURS. WHORES AND MULES.
THE CHURCH?
GONE.

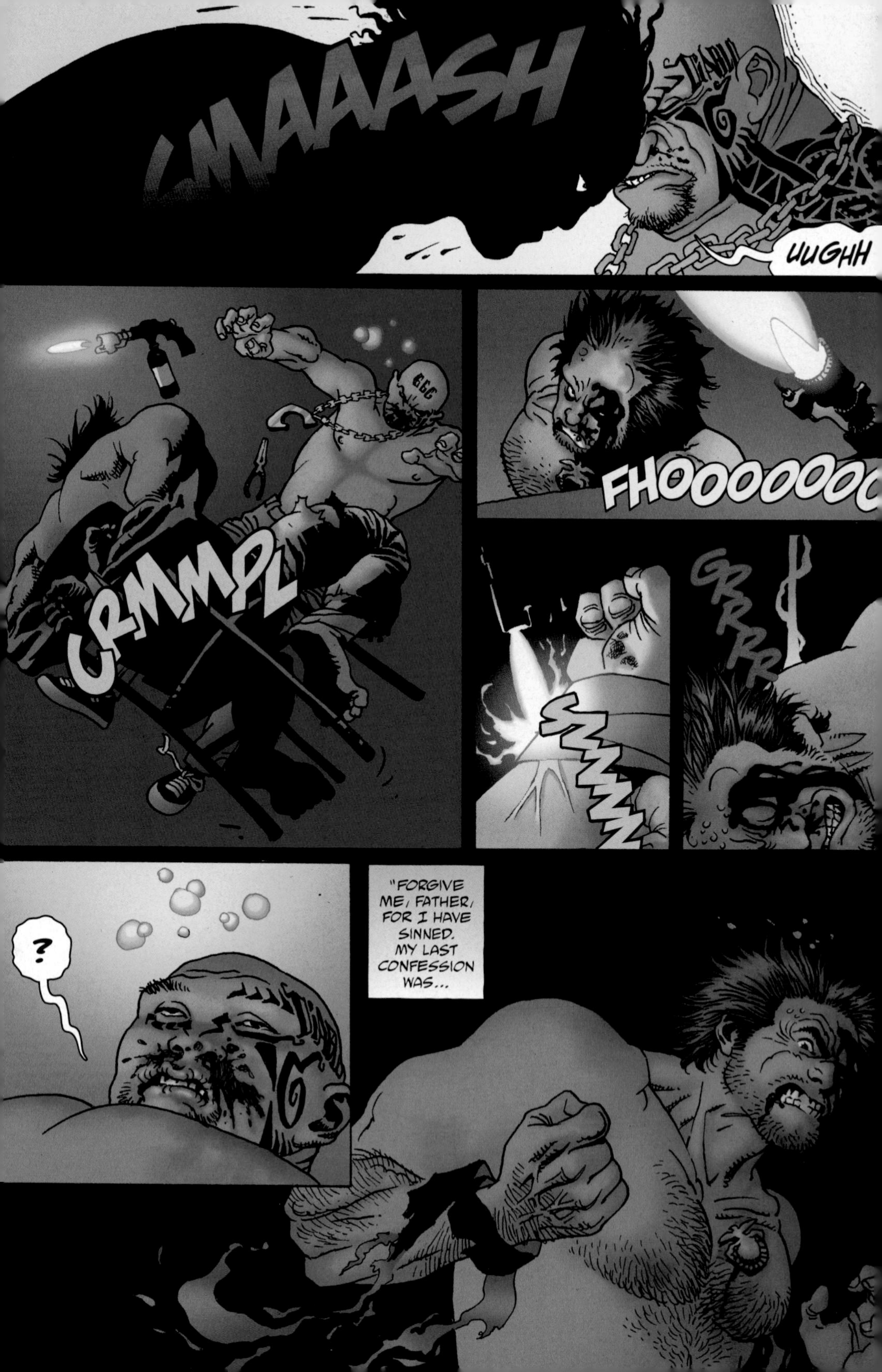

LMAAASH
UUGHH
CRMMPL
FHOOOOOOO
SSSMMMM
GRRRR
?
"FORGIVE ME, FATHER, FOR I HAVE SINNED. MY LAST CONFESSION WAS...

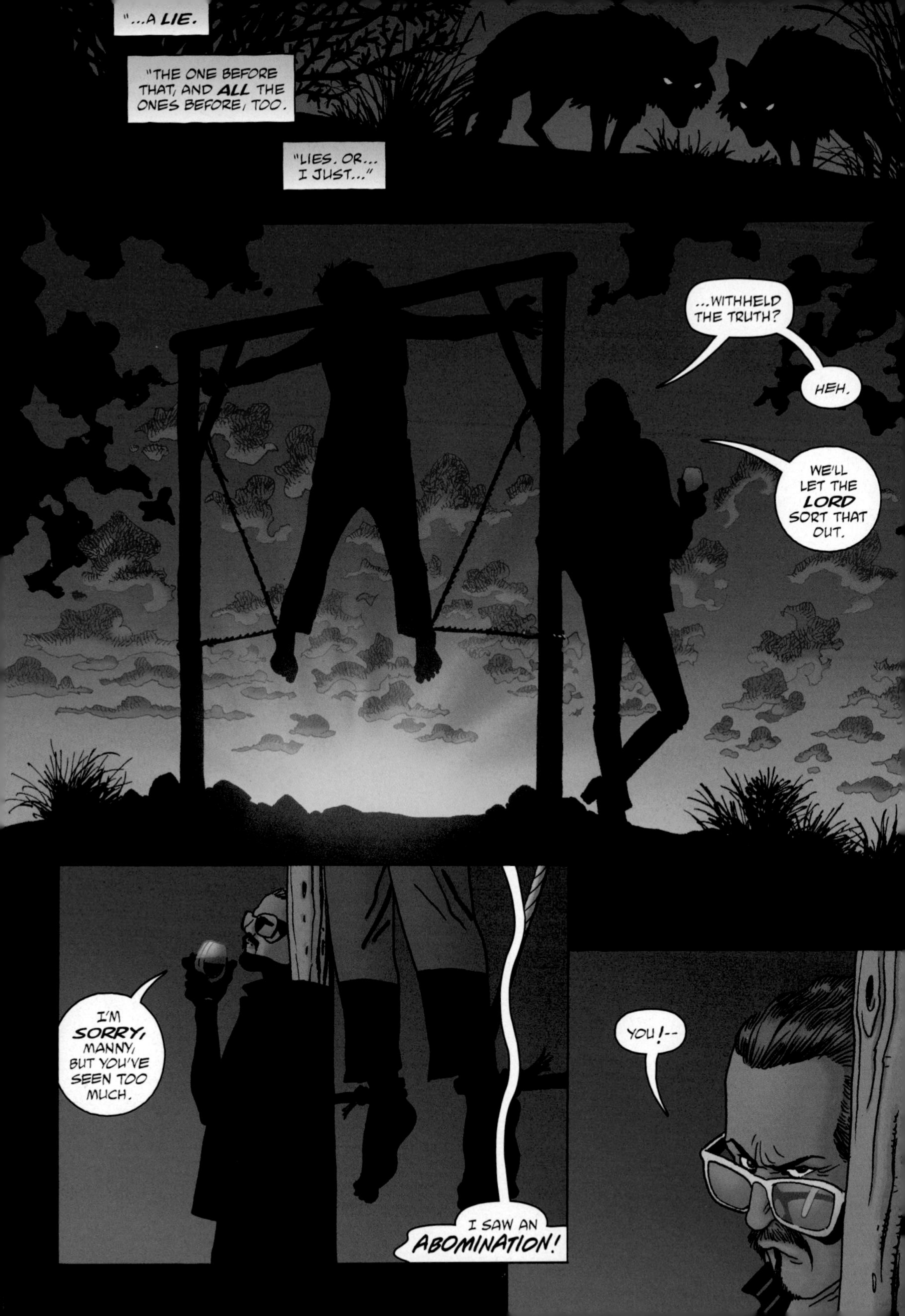

"...A LIE.
"THE ONE BEFORE THAT, AND ALL THE ONES BEFORE, TOO.
"LIES. OR... I JUST..."
...WITHHELD THE TRUTH?
HEH.
WE'LL LET THE LORD SORT THAT OUT.
I'M SORRY, MANNY, BUT YOU'VE SEEN TOO MUCH.
I SAW AN ABOMINATION!
YOU!--

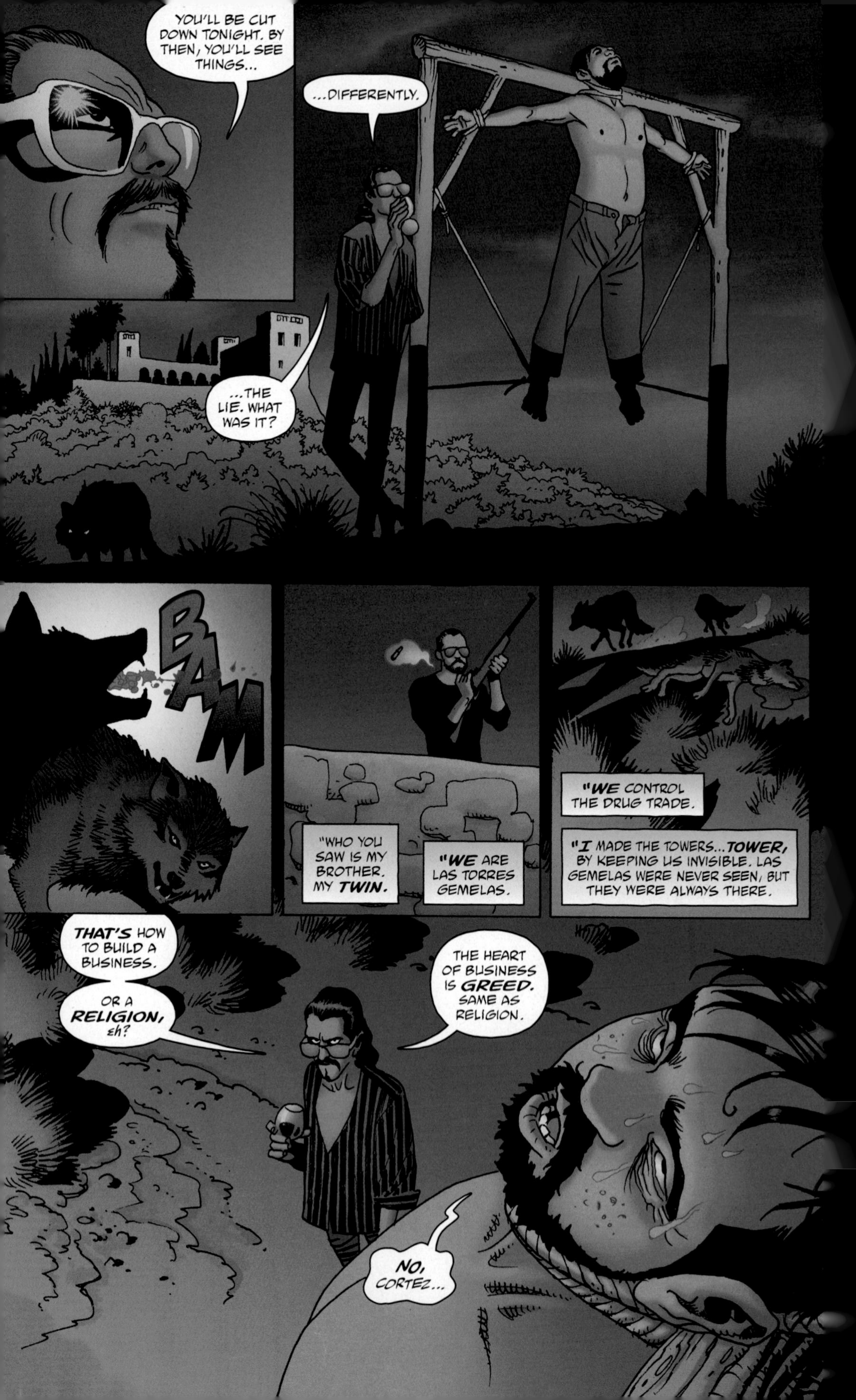

YOU'LL BE CUT DOWN TONIGHT. BY THEN, YOU'LL SEE THINGS...
...DIFFERENTLY.
...THE LIE. WHAT WAS IT?
BAM
"WHO YOU SAW IS MY BROTHER. MY TWIN.
"WE ARE LAS TORRES GEMELAS.
"WE CONTROL THE DRUG TRADE.
"I MADE THE TOWERS...TOWER, BY KEEPING US INVISIBLE. LAS GEMELAS WERE NEVER SEEN, BUT THEY WERE ALWAYS THERE.
THAT'S HOW TO BUILD A BUSINESS.
OR A RELIGION, EH?
THE HEART OF BUSINESS IS GREED. SAME AS RELIGION.
NO, CORTEZ...

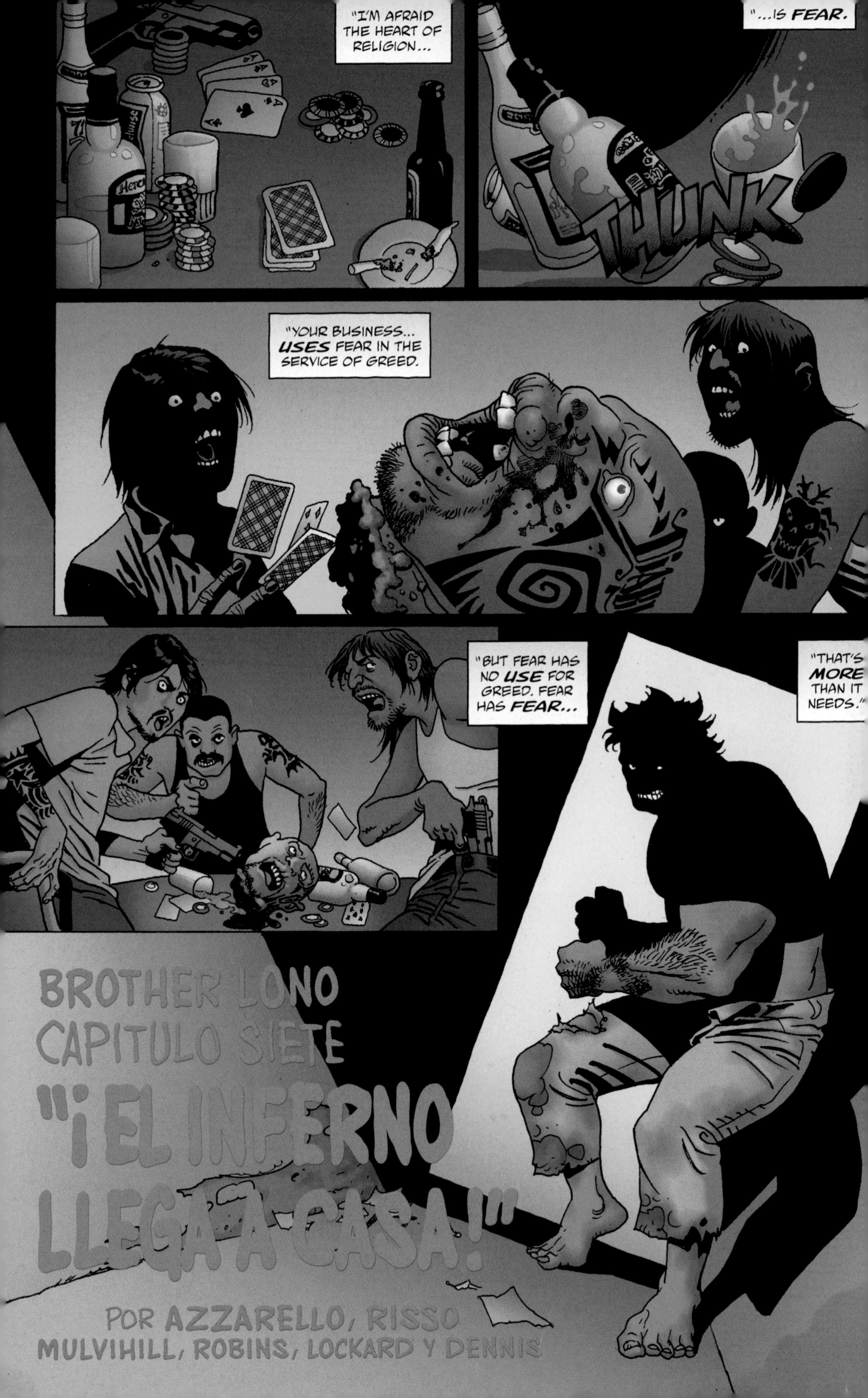
"I'M AFRAID THE HEART OF RELIGION...
"...IS FEAR.
THUNK
"YOUR BUSINESS... USES FEAR IN THE SERVICE OF GREED.
"BUT FEAR HAS NO USE FOR GREED. FEAR HAS FEAR...
"THAT'S MORE THAN IT NEEDS."
BROTHER LONO
CAPITULO SIETE
"¡EL INFERNO LLEGA A CASA!"
POR AZZARELLO, RISSO
MULVIHILL, ROBINS, LOCKARD Y DENNIS

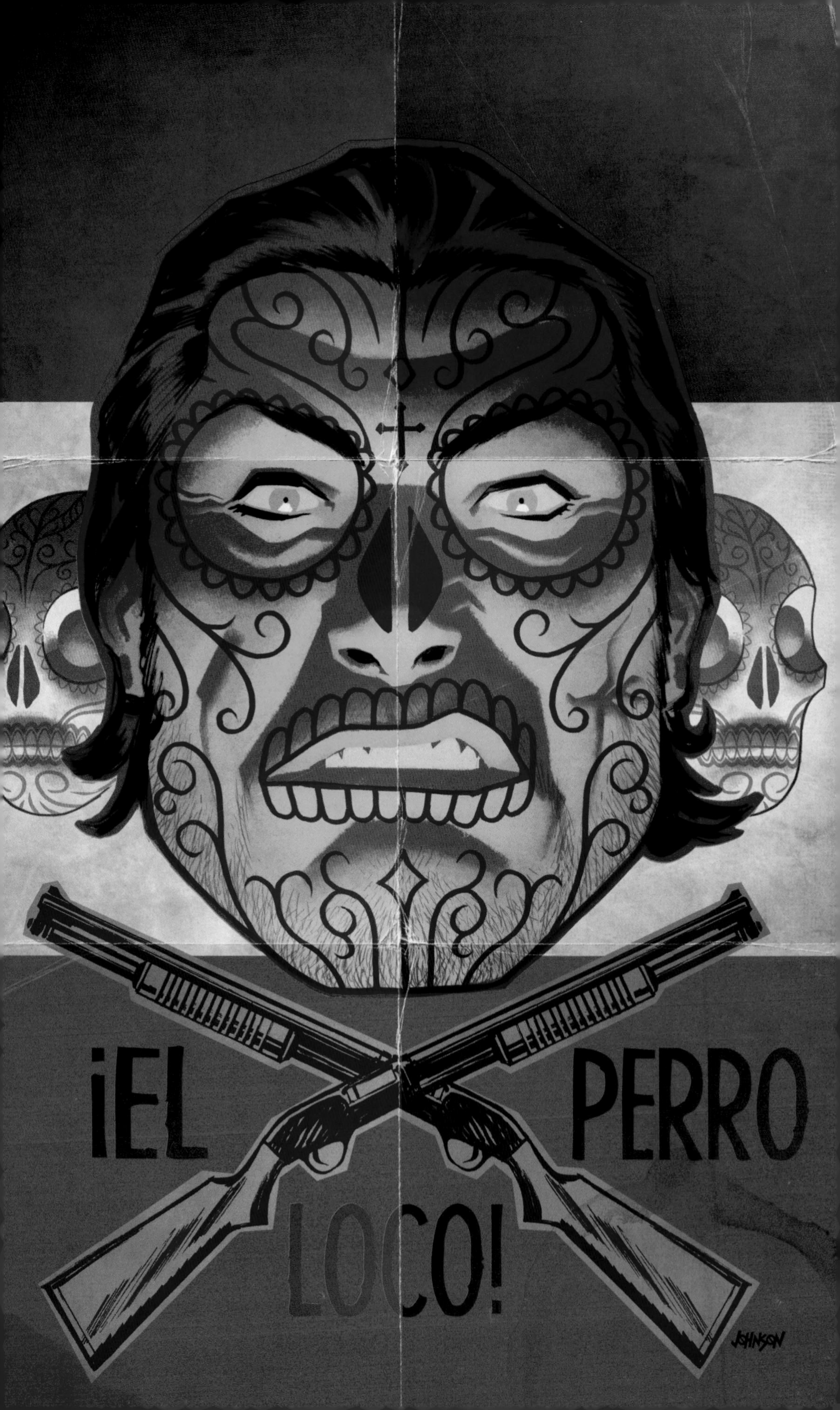
¡EL PERRO
LOCO!
JOHNSON

"The party is just getting started."

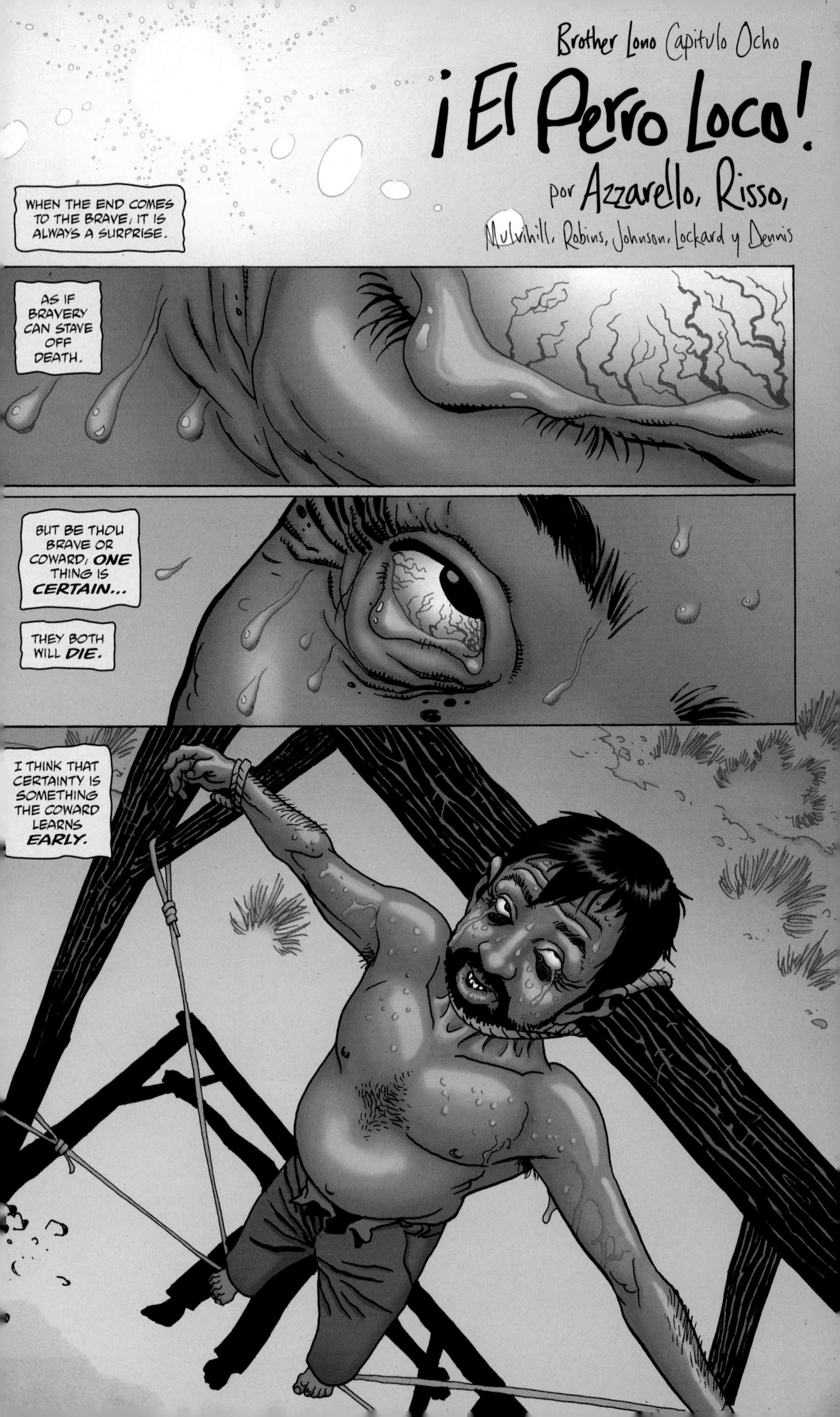
Brother Lono Capitulo Ocho
¡El Perro Loco!
por Azzarello, Risso,
Mulvihill, Robins, Johnson, Lockard y Dennis
WHEN THE END COMES TO THE BRAVE, IT IS ALWAYS A SURPRISE.
AS IF BRAVERY CAN STAVE OFF DEATH.
BUT BE THOU BRAVE OR COWARD, ONE THING IS CERTAIN...
THEY BOTH WILL DIE.
I THINK THAT CERTAINTY IS SOMETHING THE COWARD LEARNS EARLY.

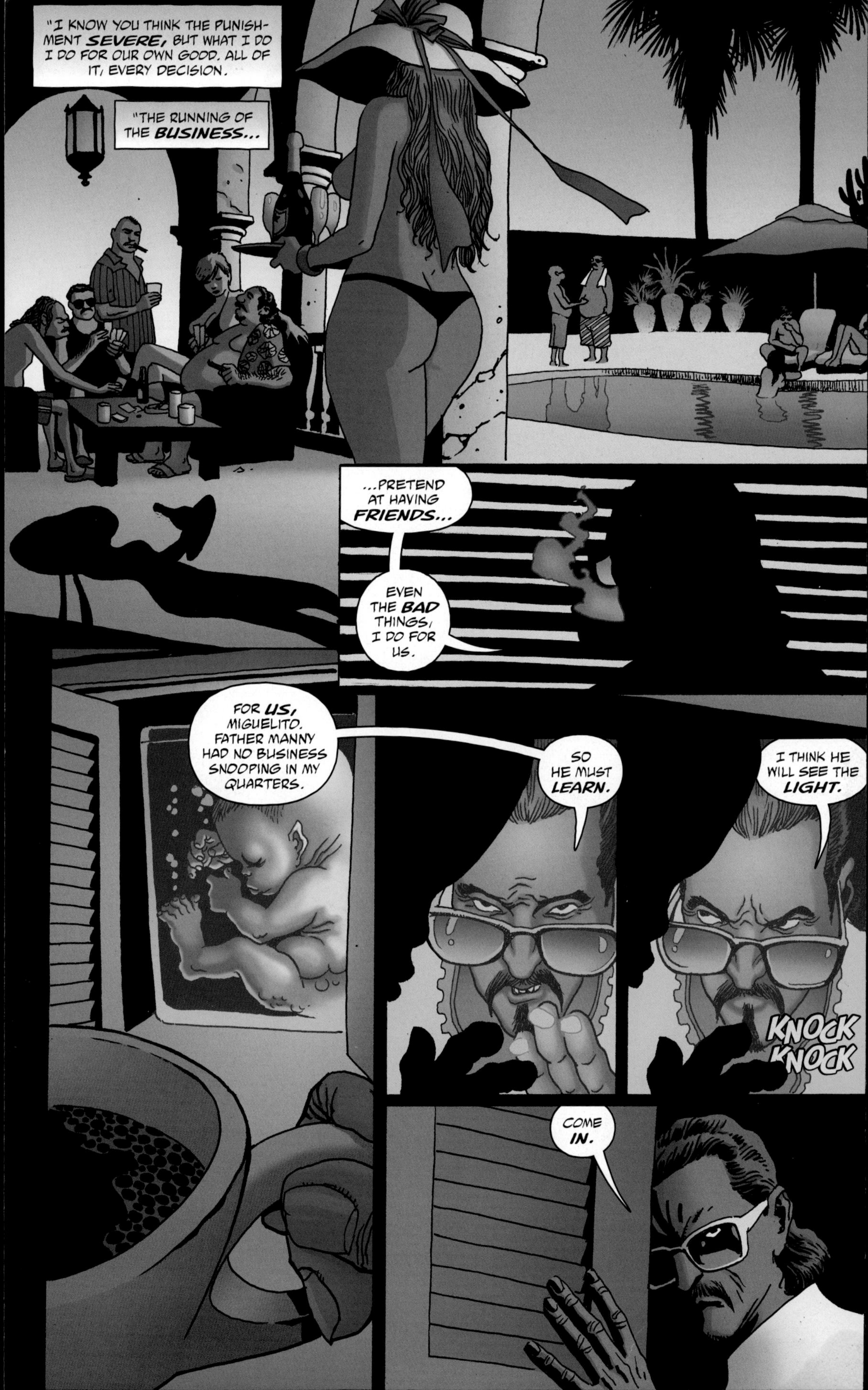
"I KNOW YOU THINK THE PUNISHMENT SEVERE, BUT WHAT I DO I DO FOR OUR OWN GOOD. ALL OF IT, EVERY DECISION.
"THE RUNNING OF THE BUSINESS...
...PRETEND AT HAVING FRIENDS...
EVEN THE BAD THINGS, I DO FOR US.
FOR US, MIGUELITO. FATHER MANNY HAD NO BUSINESS SNOOPING IN MY QUARTERS.
SO HE MUST LEARN.
I THINK HE WILL SEE THE LIGHT.
KNOCK KNOCK
COME IN.

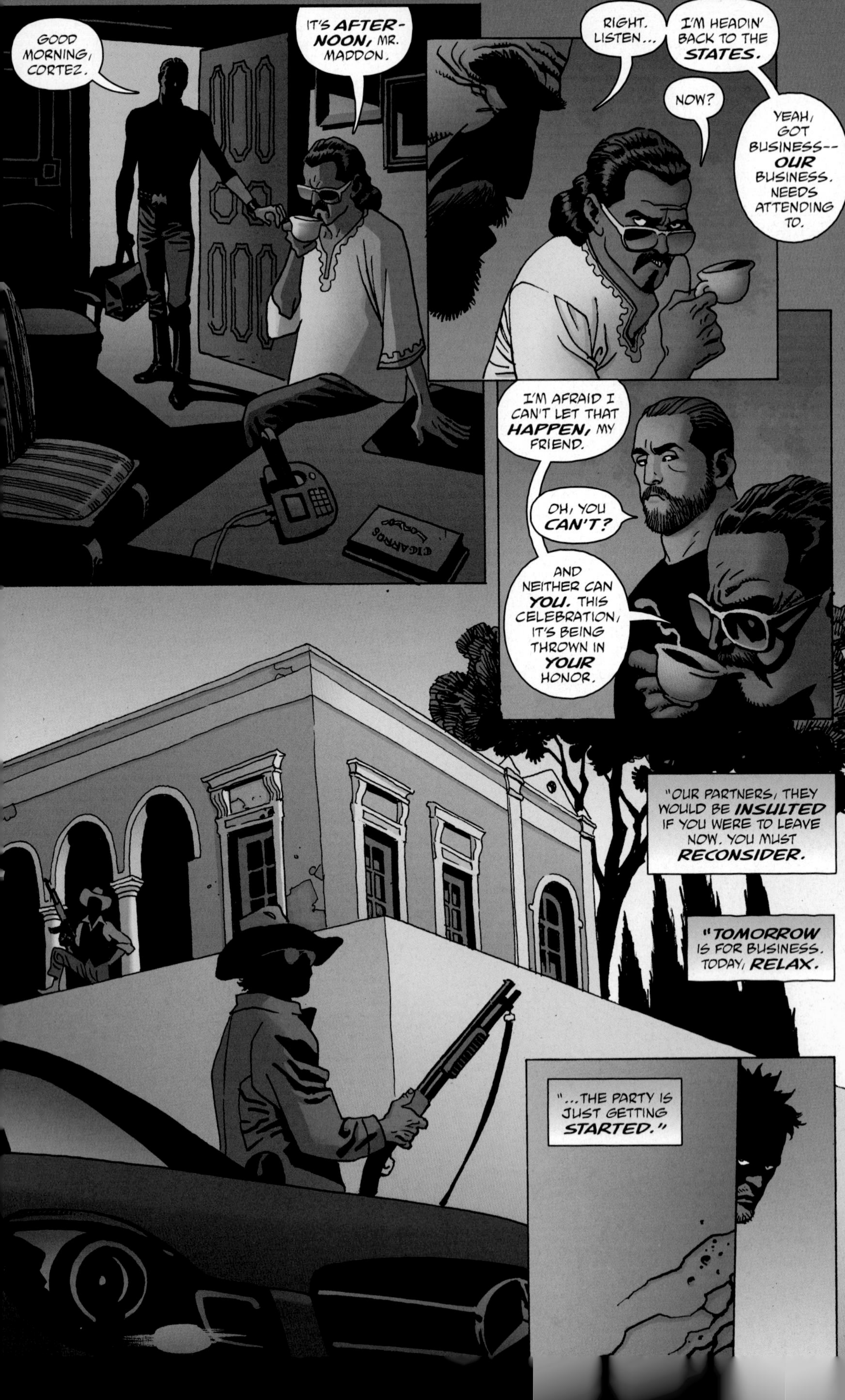
GOOD MORNING, CORTEZ.
IT'S AFTER-NOON, MR. MADDON.
CIGARROS
RIGHT. LISTEN...
I'M HEADIN' BACK TO THE STATES.
NOW?
YEAH, GOT BUSINESS-- OUR BUSINESS. NEEDS ATTENDING TO.
I'M AFRAID I CAN'T LET THAT HAPPEN, MY FRIEND.
OH, YOU CAN'T?
AND NEITHER CAN YOU. THIS CELEBRATION, IT'S BEING THROWN IN YOUR HONOR.
"OUR PARTNERS, THEY WOULD BE INSULTED IF YOU WERE TO LEAVE NOW. YOU MUST RECONSIDER.
"TOMORROW IS FOR BUSINESS. TODAY, RELAX.
"...THE PARTY IS JUST GETTING STARTED."

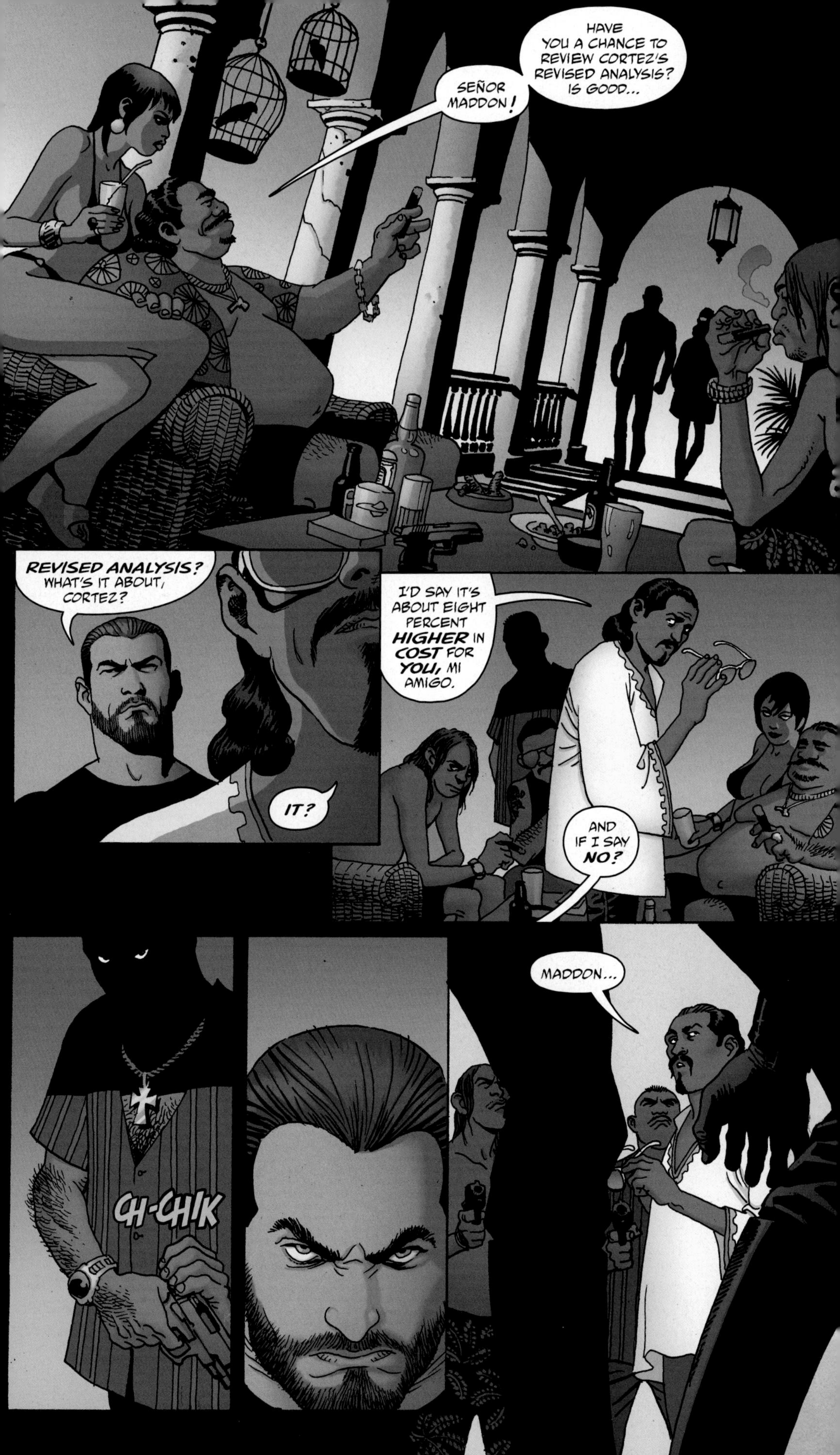
SEÑOR MADDON!
HAVE YOU A CHANCE TO REVIEW CORTEZ'S REVISED ANALYSIS? IS GOOD...
REVISED ANALYSIS? WHAT'S IT ABOUT, CORTEZ?
IT?
I'D SAY IT'S ABOUT EIGHT PERCENT HIGHER IN COST FOR YOU, MI AMIGO.
AND IF I SAY NO?
CH-CHIK
MADDON...

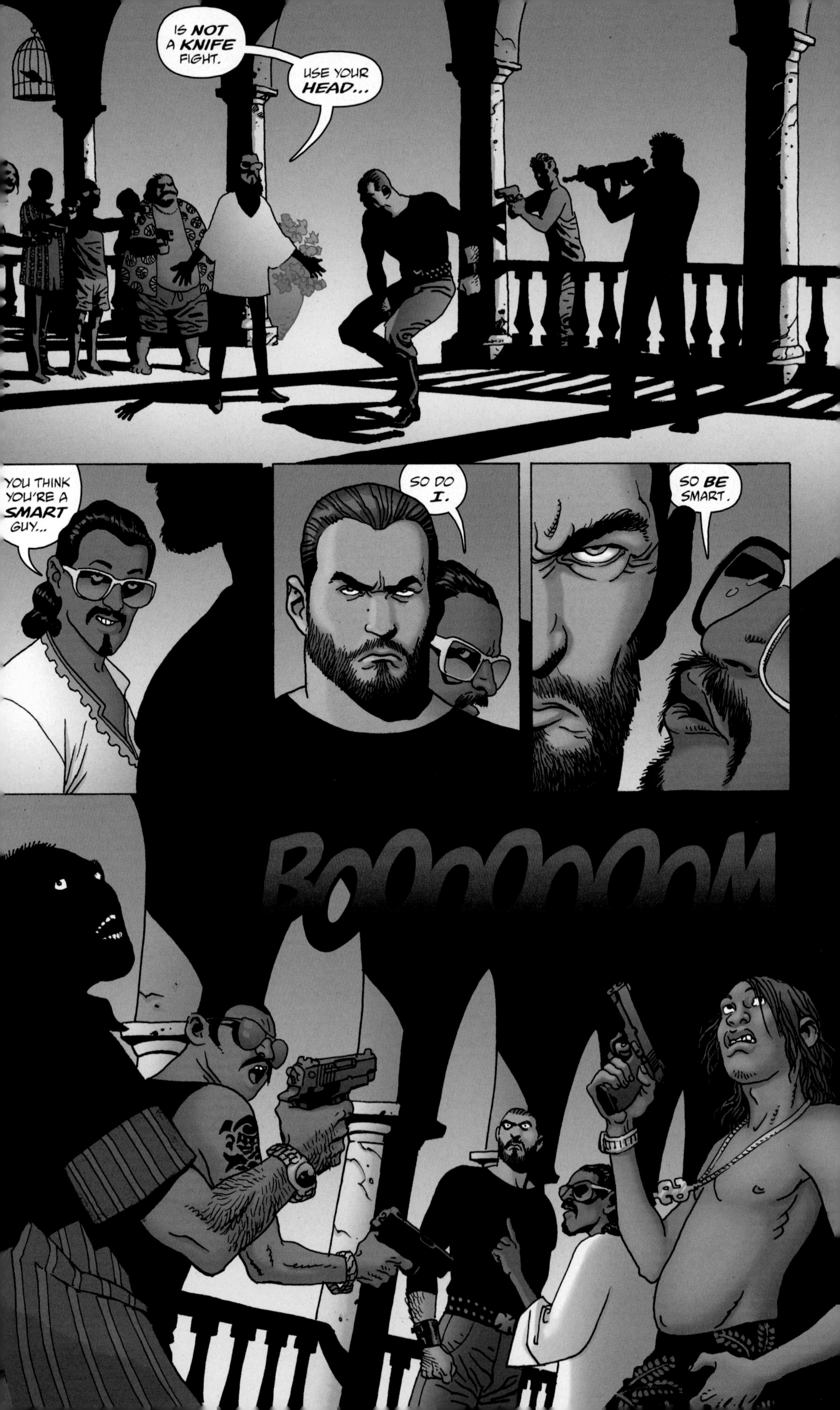
IS NOT A KNIFE FIGHT.
USE YOUR HEAD...
YOU THINK YOU'RE A SMART GUY...
SO DO I.
SO BE SMART.
BOOOOOOOM

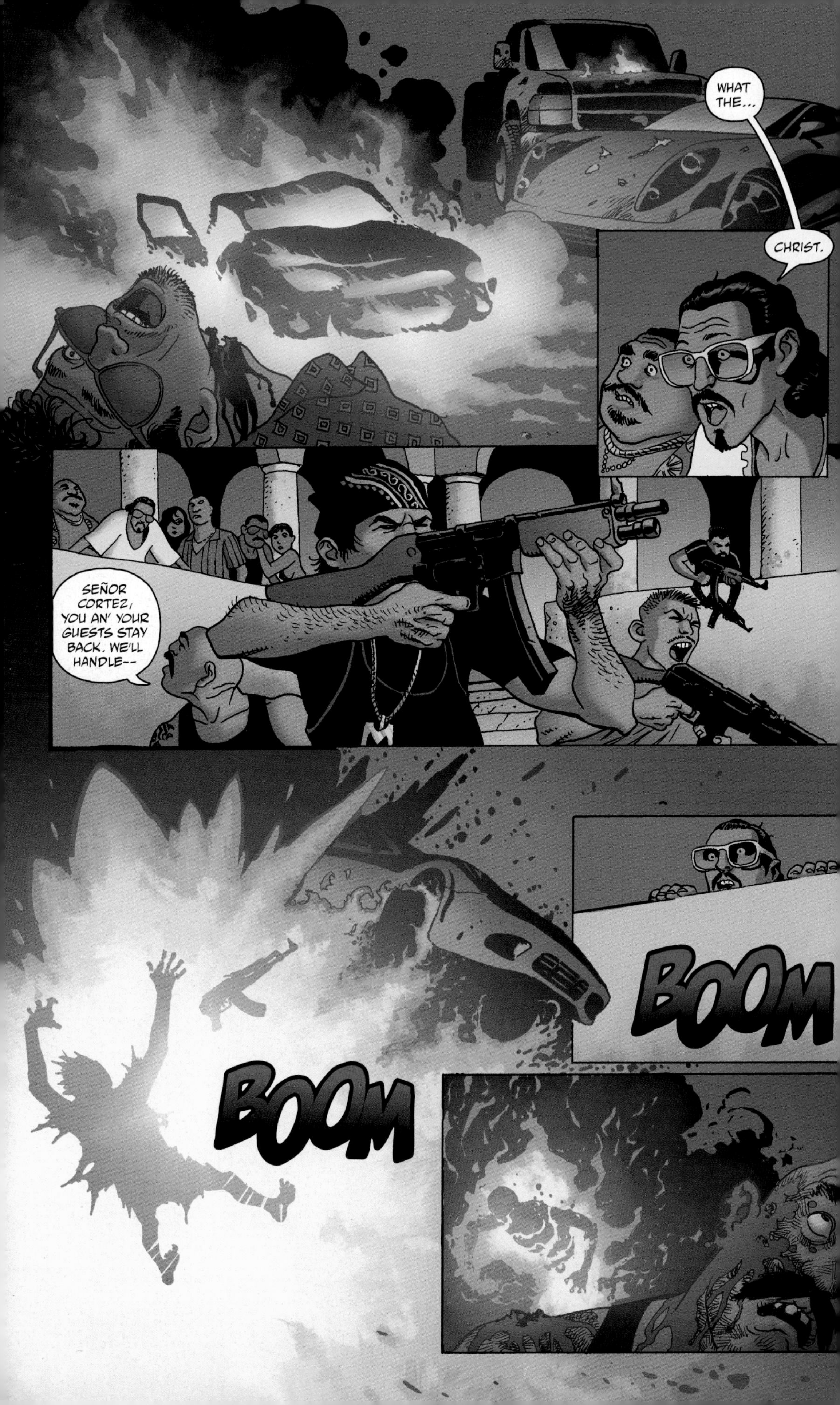
WHAT THE...
CHRIST.
SEÑOR CORTEZ, YOU AN' YOUR GUESTS STAY BACK. WE'LL HANDLE--
BOOM
BOOM

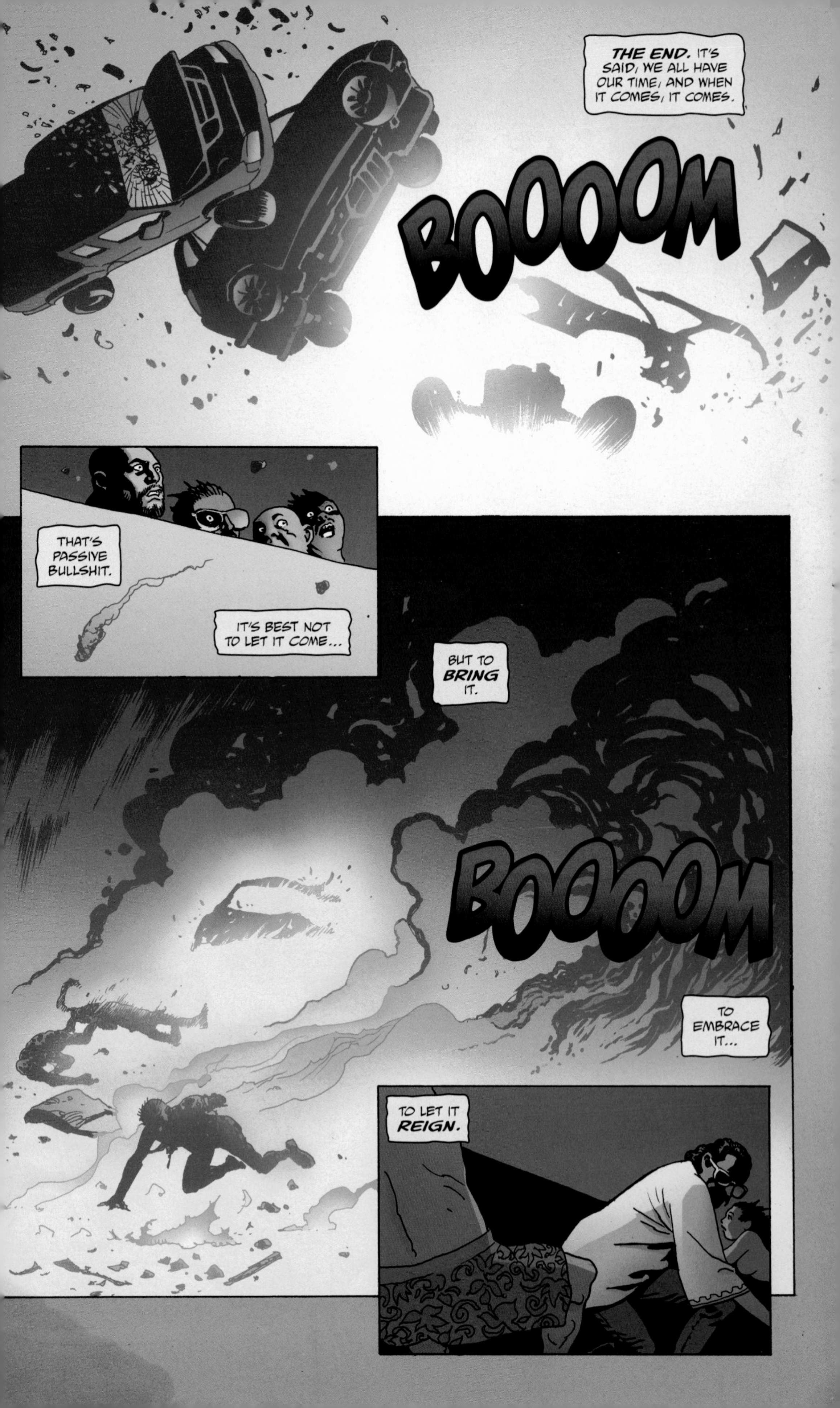
THE END. IT'S SAID, WE ALL HAVE OUR TIME, AND WHEN IT COMES, IT COMES.
BOOOOM
THAT'S PASSIVE BULLSHIT.
IT'S BEST NOT TO LET IT COME...
BUT TO BRING IT.
BOOOOM
TO EMBRACE IT...
TO LET IT REIGN.

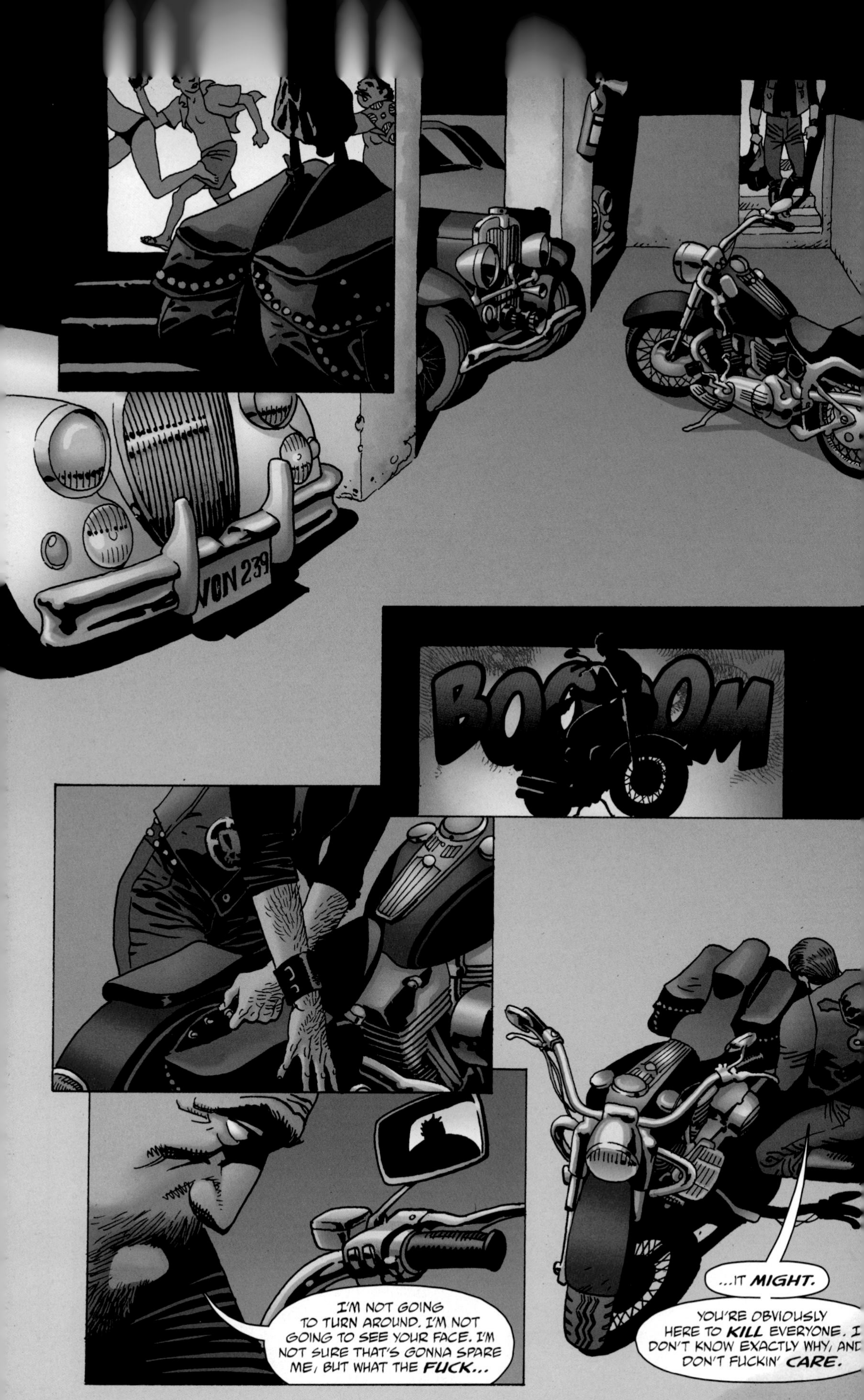
WON 239
BOOOOM
I'M NOT GOING TO TURN AROUND. I'M NOT GOING TO SEE YOUR FACE. I'M NOT SURE THAT'S GONNA SPARE ME, BUT WHAT THE FUCK...
...IT MIGHT.
YOU'RE OBVIOUSLY HERE TO KILL EVERYONE. I DON'T KNOW EXACTLY WHY, AND DON'T FUCKIN' CARE.

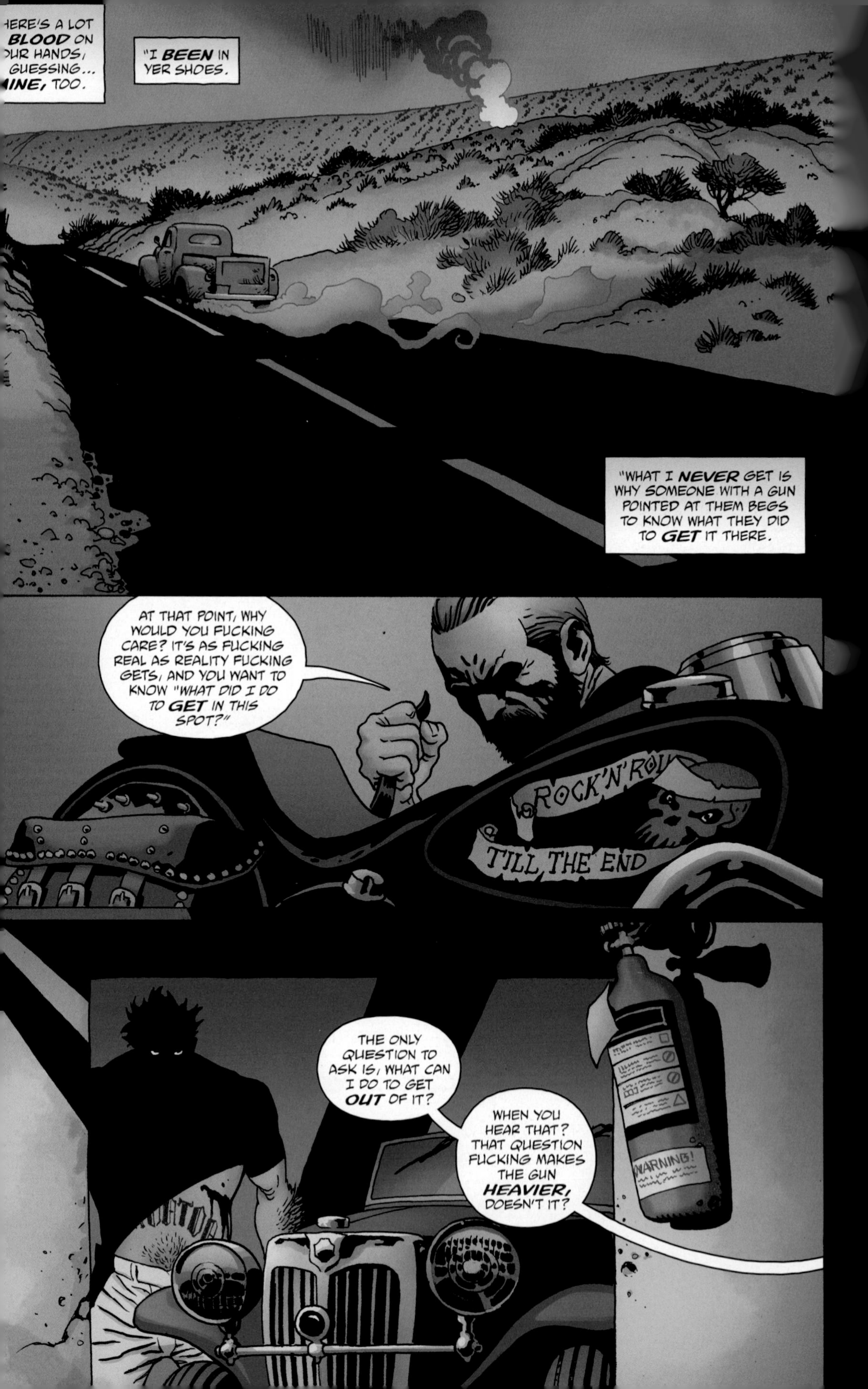
HERE'S A LOT BLOOD ON OUR HANDS, GUESSING... INE, TOO.
"I BEEN IN YER SHOES.
"WHAT I NEVER GET IS WHY SOMEONE WITH A GUN POINTED AT THEM BEGS TO KNOW WHAT THEY DID TO GET IT THERE.
AT THAT POINT, WHY WOULD YOU FUCKING CARE? IT'S AS FUCKING REAL AS REALITY FUCKING GETS, AND YOU WANT TO KNOW "WHAT DID I DO TO GET IN THIS SPOT?"
ROCK'N'ROL
TILL THE END
THE ONLY QUESTION TO ASK IS, WHAT CAN I DO TO GET OUT OF IT?
WHEN YOU HEAR THAT? THAT QUESTION FUCKING MAKES THE GUN HEAVIER, DOESN'T IT?
WARNING!

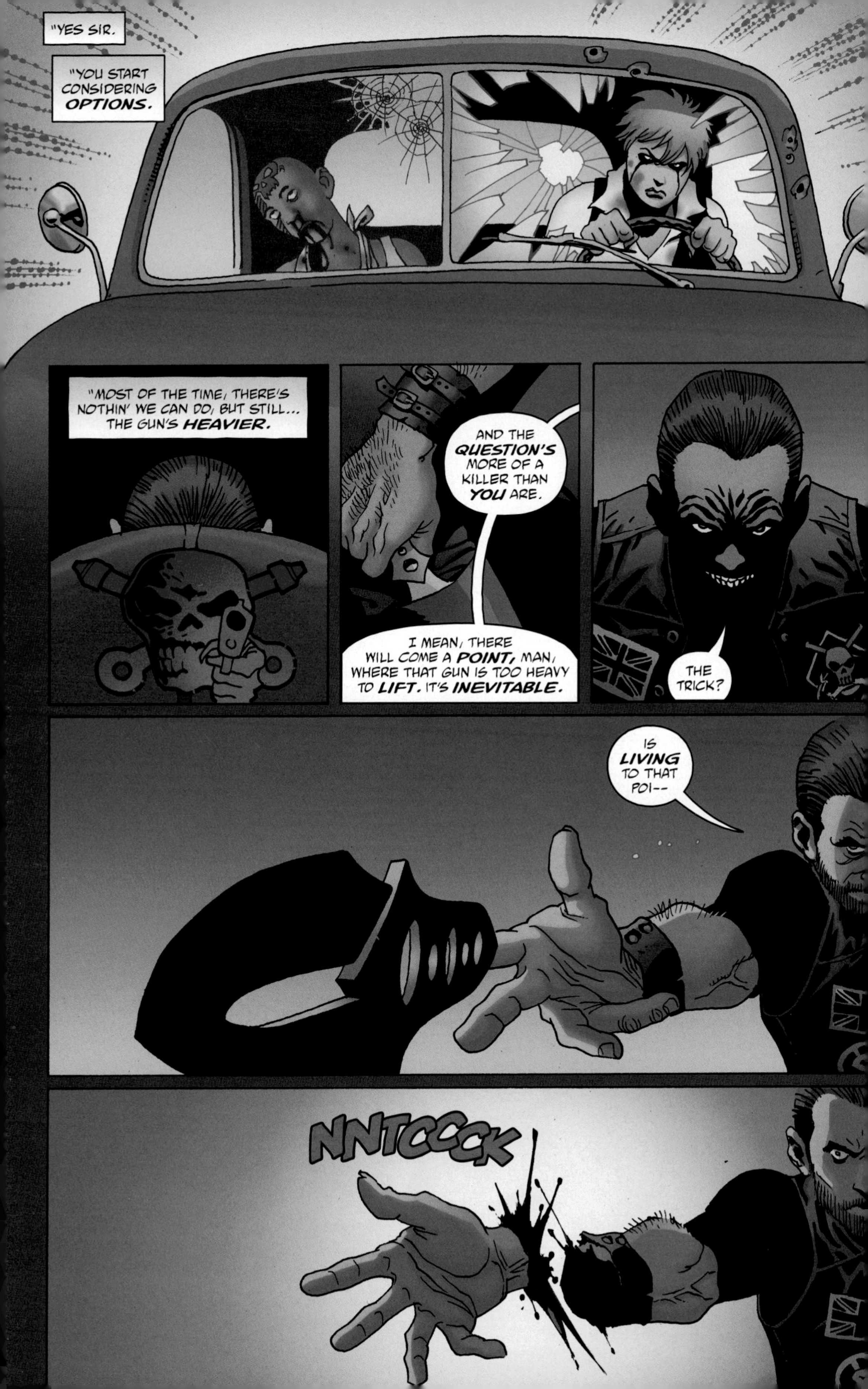
"YES SIR.
"YOU START CONSIDERING OPTIONS.
"MOST OF THE TIME, THERE'S NOTHIN' WE CAN DO, BUT STILL... THE GUN'S HEAVIER.
AND THE QUESTION'S MORE OF A KILLER THAN YOU ARE.
I MEAN, THERE WILL COME A POINT, MAN, WHERE THAT GUN IS TOO HEAVY TO LIFT. IT'S INEVITABLE.
THE TRICK?
IS LIVING TO THAT POI--
NNTCCCCK

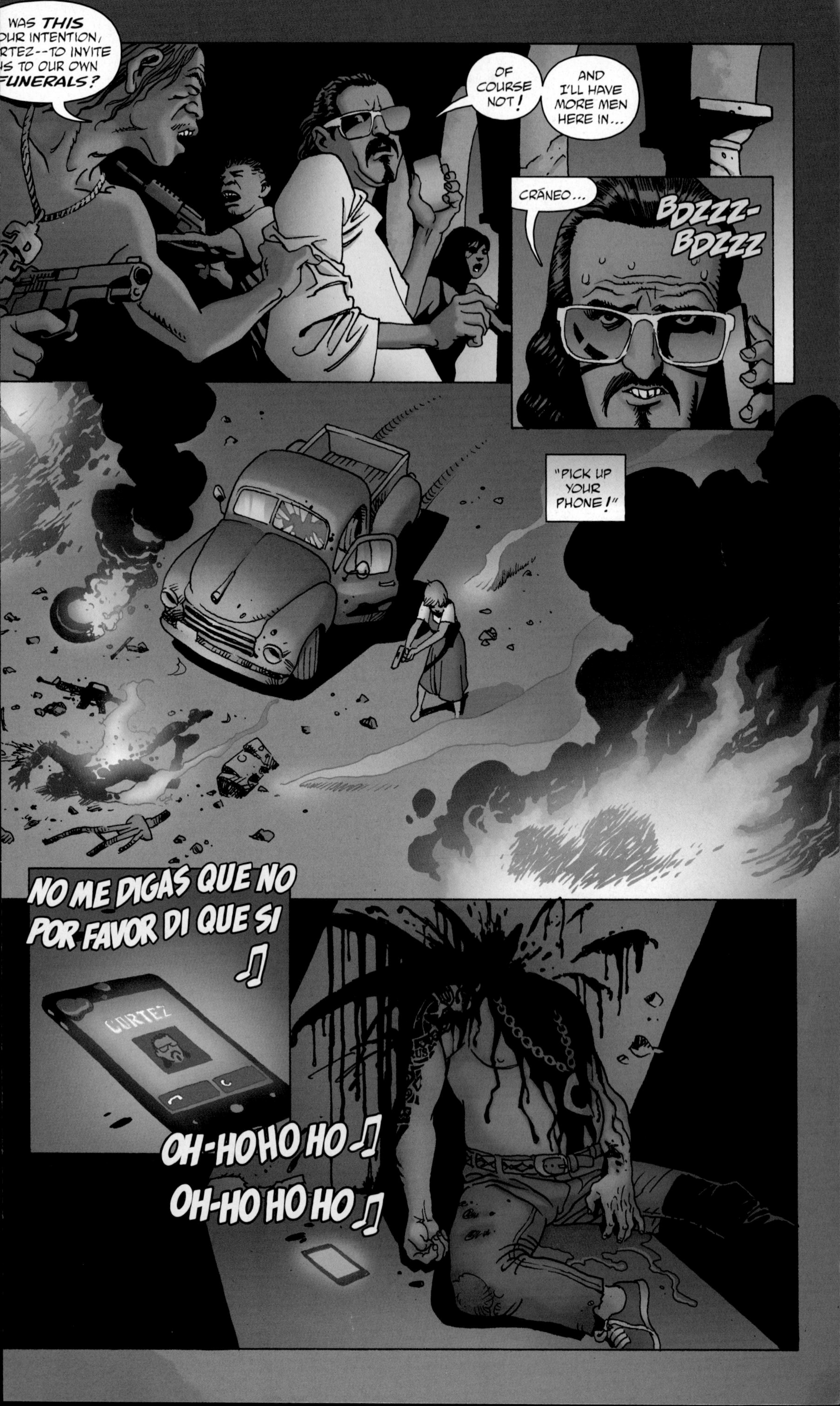
WAS THIS
OUR INTENTION,
CORTEZ--TO INVITE
US TO OUR OWN
FUNERALS?
OF COURSE NOT!
AND I'LL HAVE MORE MEN HERE IN...
CRÁNEO...
BDZZZ-BDZZZ
"PICK UP YOUR PHONE!"
NO ME DIGAS QUE NO
POR FAVOR DI QUE SI ♫
CORTEZ
OH-HOHO HO ♫
OH-HO HO HO ♫

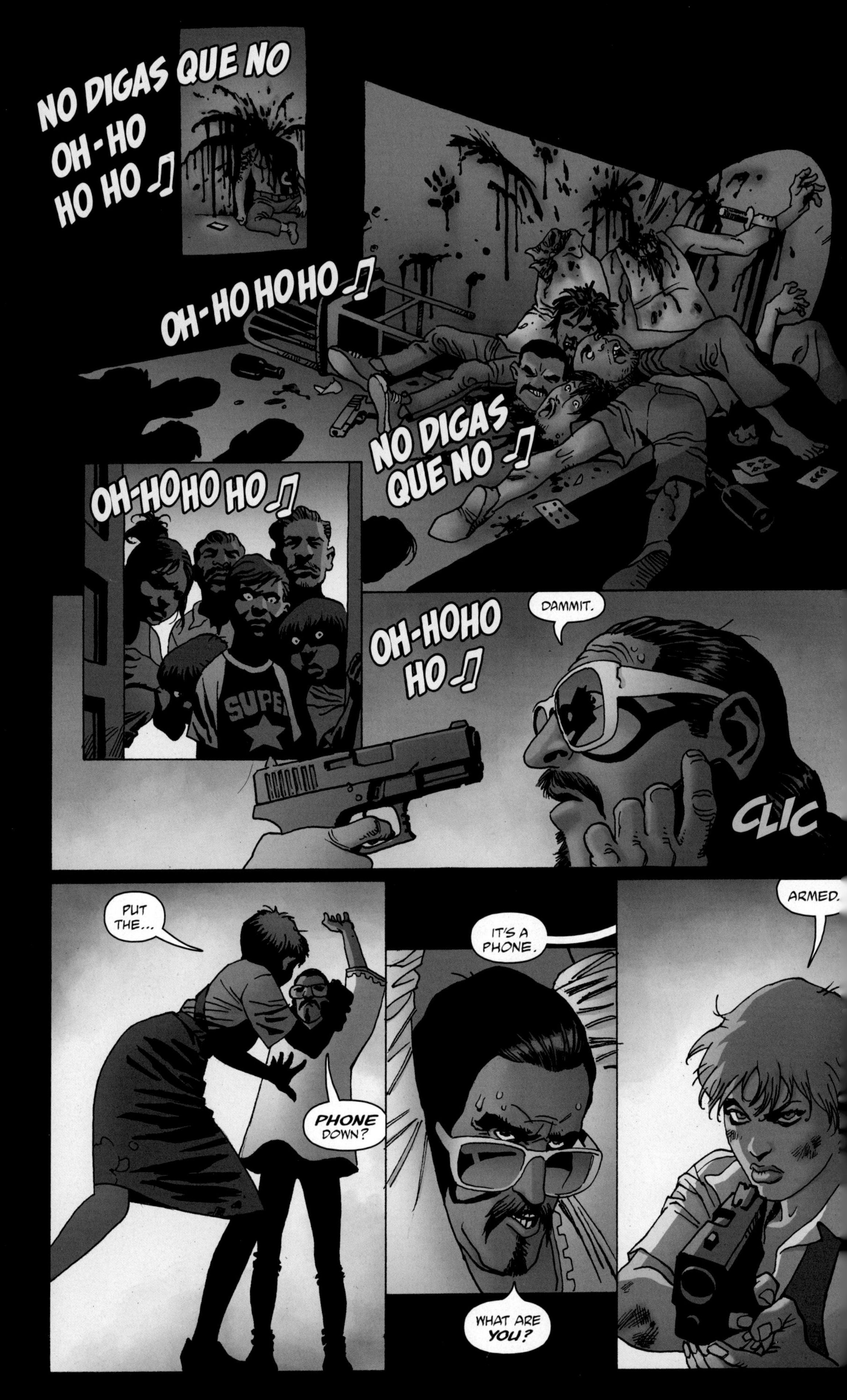
NO DIGAS QUE NO
OH-HO
HO HO ♫
OH-HO HO HO ♫
NO DIGAS
QUE NO ♫
OH-HO HO HO ♫
OH-HOHO
HO ♫
DAMMIT.
CLIC
PUT
THE...
PHONE
DOWN?
IT'S A
PHONE.
WHAT ARE
YOU?
ARMED.

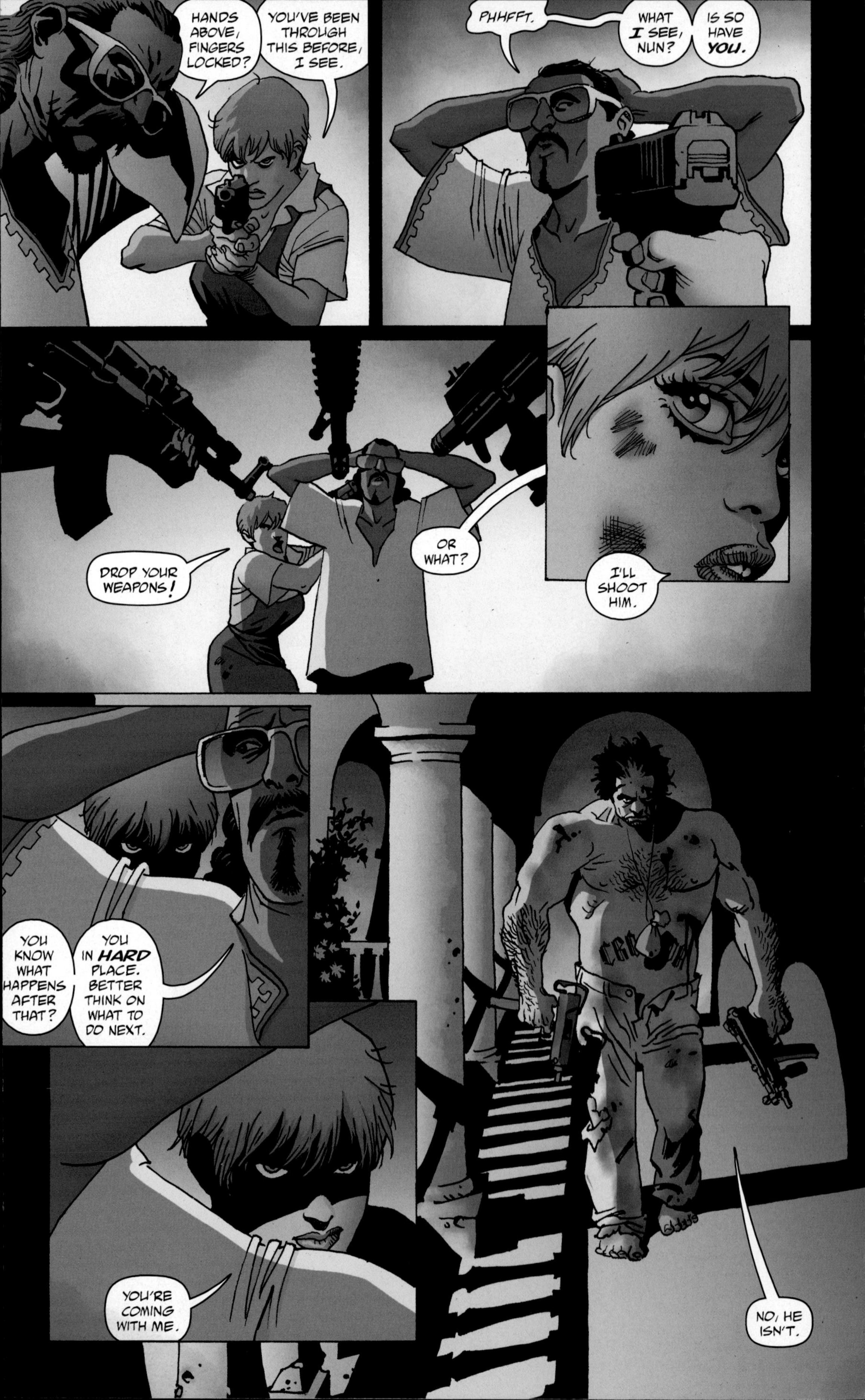

HANDS ABOVE, FINGERS LOCKED?
YOU'VE BEEN THROUGH THIS BEFORE, I SEE.
PHHFFT.
WHAT I SEE, NUN?
IS SO HAVE YOU.
DROP YOUR WEAPONS!
OR WHAT?
I'LL SHOOT HIM.
YOU KNOW WHAT HAPPENS AFTER THAT?
YOU IN HARD PLACE. BETTER THINK ON WHAT TO DO NEXT.
YOU'RE COMING WITH ME.
NO, HE ISN'T.

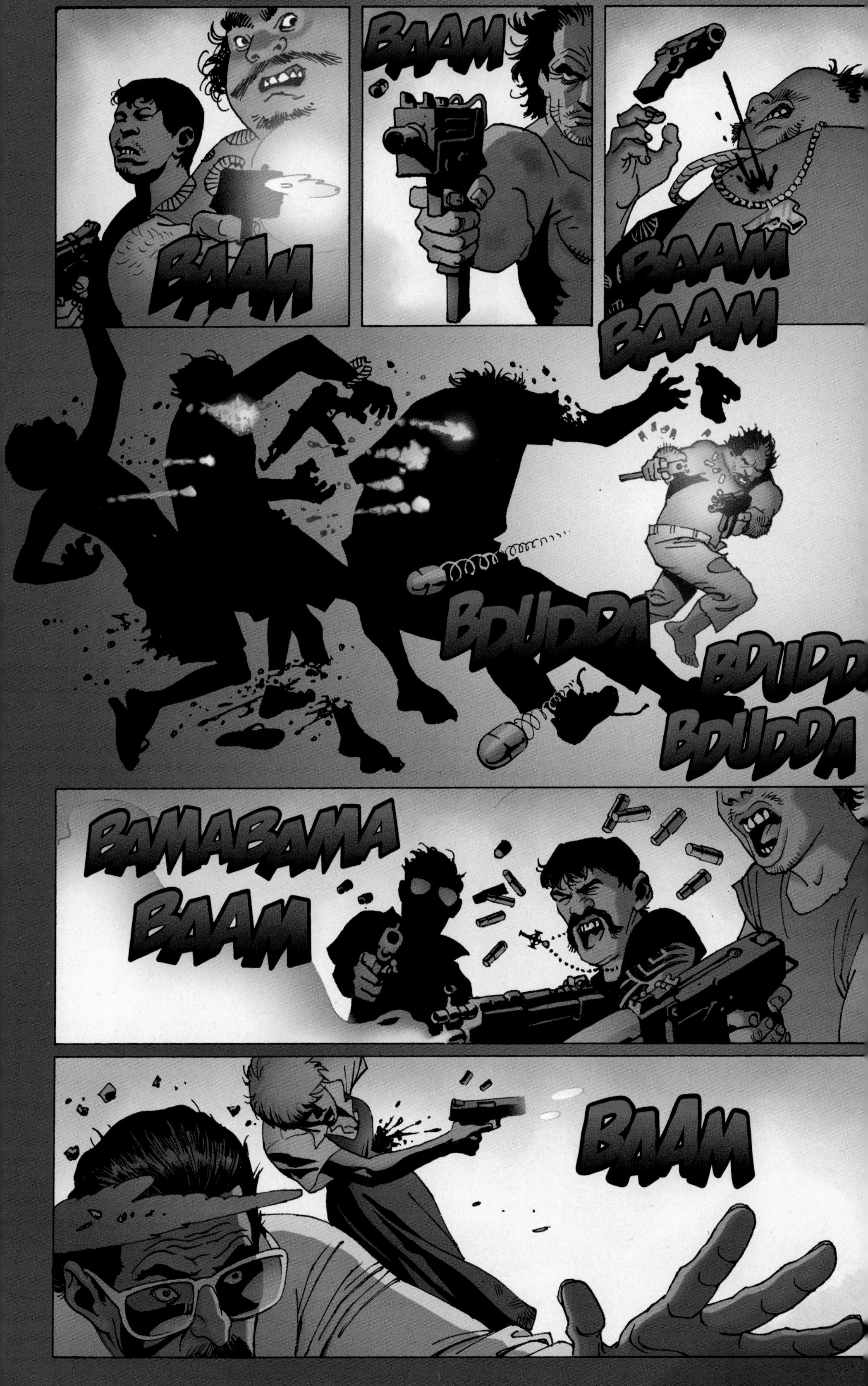
BAAM
BAAM
BAAM
BAAM
BDUDDA
BDUDDA
BDUDDA
BAMABAMA
BAAM
BAAM

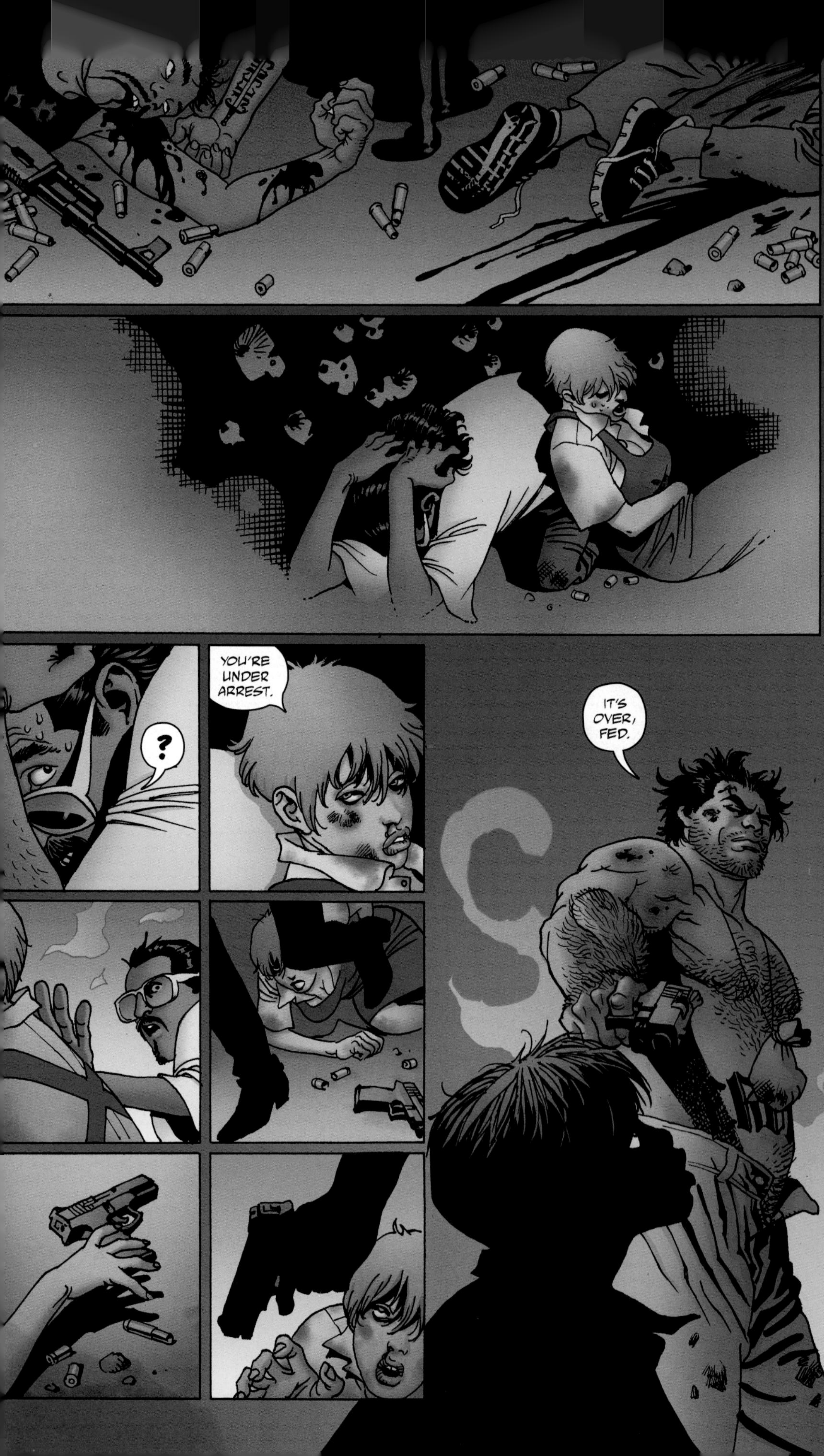
?
YOU'RE UNDER ARREST.
IT'S OVER, FED.

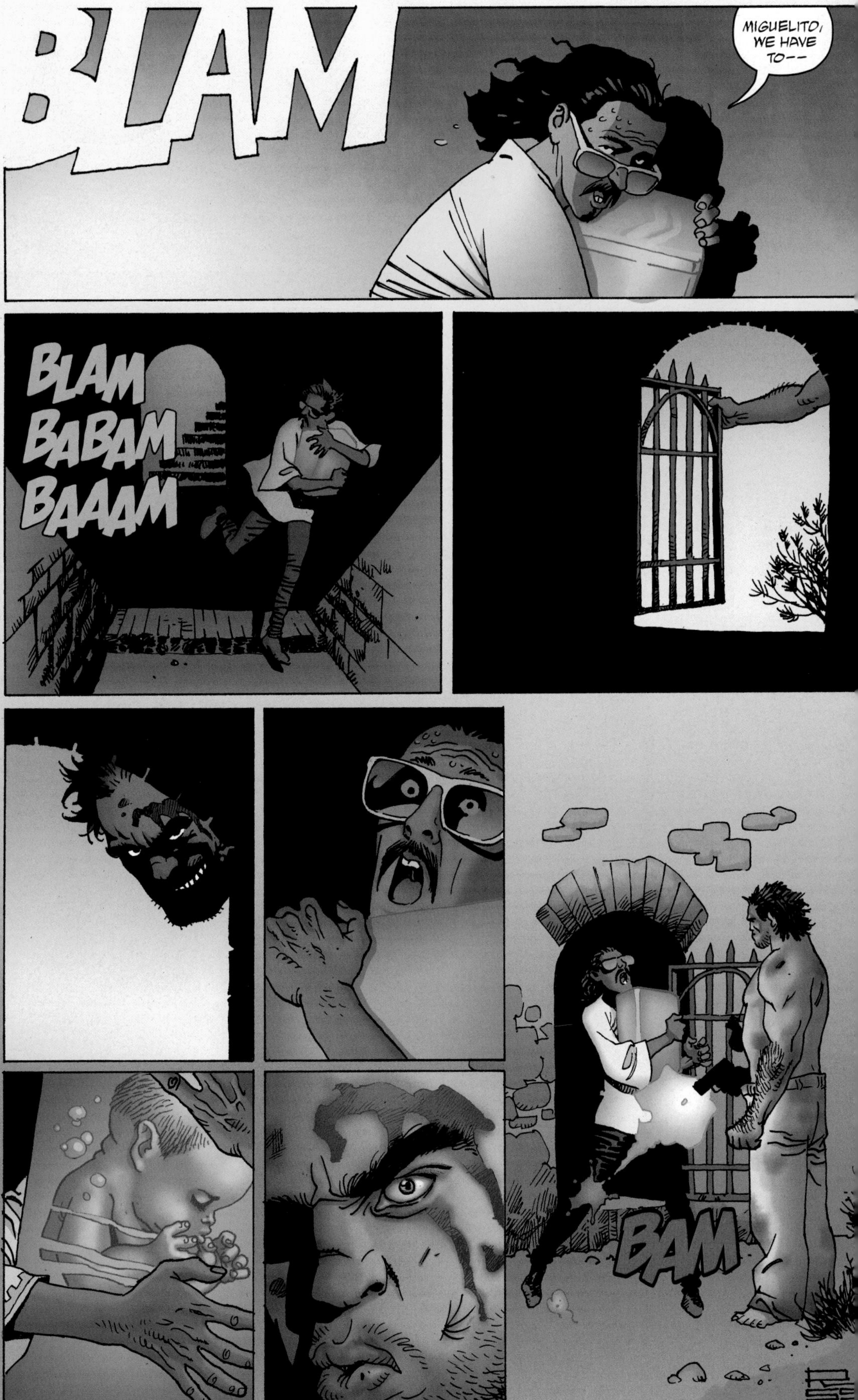
BLAM
MIGUELITO, WE HAVE TO--
BLAM
BABAM
BAAAM
BAM

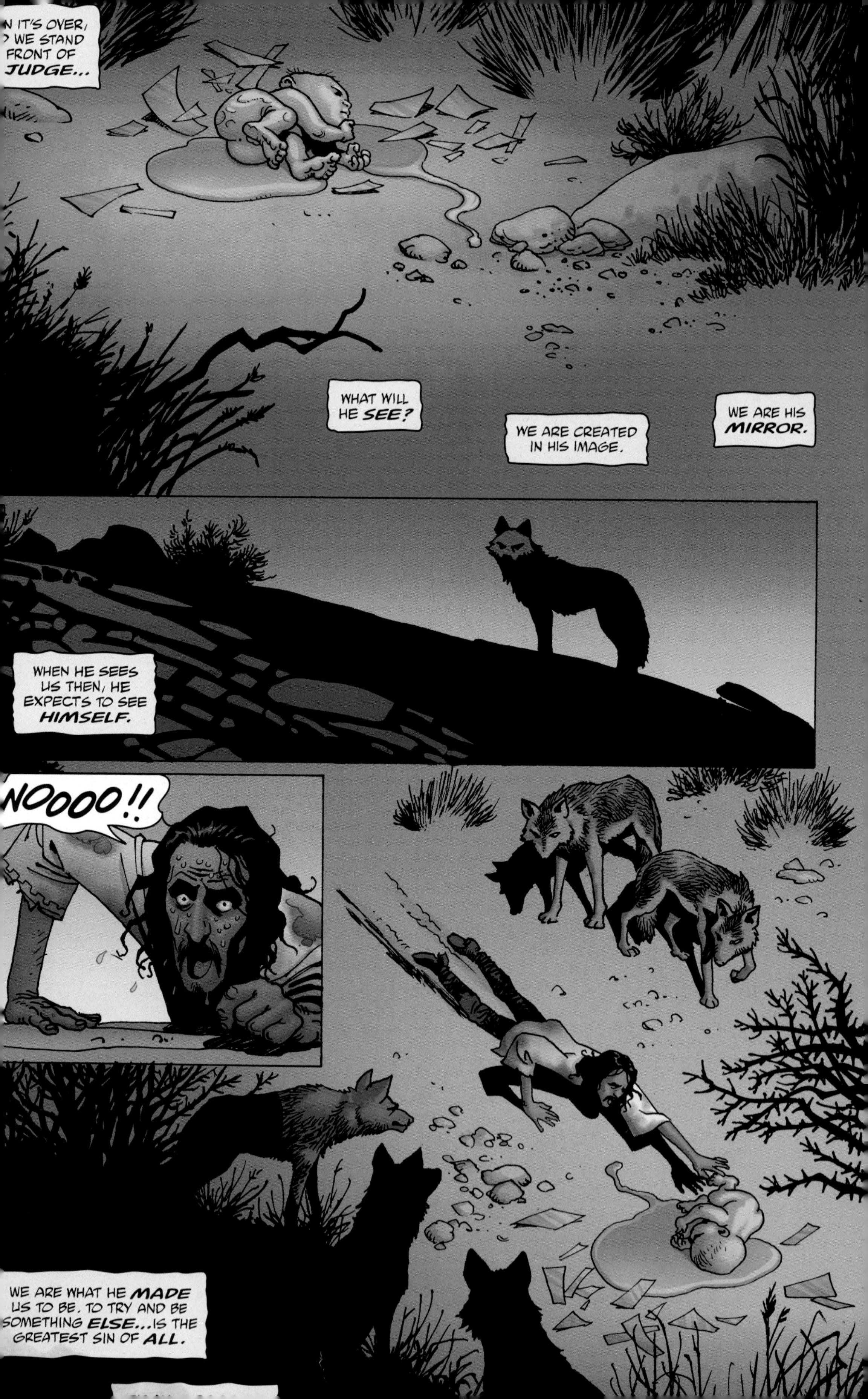
N IT'S OVER,) WE STAND FRONT OF JUDGE...
WHAT WILL HE SEE?
WE ARE CREATED IN HIS IMAGE.
WE ARE HIS MIRROR.
WHEN HE SEES US THEN, HE EXPECTS TO SEE HIMSELF.
NOOOO!!
WE ARE WHAT HE MADE US TO BE. TO TRY AND BE SOMETHING ELSE...IS THE GREATEST SIN OF ALL.

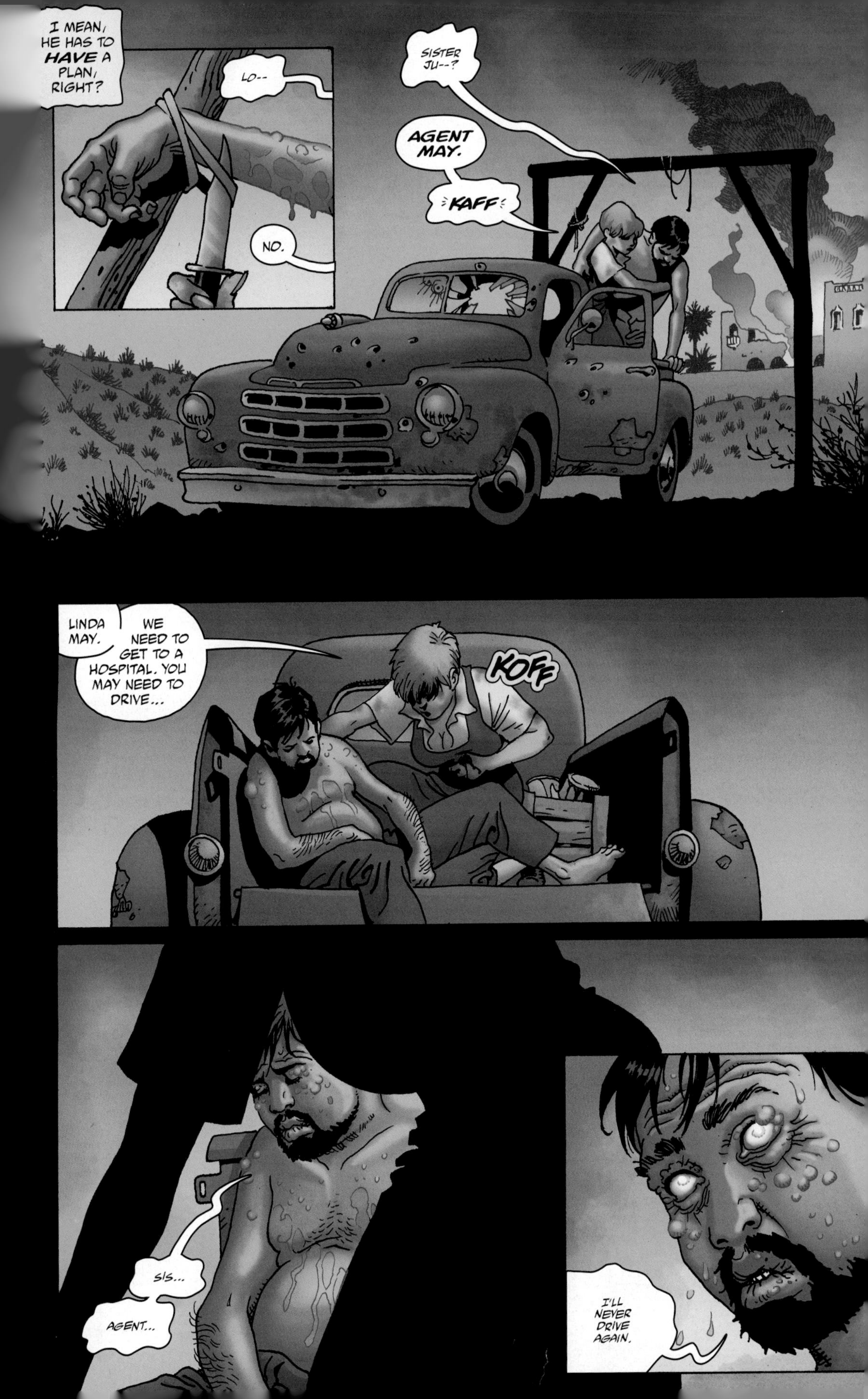
I MEAN, HE HAS TO *HAVE* A PLAN, RIGHT?
LO--
NO.
SISTER JU--?
AGENT MAY.
KAFF
LINDA MAY.
WE NEED TO GET TO A HOSPITAL. YOU MAY NEED TO DRIVE...
KOFF
SIS...
AGENT...
I'LL NEVER DRIVE AGAIN.

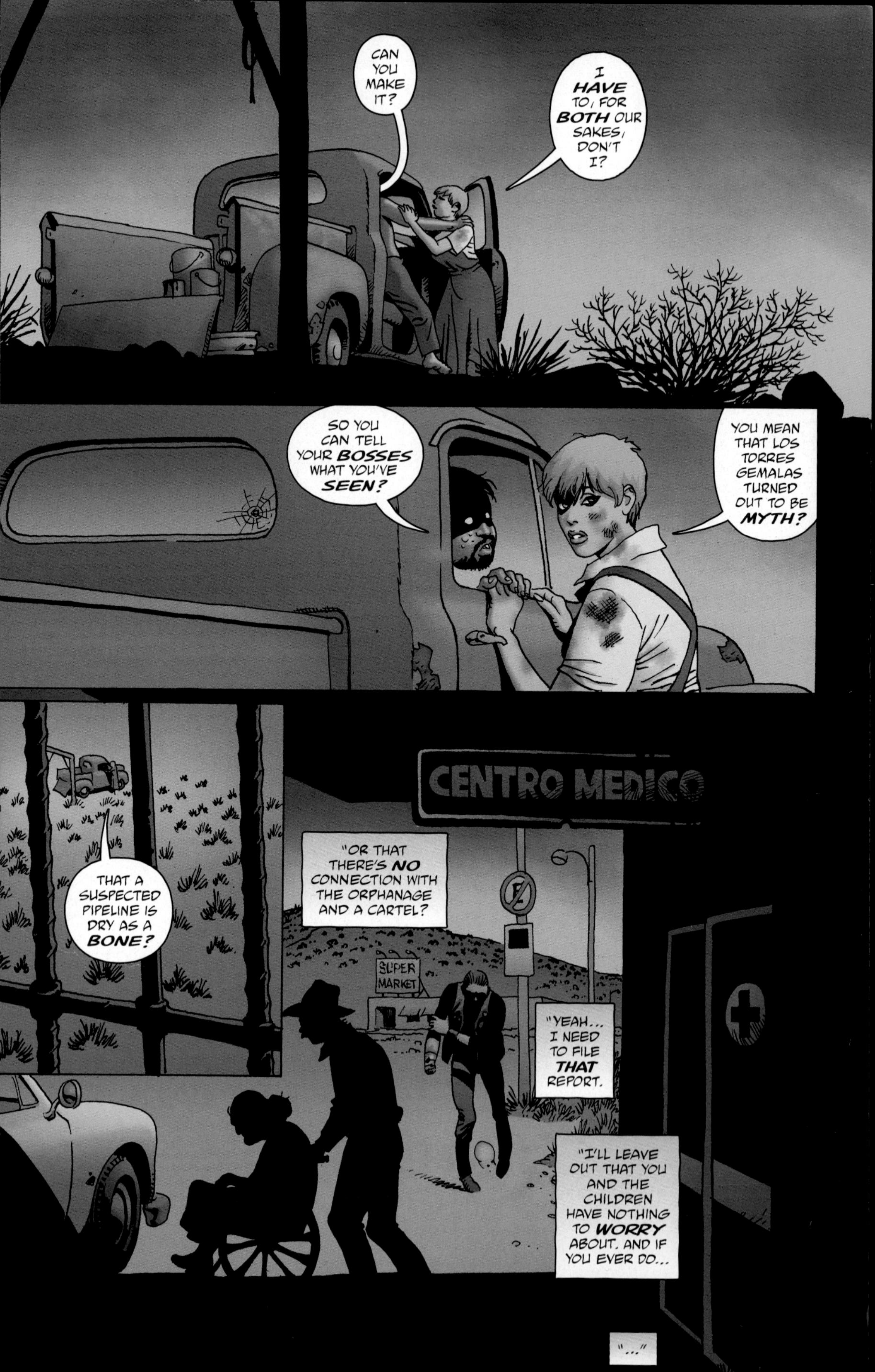
CAN YOU MAKE IT?
I HAVE TO, FOR BOTH OUR SAKES, DON'T I?
SO YOU CAN TELL YOUR BOSSES WHAT YOU'VE SEEN?
YOU MEAN THAT LOS TORRES GEMALAS TURNED OUT TO BE MYTH?
CENTRO MEDICO
THAT A SUSPECTED PIPELINE IS DRY AS A BONE?
"OR THAT THERE'S NO CONNECTION WITH THE ORPHANAGE AND A CARTEL?
SUPER MARKET
"YEAH... I NEED TO FILE THAT REPORT.
"I'LL LEAVE OUT THAT YOU AND THE CHILDREN HAVE NOTHING TO WORRY ABOUT. AND IF YOU EVER DO...
"..."

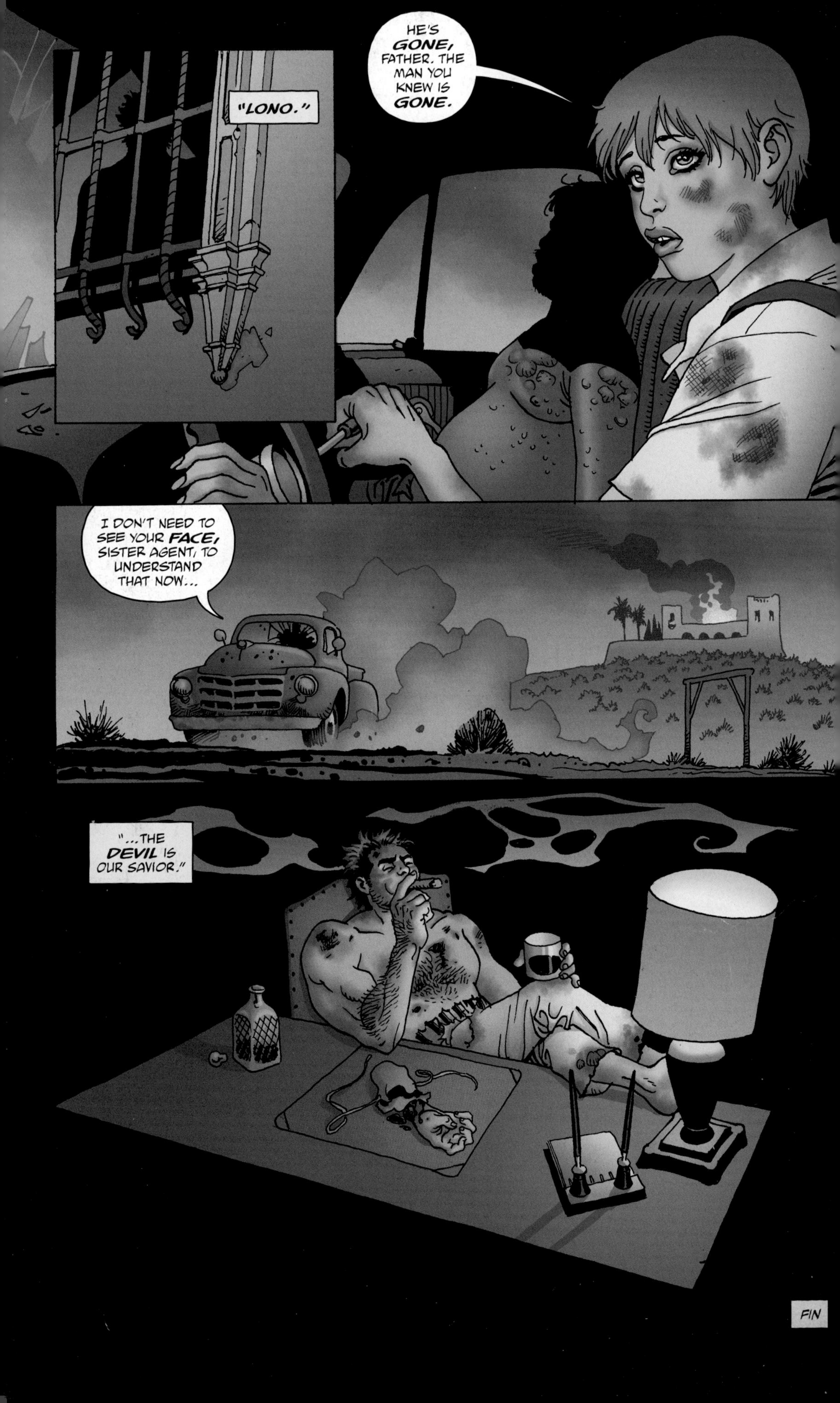
"LONO."
HE'S GONE, FATHER. THE MAN YOU KNEW IS GONE.
I DON'T NEED TO SEE YOUR FACE, SISTER AGENT, TO UNDERSTAND THAT NOW...
"...THE DEVIL IS OUR SAVIOR."
FIN

Variant cover art for issue #1 by Eduardo Risso.

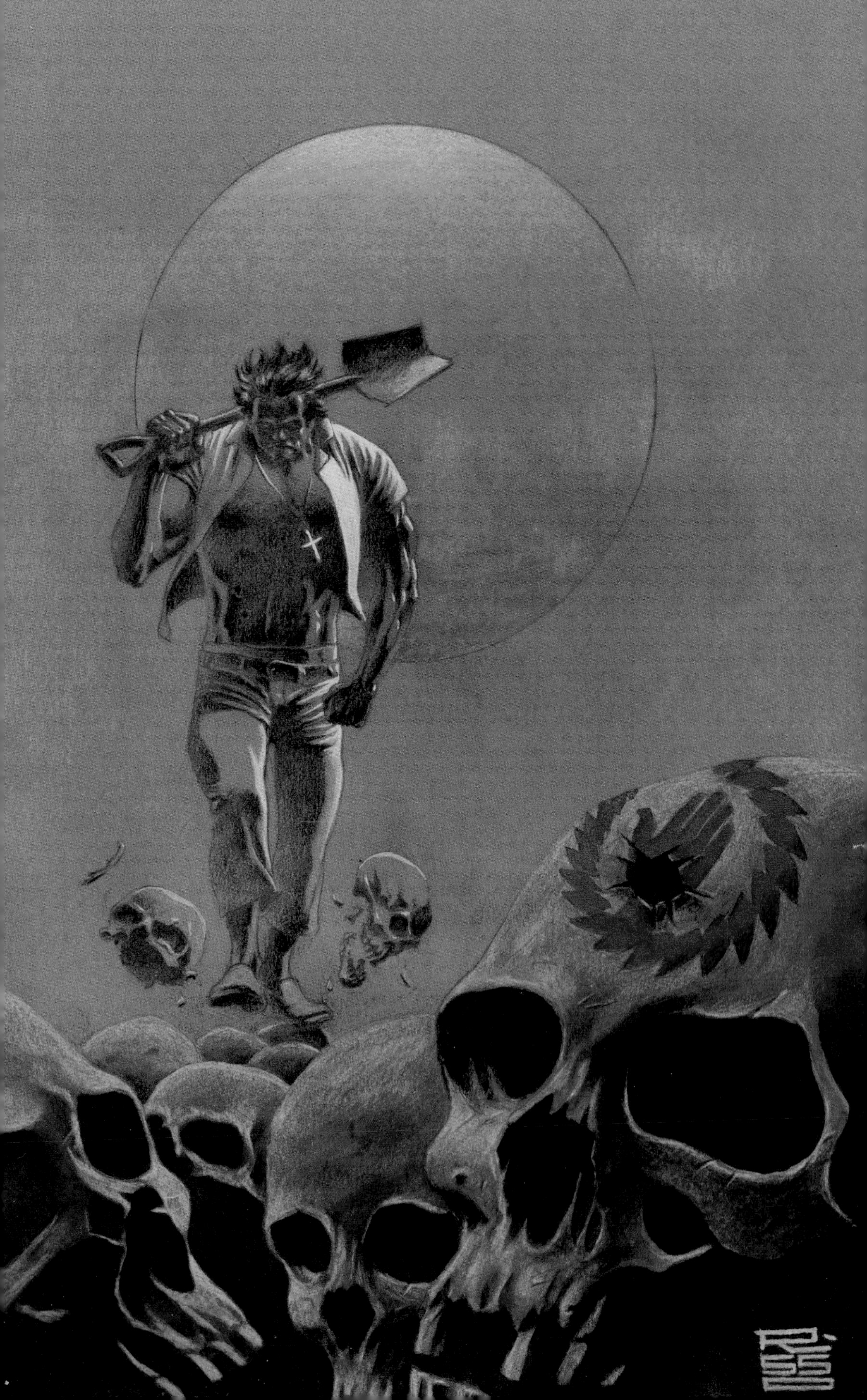

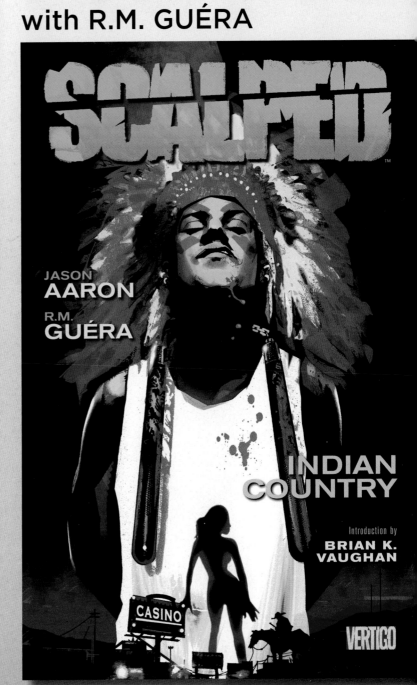

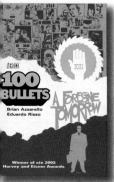

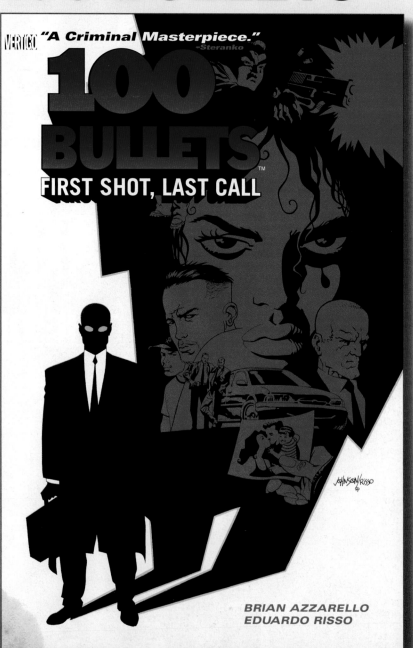

FROM THE WRITER OF *NORTHLANDERS* & *DEMO*
BRIAN WOOD
with RICCARDO BURCHIELLI

**DMZ VOL. 3:
PUBLIC WORKS**

**READ THE ENTIRE
SERIES!**

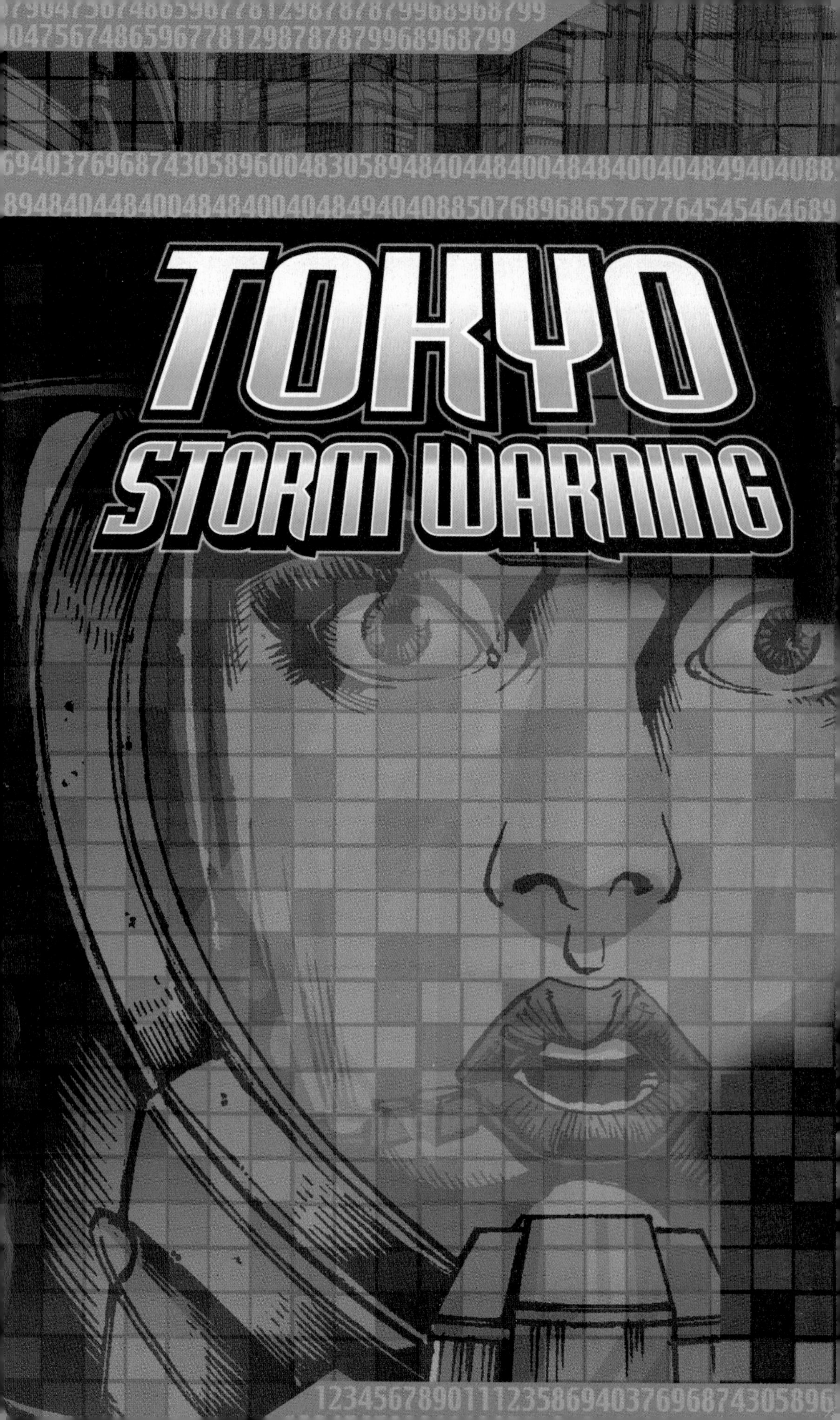
TOKYO STORM WARNING

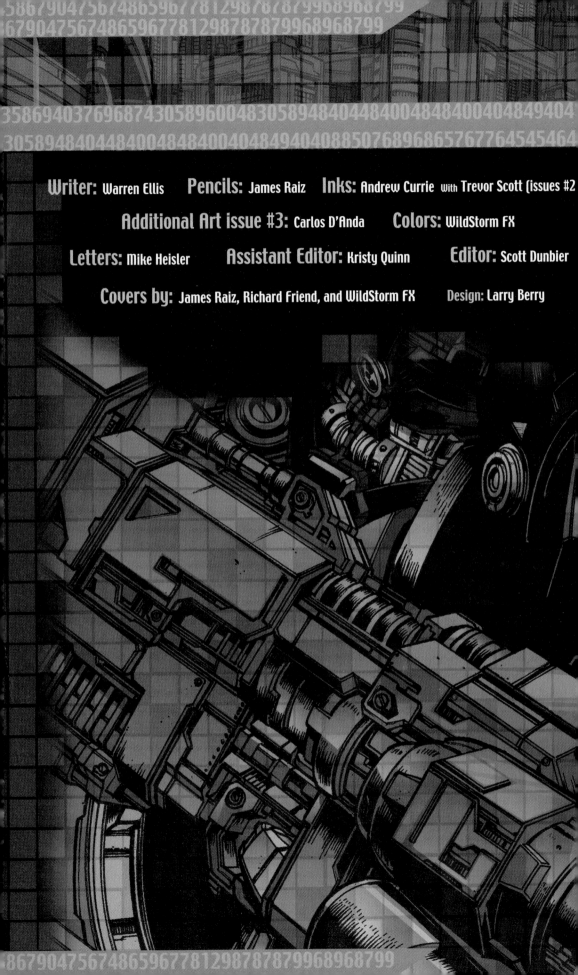

Writer: Warren Ellis **Pencils:** James Raiz **Inks:** Andrew Currie with Trevor Scott (issues #2

Additional Art issue #3: Carlos D'Anda **Colors:** WildStorm FX

Letters: Mike Heisler **Assistant Editor:** Kristy Quinn **Editor:** Scott Dunbier

Covers by: James Raiz, Richard Friend, and WildStorm FX **Design:** Larry Berry

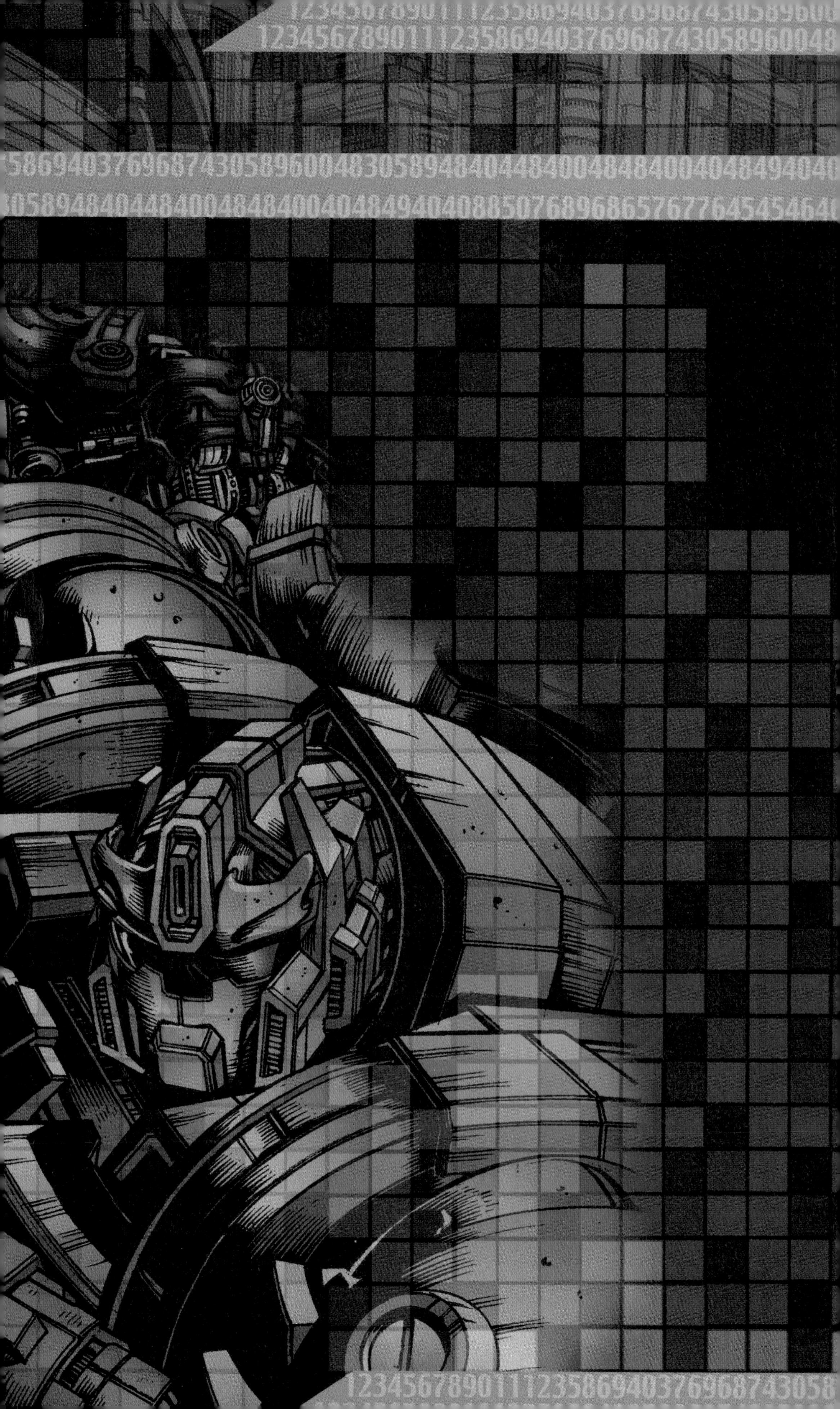

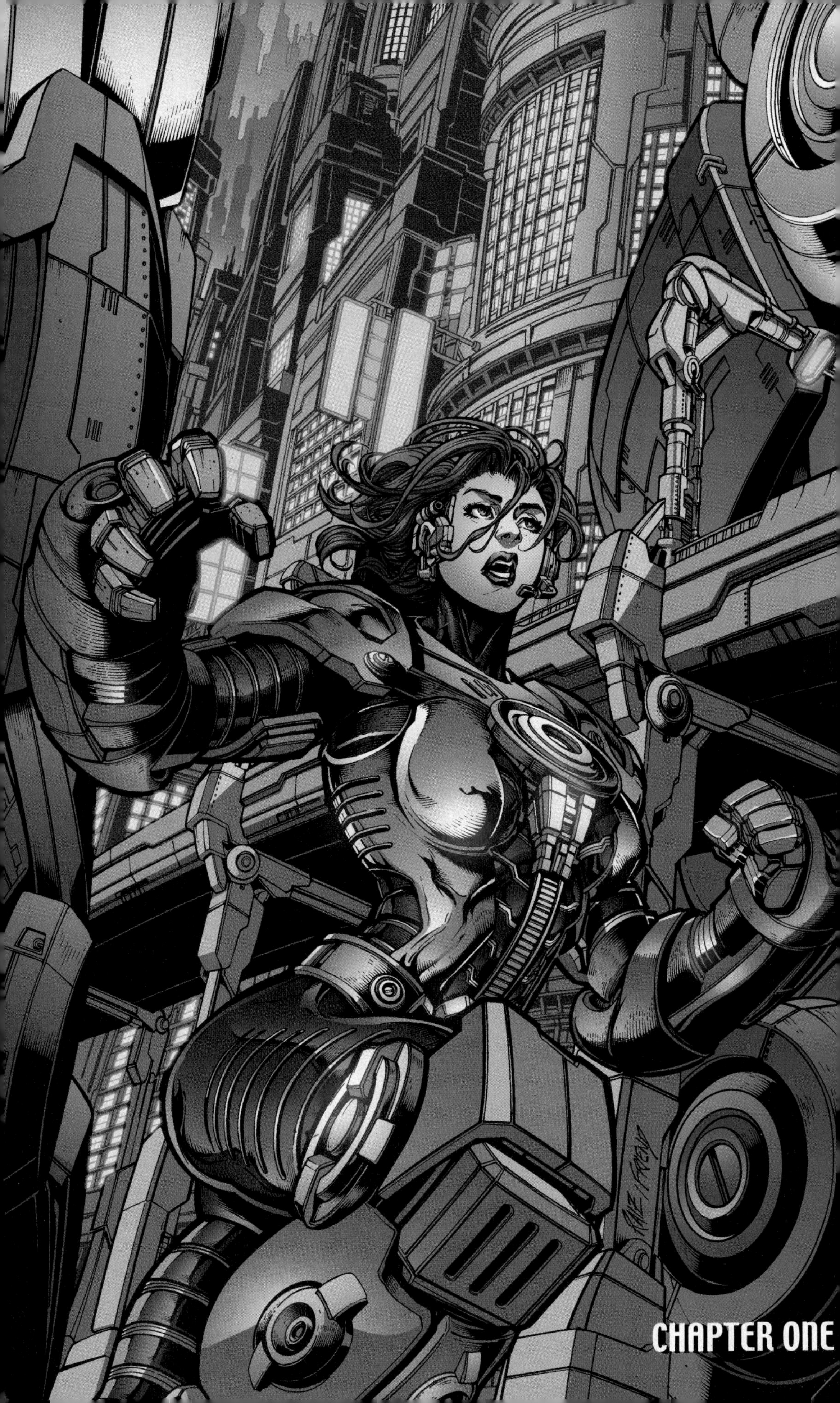
CHAPTER ONE

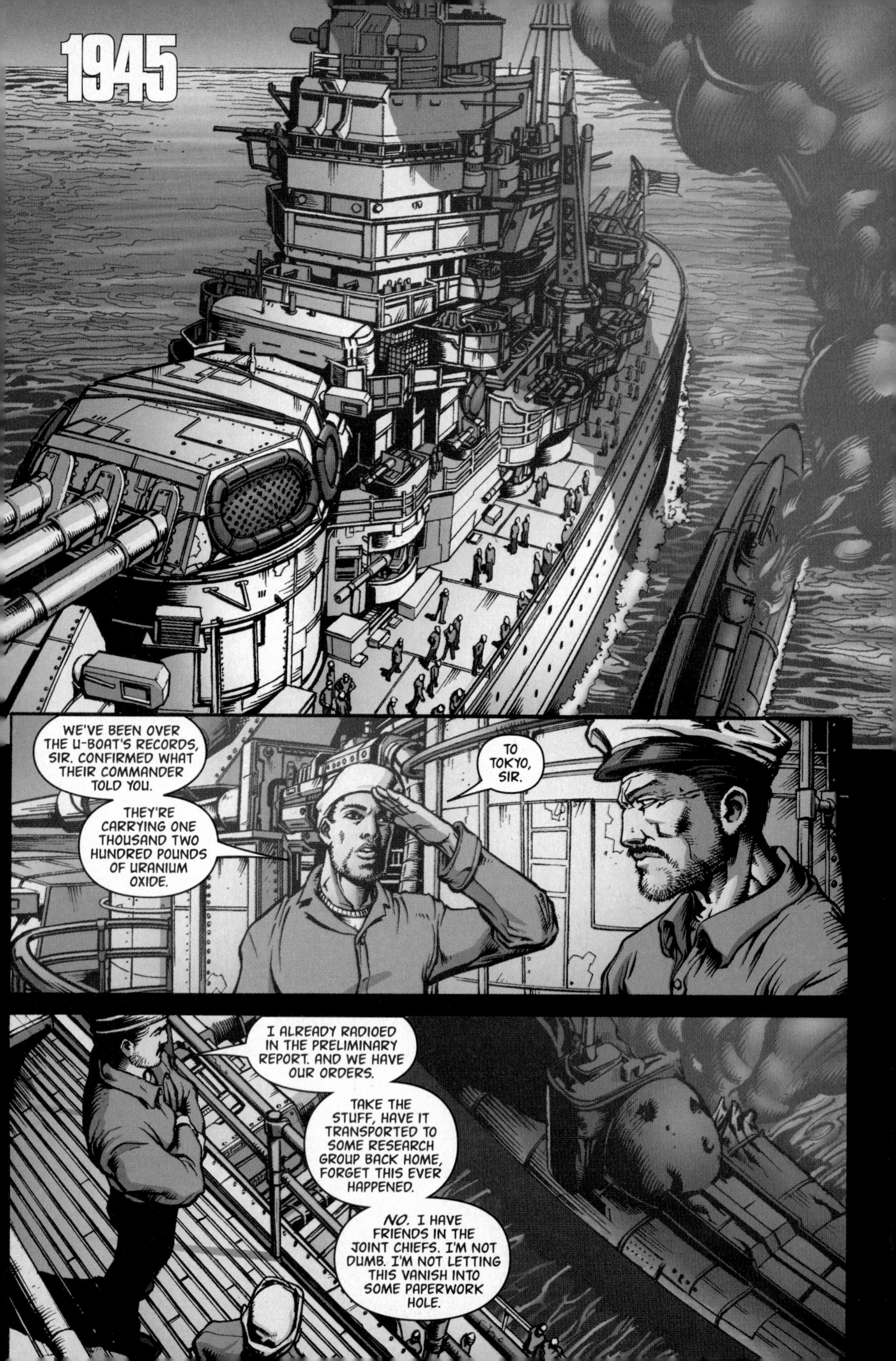
1945
WE'VE BEEN OVER THE U-BOAT'S RECORDS, SIR. CONFIRMED WHAT THEIR COMMANDER TOLD YOU.
THEY'RE CARRYING ONE THOUSAND TWO HUNDRED POUNDS OF URANIUM OXIDE.
TO TOKYO, SIR.
I ALREADY RADIOED IN THE PRELIMINARY REPORT. AND WE HAVE OUR ORDERS.
TAKE THE STUFF, HAVE IT TRANSPORTED TO SOME RESEARCH GROUP BACK HOME, FORGET THIS EVER HAPPENED.
NO. I HAVE FRIENDS IN THE JOINT CHIEFS. I'M NOT DUMB. I'M NOT LETTING THIS VANISH INTO SOME PAPERWORK HOLE.

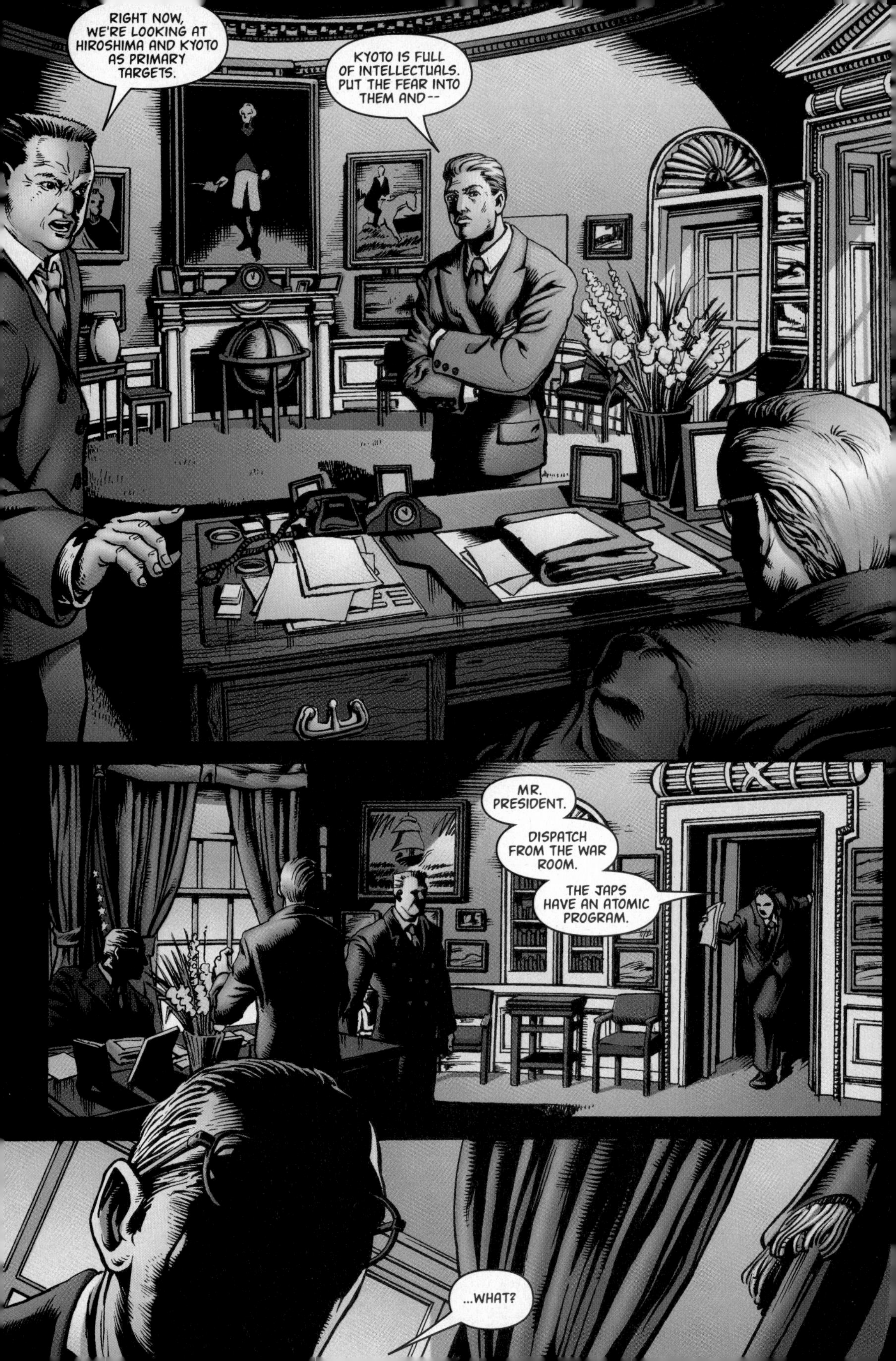
RIGHT NOW, WE'RE LOOKING AT HIROSHIMA AND KYOTO AS PRIMARY TARGETS.
KYOTO IS FULL OF INTELLECTUALS. PUT THE FEAR INTO THEM AND--
MR. PRESIDENT.
DISPATCH FROM THE WAR ROOM.
THE JAPS HAVE AN ATOMIC PROGRAM.
...WHAT?

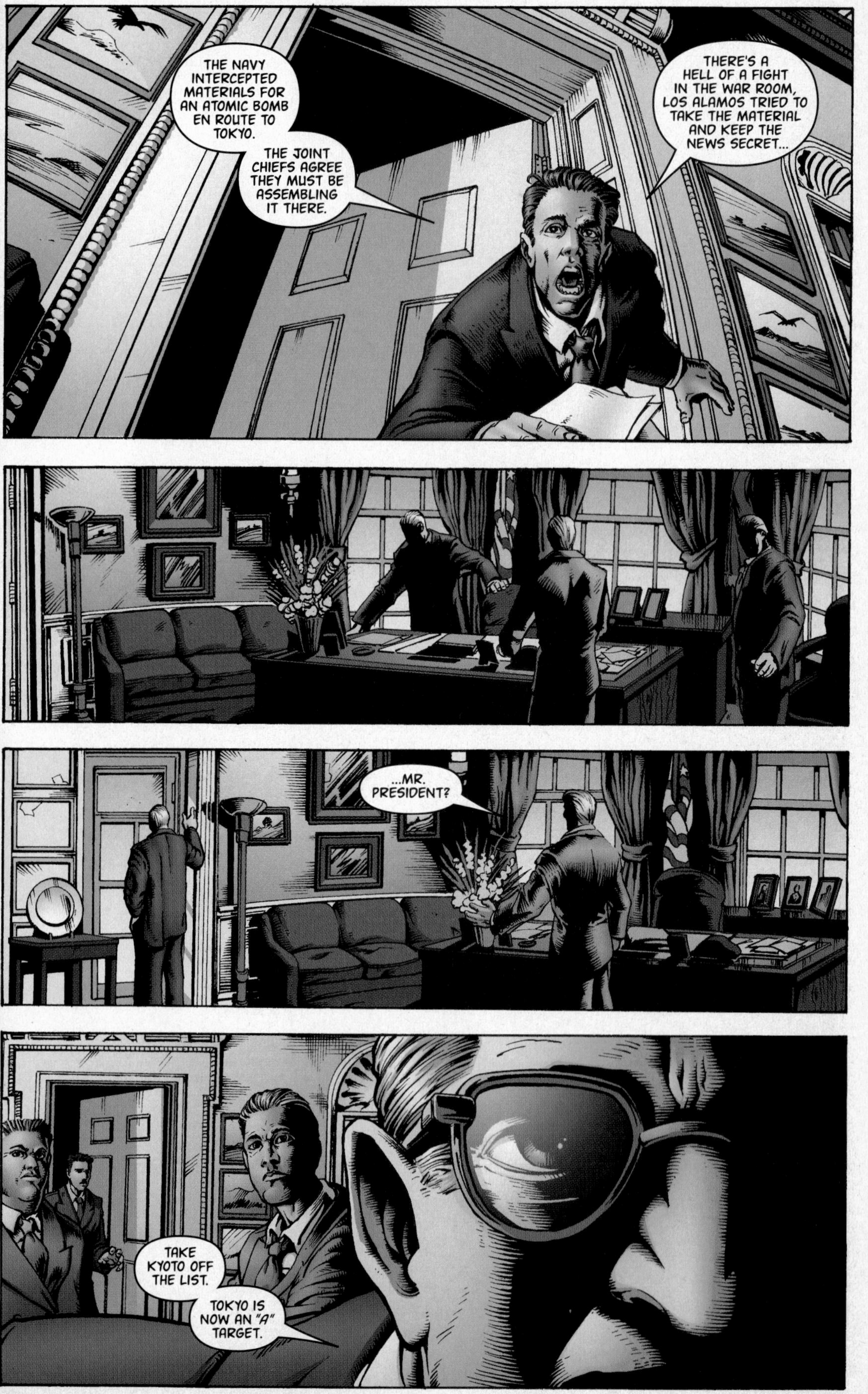
THE NAVY INTERCEPTED MATERIALS FOR AN ATOMIC BOMB EN ROUTE TO TOKYO.
THE JOINT CHIEFS AGREE THEY MUST BE ASSEMBLING IT THERE.
THERE'S A HELL OF A FIGHT IN THE WAR ROOM, LOS ALAMOS TRIED TO TAKE THE MATERIAL AND KEEP THE NEWS SECRET...
...MR. PRESIDENT?
TAKE KYOTO OFF THE LIST.
TOKYO IS NOW AN "A" TARGET.

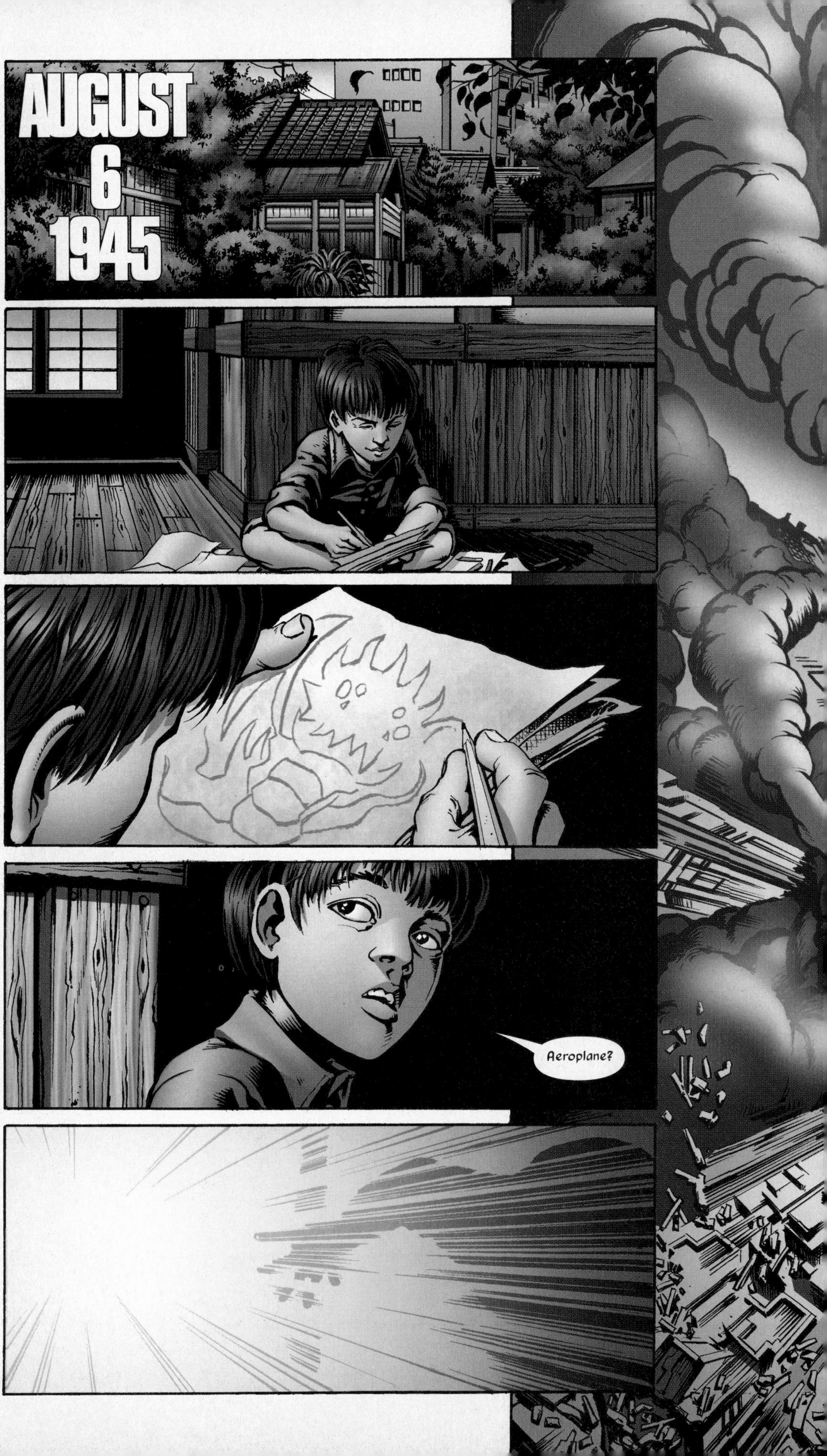
AUGUST
6
1945
Aeroplane?

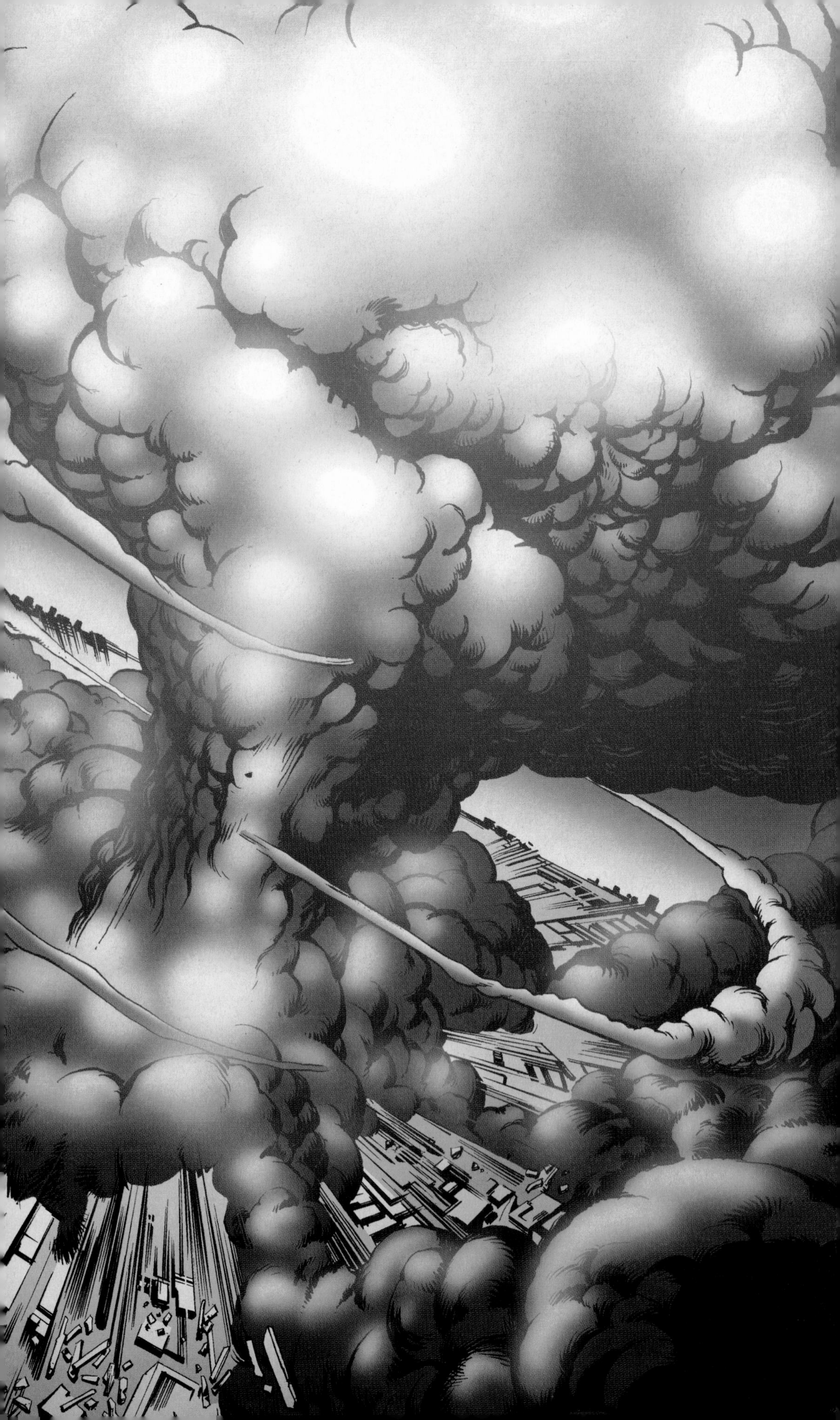

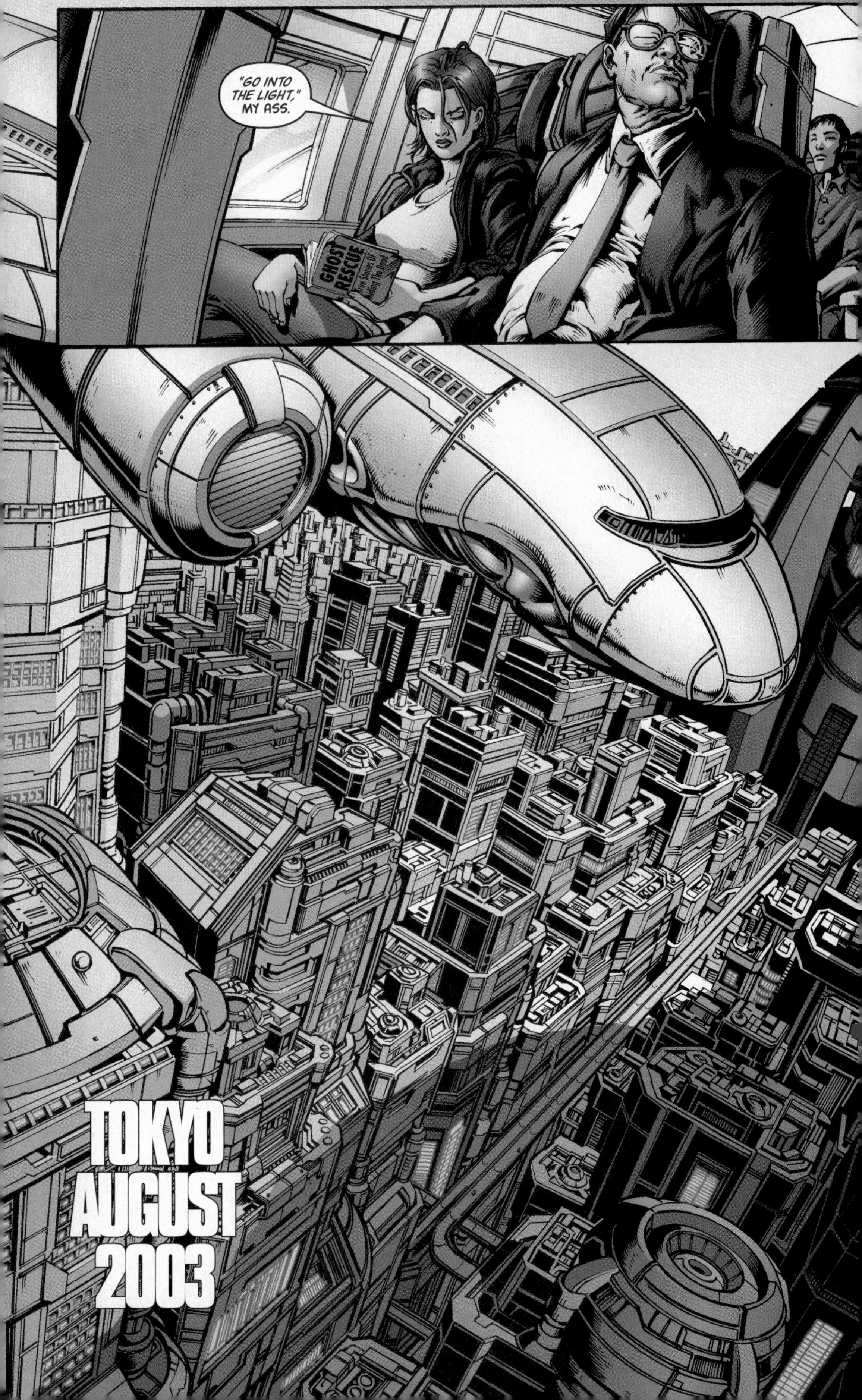
"GO INTO THE LIGHT," MY ASS.
GHOST RESCUE
True Stories Of Aiding The Dead
TOKYO AUGUST 2003

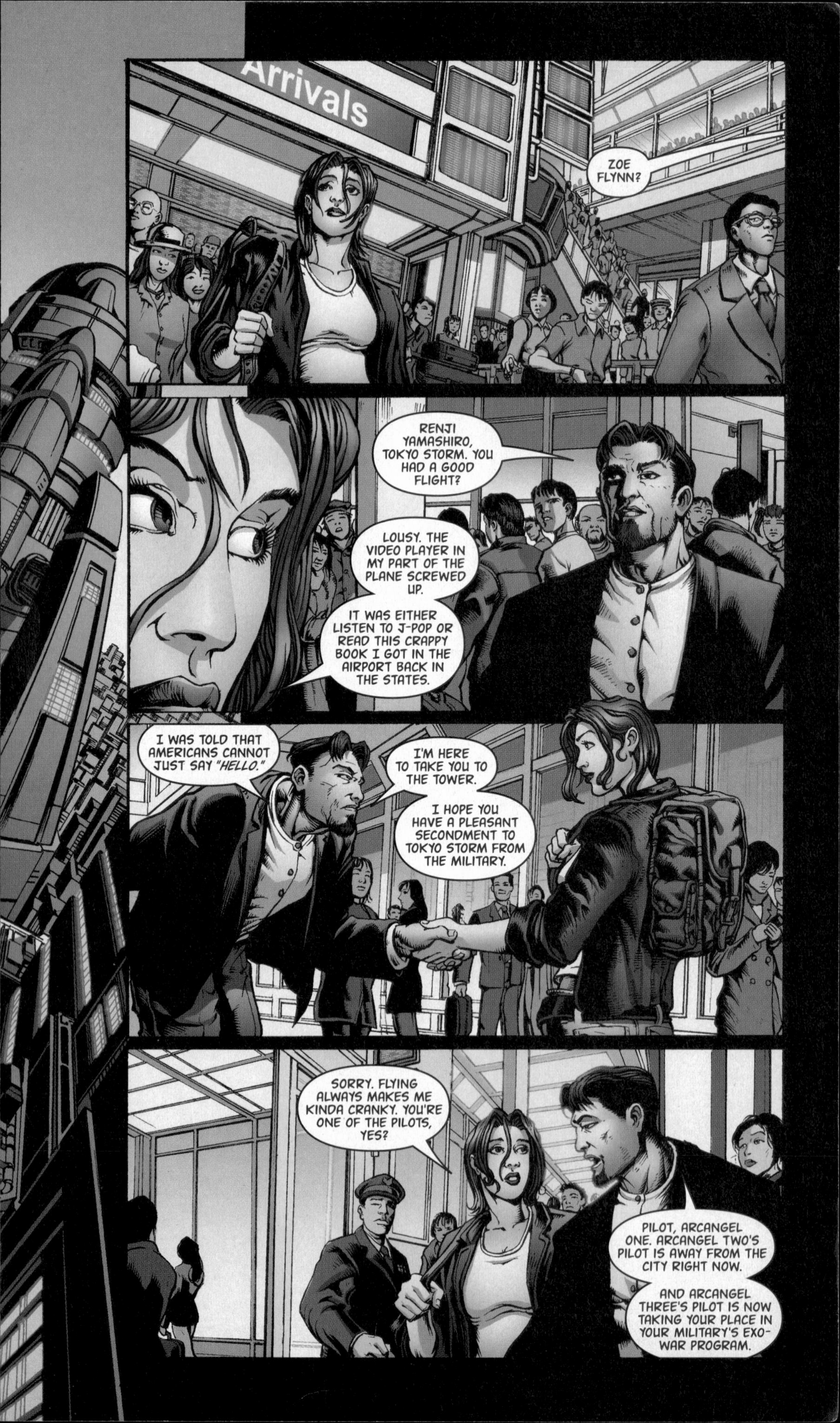
Arrivals
ZOE FLYNN?
RENJI YAMASHIRO, TOKYO STORM. YOU HAD A GOOD FLIGHT?
LOUSY. THE VIDEO PLAYER IN MY PART OF THE PLANE SCREWED UP.
IT WAS EITHER LISTEN TO J-POP OR READ THIS CRAPPY BOOK I GOT IN THE AIRPORT BACK IN THE STATES.
I WAS TOLD THAT AMERICANS CANNOT JUST SAY "HELLO."
I'M HERE TO TAKE YOU TO THE TOWER.
I HOPE YOU HAVE A PLEASANT SECONDMENT TO TOKYO STORM FROM THE MILITARY.
SORRY. FLYING ALWAYS MAKES ME KINDA CRANKY. YOU'RE ONE OF THE PILOTS, YES?
PILOT, ARCANGEL ONE. ARCANGEL TWO'S PILOT IS AWAY FROM THE CITY RIGHT NOW.
AND ARCANGEL THREE'S PILOT IS NOW TAKING YOUR PLACE IN YOUR MILITARY'S EXO-WAR PROGRAM.

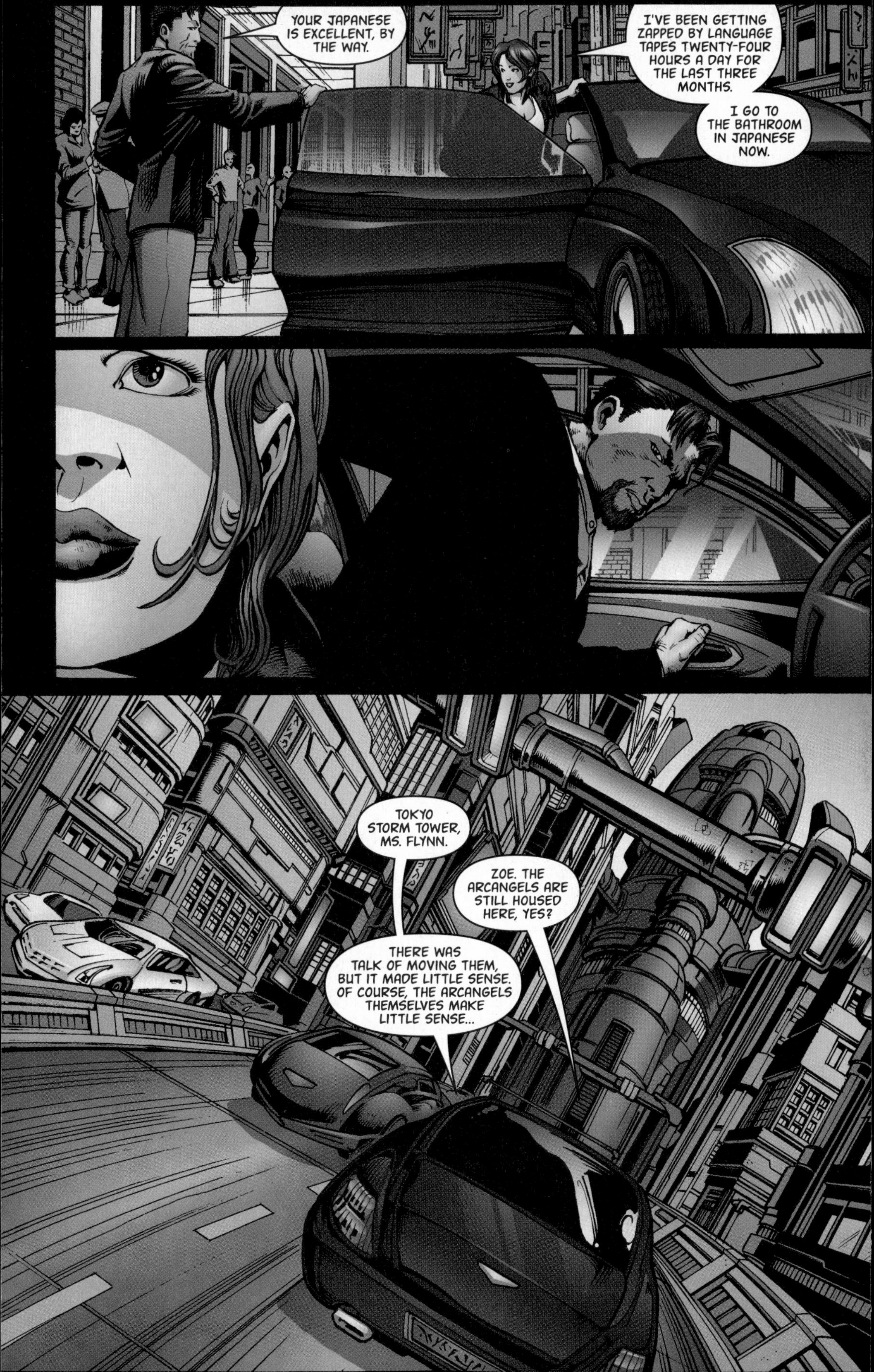
YOUR JAPANESE IS EXCELLENT, BY THE WAY.
I'VE BEEN GETTING ZAPPED BY LANGUAGE TAPES TWENTY-FOUR HOURS A DAY FOR THE LAST THREE MONTHS.
I GO TO THE BATHROOM IN JAPANESE NOW.
TOKYO STORM TOWER, MS. FLYNN.
ZOE. THE ARCANGELS ARE STILL HOUSED HERE, YES?
THERE WAS TALK OF MOVING THEM, BUT IT MADE LITTLE SENSE. OF COURSE, THE ARCANGELS THEMSELVES MAKE LITTLE SENSE...

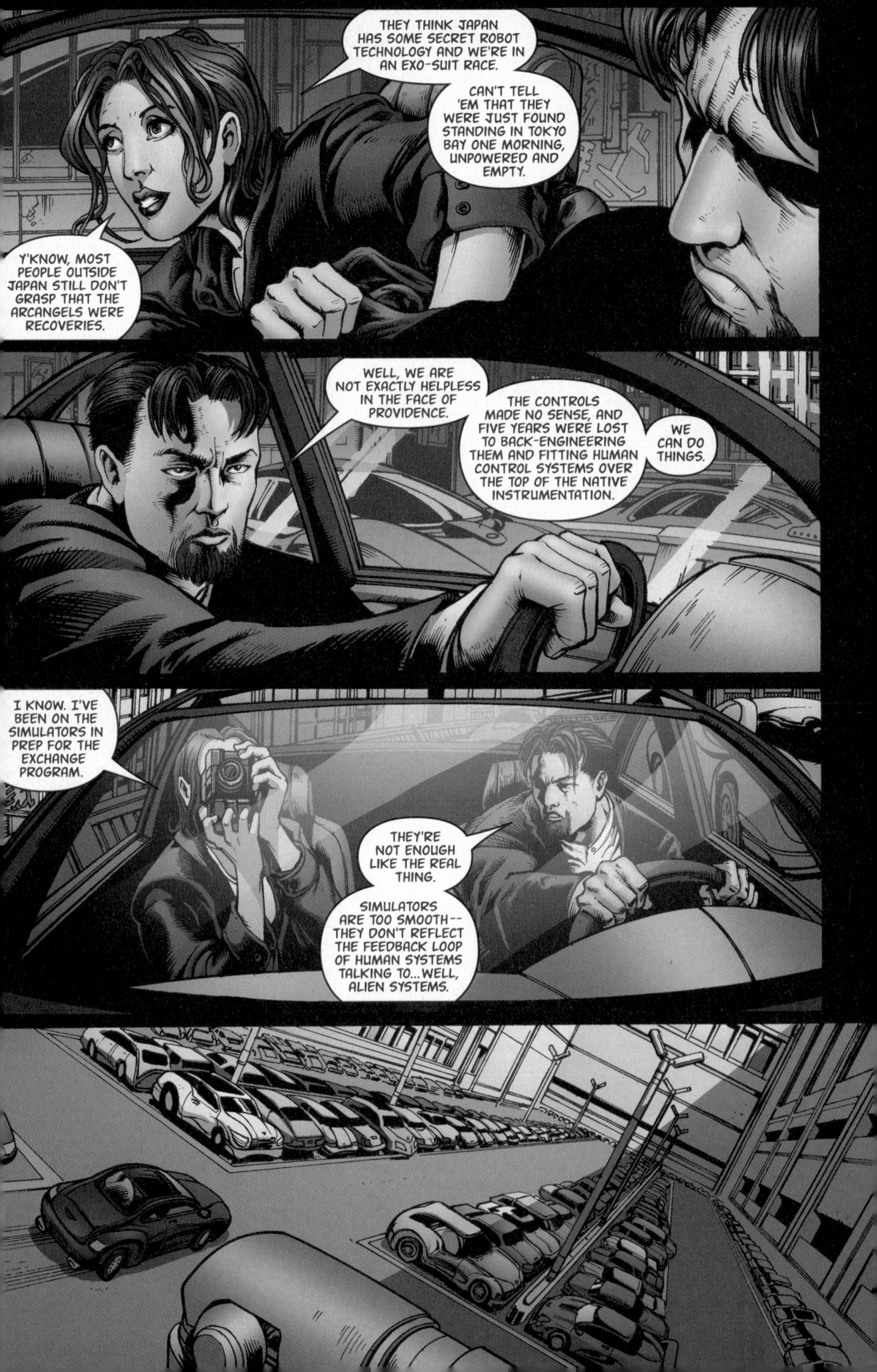
Y'KNOW, MOST PEOPLE OUTSIDE JAPAN STILL DON'T GRASP THAT THE ARCANGELS WERE RECOVERIES.
THEY THINK JAPAN HAS SOME SECRET ROBOT TECHNOLOGY AND WE'RE IN AN EXO-SUIT RACE.
CAN'T TELL 'EM THAT THEY WERE JUST FOUND STANDING IN TOKYO BAY ONE MORNING, UNPOWERED AND EMPTY.
WELL, WE ARE NOT EXACTLY HELPLESS IN THE FACE OF PROVIDENCE.
THE CONTROLS MADE NO SENSE, AND FIVE YEARS WERE LOST TO BACK-ENGINEERING THEM AND FITTING HUMAN CONTROL SYSTEMS OVER THE TOP OF THE NATIVE INSTRUMENTATION.
WE CAN DO THINGS.
I KNOW. I'VE BEEN ON THE SIMULATORS IN PREP FOR THE EXCHANGE PROGRAM.
THEY'RE NOT ENOUGH LIKE THE REAL THING.
SIMULATORS ARE TOO SMOOTH-- THEY DON'T REFLECT THE FEEDBACK LOOP OF HUMAN SYSTEMS TALKING TO...WELL, ALIEN SYSTEMS.

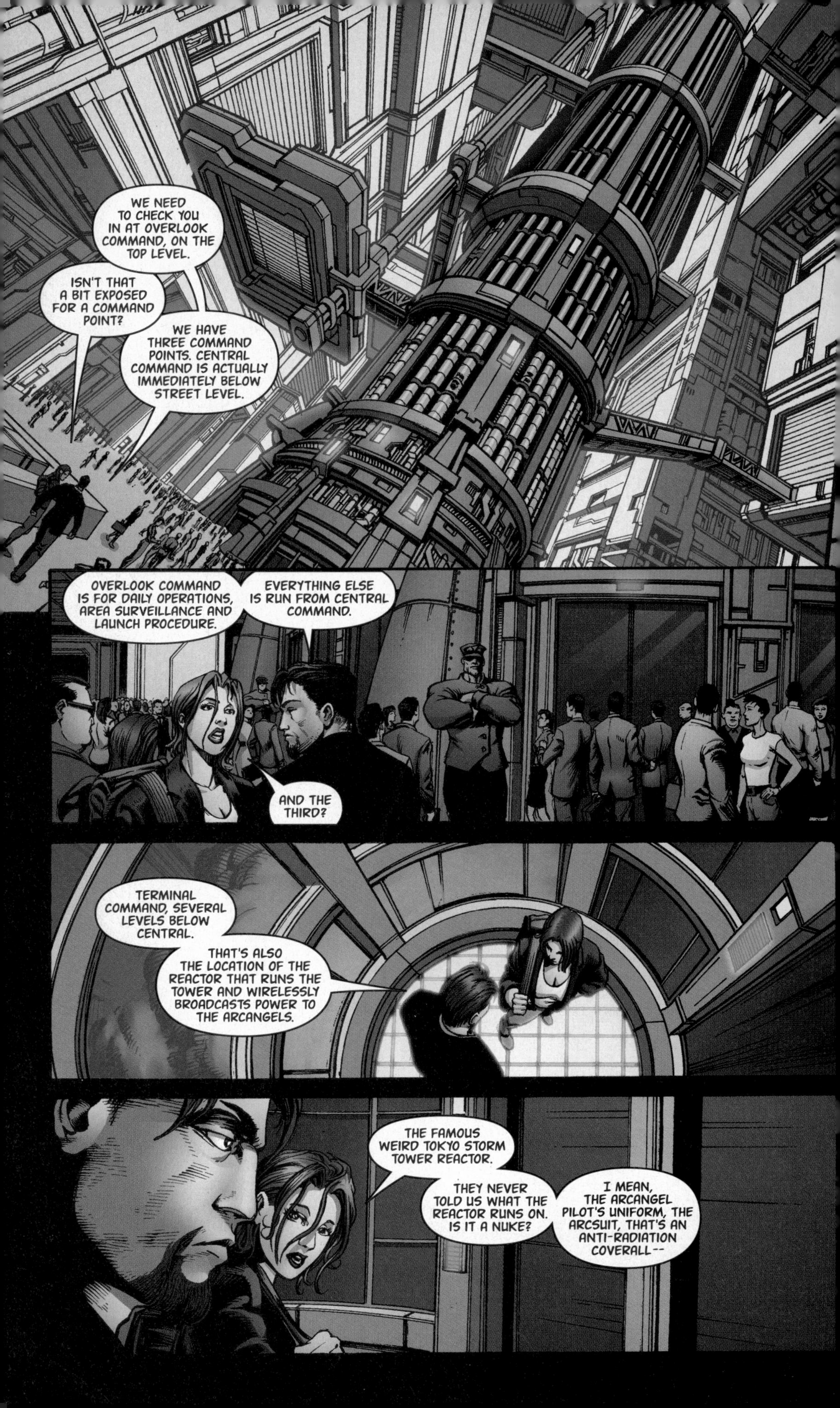
WE NEED TO CHECK YOU IN AT OVERLOOK COMMAND, ON THE TOP LEVEL.
ISN'T THAT A BIT EXPOSED FOR A COMMAND POINT?
WE HAVE THREE COMMAND POINTS. CENTRAL COMMAND IS ACTUALLY IMMEDIATELY BELOW STREET LEVEL.
OVERLOOK COMMAND IS FOR DAILY OPERATIONS, AREA SURVEILLANCE AND LAUNCH PROCEDURE.
EVERYTHING ELSE IS RUN FROM CENTRAL COMMAND.
AND THE THIRD?
TERMINAL COMMAND, SEVERAL LEVELS BELOW CENTRAL.
THAT'S ALSO THE LOCATION OF THE REACTOR THAT RUNS THE TOWER AND WIRELESSLY BROADCASTS POWER TO THE ARCANGELS.
THE FAMOUS WEIRD TOKYO STORM TOWER REACTOR.
THEY NEVER TOLD US WHAT THE REACTOR RUNS ON. IS IT A NUKE?
I MEAN, THE ARCANGEL PILOT'S UNIFORM, THE ARCSUIT, THAT'S AN ANTI-RADIATION COVERALL--

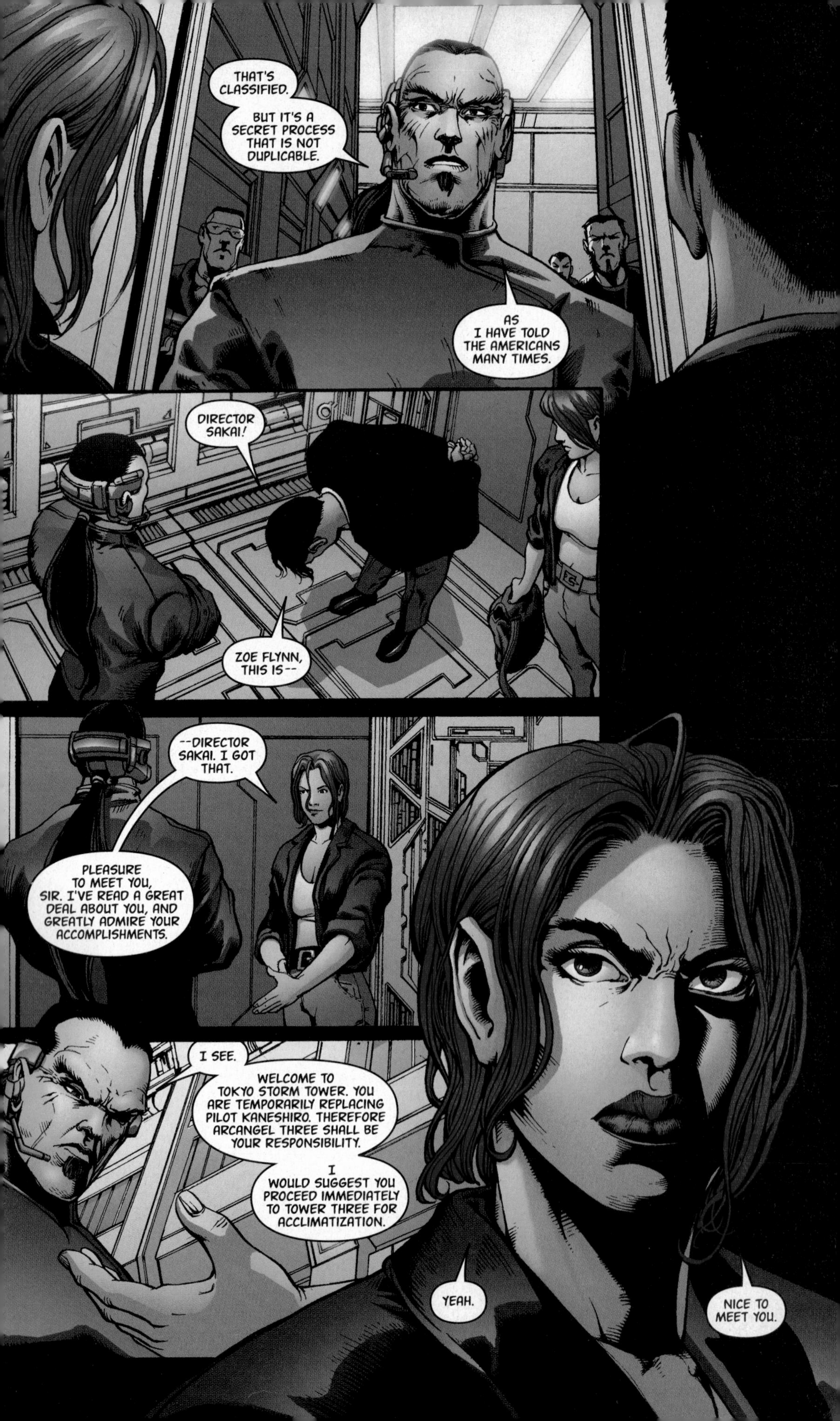

THAT'S CLASSIFIED.
BUT IT'S A SECRET PROCESS THAT IS NOT DUPLICABLE.
AS I HAVE TOLD THE AMERICANS MANY TIMES.
DIRECTOR SAKAI!
ZOE FLYNN, THIS IS--
--DIRECTOR SAKAI. I GOT THAT.
PLEASURE TO MEET YOU, SIR. I'VE READ A GREAT DEAL ABOUT YOU, AND GREATLY ADMIRE YOUR ACCOMPLISHMENTS.
I SEE.
WELCOME TO TOKYO STORM TOWER. YOU ARE TEMPORARILY REPLACING PILOT KANESHIRO. THEREFORE ARCANGEL THREE SHALL BE YOUR RESPONSIBILITY.
I WOULD SUGGEST YOU PROCEED IMMEDIATELY TO TOWER THREE FOR ACCLIMATIZATION.
YEAH.
NICE TO MEET YOU.

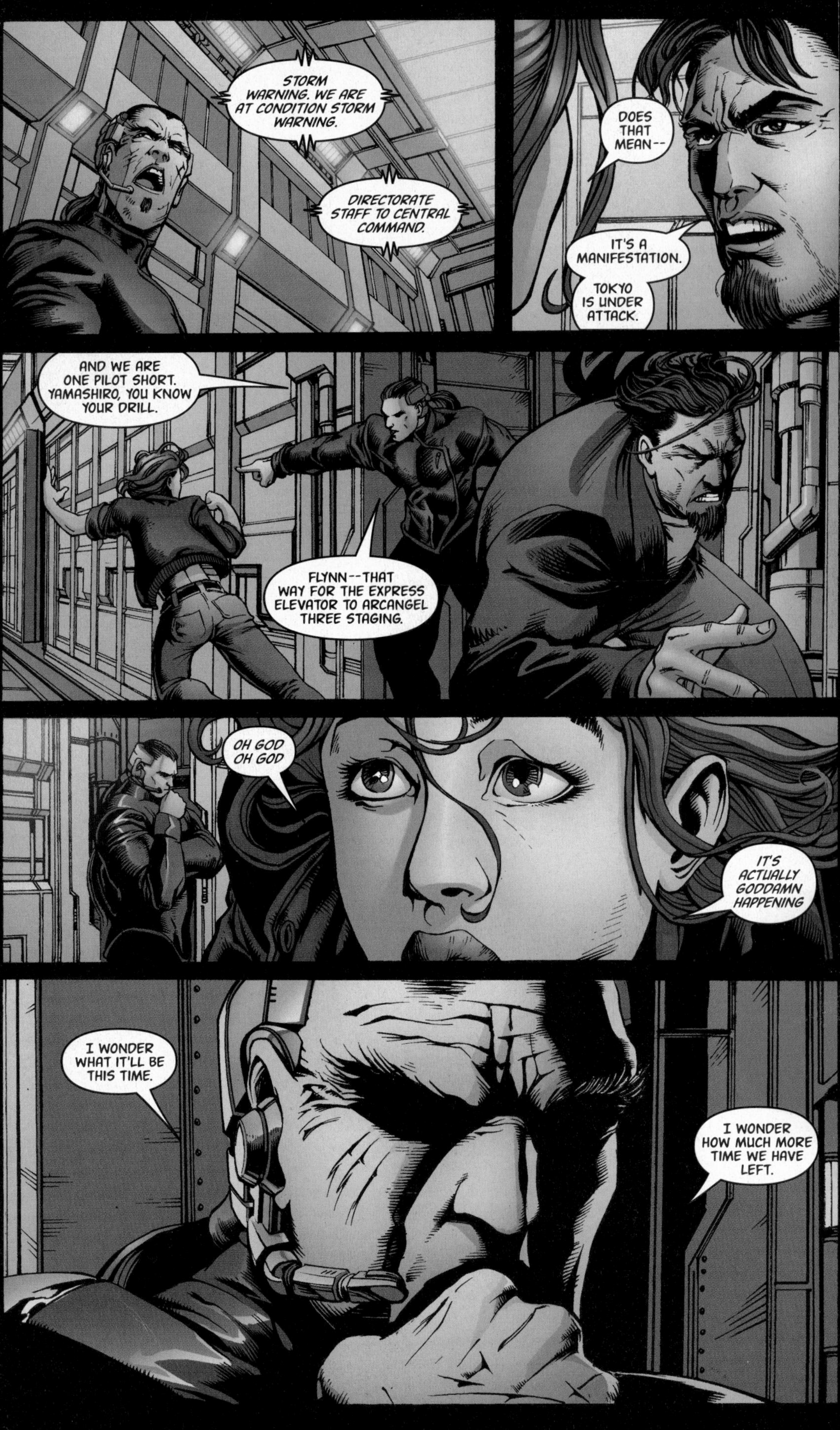
STORM WARNING. WE ARE AT CONDITION STORM WARNING.
DIRECTORATE STAFF TO CENTRAL COMMAND.
DOES THAT MEAN--
IT'S A MANIFESTATION.
TOKYO IS UNDER ATTACK.
AND WE ARE ONE PILOT SHORT. YAMASHIRO, YOU KNOW YOUR DRILL.
FLYNN--THAT WAY FOR THE EXPRESS ELEVATOR TO ARCANGEL THREE STAGING.
OH GOD OH GOD
IT'S ACTUALLY GODDAMN HAPPENING
I WONDER WHAT IT'LL BE THIS TIME.
I WONDER HOW MUCH MORE TIME WE HAVE LEFT.

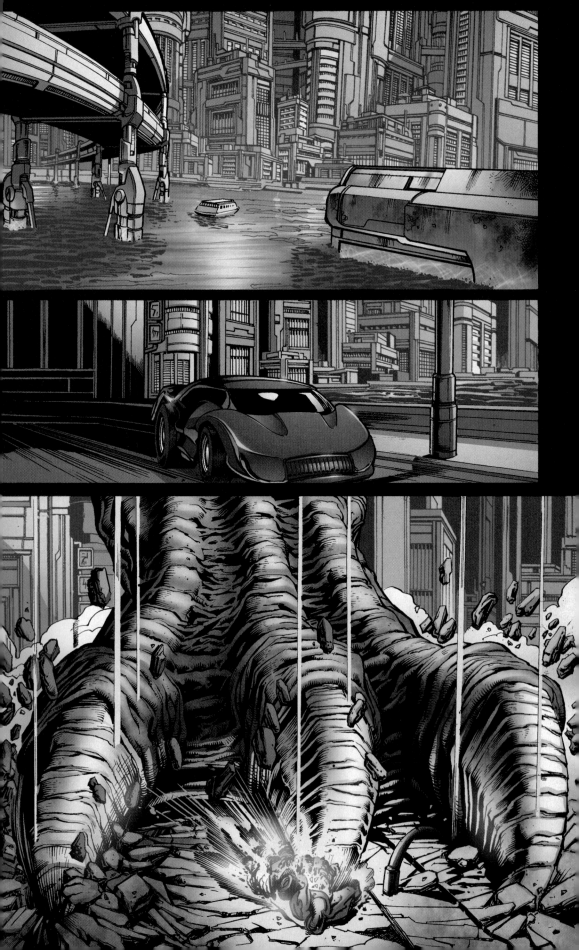

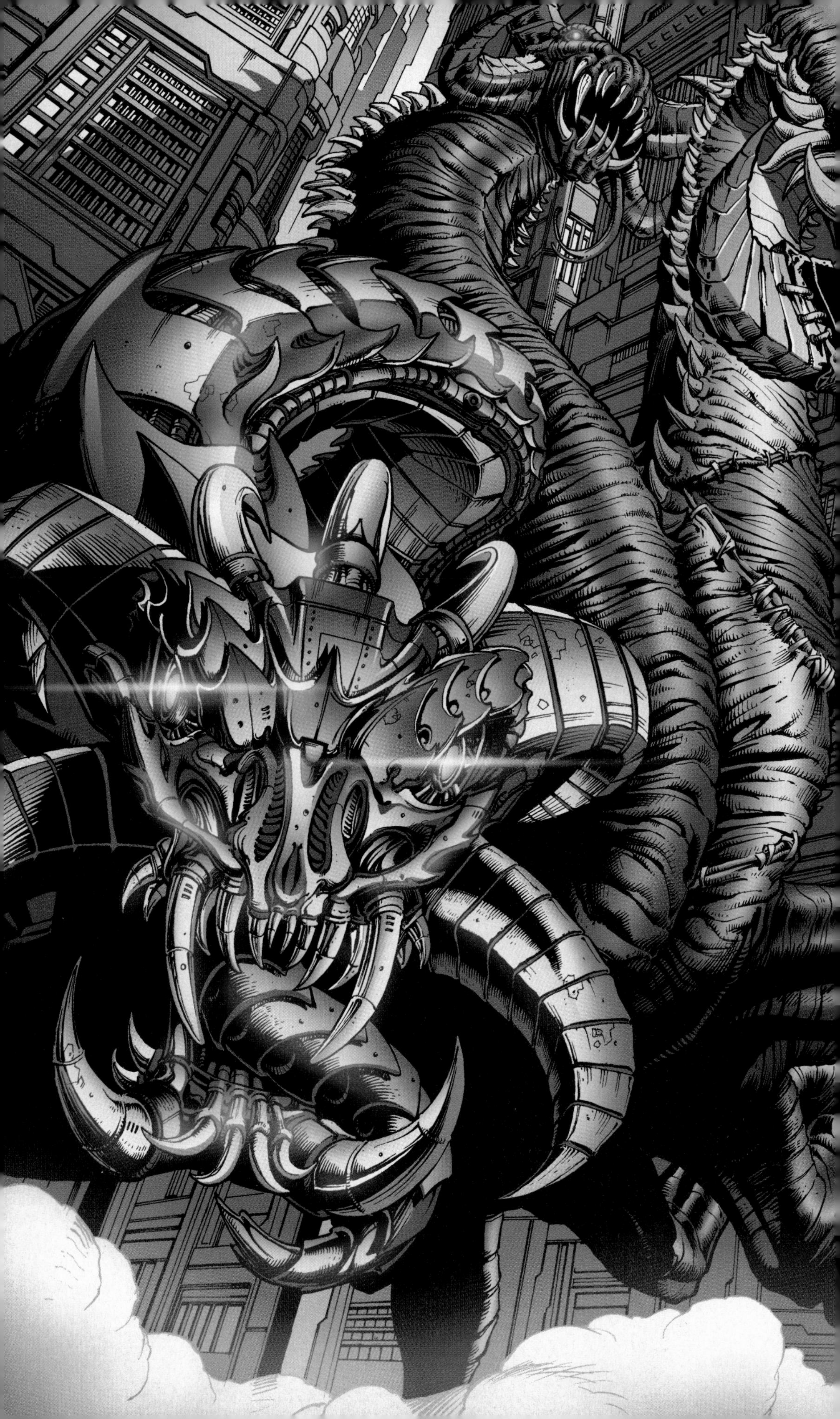

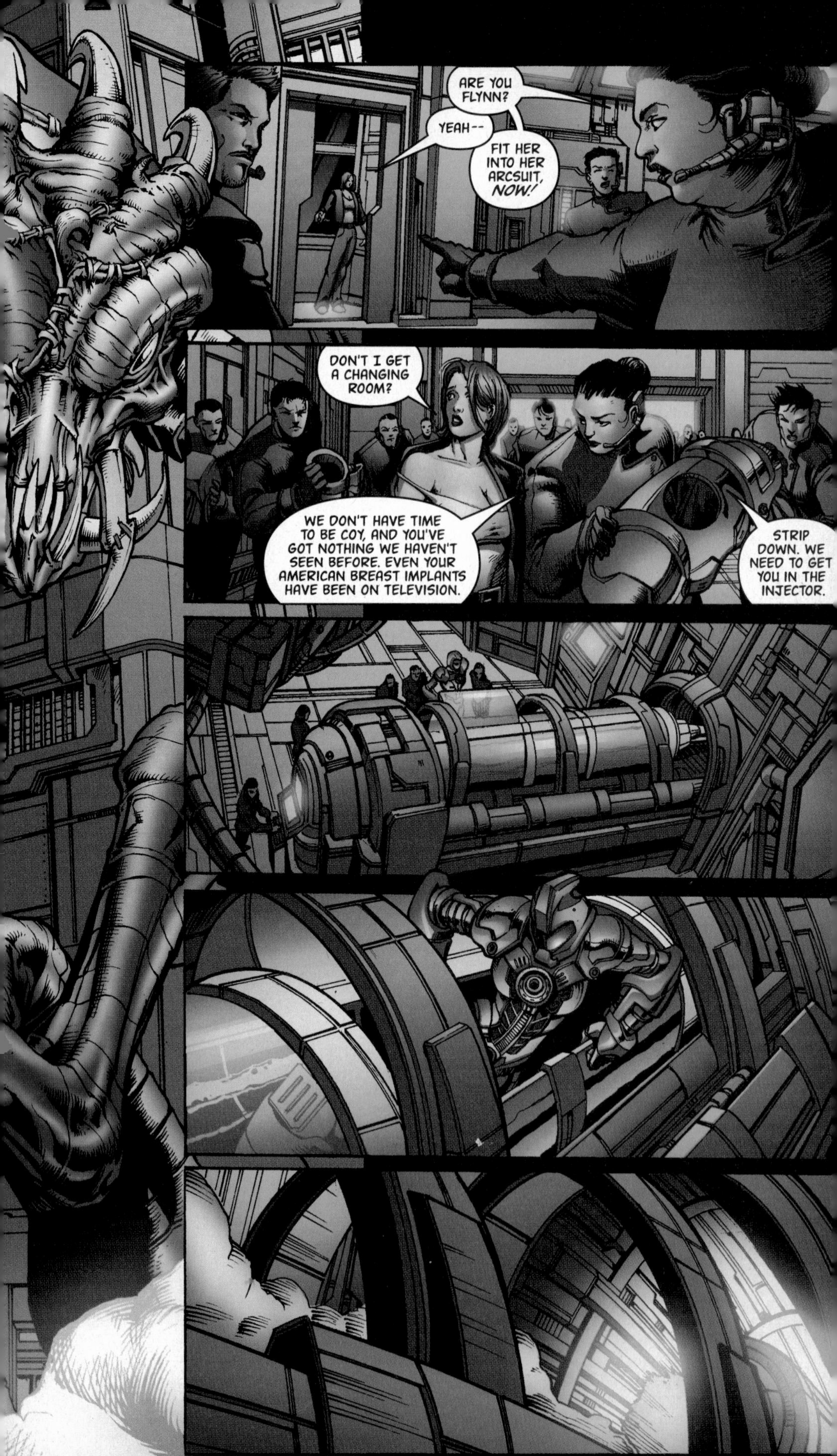
ARE YOU FLYNN?
YEAH--
FIT HER INTO HER ARCSUIT, NOW!
DON'T I GET A CHANGING ROOM?
STRIP DOWN. WE NEED TO GET YOU IN THE INJECTOR.
WE DON'T HAVE TIME TO BE COY, AND YOU'VE GOT NOTHING WE HAVEN'T SEEN BEFORE. EVEN YOUR AMERICAN BREAST IMPLANTS HAVE BEEN ON TELEVISION.

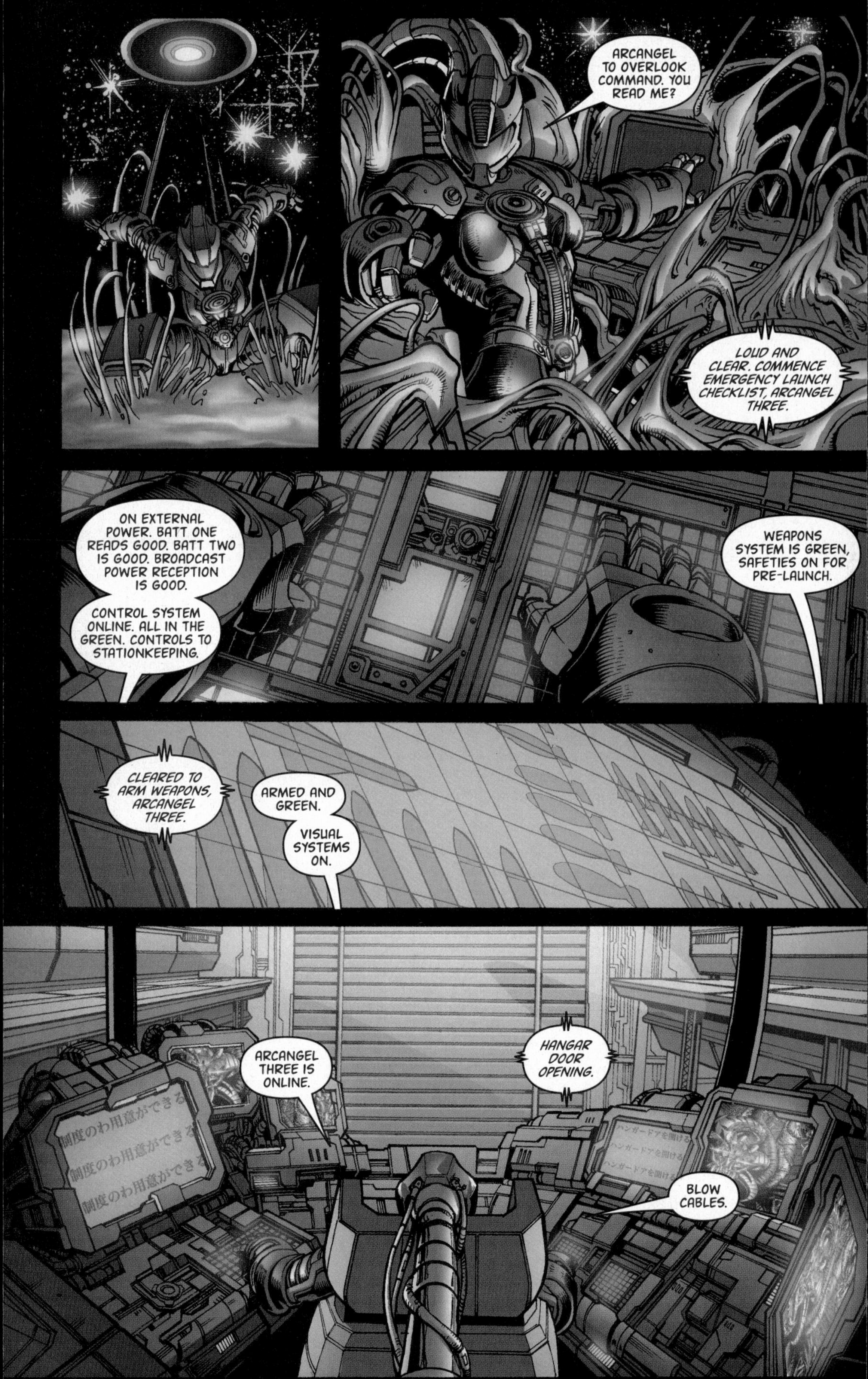
ARCANGEL TO OVERLOOK COMMAND. YOU READ ME?
LOUD AND CLEAR. COMMENCE EMERGENCY LAUNCH CHECKLIST, ARCANGEL THREE.
ON EXTERNAL POWER. BATT ONE READS GOOD. BATT TWO IS GOOD. BROADCAST POWER RECEPTION IS GOOD.
CONTROL SYSTEM ONLINE. ALL IN THE GREEN. CONTROLS TO STATIONKEEPING.
WEAPONS SYSTEM IS GREEN, SAFETIES ON FOR PRE-LAUNCH.
CLEARED TO ARM WEAPONS, ARCANGEL THREE.
ARMED AND GREEN.
VISUAL SYSTEMS ON.
ARCANGEL THREE IS ONLINE.
HANGAR DOOR OPENING.
BLOW CABLES.

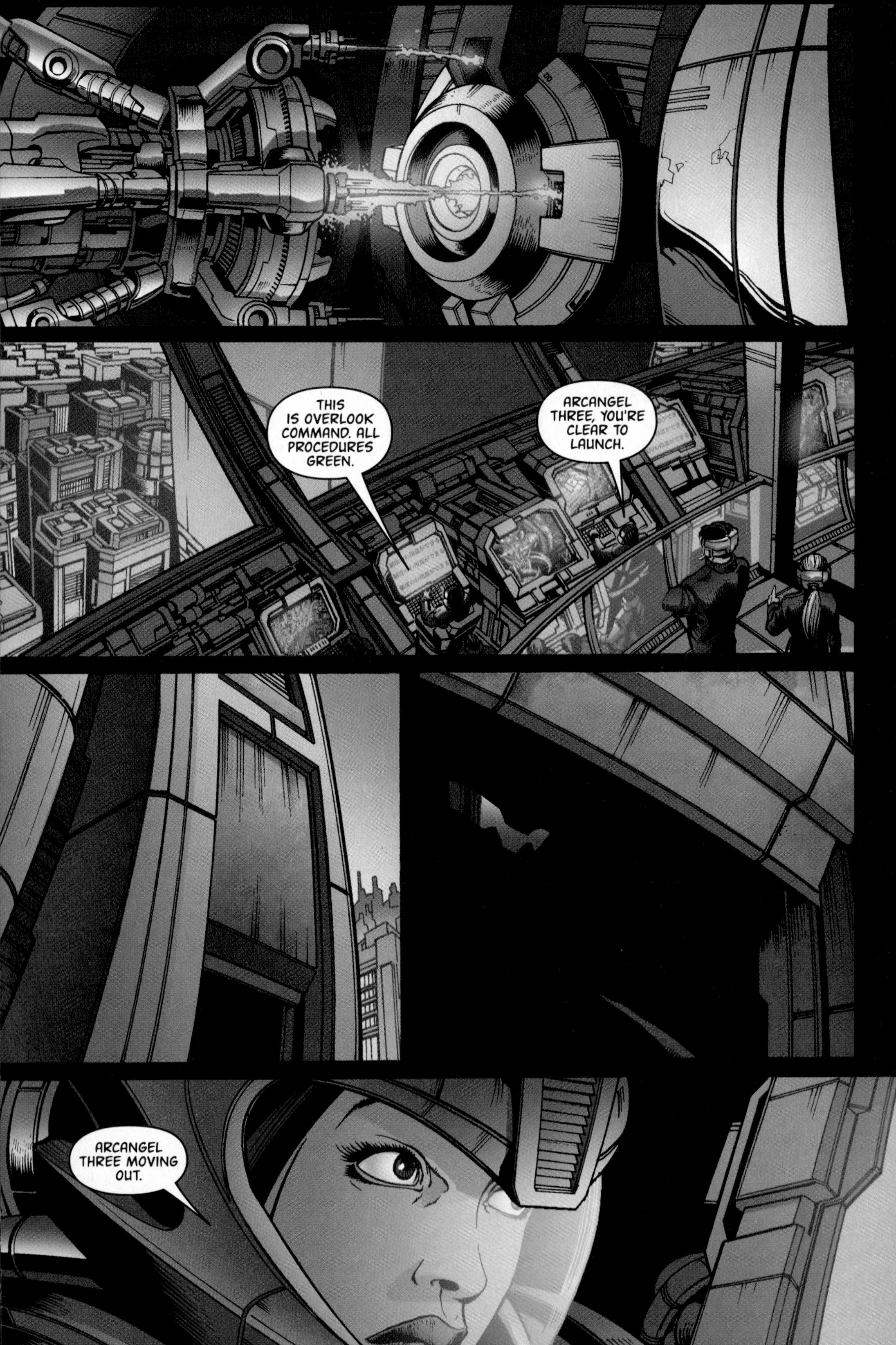
THIS IS OVERLOOK COMMAND. ALL PROCEDURES GREEN.
ARCANGEL THREE, YOU'RE CLEAR TO LAUNCH.
ARCANGEL THREE MOVING OUT.

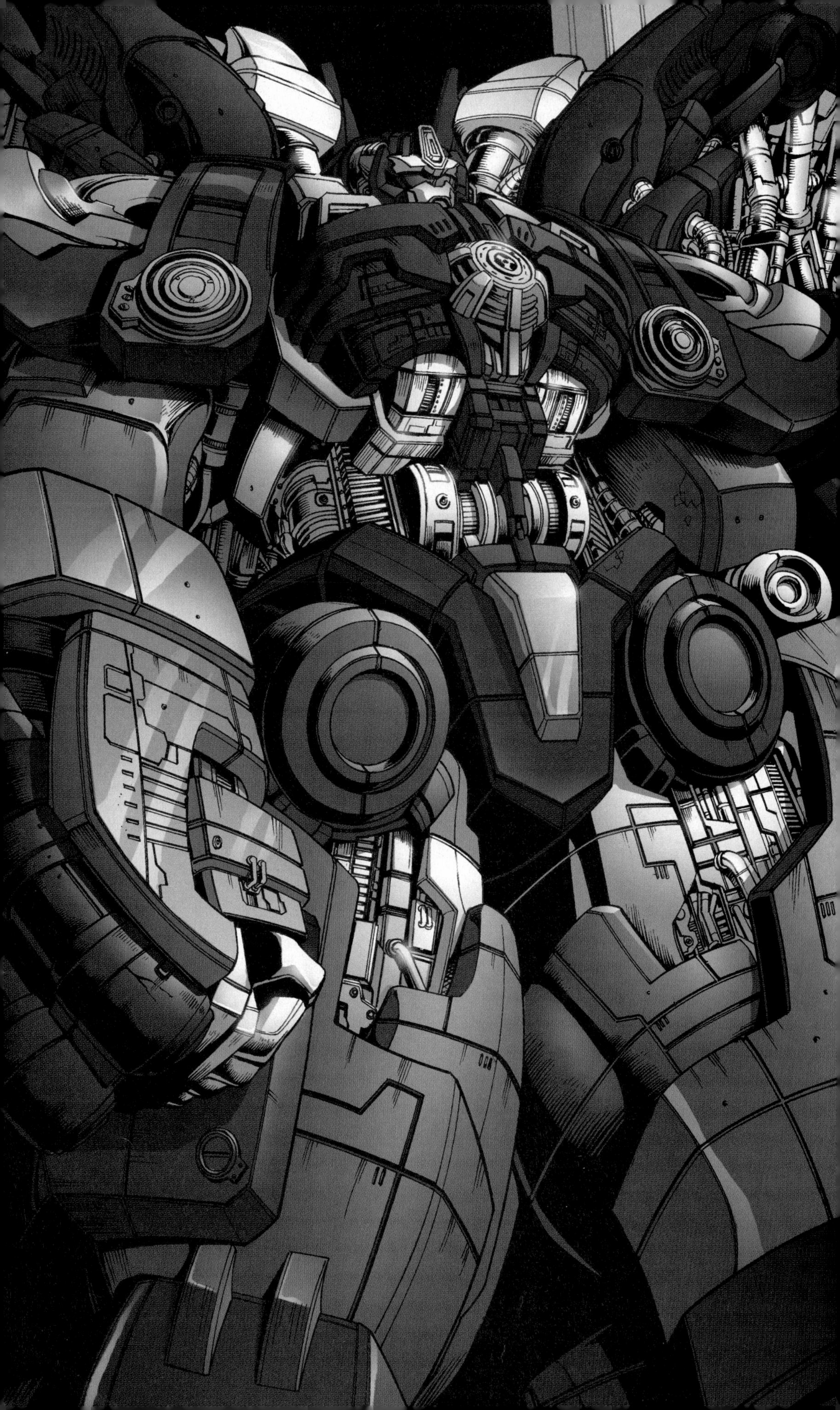

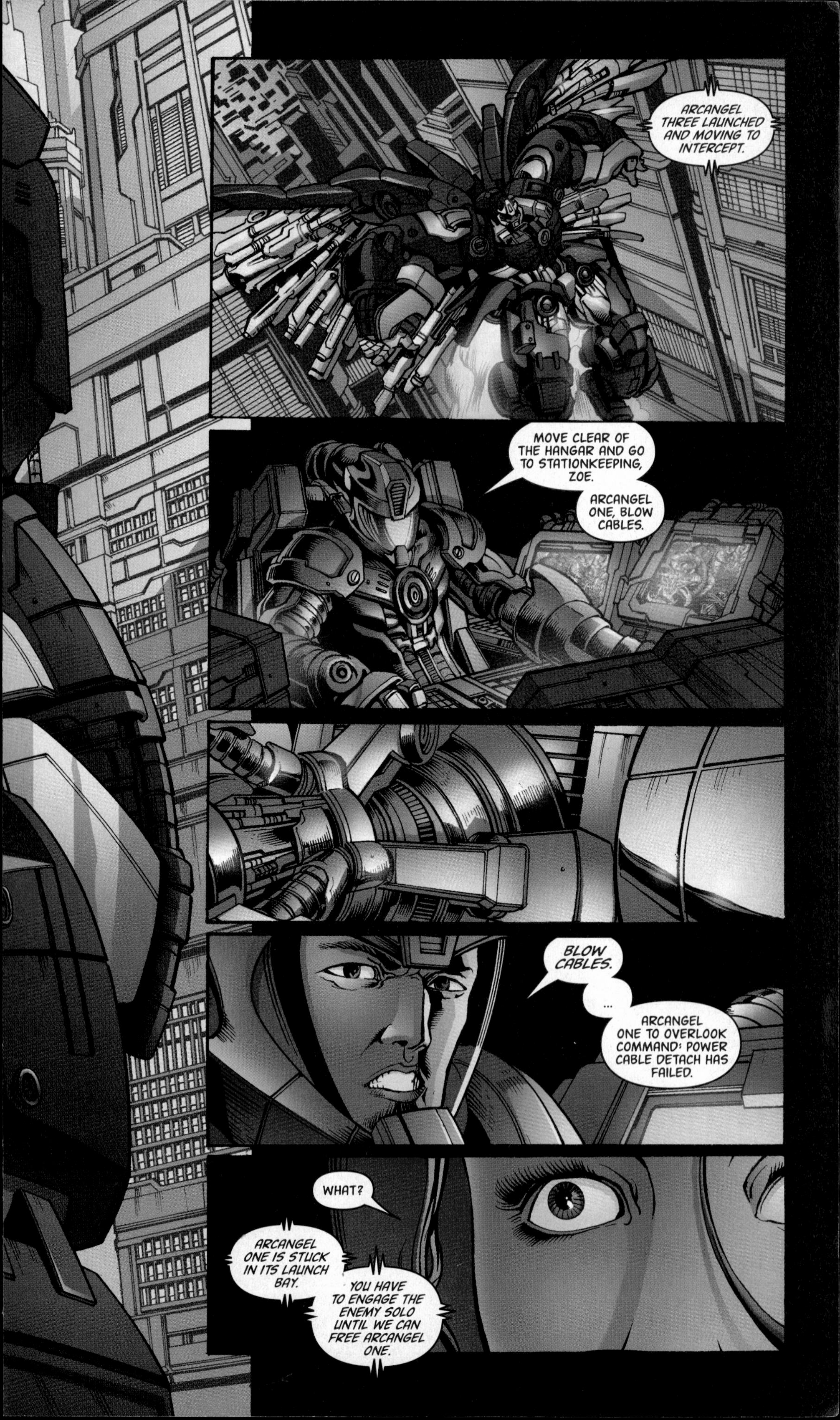

ARCANGEL THREE LAUNCHED AND MOVING TO INTERCEPT.
MOVE CLEAR OF THE HANGAR AND GO TO STATIONKEEPING, ZOE.
ARCANGEL ONE, BLOW CABLES.
BLOW CABLES.
...
ARCANGEL ONE TO OVERLOOK COMMAND: POWER CABLE DETACH HAS FAILED.
WHAT?
ARCANGEL ONE IS STUCK IN ITS LAUNCH BAY.
YOU HAVE TO ENGAGE THE ENEMY SOLO UNTIL WE CAN FREE ARCANGEL ONE.

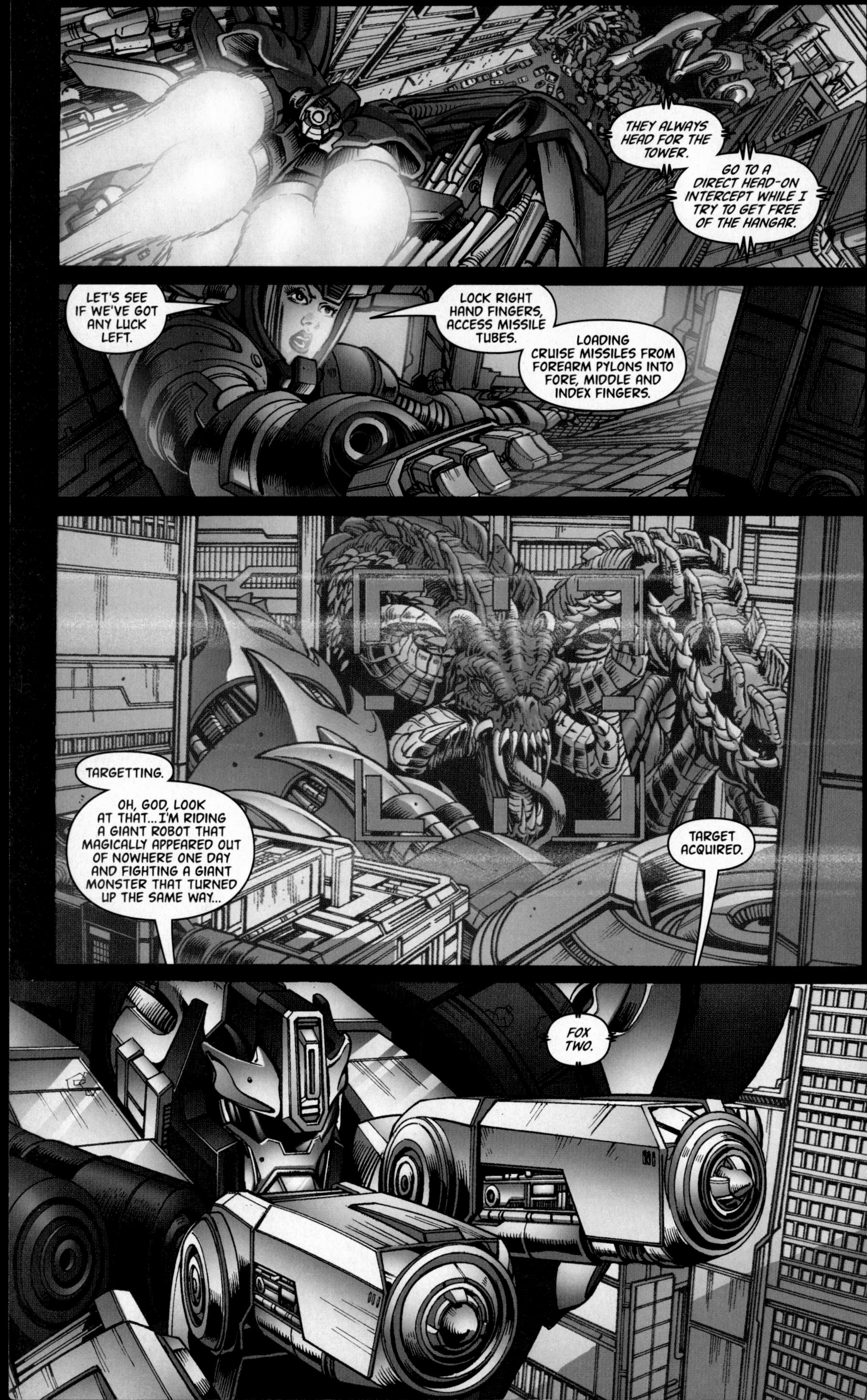
THEY ALWAYS HEAD FOR THE TOWER.
GO TO A DIRECT HEAD-ON INTERCEPT WHILE I TRY TO GET FREE OF THE HANGAR.
LET'S SEE IF WE'VE GOT ANY LUCK LEFT.
LOCK RIGHT HAND FINGERS, ACCESS MISSILE TUBES.
LOADING CRUISE MISSILES FROM FOREARM PYLONS INTO FORE, MIDDLE AND INDEX FINGERS.
TARGETTING.
OH, GOD, LOOK AT THAT...I'M RIDING A GIANT ROBOT THAT MAGICALLY APPEARED OUT OF NOWHERE ONE DAY AND FIGHTING A GIANT MONSTER THAT TURNED UP THE SAME WAY...
TARGET ACQUIRED.
FOX TWO.

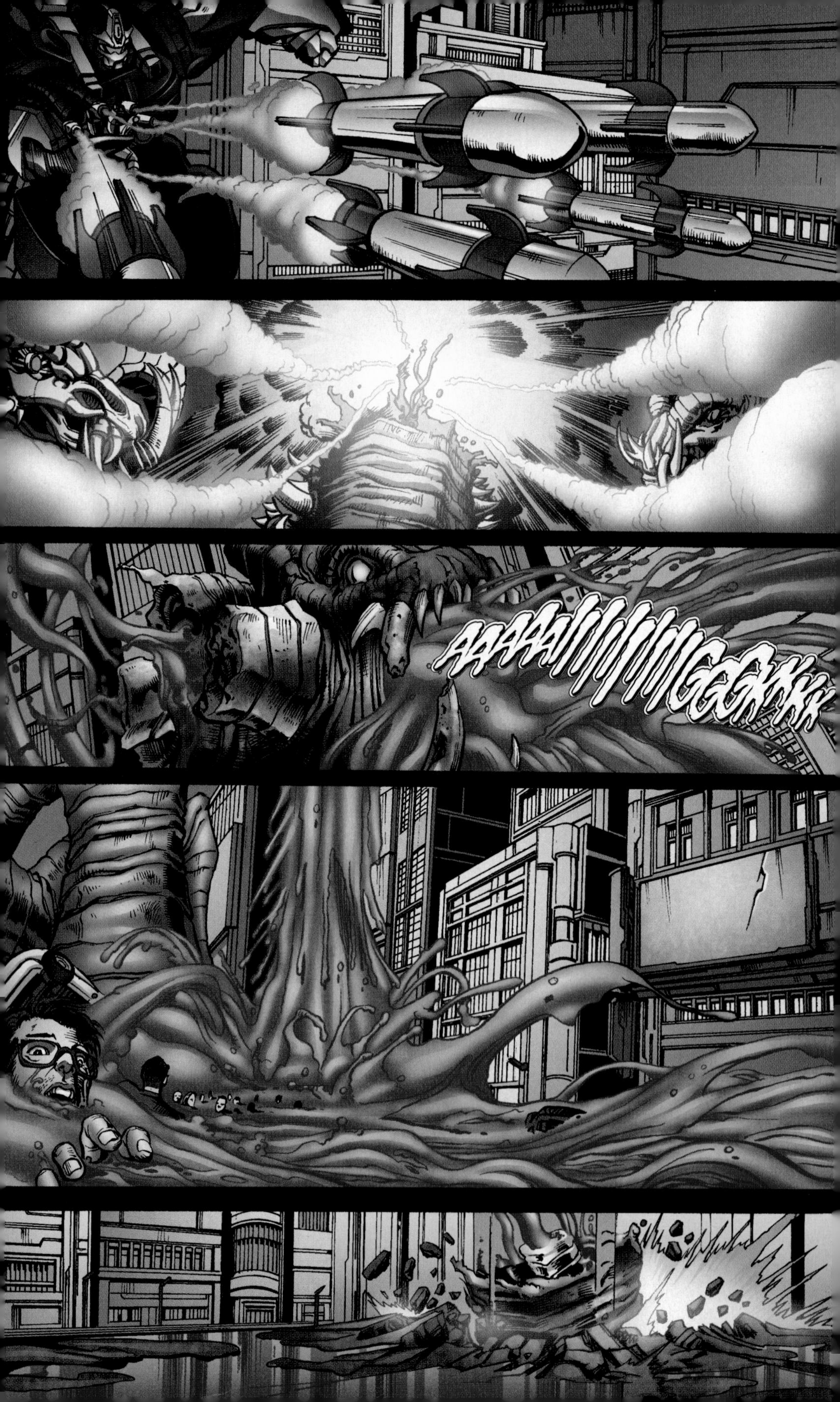
AAAAIIIIIIIIIGGGHKK

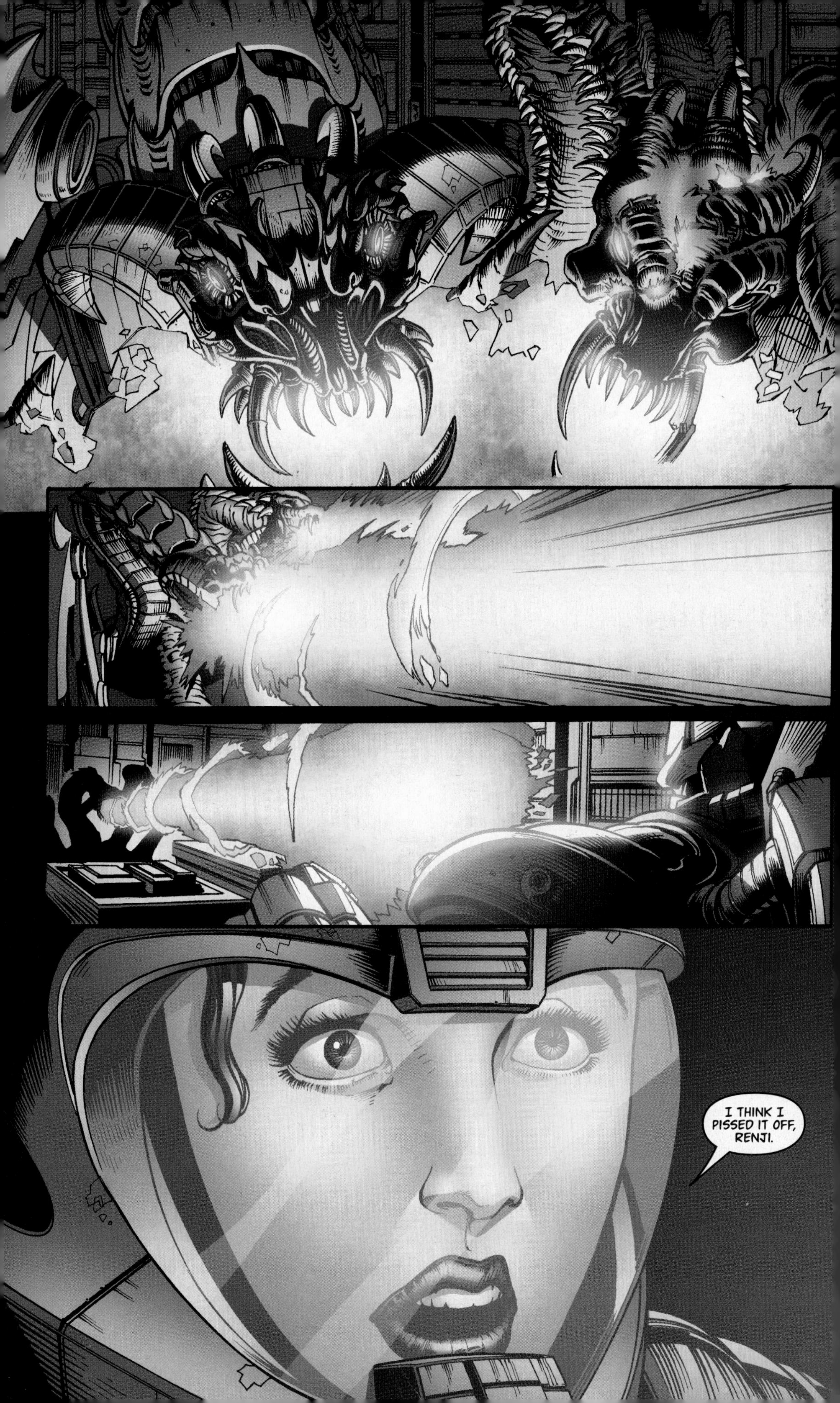
I THINK I PISSED IT OFF, RENJI.

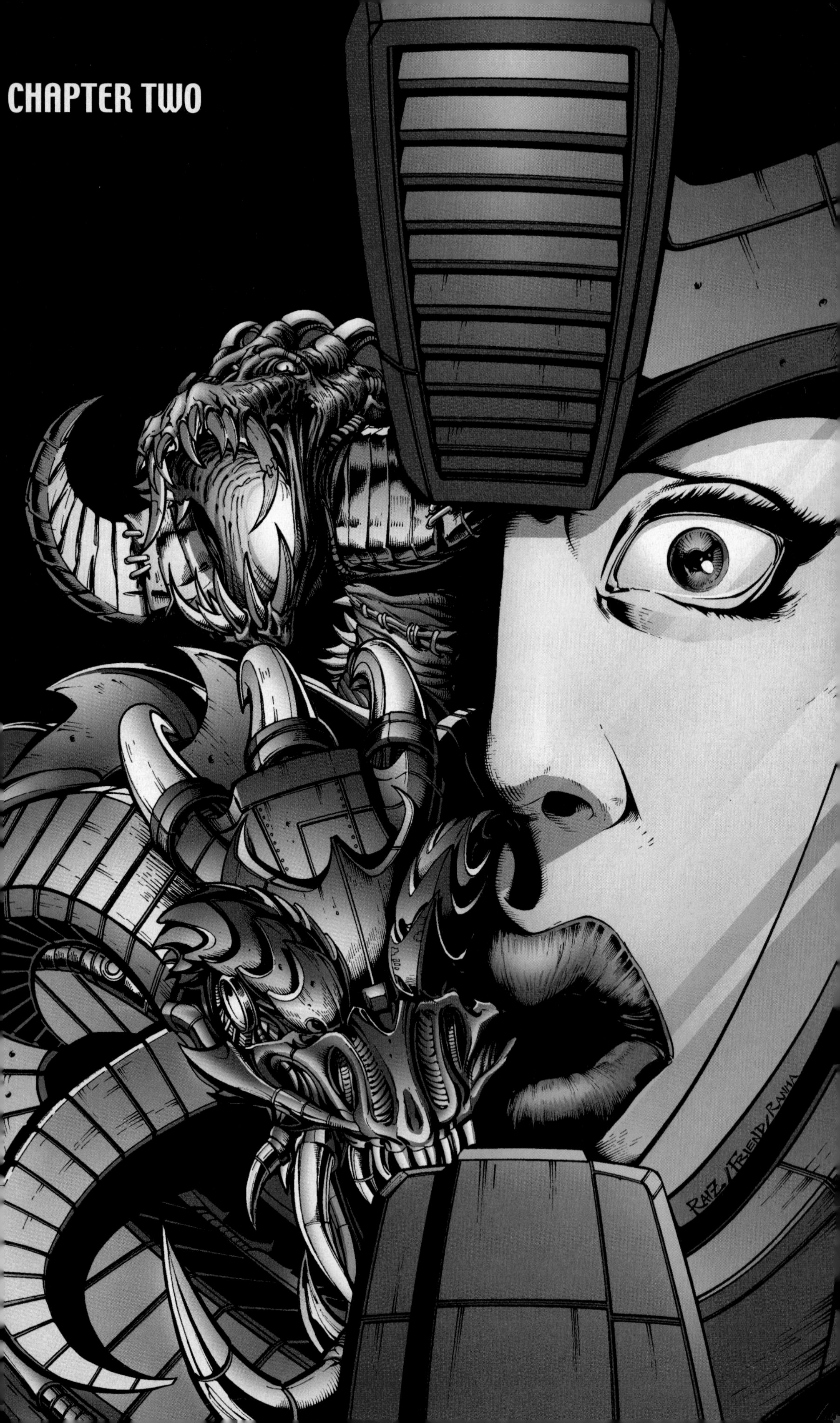
CHAPTER TWO
RAIZ./FRIEND/RANMA

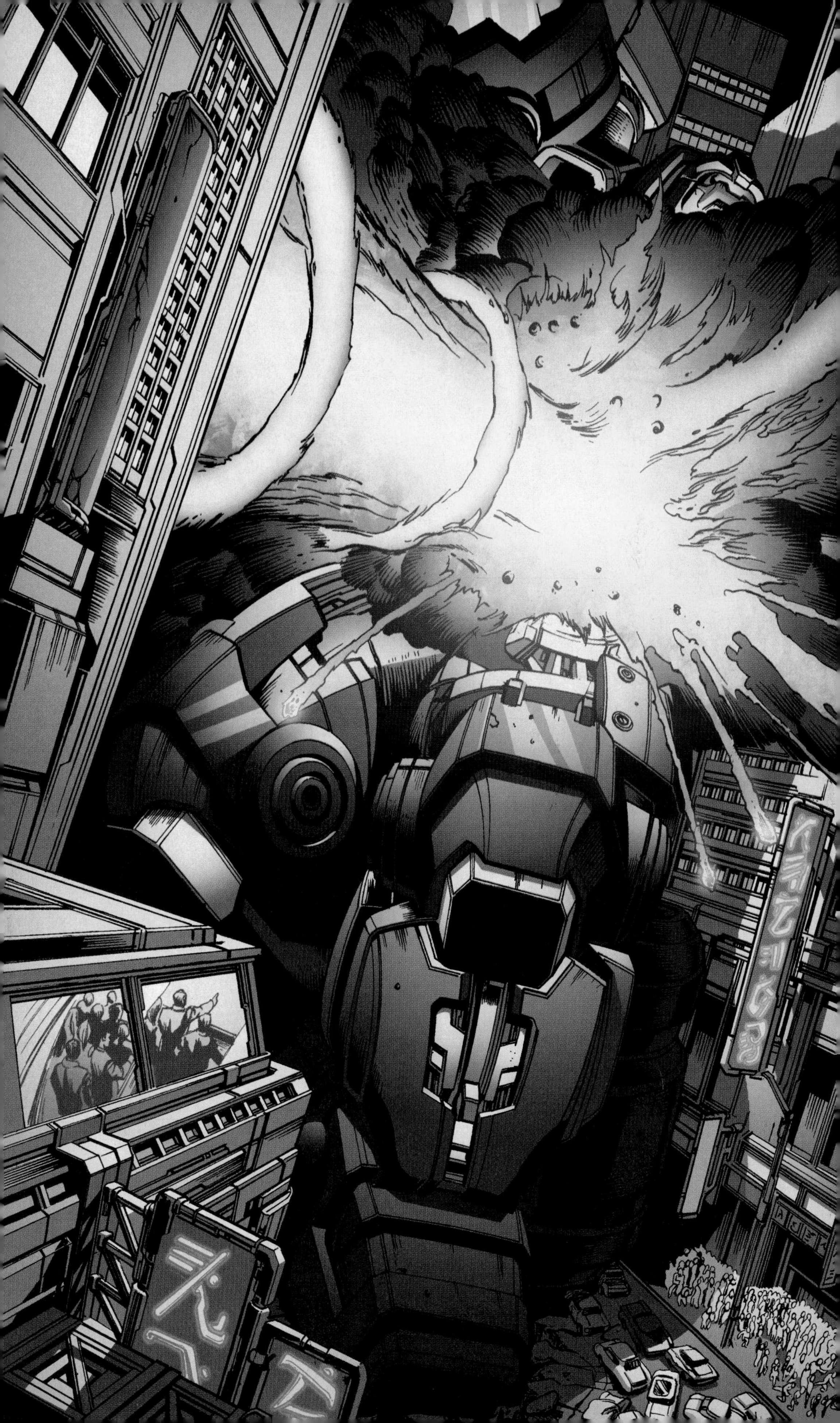

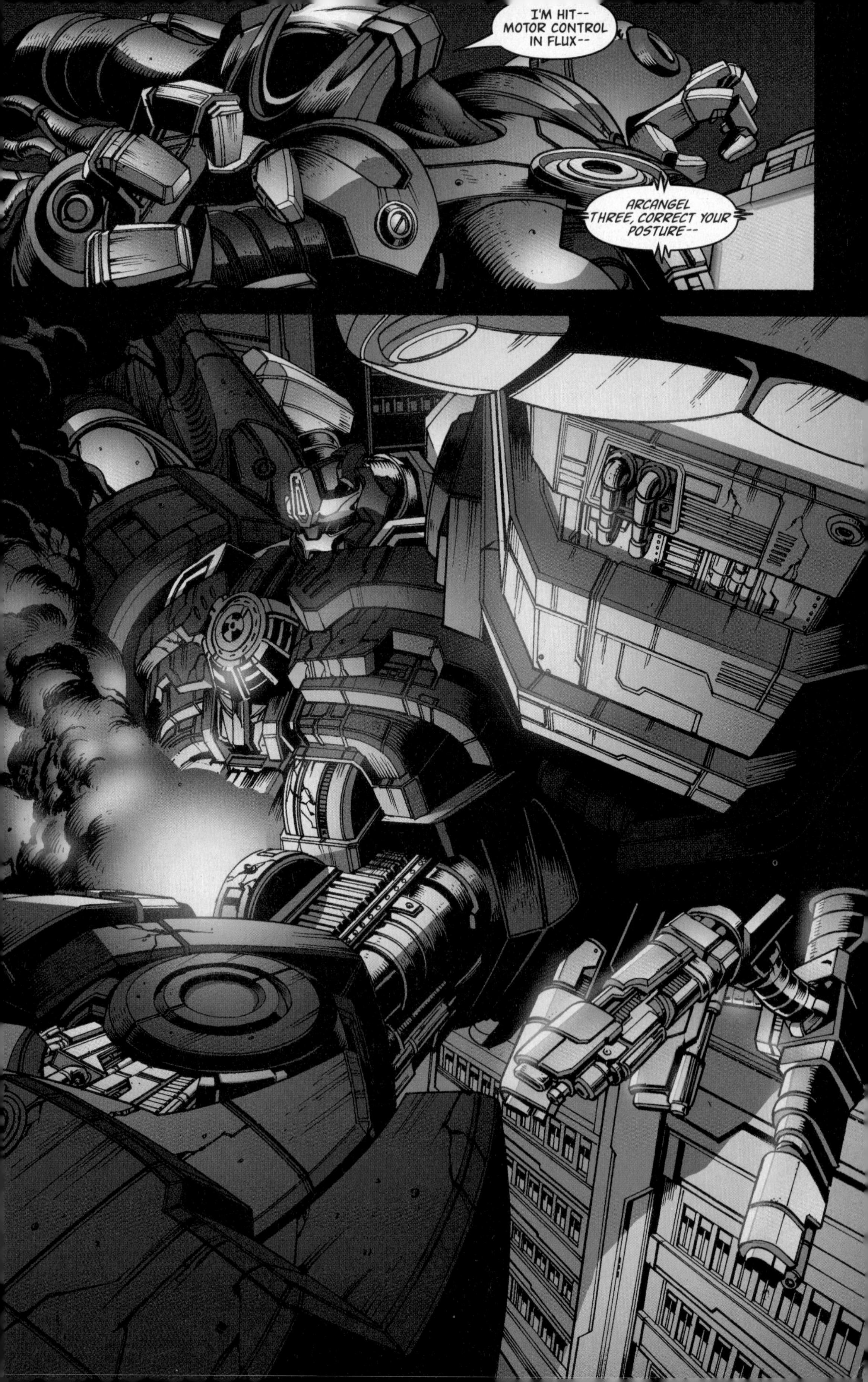
I'M HIT--
MOTOR CONTROL IN FLUX--
ARCANGEL THREE, CORRECT YOUR POSTURE--

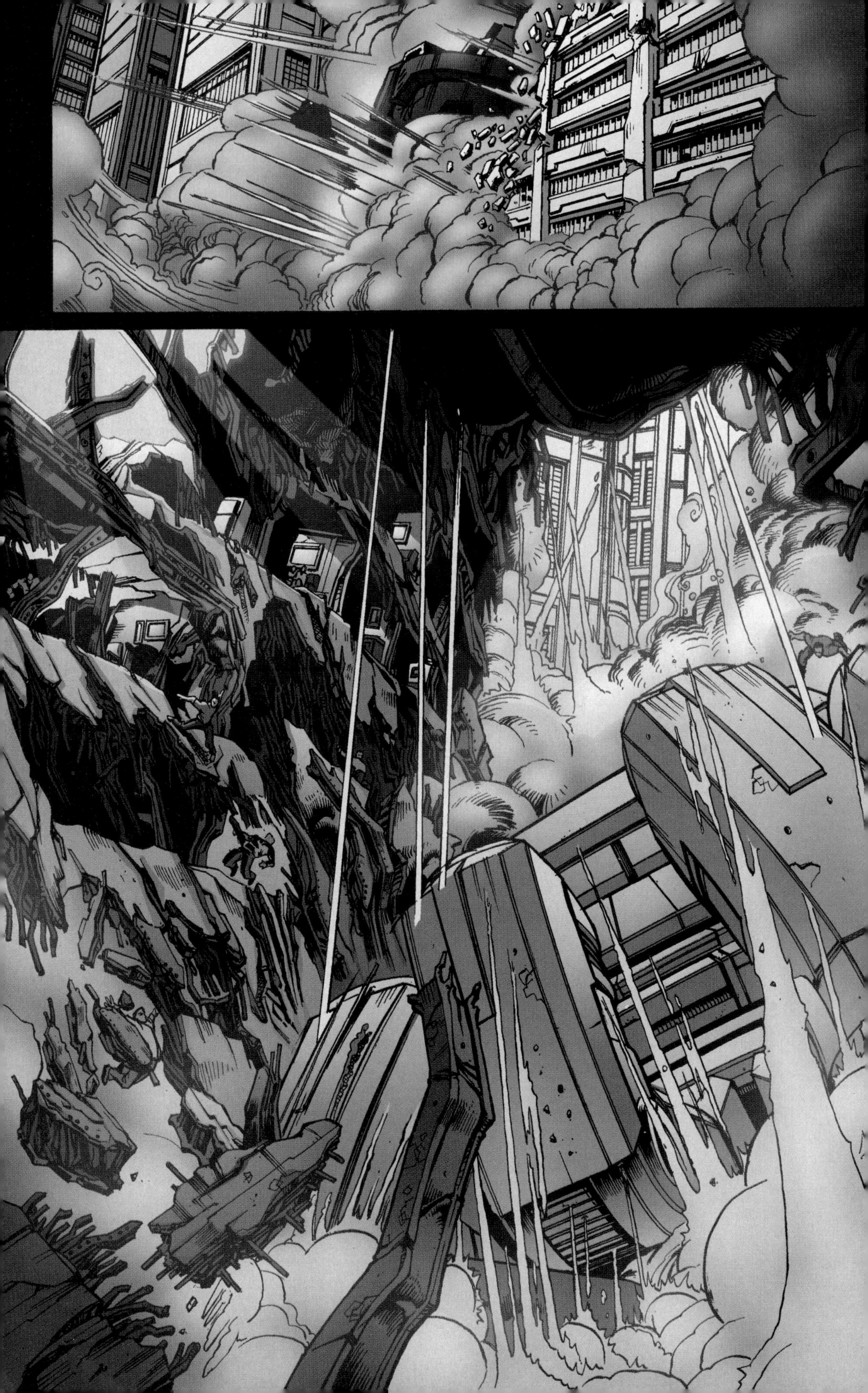

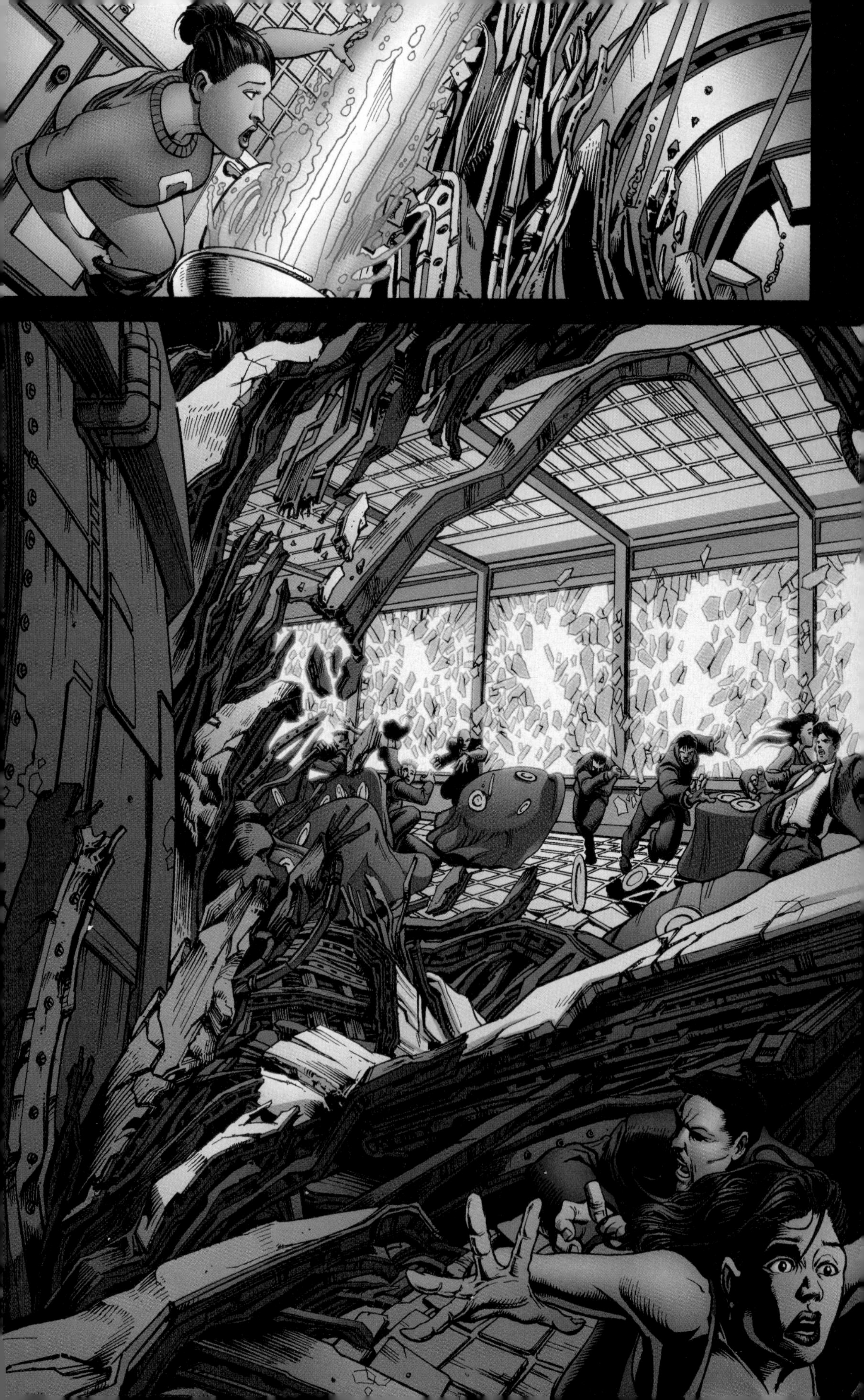

HEAT DAMAGE TO
ABDOMEN SYSTEMS--
POWER TRANSFER
EFFICIENCY DOWN
EIGHT PERCENT--

--TARGETING OFF
BY TWO DEGREES--
ADJUSTING
MANUALLY--

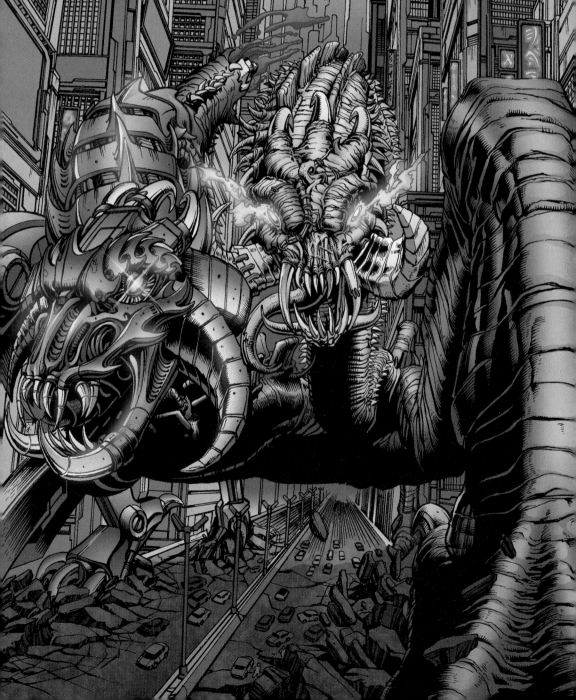

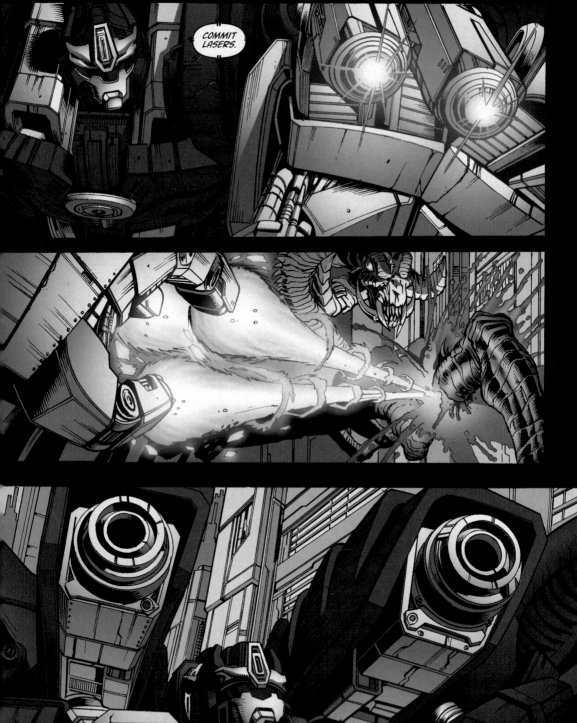

COMMIT LASERS.

MORTARS.

I'M RUNNING OUT OF TOYS HERE, RENJI...

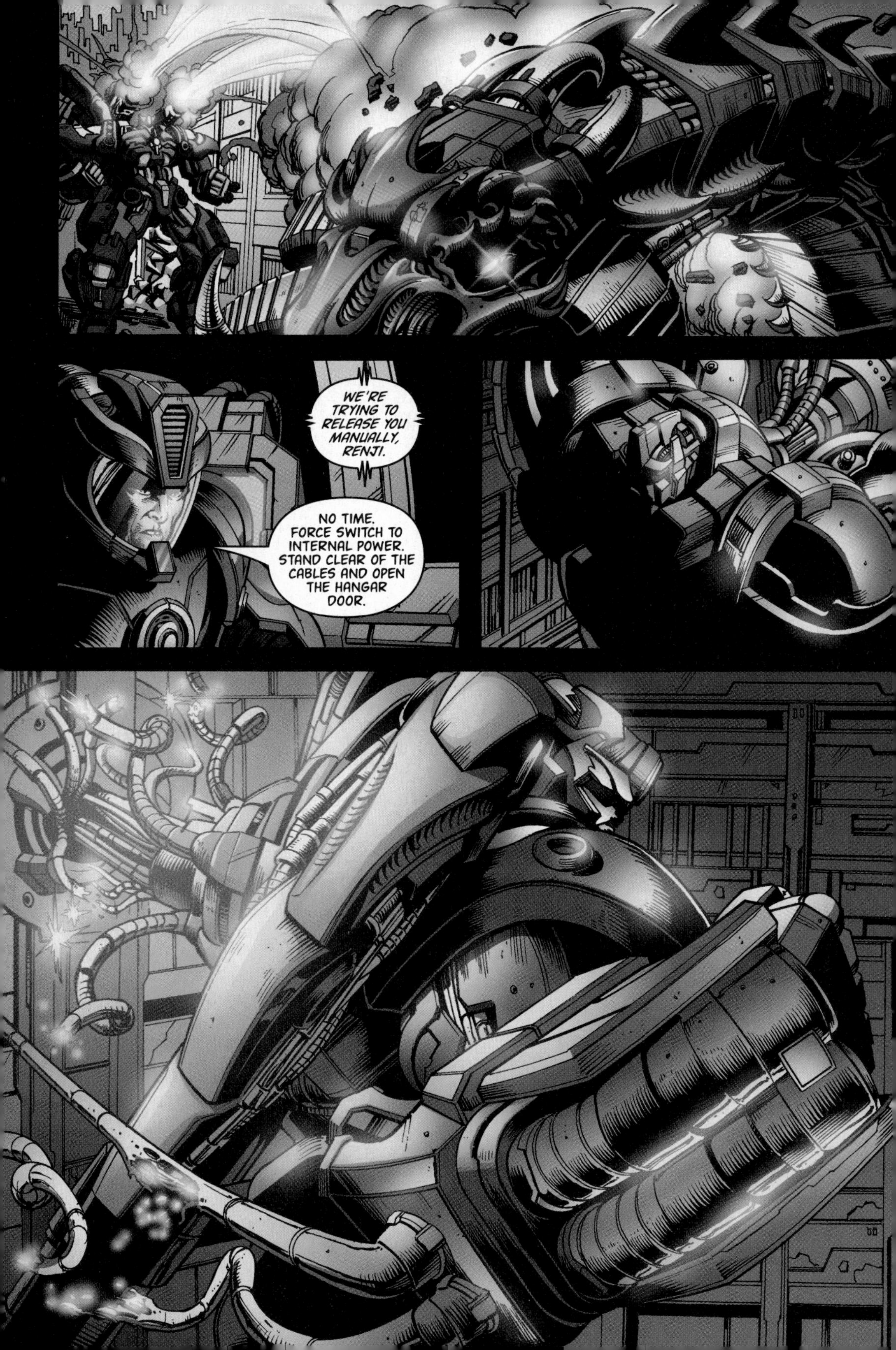
WE'RE TRYING TO RELEASE YOU MANUALLY, RENJI.
NO TIME. FORCE SWITCH TO INTERNAL POWER. STAND CLEAR OF THE CABLES AND OPEN THE HANGAR DOOR.

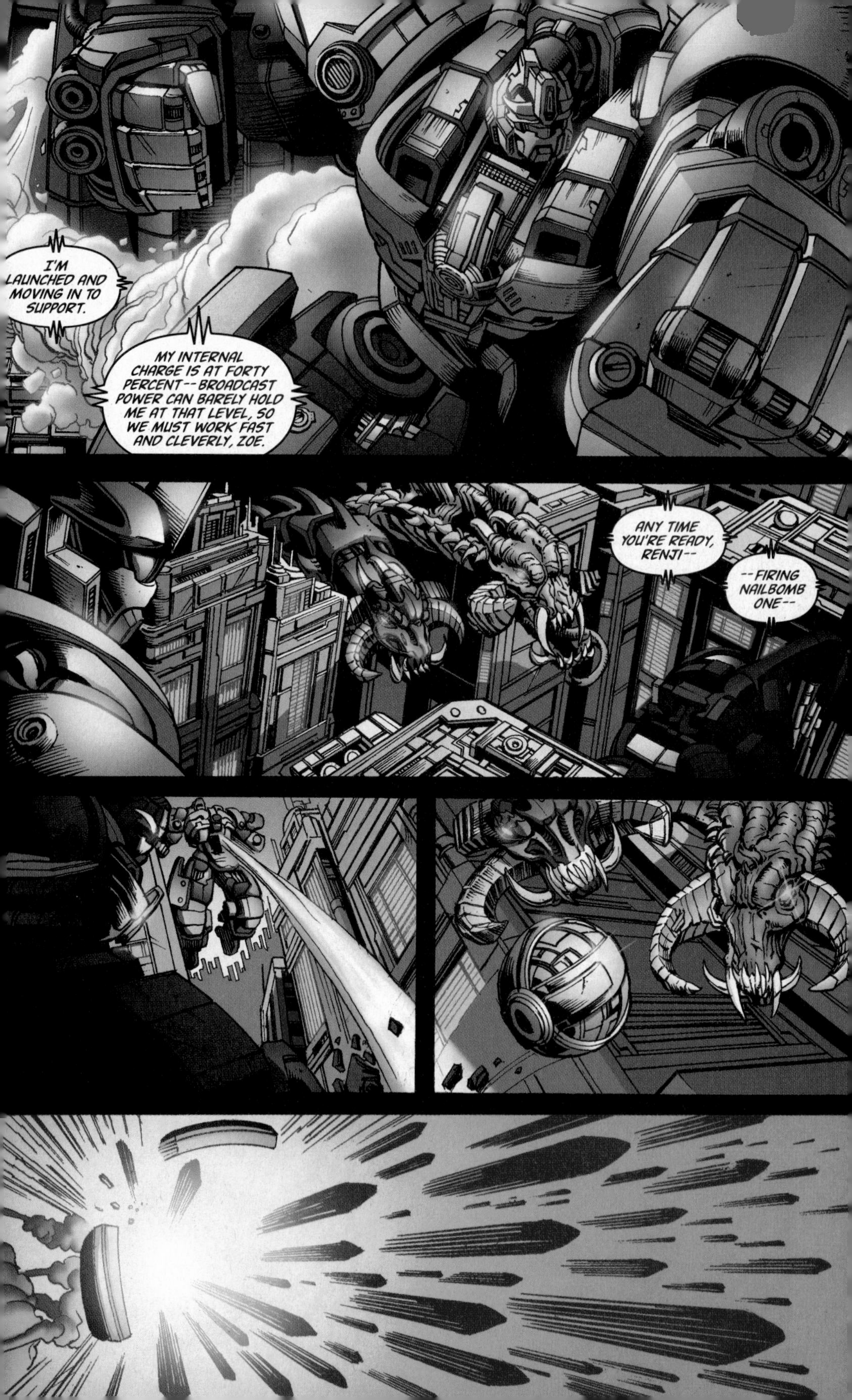
I'M LAUNCHED AND MOVING IN TO SUPPORT.
MY INTERNAL CHARGE IS AT FORTY PERCENT--BROADCAST POWER CAN BARELY HOLD ME AT THAT LEVEL, SO WE MUST WORK FAST AND CLEVERLY, ZOE.
ANY TIME YOU'RE READY, RENJI--
--FIRING NAILBOMB ONE--

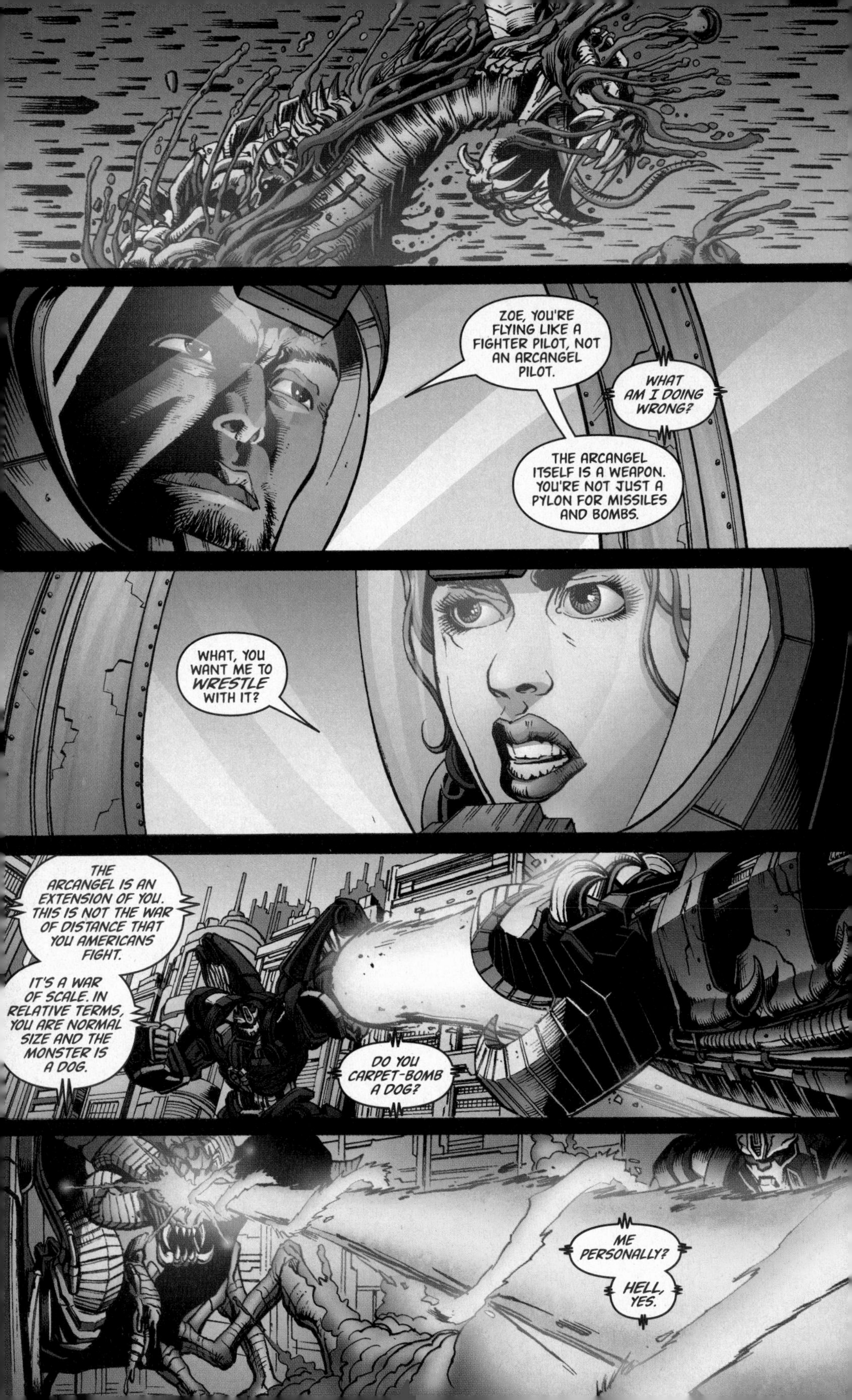
ZOE, YOU'RE FLYING LIKE A FIGHTER PILOT, NOT AN ARCANGEL PILOT.
WHAT AM I DOING WRONG?
THE ARCANGEL ITSELF IS A WEAPON. YOU'RE NOT JUST A PYLON FOR MISSILES AND BOMBS.
WHAT, YOU WANT ME TO WRESTLE WITH IT?
THE ARCANGEL IS AN EXTENSION OF YOU. THIS IS NOT THE WAR OF DISTANCE THAT YOU AMERICANS FIGHT.
IT'S A WAR OF SCALE. IN RELATIVE TERMS, YOU ARE NORMAL SIZE AND THE MONSTER IS A DOG.
DO YOU CARPET-BOMB A DOG?
ME PERSONALLY?
HELL, YES.

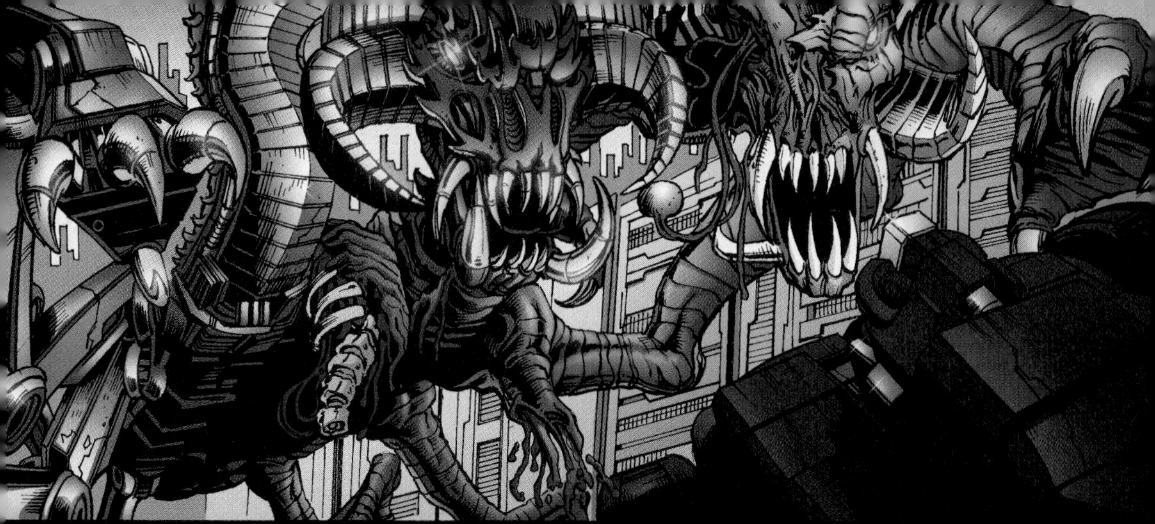
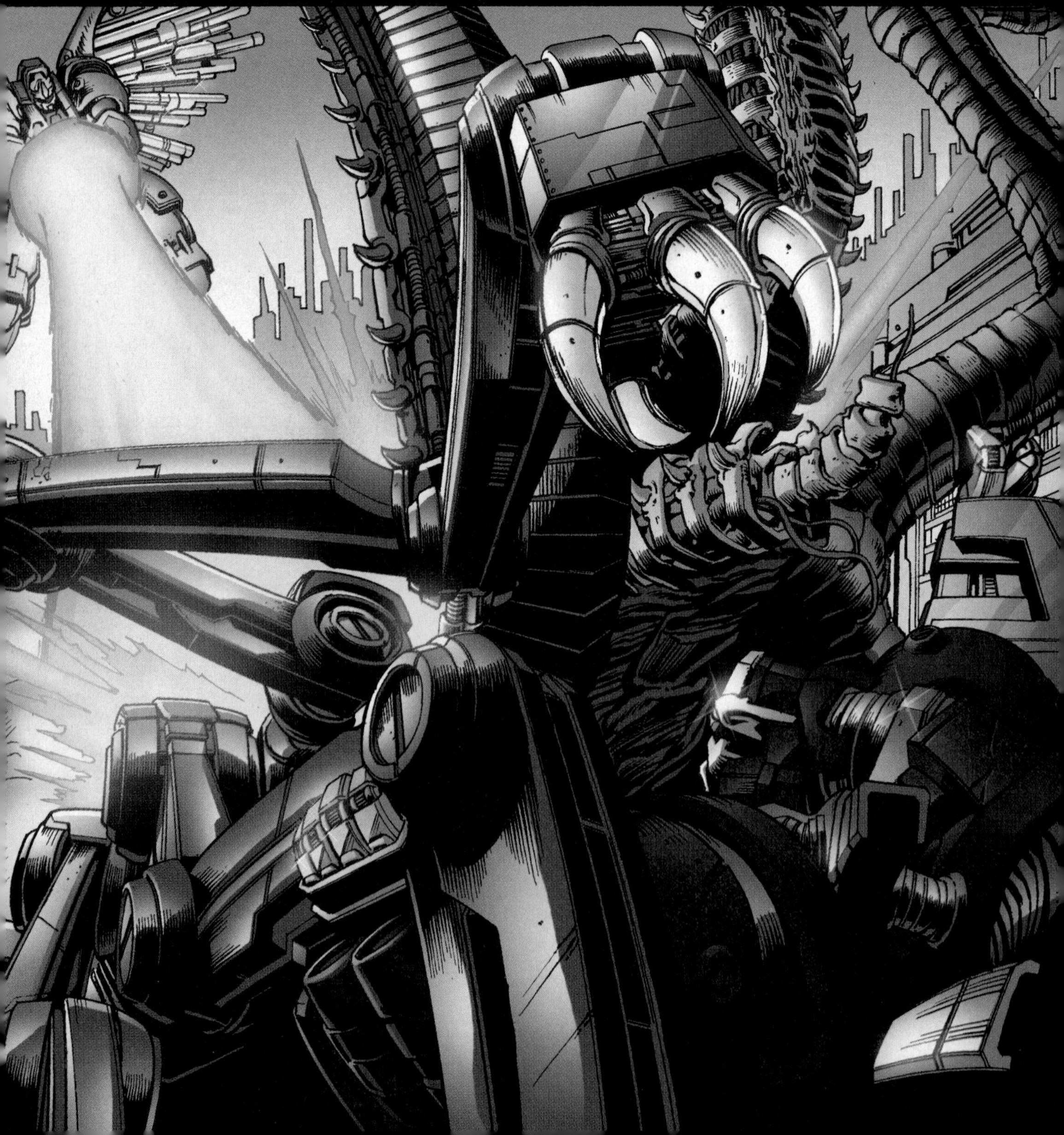

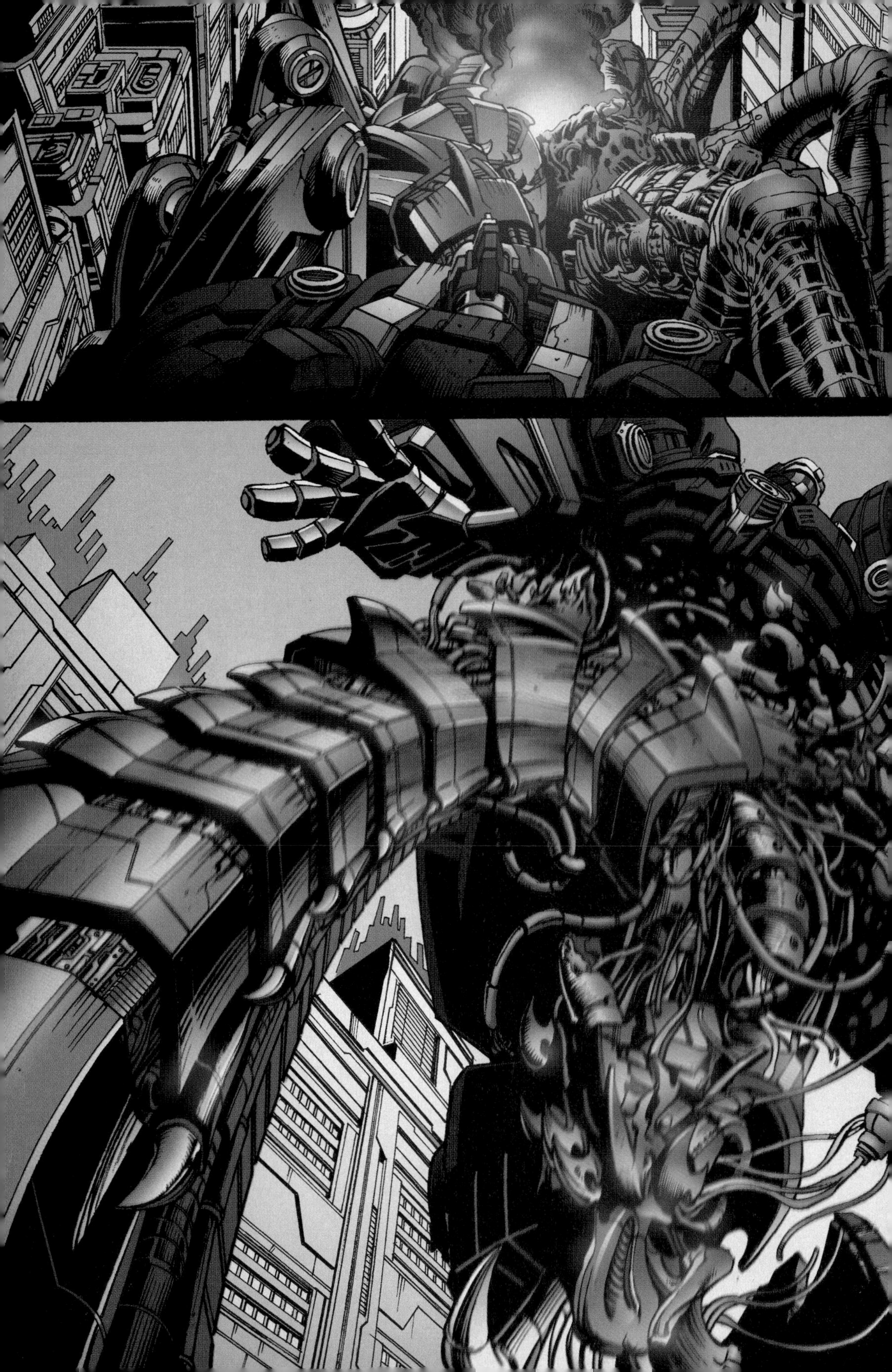

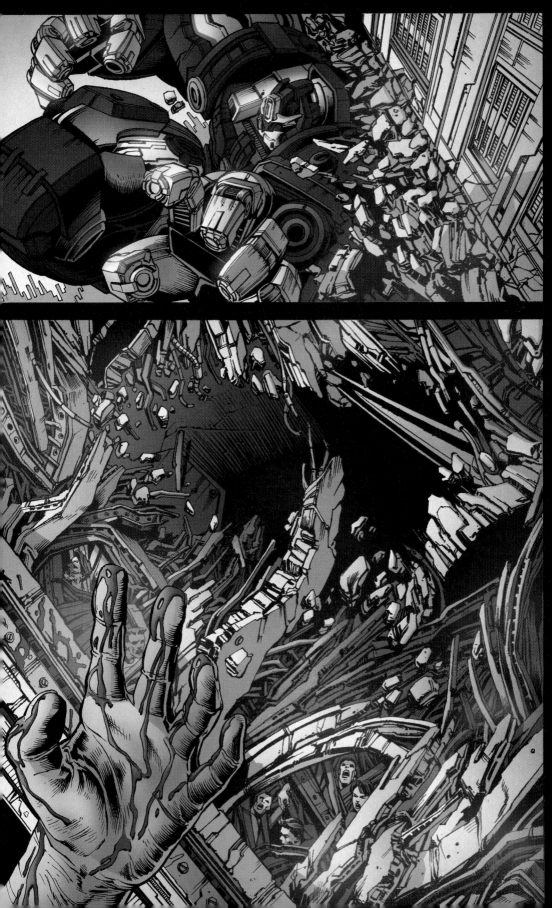

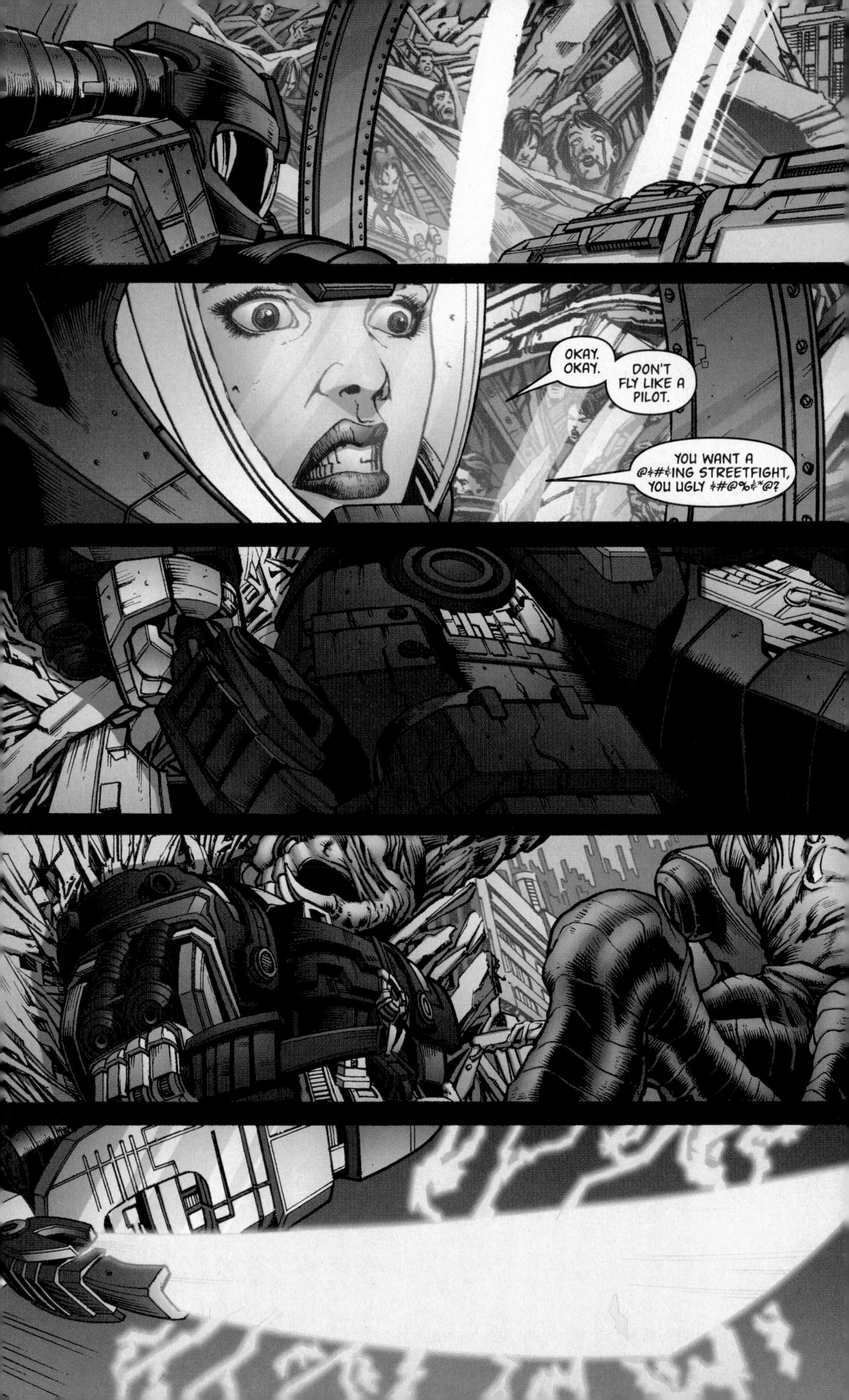
OKAY. OKAY.
DON'T FLY LIKE A PILOT.
YOU WANT A @$#$ING STREETFIGHT, YOU UGLY $#@%$*@?

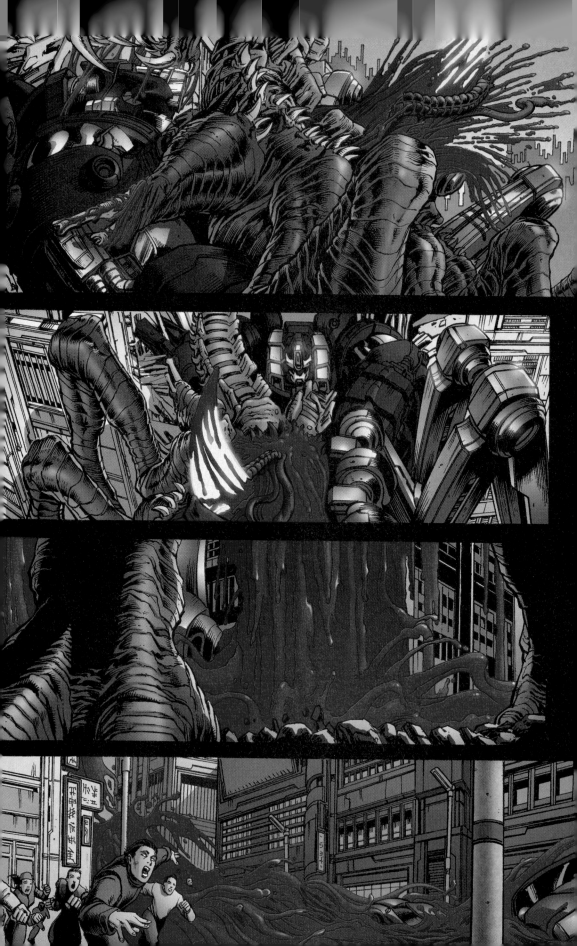

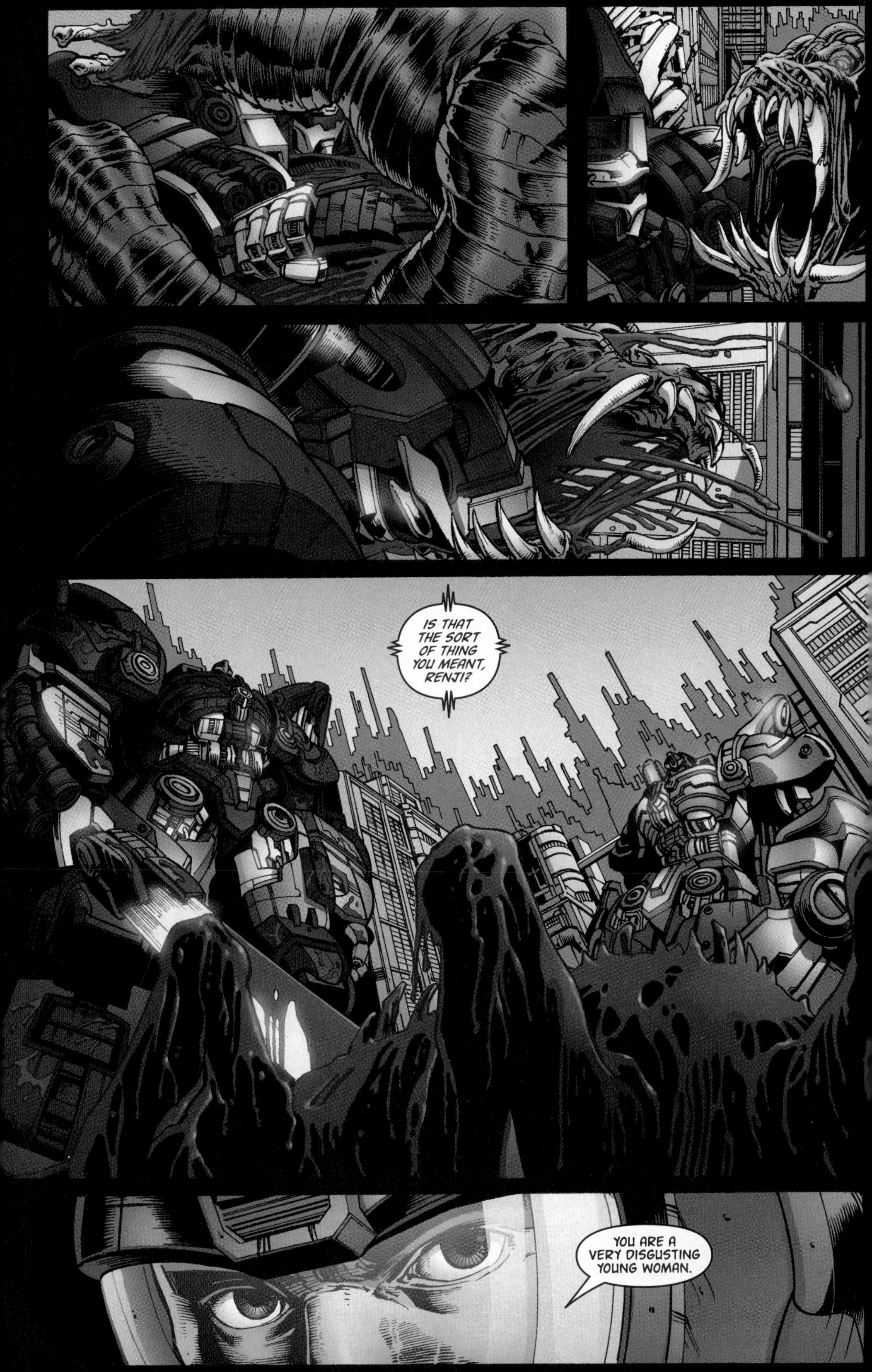
IS THAT THE SORT OF THING YOU MEANT, RENJI?
YOU ARE A VERY DISGUSTING YOUNG WOMAN.

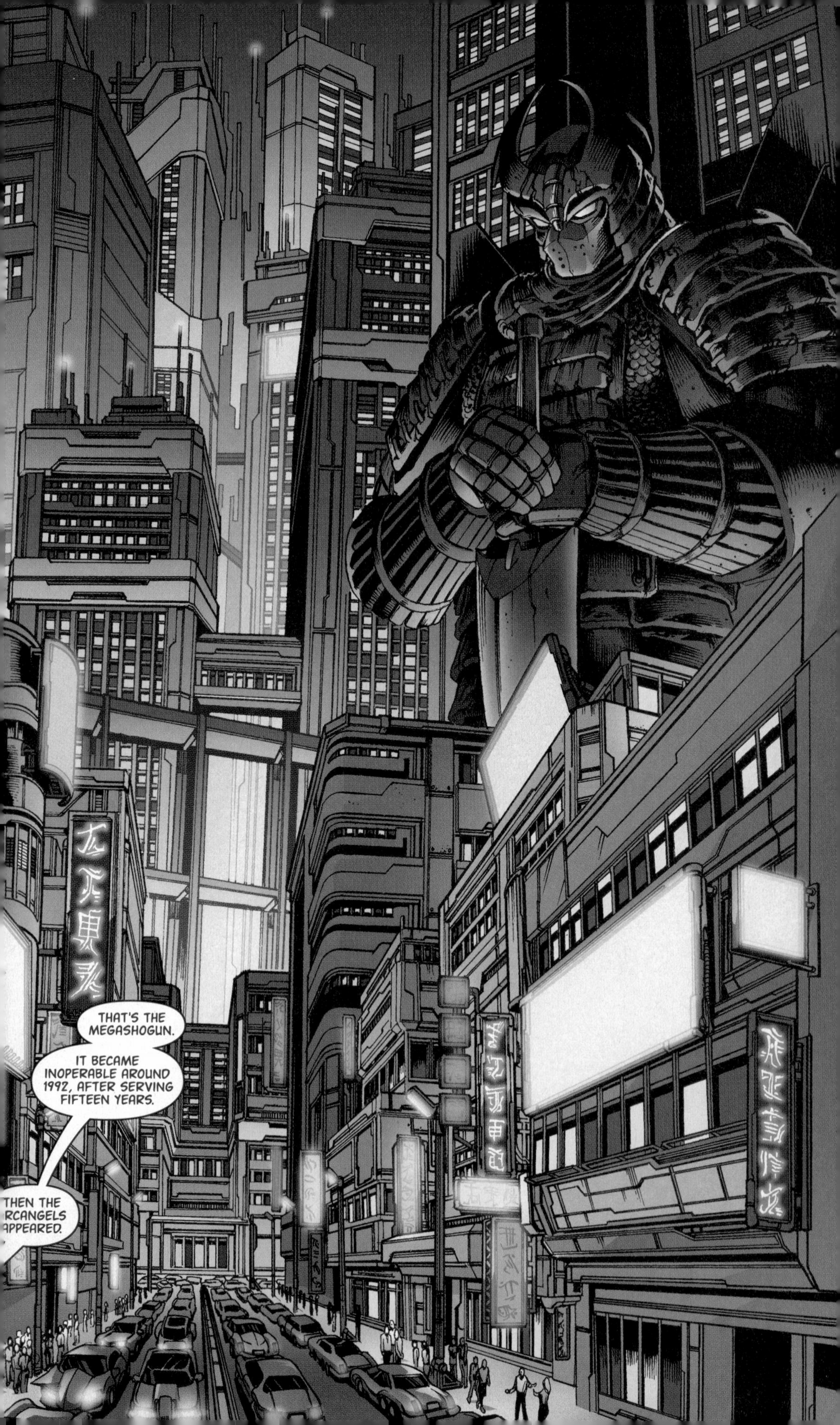
THAT'S THE MEGASHOGUN.
IT BECAME INOPERABLE AROUND 1992, AFTER SERVING FIFTEEN YEARS.
THEN THE RCANGELS APPEARED.

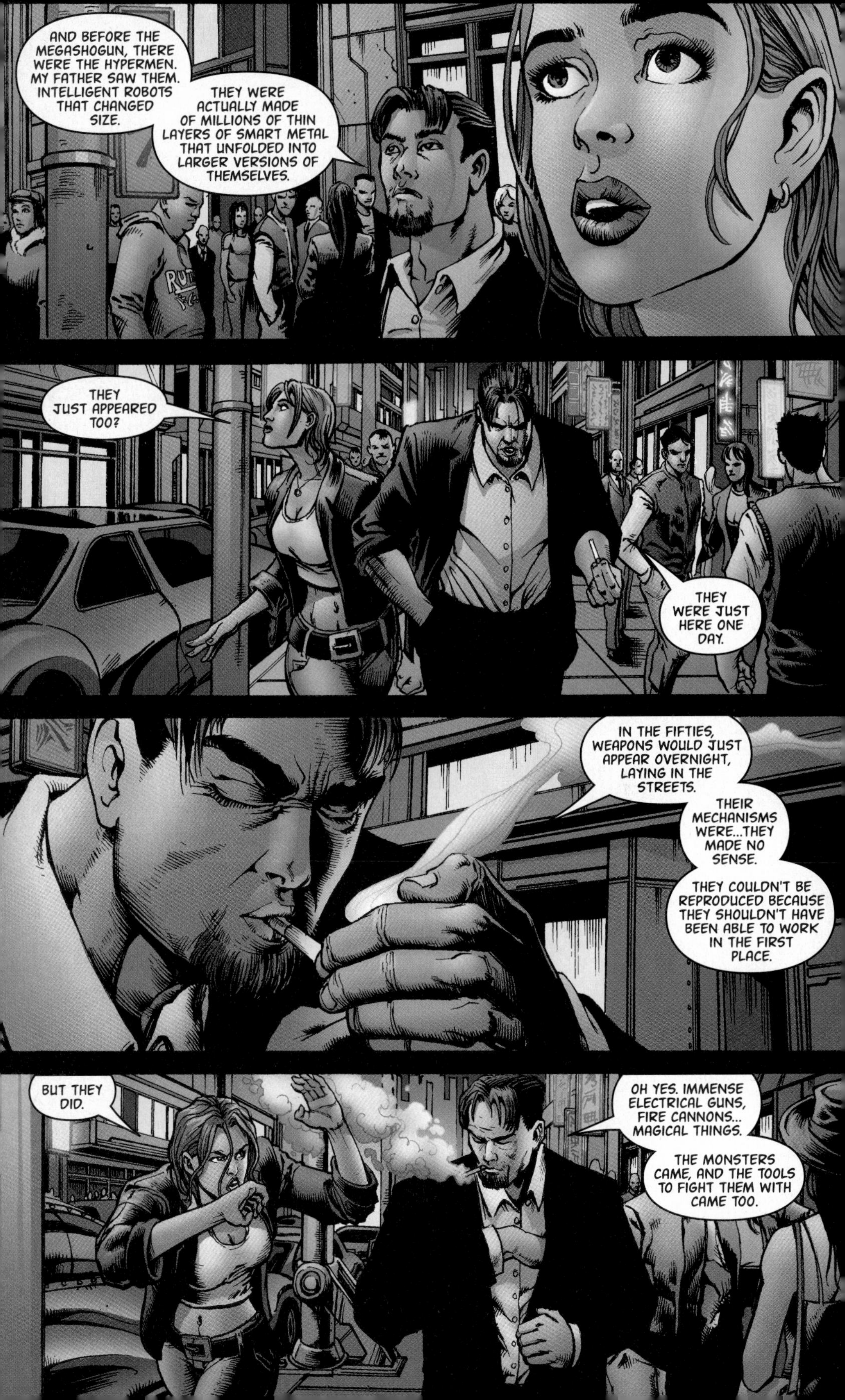
AND BEFORE THE MEGASHOGUN, THERE WERE THE HYPERMEN. MY FATHER SAW THEM. INTELLIGENT ROBOTS THAT CHANGED SIZE.
THEY WERE ACTUALLY MADE OF MILLIONS OF THIN LAYERS OF SMART METAL THAT UNFOLDED INTO LARGER VERSIONS OF THEMSELVES.
THEY JUST APPEARED TOO?
THEY WERE JUST HERE ONE DAY.
IN THE FIFTIES, WEAPONS WOULD JUST APPEAR OVERNIGHT, LAYING IN THE STREETS.
THEIR MECHANISMS WERE...THEY MADE NO SENSE.
THEY COULDN'T BE REPRODUCED BECAUSE THEY SHOULDN'T HAVE BEEN ABLE TO WORK IN THE FIRST PLACE.
BUT THEY DID.
OH YES. IMMENSE ELECTRICAL GUNS, FIRE CANNONS... MAGICAL THINGS.
THE MONSTERS CAME, AND THE TOOLS TO FIGHT THEM WITH CAME TOO.

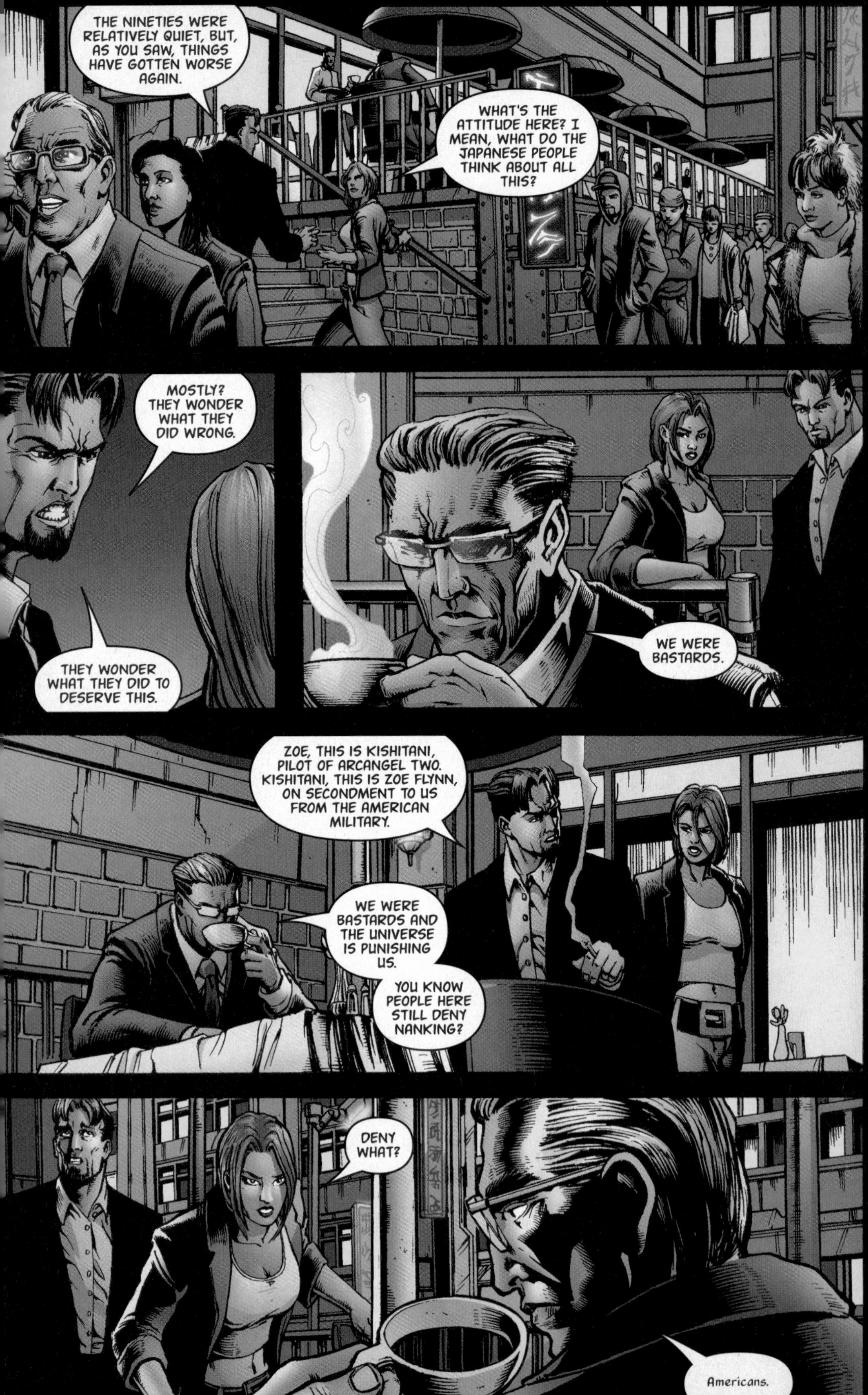
THE NINETIES WERE RELATIVELY QUIET, BUT, AS YOU SAW, THINGS HAVE GOTTEN WORSE AGAIN.
WHAT'S THE ATTITUDE HERE? I MEAN, WHAT DO THE JAPANESE PEOPLE THINK ABOUT ALL THIS?
MOSTLY? THEY WONDER WHAT THEY DID WRONG.
THEY WONDER WHAT THEY DID TO DESERVE THIS.
WE WERE BASTARDS.
ZOE, THIS IS KISHITANI, PILOT OF ARCANGEL TWO. KISHITANI, THIS IS ZOE FLYNN, ON SECONDMENT TO US FROM THE AMERICAN MILITARY.
WE WERE BASTARDS AND THE UNIVERSE IS PUNISHING US.
YOU KNOW PEOPLE HERE STILL DENY NANKING?
DENY WHAT?
Americans.

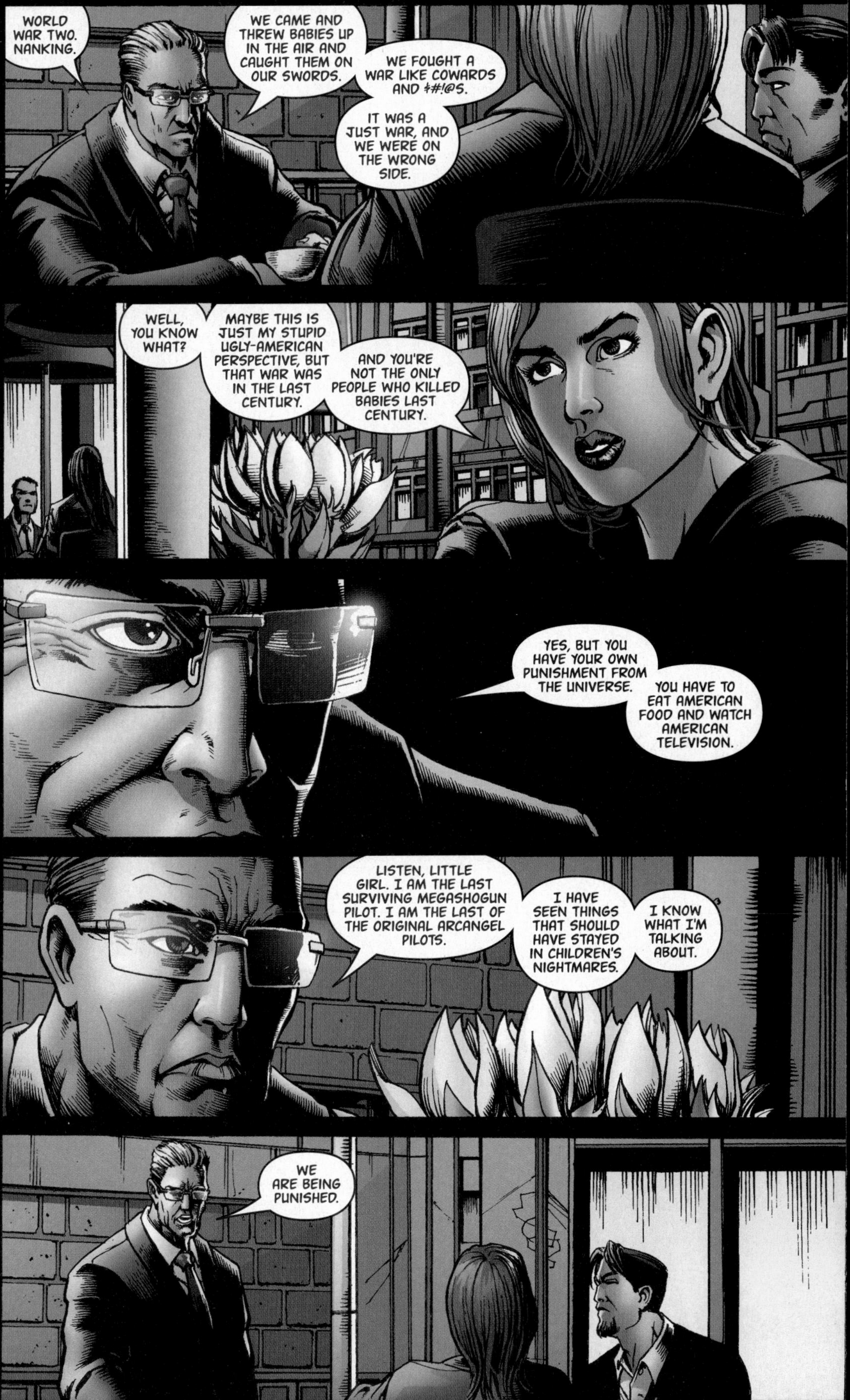
WORLD WAR TWO. NANKING.
WE CAME AND THREW BABIES UP IN THE AIR AND CAUGHT THEM ON OUR SWORDS.
WE FOUGHT A WAR LIKE COWARDS AND $#!@S.
IT WAS A JUST WAR, AND WE WERE ON THE WRONG SIDE.
WELL, YOU KNOW WHAT?
MAYBE THIS IS JUST MY STUPID UGLY-AMERICAN PERSPECTIVE, BUT THAT WAR WAS IN THE LAST CENTURY.
AND YOU'RE NOT THE ONLY PEOPLE WHO KILLED BABIES LAST CENTURY.
YES, BUT YOU HAVE YOUR OWN PUNISHMENT FROM THE UNIVERSE.
YOU HAVE TO EAT AMERICAN FOOD AND WATCH AMERICAN TELEVISION.
LISTEN, LITTLE GIRL. I AM THE LAST SURVIVING MEGASHOGUN PILOT. I AM THE LAST OF THE ORIGINAL ARCANGEL PILOTS.
I HAVE SEEN THINGS THAT SHOULD HAVE STAYED IN CHILDREN'S NIGHTMARES.
I KNOW WHAT I'M TALKING ABOUT.
WE ARE BEING PUNISHED.

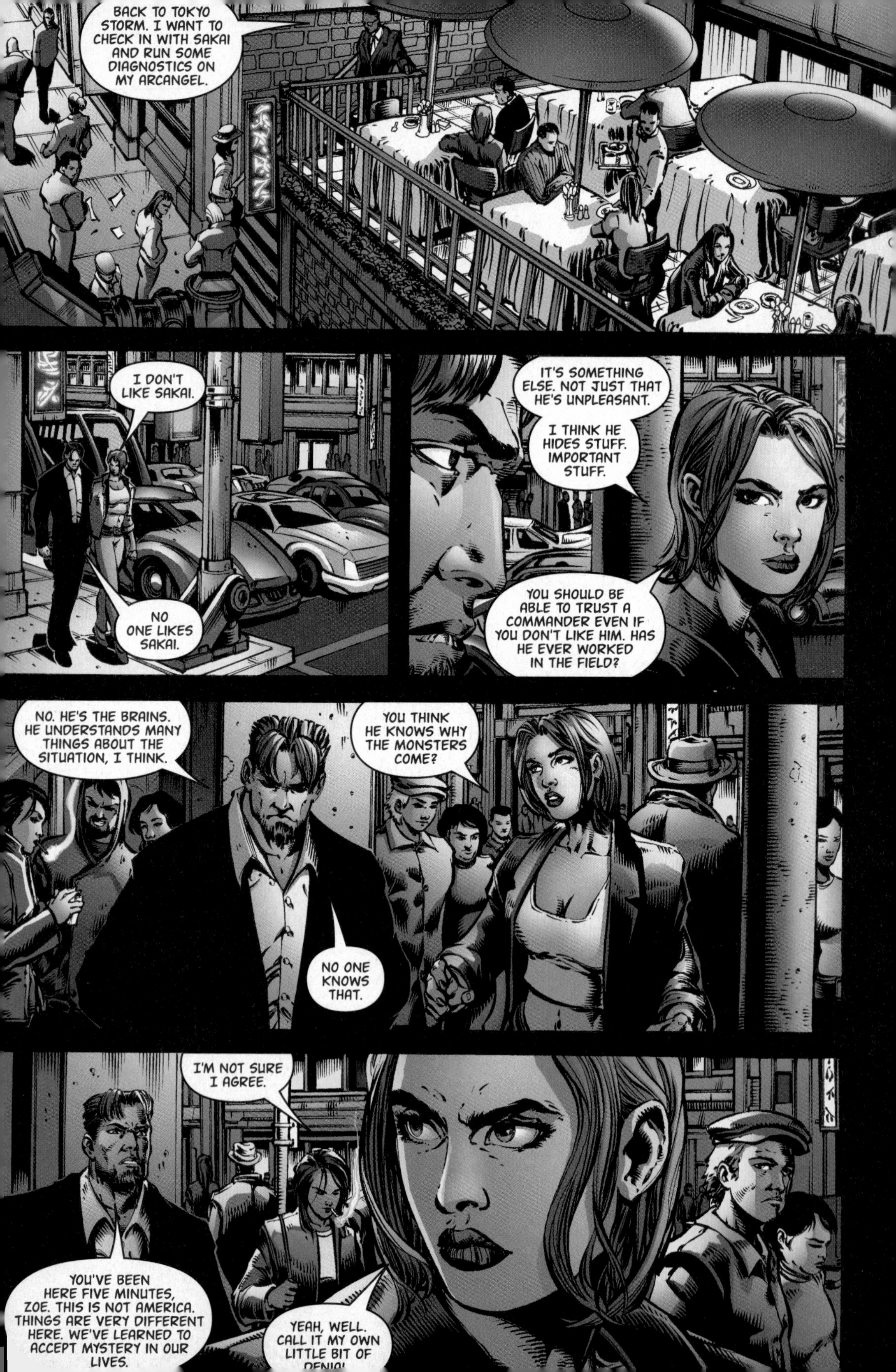
BACK TO TOKYO STORM. I WANT TO CHECK IN WITH SAKAI AND RUN SOME DIAGNOSTICS ON MY ARCANGEL.
I DON'T LIKE SAKAI.
NO ONE LIKES SAKAI.
IT'S SOMETHING ELSE. NOT JUST THAT HE'S UNPLEASANT.
I THINK HE HIDES STUFF. IMPORTANT STUFF.
YOU SHOULD BE ABLE TO TRUST A COMMANDER EVEN IF YOU DON'T LIKE HIM. HAS HE EVER WORKED IN THE FIELD?
NO. HE'S THE BRAINS. HE UNDERSTANDS MANY THINGS ABOUT THE SITUATION, I THINK.
YOU THINK HE KNOWS WHY THE MONSTERS COME?
NO ONE KNOWS THAT.
I'M NOT SURE I AGREE.
YOU'VE BEEN HERE FIVE MINUTES, ZOE. THIS IS NOT AMERICA. THINGS ARE VERY DIFFERENT HERE. WE'VE LEARNED TO ACCEPT MYSTERY IN OUR LIVES.
YEAH, WELL. CALL IT MY OWN LITTLE BIT OF

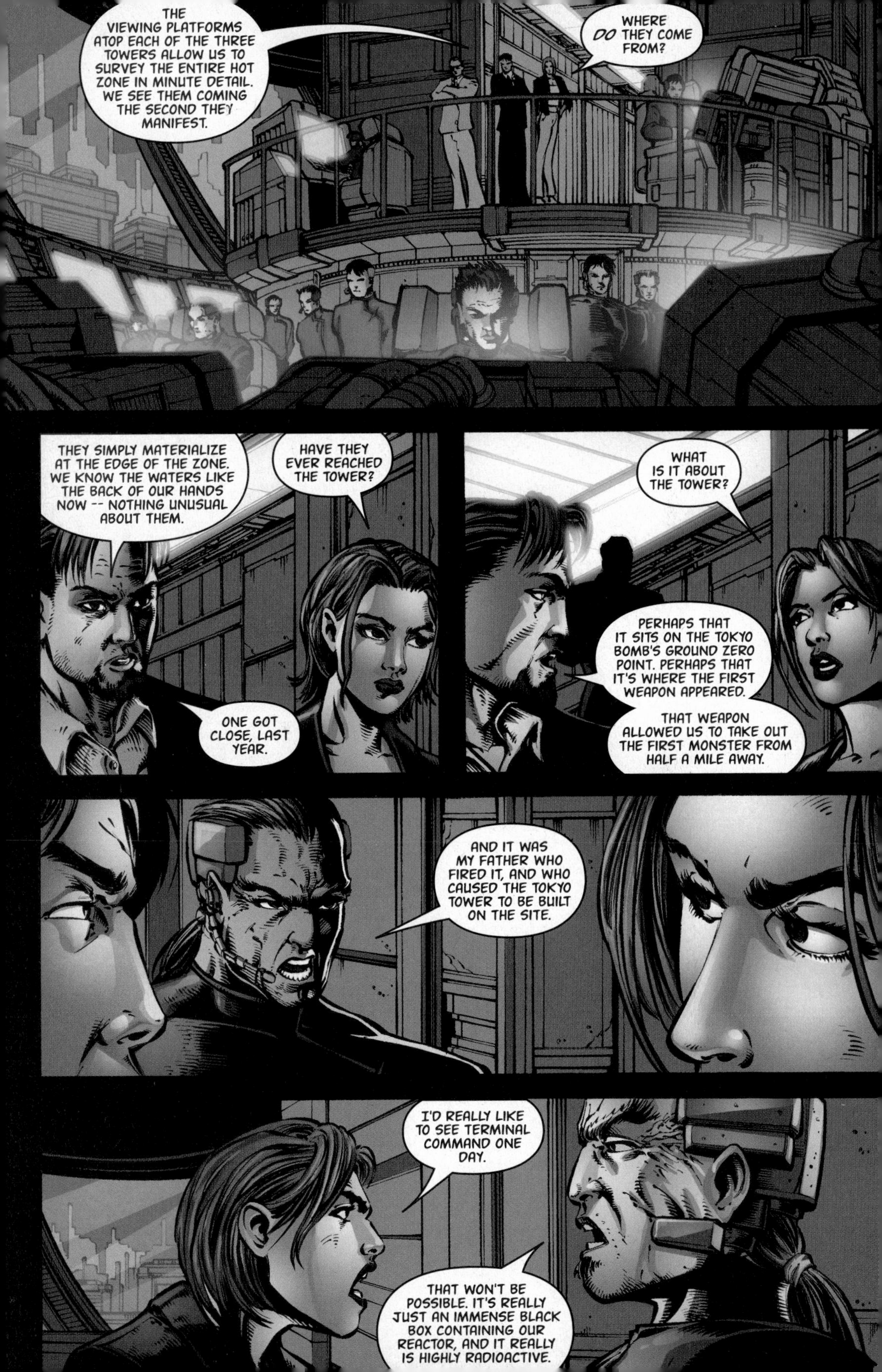
THE VIEWING PLATFORMS ATOP EACH OF THE THREE TOWERS ALLOW US TO SURVEY THE ENTIRE HOT ZONE IN MINUTE DETAIL. WE SEE THEM COMING THE SECOND THEY MANIFEST.
WHERE *DO* THEY COME FROM?
THEY SIMPLY MATERIALIZE AT THE EDGE OF THE ZONE. WE KNOW THE WATERS LIKE THE BACK OF OUR HANDS NOW -- NOTHING UNUSUAL ABOUT THEM.
HAVE THEY EVER REACHED THE TOWER?
ONE GOT CLOSE, LAST YEAR.
WHAT IS IT ABOUT THE TOWER?
PERHAPS THAT IT SITS ON THE TOKYO BOMB'S GROUND ZERO POINT. PERHAPS THAT IT'S WHERE THE FIRST WEAPON APPEARED.
THAT WEAPON ALLOWED US TO TAKE OUT THE FIRST MONSTER FROM HALF A MILE AWAY.
AND IT WAS MY FATHER WHO FIRED IT, AND WHO CAUSED THE TOKYO TOWER TO BE BUILT ON THE SITE.
I'D REALLY LIKE TO SEE TERMINAL COMMAND ONE DAY.
THAT WON'T BE POSSIBLE. IT'S REALLY JUST AN IMMENSE BLACK BOX CONTAINING OUR REACTOR, AND IT REALLY IS HIGHLY RADIOACTIVE.

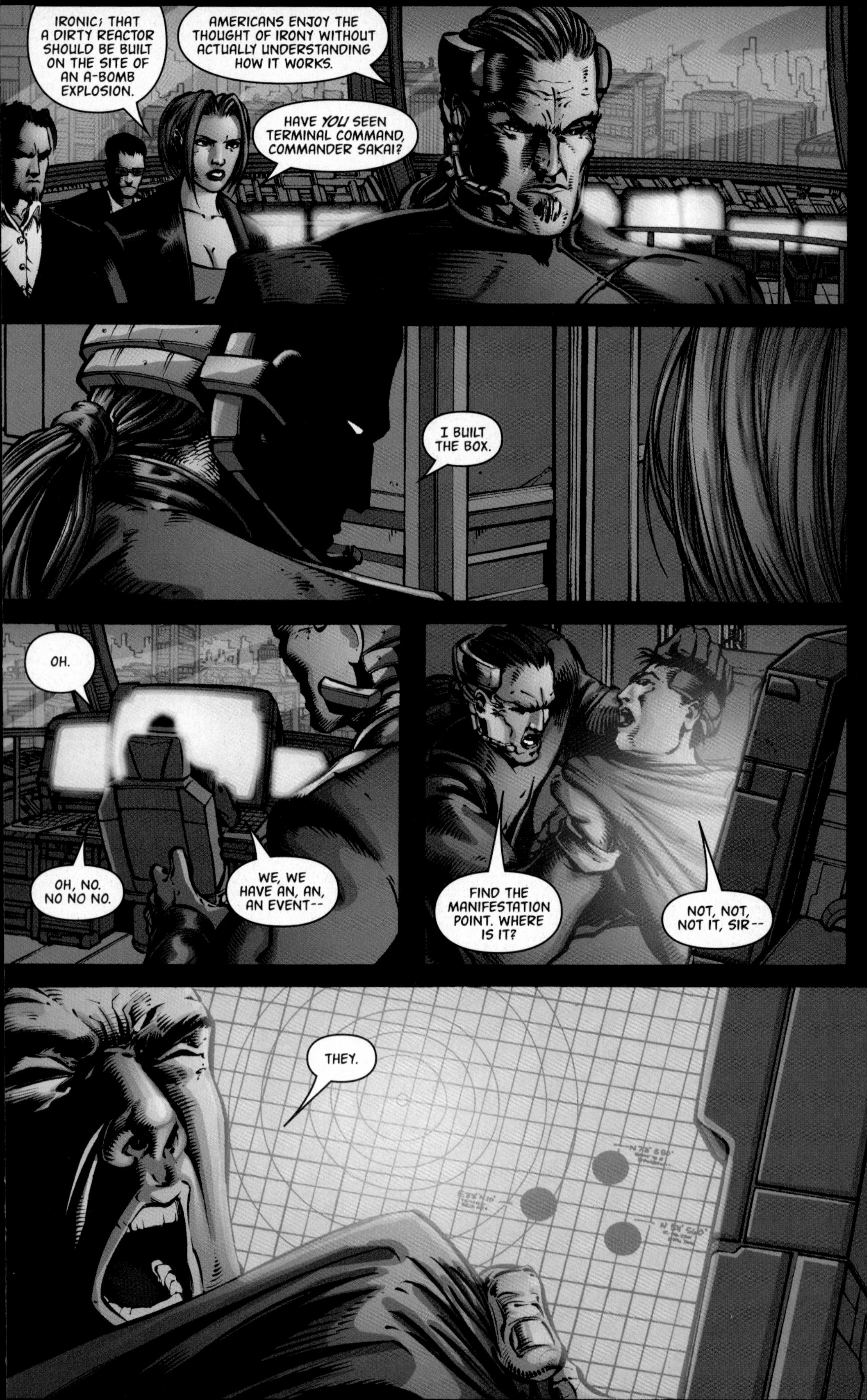
IRONIC; THAT A DIRTY REACTOR SHOULD BE BUILT ON THE SITE OF AN A-BOMB EXPLOSION.
AMERICANS ENJOY THE THOUGHT OF IRONY WITHOUT ACTUALLY UNDERSTANDING HOW IT WORKS.
HAVE *YOU* SEEN TERMINAL COMMAND, COMMANDER SAKAI?
I BUILT THE BOX.
OH.
OH, NO. NO NO NO.
WE, WE HAVE AN, AN, AN EVENT--
FIND THE MANIFESTATION POINT. WHERE IS IT?
NOT, NOT, NOT IT, SIR--
THEY.

CHAPTER THREE

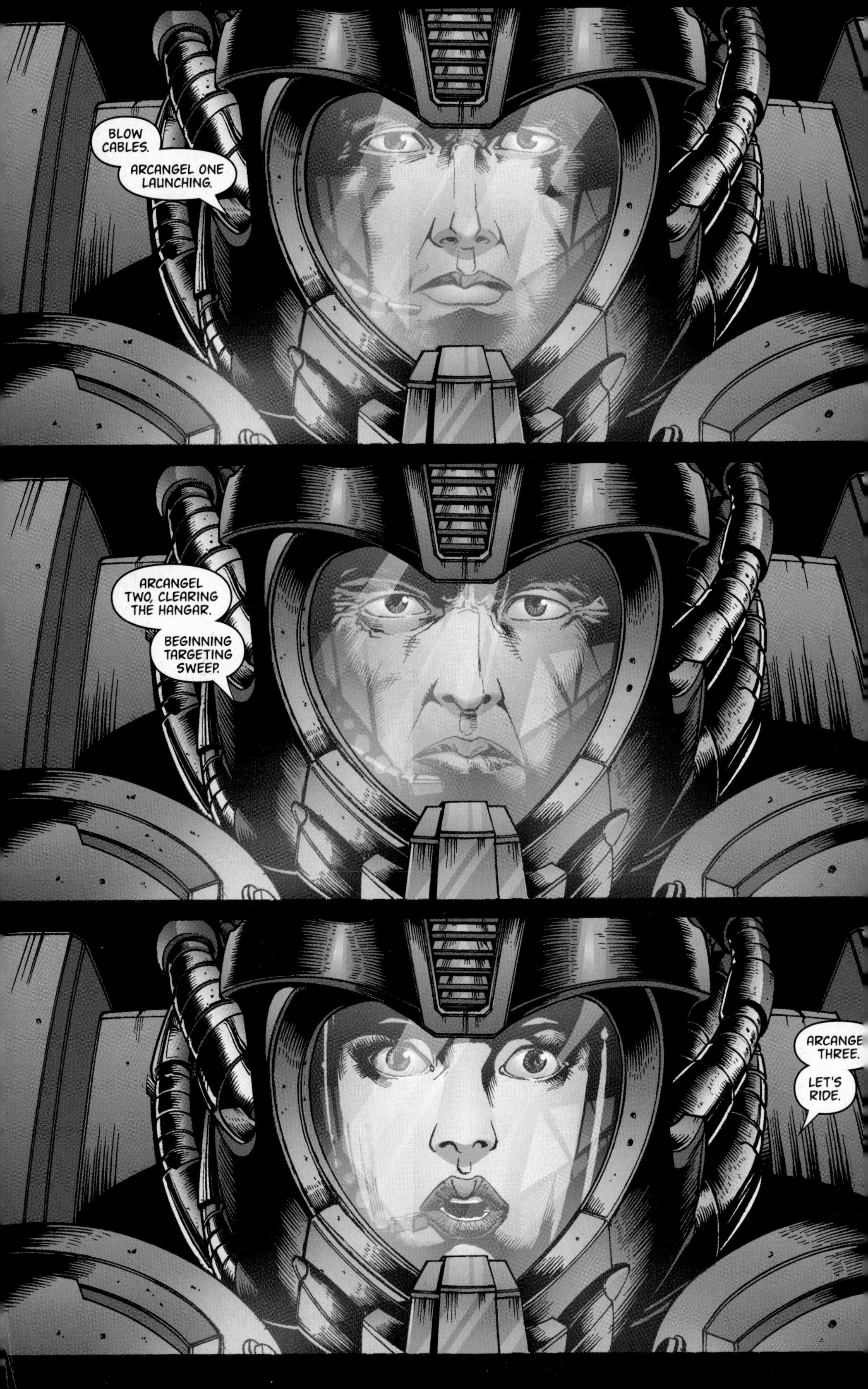

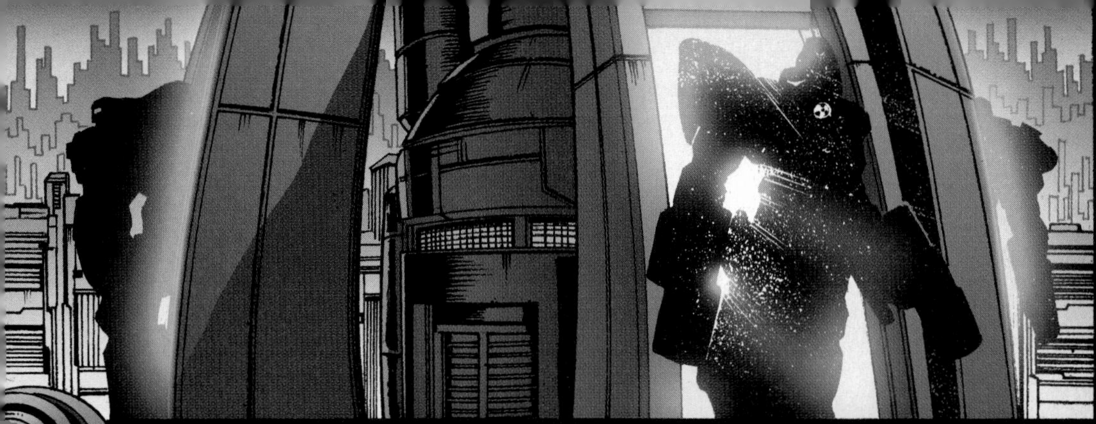
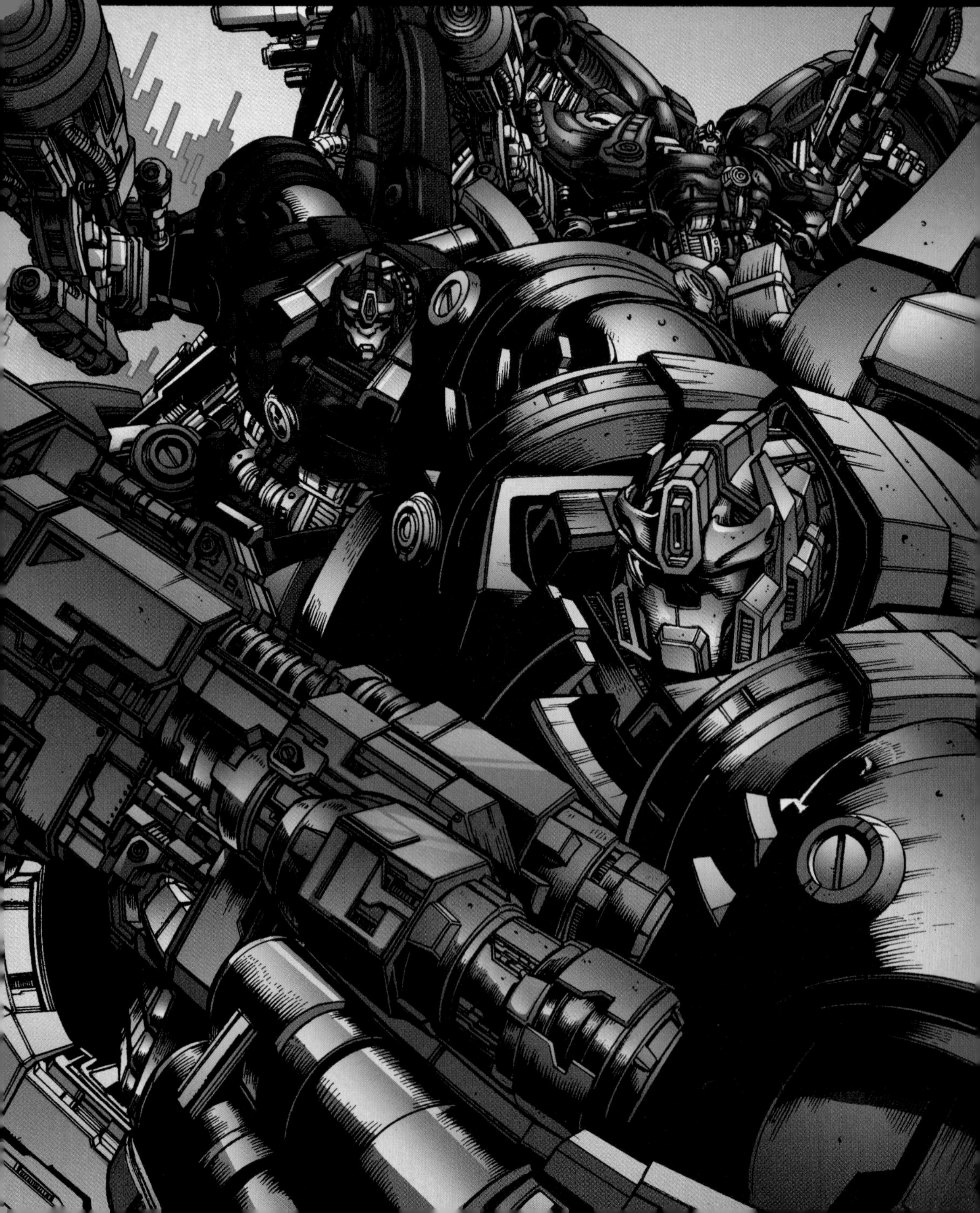

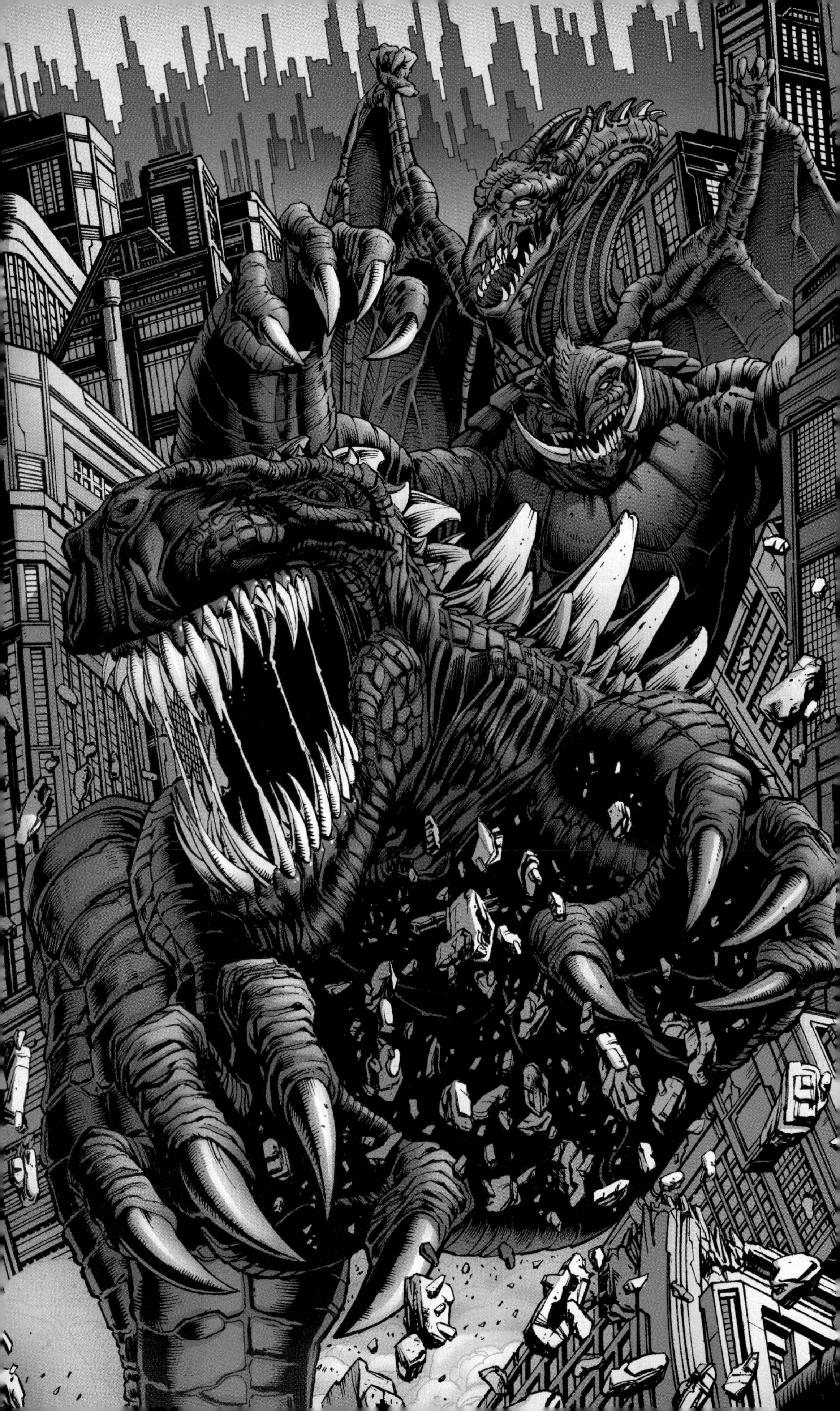

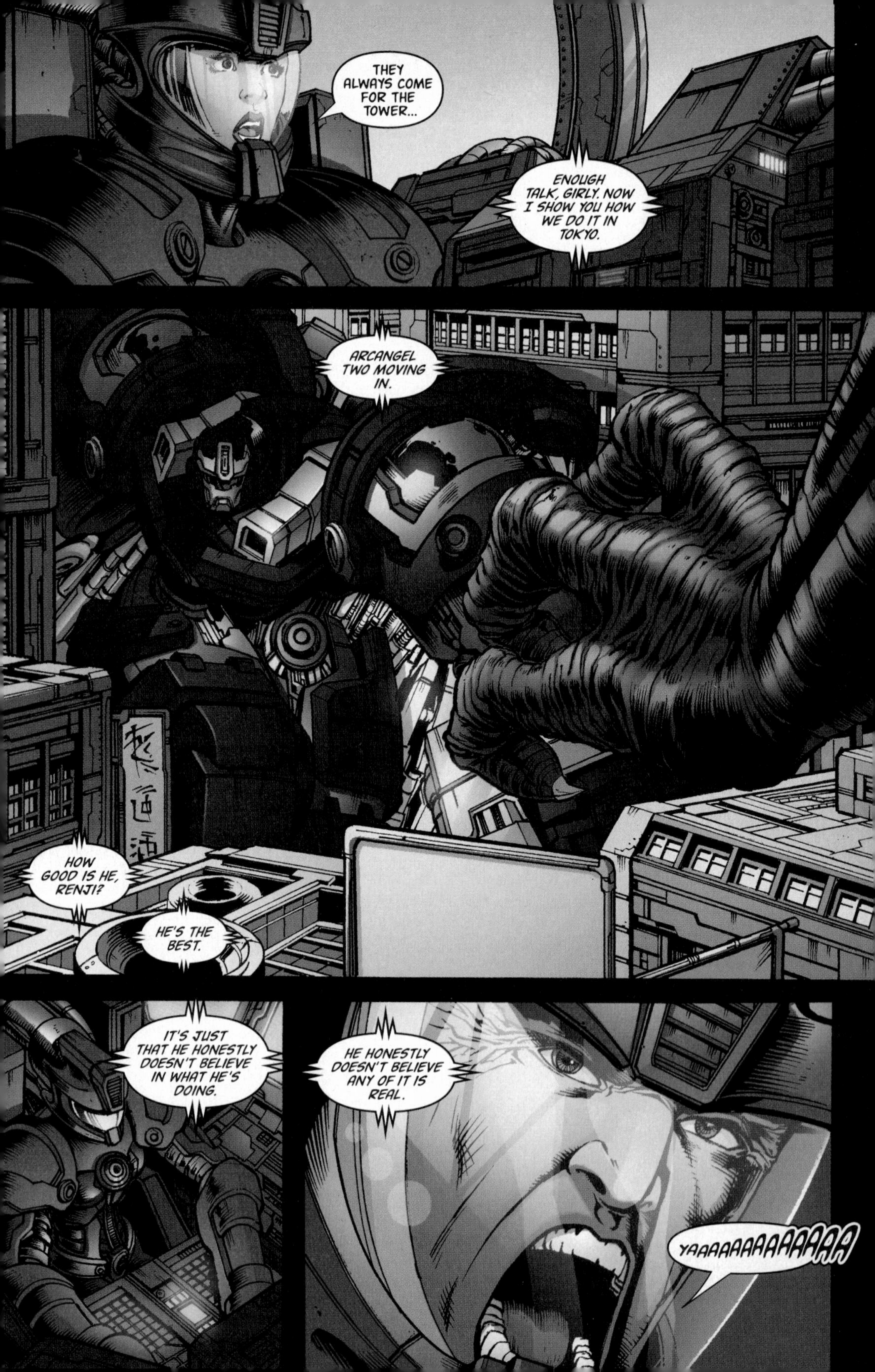
THEY ALWAYS COME FOR THE TOWER...
ENOUGH TALK, GIRLY. NOW I SHOW YOU HOW WE DO IT IN TOKYO.
ARCANGEL TWO MOVING IN.
HOW GOOD IS HE, RENJI?
HE'S THE BEST.
IT'S JUST THAT HE HONESTLY DOESN'T BELIEVE IN WHAT HE'S DOING.
HE HONESTLY DOESN'T BELIEVE ANY OF IT IS REAL.
YAAAAAAAAAAAAAA

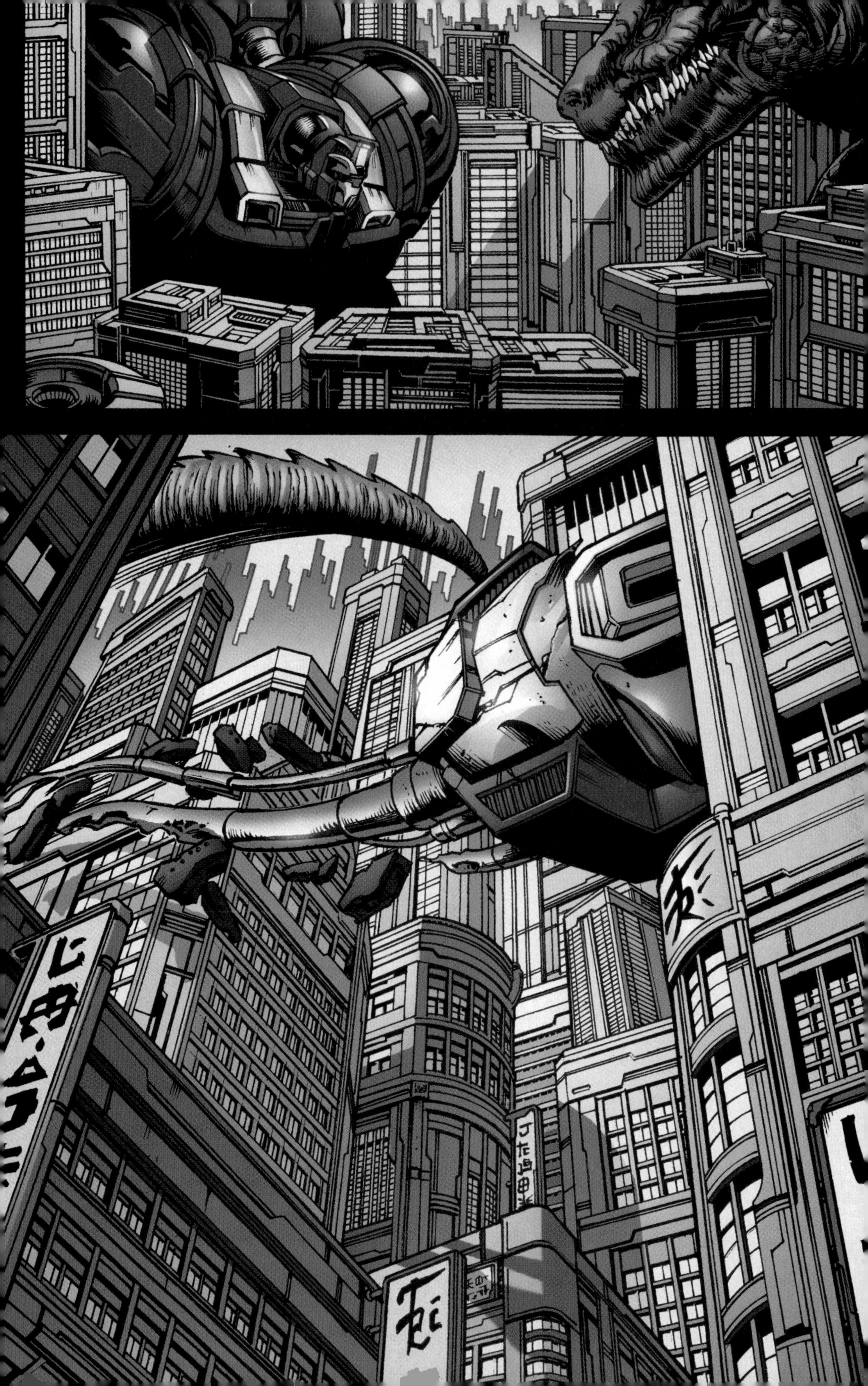

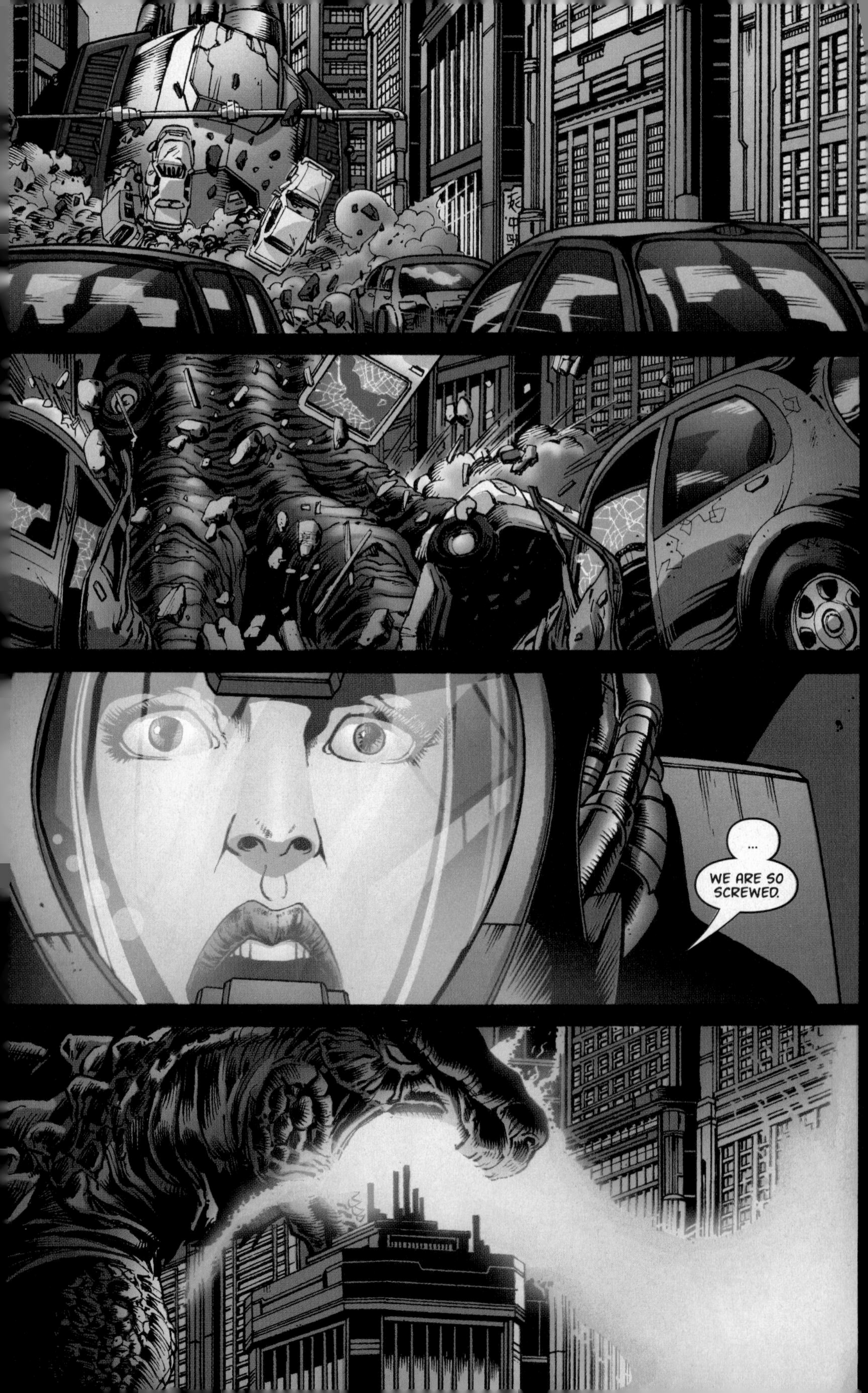
...
WE ARE SO SCREWED.

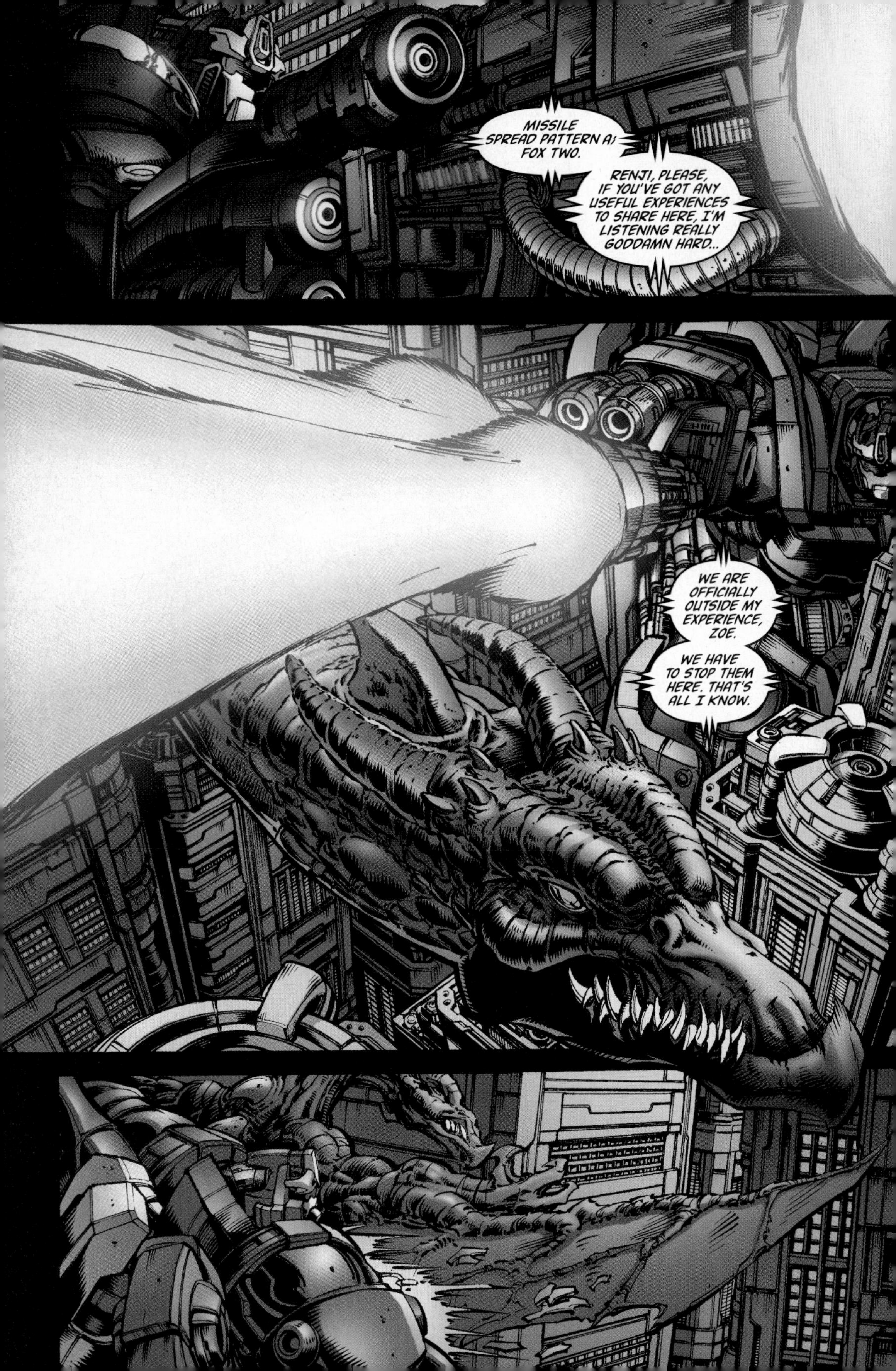
MISSILE SPREAD PATTERN A; FOX TWO.
RENJI, PLEASE, IF YOU'VE GOT ANY USEFUL EXPERIENCES TO SHARE HERE, I'M LISTENING REALLY GODDAMN HARD...
WE ARE OFFICIALLY OUTSIDE MY EXPERIENCE, ZOE.
WE HAVE TO STOP THEM HERE. THAT'S ALL I KNOW.

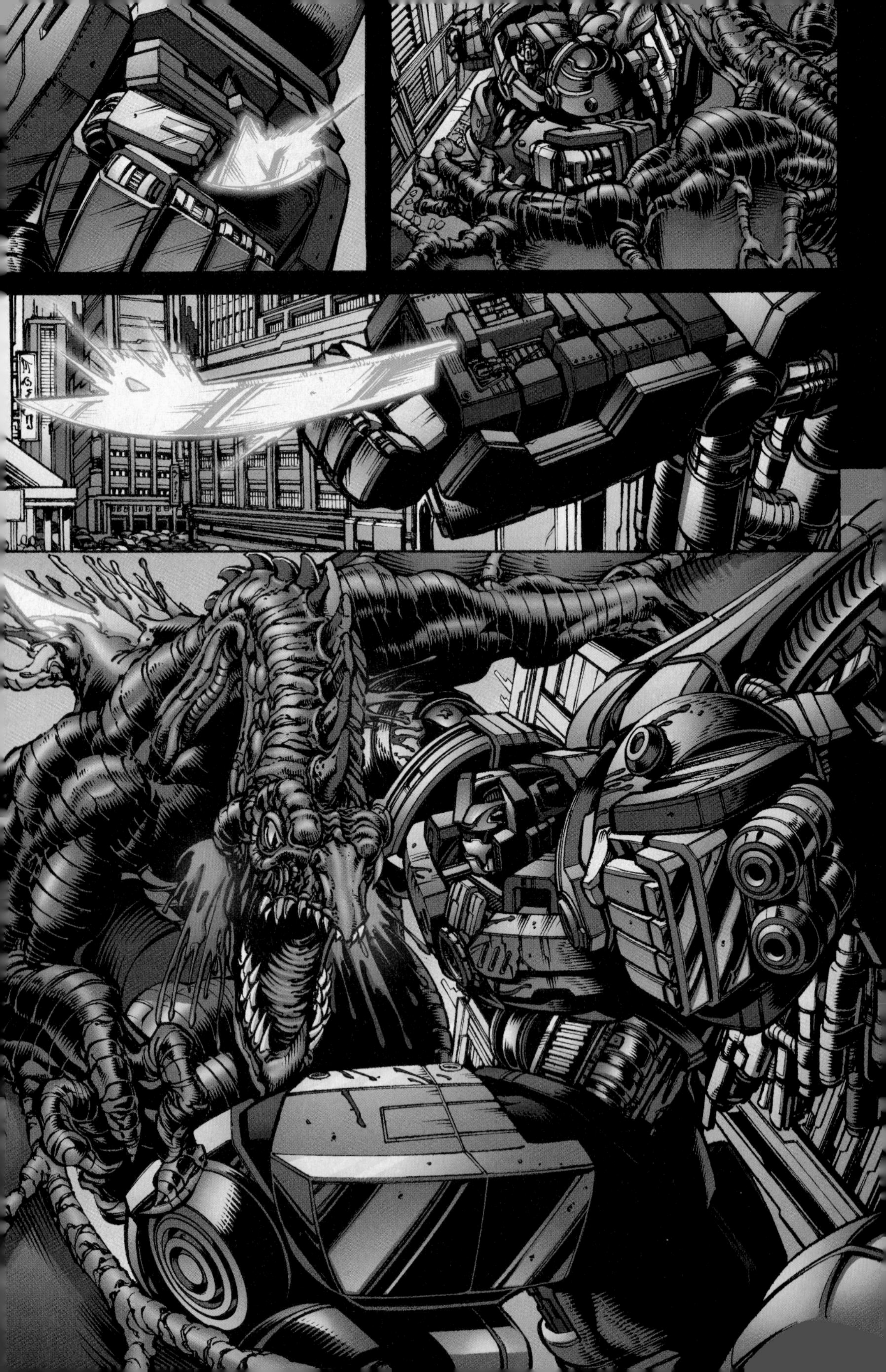

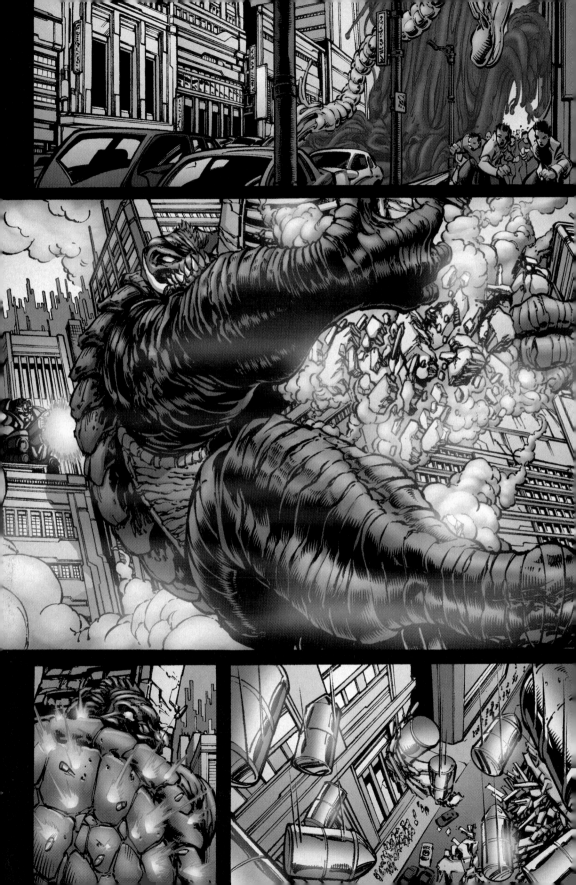

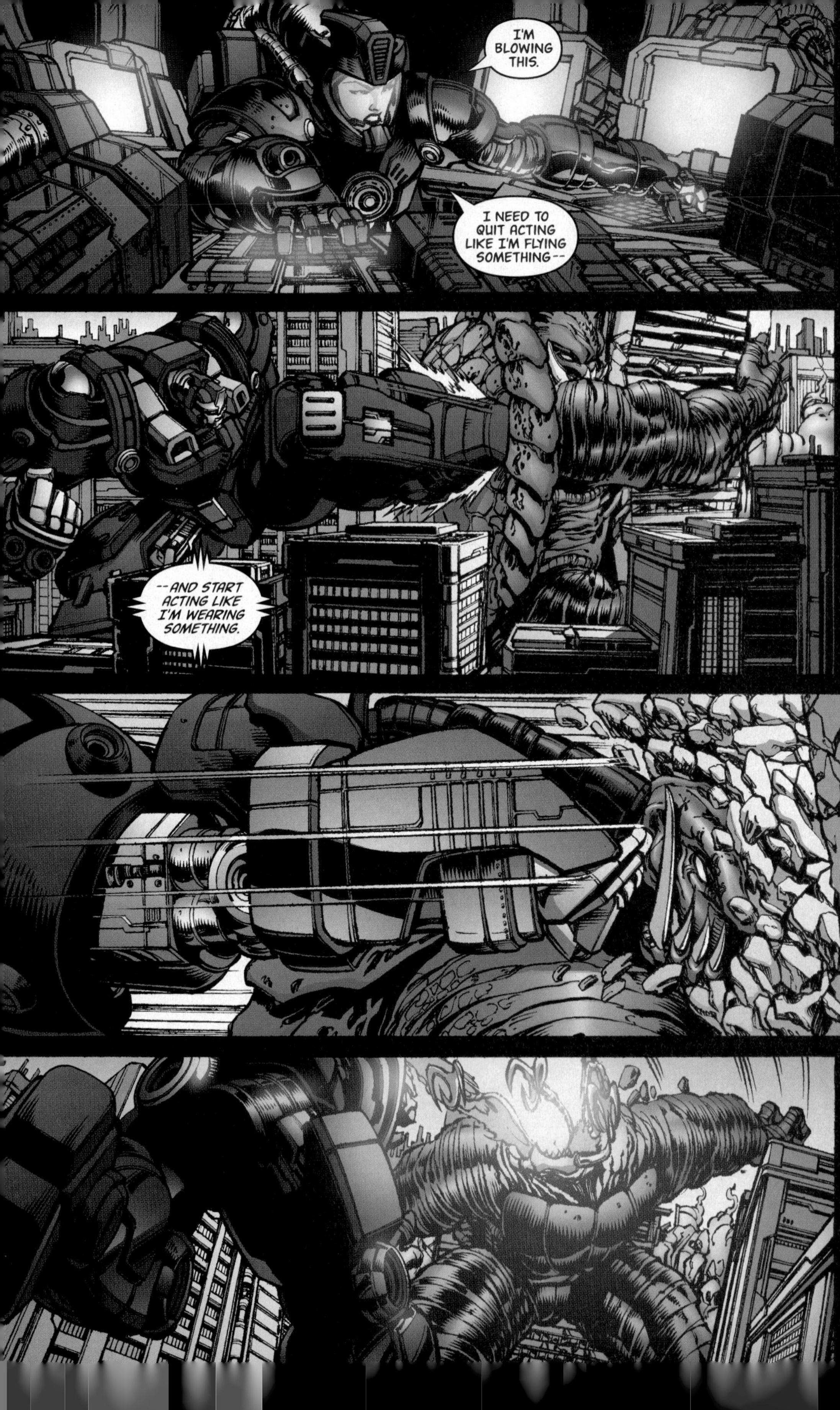
I'M BLOWING THIS.
I NEED TO QUIT ACTING LIKE I'M FLYING SOMETHING--
--AND START ACTING LIKE I'M WEARING SOMETHING.

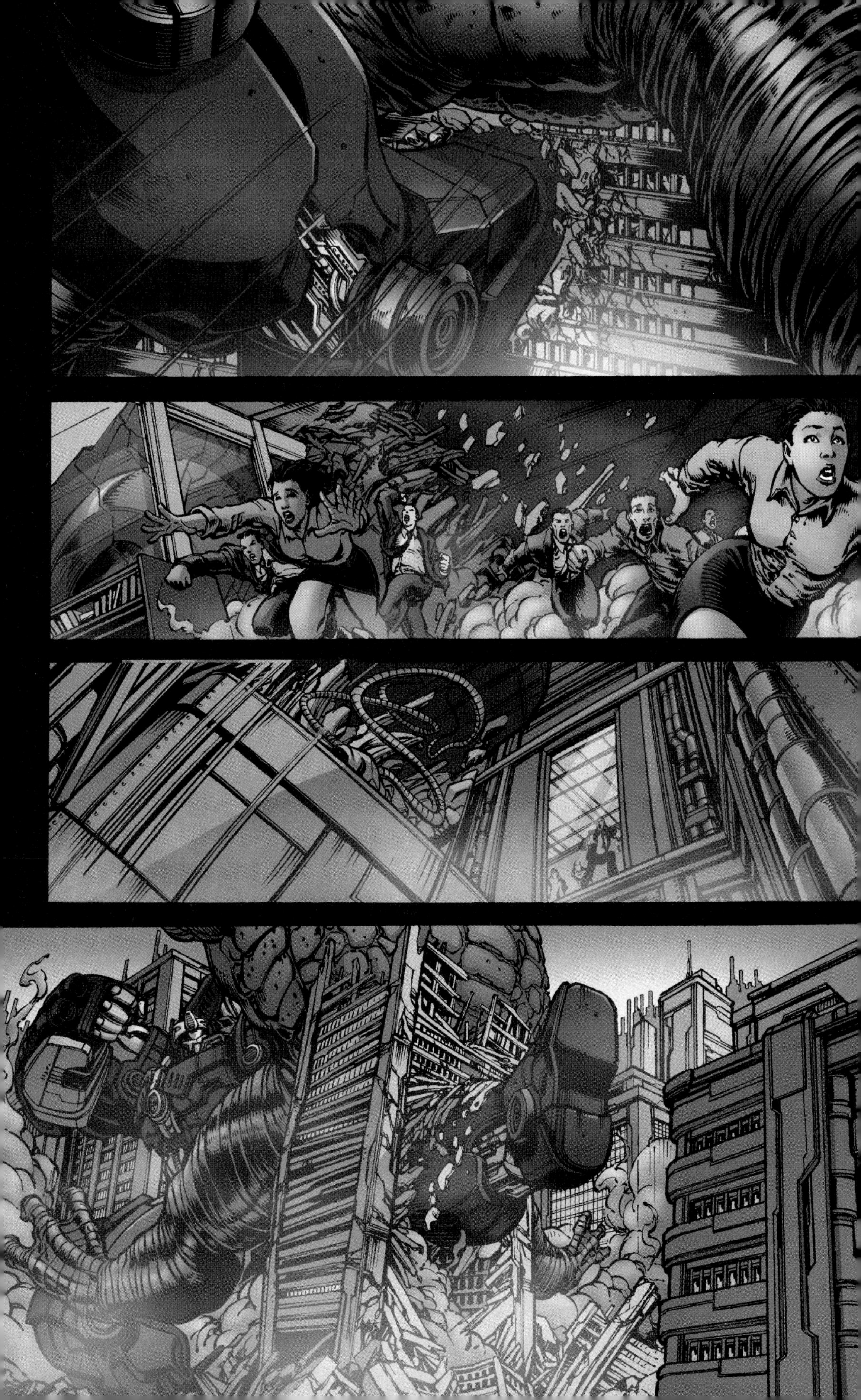

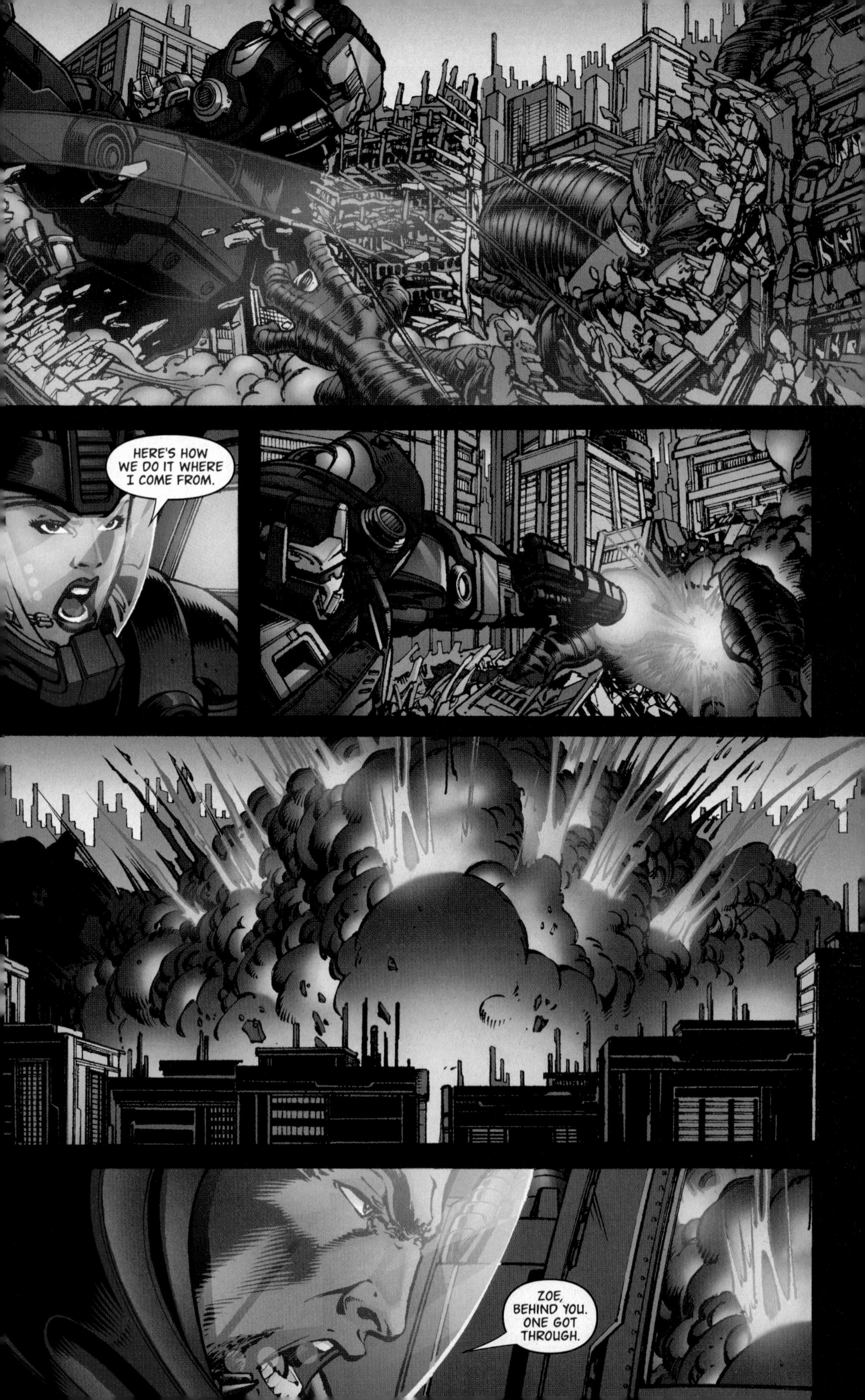
HERE'S HOW WE DO IT WHERE I COME FROM.
ZOE, BEHIND YOU. ONE GOT THROUGH.

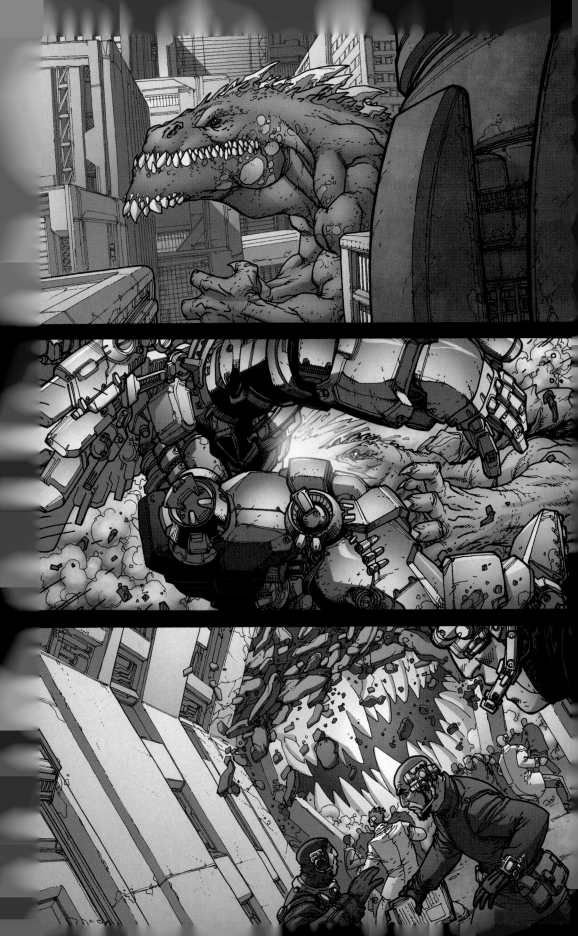

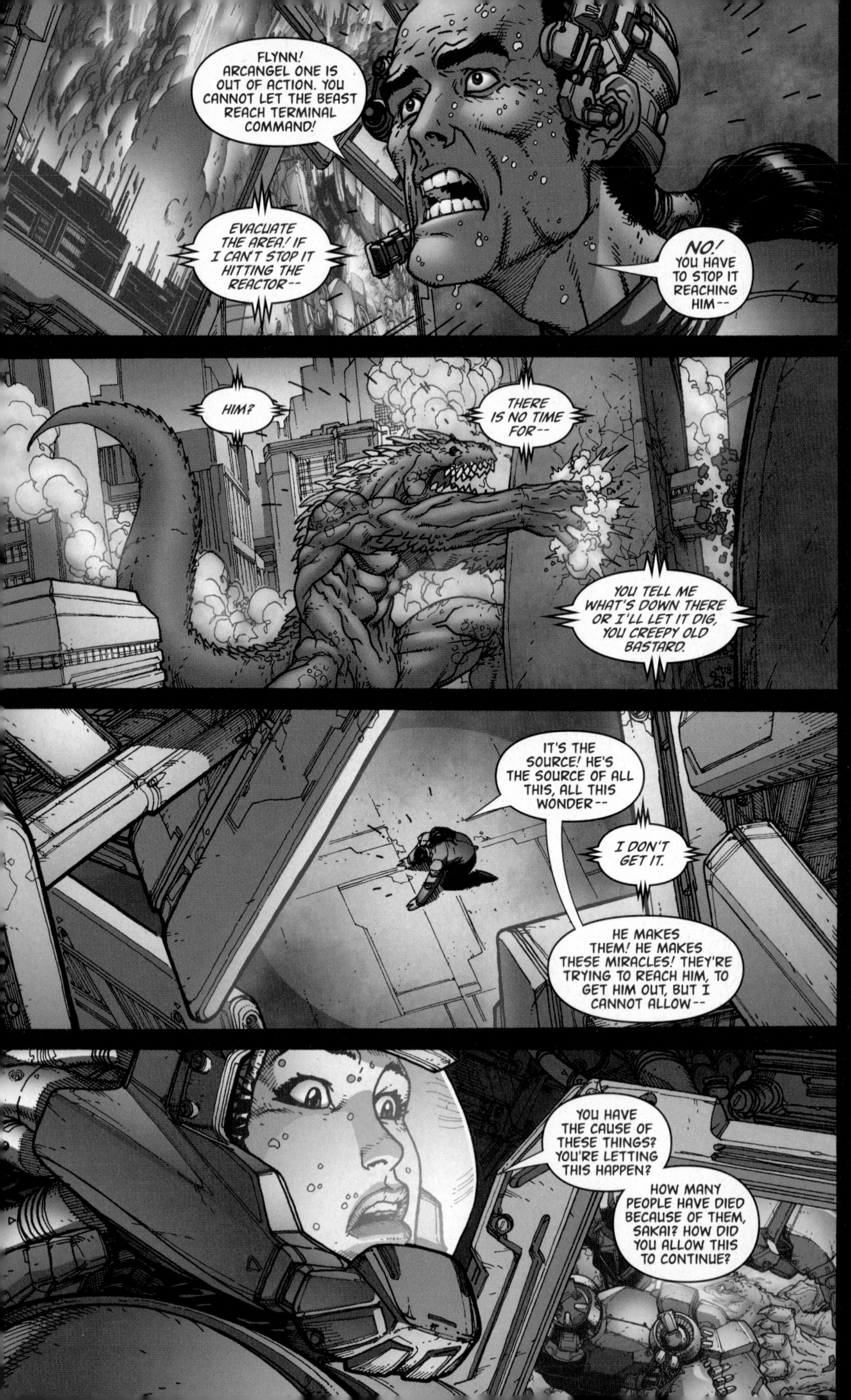
FLYNN! ARCANGEL ONE IS OUT OF ACTION. YOU CANNOT LET THE BEAST REACH TERMINAL COMMAND!
EVACUATE THE AREA! IF I CAN'T STOP IT HITTING THE REACTOR--
NO! YOU HAVE TO STOP IT REACHING HIM--
HIM?
THERE IS NO TIME FOR--
YOU TELL ME WHAT'S DOWN THERE OR I'LL LET IT DIG, YOU CREEPY OLD BASTARD.
IT'S THE SOURCE! HE'S THE SOURCE OF ALL THIS, ALL THIS WONDER--
I DON'T GET IT.
HE MAKES THEM! HE MAKES THESE MIRACLES! THEY'RE TRYING TO REACH HIM, TO GET HIM OUT, BUT I CANNOT ALLOW--
YOU HAVE THE CAUSE OF THESE THINGS? YOU'RE LETTING THIS HAPPEN?
HOW MANY PEOPLE HAVE DIED BECAUSE OF THEM, SAKAI? HOW DID YOU ALLOW THIS TO CONTINUE?

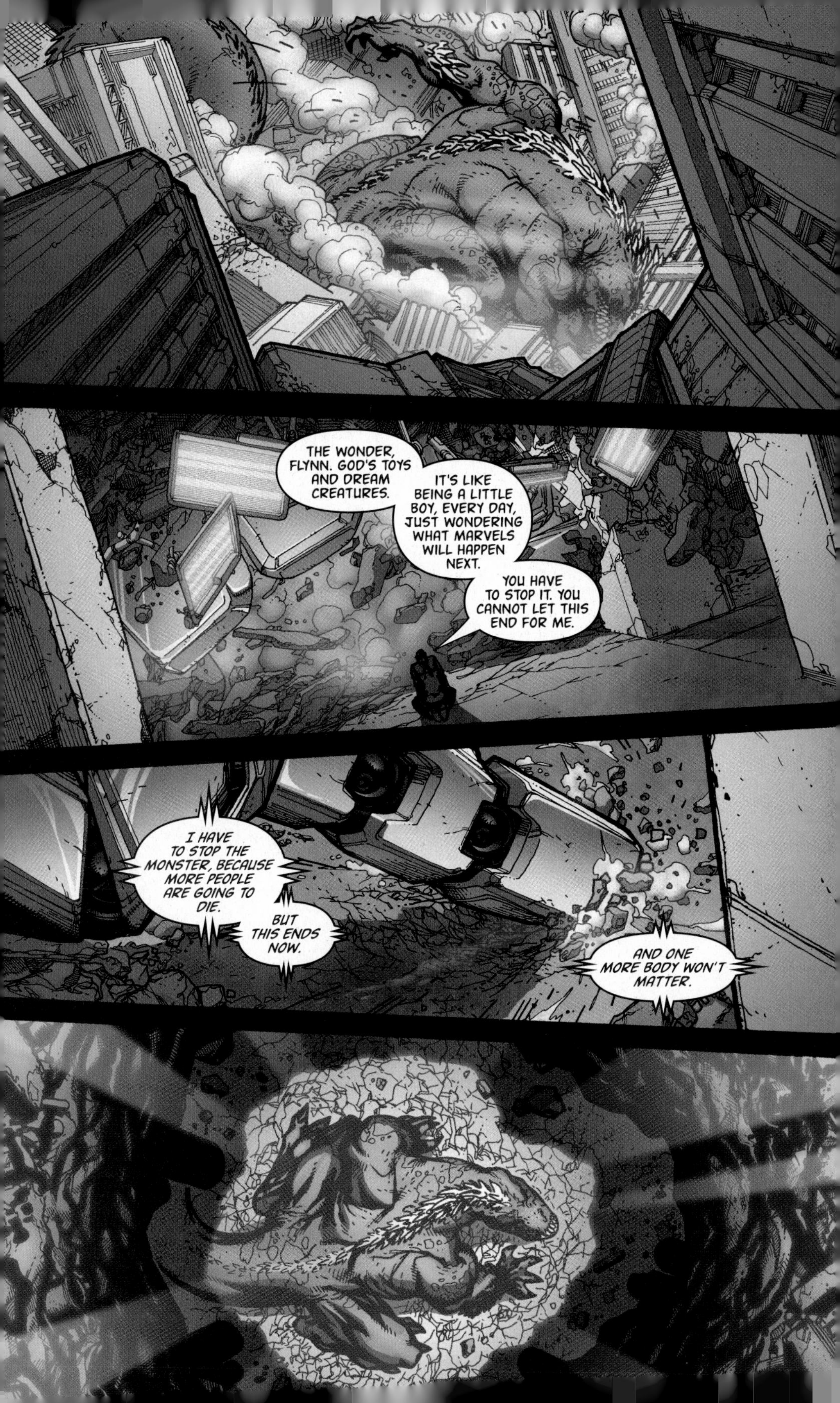
THE WONDER, FLYNN. GOD'S TOYS AND DREAM CREATURES.
IT'S LIKE BEING A LITTLE BOY, EVERY DAY, JUST WONDERING WHAT MARVELS WILL HAPPEN NEXT.
YOU HAVE TO STOP IT. YOU CANNOT LET THIS END FOR ME.
I HAVE TO STOP THE MONSTER, BECAUSE MORE PEOPLE ARE GOING TO DIE.
BUT THIS ENDS NOW.
AND ONE MORE BODY WON'T MATTER.

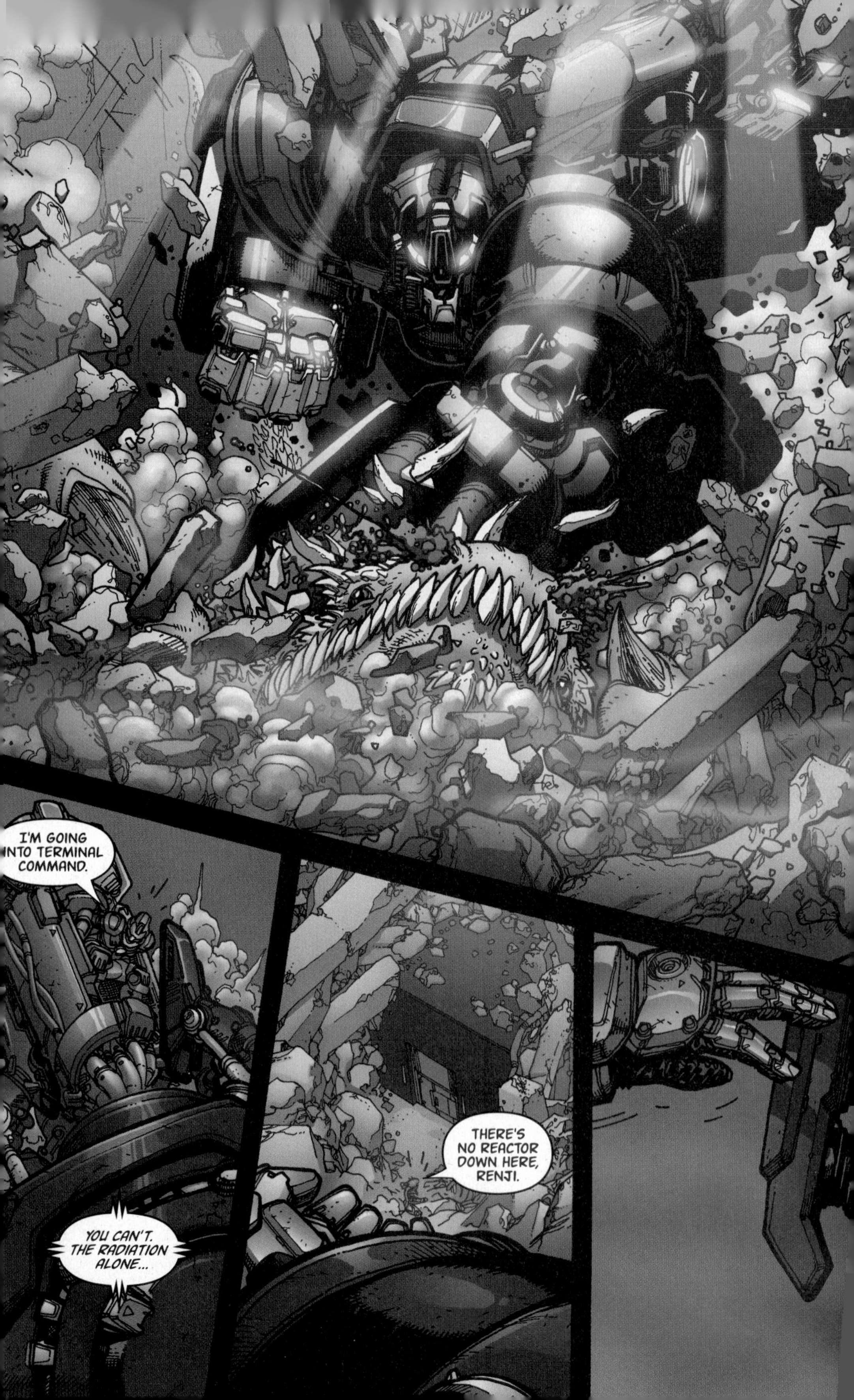

I'M GOING INTO TERMINAL COMMAND.
YOU CAN'T. THE RADIATION ALONE...
THERE'S NO REACTOR DOWN HERE, RENJI.

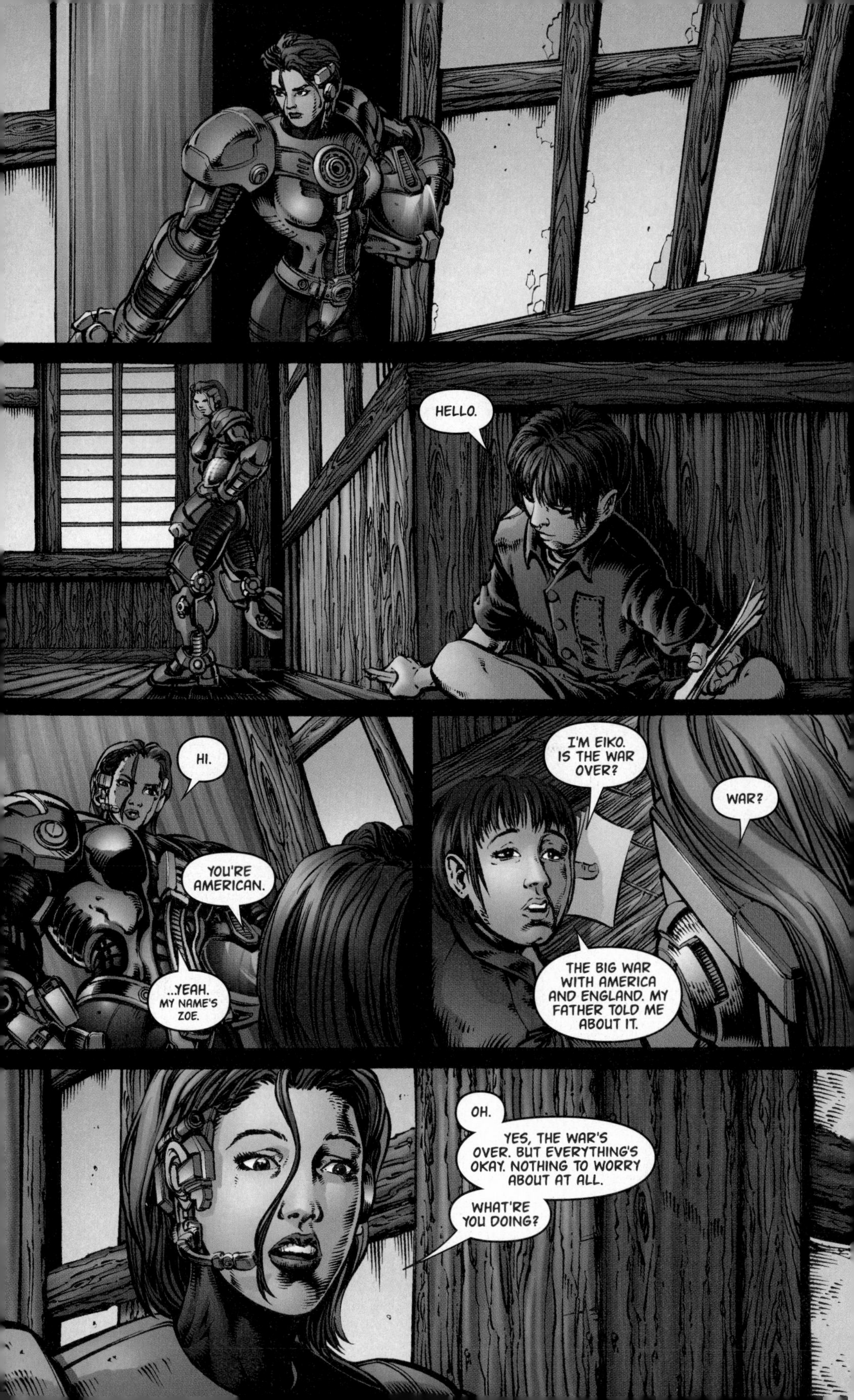
HELLO.
HI.
YOU'RE AMERICAN.
...YEAH. MY NAME'S ZOE.
I'M EIKO. IS THE WAR OVER?
WAR?
THE BIG WAR WITH AMERICA AND ENGLAND. MY FATHER TOLD ME ABOUT IT.
OH.
YES, THE WAR'S OVER. BUT EVERYTHING'S OKAY. NOTHING TO WORRY ABOUT AT ALL.
WHAT'RE YOU DOING?

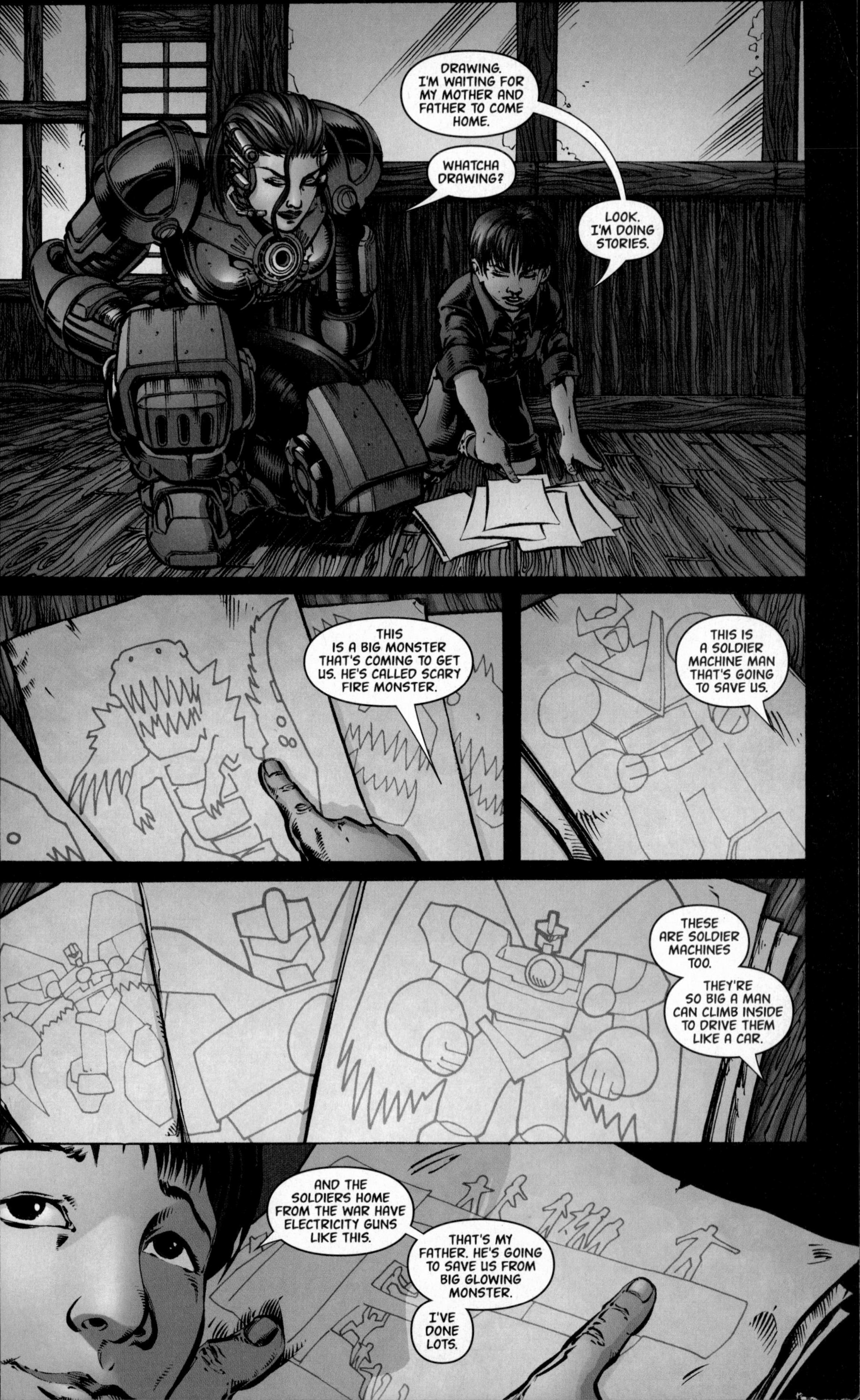
WHATCHA DRAWING?
DRAWING. I'M WAITING FOR MY MOTHER AND FATHER TO COME HOME.
LOOK. I'M DOING STORIES.
THIS IS A BIG MONSTER THAT'S COMING TO GET US. HE'S CALLED SCARY FIRE MONSTER.
THIS IS A SOLDIER MACHINE MAN THAT'S GOING TO SAVE US.
THESE ARE SOLDIER MACHINES TOO.
THEY'RE SO BIG A MAN CAN CLIMB INSIDE TO DRIVE THEM LIKE A CAR.
AND THE SOLDIERS HOME FROM THE WAR HAVE ELECTRICITY GUNS LIKE THIS.
THAT'S MY FATHER. HE'S GOING TO SAVE US FROM BIG GLOWING MONSTER.
I'VE DONE LOTS.

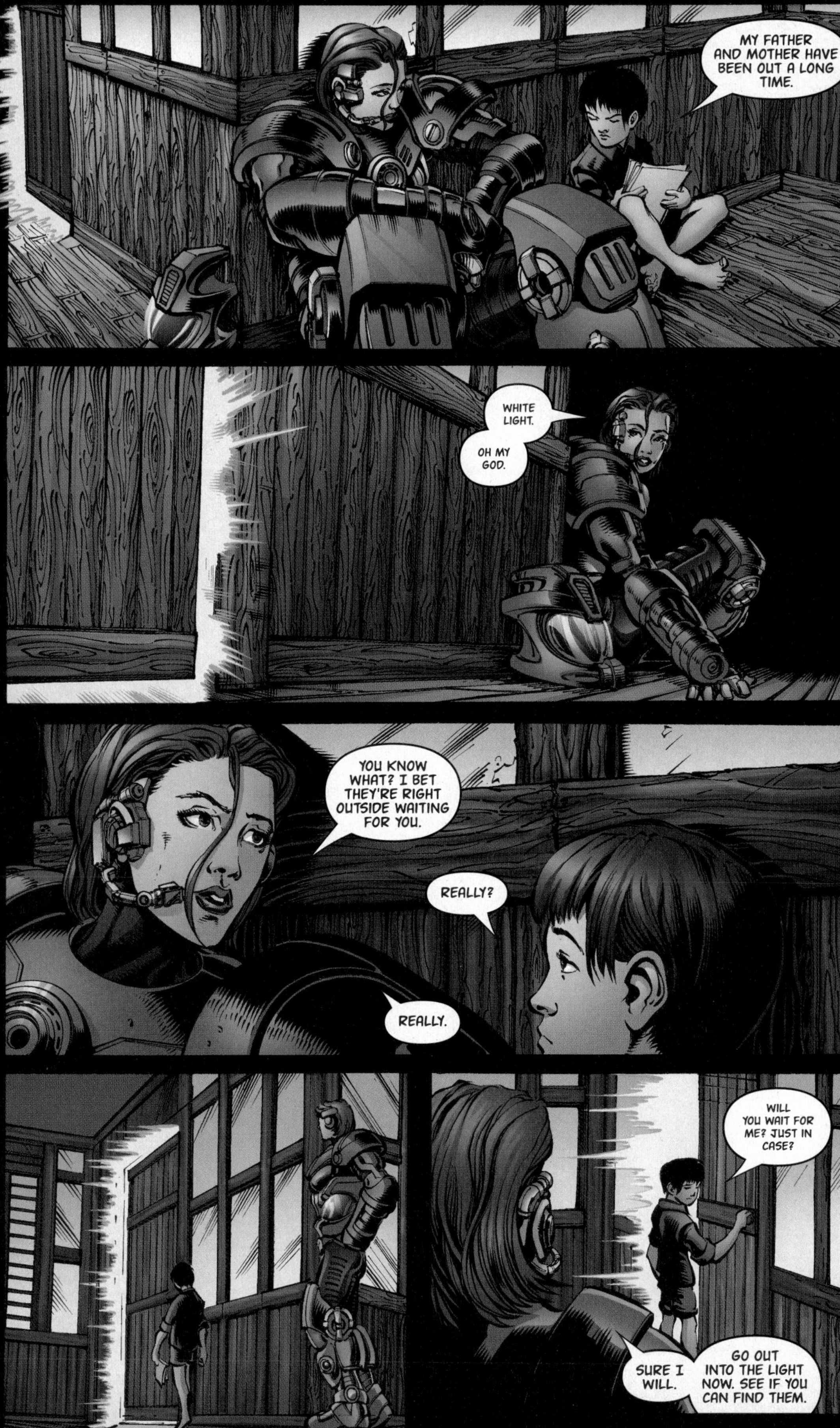
MY FATHER AND MOTHER HAVE BEEN OUT A LONG TIME.
WHITE LIGHT.
OH MY GOD.
YOU KNOW WHAT? I BET THEY'RE RIGHT OUTSIDE WAITING FOR YOU.
REALLY?
REALLY.
WILL YOU WAIT FOR ME? JUST IN CASE?
SURE I WILL.
GO OUT INTO THE LIGHT NOW. SEE IF YOU CAN FIND THEM.

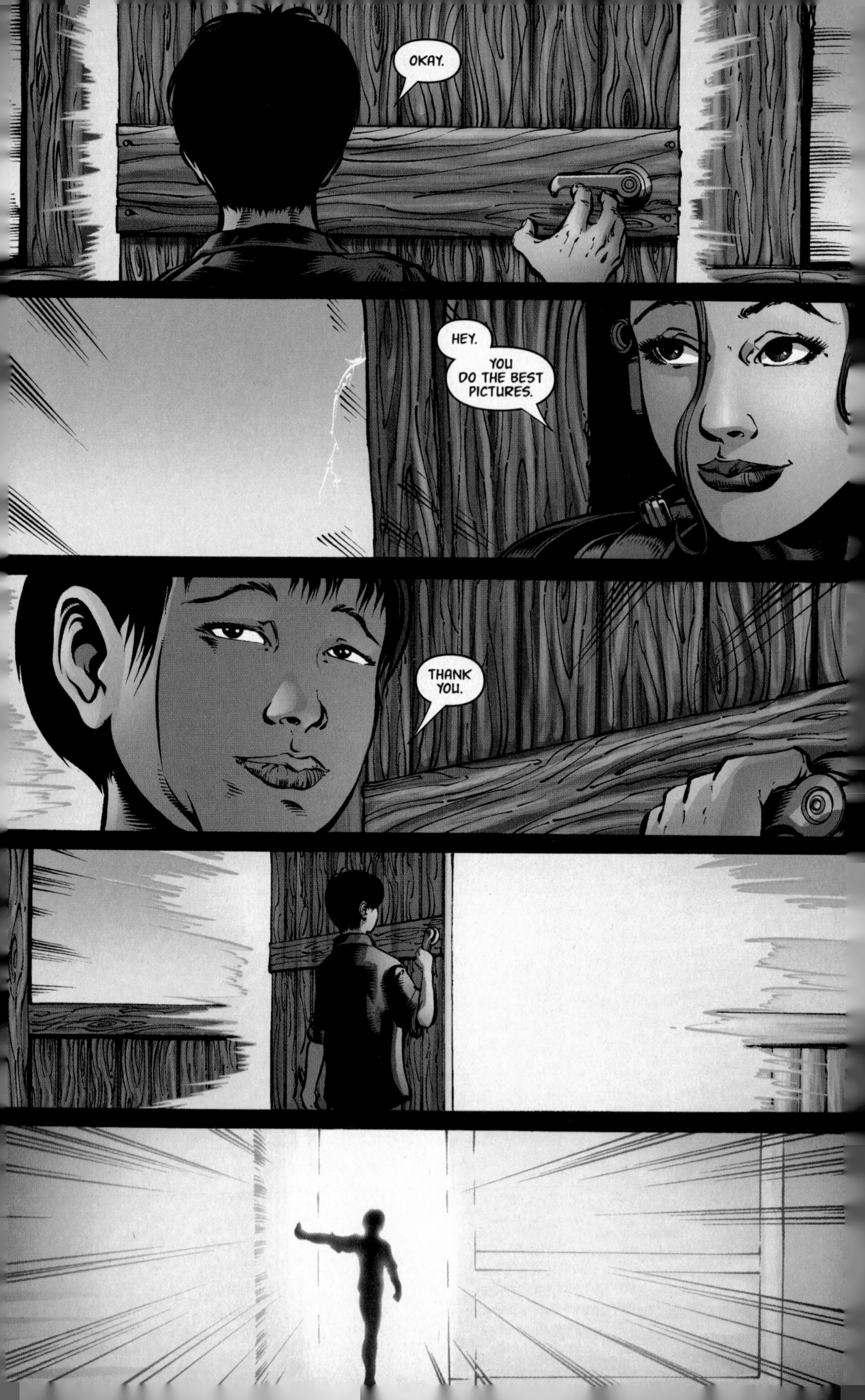
OKAY.
HEY.
YOU DO THE BEST PICTURES.
THANK YOU.

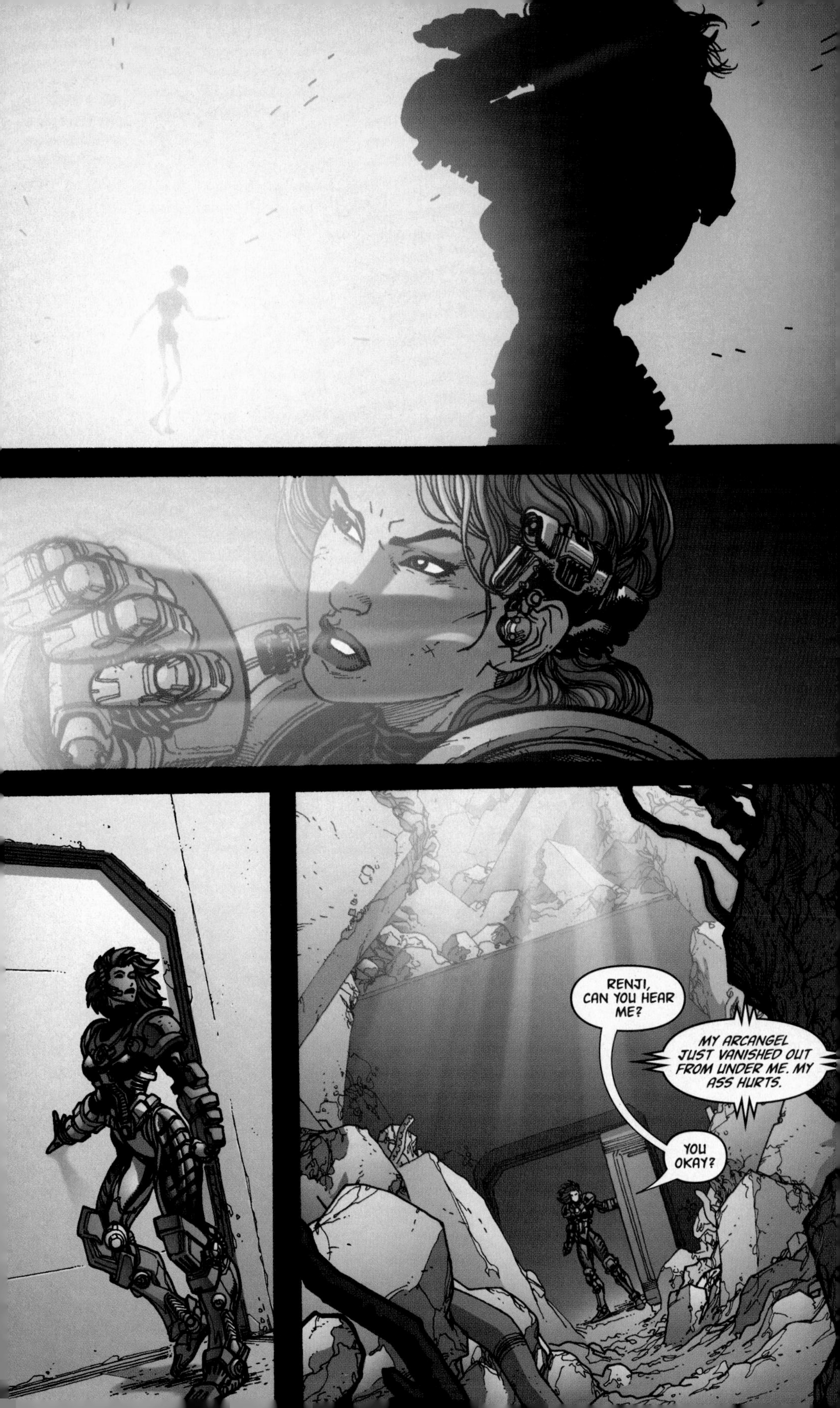
RENJI, CAN YOU HEAR ME?
MY ARCANGEL JUST VANISHED OUT FROM UNDER ME. MY ASS HURTS.
YOU OKAY?

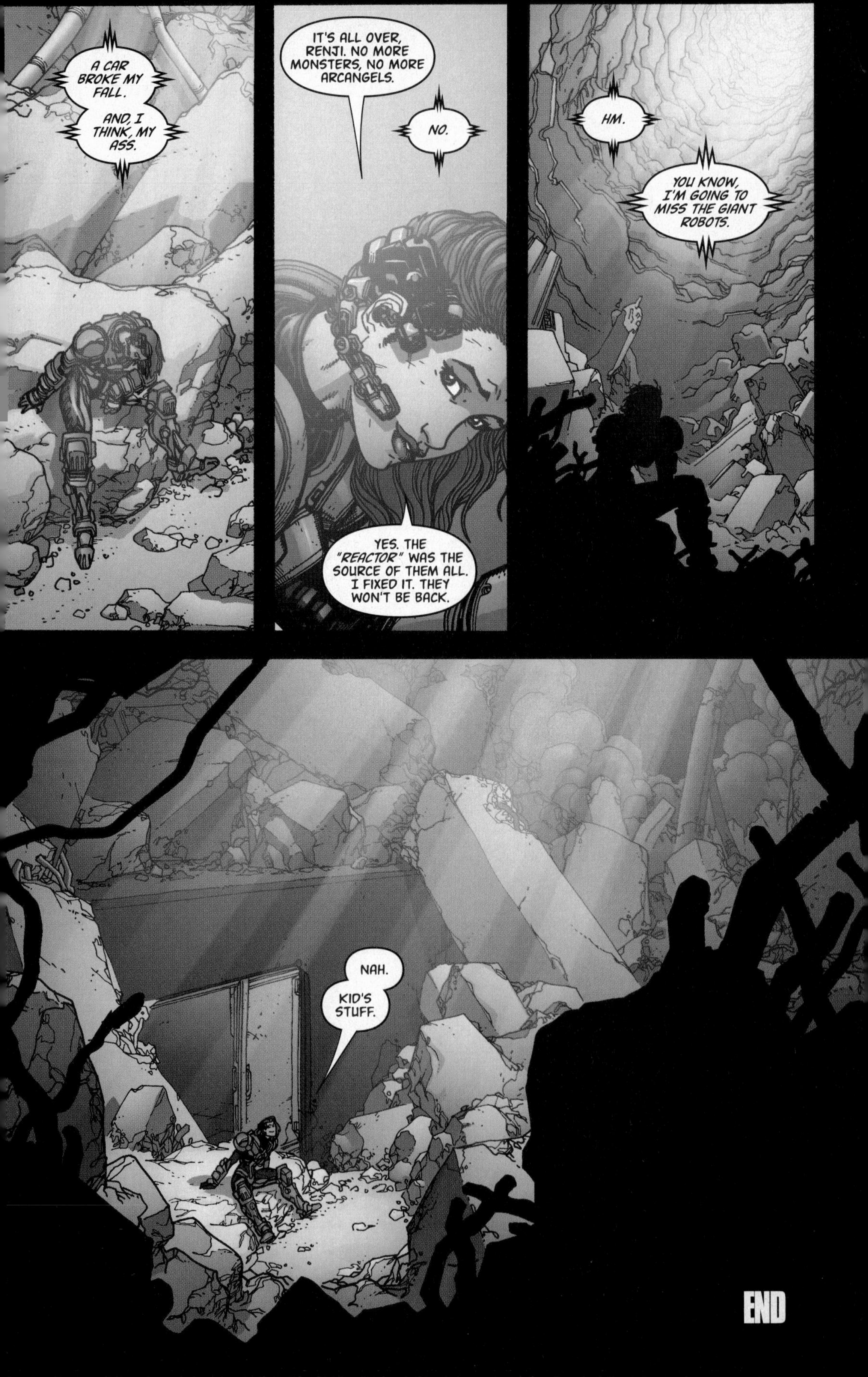
A CAR BROKE MY FALL.
AND, I THINK, MY ASS.
IT'S ALL OVER, RENJI. NO MORE MONSTERS, NO MORE ARCANGELS.
NO.
YES. THE "REACTOR" WAS THE SOURCE OF THEM ALL. I FIXED IT. THEY WON'T BE BACK.
HM.
YOU KNOW, I'M GOING TO MISS THE GIANT ROBOTS.
NAH.
KID'S STUFF.
END

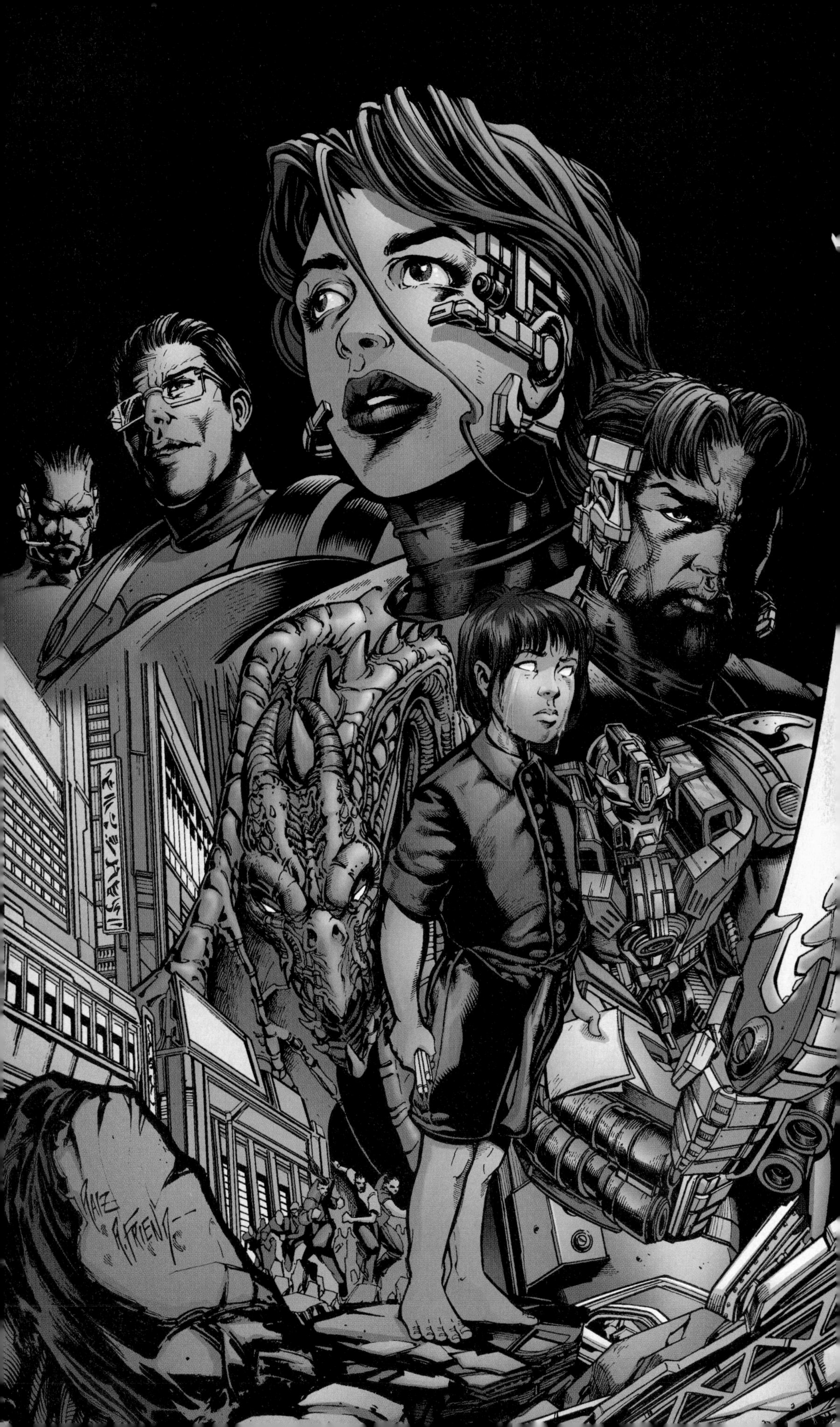